SPEEDWAY YEARBOOK 1993

Edited by

PETER OAKES

FRONT PAGE BOOKS

SPEEDWAY STAR

Still way out in front

SPEEDWAY STAR

1993 SPEEDWAY YEARBOOK

Edited by Peter Oakes

EDITOR
Peter Oakes

PHOTOGRAPHIC EDITOR
Mike Patrick

CONTRIBUTING EDITORS
Philip Rising, Bryn Williams, Wayne Swales

▲ **The 1993 SPEEDWAY YEARBOOK was first published in Great Britain, 1993, by Front Page Books, Suites 8-9, East of England Showground, Alwalton, Peterborough, PE2 0XE, England. Tel: 0733 394494. Fax: 0733 394725.**

▲ **The 1993 Speedway Yearbook was published by Front Page Books, printed by The Bath Press, England, from film prepared by Pinegen Limited, 95, Brighton Road, Surbiton, Surrey, KT6 5NF (081 399 0012) and is distributed by Front Page Books. Front cover printed by Hartham Press Limited, Unit 5A, Marshgate Trading Estate, Marshgate Drive, Hertford, SG13 7AB (0992 589334)**

ISBN 0-948882-16-6 **£11.95**

1992
WORLD CHAMPION
Gary Havelock
(Bradford & England)

KING GARY - pride of Lions

GARY Havelock put all his worst nightmares behind him as he celebrated becoming England's first World Champion in more than a decade.

The rain may have lashed down at the Olympic Stadium in Wroclaw, Poland, but nothing could pour cold water on Havvy's scintillating achievement.

He survived a heavy crash in his second ride, had to sit through a 90-minute delay while an army of track staff cleared a cloudburst that had left the track flooded, and then won his last three rides to take the title.

And, for the first time since Gothenburg, 1980, when Michael Lee was crowned King of the Track, the strains of the National Anthem accompanied the World Final prize-giving.

Gazza cried tears of joy on the rostrum...but they were also tears of relief.

Relief that he had finally won the title that had meant so much to him.

Relief that he had survived a painful route to the World Final.

And relief that he had finally put behind him the controversial past that had so dogged his climb to the top.

Within half an hour of becoming the 1992 World Champion he was admitting: "I have made mistakes in the past but that is all behind me. Now I want to help speedway get back to where it belongs as an English World Champion. The victory is not only for me – but for the whole of English speedway."

Havvy the Rebel had become Havvy the Ruler.

And who could deny him his ultimate success, an ambition he had first talked about when he was at school had finally been realised.

He said: "I have always wanted to be World Champion. That's all I have ever wanted."

No-one who was at school with him in his native Yarm was ever left in any doubt of his sporting dream.

His school reports reflected his single-mindedness with repeated references to his basic intelligence, but his reluctance to put in the necessary work effort to pass his exams.

He explained: "I always knew I would be a speedway rider. I never had any doubts. Teachers would say I would finish up without any qualifications I'd just tell them I was going to be World Speedway Champion!"

Gary was proved right and his frustrated teachers wrong in the tough classroom that was Wroclaw.

Possibly the writing had been on the World Championship blackboard all season....

For Gary's ride to glory had started with a maximum 15 points at Cradley Heath on Sunday, May 3, when he brushed aside all his British opposition in the domestic semi final.

A fortnight later he won a run-off against Martin Dugard to retain his British Championship after being afforded the luxury of losing to Bradford team-mate Paul Thorp and Mark Loram in his last ride.

He was already looking ahead, commenting: "I have never ridden in a World Final but for me this is the hardest meeting of the season for British riders. No-one gives an inch in this one. You can never take anyone for granted and that showed in my last race."

He also reflected on the bitter disappointment of going out of the 1991 title chase in the Overseas Final at his own home track at Odsal Stadium: "I only had about three bad meetings last year but one of them happened to be a World Championship round. Hopefully this year I won't have any."

While Havelock was delighted with his performance at Coventry it was a glum England colleague Jeremy Doncaster who made his way back to his Ipswich home having been the second big British name to fall by the wayside before the introduction of the overseas contenders to the domestic rounds.

Simon Cross, who had fought so bravely in his qualifying round at Exeter (he rode with a badly damaged knee), was unable to repeat that performance in the semi final and was forced to quit after coming off in his first ride at Dudley Wood.

While the list of British survivors was being whittled down to just ten at the Homefire British Final there were bigger shocks on the Continent – but more of that later!

Havelock's next stepping stone was the Ancit Commonwealth Final at King's Lynn and while the bare-bone statistics indicate another untroubled leap towards immortality it was one of the most worrying meetings of the season.

Eleven days earlier he had been buffeted about in a heavy fall in Poland and had been forced to sit out a glut of matches including the Keyline Dukes' three Bank Holiday fixtures with a series of nasty injuries.

He was in obvious pain in the Saddlebow Road pits and

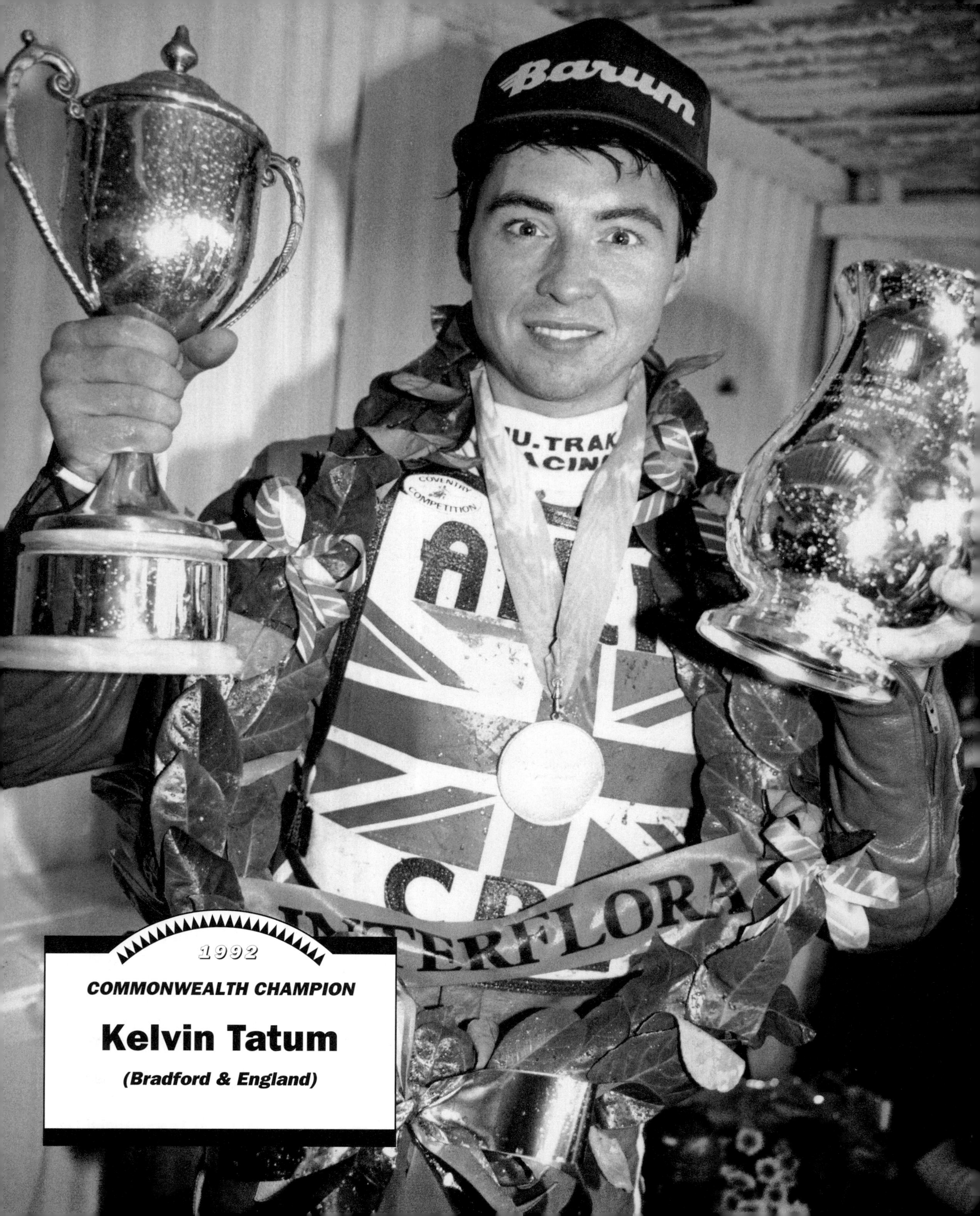

1992

COMMONWEALTH CHAMPION

Kelvin Tatum

(Bradford & England)

matters weren't helped when he crashed alarmingly after crossing the finishing line behind rival Kelvin Tatum in heat seven.

Havvy, his fingers black, blue and swollen, had lost his grip after going through the chequered flag, was unable to regain control, and careered towards the fence in front of a stunned complement of riders and pits staff.

No-one was betting on him being able to continue as he gingerly walked back to his pits place but the tough North Yorkshireman shrugged off the increased pain and even overcame mechanical problems in his next ride to force a title run-off against Tatum and the surprise package, New Zealander Mark Thorpe, the only Division Two rider in the line-up.

Not surprisingly, Havvy was content to let Tatum and Thorpe fight it out as he pulled out of the decider way before the final lap.

For once, though, he was not centre stage in the post meeting deliberations.

Instead it was the equally brave performance of Martin Dugard who won his opening ride but was then involved in a terrible tangle with Andy Smith in the first staging of heat five.

Dugard was in considerable discomfort as the track doctor warned him he had probably broken his collar bone but agreed to help strap it up and allow him to continue his challenge for a place in the Overseas Final.

Dugard, amazingly, came out for the re-run. He won both that race and his next but even though he started his two remaining rides he pulled out after failing to make the start.

He said: "I had nine points after my first three rides and only needed a couple from my last two and I would have made the rostrum. Once I got round the first turn I knew I wasn't going to get anywhere."

He had got enough points to claim a comfortable top 11 placing, an achievement made even the more remarkable when, the following day, hospital x-rays confirmed that his collar bone was fractured.

Young pretenders Chris Louis, Mark Loram and Aussie Leigh Adams were the shock non-qualifiers alongside the more predictable fall-outs David Mullett and Mark Carlson.

So it was back to Coventry, scene of his back-to-back British Final wins, for Havvy, the other 10 King's Lynn qualifiers and a controversial quintet of Americans.

The scheduled American Final had been cancelled because of squabbles States-side...and that decision provoked even more protests in England as the American Motorcycle Association twice changed their mind about who should represent them in the Homefire Overseas Final.

After a lot of to-ing and fro-ing (and a multitude of cross-Atlantic telephone calls) the in-form Greg Hancock and Bobby Ott were forced to sit on the sidelines, their World Championship hopes dashed without either of them turning a wheel in anger.

Instead 1991 American Champion Mike Faria flew across from California to join Sam Ermolenko, Ronnie Correy, Billy Hamill and Rick Miller at Brandon.

Faria and Hamill – who broke his wrist in his fourth ride when looking a likely qualifier for the next stage – were the two Yanks to miss the cut, along with Simon Wigg (one point only), Shane Parker and the Thorp(e)s, Paul and Mark!

At the other end of the scorechart there was a far more familiar look. Havvy first, Tatum third and, this time, the two Lions were separated by veteran Kiwi Mitch Shirra.

Paul Thorp made up for his disappointment at missing out by predicting: "Gary's good enough to win the World Final – but more important than that, he has the right mental approach to do it."

Havvy added: "I have gone out at this round in the last couple of seasons but I was confident and happy to have eight points at the interval. I thought that 13 or 14 would be enough, and it was."

His 13 points brought him his second World Championship title of the summer and luck favoured the brave when he was drawn at Bradford for the semi final, along with fellow Brits Andy Smith and Kelvin Tatum.

Only Martin Dugard (the last of the four home-grown survivors) would have to travel to Austria.

One big name who wouldn't be travelling anywhere was three-time World Champion Hans Nielsen who became the second of the great Danes to have been eliminated.

Nielsen, seeded to the Nordic Final after missing the Danish Final with a broken collar bone, struggled at Elgane, Norway, and scored only two points in his last three rides.

A heavy track didn't help but Nielsen offered no excuses: "From what I have read here and there the underlying message has been that I have slipped since I have changed engines from Godden to Jawa. That wasn't the reason I failed in Norway. I suppose it had to happen sooner or later, it's the first time for a very long time that I have not got through the Nordic Final."

It was, in fact, the first time that Nielsen had been eliminated at that stage since making his Scandinavian Final debut in 1979 and his run of 12 successive World Final appearances was over.

But at least he had got further than defending World Champion Jan O. Pedersen who joined the select band of title-holders who have not reached the following year's World Final.

He had suffered serious back injuries (a fractured vertebra) in an open meeting at Viborg on the eve of the two-day Danish Final.

While his Cradley Heath colleague Gert Handberg was collecting the first of his two victories, Pedersen was undergoing surgery and being told that he would not be able to ride again for the rest of the year.

With both Nielsen and Pedersen out of the World Championship the Scandinavian danger to Havelock was narrowing down to former champion Per Jonsson or one of his Swedish team-mates.

Jonsson was looking menacing as he raced through to the semi final draw. He won the Swedish qualifying round at Vetlanda, won two out of the three Swedish Final rounds and won a race-off for the silver medal at the Scandinavian

1992

NORDIC CHAMPION

Tony Rickardsson

(Ipswich & Sweden)

How Havvy hogged all the headlines

BRITISH SEMI FINAL
First, 15 points
BRITISH FINAL
First , 13 points
COMMONWEALTH FINAL
Third, 11 points
OVERSEAS FINAL
First, 13 points
SEMI FINAL
Second, 14 points
WORLD FINAL
First, 14 points

Final after stopping in his last ride when another three points would have deprived the slick-starting Handberg of the Nordic crown.

The semi final draw, made on Danish TV, threw the two favourites together at Odsal and it was Jonsson who claimed the psychological advantage.

He dropped a point to King's Lynn's Czechoslovakian international Bohumil Brhel in his opening outing but struck in heat nine with a victory over Havelock and repeated that performance when the pair of them met again in a first place run-off.

Two wins out of two for the Swede and, surely, a major boost to his chances of regaining the World Championship trophy he had lost to the unlucky Pedersen in 1991?

Unfortunately Bradford failed to live up to its 1990 World Final reputation as one of the finest racing strips of all and generally the action was lukewarm.

That is, until everyone totted up their scorecharts after heat 20 and realised that six riders had tied on eight points each...and only four of them could go through to the World Final!

A complicated elimination process saw John Jørgensen, Ronnie Correy, Zdenek Tesar and Henrik Gustafsson claim their top eight placings although Gustafsson's situation was further complicated by the performances of the three Polish semi finalists at Odsal, Miroslaw Kowalik, Piotr Swist and Piotr Paluch.

Under 1992 World Championship regulations the Poles had to have at least one World Finalist and if Kowalik's five points turned out to be better than Slawomir Drabik's return in the second semi in Vienna then Gustafsson would miss out!

After six days of worrying it was a relieved Henka who booked his World Final place as Drabik scored seven points in an Austrian semi dominated by title dark horse Gert Handberg.

The former World Under 21 Champion had competed in only four World Championship rounds on his way to Wroclaw: and won them all!

Handberg was the Austrian winner but Tommy Knudsen was the Vienna Wonder!

The Coventry skipper had been discharged from hospital only three days earlier after an operation to pin his fractured collar bone but still managed to garner enough points to climb onto the rostrum in third place, the two Danes split by American Sam Ermolenko who appeared to be coming towards his peak at a crucial time in the season.

England's Martin Dugard, who had survived a broken collar bone of his own in earlier rounds, seized an engine in his opening ride (he was still able to claim third place as Einar Kyllingstad had already been excluded) and had carburettor problems which forced him to pull out of his second.

He claimed six points from his last three rides, won a decider for the eighth qualifying slot but then missed out because of the home nation seeding ruling which saw him replaced in the last 16 by Drabik.

It left England with only two World Finalists: but one of them was Havelock!

Speedway's new order had taken over with Jonsson the only former World Champion in the field and World Final debutants in Havelock, Brian Karger, Drabik and Handberg.

In all the 16 qualifiers had only 37 previous World Final appearances between them to make it one of the most open championships of all time.

But could Havelock conquer tradition by becoming only the third rider to win the crown on his debut?

The early races, before the rains came, confirmed the belief that it could be anyone's title with six different names going down as race winners in the opening half dozen heats.

Knudsen became the first rider to win two races in heat seven and he was to remain unbeaten for nearly two hours as the meeting was halted after the cloudburst which left both the track and Wroclaw city centre awash.

At the time of the enforced stoppage the leaderboard read: Knudsen 6, Handberg 5, Ermolenko 4, Correy 4, Jonsson 3, Jørgensen 3, Havelock 3, Nilsen 3, Shirra 3, Rickardsson 3, Miller 2, Tesar 2, Karger 1, Gustafsson 1, Tatum 0, Drabik 0.

When Drabik came out to win the long-delayed re-run of heat eight the balance had swung in favour of Denmark.

A last place for Knudsen in heat 11 (won by Havvy) ended his realistic hopes but Handberg's success in heat 12 kept the pressure on the England skipper.

The title would be decided by their meeting in heat 14 and it was Havelock who speared into the first turn in front. The race was an anti-climax as Handberg trailed in third place until he was able to move past fellow Dane Brian Karger and, by then, it was too late to pressurise the leader.

Havelock was four laps away from that burning ambition and he never looked like letting the crown slip through his fingers as he had an untroubled tapes to flag victory that confirmed him as the 1992 World Champion, allowing him to watch the last three races which saw Per Jonsson leapfrog over Handberg in the shoot out for the minor placings.

AUSTRALIA

NORTHERN TERRITORY CHAMPIONSHIP (Alice Springs, Saturday, November 30, 1991): **Glen Baxter 15, Kelvin Willis 14**, Robbie Wark 13, Danny Wark 12, Murray Brown 10, Shane Aldrick 8, Marcus Gray 7, Rachael Jordan 6, Robert Harvey 6, Chris Boonstoppel 6, Daniel Leather 4, Ricky Parvinen 4, Michael Clausen 4, Kerrin Geizendanner 4, Marcus O'Cass 0.

Richard Carragher did not arrive.

Rachael Jordan became the first female rider to compete in the Australian rounds of the World Championship.

QUEENSLAND CHAMPIONSHIP (Brisbane, Sunday, December 1, 1991): **Troy Butler 14+3, Mark Carlson 14+2**, Tony Langdon 12+3, Darrin Winkler 12+2, Clinton Butler 11, Mark Pearce 10, Mick Powell 10, Darren Wade 8, Wayne Kennedy 5, Greg Davey 5, Paul Debona 5, Alan Rivett 4, Tom Smit 3, Rick Laycock 2, John Reid 1, Brian Vanerde 0. *Reserves: Tony Rose 3, Stephen Butler 0.*

The original staging of the meeting on Saturday, November 30, was abandoned because of rain.

WESTERN AUSTRALIAN CHAMPIONSHIP (Perth, Friday, December 6, 1991): **Glenn Doyle 30, Michael Carter 26**, Nigel Flatman 24.

SOUTH AUSTRALIAN CHAMPIONSHIP (North Arm, Adelaide, Friday, December 27, 1991): **Craig Hodgson 15, Shane Parker 14**, Ryan Sullivan 12, Damon Richardson 10, Scott Norman 9, Ashley Norton 9, Steve Graetz 9, Brett Tomkin 9, Darrel Branford 7, Troy Norvill 6, Mark Mitchell 4, Shaun Simpson 4, Paul Cooper 3, Paul Chevy 3, Adrian Champion 1, Russ Noble 1.

NEW SOUTH WALES CHAMPIONSHIP (Nepean, Sydney, Saturday, December 28, 1991): **Mick Poole 15, Craig Boyce 13**, Rodney Colquhoun 13, Todd Wiltshire 12, Scott Humphries 10, Matt Poole 10, Dave Edwards 9, Tony Primmer 8, Mick Holder 6, Neil Ashman 6, Jamie Plumb 5, Ty Platt 4, Darren Etheridge 3, Matt Gibson 2, Mark Unicomb 2, Matt Holder 0. *Reserve: Shane Haggerty 1.*

VICTORIAN CHAMPIONSHIP (Mildura, Sunday, December 29, 1991): **Leigh Adams 15, Jason Lyons 14**, Mark Lemon 13, Jason Hawkes 11, Jason Crump 10, Corey Alderton 10, Nigel Tremmeling 8, Gavin Sedgman 7, John McNeil 7, Reece Davison 6, Chris Barton 5, Stephen Knight 4, Nigel Alderton 3, Bob Farr 3, Shane Hamilton 2, Dean Cole 0. *Reserves: John Prior 2, Terry McGowan 0.*

Todd Wiltshire, Rodney Colquhoun, Tony Langdon and David Cheshire were seeded to the Australian Final.

AUSTRALIAN FINAL (North Arm, Adelaide, Sunday, January 26): **Leigh Adams 14, Shane Parker 13, Mark Carlson 11, Jason Lyons 10+3** Glenn Doyle 10+2, Tony Langdon 10+1, Craig Hodgson 8, Craig Boyce 8, Mick Poole 8, David Cheshire 7, Rodney Colquhoun 6, Troy Butler 6, Michael Carter 5, Glen Baxter 2, Kelvin Willis 0, Todd Wiltshire 0. *Reserves: Steve Graetz 1, Paul Schievenin 0.*

GREAT BRITAIN

QUALIFYING ROUND (Stoke, Saturday, April 11): **Dean Standing 14, Carl Blackbird 12, Nigel Crabtree 11, David Norris 11**, Alan Grahame 10, Michael Coles 9, Ray Morton 8, David Smart 8, Darren Standing 7, Gordon Kennett 6, Melvyn Taylor 6, Gary Chessell 6, Eric Monaghan 4, Mark Courtney 4, Sean Courtney 3, Mark Blackbird 0. *Reserves: Garry Stead 0, Mark Walsh 0.*

QUALIFYING ROUND (Exeter, Monday, April 13): Andrew Silver 11, Simon Cross 10, Alan Mogridge 10, Michael Warren 8+3, Richard Green 8, Alun Rossiter 7, Troy Pratt 7, Colin Cook 7, Martin Goodwin 6, Nigel Leaver 4, Andy Galvin 4, Mark Simmonds 3, Colin White 3, Paul Woods 3, Gary Tagg 2, Martin Dixon 0. Reserves: Richard Knight 2, Scott Pegler 1.

Meeting abandoned after 16 races because of a time limit at the County Ground. The result was declared by referee Barrie Richardson but reversed by the Speedway Control Board who ordered the meeting to be re-staged.

QUALIFYING ROUND (Middlesbrough, Thursday, April 16): **Paul Bentley 14, Darren Sumner 13, David Blackburn 12, Wayne Carter 11**, David Walsh 9+3, Nathan Simpson 9+2, Les Collins 8, Scott Lamb 8, Neville Tatum 7, Kenny McKinna 7, Carl Stonehewer 6, Duncan Chapman 5, Jamie Habbin 3, Andy Phillips 3, Scott Robson 3, Paul Whittaker 1. *Reserves: Jonathan Swales 1, Paul Pickering 0.*

Peter Carr and Neil Evitts withdrew.

QUALIFYING ROUND (Exeter, Monday, April 27): **Simon Cross 15, Alun Rossiter 14, Richard Green 12, Martin Goodwin 12, Troy Pratt 12**, Andrew Silver 9, Michael Warren 8, Alan Mogridge 8, Colin Cook 6, Mark Simmonds 6, Nigel Leaver 4, Gary Tagg 4, Paul Woods 4, Andy Galvin 3, David Steen 2, Colin White 1. *Reserves: Scott Pegler and Ian Humphreys, did not ride.*

Martin Dixon withdrew because of injury.

SEMI FINAL (Cradley Heath, Sunday, May 3): **Gary Havelock 15, Martin Dugard 14, Sean Wilson 11, Graham Jones 10, Andy Smith 10, Joe Screen 10, Marvyn Cox 9, Kelvin Tatum 9**, Alan Grahame 8, Darren Sumner 7, Troy Pratt 5, Martin Goodwin 5, Wayne Carter 3, Nigel Crabtree 3, Carl Blackbird 1, Simon Cross 0. *Reserves: Mark Robinson 0, Mark Meredith 0.*

John Davis withdrew because of injury; Neil Collins withdrew to ride for his club Glasgow.

SEMI FINAL (Ipswich, Sunday, May 3): **Chris Louis 15, Mark Loram 12, Jeremy Doncaster 11, David Mullett 10, Paul Thorp 9, Dean Barker 9, Simon Wigg 8+3, Alun Rossiter 8+2**, David Norris 8+1, David Blackburn 6, Richard Green 6, Dean Standing 6, Richard Knight 5, Steve Schofield 5, Paul Bentley 2, Andy Grahame 0. *Reserves: David Walsh 0, Lawrence Hare and Savalas Clouting, did not ride.*

HOMEFIRE BRITISH FINAL (Coventry, Sunday, May 17): **Gary Havelock 13+3, Martin Dugard 13+2, Andy Smith 11, Paul Thorp 10, Kelvin Tatum 10, Chris Louis 9, Marvyn Cox 9, Simon Wigg 7, Mark Loram 7, David Mullett 6+3** Dean Barker 6+2, Sean Wilson 5, Graham Jones 4, Jeremy Doncaster 4, Joe Screen 4, Alun Rossiter 1. *Track reserves: Scott Wormleighton 1, Chris Clarence 0. Reserves: David Norris and Alan Grahame, did not ride.*

> ■ ***DEAN Barker (Oxford) was the only rider to make his British Final debut in 1992.***
> ■ ***The record of number of British Final appearances is held by John Davis who competed in his SIXTEENTH British Final at Coventry in 1991.***

NEW ZEALAND

NEW ZEALAND FINAL (Napier, Saturday, January 25): Gary Allan 15, Mark Thorpe 14, Paul Atkins 13, Chris Martin 10, John Roberts 9, Mark Jamieson 9, Trevor Chapman 9, Mike Wilson 9, Steve Mudgeway 6, Barry Free 6, Dean Sullivan 6, Glen Sole 5, Robbie Price 4, Rhys Hamburger 3, Dan Ormsby 0, Justin Monk 0.

Mitch Shirra and Mark Thorpe were seeded to the Commonwealth Final.

ANCIT COMMONWEALTH FINAL (King's Lynn, England, Sunday, May 31): **Kelvin Tatum 11+3, Mark Thorpe 11+2, Gary Havelock 11+1, Marvyn Cox 10, Martin Dugard 9, Mitch Shirra 9, Simon Wigg 8, Paul Thorp 8, Jason Lyons 8, Andy Smith 7, Shane Parker 6+3**, Mark Loram 6+2, Chris Louis 5, Leigh Adams 5, David Mullett 5, Mark Carlson 1. *Track reserves: Darren Spicer and Emmerson Fairweather, did not ride.*

UNITED STATES OF AMERICA

The scheduled United States Final was cancelled. The AMA initially nominated Sam Ermolenko, Ronnie Correy, Billy Hamill, Greg Hancock and Bobby Ott for the Overseas Final after Kelly Moran had declined an invitation to compete. The selection was based on 1991 British League averages.

This decision was subsequently changed and nomination based on past performances at international and national championship level. The riders nominated were: Sam Ermolenko, Ronnie Correy, Billy Hamill, Rick Miller and Mike Faria.

HOMEFIRE OVERSEAS FINAL (Coventry, England, Sunday, June 14): **Gary Havelock 13, Mitch Shirra 11, Kelvin Tatum 11, Sam Ermolenko 10, Andy Smith 10, Martin Dugard 9, Jason Lyons 9, Rick Miller 8, Ronnie Correy 8,** Marvyn Cox 7+3, Shane Parker 7+2, Mike Faria 5, Billy Hamill 4, Paul Thorp 3, Mark Thorpe 3, Simon Wigg 1. *Reserves: Bobby Ott 0, Mark Loram, did not ride.*

DENMARK

SEMI FINAL (Korskro, Sunday, May 10): John Jørgensen 12, Brian Andersen 11, Bo Eriksen 11, Claus Jacobsen 11, Jan Andersen 10, Jan Pedersen 10, Lars Henrik Jørgensen 8+3, Rene Madsen 8+2, Jesper Olsen 8+1, Jacob Olsen 7, Henry Nielsen 6, Morten Andersen 5, Jens Peter Nielsen 4, Andre Larsen 3, Ole Hansen 2, Martin Back 0. *Reserves: Peter Larsen 4, Søren Damgård 0.*

DANISH FINAL 1 (Uhre, Saturday, May 16): Gert Handberg 14, Brian Karger 11, John Jørgensen 11, Peter Ravn 10, Tommy Knudsen 9, Brian Andersen 9, Claus Jacobsen 9, Allan Johansen 8, Bo Eriksen 8, Jan Andersen 5, Tom Knudsen 5, Jan Pedersen 4, Lars Jørgensen 4, Hans Clausen 3, Rene Madsen 3, Jan Stræchmann 1.

DANISH FINAL 2 (Holsted, Sunday, May 17): Gert Handberg 13, Brian Karger 12, John Jørgensen 12, Tommy Knudsen 12, Claus Jacobsen 10, Allan Johansen 10, Jan Stæchmann 9, Brian Andersen 9, Peter Ravn 9, Jan Andersen 5, Tom Knudsen 4, Hans Clausen 4, Jan Pedersen 4, Bo Eriksen 3, Lars Jørgensen 3, Rene Madsen 1.

Aggregate scorers: **Gert Handberg 27, Brian Karger 23+2, John Jørgensen 23+2, Tommy Knudsen 21, Claus Jacobsen 19+3,** Peter Ravn 19+2, Allan Johansen 18, Brian Andersen 18, Bo Eriksen 11, Jan Stæchmann 10, Jan Andersen 10, Tom Knudsen 9, Jan Pedersen 8, Hans Clausen 7, Lars Jørgensen 7, Rene Madsen 4.

Hans Nielsen was seeded to the Scandinavian Final. Peter Ravn went forward to a run-off at Scandinavian Final practice.

FINLAND

Vesa Ylinen and Juha Moksunen were seeded to the Scandinavian Final and Petri Kokko was nominated to a run-off at Scandinavian Final practice.

NORWAY

Lars Gunnestad and Einar Kyllingstad were seeded to the Scandinavian Final and Arnt Førland was nominated to a run-off at Scandinavian Final practice.

SWEDEN

QUALIFYING ROUND (Kumla, Saturday, May 9): **Kenneth Lindby 12, Henrik Gustafsson 12, Jimmy Nilsen 11, Christer Rohlen 10, Tony Olsson 10, Erik Stenlund 9, Patrik Olsson 8, Mikael Rittervall 8,** Joakim Karlsson 7+3, Claes Ivarsson 7+2, Lillebror Johansson 7+1, Peter Karlsson 7+0, Mikael Teurnberg 5, Magnus Oscarsson 4, Jimmy Engman 1, Stefan Lardner 1. *Reserves: Peter Johansson 1, Kent Richardsson 0.*

QUALIFYING ROUND (Vetlanda, Saturday, May 9): **Per Jonsson 12, Conny Ivarsson 12, Tony Rickardsson 11, Jörgen Johansson 11, Niklas Karlsson 11, Stefan Dannö 10, Peter Nahlin 9, Dennis Löfqvist 8,** Patrik Karlsson 6+3, Mikael Karlsson 6+2, Tommy Lindgren 5, Niklas Klingberg 5, Stefan Andersson 5, Jörgen Hultgren 4, Niklas Johansson 4, Göran Flood 1.

SWEDISH FINAL ROUND 1 (Målilla, Tuesday, May 19): Per Jonsson 14, Tony Rickardsson 13, Jimmy Nilsen 11, Peter Nahlin 10, Jörgen Johansson 9, Conny Ivarsson 9, Erik Stenlund 9, Tony Olsson 8, Kenneth Lindby 8, Mikael Rittervall 6, Christer Rohlen 6, Niklas Karlsson 5, Dennis Löfqvist 5, Patrik Olsson 4, Stefan Dannö 3, Joakim Karlsson 0.

SWEDISH FINAL ROUND 2 (Hagfors, Wednesday, May 20): Per Jonsson 14, Jimmy Nilsen 13, Peter Nahlin 12, Niklas Karlsson 11, Tony Rickardsson 10, Christer Rohlen 10, Jörgen Johansson 9, Stefan Dannö 8, Dennis Löfqvist 7, Erik Stenlund 6, Kenneth Lindby 5, Conny Ivarsson 5, Joakim Karlsson 4, Tony Olsson 3, Patrik Olsson 2, Mikael Rittervall 1.

SWEDISH FINAL ROUND 3 (Orebro, Thursday, May 21): Peter Nahlin 13, Jimmy Nilsen 12, Tony Rickardsson 12, Conny Ivarsson 11, Per Jonsson 10, Dennis Löfqvist 9, Tony Olsson 9, Jörgen Johansson 9, Christer Rohlen 7, Niklas Karlsson 6, Erik Stenlund 5, Mikael Rittervall 5, Joakim Karlsson 5, Patrik Olsson 2, Kenneth Lindby 2, Stefan Dannö 0.

*Aggregate: **Per Jonsson 38, Jimmy Nilsen 36, Tony Rickardsson 35, Peter Nahlin 35,** Jörgen Johansson 27, Conny Ivarsson 25, Christer Rohlen 23, Niklas Karlsson 22, Dennis Löfqvist 21, Tony Olsson 20, Erik Stenlund 20, Kenneth Lindby 15, Mikael Rittervall 12, Stefan Dannö 11, Joakim Karlsson 9, Patrik Olsson 8.*

Henrik Gustafsson was seeded to the Scandinavian Final. Jörgen Johansson went forward to a run off at the Scandinavian Final practice.

SCANDINAVIAN FINAL (Elgane, Norway, Sunday, June 14): **Tony Rickardsson 12, Per Jonsson 10+3, Brian Karger 10+2, John Jørgensen 10+1, Jimmy Nilsen 10+0, Henrik Gustafsson 9, Tommy Knudsen 9, Gert Handberg 9, Einar Kyllingstad 9,** Peter Nahlin 9, Lars Gunnestad 8, Hans Nielsen 6, Claus Jacobsen 4, Vesa Ylinen 3, Juha Moksunen 0, Peter Ravn 0.

The CONTINENT

PRELIMINARY ROUND 1 (Nyiregyhaza, Hungary, Sunday, April 26): **Sándor Tihanyi (Hungary) 15, László Bódi (Hungary) 12+3, Jacek Wozniak (Poland) 12+2, Zsolt Böszörmenyi (Hungary) 10, Rinat Mardanshin (CIS) 10, Oleg Kiptiev (CIS) 9, Piotr Pawlicki (Poland) 7+3, Karel Prusa (Czechoslovakia) 7+2,** Thomas Stadler (Austria) 7+1, Georgi Petranov (Bulgaria) 7+0, Heinrich Schatzer (Austria) 6, Marie Busch (Germany) 5, Roland Kolros (Germany) 4, Marius Soaita (Rumania) 3, Peter Durhammer (Austria) 1, Peter Hehlert (Germany) 1. *Reserves: Zsolt Kovacs (Hungary) 3, Attila Kovacs (Hungary) 1.*

PRELIMINARY ROUND 2 (Krsko, Slovenia, Sunday, April 26): **Andreas Bössner (Austria) 14, Igor Dubinin (CIS) 13, Armando Dal Chiele (Italy) 12, Andreas Rahn (Germany) 12, Jaroslaw Szymkowiak (Poland) 11, Piotr Paluch (Poland) 10, Kreso Omerzel (Yugoslavia) 10, Vladimir Trofimov (CIS) 10,** Gregor Pintar (Yugoslavia) 7, Massimo Mora (Italy) 6, Rob Steman (Holland) 4, Erik Drayer (Germany) 4, Torsten Berger (Germany) 3, Rudi Spitaler (Yugoslavia) 2, Gerhard Lekse (Yugoslavia) 2, Joerg Janssen (Germany) 0. *Reserve: Igor Hauptmann (Yugoslavia), did not ride.*

PRELIMINARY ROUND 3 (St. Johann i. Pongau, Austria, Friday, May 1): **René Aas (CIS) 14, Anton Pilotto (Austria) 13, Borivoj Hadek (Czechoslovakia) 12+3, Gaspar Forgac (Czechoslovakia) 12+2, Fabrizio Vesprini (Italy) 10, Walter Nebel (Austria) 8, Rainer Selb (Austria) 8, Helmut Lercher (Austria) 7+3,** Vitalj Efimov (CIS) 7+2, Thomas Meggle (Germany) 7+1, Martin Theobald (Germany) 6. Andreas Schapfl (Germany) 5, Christophe Dubernard (France) 5, Luis Albert Vallejos (Argentine) 3, Carsten Pelzmann (Germany) 2, David Ochocki (France) 1.

PRELIMINARY ROUND 4 (Ludwigslust, Germany, Sunday, April 26): **Miroslav Kowalik (Poland) 13, Phillippe Bergé (France) 12, Pavel Karnas (Czechoslovakia) 12, Jörg Pingel (Germany) 11, Andrej Korolov (Latvia) 10, Mike Ott (Germany) 10, Robert Sawina (Poland) 9, Andrea Maida (Italy) 9,** Valentino Furlanetto (Italy) 8, Thomas Diehr (Germany) 8, Sergei Kuzmini (CIS) 6, Alexei Morosov (CIS) 5, Mario Trupkovic (Germany) 2, Rene Elzinga (Holland) 1, Henk Bangma (Holland) 1, Juris Brauceje (Latvia) 0. *Reserve: Ralf Baumann (Germany) 0.*

QUALIFYING ROUND A (Stralsund, Germany, Sunday, May 24): **Sándor Tihanyi 12, Antonin Kasper (Czechoslovakia) 11+3, László Bódi 11+2, Zdenek Schneiderwind (Czechoslovakia) 10, Mikhail Starostin (CIS) 10, Jacek Wozniak (Poland) 9, Vaclav Milik (Czechoslovakia) 9, Karel Prusa 9,** Zsolt Böszörmenyi 8, Robert Barth (Germany) 7, André Pollehn (Germany) 7, Robert Csillick (Hungary) 5, Rinat Mardanshin 5, Oleg Kiptiev 3, Csaba Hell (Hungary) 2, Thomas Stadler 1. *Piotr Pawlicki withdrew because of injury.*

QUALIFYING ROUND B (Zielona Góra, Poland, Sunday, May 24): **Zoltan Adorján (Hungary) 15, Andrzej Huszcza (Poland) 13, Roman Matousek (Czechoslovakia) 12+3, Zdenek Tesar (Czechoslovakia) 12+2, Zoltan Hajdu (Hungary) 10, Slawomir Drabik (Poland) 10, Piotr Swist (Poland) 9, Piotr Paluch 7+3,** Andreas Bössner 7+2, Armando Dal Chiele 7+1, Jaroslaw Szymkowiak 6, Lubomir Jedek (Czechoslovakia) 5, Igor Dubinin 3, Andreas Rahn 3, Vladimir Trofimov 1, Kreso Omerzel 0. *Reserves: Gregor Pintar 0, Slawomir Dudek (Poland) 0.*

QUALIFYING ROUND C (Zarnovica, Czechoslovakia, Sunday, May 24): **Bohumil Brhel (Czechoslovakia) 13+3, Tomasz Gollob (Poland) 13+2, Jozsef Petrikovics (Hungary) 11+3, Petr Vandirek (Czechoslovakia) 11+2, Jacek Krzyzaniak (Poland) 11+1, Jaroslaw Olszewski (Poland) 10, Vladimir Kalina (Czechoslovakia) 9, Borivoj Hadek (Czechoslovakia) 9,** Zoltan Kovacs 8, René Aas 7, Anton Pilotto 4, Fabrizio Vesprini 4, Gaspar Forgac 4, Walter Nebel 1, Rainer Selb 1, Helmut Lercher 1.

QUALIFYING ROUND D (Neustadt-Donau, Germany, Sunday, May 24): **Gerd Riss (Germany) 14, Antal Kocso (Hungary) 13, Oleg Kurguskin (CIS) 11, Valentino Furlanetto 10, Robert Nagy (Hungary) 10, Miroslaw Kowalik (Poland) 9, Robert Sawina 9, Armando Castagna (Italy) 8,** Rif Saitgareev (CIS) 8, Mike Ott 8, Jörg Pingel 5, Tommy Dunker (Germany) 4, Franz Leitner (Austria) 4, Andrea Maida 4, Phillippe Bergé 2, Andrej Korolov (Latvia) 1. *Pavel Karnas did not ride.*

CONTINENTAL SEMI FINAL (Miskolc, Hungary, Sunday, June 14): **Zdenek Tesar 11+3, Slawomir Drabik 11+2, Roman Matousek 11+1, Antonin Kasper 11+0, Piotr Swist 10, Piotr Paluch 10, Zdenek Schneiderwind 10,** Mikhail Starostin 9, Zoltan Hajdu 8, Vaclav Milik 8, Zsolt Böszörmenyi 7, László Bód 3, Andrzej Huszcza 3, Karel Prusa 3, Zoltan Adorján 2, Jacek Wozniak 1.

CONTINENTAL SEMI FINAL (Brokstedt, Germany, Sunday, June 14): **Antal Kocso 14, Robert Nagy 12, Bohumil Brhel 9, Gerd Riss 8, Jozsef Petrikovics 8, Petr Vandirek 8, Miroslaw Kowalik 8,** Robert Sawina 8, Vladimir Kalina 7, Borivoj Hadek 6, Tomasz Gollob 6, Armando Castagna 6, Jacek Krzyzaniak 5, Jaroslaw Olszewski 5, Valentino Furlanetto 5, Oleg Kurguskin 4.

SEMI FINALS

SEMI FINAL 1 (Bradford, Sunday, August 9): **Per Jonsson 14+3, Gary Havelock 14+2, Kelvin Tatum 11, Jimmy Nilsen 9, Ronnie Correy 8+3, John Jørgensen 8+3, Zdenek Tesar 8+R+3, Henrik Gustafsson 8+1+2,** Antal Kocso 8+2+F, Bohumil Brhel 8+2+fx, Andy Smith 7, Miroslaw Kowalik 5, Jason Lyons 5, Roman Matousek 4, Piotr Swist 2, Piotr Paluch 1. *Reserves: Marvyn Cox and Robert Sawina, did not ride.*

SEMI FINAL 2 (Wiener Neustadt, Austria, Saturday, August 15): **Gert Handberg 15, Sam Ermolenko 14, Tommy Knudsen 11, Rick Miller 10, Tony Rickardsson 10, Brian Karger 9, Mitch Shirra 9,** Martin Dugard 7+3, Robert Nagy 7+2, Gerd Riss 7+1, **Slawomir Drabik 7+0,** Antonin Kasper 5, Jozsef Petrikovics 3, Einar Kyllingstad 3, Petr Vandirek 2, Zdenek Schneiderwind 1. *Reserve: Peter Nahlin 0.*

Slawomir Drabik was seeded to the World Final as the highest scoring Polish entrant.

WORLD FINAL

Olympic Stadium,
Wroclaw, Poland
Saturday, August 29, 1992

1 Gary Havelock	**3**	**2**	**3**	**3**	**3**	**14**
2 Per Jonsson	0	3	2	3	3	11
3 Gert Handberg	3	2	3	2	0	10
4 Henrik Gustafsson	1	0	2	3	3	9
4 Tommy Knudsen	3	3	0	1	2	9
6 John Jørgensen	2	1	0	3	2	8
7 Jimmy Nilsen	3	X	3	0	1	7
8 Sam Ermolenko	1	3	1	X	2	7
9 Kelvin Tatum	0	0	3	1	2	6
10 Slawomir Drabik	E	3	2	1	X	6
11 Rick Miller	0	2	2	2	E	6
12 Ronnie Correy	2	2	0	1	1	6
12 Mitch Shirra	2	1	1	2	0	6
14 Zdenek Tesar	1	1	1	2	0	5
14 Tony Rickardsson	2	1	1	0	1	5
16 Brian Karger	1	0	0	0	3	4

Reserves: Martin Dugard and Antal Kocso did not ride.

WINNERS ALL ... Gary Havelock, Per Jonsson and Gert Handberg celebrate their rostrum placings in the longest-ever World Final

1991

WORLD CHAMPION

Jan O. Pedersen

(Cradley Heath & Denmark)

1936 (Wembley, England)
1 LIONEL VAN PRAAG 26 (14:12), 2 Eric Langton 26 (13:13), 3 Bluey Wilkinson 25 (15:10), 4 Cordy Milne 20 (11:9), 5 Frank Charles 20 (8:12), 6 Dick Case 17 (8:9), 7 Jack Ormston 17 (8:9), 8 Vic Huxley 17 (7:10), 9 George Newton 16 (4:12), 10 Jack Milne 15 (6:9), 11 Bob Harrison 15 (5:10), 12 Morian Hansen 15 (5:10), 13 Wal Phillips 12 (5:7), 14 Ginger Lees 11 (4:7), 15 Arthur Atkinson 9 (3:6), 16 Bill Pitcher 8 (2:6) 17 Norman Parker, reserve, 7 (1:6).
Balzer Hansen, reserve, did not ride.
Jack Parker (12 BP) and Joe Abbott (7 BP) qualified for World Final. Ron Johnson (7BP) should have stepped up from reserve but was unfit to ride.

1937 (Wembley, England)
1 JACK MILNE 28 (15:13), 2 Wilbur Lamoreaux 25 (13:12), 3 Cordy Milne 23 (12:11), 4 Jack Parker 21 (10:11), 5 Ginger Lees 19 (9:10), 6 Frank Charles 17 (7:10), 7 Lionel Van Praag 17 (6:11), 8 Bill Kitchen 16 (9:7), 9 George Newton 16 (5:11), 10 Eric Langton 16 (4:12), 11 Morian Hansen 15 (8:7), 12 Eric Chitty 15 (4:11), 13 Joe Abbott 14 (6:8), 14 Arthur Atkinson 14 (6:8), 15 Frank Varey 11 (3:8), 16 Tommy Croombs 2 (2:0), 17 Alec Statham, reserve, 0 (0:0).
Ron Johnson, reserve, did not ride.
Bob Harrison (7BP) qualified for World Final. Stan Greatrex qualified as reserve.

1938 (Wembley, England)
1 BLUEY WILKINSON 22 (14:8), 2 Jack Milne 21 (14:7), 3 Wilbur Lamoreaux 20 (13:7), 4 Lionel Van Praag 18 (11:7), 5 Bill Kitchen 15 (9:6), 6 Cordy Milne 15 (8:7), 7 Alec Statham 13 (8:5), 8 Eric Langton 13 (8:5), 9 Benny Kaufman 12 (7:5), 10 Jack Parker 10 (6:4), 11 Arthur Atkinson 10 (5:5), 12 Tommy Price 8 (4:4), 13 Tommy Croombs 8 (4:4), 14 George Newton 7 (2:5), 15 Geoff Pymar 7 (2:5), 16 Jack Ormston, reserve, 5 (5:0), 17 Frank Varey 4 (0:4).
Jimmy Gibb, reserve, did not ride.

1939 (Wembley, England)
Meeting abandoned because of the outbreak of war.
Finalists with their qualifying points and bonus points were: Cordy Milne 53:8, Eric Langton 51:7, Wilbur Lamoreaux 50:7, Bill Kitchen 47:7, Vic Duggan 45:6, Lionel Van Praag 44:6, Arthur Atkinson 40:6, Jack Milne 40:6, Alec Statham 36:5, Jack Parker 34:5, Benny Kaufman 33:5, Eric Chitty 32:5, Ron Johnson 32:5, Frank Varey 31:4, Eric Collins 30:4, Aub Lawson 30:4. Reserves: Gil Craven 26:3, Frank Goulden 24.3.

Pre-war finalists carried forward bonus points based on their qualifying totals and these were included in their overall World Final score. Bonus points are listed in the results above after the World Final score.
From 1937-1938 bonus points were NOT carried forward by riders who did not finish among the 16 World Final qualifiers therefore, in 1937, Tommy Croombs and Alec Statham had no bonus points on World Final night and a similar situation applied to Jack Ormston in 1938.

1949 (Wembley, England)
1 TOMMY PRICE 15, 2 Jack Parker 14, 3 Louis Lawson 13, 4 Norman Parker 10, 5 Wilbur Lamoreaux 9, 6 Bill Kitchen 9, 7 Ron Clarke 8, 8 Aub Lawson 8, 9 Bill Longley 8, 10 Cyril Roger 7 11 Bill Gilbert 6, 12 Graham Warren 5, 13 Ken Le Breton 4, 14 Lloyd Goffe 2, 15 Cliff Watson 1, 16 Oliver Hart, reserve, 1, 17 Dent Oliver 0.
Alec Statham, reserve, did not ride.

1950 (Wembley, England)
1 FREDDIE WILLIAMS 14, 2 Wally Green 13, 3 Graham Warren 12, 4 Aub Lawson 10, 5 Tommy Price 8, 6 Jack Parker 8, 7 Split Waterman 8, 8 Ronnie Moore 7, 9 Jack Young 7, 10 Cyril Brine 7, 11 Dent Oliver 6, 12 Cyril Roger, reserve, 5, 13 Danny Dunton 5, 14 Vic Duggan 4, 15 Jack Biggs 3, 16 Ron Clarke 3,17 Arthur Payne 0, 18 Mike Erskine, reserve, 0.
Arthur Forrest qualified as first reserve.

1951 (Wembley, England)
1 JACK YOUNG 12, 2 Split Waterman 12, 3 Jack Biggs 12, 4 Ronnie Moore 11, 5 Jack Parker 10, 6 Louis Lawson 10, 7 Eddie Rigg 8, 8 Bob Leverenz 7, 9 Freddie Williams 7, 10 Aub Lawson 7, 11 Jeff Lloyd 6, 12 Eric Williams 6, 13 Cyril Brine 3, 14 Norman Parker 3 ,15 Dick Bradley, reserve, 2, 16 Ernie Roccio 2, 17 Alan Hunt 2.
Geoff Mardon, reserve, did not ride.

1952 (Wembley, England)
1 JACK YOUNG 14, 2 Freddie Williams 13, 3 Bob Oakley 12, 4 Ronnie Moore 10, 5 Dick Bradley 9, Dan Forsberg 9, Arthur Payne 9, 8 Arthur Forrest 7, 9 Henry Long 7, 10 Jeff Lloyd 7, 11 Brian Crutcher 6, 12 Split Waterman 6, 13 Graham Warren 5, 14 Derek Close 4, 15 Cyril Roger 2 ,16 Ron How 0.
Trevor Redmond and Basse Hveem reserves, did not ride.
Bert Roger and Alan Hunt qualified.

1953 (Wembley, England)
1 FREDDIE WILLIAMS 14, 2 Split Waterman 13, 3 Geoff Mardon 12, 4 Olle Nygren 12, 5 Jack Young 10, 6 Ronnie Moore 9, 7 Jeff Lloyd 8, 8 Arthur Forrest 7, 9 Aub Lawson 7, 10 Brian Crutcher 6, 11 Rune Sörmander 5, 12 Graham Warren 5, 13 Eric Williams 4, 14 Alan Hunt 3, 15 Dick Bradley 2, 16 Jack Biggs 2, 17 Dent Oliver, reserve 1.
Arthur Payne, reserve, did not ride.

1954 (Wembley, England)
1 RONNIE MOORE 15, 2 Brian Crutcher 13, 3 Olle Nygren 13, 4 Jack Young 11, 5 Split Waterman 9, 6 Barry Briggs 9, 7 Eddie Rigg 7, 8 Fred Brand 7, 9 Jack Biggs 7, 10 Arthur Forrest 5, 11 Tommy Price 5, 12 Geoff Mardon 5, 13 Trevor Redmond 5, 14 Aub Lawson 4, 15 Peter Craven 3, 16 Ove Fundin 2.
Alan Hunt and Freddie Williams, reserves, did not ride.

1955 (Wembley, England)
1 PETER CRAVEN 13, 2 Ronnie Moore 12, 3 Barry Briggs 12, 4 Eric Williams 12, 5 Brian Crutcher 10, 6 Jack Young 10, 7 Ove Fundin 10, 8 Olle Nygren 9, 9 Arthur Forrest 7, 10 Arthur Wright 6, 11 Billy Bales 6, 12 Ron Johnson 6, 13 Kjell Carlsson 3,14 Phil Clarke 2,15 Henry Andersen 2, 16 Cyril Roger 0.
Ken McKinlay and Gerry Hussey, reserves, did not ride.

1956 (Wembley, England)
1 OVE FUNDIN 13, 2 Ronnie Moore 12, 3 Arthur Forrest 11, 4 Peter Craven 11, 5 Peo Söderman 10, 6 Ken McKinlay 10, 7 Barry Briggs 10, 8 Brian Crutcher 9, 9 Peter Moore 8, 10 Eric Boothroyd 7, 11 Alan Hunt 6, 12 Dick Fisher 5, 13 Doug Davies 4,14 Olle Andersson 2, 15 Ulf Ericsson 2, 16 Gerry Hussey 0.
Jack Biggs and Nigel Boocock, reserves, did not ride.

1957 (Wembley, England)
1 BARRY BRIGGS 14, 2 Ove Fundin 14, 3 Peter Craven 11, 4 Aub Lawson 11, 5 Rune Sörmander 11, 6 Ron Johnston 9, 7 Ken McKinlay 8, 8 Bob Roger 8, 9 Peo Söderman 7, 10 Jack Geran 7,11 Ron How 7, 12 Aage Hansen 4, 13 George White 4,14 Ian Williams 3, 15 Dan Forsberg 2, 16 Josef Hofmeister 0.
Brian Crutcher and Jack Biggs, reserves, did not ride.

1958 (Wembley, England)
1 BARRY BRIGGS 15, 2 Ove Fundin 13, 3 Aub Lawson 11, 4 Peter Craven 11, 5 Ken McKinlay 11, 6 Ronnie Moore 9, 7 Olle Nygren 9, 8 Ron Johnston 8, 9 Gerry Hussey 7, 10 Ron How 7, 11 Peter Moore 5, 12 Mike Broadbank 5, 13 Rune Sörmander 4, 14 Jack Geran 3, 15 Josef Hofmeister 2, 16 Joel Jansson 0.
Brian Crutcher and Peo Söderman, reserves, did not ride.

1959 (Wembley, England)
1 RONNIE MOORE 15, 2 Ove Fundin 13, 3 Barry Briggs 11, 4 Olle Nygren 11, 5 Aub Lawson 11, 6 Brian Crutcher 10, 7 Arne Carlsson 8, 8 George White 7, 9 Peter Craven 7, 10 Geoff Mardon 6, 11 Rune Sörmander 6, 12 Mieczyslaw Polukard 5, 13 Josef Hofmeister 4, 14 Peter Moore 3, 15 Ron How 3, 16 Cyril Roger 0.
Ken McKinlay and Florian Kapala, reserves, did not ride.

1960 (Wembley, England)
1 OVE FUNDIN 14, 2 Ronnie Moore 14, 3 Peter Craven 14, 4 Peter Moore 12, 5 Ron Johnston 10, 6 Barry Briggs 9, 7 Stefan Kwoczala 8, 8 Josef Hofmeister 6, 9 Ken McKinlay 6, 10 Jack Young 6, 11 Chum Taylor 5, 12 Rune Sörmander 5, 13 Henryk Zyto 4, 14 Aub Lawson 4, 15 Bob Andrews, reserve, 2, 16 Marian Kaiser 1, 17 Bryan Elliott 0.
Mieczyslaw Polukard, reserve, did not ride.

1961 (Malmö, Sweden)
1 OVE FUNDIN 14, 2 Björn Knutsson 12, 3 Göte Nordin 12, 4 Barry Briggs 12, 5 Ronnie Moore 10, 6 Bob Andrews 10, 7 Florian Kapala 8, 8 Rune Sörmander 7, 9 Ron How 7, 10 Peter Craven 6, 11 Ken McKinlay 5, 12 Cyril Maidment 4, 13 Igor Plechanov 4, 14 Ray Cresp 3, 15 Stanislaw Tkocz 3, 16 Mike Broadbank 2.
Jack Young and Leif Larsson, reserves, did not ride.
Josef Hofmeister qualified.

1962 (Wembley, England)
1 PETER CRAVEN 14, 2 Barry Briggs 13, 3 Ove Fundin 10, 4 Björn Knutsson 10, 5 Ronnie Moore 9, 6 Bob Andrews 9, 7 Ken McKinlay 9, 8 Göte Nordin 9, 9 Sören Sjösten 8, 10 Igor Plechanov 7, 11 Rune Sörmander 7, 12 Ron How 6, 13 Arne Carlsson 3, 14 Mike Broadbank 2, Ron Mountford 2, Pawel Waloszek 2.
Nigel Boocock and Henryk Zyto, reserves, did not ride.

1963 (Wembley, England)
1 OVE FUNDIN 14, 2 Björn Knutsson 13, 3 Barry Briggs 12, 4 Boris Samorodov 11, 5 Göte Nordin 10, 6 Sverre Harrfeldt 10, 7 Nigel Boocock 8, 8 Leo McAuliffe 7, 9 Ron How 7, 10 Peter Craven 6, 11 Peter Moore 6, 12 Peo Söderman 5, 13 Dick Fisher 5, 14 Jim Lightfoot 4, 15 Per Tage Svensson 1, 16 Arne Carlsson 1.
Tadeusz Teodorowicz and Ron Mountford, reserves, did not ride.
Antonin Kasper (sen), qualified as reserve.

1964 (Gothenburg, Sweden)
1 BARRY BRIGGS 15, 2 Igor Plechanov 13, 3 Ove Fundin 13, 4 Boris Samorodov 11, 5 Björn Knutsson 10, 6 Ron How 10, 7 Cyril Maidment 8, 8 Gennady Kurilenko 7, 9 Mike Broadbank 6, 10 Nigel Boocock 6, 11 Ken McKinlay 6, 12 Andrzej Wyglenda 4, 13 Bob Andrews 4, 14 Zbigniew Podlecki 3, 15 Jaroslav Volf 3, 16 Dick Fisher 1.
Jim Lightfoot and Göte Nordin, reserves, did not ride.

1965 (Wembley, England)
1 BJÖRN KNUTSSON 14, 2 Igor Plechanov 13, 3 Ove Fundin 13, 4 Barry Briggs 10, 5 Bengt Jansson 10, 6 Brian Brett 9, 7 Sören Sjösten 9, 8 Nigel Boocock 8, 9 Andrzej Pogorzelski 7, 10 Antonin Woryna 6, 11 Leif Larsson 5, 12 Reg Luckhurst 5, 13 Ken McKinlay 4, 14 Jimmy Gooch 3, 15 Andrzej Wyglenda 2, 16 Lubos Tomicek 2.
Mike Broadbank and Marian Rose, reserves, did not ride.

1966 (Gothenburg, Sweden)
1 BARRY BRIGGS 15, 2 Sverre Harrfeldt 14, 3 Antonin Woryna 13, 4 Ivan Mauger 11, 5 Torbjörn Harrysson 10, 6 Göte Nordin 9, 7 Leif Enecrona 8, 8 Igor Plechanov 8, 9 Stanislaw Tkocz 7, 10 Björn Knutsson 5, 11 Marian Kaiser 5, 12 Andrzej Pogorzelski 5, 13 Mike Broadbank 4, 14 Leif Larsson 3, 15 Nigel Boocock 2, 16 Peo Söderman 1.
Bengt Brannefors and Ken McKinlay, reserves, did not ride.

1967 (Wembley, England)
1 OVE FUNDIN 14, 2 Bengt Jansson 14, 3 Ivan Mauger 13, 4 Igor Plechanov 12, 5 Barry Briggs 11, 6 Anders Michanek 9, 7 Eric Boocock 9, 8 Ray Wilson 7, 9 Andrzej Pogorzelski 6, 10 Bernt Persson 6, 11 Antonin Woryna 5, 12 Rick France 5, 13 Colin Pratt 4, 14 Jerzy Trzeszkowski 3, 15 Andrzej Wyglenda 2, 16 Jochen Dinse 0.
Mike Broadbank and Jan Holub, reserves, did not ride.

1968 (Gothenburg, Sweden)
1 IVAN MAUGER 15, 2 Barry Briggs 12, 3 Edward Jancarz 11, 4 Gennady Kurilenko

11, 5 Pawel Waloszek 10, 6 Torbjörn Harrysson 10, 7 Anders Michanek 9, 8 Hasse Holmkvist 9, 9 Ove Fundin 7, 10 Gunnar Malmkvist 7, 11 Martin Ashby 5, 12 Antonin Woryna 5, 13 Reidar Eide 3, 14 Jerzy Trzeszkowski 3, 15 Nigel Boocock 1, 16 Bernt Persson 1.

Bengt Jansson and Igor Plechanov, reserves, did not ride.

1969 (Wembley, England)
1 IVAN MAUGER 14, 2 Barry Briggs 11, 3 Sören Sjösten 11, 4 Nigel Boocock 10, 5 Hasse Holmkvist 10, 6 Edward Jancarz 9, 7 Ove Fundin 9, 8 Ken McKinlay 7, 9 Andrzej Pogorzelski 7, 10 Jan Mucha 7, 11 Ronnie Moore 6, 12 Henryck Glucklich 5, 13 Valeri Klementiev 4, 14 Torbjörn Harrysson 4, 15 Zbigniew Podlecki, reserve, 3, 16 Andrzej Wyglenda 2, 17 Howard Cole 1.

Arnold Haley, reserve, did not ride.

1970 (Wroclaw, Poland)
1 IVAN MAUGER 15, 2 Pawel Waloszek 14, 3 Antonin Woryna 13, 4 Sören Sjösten 9, 5 Henryck Glucklich 9, 6 Valeri Klementiev 8, 7 Barry Briggs 7, 9 Andrzej Wyglenda 7, 9 Anders Michanek 7, 10 Ole Olsen 6, 11 Jan Mucha 6, 12 Hans Jurgen Fritz 5, 13 Vladimir Gorceev 5, 14 Edmund Migos, reserve, 4, 15 Zygfryd Friedek 2, 16 Gennady Kurilenko 2, 17 Trevor Hedge 0.

Juri Dubinin and Jerzy Szczakiel qualified. Ronnie Moore qualified as reserve.

1971 (Gothenburg, Sweden)
1 OLE OLSEN 15, 2 Ivan Mauger 12, 3 Bengt Jansson 12, 4 Ray Wilson 11, 5 Anders Michanek 11, 6 Bernt Persson 9, 7 Jim Airey 8, 8 Sören Sjösten 8, 9 Nigel Boocock 6, 10 Ronnie Moore 5, 11 Eric Boocock 4, 12 Leif Enecrona 4, 13 Jiri Stancl 3, 14 Tommy Jansson 1 15 Jerzy Szczakiel 0.

Tony Lomas and Göte Nordin, reserves, did not ride.

■ *Vladimir Gordeev finished fifth on 11 points but was subsequently disqualified by the FIM after tests showed he had used the banned fuel additive nitro-methane.*

1972 (Wembley, England)
1 IVAN MAUGER 13, 2 Bernt Persson 13, 3 Ole Olsen 12, 4 Christer Löfqvist 11, 5 John Louis 11, 6 Alexander Pavlov 8, 7 Anders Michanek 8, 8 Pawel Waloszek 6, 9 Viktor Trofimov 6, 10 Nigel Boocock 6, 11 Viktor Kalmykov 6, 12 Antoli Kuzmin 4, 13 Grigori Khlinovski 4, 14 Barry Briggs 3, 15 Eric Boocock 2, Jan Simensen, reserve, 2, 17 Valeri Gordeev 2, Jim McMillan, reserve, 2.

1973 (Katowice, Poland)
1 JERZY SZCZAKIEL 13, 2 Ivan Mauger 13, 3 Zenon Plech 12, 4 Ole Olsen 11, 5 Grigori Khlinovski 10, 6 Vladimir Paznikov 8, 7 Pawel Waloszek 8, 8 Valeri Gordeev 7, 9 Jan Mucha 7, 10 Anders Michanek 6, 11 Edward Jancarz 6, 12 Peter Collins 6, 13 John Boulger 6, 14 Ray Wilson 5, 15 Vladimir Zaplecznу 2, 16 Tommy Jansson, reserve, 0, Andrzej Wyglenda, reserve, 0, Bernt Persson 0.

1974 (Gothenburg, Sweden)
1 ANDERS MICHANEK 15, 2 Ivan Mauger 11, 3 Sören Sjösten 11, 4 John Louis 9, 5 Bengt Jansson 8, 6 Peter Collins 9, 7 Tommy Johansson 8, 8 Zenon Plech 8, 9 Christer Löfqvist 8, 10 Grigori Khlinovski 6, 11 Dag Lövaas 6, 12 Terry Betts 6, 13 Dave Jessup 5, 14 Tommy Jansson, reserve, 3, 15 Mikhail Krasnov 3, 16 Ole Olsen 2, 17 Edward Jancarz, reserve, 1, 18 Vladimir Gordeev 0.

1975 (Wembley, England)
1 OLE OLSEN 15, 2 Anders Michanek 13, 3 John Louis 12, 4 Ivan Mauger 12, 5 Peter Collins 10, 6 Phil Crump 10, 7 Malcolm Simmons 10, 8 Viktor Trofimov 8, 9 Tommy Jansson 7, 10 Bernt Persson 5, 11 Ray Wilson 5, 12 Edward Jancarz 4, 13 Valeri Gordeev 4, 14 Zenon Plech 4, 15 Marek Cieslak 1, 16 Vladimir Gordeev, reserve, 0, Henryck Glucklich 0.

Martin Ashby, reserve, did not ride.

1976 (Katowice, Poland)
1 PETER COLLINS 14, 2 Malcolm Simmons 13, 3 Phil Crump 12, 4 Ivan Mauger 11, 5 Zenon Plech 11, 6 John Louis 9, 7 Doug Wyer 8, 8 Egon Müller 8, 9 Scott Autrey 7, 10 Jiri Stancl 6, 11 Chris Morton 6, 12 Edward Jancarz 5, 13 Marek Cieslak 4, 14 Jerzy Rembas 3, 15 Anders Michanek 2, 16 Valeri Gordeev 1, 17 Vladimir Gordeev 0.

Grigori Khlinovski, reserve, did not ride.

1977 (Gothenburg, Sweden)
1 IVAN MAUGER 14, 2 Peter Collins 13, 3 Ole Olsen 12, 4 Michael Lee 12, 5 Finn Thomsen 10, 6 Bengt Jansson 9, 7 Egon Müller 8, 8 Anders Michanek 8, 9 Billy Sanders 6, 10 Tommy Nilsson 6, 11 Bernt Persson 6, 12 John Boulger 5, 13 Edward Jancarz 4, 14 Jiri Stancl 3, 15 Jan Mucha 1, Jan Verner 1.

John Davis, Sören Karlsson and Boguslaw Nowak, reserves, did not ride.

Vladimir Rozanczuk qualified as reserve.

1978 (Wembley, England)
1 OLE OLSEN 13, 2 Gordon Kennett 12, 3 Scott Autrey 11, 4 Dave Jessup 11, 5 Jerzy Rembas 11, 6 Malcolm Simmons 10, 7 Michael Lee 9, 8 Ivan Mauger 8, 9 John Titman 7, 10 Anders Michanek 7, 11 Ilkka Teromaa 6, 12 Marek Cieslak 5, 13 Jan Verner 5, 14 Jan Andersson 3, 15 Jiri Stancl 2, 16 Petr Ondrasik 0.

Steve Bastable, Zdenek Kudrna and Bernt Persson, reserves, did not ride.

Hans Wassermann qualified.

1979 (Katowice, Poland)
1 IVAN MAUGER 14, 2 Zenon Plech 13, 3 Michael Lee 11, 4 Kelly Moran 11, 5 Billy Sanders 11, 6 Ole Olsen 11, 7 Zdenek Kudrna 8, 8 Dave Jessup 8, 9 Edward Jancarz 7, 10 Finn Thomsen 6, 11 Peter Collins 6, 12 John Titman 6, 13 Mikhail Starostin 3, 14 Robert Slabon 2, Christoph Betzl 2, 16 Alois Wiesböck 1.

Petr Ondrasik and Larry Ross, reserves, did not ride.

1980 (Gothenburg, Sweden)
1 MICHAEL LEE 14, 2 Dave Jessup 12, 3 Billy Sanders 12, 4 Jan Andersson 11, 5 Bruce Penhall 9, 6 John Davis 9, 7 Kai Niemi 8, 8 Chris Morton 8, 9 Peter Collins 8, 10 Finn Thomsen 7, 11 Hans Nielsen 7, 12 Ales Dryml 5, 13 Jiri Stancl 5, 14 Egon Müller 4, 15 Zenon Plech 1, 16 Petr Ondrasik 0.

Hasse Danielsson, Ole Olsen and Vaclav Verner, reserves, did not ride.

1981 (Wembley, England)
1 BRUCE PENHALL 14, 2 Ole Olsen 12, 3 Tommy Knudsen 12, 4 Erik Gundersen 11, 5 Kenny Carter 11, 6 Jan Andersson 9, 7 Egon Müller 9, 8 Dave Jessup 7, 9 Hans Nielsen 6, 10 Michael Lee 5, 11 Chris Morton 5, 12 Edward Jancarz 5, 13 Larry Ross 4, 14 Ales Dryml 3, 15 Zenon Plech 3, 16 Jiri Stancl 3, 17 Henryck Olszak, reserve, 0.

Preben Eriksen, reserve, did not ride.

1982 (Los Angeles, United States of America)
1 BRUCE PENHALL 14, 2 Les Collins 13, 3 Dennis Sigalos 12, 4 Kelly Moran 11, 5 Kenny Carter 10, 6 Dave Jessup 8, 7 Hans Nielsen 8, 8 Jan Andersson 8, 9 Jiri Stancl 7, 10 Edward Jancarz 7, 11 Georg Hack 6, 12 Kai Niemi 5, 13 Peter Collins 5, 14 Phil Crump 4, 15 Vaclav Verner 2, 16 Mikhail Starostin 0.

Andy Grahame and Emil Sova, reserves, did not ride.

1983 (Norden, West Germany)
1 EGON MÜLLER 15, 2 Billy Sanders 12, 3 Michael Lee 11, 4 Erik Gundersen 10, 5 Kenny Carter 10, 6 Ole Olsen 10, 7 Hans Nielsen 9, 8 Dennis Sigalos 8, 9 Karl Maier 8, 10 Chris Morton 7, 11 Mitch Shirra 7, 12 Lance King 4, 13 Phil Collins 4, 14 Antonin Kasper (jun) 3, 15 Zenon Plech 1, 16 Jiri Stancl 1.

Henny Kroeze and Peter Ravn, reserves, did not ride.

Petr Ondrasik qualified.

1984 (Gothenburg, Sweden)
1 ERIK GUNDERSEN 14, 2 Hans Nielsen 13, 3 Lance King 13, 4 Kelly Moran 11, 5 Mitch Shirra 10, 6 Simon Wigg 9, 7 Bo Petersen 9, 8 Shawn Moran 7, 9 Karl Maier 7, 10 Jan Andersson 6, 11 Alan Grahame, reserve, 5, 12 Billy Sanders 5, 13 Kai Niemi 4, 14 Petr Ondrasik 3, 15 Egon Müller 3, 16 Jiri Stancl 1, 17 Vaclav Verner 0.

Tommy Nilsson, reserve, did not ride.

Edward Jancarz qualified.

1985 (Bradford, England)
1 ERIK GUNDERSEN 13, 2 Hans Nielsen 13, 3 Sam Ermolenko 13, 4 Kai Niemi 10, 5 Shawn Moran 10, 6 Tommy Knudsen 10, 7 John Cook 9, 8 Kelvin Tatum 8, 9 Jan O. Pedersen 7, 10 Jan Andersson 7, 11 Lance King 6, 12 Egon Müller 5, 13 Armando Castagna 4, 14 Zoltán Adorján 2, 15 Viktor Kuznetsov 2, 16 Karl Maier 1.

Phil Collins and Grzegorz Dzikowski, reserves, did not ride.

1986 (Katowice, Poland)
1 HANS NIELSEN 14, 2 Jan O. Pedersen 13, 3 Kelvin Tatum 12, 4 Jimmy Nilsen 11, 5 Tommy Knudsen 10, 6 Viktor Kuznetsov 10, 7 Sam Ermolenko 9, 8 Chris Morton 8, 9 Neil Evitts 8, 10 Erik Gundersen 7, 11 Ryszard Dolomisiewicz 6, 12 Marvyn Cox 3, 13 Karl Maier 3, 14 Antonin Kasper (jun) 2, 15 Armando Castagna 2, 16 Mitch Shirra 1, 17 Petr Vandirek, reserve, 1.

Jan Andersson, reserve, did not ride.

1987 (Amsterdam, Holland)
1 HANS NIELSEN 27 (12:15), 2 Erik Gundersen 24 (13:11), 3 Sam Ermolenko 24 (13:11), 4 Jimmy Nilsen 22 (9:13), 5 Per Jonsson 22 (11:11), 6 Jeremy Doncaster 20 (12:8), 7 Jan O. Pedersen 19 (10:9), 8 John Cook 15 (7:8), 9 Mitch Shirra 12 (7:5), 10 Gerd Riss 12 (4:8), 11 Simon Cross 10 (7:3), 12 Antonin Kasper (jun) 9 (5:4), 13 Chris Morton 9 (5:4), 14 Roman Jankowski 8 (0:8), 15 Roman Matousek 5 (3:2), 16 Henny Kroeze 1 (1:0), 17 Peter Ravn, reserve, 1 (1:N).

Vladimir Trofimov and Peter Seur, reserves, did not ride.

1988 (Vojens, Denmark)
1 ERIK GUNDERSEN 14, 2 Hans Nielsen 14, 3 Jan O. Pedersen 13, 4 Sam Ermolenko 12, 5 Per Jonsson 9, 6 Simon Wigg 9, 7 Roman Matousek 8, 8 Kelvin Tatum 8, 9 Conny Ivarsson 7, 10 Chris Morton 6, 11 Antal Kocso 6, 12 John Davis 3, 13 John Jørgensen 3, 14 Zenon Kasprzak 3, 15 Sándor Tihanyi 3, 16 Roman Jankowski 2.

Simon Cross and Andrzej Huszcza, reserves, did not ride.

1989 (Munich, West Germany)
1 HANS NIELSEN 15, 2 Simon Wigg 12, 3 Jeremy Doncaster 12, 4 Erik Gundersen 11, 5 Kelvin Tatum 10, 6 Mitch Shirra 10, Andy Smith 10, 8 Tony Olsson 8, 9 Gerd Riss 5, 10 Roman Matousek 5, 11 Karl Maier 5, 12 Troy Butler 4, Olli Tyrvainen 4, 14 Ronnie Correy 4, 15 Zoltán Adorján 4, 16 Bohumil Brhel 1.

Jozsef Petrikovics and Peter Ravn, reserves, did not ride.

Jan O. Pedersen qualified. Andy Grahame qualified as reserve but did not travel.

1990 (Bradford, England)
1 PER JONSSON 13, 3 Todd Wiltshire 12, 4, Hans Nielsen 11, 5 Jimmy Nilsen 10, 6 Henrik Gustafsson 9, 6 Kelvin Tatum 9, 8 Armando Castagna 8, 8 Rick Miller 8, 10 Richard Knight 7, 11 Martin Dugard 6, 12 Roman Matousek 5, 13 Zoltán Adorján 2, 13 Zdenek Tesar 2, 15 Ronnie Correy 2, 15 Antonin Kasper 2.

Dennis Löfqvist and Sándor Tihanyi, reserves, did not ride.

Jan O. Pedersen and Gerd Riss qualified.

■ *Shawn Moran competed in the World Final, scored 13 points and lost a run-off for the title. He was subsequently stripped of his placing after giving a positive drugs test at the Overseas Final. The FIM decided not to upgrade the remaining finalists and the records will show no silver medal issued.*

1991 (Gothenburg, Sweden)
1 JAN O. PEDERSEN 15, 2 Tony Rickardsson 12, 3 Hans Nielsen 11 +3, 4 Tommy Knudsen 11 +2, 5 Jimmy Nilsen 10, 6 Paul Thorp 10, 7 Sam Ermolenko 9, 8 Kelvin Tatum 8, 9 Per Jonsson 7, 10 Ronnie Correy 6, 11 Armando Castagna 6, 12 Billy Hamill 6, 13 Mitch Shirra 4, 14 Roman Matousek 2, 14 Jeremy Doncaster 2, 16 Gerd Riss 1, 17 Michael Blixt 0.
Gert Handberg, reserve, did not ride.

1992 (Wroclaw, Poland)
1 GARY HAVELOCK 14, 2 Per Jonsson 11, 3 Gert Handberg 10, 4 Henrik Gustafsson 9, Tommy Knudsen 9, 6 John Jørgensen 8, 7 Jimmy Nilsen 7, 8 Sam Ermolenko 7, 9 Kelvin Tatum 6, 10 Slawomir Drabik 6, 11 Rick Miller 6, 12 Ronnie Correy 6, Mitch Shirra 6, 14 Zdenek Tesar 5, Tony Rickardsson 5, 16 Brian Karger 4.
Martin Dugard and Antal Kocso, reserves, did not ride.

● *Where available official placings are taken from FIM records.*

WORLD FINAL RECORDS...WORLD FINAL RECORDS

Wins:* *Six, Ivan Mauger, 1968, 1969, 1970, 1972, 1977, 1979.

Appearances:* *Eighteen, Barry Briggs, 1954, 1955, 1956, 1957, 1958, 1959, 19670, 1961, 1962, 1963, 1964, 1965, 1966, 1967, 1968, 1969, 1970, 1972.

Points: 201, Barry Briggs (see above).

Winning on Debut: Lionel Van Praag (1936), Freddie Williams (1950), Gary Havelock (1992).

Disqualifications: Shawn Moran, 1990, failing drugs test at earlier round. Vladimir Gordeev, 1971, using an additive in his fuel.

ENGLAND'S WORLD CHAMPIONS

KINGS OF THE TRACK

↖ **TOMMY PRICE**
England's first World Champion in 1949

↙ **PETER CRAVEN**
The only two time winner, successful in 1955 and 1962

↗ **PETER COLLINS**
He ended a barren 13 years with his 1976 victory

↘ **MICHAEL LEE**
Victorious in Sweden in 1980

STARRY-EYED

JOHN Scott took the biggest gamble of his career in charge of American team affairs when he ignored the World Team Cup claims of newly-crowned Swedish Champion John Cook.

Cowboy Cookie, racing regularly in Sweden, had been crowned national champion only a fortnight before the World Team Cup Final...with a 15-point maximum at staging track Kumla.

It was a performance that tempted the urbane Scott to pick him for the final five-rider squad but he resisted that temptation explaining: "It would be morally wrong because all the riders racing in Britain have been aiming their sights on the World Team Cup Final.

"It would be bad for their morale and ethically bad to bring Cookie in, as well as he has been riding in Sweden."

But in the end Cook did have a vital role to play in America's second victory in three seasons as he ignored any disappointment he may have felt to be on hand in the pits with careful advice and invaluable knowledge.

Gold medal winner Greg Hancock said: "We owe a lot to Cookie. He passed on hints and told us what the track does."

That advice turned out to be golden as the Americans recovered from an unimpressive start to storm through to a relatively comfortable win with a string of mid and late-meeting race winners.

Hancock began with a new track record in heat one and picked up another race win in his second ride but he was the only Californian charmer in the first nine races!

After four races England had dropped only two points to lead with 10 points, Sweden were second on seven, America third with five, and a sadly depleted Denmark (without the injured Jan O. Pedersen and Tommy Knudsen) had only two points, courtesy of a Hans Nielsen second place.

Eight heats gone and England still led from Sweden with the Yanks in third and Denmark a poor fourth with only Nielsen (five points) on the scoresheet!

And that became the turning point of the entire afternoon as the organisers held an interval during which the tractors came out and dragged away much of the loose dirt that had been so to the liking of the youngest ever Homefire Lions World Team Cup squad.

Martin Dugard kept the flag flying with race wins in both heats nine and 13 but the intervening three heats brought England a mere three points with reserve Kelvin Tatum replacing Joe Screen.

After starting off so well England didn't provide a single three-pointer in any of the last seven races as America and Sweden fought it out for first place.

Successive victories from Sam Ermolenko, Ronnie Correy and Billy Hamill in heats 16, 17 and 18, virtually sealed it and the celebrations began before the last race was over when hero Hancock could afford to finish in third place and still step up for his second gold medal of the season.

While America were celebrating another success – to add to their World Pairs triumph – one can only imagine the thoughts of former World Champion Erik Gundersen as he witnessed, first hand, the demise of Denmark.

Ravaged by injuries to Gundersen, Jan O. Pedersen and Tommy Knudsen, the Danes were a one man band and this was one occasion when not even Hans Nielsen could inspire his team-mates.

The Main Dane won three of his five races, scored 11 of his country's paltry 17 points and will now have to start his 1993 World Team Cup challenge in Group A alongside Australia, Czechoslovakia and the Group B winners.

That's where England's 1992 challenge had begun following their demotion the previous season.

Whether the Danes can make such light work of the task as the Brits did remains to be seen.

England, boosted by home track advantage with the single Group A round being held at King's Lynn, never looked anything other than winners.

Mark Loram won the opening race on his home track and that set the pattern for the rest of the meeting with only Martin Dugard struggling to make a real impact.

Joe Screen, in his World Team Cup debut, relished the heavy going with a spectacular 13 points (beaten only by Bohumil Brhel in his first ride and Antal Kocso in his second) while Loram was beaten twice by Jason Lyons and skipper Gary Havelock picked up 14 points from his five rides, being beaten by only Brhel who used his home track knowledge to his best advantage.

Australia consolidated their ranking in the world's top six nations with a fine performance, highlighted by consistent all-round scoring from each of their five selected riders, but neither Czechoslovakia nor Hungary were at the races.

The Czechs carried too many passengers to be any real threat and the Magyars were anything but magical on an afternoon when a wet track was obviously more to the liking of the home riders than anyone else.

The growing internationalism of speedway had been reflected in the early rounds of the World Team Cup with France staging a meeting in Group D and Latvia and Slovenia entering teams following the Iron Curtain revolution.

Neither progressed beyond the preliminary stages with Austria winning Group D, and then returning to the opening round when they were hopelessly outclassed by Poland, Italy and Finland in the following stage of the competition. Poland survived in a higher group (principally due to the 28 out of 30 points scored by Tomasz Gollob) but Germany continued their slide backwards with relegation to Group C in 1993.

1992

WORLD TEAM CHAMPIONS

U.S.A.

Bobby Ott, Billy Hamill, John Scott (manager), Ronnie Correy, Greg Hancock, John Cook, Sam Ermolenko

WORLD TEAM CUP GROUP D

ROUND 1 (Marmande, France, Monday, April 20):1 AUSTRIA 33 (Andreas Bössner 17, Heinrich Schatzer 9, Walter Nebel 7) 2 HOLLAND 27 (Rob Steman 16, Ronnie Koppe 7, Rene Elzinga 4) 3 FRANCE 22 (Phillippe Bergé 15, David Ochocki 4, Christophe Dubernard 3) 4 LATVIA 20 (Andrej Korolov 12, Juris Brauceje 6, Valeri Sokolov 2) 5 SLOVENIA17 (Gregor Pintar 9, Kreso Omerzel 5, Igor Hauptmann 3).

ROUND 2 (Ljubljana, Slovenia, Sunday, May 3):1 AUSTRIA 43 (Andreas Bössner 18, Walter Nebel 16, Heinrich Schatzer 9) 2 FRANCE 23 (Phillippe Bergé 11, Christophe Dubernard 9, David Ochocki 3) and SLOVENIA 23 (Gerhard Lekse 11, Gregor Pintar 8, Kreso Omerzel 4) 4 HOLLAND 15 (Rene Elzinga 6, Rob Steman 5, Henk Bangma 4) and LATVIA 15 (Andrej Korolov 9, Valeri Sokolov 4, Juris Brauceje 2).

*Aggregate: **AUSTRIA 76,** France 45, Holland 42, Slovenia 40, Latvia 35. AUSTRIA progress to Group C.*

WORLD TEAM CUP GROUP C

ROUND 1 (Leszno, Poland, Sunday, May 10):1 POLAND 53 (Tomasz Gollob 15, Piotr Swist 15, Piotr Pawlicki 11, Miroslaw Kowalik 9, Jaroslaw Olszewski 3) 2 ITALY 31 (Armando Dal Chiele 9, Valentino Furlanetto 8, Andrea Maida 7, Paolo Salvatelli 7, Fabrizio Vesprini 0) 3 FINLAND 24 (Vesa Ylinen 9, Juha Moksunen 9, Mika Pellinen 4, Petri Nurmesniemi 2, Tomi Havu 0) 4 AUSTRIA 12 (Heinrich Schatzer 6, Andreas Bössner 4, Franz Leitner 2, Walter Nebel 0).

ROUND 2 (Seinajoki, Finland, Sunday, May 31):1 POLAND 50 (Piotr Swist 14, Tomasz Gollob 12, Jacek Krzyzaniak 11, Miroslaw Kowalik 9, Jaroslaw Olszewski 4) 2 ITALY 33 (Paolo Salvatelli 9, Armando Castagna 9, Armando Dal Chiele 5, Andrea Maida 5, Valentino Furlanetto 5) 3 FINLAND 24 (Vesa Ylinen 9, Juha Moksunen 6, Olli Tyrvainen 6, Marko Hyyrylainen 2, Petri Nurmesniemi 1) 4 AUSTRIA 13 (Andreas Bössner 8, Heinrich Schatzer 3, Thomas Stadler 1, Franz Leitner 1).

*Aggregate: **POLAND 103,** Italy 64, Finland 48, Austria 25. POLAND progress to Group B. Austria relegated to Group D in 1993.*

WORLD TEAM CUP GROUP B

ROUND 1 (Elgane, Norway, Sunday, June 21):1 NORWAY 35 (Lars Gunnestad 12, Arnt Førland 11, Einar Kyllingstad 10, Atle Knudsen 1, Robert Langeland 1) 2 HUNGARY 31 (Zoltan Hajdu 9, Jozsef Petrikovics 9, Zoltan Adorján 7, László Bódi 6) 3 POLAND 30 (Tomasz Gollob 14, Jacek Krzyzaniak 6, Slawomir Drabik 5, Miroslaw Kowalik 3, Piotr Paluch 2) 4 GERMANY 25 (Gerd Riss 9, Robert Barth 7, Carsten Pelzmann 5, Thomas Meggle 4).

ROUND 2 (Landshut, Germany, Saturday, June 27):1 HUNGARY 38 (Jozsef Petrikovics 9, Zoltan Adorján 9, Zoltan Hajdu 8, László Bódi 6, Antal Kocso 6) 2 POLAND 36 (Tomasz Gollob 14, Piotr Swist 8, Jacek Krzyzaniak 8, Slawomir Drabik 5, Robert Sawina 1) 3 GERMANY 27 (Gerd Riss 9, Klaus Lausch 7, Robert Barth 6, Thomas Meggle 3, Carsten Pelzmann 2) 4 NORWAY 19 (Lars Gunnestad 9, Einar Kyllingstad 6, Atle Knudsen 2, Robert Langeland 2, WIlli Tjessem 0).

*Aggregate: **HUNGARY 69,** Poland 66, Norway 54, Germany 52. HUNGARY progress to Group A. Germany relegated to Group C in 1993.*

WORLD TEAM CUP GROUP A

ROUND 1 (King's Lynn, England, Sunday, September 6):1 ENGLAND 48 (Gary Havelock 14, Joe Screen 13, Mark Loram 13, Kelvin Tatum 5, Martin Dugard 3) 2 AUSTRALIA 35 (Jason Lyons 11, Leigh Adams 9, Glenn Doyle 8, Craig Boyce 4, Shane Parker 3) 3 CZECHOSLOVAKIA 23 (Bohumil Brhel 8, Zdenek Tesar 7, Roman Matousek 4, Petr Vandirek 4, Vaclav Milik 0) 4 HUNGARY 14 (Antal Kocso 7, Robert Nagy 3, Zoltan Adorján 2, Jozsef Petrikovics 2, Sándor Tihanyi 0).

ENGLAND progress to the World Team Cup Final. Hungary relegated to Group B in 1993.

WORLD TEAM CUP FINAL
Kumla, Sweden, Saturday, September 19

1 UNITED STATES OF AMERICA 39						
Sam Ermolenko	1	1	3	3	2	10
Ronnie Correy	1	N	1	N	3	5
Billy Hamill	0	2	3	2	3	10
Greg Hancock	3	3	2	2	1	11
Bobby Ott	2	1				3
2 SWEDEN 33						
Tony Rickardsson	2	1	2	0	2	7
Per Jonsson	3	3	0	3	2	11
Henrik Gustafsson	1	2	3	3	3	12
Jimmy Nilsen	1	N	N	N	0	1
Peter Nahlin	1	1	X			2
3 ENGLAND 31						
Gary Havelock	2	1	2	1	1	7
Mark Loram	3	2	0	2	0	7
Joe Screen	2	F	N	N	N	2
Martin Dugard	3	3	3	3	0	12
Kelvin Tatum	1	1	1			3
4 DENMARK 17						
Hans Nielsen	2	3	1	2	3	11
Gert Handberg	0	X	0	0		0
Brian Karger	0	0	2	0	1	3
John Jørgensen	0	0	N	1	0	1
Morten Andersen	0	2				2

Denmark relegated to Group A in 1993.

CALLED UP ... Eastbourne's Peter Nahlin

1960 (Gothenburg, Sweden)
1 SWEDEN 44 (Ove Fundin 12, Olle Nygren 12, Rune Sörmander 11, Björn Knutsson 9) 2 Great Britain 30 (Peter Craven 8, Ken McKinlay 8, Ron How 7, George White 6, Nigel Boocock 1) 3 Czechoslovakia 15 (Antonin Kasper 5, Lubos Tomicek 4, Jaroslav Machac 3, Frantisek Richter 3) 4 Poland 7 (Konstanty Pociejkowicz 3, Marian Kaiser 2, Mieczyslaw Polukard 2, Jan Malinowski 0, Bronislaw Rogal 0).

UNBEATEN ... Ove Fundin led Sweden to victory in the first ever World Team Cup Final

1961 (Wroclaw, Poland)
1 POLAND 32 (Marian Kaiser 10, Henryk Zyto 7, Florian Kapala 6, Mieczyslaw Polukard 5, Stanislaw Tkocz 4) 2 Sweden 31 (Ove Fundin 11, Rune Sörmander 10, Björn Knutsson 7, Per Tage Svensson 3) 3 Great Britain 21 (Peter Craven 8, Bob Andrews 6, Ken McKinlay 4, Ron How 3) 4 Czechoslovakia 12 (Lubos Tomicek 7, Antonin Kasper 4, Bohumil Bartonek 1, Stanislav Svoboda 0).

1962 (Slany, Czechoslovakia)
1 SWEDEN 36 (Björn Knutsson 10, Sören Sjösten 10, Ove Fundin 9, Göte Nordin 4, Rune Sörmander 3) 2 Great Britain 24 (Ronnie Moore 10, Barry Briggs 8, Peter Craven 6, Ron How 0, Cyril Maidment 0) 3 Poland 20 (Marian Kaiser 9, Florian Kapala 5, Joachim Maj 4, Pawel Waloszek 2, Mieczyslaw Polukard 0) 4 Czechoslovakia 16 (Lubos Tomicek 7, Bedrich Slany 4, Jaroslav Volf 3, Karel Prusa 2).

1963 (Vienna, Austria)
1 SWEDEN 37 (Björn Knutsson 11, Peo Söderman 10, Ove Fundin 7, Göte Nordin 6, Rune Sörmander 3) 2 Czechoslovakia 27 (Antonin Kasper 10, Stanislaw Kubicek 7, Miroslaw Smid 5, Lubos Tomicek 5) 3 Great Britain 25 (Barry Briggs 12, Peter Craven 8, Dick Fisher 4, Peter Moore 1) 4 Poland 7 (Henryk Zyto 4, Marian Kaiser 1, Stanislaw Tkocz 1, Joachim Maj 1, Andrzej Pogorzelski 0).

1964 (Abensberg, West Germany)
1 SWEDEN 34 (Björn Knutsson 11, Göte Nordin 10, Rune Sörmander 7, Ove Fundin 6, Sören Sjösten 0) 2 Soviet Union 25 (Igor Plechanov 8, Gennady Kurilenko 8, Yuri Czekranov 6, Boris Samorodov 3) 3 Great Britain 21 (Barry Briggs 9, Ken McKinlay 7, Nigel Boocock 3, Ron How 2, Brian Brett 0) 4 Poland 16 (Andrzej Wyglenda 8, Andrzej Pogorzelski 3, Zbigniew Podlecki 3, Marian Rose 2, Marian Kaiser 0).

1965 (Kempten, West Germany)
1 POLAND 38 (Andrzej Wyglenda 11, Andrzej Pogorzelski 11, Antonin Woryna 9, Zbigniew Podlecki 7) 2 Sweden 33 (Björn Knutsson 11, Ove Fundin 8, Bengt Jansson 8, Göte Nordin 6) 3 Great Britain 18 (Ken McKinlay 7, Nigel Boocock 6, Jimmy Gooch 3, Barry Briggs 1, Charlie Monk 1) 4 Soviet Union 7 (Vladimir Sokolov 2, Yuri Czekranov 2, Gennady Kurilenko 2, Igor Plechanov 1, Viktor Trofimov 0).

1966 (Wroclaw, Poland)
1 POLAND 41 (Andrzej Wyglenda 11, Antonin Woryna 11, Marian Rose 11, Andrzej Pogorzelski 8, Edmund Migos 0) 2 Soviet Union 25 (Boris Samorodov 9, Viktor Trofimov 6, Igor Plechanov 6, Farid Szajnurow 4) 3 Sweden 22 (Björn Knutsson 11, Leif Enecrona 4, Göte Nordin 3, Ove Fundin 2, Leif Larsson 2) 4 Great Britain 8 (Nigel Boocock 4, Ivan Mauger 3, Barry Briggs 1, Terry Betts 0, Colin Pratt 0).

1967 (Malmö, Sweden)
1 SWEDEN 32 (Göte Nordin 11, Bengt Jansson 9, Ove Fundin 6, Torbjörn Harrysson 6) 2 Poland 26 (Antonin Woryna 10, Andrzej Wyglenda 9, Jerzy Trzeszkowski 4, Zbigniew Podlecki 3, Andrzej Pogorzelski 0) 3 Great Britain 19 (Barry Briggs 8, Eric Boocock 5, Ray Wilson 4, Ivan Mauger 2, Colin Pratt 0) and Soviet Union 19 (Igor Plechanov 9, Viktor Trofimov 4, Boris Samorodov 3, Gabdrahman Kadirov 2, Farid Szajnurow 1).

1968 (Wembley, England)
1 GREAT BRITAIN 40 (Ivan Mauger 12, Nigel Boocock 10, Martin Ashby 8, Barry Briggs 7, Norman Hunter 3) 2 Sweden 30 (Ove Fundin 11, Bengt Jansson 7, Anders Michanek 7, Olle Nygren 3, Torbjörn Harrysson 2) 3 Poland 19 (Edmund Migos 8, Edward Jancarz 6, Andrzej Wyglenda 2, Henryck Glucklich 2, Pawel Waloszek 1) 4 Czechoslovakia 7 (Antonin Kasper 3, Lubos Tomicek 2, Jaroslav Volf 1, Jan Holub 1).

1969 (Rybnik, Poland)
1 POLAND 31 (Andrzej Wyglenda 11, Edward Jancarz 11, Stanislaw Tkocz 4, Henryck Glucklich 3, Andrzej Pogorzelski 2) 2 Great Britain 27 (Ivan Mauger 9, Barry Briggs 8, Nigel Boocock 5, Martin Ashby 5) 3 Soviet Union 23 (Vladimir Smirnov 9, Gennady Kurilenko 8, Valeri Klementiev 5, Yuri Dubinin 1, Viktor Trofimov 0) 4 Sweden 12 (Anders Michanek 7, Ove Fundin 2, Sören Sjösten 2, Bengt Jansson 1).

1970 (Wembley, England)
1 SWEDEN 42 (Ove Fundin 11, Bengt Jansson 11, Anders Michanek 10, Sören Sjösten 10) 2 Great Britain 31 (Barry Briggs 11, Ivan Mauger 9, Eric Boocock 5, Ray Wilson 4, Nigel Boocock 2) 3 Poland 20 (Jan Mucha 6, Antonin Woryna 5, Edmund Migos 4, Henryck Glucklich 3, Pawel Waloszek 2) 4 Czechoslovakia 3 (Vaclav Verner 3, Miroslav Verner 0, Jiri Stancl 0, Zdenek Majstr 0, Jan Holub 0).

1971 (Wroclaw, Poland)
1 GREAT BRITAIN 37 (Ray Wilson 12, Ivan Mauger 10, Jim Airey 9, Barry Briggs 6) 2 Soviet Union 22 (Grigori Khlinovski 8, Vladimir Smirnov 7, Vladimir Gordeev 4, Anatoli Kuzmin 3) 3 Poland 19 (Pawel Waloszek 5, Henryck Glucklich 4, Antonin Woryna 4, Edward Jancarz 4, Andrzej Wyglenda 2) 4 Sweden 18 (Anders Michanek 9, Sören Sjösten 3, Bengt Jansson 3, Leif Enecrona 3, Bernt Persson 0).

1972 (Olching, West Germany)
1 GREAT BRITAIN 36 (Ivan Mauger 11, John Louis 9, Ray Wilson 8, Terry Betts 8) 2 Soviet Union 21 (Anatoli Kuzmin 6, Grigori Khlinovski 5, Viktor Trofimov 5, Viktor Kalmykov 5) 3 Poland 21 (Zenon Plech 7, Henryck Glucklich 6, Pawel Waloszek 5, Zdislaw Dobrucki 3, Marek Cieslak 0) 4 Sweden 18 (Christer Löfqvist 6, Anders Michanek 4, Tommy Jansson 4, Jan Simensen 3, Göte Nordin 1). /

■ *In two races to decide second place the Soviet Union scored 7 points and Poland 5. Individual scorers: Kalmykov 3, Kuzmin 2, Khlinovski 1, Trofimov 1; Waloszek 3, Plech 2, Glucklich 0, Dobrucki 0.*

1973 (Wembley, England)
1 GREAT BRITAIN 37 (Peter Collins 12, Terry Betts 9, Malcolm Simmons 8, Ray Wilson 8) 2 Sweden 31 (Anders Michanek 11, Bernt Persson 9, Bengt Jansson 6, Tommy Jansson 5) 3 Soviet Union 20 (Vladimir Gordeev 7, Vladimir Paznikov 5, Grigori Khlinovski 4, Alexander Pavlov 2, Viktor Trofimov 2) 4 Poland 8 (Zenon Plech 5, Edward Jancarz 2, Pawel Waloszek 1, Jerzy Szczakiel 0).

1974 (Chorzow, Poland)
1 ENGLAND 42 (Peter Collins 12, John Louis 12, Dave Jessup 10, Malcolm Simmons 8) 2 Sweden 31 (Sören Sjösten 10, Anders Michanek 9, Tommy Jansson 7, Christer Löfqvist 5) 3 Poland 13 (Zenon Plech 4, Jan Mucha 4, Andrzej Jurczynski 3, Andrzej Tkocz 2, Jerzy Szczakiel 0) 4 Soviet Union 10 (Mikhail Krasnov 5, Valeri Gordeev 4, Viktor Kalmykov 1, Anatoli Kuzmin 0).

1975 (Norden, West Germany)
1 ENGLAND 41 (Peter Collins 12, Malcolm Simmons 11, Martin Ashby 10, John Louis 8) 2 Soviet Union 29 (Valeri Gordeev 8, Viktor Trofimov 8, Grigori Khlinovski 8, Vladimir Gordeev 5) 3 Sweden 17 (Anders Michanek 8, Tommy Jansson 4, Bernt Persson 2, Sören Sjösten 2, Sören Karlsson 1) 4 Poland 9 (Marek Cieslak 4, Henryck Glucklich 2, Jerzy Rembas 2, Edward Jancarz 1, Zenon Plech 0).

1976 (White City, England)
1 AUSTRALIA 31 (Phil Crump 11, Billy Sanders 7, Phil Herne 7, John Boulger 6) 2 Poland 28 (Edward Jancarz 9, Marek Cieslak 7, Zenon Plech 6, Jerzy Rembas 5, Boleslaw Proch 1) 3 Sweden 26 (Anders Michanek 11, Bernt Persson 8, Lars-Ake Andersson 5, Bengt Jansson 1, Christer Löfqvist 1) 4 Soviet Union 11 (Valeri Gordeev 5, Grigori Khlinovski 2, Vladimir Gordeev 2, Vladimir Paznikov 2, Viktor Trofimov 0).

HUR-ROO ... Phil Crump led Australia to their one and only World Team Cup victory

1977 (Wroclaw, Poland)
1 ENGLAND 37 (Peter Collins 10, Michael Lee 9, Dave Jessup 9, John Davis 6, Malcolm Simmons 3) 2 Poland 25 (Edward Jancarz 10, Jerzy Rembas 6, Boguslaw Nowak 6, Marek Cieslak 2, Ryszard Fabiszewski 1) 3 Czechoslovakia 23 (Jiri Stancl 8, Vaclav Verner 5, Jan Verner 5, Ales Dryml 5) 4 Sweden 11 (Anders Michanek 5, Bernt Persson 4, Bengt Jansson 2, Tommy Nilsson 0, Sören Karlsson 0).

1978 (Landshut, West Germany)
1 DENMARK 37 (Hans Nielsen 11, Ole Olsen 10, Mike Lohmann 9, Finn Thomsen 7) 2 England 27 (Malcolm Simmons 8, Peter Collins 6, Dave Jessup 5, Michael Lee 5, Gordon Kennett 3) 3 Poland 16 (Edward Jancarz 6, Marek Cieslak 5, Jerzy Rembas 3, Zenon Plech 1, Andrzej Huszcza 1) 4 Czechoslovakia 16 (Jiri Stancl 7, Jan Verner 5, Vaclav Verner 2, Ales Dryml 2).

Jancarz beat Stancl in a run-off for third place.

1979 (White City, London)
1 NEW ZEALAND 35 (Larry Ross 11, Mitch Shirra 10, Ivan Mauger 9, Bruce Cribb 5) 2 Denmark 31 (Ole Olsen 12, Hans Nielsen 9, Mike Lohmann 6, Finn Thomsen 4, Bo Petersen 0) 3 Czechoslovakia 19 (Jiri Stancl 6, Ales Dryml 5, Zdenek Kudrna 4, Vaclav Verner 4) 4

Poland 11 (Piotr Pyszny 4, Zenon Plech 4, Robert Slabon 2, Marek Cieslak 1, Andrzej Tkocz 0).

1980 (Wroclaw, Poland)
1 ENGLAND 40 (Michael Lee 11, Chris Morton 11, Peter Collins 10, Dave Jessup 8) 2 United States of America 29 (Bruce Penhall 12, Scott Autrey 9, Dennis Sigalos 5, Bobby Schwartz 3, Ron Preston 0) 3 Poland 15 (Roman Jankowski 5, Zenon Plech 5, Edward Jancarz 3, Andrzej Huszcza 2 Jerzy Rembas 0) 4 Czechoslovakia 12 (Jiri Stancl 4, Vaclav Verner 3, Petr Ondrasik 3, Ales Dryml 1, Zdenek Kudrna 1).

1981 (Olching, West Germany)
1 DENMARK 36 (Hans Nielsen 11, Erik Gundersen 9, Tommy Knudsen 9, Ole Olsen 6, Finn Thomsen 1) 2 England 29 (Chris Morton 11, Kenny Carter 9, John Davis 5, Dave Jessup 3, Gordon Kennett 1) 3 West Germany 28 (Egon Müller 10, Karl Maier 8, Georg Hack 5, Georg Gilgenreiner 5) 4 Soviet Union 3 (Viktor Kuznetsov 2, Anatoli Maximov 1, Valeri Gordeev 0, Mikhail Starostin 0, Nikolai Kornev 0).

WONDER GUNDER ... Erik Gundersen collected the first of seven World Team Cup gold medals in 1984

1982 (White City, London)
1 UNITED STATES OF AMERICA 37 (Kelly Moran 10, Bruce Penhall 10, Bobby Schwartz 9, Shawn Moran 8, Scott Autrey 0) 2 Denmark 24 (Hans Nielsen 11 Erik Gundersen 7, Preben Eriksen 4, Tommy Knudsen 1, Ole Olsen 1) 3 West Germany 18 (Karl Maier 7, Egon Müller 5, Georg Hack 5, Georg Gilgenreiner 1, Alois Wiesböck 0) 4 Czechoslovakia 17 (Ales Dryml 7, Vaclav Verner 6, Jiri Stancl 4, Petr Ondrasik 0, Antonin Kasper [jun] 0).

1983 (Vojens, Denmark)
1 DENMARK 37 (Erik Gundersen 12, Hans Nielsen 11, Ole Olsen 7, Peter Ravn 7, Finn Thomsen 0) 2 England 29 (Michael Lee 11, Kenny Carter 8, Chris Morton 7, Dave Jessup 2, Peter Collins 1) 3 United States of America 27 (Dennis Sigalos 9, Bobby Schwartz 6, Kelly Moran 6, Lance King 6) 4 Czechoslovakia 3 (Jiri Stancl 2, Vaclav Verner 1, Antonin Kasper [jun] 0, Petr Ondrasik 0, Ales Dryml 0).

1984 (Leszno, Poland)
1 DENMARK 44 (Erik Gundersen 12, Bo Petersen 12, Hans Nielsen 11, Preben Eriksen 9) 2 England 24 (Simon Wigg 9, Phil Collins 7, Chris Morton 4, Peter Collins 2, Neil Collins 2) 3 United States of America 20 (Shawn Moran 6, Kelly Moran 5, Lance King 5, Bobby Schwartz 2, John Cook 2) 4 Poland 8 (Zenon Plech 4, Leonard Raba 2, Roman Jankowski 1, Zenon Kasprzak 1, Boleslaw Proch 0).

1985 (Long Beach, United States of America)
1 DENMARK 37 (Tommy Knudsen 12, Erik Gundersen 10, Hans Nielsen 10, Preben Eriksen 5, Bo Petersen 0) 2 United States of America 35 (Shawn Moran 11, Bobby Schwartz 11, Lance King 9, Sam Ermolenko 3, John Cook 1) 3 England 13 (Jeremy Doncaster 6, Kelvin Tatum 3, Phil Collins 2, Richard Knight 2, John Davis 0) 4 Sweden 10 (Jan Andersson 5, Tommy Nilsson 3, Jimmy Nilsen 2, Per Jonsson 0, Pierre Brannefors 0).

1986 (Vetlanda, Sweden)
1 DENMARK 39 (Erik Gundersen 11, Hans Nielsen 10, Jan O. Pedersen 10, Tommy Knudsen 8) 2 Sweden 35 (Jan Andersson 11, Per Jonsson 10, Jimmy Nilsen 9, Tommy Nilsson 5) 3 England 29 (Chris Morton 8, Neil Evitts 8, Simon Wigg 7, Kelvin Tatum 4, Jeremy Doncaster 2) United States of America 17 (Shawn Moran 9, Bobby Schwartz 4, Sam Ermolenko 3, Lance King 1).

1986 (Vojens, Denmark)
1 DENMARK 48 (Erik Gundersen 14, Hans Nielsen 13, Tommy Knudsen 12, John Jørgensen 8, Jan O. Pedersen 1) 2 United States of America 29 (Sam Ermolenko 11, Shawn Moran 10, Lance King 7, Rick Miller 1, Bobby Schwartz 0) 3 England 23 (Simon Wigg 10, Kelvin Tatum 7, Chris Morton 5, Jeremy Doncaster 1, Neil Evitts 0) 4 Sweden 19 (Per Jonsson 8, Jan Andersson 7, Jimmy Nilsen 2, Tommy Nilsson 2, Erik Stenlund 0).

1986 (Bradford, England)
1 DENMARK 42 (Tommy Knudsen 13, Hans Nielsen 12, Jan O. Pedersen 9, Erik Gundersen 8) 2 United States of America 30 (Lance King 11, Sam Ermolenko 9, Shawn Moran 8, Bobby Schwartz 1, Rick Miller 1) 3 England 29 (Kelvin Tatum 8, Chris Morton 7, Simon Wigg 7, Jeremy Doncaster 7, Marvyn Cox 0) 4 Sweden 19 (Jan Andersson 10, Jimmy Nilsen 5, Per Jonsson 3, Erik Stenlund 1, Tony Olsson 0).

In 1986 the competition was extended to 20 heats and World Final placings were decided on a league points basis 3-2-1-0 and the final finishing positions were as follows
1 DENMARK 9, 2 United States of America 4, 3 England 3, 4 Sweden 2.

1987 (Fredericia, Denmark)
1 DENMARK 47 (Hans Nielsen 15, Jan O. Pedersen 12, Erik Gundersen 10, Tommy Knudsen 10) 2 England 37 (Jeremy Doncaster 13, Simon Wigg 9, Simon Cross 8, Kelvin Tatum 7) 3 United States of America 24 (Sam Ermolenko 9, Rick Miller 8, Shawn Moran 4, Lance King 3) 4 Czechoslovakia 12 (Antonin Kasper [jun] 4, Lubomir Jedek 4, Roman Matousek 3, Petr Vandirek 1, Zdenek Schneiderwind 0).

1987 (Coventry, England)
1 UNITED STATES OF AMERICA 43 (Shawn Moran 14, Sam Ermolenko 11, Rick Miller 9, Lance King 5, Kelly Moran 4) 2 Denmark 37 (Hans Nielsen 11, Jan O. Pedersen 10, Erik Gundersen 9, Tommy Knudsen 7) 3 England 33 (Simon Wigg 11, Kelvin Tatum 9, Jeremy Doncaster 6, Simon Cross 5, Marvyn Cox 2) 4 Czechoslovakia 7 (Antonin Kasper [jun] 3, Roman Matousek 2, Petr Vandirek 1, Lubomir Jedek 1, Zdenek Schneiderwind 0).

1987 (Prague, Czechoslovakia)
1 DENMARK 46 (Erik Gundersen 14, Hans Nielsen 12, Jan O. Pedersen 10, Tommy Knudsen 10) 2 England 31 (Kelvin Tatum 9, Simon Wigg 9, Simon Cross 8, Jeremy Doncaster 5, Marvyn Cox 0) 3 United States of America 26 (Kelly Moran 10, John Cook 6, Rick Miller 5, Shawn Moran 5) 4 Czechoslovakia 17 (Roman Matousek 9, Zdenek Schneiderwind 3, Antonin Kasper [jun] 3, Petr Vandirek 2, Lubomir Jedek 0).

World Final 1987 placings were decided on aggregate race points and the final finishing positions were as follows: 1 DENMARK 130, 2 England 101, 3 United States of America 93, 4 Czechoslovakia 36.

1988 (Long Beach, United States of America)
1 DENMARK 44 (Hans Nielsen 14, Jan O. Pedersen 12, Erik Gundersen 8, Tommy Knudsen 8, John Jørgensen 2) 2 United States of America 32 (Sam Ermolenko 13, Shawn Moran 8, Lance King 6, Kelly Moran 5, Rick Miller 0) 3 Sweden 22 (Per Jonsson 9, Jimmy Nilsen 5, Tony Olsson 4, Henrik Gustafsson 4, Conny Ivarsson 0) 4 England 22 (Gary Havelock 8, Kelvin Tatum 7, Chris Morton 4, Simon Cross 3, Simon Wigg 0). *Jonsson beat Tatum in a run-off for third place.*

Sweden relegated to Group A in 1989 as England are seeded as hosts to the 1989 World Final.

1989 (Bradford, England)
1 ENGLAND 48 (Jeremy Doncaster 13, Paul Thorp 12, Kelvin Tatum 12, Simon Wigg 11, Simon Cross 0) 2 Denmark 34 (Hans Nielsen 11, Gert Handberg 9, John Jørgensen 7, Brian Karger 7, Erik Gundersen 0) 3 Sweden 30 (Mikael Blixt 10, Per Jonsson 8, Tony Olsson 7, Erik Stenlund 5, Jimmy Nilsen 0) 4 United States of America 8 (Kelly Moran 6, Greg Hancock 2, Ronnie Correy 0, Rick Miller 0, Lance King 0).

Sweden and United States of America relegated to Group A in 1990 as Czechoslovakia are seeded as hosts to the 1990 World Final.

1990 (Prague, Czechoslovakia)
1 UNITED STATES OF AMERICA 37 (Kelly Moran 12, Sam Ermolenko 11, Shawn Moran 10, Billy Hamill 4, Rick Miller 0) 2 England 34 (Kelvin Tatum 11, Simon Wigg 8, Jeremy Doncaster 8, Gary Havelock 5, Marvyn Cox 2) 3 Denmark 30 (Hans Nielsen 13, Brian Karger 5, John Jørgensen 4, Bo Petersen 4, Tommy Knudsen 4) 4 Czechoslovakia 19 (Zdenek Tesar 6, Bohumil Brhel 6, Roman Matousek 3, Antonin Kasper [jun] 3, Vladimir Kalina 1).

Czechoslovakia relegated to Group A in 1991.

1991 (Vojens, Denmark)
1 DENMARK 51 (Jan O. Pedersen 15, Hans Nielsen 14, Tommy Knudsen 13, Gert Handberg 8, Brian Karger 1) 2 Sweden 30 (Per Jonsson 9, Tony Rickardsson 7, Henrik Gustafsson 7, Jimmy Nilsen 7) 3 United States of America 28 (Sam Ermolenko 9, Billy Hamill 9, Greg Hancock 6, Rick Miller 4, Ronnie Correy 0) 4 England 11 (Martin Dugard 4, Gary Havelock 3, Marvyn Cox 3, Chris Louis 1, Paul Thorp 0).

England relegated to Group A in 1992.

1992 (Kumla, Sweden)
1 UNITED STATES OF AMERICA 39 (Greg Hancock 11, Sam Ermolenko 10, Billy Hamill 10, Ronnie Correy 5, Bobby Ott 3) 2 Sweden 33 (Henrik Gustafsson 12, Per Jonsson 11, Tony Rickardsson 7, Peter Nahlin 2, Jimmy Nilsen 1) 3 England 31 (Martin Dugard 12, Gary Havelock 7, Mark Loram 7, Kelvin Tatum 3, Joe Screen 2) 4 Denmark 17 (Hans Nielsen 11, Brian Karger 3, Morten Andersen 2, John Jørgensen 1, Gert Handberg 0).

Denmark relegated to Group A in 1993.

FIM GOLD MEDAL RANKINGS

9 ... Denmark 6 ... Sweden 5 ... England 4 ... Great Britain and Poland 3 ... United States of America 1 ... Australia and New Zealand

Pasta-master Greg

GREG Hancock was ignored by the American selectors for the individual World Championship – but provided his own stinging rebuke.

For Hancock emerged from the pits in heat nine of the World Pairs Final in Lonigo, Italy, to become the Midnight Marvel as he steered his country to the gold medal.

He replaced a strangely subdued Ronnie Correy after the Wolverhampton star had scored only three points from his first two outings and turned in a stunning solo display.

In four rides he dropped only one point – to home favourite Armando Castagna – and then came out for a fifth time to defeat England's Gary Havelock in a race-off for the title.

No wonder Hancock took great glee in sending off a fax to the American Motorcycle Association telling them of his Italian exploits after his World Championship snub.

He admitted: "I was so pumped up before the run-off because I wanted to win the title so bad and make a point to the AMA." Point made!

It was a last gasp victory for the Yankee Doodle Dandies as they came from behind to pip England at the final chequered flag.

The Lions, with Kelvin Tatum and Martin Dugard replacing semi-final selections Paul Thorp and Chris Louis as Gary Havelock's back-up, had started off confidently with Havvy setting a new track record in heat two.

But with his partner Kelvin Tatum surprisingly sluggish in his first three rides it was always going to be tight.

England and Sweden – unlike the remaining nations – relied solely on their first string riders.

Dugard was a pits passenger despite Tatum's inconsistency and the Swedes relied on Per Jonsson and Henrik Gustafsson with Tony Rickardsson their spectator. The Swedish plan almost paid off and would have done but for a 2-4 reverse in their final ride when they were within touching distance of the crown.

But America's willingness to ring the changes proved to be the winning gamble...with Hancock the real pasta-master on a balmy Italian evening.

STARS AND SMILES ... triumphant Americans Ronnie Correy, Sam Ermolenko, team manager John Scott and Greg Hancock

WORLD PAIRS CHAMPIONSHIP

QUALIFYING ROUND (Wroclaw, Poland, Sunday, May 17): **1 POLAND 26 (Piotr Swist 11, Slawomir Drabik 8, Miroslaw Kowalik 7) 2 CIS 24 (Rif Saitgareev 13, Mikhail Starostin 11, Oleg Kurguskin, did not ride) 3 FINLAND 23 (Juha Moksunen 13, Vesa Ylinen 10) 4 AUSTRIA 22 (Andreas Bössner 12, Heinrich Schatzer 9, Franz Leitner 1)** 5 SLOVENIA 12 (Gregor Pintar 6, Kreso Omerzel 6) 6 LATVIA 12 (Andrej Korolov 8, Juri Sokolov 3, Oleg Bucko 1) 7 HOLLAND 7 (Henk Bangma 7, Rob Steman 0).

SEMI FINAL (Pardubice, Czechoslovakia, Sunday, June 7): **1 UNITED STATES OF AMERICA 26 (Ronnie Correy 16, Sam Ermolenko 10, Greg Hancock, did not ride) 2 SWEDEN 22 (Per Jonsson 15, Tony Rickardsson 4, Jimmy Nilsen 3) 3 AUSTRALIA 19 (Leigh Adams 13, Shane Parker 4, Craig Boyce 2)** 4 CZECHOSLOVAKIA 18 (Bohumil Brhel 12, Roman Matousek 4, Antonin Kasper 2) 5 HUNGARY 14 (Zoltan Adorján 10, Sándor Tihanyi 2, Antal Kocso 2) 6 POLAND 14 (Tomasz Gollob 9, Piotr Swist 4, Slawomir Drabik 1) 7 FINLAND 13 (Vesa Ylinen 9, Juha Moksunen 4).

SEMI FINAL (Norden, Germany, Sunday, June 7): **1 ENGLAND 28 (Gary Havelock 18, Paul Thorp 10, Chris Louis, did not ride) 2 DENMARK 26 (Tommy Knudsen 14, Hans Nielsen 12, Gert Handberg, did not ride) 3 NEW ZEALAND 21 (Mitch Shirra 11, Mark Thorpe 10, David Bargh, did not ride)** 4 NORWAY 18 (Lars Gunnestad 11, Einar Kyllingstad 7, Arnt Førland, did not ride) 5 Germany 14 (Gerd Riss 11, Tommy Dunker 3, André Pollehn 0) 6 CIS 11 (René Aas 6, Rinat Mardanshin 5) 7 Austria 8 (Andreas Bössner 6, Heinrich Schatzer 2, Franz Leitner, did not ride).

WORLD PAIRS FINAL

Lonigo, Italy, Saturday, July 18

1 UNITED STATES OF AMERICA 23+3							
Sam Ermolenko	1	2	2	1	1	2	9:4
Ronnie Correy	2	1	N	N	N	N	3:1
Greg Hancock	3	2	3	3			11
2 ENGLAND 23+2							
Gary Havelock	3	3	1	3	3	2	15:2
Kelvin Tatum	0	1	2	2	0	3	8:1
Martin Dugard	did not ride						
3 SWEDEN 22							
Per Jonsson	2	2	3	3	2	2	14:2
Henrik Gustafsson	3	0	0	2	3	0	8:1
Tony Rickardsson	did not ride						
4 ITALY 18							
Armando Castagna	3	3	2	3	2	3	16
Valentino Furlanetto	1	0	N	0	1	X	2:1
Armando dal Chiele	0						0
5 DENMARK 16							
Hans Nielsen	3	3	3	2	1	1	13
Tommy Knudsen	1	N	N	N	fx	N	1
Brian Karger	fx	1	1	0			2:1
6 NEW ZEALAND 14							
Mitch Shirra	1	2	1	3	3	2	12
Mark Thorpe	0	0	0	N	N	N	0
David Bargh	0	1	1				2:1
7 AUSTRALIA 10							
Leigh Adams	2	1	1	0	N	0	4:1
Craig Boyce	0	2	0	N	2	1	5
Shane Parker	1	R					1

Greg Hancock (USA) defeated Gary Havelock in a run-off for title.

***1969 (Stockholm, Sweden)**
1 NEW ZEALAND 28 (Ivan Mauger 18, Bob Andrews 10) 2 Sweden 27 (Ove Fundin 14, Göte Nordin 13) 3 England 21 (Nigel Boocock 11, Martin Ashby 10) 4 Denmark 17 (Ole Olsen 13 Bent Norregaard Jensen 4) 5 Czechoslovakia 15 (Jan Holub 9, Zdenek Majstr 6) 6 East Germany 9 (Gerhard Uhlenbrock 8, Jochen Dinse 1) 7 Bulgaria 8 (Petr Petkov 6, Petr Iliev 2).

1970 (Malmö, Sweden)
1 NEW ZEALAND 28 (Ronnie Moore 16, Ivan Mauger 12) 2 Sweden 25 (Ove Fundin 15, Bengt Jansson 10) 3 England 19 (Eric Boocock 13, Nigel Boocock 6) 4 Scotland 18 (Jim McMillan 10, Bert Harkins 8) 5 Czechoslovakia 11 (Jiri Stancl 6, Vaclav Verner 5) 6 Yugoslavia 8 (Drasko Orsic 5, Ivan Kos 3).
Denmark 17 (Ole Olsen 12, Bent Norregaard Jensen 5) replaced Poland but their points did not count in final placings.

1971 (Rybnik, Poland)
1 POLAND 30 (Jerzy Szczakiel 15, Andrzej Wyglenda 15) 2 New Zealand 25 (Barry Briggs 13, Ivan Mauger 12) 3 Sweden 22 (Anders Michanek 13, Bernt Persson 9) 4 Czechoslovakia 17 (Vaclav Verner 9, Pavel Mares 8) 5 Scotland 16 (Jim McMillan 11, George Hunter 5) 6 Yugoslavia 10 (Drasko Orsic 5 Ivan Molan 5) 7 Austria 6 (Josef Haider 3, Heinz Zimmerman 3).

1972 (Borås, Sweden)
1 ENGLAND 24 (Ray Wilson 15, Terry Betts 9) 2 New Zealand 24 (Ivan Mauger 14, Ronnie Moore 10) 3 Sweden B 22 (Bernt Persson 13, Hasse Holmkvist 9) 4 Sweden A 22 (Anders Michanek 15, Bengt Jansson 7), 5 Poland 15 (Zbigniew Marcinkowski 13, Wiktor Jastrzebski 2) 6 Czechoslovakia 12 (Jiri Stancl 7, Jan Holub 5) 7 Hungary 6 (Ferenc Radacsi 6, Pal Perenyi 0).
Wilson beat Mauger in a run-off for first place; Persson beat Michanek in third place run off.

1973 (Borås, Sweden)
1 SWEDEN 24 (Anders Michanek 15, Tommy Jansson 9) 2 Denmark 21 (Ole Olsen 18, Kurt Bøgh 3) 3 Poland 21 (Zenon Plech 14, Zbigniew Marcinkowski 7) 4 Soviet Union 20 (Vladimir Gordeev 10, Anatoli Kuzmin 10) 5 Norway 17 (Reidar Eide 9, Dag Lovaas 8) 6 Czechoslovakia 11 (Jiri Stancl 9, Petr Ondrasik 2) 7 New Zealand 10 (Ivan Mauger 8, Graeme Stapleton 2).
Olsen beat Plech in run off for second place.

1974 (Belle Vue, Manchester, England)
1 SWEDEN 28 (Anders Michanek 14, Sören Sjösten 14) 2 Australia 23 (Phil Crump 14, John Boulger 9) 3 New Zealand 21 (Ivan Mauger 17, Barry Briggs 4) 4 England 20 (Peter Collins 12, Dave Jessup 8) 5 Poland 18 (Zenon Plech 12, Edward Jancarz 6) 6 Soviet Union 10 (Grigori Khlinovski 6, Vladimir Gordeev 4) 7 Czechoslovakia 6 (Jan Holub 3, Jan Hadek 3).

1975 (Wroclaw, Poland)
1 SWEDEN 24 (Anders Michanek 17, Tommy Jansson 7) 2 Poland 23 (Edward Jancarz 15, Piotr Bruzda 8) 3 Denmark 20 (Ole Olsen 18, Jan Henningsen 2) 4 England 20 (John Louis 12, Peter Collins 8) 5 Australia 19 (Phil Crump 10, John Boulger 9) 6 West Germany 10 (Christoph Betzl 7, Frits Baur 3) 7 Austria 10 (Adi Funk 6, Herbert Szerecz 4).
Olsen beat Louis in run off for third place.

1976 (Eskilstuna, Sweden)
1 ENGLAND 27 (John Louis 17, Malcolm Simmons 10) 2 Denmark 24 (Ole Olsen 16, Finn Thomsen 8) 3 Sweden 22 (Bengt Jansson 11, Bernt Persson 11) 4 Australia 16 (Phil Crump 10, Billy Sanders 6) 5 New Zealand 15 (Ivan Mauger 8, Barry Briggs 7) 6 Scotland 12 (Jim McMillan 10, George Hunter 2) 7 Poland 10 (Edward Jancarz 7, Zenon Plech 3).

1977 (Belle Vue, Manchester, England)
1 ENGLAND 28 (Peter Collins 15, Malcolm Simmons 13) 2 Sweden 18 (Anders Michanek 16, Bernt Persson 2) 3 West Germany 18 (Egon Müller 11, Hans Wassermann 7) 4 Czechoslovakia 17 (Jiri Stancl 11, Jan Verner 6) 5 New Zealand 17 (Ivan Mauger 16, Larry Ross 1) 6 Finland 14 (Ilkka Teromaa 7, Kai Niemi 7) 7 Australia 12 (Phil Crump 10, Billy Sanders 2).

1978 (Chorzow, Poland)
1 ENGLAND 24 (Malcolm Simmons 15, Gordon Kennett 9) 2 New Zealand 24 (Ivan Mauger 12, Larry Ross 12) 3 Denmark 21 (Ole Olsen 16, Finn Thomsen 5) 4 Czechoslovakia 18 (Jiri Stancl 9, Jan Verner 9) 5 Poland 15 (Edward Jancarz 13, Boleslaw Proch 2) 6 West Germany 13 (Georg Hack 8, Hans Wassermann 5) 7 Sweden 11 (Jan Andersson 10, Börje Klingberg 1).
Simmons beat Mauger in run off for first place.

1979 (Vojens, Denmark)
1 DENMARK 25 (Ole Olsen 15, Hans Nielsen 10) 2 England 24 (Michael Lee 15, Malcolm Simmons 9) 3 Poland 20 (Edward Jancarz 13, Zenon Plech 7) 4 Australia 19 (Phil Crump 13, John Titman 6) 5 United States of America 14 (Bruce Penhall 14, no partner) 6 New Zealand 12 (Ivan Mauger 6, Larry Ross 6) 7 Finland 7 (Kai Niemi 7, Ilkka Teromaa 0).

1980 (Krsko, Yugoslavia)
1 ENGLAND 29 (Dave Jessup 15, Peter Collins 14) 2 Poland 22 (Edward Jancarz 15, Zenon Plech 7) 3 Denmark 21 (Ole Olsen 13, Hans Nielsen 8) 4 Sweden 18 (Jan Andersson 9, Richard Hellsén 9) 5 New Zealand 16 (Ivan Mauger 11, Larry Ross 5) 6 Finland 14 (Ilkka Teromaa 8, Kai Niemi 6) 7 Yugoslavia 6 (Stefan Kekec 6, Vlado Kocuvan 0).

1981 (Katowice, Poland)
1 UNITED STATES OF AMERICA 23 (Bruce Penhall 14, Bobby Schwartz 9) 2 New Zealand 22 (Ivan Mauger 12, Larry Ross 10) 3 Poland 21 (Zenon Plech 15, Edward Jancarz 6) 4 Czechoslovakia 18 (Ales Dryml 12, Jan Verner 6) 5 Denmark 17 (Ole Olsen 10, Hans Nielsen 7) 6 England 17 (Chris Morton 10, Dave Jessup 7) 7 West Germany 3 (Egon Müller 2, Georg Gilgenreiner 1).

1982 (Liverpool, Australia)
1 UNITED STATES OF AMERICA 30 (Dennis Sigalos 18, Bobby Schwartz 12) 2 England 22 (Peter Collins 15, Kenny Carter 7) 3 Denmark 21 (Hans Nielsen 11, Ole Olsen 10) 4 Australia 16 (Billy Sanders 11, Gary Guglielmi 5) 5 Finland 16 (Kai Niemi 12, Ari Koponen 4) 6 New Zealand 13 (Mitch Shirra 8, Larry Ross 5) 7 Czechoslovakia 8 (Jiri Stancl 5, Ales Dryml 3).

1983 (Gothenburg, Sweden)
1 ENGLAND 25 (Kenny Carter 15, Peter Collins 10) 2 Australia 24 (Billy Sanders 15, Gary Guglielmi 9) 3 Denmark 19 (Hans Nielsen 11, Erik Gundersen 8) 4 United States of America 18 (Dennis Sigalos 10, Bobby Schwartz 8) 5 Sweden 16 (Jan Andersson 11, Pierre Brannefors 5) 6 West Germany 12 (Egon Müller 6, Karl Maier 6) 7 New Zealand 11 (Ivan Mauger 7, Larry Ross 4).

1984 (Lonigo, Italy)
1 ENGLAND 27 (Chris Morton 14, Peter Collins 13) 2 Denmark 25 (Hans Nielsen 15, Erik Gundersen 10) 3 New Zealand 25 (Mitch Shirra 15, Ivan Mauger 10) 4 United States of America 19 (Bobby Schwartz 11, Shawn Moran 8) 5 Australia 14 (Gary Guglielmi 8, Billy Sanders 6) 6 Czechoslovakia 10 (Ales Dryml 5, Jiri Stancl 5) 7 Italy 6 (Armando Castagna 5, Armando dal Chiele 1).
Nielsen beat Shirra in run off for second place.

1985 (Rybnik, Poland)
1 DENMARK 29 (Erik Gundersen 16, Tommy Knudsen 13) 2 England 27 (Kenny Carter 14, Kelvin Tatum 13) 3 United States of America 22 (Shawn Moran 13, Bobby Schwartz 9) 4 New Zealand 15 (Ivan Mauger 8, Mitch Shirra 7) 5 Sweden 14 (Jan Andersson 10, Per Jonsson 4) 6 Australia 11 (Steve Regeling 6, Phil Crump 5) 7 Poland 8 (Andrzej Huszcza 4, Grzegorz Dzikowski 4).

1986 (Pocking, West Germany)
1 DENMARK 46 (Hans Nielsen 27, Erik Gundersen 19) 2 United States of America 46 (Kelly Moran 23, Sam Ermolenko 23) 3 Czechoslovakia 32 (Antonin Kasper 22, Roman Matousek 10) 4 Sweden 32 (Jan Andersson 17, Tommy Nilsson 15) 5 New Zealand 32 (Larry Ross 20, Mitch Shirra 12) 6 West Germany 27 (Karl Maier 22, Klaus Lausch 5) 7 England 23 (Jeremy Doncaster 12, Simon Wigg 11) 8 Italy 15 (Valentino Furlanetto 8, Armando Castagna 7) 9 Australia 15 (Phil Crump 10, Steve Regeling 5).
Nielsen beat Moran in run off for first place.

1987 (Pardubice, Czechoslovakia)
1 DENMARK 52 (Erik Gundersen 26, Hans Nielsen 26) 2 England 44 (Kelvin Tatum 24, Simon Wigg 20) 3 United States of America 36 (Sam Ermolenko 18, Kelly Moran 18) 4 New Zealand 36 (David Bargh 20, Mitch Shirra 16) 5 Czechoslovakia 30 (Roman Matousek 16, Antonin Kasper 14) 6 Finland 19 (Olli Tyrvainen 11, Kai Niemi 8) 7 Australia 21 (Steve Baker 16, Steve Regeling 5) 8 Italy 18 (Armando Castagna 11, Valentino Furlanetto 7) 9 Poland 14 (Wojciech Zabialowicz 8, Roman Jankowski 6).

1988 (Bradford, England)
1 DENMARK 45 (Hans Nielsen 27, Erik Gundersen 18) 2 England 41 (Kelvin Tatum 21, Simon Cross 20) 3 United States of America 39 (Shawn Moran 23, Sam Ermolenko 16) 4 New Zealand 32 (Mitch Shirra 24, Alan Rivett 8) 5 Sweden 29 (Jimmy Nilsen 17, Per Jonsson 12) 6 Hungary 25 (Antal Kocso 15, Zoltán Adorján 10) 7 Italy 21 (Armando Castagna 17, Valentino Furlanetto 4) 8 West Germany 21 (Gerd Riss 17, Tommy Dunker 4) 9 Poland 17 (Piotr Swist 9, Roman Jankowski 8).

1989 (Leszno, Poland)
1 DENMARK 48 (Hans Nielsen 28, Erik Gundersen 20) 2 Sweden 44 (Jimmy Nilsen 23, Per Jonsson 21) 3 England 37 (Kelvin Tatum 21, Paul Thorp 16) 4 West Germany 36 (Karl Maier 22, Gerd Riss 14) 5 Finland 31 (Kai Niemi 18, Olli Tyrvainen 13) 6 Hungary 22 (Antal Kocso 14, Zoltán Adorján 8) 7 Czechoslovakia 25 (Bohumil Brhel 14, Zdenek Tesar 11) 8 Italy 15 (Armando dal Chiele 9, Valentino Furlanetto 6) 9 Poland 11 (Piotr Swist 11, Roman Jankowski 0).

1990 (Landshut, West Germany)
1 DENMARK 43 (Jan O. Pedersen 24, Hans Nielsen 19) 2 Australia 41 (Todd Wiltshire 25, Leigh Adams 16) 3 Hungary 33 (Zoltán Adorján 21, Sándor Tihanyi 12) 4 Sweden 33 (Jimmy Nilsen 17, Per Jonsson 16) 5 New Zealand 32 (Mitch Shirra 23, David Bargh 9) 6 United States of America 28 (Ronnie Correy 15, Kelly Moran 13) 7 Czechoslovakia 21 (Antonin Kasper 11, Roman Matousek 10) 8 England 20 (Kelvin Tatum 20, Simon Cross 0) 9 West Germany 15 (Klaus Lausch 15, Gerd Riss 0). Reserve: Alois Bachhuber 3.

1991 (Poznan, Poland)
1 DENMARK 28 (Hans Nielsen 14, Jan O. Pedersen 14, Tommy Knudsen, did not ride) 2 Sweden 24 (Henrik Gustafsson 9, Jimmy Nilsen 8, Per Jonsson 7) 3 Norway 19 (Lars Gunnestad 11, Einar Kyllingstad 8, Tor Einar Hjelm, did not ride) 4 Germany 18 (Gerd Riss 9, Klaus Lausch 9, Tommy Dunker, did not ride) 5 Czechoslovakia 18 (Bohumil Brhel 12, Roman Matousek 6, Zdenek Tesar 0) 6 Italy 10 (Armando Castagna 9, Valentino Furlanetto 1, Fabrizio Vesprini 0) 7 Poland 9 (Ryszard Dolomisiewicz 5, Piotr Swist 3, Wojciech Zaluski 1).

1992 (Lonigo, Italy)
1 UNITED STATES OF AMERICA 23+3 (Greg Hancock 11+3, Sam Ermolenko 9, Ronnie Correy 3) 2 England 23+2 (Gary Havelock 15+2, Kelvin Tatum 8, Martin Dugard, did not ride) 3 Sweden 22 (Per Jonsson 14, Henrik Gustafsson 8, Tony Rickardsson, did not ride), 4 Italy 18 (Armando Castagna 16, Valentino Furlanetto 2, Armando dal Chiele 0) 5 Denmark 16 (Hans Nielsen 13, Brian Karger 2, Tommy Knudsen 1) 6 New Zealand 14 (Mitch Shirra 12, David Bargh 2, Mark Thorpe 0) 7 Australia 10 (Craig Boyce 5, Leigh Adams 4, Shane Parker 1).

■ **The 1969 World Final is no longer recognised by the FIM even though official FIM medals were issued to the three top nations.**

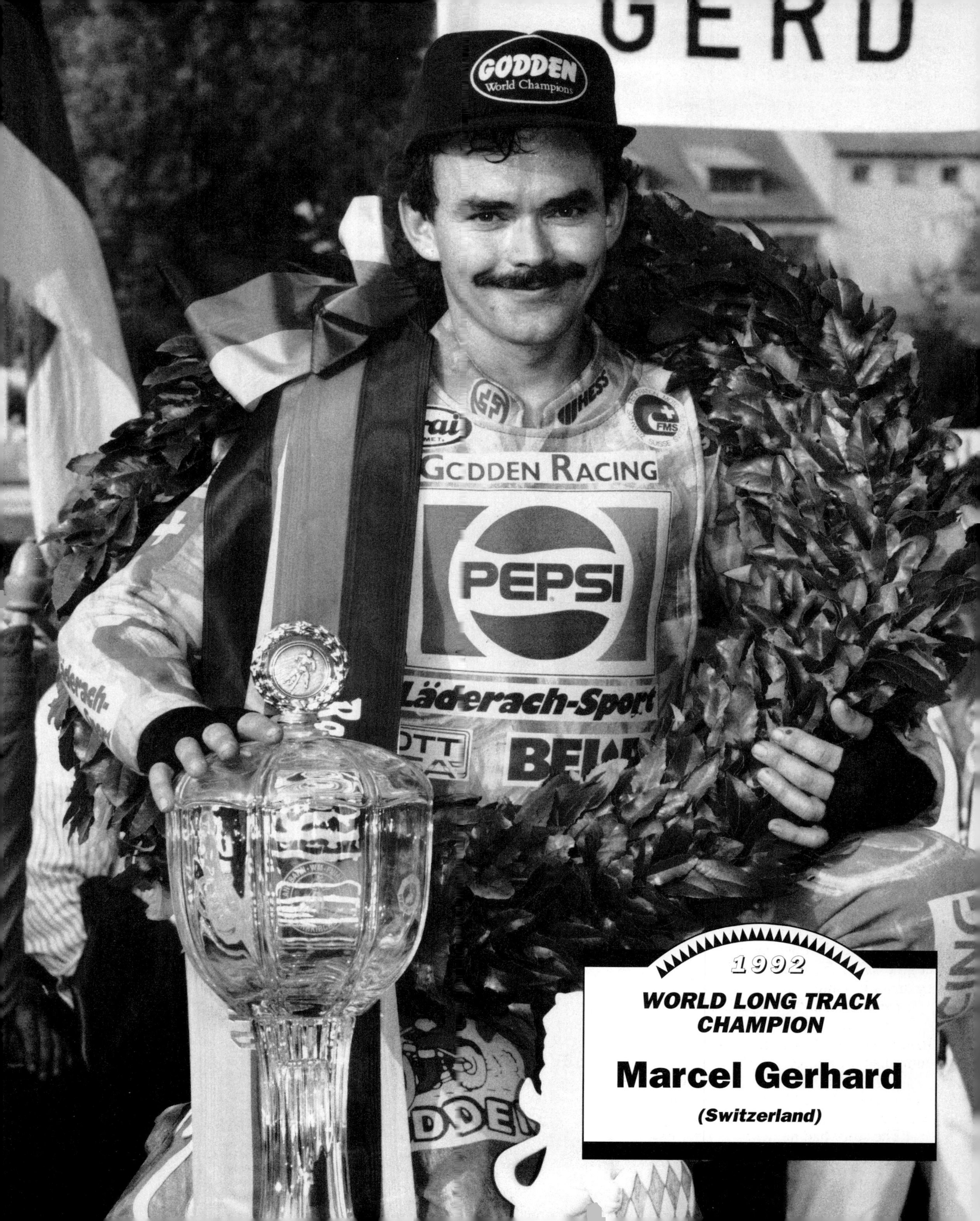

1992

WORLD LONG TRACK CHAMPION

Marcel Gerhard

(Switzerland)

Tragedy for Andy

ANDY SMITH and former Hackney signing Uwe Gessner were airlifted to hospital after tragedy struck in the World Long Track Final.

The Coventry star, through to his second successive Final, was bidding to overtake race leader and defending title-holder Gerd Riss on the long back straight at Pfarrkirchen when the German appeared to drift into his path.

They both came down and Smith's riderless machine was struck by Gessner who ended up critically injured on the centre green.

Initially there were fears for Gessner's life as he was taken by helicopter to a special clinic where he was put on a life support machine.

Smith, with a suspected broken leg and badly damaged hand, was taken to the local hospital but subsequently airlifted back to England where he was admitted to the Coventry and Warwickshire Hospital.

Remarkably it was Gessner who appeared to escape with less serious injuries while Smith spent weeks in hospital with damaged knee ligaments that ruled him out for the season.

When the semi-final race was re-run, Riss took the five points to go into the final just one point behind meeting leader Marcel Gerhard, bidding to give Switzerland a first ever FIM medal in track racing.

There was everything to race for in the final heat with Gerhard and four-time champion Karl Maier on 18 points, Riss and Kiwi Mitch Shirra on 17, England's Mark Loram on 15 and the sixth qualifier Ales Dryml with 13 points.

Mathematically all but the Czech Dryml had a chance of taking the title!

But it was all over coming out of the first turn as brave Gerhard (who rode with a broken collar bone he kept a secret from the medical staff until after the meeting) hit the front and held off Shirra's darting moves to repeat his semi-final mastery.

Shirra's second place in the last race was enough to give him the silver medal while Loram had to be content with fourth place even though he finished in front of bronze medallist Maier, Riss and Dryml in the last race – a fine achievement for a relatively inexperienced long-tracker even though he was competing in his third Final.

England's pre-meeting favourite had been triple champion Simon Wigg but he touched the tapes in his opening heat, punctured in his second and then seized an expensive engine in his third outing to be eliminated without a point against his name.

He admitted: "The whole day was just a mess."

And it could have been the same for Australian Shane Parker whose bikes didn't arrive until after official and compulsory practice had finished.

Fortunately for the Ipswich star the FIM jury were lenient and allowed him a four-minute solo session which was enough to qualify for the meeting.

The story had no happy ending though, as he claimed only one point from three races.

QUALIFYING ROUND (Mühldorf, Germany, Sunday, June 21): **Henrik Gustafsson (Sweden) 25, Shane Parker (Australia) 22, Antal Kocso (Hungary) 22, Luis Vallejos (Argentine) 17, Tony Briggs (New Zealand) 15, Valentino Furlanetto (Italy) 11,** Phillippe Bergé (France) 10, Roland Kolros (Germany) 10, Jaroslav Ptek (Czechoslovakia) 9, Andreas Schöpfl (Germany) 6, Paul Fry (Great Britain) 6, Stephen Davies (Australia) 4, Christian Cigane (France) 4, Franco Mozzato (Italy) 3, Jesse Inauen (Switzerland) 3, Oleg Volokov (CIS) 3, René Aas (CIS) 2, Peter Schroeck (Germany) 0.

SEMI FINAL (Ludwigslust, Germany, Sunday, July 5): **Marvyn Cox (Great Britain) 22, Uwe Gessner (Germany) 21, Mitch Shirra (New Zealand) 19, Andy Smith (Great Britain) 18, Klaus Lausch (Germany) 18**, Jeremy Doncaster (Great Britain) 13, **Borivoj Hadek (Czechoslovakia) 9**, Luis Vallejos 9, Robert Barth (Germany) 8, Peter Nahlin (Sweden) 8, Hans Otto Pingel (Germany) 7, Jan Pedersen (Denmark) 5, Gjermund Aas (Norway) 5, Jan Holub (Czechoslovakia) 4, Clayton Williams (Great Britain) 4, Antal Kocso 4, Kjetil Tveitdal (Norway) 1, Bengt Fogelberg (Sweden) 1. *Reserve: Ralf Baumann (Germany) 2.*

Jeremy Doncaster does not go forward to the World Final because two other British riders had already qualified from this semi final.

SEMI FINAL (Harsewinkel, Germany, Sunday, July 26): **Karl Maier (Germany) 25, Simon Wigg (Great Britain) 23, Mark Loram (Great Britain) 19, Egon Müller (Germany) 17, Stefan Dannö (Sweden) 14, Shane Parker 14** Vlastimil Cervenka (Czechoslovakia) 10, Henry Nielsen (Denmark) 10, Erik Stenlund (Sweden) 9, Jens Peter Nielsen (Denmark) 8, Ari Koponen (Finland) 7, André Pollehn (Germany) 6, Leigh Adams (Australia) 6, Mario Trupkovic (Germany) 5, Pavel Karnas (Czechoslovakia) 4, Will James (Great Britain) 1, Chris McGee (America) 0, Tony Briggs 0.

SEMI FINAL (Marianske-lazne, Czechoslovakia, Saturday, August 22): **Marcel Gerhard (Switzerland) 25, Ales Dryml (Czechoslovakia) 23, Gerd Riss (Germany) 21, Henrik Gustafsson 18, Steve Schofield (Great Britain) 15, Bernd Diener (Germany) 14,** Kai Niemi (Finland) 11, Rinat Mardanshin (Russia) 10, Joe Screen (Great Britain) 10, Petr Vandirek (Czechoslovakia) 10, Andreas Bössner (Austria) 5, Valentino Furlanetto 4, Zoltan Adorján (Hungary) 3, Martin Theobald (Germany) 2, Vaclav Maxim (Czechoslovakia) 2, Juha Moksunen (Finland) 2, Christian Strobel (Germany) 2, Igor Stoliarov (Russia) 2, Gaspar Forgac (Czechoslovakia) 1.

The semi final was allocated to Marianske-lazne, Czechoslovakia, but rained off on Sunday, July 5 and Monday, July 6. The organisers notified the FIM they could not afford to stage the meeting but later reversed that decision.

WORLD FINAL

Pfarrkirchen Langbahn, Germany
Sunday, September 13, 1992

1	**Marcel Gerhard**	**5**	**3**	**5**	**5**	**5**	**23**
2	Mitch Shirra	4	4	5	4	4	21
3	Karl Maier	5	5	4	4	2	20
4	Mark Loram	4	4	4	3	3	18
5	Gerd Riss	5	5	2	5	1	18
6	Ales Dryml	2	5	3	3	0	13
7	Henrik Gustafsson	3	3	3	2		11
8	Klaus Lausch	3	1	5	1		10
9	Uwe Gessner	4	4	1	F		9
10	Stefan Dannö	1	2	4	2		9
11	Egon Müller	2	2	2	R		6
12	Andy Smith	2	3	0	F		5
13	Borivoj Hadek	3	2	0			5
14	Marvyn Cox	1	1	3			5
15	Bernd Diener	0	0	2			2
16	Steve Schofield	0	1	1			2
17	Shane Parker	0	0	1			1
18	Simon Wigg	E	0	R			0
	Reserve: Luis Vallejos	*1*					*1*

1971 (Oslo, Norway)
1 IVAN MAUGER 27, 2 Manfred Poschenrieder 26, 3 Runo Wedin 22, 4 Jan Kater 15, 5 Bent Norregaard Jensen 13, 6 Barry Briggs 10, 7 Don Godden 10, 8 Hans Siegl 9, Sven Sigurd 9, Willihard Thomsson 9, 11 Josef Unterholzner 8, 12 Kurt Petersen 7, 13 Bernt Hornfeld 6, Jan Holm Nielsen 6, Jon Odegard 6, 16 Walter Matl 4, 17 Reijo Koski 3, 18 Hans Zierk 0.

1972 (Mühldorf, West Germany)
1 IVAN MAUGER 30, 2 Manfred Poschenrieder 23, 3 Jon Odegard 18, 4 Hans Siegl 17, Bent Norregaard Jensen 17, 6 Antonin Svab 14, 7 Hans Zierk 13, 8 Josef Angermüller 11, Willihard Thomsson 11, 10 Don Godden 9, Rudi Kastl 9, 12 Jan Kater 6, 13 Heinrich Sprenger 4, 14 Gottfried Schwarze 3, Henning Hansen 3, 16 Matti Olin 2, 17 Nils Haraldsen 1, Runo Wedin 1.

1973 (Oslo, Norway)
1 OLE OLSEN 24, 2 Hans Siegl 20, 3 Manfred Poschenrieder 20, 4 Don Godden 19, 5 Jan Kater 15, Josef Angermüller 15, 7 Runo Wedin 11, Willihard Thomsson 11, 9 Egon Müller 10, 10 Milan Spinka 7, 11 Einar Egedius 6, Sture Lindblom 6, 13 Zdenek Májstr 3, Bernt Hornfeld 3, 15 Bent Norregaard Jensen 2, 16 Jon Odegard 0, Conny Samuelsson 0, Hakan Storm 0.

1974 (Scheeßel, West Germany)
1 EGON MÜLLER 30, 2 Ivan Mauger 26, 3 Alois Wiesböck 21, 4 Anders Michanek 15, 5 Don Godden 13, Josef Angermüller 13, 7 Peter Collins 11, Jon Odegard 11, 9 Manfred Poschenrieder 10, 10 Preben Bollerup 9, Jiri Stancl 9, 12 Christoph Betzl 8, 13 Preben Rosenkilde 5, 14 Milan Spinka 4, 15 Hans Zierk 3, 16 Stanislaw Kubicek 2, 17 Gottfried Schwartze 1, 18 Edgar Stangeland 0.
Jan Kater and Ole Olsen qualified, did not ride.

1975 (Radgona, Yugoslavia)
1 EGON MÜLLER 27, 2 Ivan Mauger 22, 3 Ole Olsen 19, 4 Barry Briggs 19, 5 Christoph Betzl 17, 6 Anders Michanek 13, 7 Hans Wassermann 11, Don Godden 11, Peter Collins 11, 10 Manfred Poschenrieder 9, Jiri Stancl 9, 12 Vaclav Verner 8, 13 Hans Zierk 5, 14 Joachim Kall 4, Vlado Kocuvan 4, 16 Runo Wedin 2, 17 Kristian Præstbro 1, 18 Stefan Kekec 0.
Zdenek Kudrna and Edgar Stangeland, reserves, did not ride.

1976 (Marianske-lazne, Czechoslovakia)
1 IVAN MAUGER 26, 2 Ole Olsen 25, 3 Egon Müller 21, 4 Alois Wiesböck 21, 5 Jiri Stancl 16, 6 Zdenek Kudrna 14, 7 Anders Michanek 12, 8 Christoph Betzl 10, 9 Josef Angermüller 9, 10 Vaclav Verner 8, 11 Barry Briggs 7, 12 Don Godden 5, 13 Emil Sova, reserve, 5, 14 Hans Wassermann 4, Wilhelm Duden 4, 16 Edgar Stangeland 3, 16 Conny Samuelsson 1, Stanislaw Kubicek 1, 18 Jan Verner, reserve, 0.

1977 (Aalborg, Denmark)
1 ANDERS MICHANEK 20, 2 Hans Siegl 18, 3 Ole Olsen 18, 4 Jiri Stancl 15, 5 Joachim Kall 14, 6 Alois Wiesböck 13, 7 Ales Dryml 12, 8 Ivan Mauger 12, Kristian Praestbro 12, 10 Georg Hack 11, 11 Christoph Betzl 9, 12 Zdenek Kudrna 8, 13 Hans Wassermann 5, 14 Jan Verner 4, 15 Vaclav Verner 3, 16 Jan Kater 2, 17 Otto Lantenhammer 2, 18 Egon Müller 0.
Peter Collins and Hans Zierk, qualified, did not ride.
Francesco Biginato, reserve, did not ride.

1978 (Mühldorf, West Germany)
1 EGON MÜLLER 26, 2 Alois Wiesböck 26, 3 Peter Collins 24, 4 Ivan Mauger 24, 5 Ole Olsen 23, 6 Georg Hack 19, 7 Karl Maier 17, 8 Jiri Jirout 12, 9 Jiri Stancl 11, 10 Ales Dryml 10, 11 Scott Autrey 9, Kristian Praestbro 9, Jan Verner 9, 14 Don Godden 8, 15 Zdenek Kudrna 7, 16 Wilhelm Duden, 17 Otto Lantenhammer, reserve, 1.
Anders Michanek, reserve, did not ride.

1979 (Marianske-lazne, Czechoslovakia)
1 ALOIS WIESBÖCK 21, 2 Anders Michanek 20, 3 Ole Olsen 19, 4 Jiri Stancl 17, 5 Georg Hack 16, 6 Karl Maier 13, 7 Egon Müller 12, 8 Kristian Praestbro 11, 9 Michael Lee 9, 10 Ales Dryml 8, Ivan Mauger 8, 12 Peter Collins 7, 13 Christoph Betzl 6, Wilhelm Duden 6, 15 Alf Busk 3, 16 Zdenek Kudrna 2, 17 Francesco Biginato 1, Walter Grubmüller 1.
Don Godden and Hubert Sprenger, reserves, did not ride.

1980 (Scheeßel, West Germany)
1 KARL MAIER 23, 2 Egon Müller 18, 3 Josef Aigner and Christoph Betzl 16, 5 Georg Hack 14, 6 Wilhelm Duden 11, 7 Ivan Mauger 9, 8 Zdenek Kudrna 9, 9 Ole Olsen 8, 10 Michael Lee 8, 11 Peter Collins 7, 12 Jiri Stancl 6, 13 Chris Morton 5, 14 Milan Spinka 5, 15 Frits Koning 3, 16 Anders Michanek 2, 17 Bruce Penhall 0.

Alois Wiesböck scored 18 points to finish third but was later disqualified after it was found his engine was over the prescribed limit. The FIM awarded bronze medals to both Aigner and Betzl.

Kai Niemi and Erik Pedersen, reserves, did not ride.

1981 (Radgona, Yugoslavia)
1 MICHAEL LEE 23, 2 Christoph Betzl 20, 3 Anders Michanek 19, 4 Georg Gilgenreiner 19, 5 Egon Müller 16, 6 Phil Collins 14, 7 Josef Aigner 13, 8 Hans Otto Pingel 12, 9 Peter Collins 10, 10 Ivan Mauger 6, 11 Jiri Stancl 6, 12 Georg Hack 5, 13 Karl Maier 5, 14 Zdenek Kudrna 4, 15 Stefan Kekec 3, 16 Alois Wiesböck 1, Vlado Kocuvan 1, 18 Wilhelm Duden 0.
Bruce Penhall and Steve Bastable, reserves, did not ride.

1982 (Korskro, Denmark)
1 KARL MAIER 24, 2 Alois Wiesböck 22, 3 Egon Müller 21, 4 Georg Gilgenreiner 15, 5 Peter Collins 15, 6 Ivan Mauger 14, 7 Ole Olsen 11, 8 Anders Michanek 9, 9 Hans Nielsen 8, 10 Christoph Betzl 7, Georg Hack 7, 12 Marcel Gerhard 6, 13 Simon Wigg 5, 14 Bobby Schwartz 4, 15 Jiri Stancl 4, 16 Chris Morton 4, 17 Josef Aigner 4, 18 Phil Collins 0.
Petr Ondrasik and Hans Otto Pingel, reserves, did not ride.

1983 (Marianske-lazne, Czechoslovakia)
1 SHAWN MORAN 22, 2 Jiri Stancl 20, 3 Karl Maier 18, 4 Alois Wiesböck 16, 5 Finn Rune Jensen 16, 6 Ales Dryml 15, 7 Simon Wigg 11, 8 Egon Müller 11, 9 Ivan Mauger 10, 10 Georg Hack 9, 11 John Titman 9, 12 Hans Nielsen 7, 13 Bobby Schwartz 4, 14 Les Collins 3, 15 Marcel Gerhard 3, 16 Ole Olsen 3, 17 Hans Otto Pingel 2, 18 Heinrich Diener 1.
Klaus Lausch and Michael Lee, reserves, did not ride.

1984 (Herxheim, West Germany);
1 ERIK GUNDERSEN 23, 2 Egon Müller 19, 3 Karl Maier 17, 4 Peter Collins 16, 5 Finn Rune Jensen 16, 6 Gerd Riss 13, 7 Ales Dryml 10, 8 Jiri Stancl 9, 9 Marcel Gerhard 9, 10 John Titman 8, 11 Jeremy Doncaster 7, 12 Hans Nielsen 7, 13 Ivan Mauger 5, 14 Josef Aigner 5, 15 Hans Otto Pingel 4, 16 Kai Niemi 4, 17 Les Collins 4, 18 Shawn Moran 3.
Günter Bünning and Bo Petersen, reserves, did not ride.

1985 (Korskro, Denmark)
1 SIMON WIGG 22, 2 Jiri Stancl 19, 3 Peter Collins 18, 4 Shawn Moran 17, 5 Egon Müller 17, 6 Bobby Schwartz 15, 7 Martin Hagon 12, 8 Gerd Riss 11, 9 Jeremy Doncaster 9, 10 Georg Hack 7, 11 Klaus Lausch 6, 12 Finn Rune Jensen 5, 13 Vaclav Verner 5, 14 Ivan Mauger 4, 15 Ales Dryml 4, Petr Ondrasik 4, 17 Heinrich Diener 2, 18 Brian Jakobsen, reserve, 2, 19 Marcel Gerhard 0, Chris Morton, reserve, 0.

1986 (Pfarrkirchen, West Germany)
1 ERIK GUNDERSEN 25, 2 Peter Collins 18, 3 Marcel Gerhard 18, 4 Gerd Riss 17, 5 Hans Nielsen 14, 6 Karl Maier 11, 7 Bernd Diener 10, 8 Kai Niemi 10, 9 Petr Vandirek 9, 10 Shawn Moran 8, 11 Hans Otto Pingel 8, Emil Sova 8, 13 Phil Collins 5, 14 Roland Dannö 4, 15 Pavel Karnas 4, 16 Heinrich Diener 4, 17 Trevor Banks 3, 18 Alois Wiesböck 0.
Ari Koponen and Jiri Svoboda, reserves, did not ride.

1987 (Mühldorf, West Germany)
1 KARL MAIER 22, 2 Simon Wigg 21, 3 Shawn Moran 19, 4 Martin Hagon 19, 5 Egon Müller 15, 6 Heinz Huber 14, 7 Erik Gundersen 10, 8 Steve Baker 10, 9 Gerd Riss 9, 10 Lubomir Jedek 9, 11 Finn Rune Jensen 6, 12 Alois Wiesböck 6, 13 Trevor Banks 5, 14 Klaus Lausch 4, 15 Kai Niemi 3, 16 Erik Stenlund 3, 17 Pavel Karnas 2, Simon Cross, reserve, 2, 19 Chris Morton 2, 20 Petr Vandirek, reserve, 0.

1988 (Scheeßel, West Germany)
1 KARL MAIER 42, 2 Klaus Lausch 32, 3 Chris Morton 31, 4 Hans Nielsen 27, 5 Gerd Riss 26, 6 Heinrich Diener 26, 7 Roland Dannö 24, 8 Simon Wigg 21, 9 Jens Henry Nielsen 15, 10 Egon Müller 15, 11 Sam Ermolenko 13, 12 Petr Vandirek 9, 13 Kai Niemi 9, 14 Steve Schofield 6, 15 Antonin Kasper 4, 16 Simon Cross 3.
Steve Baker and Ari Koponen, reserves, did not ride.

1989 (Marianske-lazne, Czechoslovakia)
1 SIMON WIGG 38, 2 Ales Dryml 37, 3 Karl Maier 33, 4 Erik Stenlund 28, 5 Egon Müller 22, 6 Hans Nielsen 20, 7 André Pollehn 19, 8 Mario Trupkovic 19, 9 Marcel Gerhard 17, 10 Marvyn Cox 16, 11 Gerd Riss 12, 12 Steve Schofield 12, 13 Borivoj Hadek 12, 14 Petr Vandirek 9, 15 Chris Morton 8, 16 Klaus Lausch 1.
Finn Rune Jensen and Antonin Kasper, reserves, did not ride.

1990 (Herxheim, West Germany)
1 SIMON WIGG 37, 2 Karl Maier 30, 3 Hans Otto Pingel 30, 4 Marcel Gerhard 28, 5 Klaus Lausch 28, 6 Marvyn Cox 23, 7 Erik Stenlund 21, 8 Borivoj Hadek 19, 9 Georg Limbrunner 15, 10 Mark Loram 15, 11 Petr Vandirek 14, 12 Ales Dryml 10, 13 Gerd Riss 9, 14 Steve Schofield 9, 15 Pavel Karnas 8, 16 Mario Trupkovic 4, 17 Jens Henry Nielsen, reserve, 3, 18 Finn Rune Jensen, reserve, 2.
Jan O. Pedersen, qualified, did not ride.

1991 (Marianske-lazne, Czechoslovakia)
1 GERD RISS 24, 2 Ales Dryml 21, 3 Jan O. Pedersen 21, 4 Marcel Gerhard 18, 5 Mitch Shirra 17, 6 Stefan Dannö 12, 7 Karl Maier 10, 8 Andy Smith 10, 9 Simon Wigg 10, 10 Mark Loram 8, 11 Klaus Lausch 7, 12 Marvyn Cox 7, 13 Steve Schofield 5, 14 Erik Stenlund 4, 15 Hans-Otto Pingel 3, 16 Walter Scherwitzki 1, 17 Jan Holub 1, 18 Borivoj Hadek 1.
Andreas Bössner and Mario Trupkovic, reserves, did not ride.

1992 (Pfarrkirchen, Germany)
1 MARCEL GERHARD 23, 2 Mitch Shirra 21, 3 Karl Maier 20, 4 Mark Loram 18, 5 Gerd Riss 18, 6 Ales Dryml 13, 7 Henrik Gustafsson 11, 8 Klaus Lausch 10, 9 Uwe Gessner 9, 10 Stefan Dannö 9, 11 Egon Müller 6, 12 Andy Smith 5, 13 Borivoj Hadek 5, 14 Marvyn Cox 5, 15 Bernd Diener 2, 16 Steve Schofield 2, 17 Shane Parker 1, 18 Luis Vallejos, reserve,1, 19 Simon Wigg 0.
Vlastimil Cervenka and Kai Niemi, reserves, did not ride.

- **MARCEL Gerhard's victory in the 1992 World Long Track Final brought Switzerland a first-ever FIM shale medal.**
- ***EGON Müller, 43, qualified for a record SEVENTEENTH World Long Track Final in 1992 – 19 years after making his debut. In his 17 appearances, Müller has won the championship three times, finished second twice and also picked up two bronze medals.***
- **LUIS Vallejos became the first Argentinian rider to reach a World shale final when he rode as reserve in the 1992 World Long Track Final.**
- ***GERMANY has provided nine winners in the competition's 22 stagings.***

Mark's costly miss

MARK LORAM missed out on the biggest pay-day of his life as Leigh Adams took the rich pickings on a World title.

When the two Homefire League rivals came to the tapes for a run-off for the World Under 21 title, Loram knew that victory would not only bring him the crown but also a £10,000 bonus on offer from the sport's major sponsors Coal Products Limited for any Englishman winning an individual world title.

And scarcely a week later the cost of missing the start on a rain-soaked Pfaffenhofen track had risen by a further £15,000 as Gary Havelock's World Final victory would have qualified Loram for a half share of the additional £30,000 offered if a British rider won both the major titles!

It was Loram's second defeat against the Swindon number one, as he had also given second best to the Victorian in the opening race and only got his second chance thanks to Homefire Lions' team-mate Joe Screen's heat 14 victory over the otherwise unbeaten Adams.

Screen's own chances had been hit by a shock second place to Sweden's Jörgen Hültgren in his opening ride and he was shut out of a run-off when he couldn't make up enough ground to catch Loram in heat 18 – a crucial race that also embraced Norwegian Champion Lars Gunnestad who won three races but was surprisingly pegged back in last place in his second ride.

Britain departed from tradition by running a domestic qualifying round at Long Eaton although the Speedway Control Board reserved the right to nominate riders to fill the four available places in the World qualifier at Belle Vue.

It was a wise move as a clash of dates saw Ipswich in Gold Cup action at Poole the same evening, ruling out both David Norris and Ben Howe.

Defending British Under 21 champion Screen was everyone's favourite to win at Station Road – the track closest to his Chesterfield home – but when he failed to finish his last race the title went to Cradley Heath's Scott Smith with Mark Loram in second place.

Screen had to be content with third place but as the top three all went through to Belle Vue he was on his way.

The fourth slot went to Norris, much to the disappointment of Eastbourne's Paul Dugard who had recovered from a traumatic experience immediately before the Long Eaton meeting got underway.

He was one of half a dozen riders who appeared to fail an alcohol test and actually missed the parade while he was taking a second test away from the pits exhaust fumes.

He passed that without a blink and it was generally accepted that the meter had been giving false readings although Dugard still seemed slightly bemused as he collected only three points from his two opening rides but then emerged as a genuine rostrum contender.

Smith lost a run-off at Belle Vue and had to accept a non-riding reserve rôle at the semi final stage but the three remaining Brits all won through to the World Final where 16-year-old Pole Tomasz Bajerski became the youngest-ever rider to win a World Final race.

QUALIFYING ROUND 1 (Belle Vue, England, Sunday, May 24): **Joe Screen (England) 15, Leigh Adams (Australia) 13, Niklas Klingberg (Sweden) 12, David Norris (England) 11, Mark Loram (England) 11, Jacob Olsen (Denmark) 11, Stefan Andersson (Sweden) 7, Rene Madsen (Denmark) 6+3**, Scott Smith (England) 6+2, Allan Nielsen (Denmark) 5, Jan Schelde (Denmark) 4, Stefan Ekberg (Sweden) 4, Johnny Andersen (Denmark) 3, Jim Groen (Holland) 3, Henk Bangma (Holland) 1, Mark Lemon (Australia) 0. *Reserves: Carl Stonehewer 6, Peter Scully 0.*

QUALIFYING ROUND 2 (Meißen, Germany, Sunday, May 17): **Tomasz Gollob (Poland) 14, Zsolt Kovacs (Hungary) 12, Lars Gunnestad (Norway) 11, Tomasz Topinka (Czechoslovakia) 11, Vladimir Visvader (CIS) 10, Joachim Kugelmann (Germany) 10, Jacek Rempala (Poland) 9, Andrzej Zarzecki (Poland) 8,** Robert Sawina (Poland) 8, Csaba Csoban (Hungary) 8, Oleg Kiptev (CIS) 6, Sergei Kusin (CIS) 5, Fanel Popa (Romania) 4, Ingar Hvamstadt (Norway) 3, Peter Würsch (Germany) 1, Marian Stefan (Romania) 0.

QUALIFYING ROUND 3 (Mariestad, Sweden, Saturday, May 30): **Viktor Gaidym (CIS) 15, Mikael Karlsson (Sweden) 14, Hans Clausen (Denmark) 12, Jörgen Hültgren (Sweden) 10, Allan Fog (Denmark) 10, Kim Brandt (Denmark) 9, Robert Johansson (Sweden) 7+3, Mattias Koch (Germany) 7+2,** Aleksander Biznja (Latvia) 7+1, Marcus Andersson (Sweden) 7+0, Petri Vaatsio (Finland) 5, Toni Havu (Finland) 5, Vitaly Smirnitskih (CIS) 5, Björn A. Tönnesen (Norway) 4, Jörn Arve Ardal (Norway) 2, Niklas Finne (Finland) 1.

QUALIFYING ROUND 4 (Wolfslake, Germany, Sunday, June 28): **Grzegorz Rempala 15, Antonin Svab 14, Norbert Magosi (Hungary) 11, Thomas Hopp (Germany) 10, Tomasz Bajerski (Poland) 10, Jiri Staricek (Czechoslovakia) 9, Massimo Mora (Italy) 8+3, Gabor Rôth (Hungary) 8+2**, Christophe Dubernard (France) 8+1, Sascha Wehrle (Germany) 6, Henry Sievers (Germany) 3, Stephane Tresarieu (France) 2, Luca Taccini (Italy) 2, Rene Kuhr (Austria) 1, Antonin Hrubant (Czechoslovakia) 0, Rene Pfeiffer (Austria) 0. *Reserves: Heiko Mülle (Germany) 8, Johann Rieder (Germany) 4.*

SEMI FINAL 1 (Tarnow, Poland, Sunday, July 12): **Joe Screen 14, Mark Loram 12+3, Leigh Adams 12+2, Tomasz Gollob 11, Lars Gunnestad 10, Niklas Klingberg 10, Robert Sawina 10, David Norris 8,** Rene Madsen 7, Andrzej Zarzecki 6, Jacek Rempala 6, Jacob Olsen 4, Stefan Andersson 4, Joachim Kugelmann 2, Vladimir Visvader 2, Zsolt Kovacs 2.

SEMI FINAL 2 (Brovst, Denmark, Sunday, July 12): **Mikael Karlsson 15, Hans Clausen 14, Viktor Gaidym 11, Robert Johansson 11, Tomasz Bajerski 11, Jörgen Hültgren 11, Kim Brandt 9,** Jiri Staricek 8, Massimo Mora 7, Allan Fog 4, Grzegorz Rempala 4, Gabor Röth 4, Christophe Dubernard 3, **Mattias Koch 3,** Thomas Hopp 2, Antonin Svab 2.

Mattias Koch seeded to the World Final as the highest scoring German entrant.

WORLD FINAL

Pfaffenhofen, Germany

Sunday, August 23, 1992

1 LEIGH ADAMS	**3**	**3**	**3**	**2**	**3**	**14 +3**
2 Mark Loram	2	3	3	3	3	14 +2
3 Joe Screen	2	3	3	3	2	13
4 Lars Gunnestad	3	0	3	3	1	10
5 Tomasz Gollob	1	2	1	3	3	10
6 David Norris	1	2	2	1	3	9
7 Niklas Klingberg	2	2	1	2	2	9
8 Jörgen Hültgren	3	1	1	1	2	8
9 Hans Clausen	3	1	2	1	1	8
10 Mikael Karlsson	0	2	2	2	2	8
11 Tomasz Bajerski	0	3	2	0	1	6
12 Viktor Gaidym	E	1	0	2	1	4
13 Robert Johansson	fx	1	1	1	R	3
14 Kim Brandt	2	0	X	0	0	2
15 Robert Sawina	1	fx	-	-	-	1
16 Matthias Koch	0	0	0	0	0	0
Reserves						
Rene Madsen	0	0	0			0
Jiri Staricek	F	E	F			0

1992

WORLD UNDER 21 CHAMPION

Leigh Adams

(Swindon and Australia)

THE FIM launched the first Junior Championship in 1977 under the label of the European Junior Championship although the event has always been open to riders from both the Americas and Australasia.

In 1988 it was officially given full status as the World Junior Championship for riders under the age of 21.

One of the rules which applied until the end of the 1991 season was that if any competitor reached the semi-final stage of the World Championship (i.e. the Inter Continental Final, the Continental Final or, in 1991, the Semi Finals) then he had to choose between continuing in that competition or withdrawing and continuing in the Junior Championship. From 1992 riders were allowed to compete in both competitions without any restriction.

EUROPEAN JUNIOR CHAMPIONSHIP

1977 (Vojens, Denmark)
1 ALF BUSK 9, 2 Joe Owen 8, 3 Les Collins 7, 4 Lars Ericsson 6, Zytun Gafurov 6, Hans Nielsen 6, Peter Lempenauer 6, 8 Lillebror Johansson 4, Marek Okoniewski 4, 10 Alexander Chaljavin 3, Jiri Svoboda 3, Andrzej Huszcza 3, Franz Kreimoser 3, 14 Rudi Muts 2, Nikolai Manev 2, 16 Paolo Noro 0.

Meeting abandoned after 12 heats. Result to stand.

1978 (Lonigo, Italy)
1 FINN RUNE JENSEN 13, 2 Kevin Jolly 12, 3 Neil Middleditch 12, 4 Steve Finch 12, 5 Erik Gundersen 11, 6 Hans Nielsen 10, 7 Josef Juza 8, Pavel Karnas 8, 9 Henryk Olszak 6, Ryszard Romaniak 6, 11 Fausto Birbini 5, Leif Johansson 5, 13 Nikolai Manev 4, Mieczyslaw Kmieciak 4, 15 Armando Giglioli 2, Roman Jankowski 2.

1979 (Leningrad, Soviet Union)
1 RON PRESTON 13, 2 Airat Faljzulin 12, 3 Ari Koponen 11, 4 Knud Ellegaard 10, 5 Anders Eriksson 9, Stanislav Urban 9, 7 Trond Skretting 8, Marek Kempa 8, 9 Zbyszek Holy 7, Vladimir Pankin 7, 11 Jaromir Bartos 6, Hans Albert Klinge 6, 13 Stefan Berec 5, 14 Josef Aigner 4, 15 Jan Eriksson 3, 16 Fausto Birbini 1.

1980 (Pocking, West Germany)
1 TOMMY KNUDSEN 14, 2 Tony Briggs 12, 3 Dennis Sigalos 11, 4 Erik Gundersen 11, 5 Ari Koponen 9, Marek Kepa 9, Nei Collins 9, 8 Nigel Flatman 8, 9 Antonin Kasper 8, 10 Josef Aigner 6, 11 Lars Hammarberg 5, Christian Brandt 5, Rif Saitgareev 5, 14 Hans Albert Klinge 4, 15 Miroslav Berlinski 3, 16 Shawn Moran 2.

1981 (Slany, Czechoslovakia)
1 SHAWN MORAN 15, 2 Antonin Kasper 14, 3 Jiri Hnidak 13, 4 Roman Matousek 10, 5 Mark Courtney 10, 6 Piotr Podrzycki 9, Kent Noer 9, 8 Miroslav Berlinski 8, Lubomir Jedek 8, 10 Georg Greif 5, 11 Hans Albert Klinge 4, Peter Ravn 4, 13 Anders Eriksson 3, 14 Zoltán Hajdú reserve, 2, 15 Roger Gustafsson 1, Flemming Pedersen 1, Peter Nieder, reserve, 1, 18 Zoltán Adorján 0.

1982 (Pocking, West Germany)
1 ANTONIN KASPER 14, 2 Mark Courtney 12, 3 Peter Ravn 12, 4 Lance King 11, 5 Jan O. Pedersen 10, 6 Zoltán Hajdú 9, Oleg Volokhov 9, John Jørgensen 9, 9 David Bargh 8, 10 Giorgio Zaramella 6, Zoltán Adorján 6, 12 Georg Greif 4, 13 Vladimir Trofimov 3, Klaus Lausch 3, Brian Jacobsen 3, 16 Sándor Tihanyi 0.

1983 (Lonigo, Italy)
1 STEVE BAKER 13, 2 David Bargh 12, 3 Marvyn Cox 11, 4 John Jørgensen 10, Oleg Volokhov 10, Neil Evitts 10, 7 Jozsef Petrikovics 9, 8 Valentino Furlanetto 8, 9 Peter Carr 7, 10 Zenon Kasprzak 6, 11 Sándor Tihanyi 5, Jan O. Pedersen 5, Vladimir Trofimov 5, 14 Heinz Huber 4, 15 Andras Kovacs 3, 16 Giorgio Zaramella 1.

1984 (King's Lynn, England)
1 MARVYN COX 12, 2 Neil Evitts 11, 3 Steve Lucero 11, 4 Hans Wahlstrom 11 5 Jozsef Petrikovics 10, Andy Smith 10, Frank Andersen 10, 8 Lars Andersson 9, 9 Armando Castagna 8, 10 Oleg Volokhov 6, 11 Leif Wahlmann 5, 12 Giorgio Zaramella 5, 13 Flemming Rasmussen 4, 14 Valentino Furlanetto 3, 15 Wojciech Zaluski 2, 16 Klaus Lausch 1, Kurt Hansen, reserve, 1, 18 Jiri Broz, reserve, 0, Paul Clarke, reserve, 0.

†Leif Wahlmann died of injuries received in a Heat 13 crash.

1985 (Abensberg, West Germany)
1 PER JONSSON 15, 2 Jimmy Nilsen 13, 3 Ole Hansen 11, 4 Kenneth Nyström 11, 5 Gerd Riss 9, Juha Moksunen 9, Roman Matousek 9, 8 Valentino Furlanetto 8, Kurt Hansen 8, 10 Miroslav Prager 6, Igor Marko 6, 12 Einar Kyllingstad 5, 13 Mikael Teurnberg 4, Heinz Huber 4, 15 Barnabas Gyepes 1, Peter Schroeck, reserve, 1, Peter Hehlert, reserve, 0.
Michael Datzmann qualified, did not ride.

1986 (Rovno, Soviet Union)
1 IGOR MARKO 13, 2 Tony Olsson 12, 3 Brian Karger 11, 4 Bohumil Brhel 10, 5 Jan Jakobsen 10, Conny Ivarsson 10, 7 Jan Stæchmann 8, 8 Mikael Teurnberg 8, 9 Andrew Silver 7, 10 Zbigniew Blazejczak 7, 11 Nigel De'ath 5, David Cheshire 5, 13 Gerd Riss 4, 14 Allan Johansen 3, 15 Jan Holub, reserve, 3, 16 Robert Nagy 2, 17 Igor Zverev 1, Josef Fejfar, reserve, 1.

1987 (Zielona Gora, Poland)
1 GARY HAVELOCK 13, 2 Piotr Swist 11, 3 Sean Wilson 11, 4 Bo Arrhen 11, 5 Tommy Dunker 11, 6 Peter Nahlin, reserve, 9, 7 Gaspar Forgac 8, 8 Vladimir Kalina 7, 9 Niklas Karlsson 6, 10 Tor Einar Helm 6, 11 Ronnie Correy 5, 12 Borivoj Hadek 5, 13 Cezary Owizyc 5, 14 Oleg Kurguskin 4, 15 Torben Hansen 4, 16 Slawomir Drabik 2, Allan Johansen 2.

WORLD JUNIOR CHAMPIONSHIP

1988 (Slany, Czechoslovakia)
1 PETER NAHLIN 14, 2 Henrik Gustafsson 11, 3 Brian Karger 11, 4 Kenneth Arnfred 11, 5 Krister Karlsson 10, 6 Niklas Karlsson 10, 7 Tommy Dunker 9, 8 Piotr Swist 9, 9 Troy Butler 8, 10 Waldemar Ciesewicz 8, 11 Rusian Koval 6, 12 Zbigniew Blazejczak 4, 13 Jan Schinagl 3, 14 Slawomir Dudek 3, 14 Jaroslaw Olszewski 3, 16 Vladimir Kalina 0.

1989 (Lonigo, Italy)
1 GERT HANDBERG 13, 2 Chris Louis 13, 3 Niklas Karlsson 12, 4 Henrik Gustafsson 11, 5 Mark Loram 10, 6 Frede Schøtt 9, 7 Leigh Adams 9, 8 Claus Jacobsen 6, 9 René Aas 6, 10 Craig Hodgson 5, 11 Kenneth Lindby 5, 12 Dean Standing, reserve, 5, 13 Jan Holub, reserve, 4, 14 Peter Karlsson 4, 15 Piotr Swist 3, 16 Jaroslaw Olszewski 2, 17 Slawomir Dudek 1, 18 Riccardo Salamon 0.

1990 (Lvov, Soviet Union)
1 CHRIS LOUIS 14, 2 René Aas 13, 3 Tony Rickardsson 10, 4 Jaroslaw Olszewski 10, 5 Shane Parker 9, 6 Lars Gunnestad 9, 7 Brian Andersen 8, 8 Shane Bowes 7, 9 Jaroslaw Szymkowiak 6, 10 Dean Standing 6, 11 Massimo Mora 6, 12 Dariusz Sledz 5, 13 Zsolt Böszörmányi 5, 14 Georgi Petranov 4, 15 Andrej Korolev 3, 16 Viktor Gaidym 2, 17 Attila Kovács 1, 17 Peter Karlsson 0.

1991 (Coventry, England)
1 BRIAN ANDERSEN 14, 2 Morten Andersen 14, 3 Jason Lyons 11, 4 Shane Parker 10, 5 Joe Screen 10, 6 Jacob Olsen 9, 7 Niklas Klingberg 8, 8 Frede Schøtt 8, 9 Joakim Karlsson 6, 10 Jimmy Engman 6, 11 Viktor Gaidym 6, 12 Piotr Paluch 5, 13 Robert Kuzdzal 4, 14 Marek Hucko 3, 15 Zsolt Böszörmenyi 2, 16 Dean Barker, reserve, 2, Jacek Rempala, reserve, 2, 18 Adam Labedzki 0.

1992 (Pfaffenhofen, Germany)
1 LEIGH ADAMS 14+3, 2 Mark Loram 14+2, 3 Joe Screen 13, 4 Lars Gunnestad 10, 5 Tomasz Gollob 10, 6 David Norris 9, 7 Niklas Klingberg 9, 8 Jörgen Hültgren 8, 9 Hans Clausen 8, 10 Mikael Karlsson 8, 11 Tomasz Bajerski 6, 12 Viktor Gaidym 4, 13 Robert Johansson 3, 14 Kim Brandt 2, 15 Robert Sawina 1, 16 Mattias Koch 0.
Reserves: Rene Madsen 0 and Jiri Staricek 0.

DANISH DELIGHT ... Brian Andersen (centre) and Morten Andersen (right) made it a Scandinavian 1-2 when they finished first and second after a run-off in the 1991 World Under 21 Final. Australia's Jason Lyons was third

CRACKER CHRIS ... Chris Louis became the first rider to win a conventional speedway World Final in the old Soviet Union

Gert's title warning

CRADLEY Heath's young Danish star Gert Handberg fired a World Championship message to his rivals...when he won the Champions Cup.

Handberg was pegged back to third place in his second ride but still maintained Scandinavia's dominance of the championship and to add another title to his 1989 World Under 21 crown.

Hungary's Zoltán Adorján remains the only non-Nordic winner of a meeting supposed to embrace the national champion from all major speedway nations.

British Champion Gary Havelock experienced problems in two of his races but won the remaining three at Rovno, scene of Chris Louis's World Under 21 Championship success.

Roll of Honour

1986 (Pardubice, Czechoslovakia)
1 ERIK STENLUND 14, 2 Viktor Kuznetsov 13 (+3), 3 Antonin Kasper 13 (+2), 4 Armando Castagna 12, 5 Roman Matousek 10, 6 Zoltán Adorján 8, 7 Petr Vandirek 7, 8 Pavel Karnas 7, 9 Nikolai Manev 7, 10 Zenon Plech 6, 11 John Davis 6, 12 Siegfried Eder 6, 13 Kreso Omerzel 4, 14 Juha Moksunen 4, 15 Henny Kroeze 2, 16 Petr Kucera, reserve 1, 17 Diethelm Triemer 0.

1987 (Miskolc, Hungary)
1 ZOLTÁN ADORJÁN 12 (+3), 2 Armando Castagna 12 (+2), 3 Antonin Kasper 11 (+3), 4 Neil Evitts 11 (+2), 5 Per Jonsson 11 (+1), 6 Erik Stenlund 10, 7 Gerd Riss 9, 8 Diethelm Triemer 8, 9 Jens Peter Nielsen 6, 10 Wojciech Zabialowicz 6, 11 Valeri Gordeev 5, 12 Heinrich Schatzer 5, 13 Nikolai Manev 4, 14 Juha Moksunen 3, 15 Henny Kroeze 2, 16 Artur Horvat 2.

1988 (Krsko, Yugoslavia)
1 PER JONSSON 14, 2 Gerd Riss 13 (+2), 3 Zoltán Adorján 13 (+2), 4 Heinrich Schatzer 11, 5 Per Sørensen 10, 6 Antonin Kasper 9, 7 Zenon Kasprzak 9, 8 Valentino Furlanetto 8, 9 Valeri Gordeev 8, 10 Kelvin Tatum 6, 11 Ari Koponen 5, 12 Zvenko Pavlic 4, 13 Henk Steman 3, 14 Nikolai Manev 3, 15 Artur Horvat 2, 16 Einar Tor Hjelm 2.

1989 (Natschbach-Loipersbach, Austria)
1 JAN O. PEDERSEN 15, 2 Mitch Shirra 13, 3 Kai Niemi 10, 4 Simon Wigg 9, 5 Sam Ermolenko 9, Roman Matousek 9, Zoltán Adorján 9, Klaus Lausch 9, 9 Lars Gunnestad 8, 10 Vladimir Trofimov 7, 11 Per Jonsson 5, Armando Castagna 5, 13 Nikolai Manev 4, 14 Robert Funk, reserve, 3, 15 Zenon Kasprzak 2, 16 Artur Horvat 1, Heinrich Schatzer 1.

1990 (Lonigo, Italy)
1 HANS NIELSEN 14, 2 Zoltán Adorján 14 (+2), 3 Simon Wigg 12, 4 Klaus Lausch 11, 5 Arnt Førland 11, 6 Peter Karlsson 10, 7 Rif Saitgareev 10, 8 Juha Moksunen 8, 9 Petr Vandirek 7, 10 Wojciech Zaluski 6, 11 Valentino Furlanetto 5, 12 Toni Pilotto 5, 13 Gregor Pintar 3, 14 Nikolai Manev 2, 15 Gianni Famari 1, 16 René Elzinga 1.
■ *Ronnie Correy did not arrive and was replaced by a second Italian rider Gianni Famari.*

1991 (Elgane, Norway)
1 LARS GUNNESTAD 14, 2 Antonin Kasper 13, 3 Hans Nielsen 12, 4 Tony Rickardsson 11, 5 Mikhail Starostin 11, 6 Armando Castagna 10, 7 Zoltan Hajdu 8, 8 Klaus Lausch 8, 9 Tor Einar Hjelm 7, 10 Kelvin Tatum 6, 11 Zenon Kasprzak 5, 12 Heinrich Schatzer 3, 13 Gregor Pintar 2

■ *Kai Niemi (Finland) did not ride because of injury but was not replaced by his Federation. René Elzinga (Holland), did not arrive. The United States of America did not send a representative.*

LONE STAR ... 1991 Champions Cup winner Lars Gunnestad, Norway's only world class performer

1992 (Rovno, Ukraine)
1 GERT HANDBERG (Denmark) 13, 2 Zoltan Adorján (Hungary) 12, 3 Peter Karlsson (Sweden) 11, 4 Vaclav Milik (Czechoslovakia) 10, 5 Armando Castagna (Italy) 10, 6 Andreas Bössner (Austria) 10, 7 Mike Faria (America) 9, 8 Gary Havelock (Great Britain) 8, 9 Andrej Korolov (Latvia) 5, 10 Roland Kolros (Germany) 5, 11 Matti Pellinen (Finland) 4, 12 Sergei Kusin (Russia) 4, 13 Einar Kyllingstad (Norway) 4, 14 Gregor Pintar (Slovenia) 2, 15 Slawomir Drabik (Poland) 2, 16 Rob Steman (Holland) 0. *Reserves: Vladimir Trofimov (Russia) 6, Viktor Gaidym (Russia) 4.*

CHAMPIONS CUP
Rovno, Ukraine, Sunday, August 2

1 GERT HANDBERG (Denmark) 13, 2 Zoltán Adorján (Hungary) 12, 3 Peter Karlsson (Sweden) 11, 4 Vaclav Milik (Czechoslovakia) 10, 5 Armando Castagna (Italy) 10, 6 Andreas Bössner (Austria) 10, 7 Mike Faria (America) 9, 8 Gary Havelock (Great Britain) 8, 9 Andrej Korolov (Latvia) 5, 10 Roland Kolros (Germany) 5, 11 Matti Pellinen (Finland) 4, 12 Sergei Kusin (Russia) 4, 13 Einar Kyllingstad (Norway) 4, 14 Gregor Pintar (Slovenia) 2, 15 Slawomir Drabik (Poland) 2, 16 Rob Steman (Holland) 0.
Reserves: Vladimir Trofimov (Russia) 6, Viktor Gaidym (Russia) 4.

EUROPEAN GRASS TRACK CHAMPIONSHIP

QUALIFYING ROUND 1 (Vechta, Germany, Sunday, May 10): **Olaf Brüggemann (Germany) 23, Jörg Pingel (Germany) 21, Vaclav Milik (Czechoslovakia) 20, Benny Tögersen (Denmark) 18, Peter Lloyd (Great Britain) 17, Viktor Gaidym (Russia) 13, Daniel Bohac (Czechoslovakia) 12, Rob Fortune (Great Britain) 11, Rias Cazemier (Holland) 8**, Erik Eijbergen (Holland) 8, Klaus-Peter Gerdemann (Germany) 7, Sergei Kusin (Russia) 4, Patrick Goret (France) 4, Richard Musson (Great Britain) 3, Esa Einola (Finland) 3, Janne Moksunen (Finland) 3, Hans-Jürgen Brikey (Germany) 3, Siegfried Eder (Austria) 2.

QUALIFYING ROUND 2 (Eenrum, Holland, Sunday, May 17): **Kent Noer (Denmark) 24, Anne van der Helm (Holland) 24, Christophe Dubernard (France) 17, Helmut Zapf (Germany) 17, Jan Schinagl (Czechoslovakia) 15, Jim Groen (Holland) 12, David Ochocki (France) 11, Wolfgang Buske (Germany) 11, Gerard Kok (Holland) 10, John Petersen (Denmark) 8**, Christian Ianotto (France) 8, Steven van der Helm (Holland) 8, Pieter Visser (Holland) 4, Aki Ala-Rihimaki (Finland) 3, Roger Söderberg (Sweden) 3, Ralf Baumann (Germany) 2, Jaromir Lach (Czechoslovakia) 1, Stefan Hedstrom (Sweden) 0.

SEMI FINAL 1 (Stadskanaal, Holland, Monday, June 1 - Monday, June 8): **Oleg Kurguskin 24, Rif Saitgareev 22, Paulus Ellens 18, Henk Snijder 14, Vaclav Milik 14, Uppie Bos 14, Armando dal Chiele 12, Trevor Banks 12, Jörg Pingel 10**, Rob Fortune 10, Peter Lloyd 7, Daniel Rohac 7, Rias Cazemier 5, Viktor Gaidym 4, Benny Tögersen 3, Ola Westlund 3, Rene Mortensen 1, Olaf Brüggeman 0.

SEMI FINAL 2 (Cloppenburg, Germany, Saturday, July 18-Sunday, July 19): **Kent Noer 25, Anne van der Helm 19, Zdenek Schneiderwind 17, Klaus Ziegler 16, Detlef Conradi 15, Christophe Dubernard 15, Helmut Zapf 10, Gerard Kok 10, Peter Read 9**, Andy Riley 8, Jim Groen 8, Ralf Strach 7, Christian Ianotto 6, Tony Forward 5, Thomas Meggle 5, Jan Schinagl 3, Massimo Mora 1, David Ochocki 1.

FINAL (Alken, Belgium, Saturday July 24-Sunday, July 25): 1 Anne van der Helm 21, 2 Vaclav Milik 20, 3 Paulus Ellens 19, 4 Helmut Zapf 18, 5 Henk Snijder 15, 6 Kent Noer 13, 7 Trevor Banks 13, Peter Read 12, Rob Fortune 9, Christophe Dubernard 9, Jörge Pingel 6, Andy Riley 6, Armando dal Chiele 6, Rif Saitgareev 4, Zdenek Schneiderwind 3, Klaus Ziegler 3, Detlef Conradi 2, Gerard Kok 1.

Roll of Honour

1978 (Hereford, England):	**1 Chris Baybutt**	**2 Franz Kolbeck**	**3 Don Godden**
1979 (Assen, Holland)	**1 Gerald Short**	**2 Gunther Brackland**	**3 John Britcher & Tjalle Reitsma**
1980 (Bad Waldsee, Germany)	**1 Willi Stauch**	**2 Gerald Short**	**3 Sture Lindblom**
1981 (A. de Lussac, France)	**1 Neil Farnish**	**2 Bernie Leigh**	**3 Skjold Larsen**
1982 (Damme, Germany)	**1 Jeremy Doncaster**	**2 Mike Beaumont**	**3 Josef Maucher**
1983 (Nandlstad, Germany)	**1 Christian Brandt**	**2 Erich Schäfferer**	**3 Gerald Short**
1984 (Eenrum, Holland)	**1 Martin Hagon**	**2 Vaclav Verner**	**3 Kent Noer**
1985 (La Reole, France)	**1 Clayton Williams**	**2 Harm Horstede**	**3 Tommy Broch**
1986 (Eenrum, Holland)	**1 Simon Cross**	**2 Steve Schofield**	**3 Joachim Reitzel**
1987 (Nandlstad, Germany)	**1 Roman Matousek**	**2 Joachim Reitzel**	**3 Robert Dolman**
1988 (Joure, Holland)	**1 Frank Kehlenbeck**	**2 Will James**	**3 Kent Noer**
1989 (La Reole, France)	**1 Robert Barth**	**2 Kent Noer**	**3 John Bostin**
1990 (Uithuizen, Holland)	**1 Robert Barth**	**2 Kent Noer**	**3 Henk Snijder**
1991 (Werlte, Germany)	**1 Rif Saitgareev**	**2 Thomas Diehr**	**3 Trevor Banks**
1992 (Alken, Belgium)	**1 Anne van der Helm**	**2 Vaclav Milik**	**3 Paulus Ellen**

Right Royal Year

BUCKINGHAM Palace must have seemed like home from home for Chris Morton in 1992.

He made two trips down The Mall. Firstly when he became the first English rider to be awarded the M.B.E. for his services to speedway and then, later in the summer, as one of this country's World Champions.

To celebrate her 30 years on the throne, The Queen invited all this country's sporting World Champions to the Palace for a special Garden Party.

Photographer Mike Patrick was on hand to record both occasions for posterity.

Mike snapped Chris in suitable dress for his inauguration as a Member of the British Empire.

And the main picture below is a group photograph of 16 British World Champions who were guests at the Palace.

Left to right: Malcolm Simmons, Ray Wilson, Martin Ashby, Chris Louis, Dave Jessup, Jeremy Doncaster, Peter Collins, John Davis, John Louis, Simon Wigg, Chris Morton, Michael Lee, Simon Cross, Paul Thorp, Terry Betts and Norman Hunter.

▲ ***CRASH ... Australia's Jason Lyons ploughs into Martin Dugard (who sustained a fractured collar bone) to provide photographer Kevin Gipp with one of the action pix of the decade***

☛ ***WINNERS ... the Homefire Lions' squad that won the series against Australia: David Norris, team manager Eric Boocock, Mark Loram, Graham Jones, Chris Louis, Gary Havelock, Dean Barker and Sean Wilson. The injured Martin Dugard is missing from the celebrations***

Lions let it slip slide away...

ENGLAND began their international season with high hopes...but ended in deep dungeon!

Joint managers Eric Boocock and Colin Pratt saw the Homefire Lions demolish Australia in the opening Test of the first domestic series between the two countries since 1969 with an overwhelming victory at

1992 Results

First Test, Oxford, Friday, April 10

ENGLAND 73			
1 †Gary Havelock	3 3 **2** 3 N 3	14	1
2 Chris Louis	**2 2** 0 N 3 **2**	9	3
3 Martin Dugard	**3 3 3 3 3 3**	**18**	
4 Dean Barker	1 **2 2 2 2** 1	10	4
5 Mark Loram	1 2 **1** N **2 1**	7	3
6 Marvyn Cox	3 **1** 2 2 3 N	11	1
7 David Norris	0 1	1	
8 Dean Standing	**1** 2	3	1
AUSTRALIA 35			
1 Leigh Adams	1 1 3 2 1 3	11	
2 Steve Regeling	0 0 N **1** 0 N	1	1
3 Shane Parker	2 3 3 1 1 0	10	
4 Glenn Doyle	R 0 1 0 N 1	2	
5 Craig Boyce	2 1 1 3 2 0	9	
6 Mark Carlson	0 0 0 N 0 2	2	
7 Trevor O'Brien	0 0	0	
8 Tony Langdon	0 fx	0	

Second Test, Reading, Monday, June 15

ENGLAND 55			
1 †Jeremy Doncaster	**1 2** 0 1 **2** N	6	3
2 §David Mullett	2 3 2 3 3 1	14	
3 Andy Smith	1 fx N N N N	1	
4 Ray Morton	3 2 1 **1** 2 2	11	1
5 Mark Loram	**1** 3 1 2 3 2	12	1
6 Chris Louis	2 1 0 **1** 1 **1**	6	2
7 Dean Standing	2 0 0 0	2	
8 Dean Barker	3 fn	3	
AUSTRALIA 53			
1 Leigh Adams	3 3 3 2 3 3	17	
2 Jason Lyons	0 1 N N N N	1	
3 Shane Parker	0 2 3 fx R **2**	7	1
4 Troy Butler	2 0 1 3 2 3	11	
5 Craig Boyce	3 1 2 3 1 3	13	
6 †Stephen Davies	0 0 N N N N	0	
7 David Cheshire	0 F R	0	
8 Shane Bowes	**2** 0 1 0 1	4	1

Third Test, Peterborough, Sunday, July 5

ENGLAND 49			
1 Martin Dugard	3 2 fn N N N	5	
2 Mark Loram	1 **1** 2 2 2 2	10	1
3 †Gary Havelock	1 1 3 3 3 1	12	
4 Chris Louis	0 0 N 1 0 3	4	
5 Graham Jones	1 3 0 0 0 N	4	
6 Sean Wilson	3 1 3 2 2 1	12	
7 David Norris	**1** 0 **1** 0	2	2
8 Dean Barker	0 0	0	
AUSTRALIA 59			
1 Craig Boyce	2 3 2 1 **1** 3	12	1
2 †Mick Poole	0 **2 1** 3 2 **2**	10	3
3 Leigh Adams	**2** 2 3 0 3 3	13	1
4 Jason Lyons	3 0 fn N N N	3	
5 Shane Parker	0 3 2 3 3 0	11	
6 Troy Butler	2 fx N 1 0 2	5	
7 Stephen Davies	**1** 2 1 1	5	1
8 David Cheshire	0	0	

England win the series 2-1.
Australia Team Manager: Neil Street

Oxford.

So comprehensive was the winning margin (and the manner of the victory) that representations were made to Australian team manager Neil Street asking him to pick a stronger side for the two remaining Tests.

By the end of the series the Kangaroos had recorded their first win over England in this country since 1953 and came within two points of taking the series!

England's results deteriorated after their shock defeat at Peterborough – the first English Division Two track to host a senior international.

America piled on the agony in the second Homefire series of the summer with three wins in a row.

Bobby Ott was an international revelation in the opening match at his home track and England's lack of depth must have worried the two men in charge.

It was the first time since they had taken over at the beginning of 1986 that Boocock and Pratt had been on the receiving end of a home white-wash but there were no recriminations, a startling contrast to an earlier decade when the England managers faced an automatic chop if results went against them!

The two former World Finalists were confirmed as the 1993 managers.

1992 Results

First Test, Belle Vue, Sunday, July 12

ENGLAND 40

1 †Gary Havelock	2 2 1 2 2 2	11	1
2 Sean Wilson	1 1 0 3 X 0	5	2
3 Chris Louis	2 1 2 1 1 2	9	
4 Andy Smith	fx 0 1 0 N N	1	1
5 Kelvin Tatum	3 2 0 2 0 0	7	
6 Graham Jones	2 0 1 1 1 1	6	2
7 §Carl Stonehewer	1	1	1
8 Dean Standing	0	0	

UNITED STATES OF AMERICA 68

1 Ronnie Correy	0 2 2 1 2 2	9	4
2 Greg Hancock	3 3 3 0 3 3	15	
3 Bobby Ott	**3 3 3 3 3 3**	**18**	
4 Kelly Moran	1 1 2 2 2 1	9	3
5 †Sam Ermolenko	1 3 3 3 3 3	16	
6 Rick Miller	F N N N N N	0	
7 Charles Ermolenko	0 R 1 0	1	
8 §Josh Larsen	0	0	

Second Test, Wolverhampton, Monday, August 17

ENGLAND 47

1 †Gary Havelock	2 2 1 3 1 2	11	2
2 Andrew Silver	1 1 2 2 2 0	8	3
3 Kelvin Tatum	1 0 1 0 N R	2	1
4 Marvyn Cox	0 2 2 1 1 1	7	1
5 Joe Screen	2 3 3 2 2 2	14	
6 Chris Louis	1 1 0 N N 0	2	1
7 David Norris	2 0	2	
8 Sean Wilson	1	1	1

UNITED STATES OF AMERICA 61

1 Ronnie Correy	3 1 2 0 0 3	9	
2 Bobby Ott	0 3 1 1 3 1	9	1
3 Greg Hancock	2 2 3 3 1 3	14	1
4 Billy Hamill	3 0 0 2 3 1	9	1
5 †Sam Ermolenko	**3 3 3 3 3 2**	**17**	**1**
6 Kelly Moran	0 0 N N N N	0	
7 Charles Ermolenko	0 0 0	0	
8 Josh Larsen	3	3	

Third Test, Swindon, Sunday, September 17

ENGLAND 50

1 †Gary Havelock	2 2 1 3 2 0	10	2
2 Mark Loram	3 1 2 2 1 3	12	3
3 Martin Dugard	0 0 N N N 0	0	
4 Joe Screen	3 2 1 2 R 1	9	
5 §Steve Schofield	0 2 0 3 1 1	7	2
6 Simon Cross	2 3 1 R 2 0	8	
7 Andrew Silver	1	1	
8 Sean Wilson	3 0	3	

UNITED STATES OF AMERICA 58

1 Ronnie Correy	1 1 3 1 3 3	12	
2 Charles Ermolenko	fx N N N N N	0	
3 †Kelly Moran	1 0 0 1 0 1	3	2
4 Greg Hancock	2 1 3 3 3 2	14	
5 Bobby Ott	3 3 2 2 3 3	16	
6 Josh Larsen	1 0 0 1 0 N	2	1
7 Doug Nicol	*did not ride*		
8 Sam Ermolenko	3 2 0 2 2 2	11	4

United States of America win the series 3-0.
USA Team Manager: John Scott

Roll of Honour

1961	
Cardiff	**England C 64 USA 44**
Poole	**England C 46 USA 52**
Dublin	**England C 42 USA 66**
Aldershot	**England C 76 USA 32**
Swindon	**England C 57 USA 58**

■ ***The above series took place on Third Division tracks and at Shelbourne Park, Dublin, Republic of Ireland where the Americans were based throughout the summer.***

1980	
Wimbledon	**England 54 USA 54**
Cradley Heath	**England 62 USA 46**
Hull	**England 47 USA 61**
Poole	**England 44 USA 63**
Swindon	**England 49 USA 59**
1981	
Belle Vue	**England 60 USA 48**
Poole	**England 55 USA 53**
Swindon	**England 64 USA 43**
Ipswich	**England 44 USA 52**
Cradley Heath	**England 69 USA 38**
1982	
Wimbledon	**England 63 USA 45**
Swindon	**England 47 USA 60**
Ipswich	**England 42 USA 66**
Belle Vue	**England 61 USA 47**
Poole	**England 39 USA 69**
1983	
Wimbledon	**England 43 USA 64**
Swindon	**England 57 USA 51**
Poole	**England 63 USA 45**
Ipswich	**England 42 USA 66**
Sheffield	**England 58 USA 50**
1984	
Swindon	**England 50 USA 58**
Sheffield	**England 58 USA 50**
Cradley Heath	**England 49 USA 59**
Ipswich	**England 36 USA 72**
Poole	**England 50 USA 58**
1985	
Belle Vue	**England 48 USA 58**
Ipswich	**England 50 USA 58**
Swindon	**England 42 USA 66**
1986	
Sheffield	**England 60 USA 48**
Oxford	**England 60 USA 47**
Ipswich	**England 62 USA 43**
1987	
Ipswich	**England 55 USA 52**
Sheffield	**England 59 USA 49**
1988	
◆ ***Bradford***	**England 57 USA 33**
◆ **1988 Diamond Jubilee Series**	
1989	
Cradley Heath	**England 64 USA 44**
Belle Vue	**England 53 USA 54**
Swindon	**England 75 USA 32**
1991	
Bradford	**England 64 USA 44**
Wolverhampton	**England 56 USA 52**
Swindon	**England 57 USA 51**
1992	
Belle Vue	**England 40 USA 68**
Wolverhampton	**England 47 USA 61**
Swindon	**England 50 USA 58**

THREE touring sides – two from Sweden and regular visitors Slangerup from Denmark – provided an early season curtain raiser for a variety of First and Second Division clubs.

Rospiggarna, with Erik Stenlund and Vesa Ylinen impressive, were beaten only once, by the side that subsequently went on to dominate the Division Two honours.

Sunday, March 22

RYE HOUSE 41

1 †Martin Goodwin	2 2 3 2 2 0	11	1
2 Sean Courtney	1 1 1 1	4	2
3 Jan Pedersen	1 2 1 1	5	1
4 Trevor O'Brien	1 1 fx3	5	1
5 Mark Courtney	3 2 2 0 1	8	
6 John Wainwright	3 2 0 0	5	
7 Wayne Baxter	0 3 0 T	3	

SLANGERUP 49

1 †Bo Petersen	**3 3 3 3 2**	**14**	**1**
2 Per Sørensen	0 R 2 2	4	1
3 Brian Karger	**3 3 3 3 3**	**15**	
4 Lars Munkedal	0 3 2 2	7	1
5 Allan Johansen	2 1 1 fx	4	
6 Jesper Olsen	1 R 1 fn	2	1
7 Bo Sørensen	2 0 0 0 1	3	

Monday, March 23

WOLVERHAMPTON 51

1 Ronnie Correy	2 2 3 3	10	
2 Charles Ermolenko	1 1 2 2	6	3
3 †Sam Ermolenko	2 3 3 3 2	13	
4 Graham Jones	3 3 1 2 0	9	
5 Peter Karlsson	fx1 fnN	1	
6 Wayne Carter	3 1 2 2 1	9	3
7 Stephen Morris	1 1 0 fx1 N	3	1

INDIANERNA 38

1 †Henrik Gustafsson	3 2 3 2 2 1	13	
2 Stefan Dannö	0 0 0 1	1	1
3 Bo Petersen	3 3 3 2 3 3	17	
4 Magnus Oscarsson	F 0 1 0	1	
5 Dennis Löfqvist	fnN N T	0	
6 Tommy Lindgren	2 2 0 1 0	5	
7 Mikael Håglund	0 0 1 T 0 0	1	

Thursday, March 25

MIDDLESBROUGH 41

1 †Steve Regeling	2 2 F 0 3 1	8	1
2 Mark Lemon	fx1 1 R	2	1
3 Darren Sumner	3 2 3 3	11	
4 Donny Odom	3 2 1 0	6	1
5 David Cheshire	0 3 1 1 2	7	
6 Duncan Chapman	3 1 0 3 N	7	
7 Paul Pickering	E E 0 0 N	0	

SLANGERUP 47

1 †Jan Stæchmann	fnR 1 R	1	1
2 Per Sørensen	3 1 2 2 0	8	
3 Jan Pedersen	R 3 3 2	8	1
4 Lars Munkedal	1 1 3 2	7	1
5 Peter Ravn	2 3 3 2 3	13	
6 Jesper Olsen	F 2 0 2 1	5	2
7 Bo Sørensen	1 2 0 2	5	2

Thursday, March 26

IPSWICH 46

1 †Chris Louis	1 0 3 2 0	6	1
2 Jacek Rempala	2 1 1 2	6	1
3 Tony Rickardsson	1 R 1 3	5	
4 Shane Parker	R R 1 0	1	1
5 Zdenek Tesar	2 2 3 2 1	10	1
6 Ben Howe	2 2 3 2	9	2
7 David Norris	3 3 0 3	9	

INDIANERNA 43

1 †Henrik Gustafsson	3 3 3 1 3	13	
2 Stefan Dannö	0 fx2 T	2	
3 Bo Petersen	3 3 1 2 3 2	14	2
4 Magnus Oscarsson	1 1 0 N	2	1
5 Tony Olsson	3 2 0 1	6	1
6 Tommy Lindgren	1 2 0 2	5	1
7 Kenneth Johansson	0 0 N N 0	0	
8 Mikael Håglund	0 1	1	

Friday, March 27

PETERBOROUGH 49

1 Mick Poole	3 3 3 3 2	14	
2 Mark Blackbird	0 1 1 1	3	
3 †Stephen Davies	3 2 3 1 1	10	2
4 Paul Whittaker	1 0 0 2	3	1
5 Rodney Colquhoun	2 2 3 2	9	
6 Jason Crump	3 2 1 2	8	3
7 Paul Hurry	1 0 0 1	2	1

ROSPIGGARNA 41

1 †Tony Rickardsson	2 3 3 2 3 3	16	
2 Vesa Ylinen	1 1 2 1 0	5	3
3 Mikael Teurnberg	1 2 1 1	5	1
4 Stefan Lardner	0 0 0 N	0	
5 Erik Stenlund	3 3 2 2 3	13	
6 Patrik Karlsson	2 0 0 0	2	
7 Mikael Messing	0 0 T T 0	0	

Sunday, March 29

MILDENHALL 43

1 †David Smart	2 1 1 3	7	
2 Nigel Leaver	0 3 3 3 0	9	
3 Melvyn Taylor	R 3 3 3 3	12	
4 Gary Tagg	1 1 0 0	2	
5 Ian Barney	3 0 1 1	5	1
6 Jamie Habbin	3 1 0 2 1	7	
7 Savalas Clouting	1 0 0 N	1	

ROSPIGGARNA 47

1 †Tony Olsson	3 3 1 2	9	1
2 Vesa Ylinen	1 2 1 2 2	8	2
3 Mikael Teurnberg	3 2 3 2 1	11	1
4 Stefan Lardner	R 1 2 0	3	1
5 Erik Stenlund	2 2 1 3	8	1
6 Patrik Karlsson	2 0 2 R 2	6	1
7 Mikael Messing	0 2 E 0	2	1

Monday, March 30

EXETER 35

1 †Peter Jeffery	1 3 2 0 1	7	
2 Paul Fry	R R 2 1 0	3	1
3 Tony Olsson	3 2 R 0	5	
4 Colin Cook	1 R 1 2	4	1
5 Richard Green	2 2 3 3 1	11	1
6 Mark Simmonds	2 1 1 1 0	5	2
7 Ian Humphreys	N N N N	0	

ROSPIGGARNA 53

1 †Henrik Gustafsson	2 3 3 2	10	1
2 Vesa Ylinen	3 1 3 2 2	11	2
3 Mikael Teurnberg	2 2 2 3	9	
4 Stefan Lardner	0 0 3 1 3	7	1
5 Erik Stenlund	**3 3 2 3**	**11**	**1**
6 Patrik Karlsson	fx1 1 0	2	2
7 Mikael Messing	3 0 0 0	3	

Tuesday, March 31

MILTON KEYNES 34

1 Gordon Kennett	2 2 3 1 1 3	12	
2 Frank Smart	1 1 0 0	2	2
3 Richard Hellsén	F 2 1 1	4	1
4 †Peter Glanz	1 1 0 3	5	
5 Lars Munkedal	0 0 1 2	3	1
6 David Steen	2 3 0 2 F	7	
7 Justin Walker	1 T R R	1	1

ROSPIGGARNA 56

1 †Tony Rickardsson	**3 3 3 3 2**	**14**	**1**
2 Vesa Ylinen	0 2 2 2	6	2
3 Mikael Teurnberg	2 3 3 3 3	14	
4 Stefan Lardner	2 1 2 0	5	1
5 Erik Stenlund	3 3 2 1	9	2
6 Patrik Karlsson	3 0 0 2	5	
7 Mikael Messing	0 1 1 1	3	3

The Swedish side began their British tour at Long Eaton on Wednesday, March 25, but the meeting was abandoned after eight races. The scorers were: LONG EATON 19 (†Jan Stæchmann f x - R- 0, Colin White fn-2-1-3:1, Martin Dixon 2-1-3, Carl Blackbird 2-F- 2:1, Gary O'Hare 3-2- 5, Paul Blackbird 1-1-R- 2:2, Deon Prinsloo 2-2- 4) ROSPIGGARNA 28 (†Tony Rickardsson 3-3- 6, Vesa Ylinen 2-1-3- 6:1, Mikael Teurnberg 3-1- 4, Stefan Lardner 0-2- 2:1, Erik Stenlund 1-3- 4, Patrik Karlsson 3-3- 6, Mikael Messing E-0-0- 0).

1992 Diary JAN

DAY BY DAY

JANUARY

1 ICE expert Andy Campbell is named in the England squad to take on the Rest of the World at Telford ice rink.

2 TOMMY RANDER confirms that he is hoping to make an official application to promote at Hackney. He has until the end of the month to make a formal bid for a Second Division licence.

3 *AUDREY Hoskins, widow of the founder of speedway Johnnie Hoskins is buried alongside her late husband at St. Bartholomew's Church, Herne Bay, Kent, after passing away on Boxing Day, aged 97.*

4 ***MIDDLESBROUGH hope to have talks with American Donny Odom about joining the Bears – Oxford indicate they would be willing to let Australian Champion Craig Boyce move on after only one season at Sandy Lane – Long Eaton make a firm approach for Cradley Heath's transfer-listed Alan Grahame.***

5 *ARENA Essex are set to give Troy Pratt his chance in the First Division, partnering Andy Galvin at reserve in their line-up – Wolverhampton place a near £15,000 fee on the head of former England international Neil Collins who spent 1991 on loan to Belle Vue. Promoter Chris Van Straaten says he is not willing to loan out the rider for another year and will be looking for a full transfer.*

6 MILTON Keynes's future is likely to be decided shortly as promoter Terry Cheney continues secret negotiations to lease out the speedway rights at Elfield Park – American Ronnie Correy wants to stay at Wolverhampton despite interest from First Division newcomers Arena Essex – Peter Jeffery and Frank Smart sign 1992 contracts for Exeter.

7 ***COVENTRY make a move to sign World Under 21 Champion Brian Andersen, who spent the final weeks of 1991 with Second Division Newcastle although there was a clause in their agreement that he would be free to move to a Division One club.***

8 WOLVERHAMPTON transfer list former Commonwealth Finalist Andy Phillips.

9 *COVENTRY make an official approach for Middlesbrough's Paul Bentley, and also express an interest in Bradford's Andy Smith – Reading promoter Pat Bliss is appointed president of the newly-formed Sidecar Speedway Association in recognition of her past interest in the sport.*

10 JAMES Easter and Peter Oakes announce they will run Peterborough following the financial collapse of the previous promoting company. They tell a public meeting of fans: "We want to renew faith in the club."

11 *FORMER World Finalist Edward Jancarz, 45. dies in a stabbing incident at his home in Poland. His wife is arrested and charged with his murder. Jancarz spent six seasons racing in Britain for Wimbledon, rode in 10 World Finals and finished third in 1968 – David Walsh confirms he will stay at Berwick – Bradford's Michael Graves is to face an assault charge after an alleged attack on Berwick official Neil Grant during the 1991 summer.*

12 ***JOHN Cook, a former junior with the club, is appointed Eastbourne's new commercial manager and one of his first decisions is to drop the Dons nickname. The Sussex side will now revert to their traditional Eastbourne Eagles, ending their links with the old Wimbledon club – Australian Dave Hamnett warns Newcastle he may not return to Britain after suffering a nasty back injury at Milton Keynes. He awaits a further medical examination in February before deciding his future.***

13 HUNGARIAN Robert Nagy turns down the chance of joining Second Division Glasgow in favour of racing regularly in the Polish League – World Finalist Armando Castagna is to return to his old club Reading – King's Lynn fail in a bid to sign Ray Morton as the Racers offer him a new contract – Hans Nielsen switches to Jawa machinery – The BSPA confirm that Swindon are relegated.

14 TOP referee Frank Ebdon will be in charge of the World Pairs Final.

15 *RICHARD Knight opens contract talks to stay at Berwick – Dean Barker wants to leave Oxford – Wayne Garratt is released by Cradley Heath – Peterborough sign Ade Hoole on loan from Wolverhampton and open talks with Long Eaton's Mark Blackbird.*

16 THE FIM scrap the already agreed World Final calendar – throwing doubts on whether the 1994 meeting, scheduled for England, will take place – Ivan Mauger accepts the post of scout for Peterborough.

17 ADT Auctions will hold a board meeting early next month to decide whether to keep speedway at Blunsdon following the decision to relegate Swindon to Division Two.

18 TEENAGER Jason Crump indicates he wants to join a Division Two club rather than take his chance in the top flight – Bradford confirm they want to sign loanee Simon Wigg on a permanent basis.

19 *RYE HOUSE want to sign Danish star Jan Pedersen as a replacement for transfer-listed Melvyn Taylor – A Save Our Speedway campaign is launched in Swindon – Joe Screen agrees a new Belle Vue contract – Peter McBride is to quit as a major shareholder at Glasgow – he has agreed to sell his interest to local businessman Douglas Hopes.*

20 ***LONG Eaton complete the formal signing of Carl Blackbird, who spent 1991 on loan from Edinburgh – There are now real doubts about the future of Hackney following the failure of Tommy Rander to gather a consortium to take the track back into League racing – Coventry will release Sean Wilson to spend another loan season at Bradford – Poole make a firm approach for Oxford's unsettled Craig Boyce.***

21 EASTBOURNE are given permission to talk with Swindon's Andrew Silver – Travel Plus Tours, owned by James Easter, are appointed sole European ticket agents for the 1992 World Final.

22 *RICHARD Juul gets an unexpected contract offer from his 1991 club Newcastle – King's Lynn express an interest in Dean Barker.*

23 PETERBOROUGH drop plans to sign Polish star Jaroslav Olszewski, fourth in the 1991 World Under 21 Final – Ex-World Champion Michael Lee rules out a 1992 comeback with Poole – Sheffield promoter Cliff Carr warns his riders they will not be offered improved financial terms.

24 ALLAN Johansen is returning to British racing after nearly two year's absence. He will join Arena Essex – Coventry sign Andy Smith on loan from Bradford – with Sean Wilson remaining at Odsal.

25 GARY Allan (above) becomes the 1992 New Zealand Champion, one point ahead of Mark Thorpe.

26 LEIGH Adams wins the Australian Final with 14 points. Shane Parker, Mark Carlson and Jason Lyons join him in the Commonwealth Final but Todd Wiltshire's World Championship dream is over as he fractures his

pelvis in a first race crash.

27 *SWINDON are back in Division One after an Extraordinary General Council of the BSPA accepts Mildenhall and Milton Keynes into the 1992 Second Division. Former second halfer Dick Partridge and ex-Norwich rider Derek Hewitt are the men behind the Fen Tigers' revival after a two year absence from League racing – Under the Constitution which stipulates that Divisions should be of an equal strength if there are an even number of League tracks, Swindon are allowed to remain in Division One – Gary Allan (Poole) agrees a loan deal with King's Lynn.*

28 PAUL WHITTAKER and Paul Hurry agree to join Peterborough – Poole axe skipper Alun Rossiter and Aussie Mick Poole.

29 ***EXETER promoter Colin Hill officially announces that he and Roger Jones have taken over at Milton Keynes.***

30 ENGLAND star Kelvin Tatum is joining Bradford – Swedish star Jimmy Nilsen claims he is still owed £10,000 by Berwick.

31 *JASON Lyons asks Glasgow for a transfer – Middlesbrough slap a £10,000 fee on Paul Bentley, who wants to join Coventry.*

FEBRUARY

1 **GLASGOW open contract talks with Kenny McKinna, who spent the latter part of 1991 on loan to Middlesbrough.**

2 POOLE make an offer for Sheffield's transfer-listed Norwegian star Lars Gunnestad.

3 **WORLD Champion Per Jonsson will be returning to his old club Reading – Arena Essex pursue their interest in Swindon's Brian Karger.**

4 *THE Speedway Riders' Association are to become part of the 930,000-strong GMB union which already has Scottish footballers and Rugby League players among its members.*

5 **THE BSPA set up a working party to examine the contentious promotion and relegation issue – Ipswich tell Eastbourne they are not willing to pay a £10,000 fee for Neville Tatum, who spent part of 1991 on loan to the Connells' Witches.**

6 SWINDON switch their race-night from a Saturday to a Thursday – to allow greyhounds to move to the weekend.

7 ***BELLE VUE, Swindon and Poole are given the okay to talk with Glasgow's want-away Jason Lyons.***

8 AMERICAN Donny Odom (right) accepts Middlesbrough's offer of a team place – Dean Barker is ready to settle his differences with Oxford and sign a new contract – Leigh Adams wins the Australian Under 21 Championship for the fourth time – John Cearns, President of Wimbledon Stadium and whose father launched speedway at Plough Lane in 1928, dies.

9 **AUSTRALIAN Stephen Davies agrees to stay at Peterborough under the new promotion – Bradford are interested in Berwick's Kevin Little.**

10 NEWCASTLE rule Scott Lamb out of their team plans after he turns down their financial terms.

11 **POOLE sign Swedish international Mikael Blixt even though he is still recovering from a badly damaged wrist – Swindon and Eastbourne show interest in Berwick's Richard Knight.**

12 *RYE HOUSE'S Jens Rasmussen is told he will be able to race again after visiting hospital for a check-up on his broken leg.*

13 ***BRADFORD complete their team-building by signing Kevin Little on loan from Berwick – Dane Peter Ravn looks like being the odd rider out at Coventry – Aussie Steve Regeling fails to agree terms with Exeter and is likely to move to Middlesbrough in a deal that will see Lars Munkedal join Milton Keynes.***

14 ALAN Grahame and Neil Collins turn down offers from Long Eaton – Collins opts for Glasgow and Grahame signs for Stoke.

15 **SWINDON and Arena Essex agree terms for Brian Karger's move to Purfleet.**

'Ice one, Jonah

ANDY Campbell's three year reign as England's Ice King ended...spiked by the local hero!

Wolverhampton's Graham Jones finally overtook Campbell in the battle of the Brits and was given a thunderous reception by another full house at Telford.

The battling Jones claimed a rare victory over Campbell in heat 10 and then went on to complete an unbeaten day as he scored a 12 point maximum in England's third in a row win against the Rest of the World.

The only blot was in the Speedway Star Pairs where he failed to reach the semi finals even though he won his heat. With partner Shawn Venables in last place, opponents Garry Stead and Mark Loram went through to the next stage in a Knock Out competition.

Biggest disappointment for the sell-out crowd was the absence of Swiss butcher Jessy Inauen who had to withdraw after slicing off the top of his finger in an accident the day before the meeting!

INTERNATIONAL (Telford, Sunday, February 16)
ENGLAND 39 (Andy Campbell 3-3-3-1-10, Joe Screen **2**-1-3-0- 6:1, Simon Cross 1-1-**1**-0- 3:1, **Graham Jones 3-3-3-3- 12**, Alun Rossiter R-1-**2**-1- 4:1, Mark Loram 1-0-0- 1, Eric Monaghan X-1-2- 3) **REST OF THE WORLD 38** (Richard Hellsén X-2-3-3- 8, Steve Regeling X-0-X-0- 0, Tony Briggs 3-R-R-2- 5, Jan Stæchmann 2-**2**-**1**-**2**- 7:3, Peter Glanz **1**-3-2-0- 6:1, Shawn Venables 3-2-1- 6, David Steen **2**-**2**-2- 6:2)

Roll of Honour

1986	England 25 Rest of the World 52
	England 37 Rest of the World 52
1988	England 38 Rest of the World 40
1989	England 56 Rest of the World 34
1991	England 45 Rest of the World 32
1992	England 39 Rest of the World 38

SPEEDWAY STAR BEST PAIRS
1 JAN STÆCHMANN & PETER GLANZ
2 Eric Monaghan & Simon Cross
3 Andy Campbell & Joe Screen
3 Mark Loram & Garry Stead

BRITISH OPEN CHAMPIONSHIP
(Telford, Sunday, February 16)

1 GRAHAM JONES	**3**	**3**	**3**	**3**	**3**	**15**
2 Andy Campbell	3	3	2	3	3	14
3 Richard Hellsén	3	3	3	2	2	13
4 Jan Stæchmann	2	X	3	2	3	10
5 Tony Briggs	3	1	3	1	2	10
6 Joe Screen	R	2	2	3	2	9
7 Peter Glanz	2	3	2	1	1	9
8 Garry Stead	1	2	0	3	1	7
9 Eric Monaghan	2	1	1	2	0	6
10 Simon Cross	2	R	1	2	1	6
11 Alun Rossiter	X	2	1	0	2	5
12 David Steen	R	R	F	1	3	4
13 Steve Regeling	F	2	1	0	0	3
14 Shawn Venables	F	1	2	0	N	3
15 Mark Loram	0	0	0	1	1	2
16 Nigel Crabtree	1	0	0	0	0	1

Roll of Honour

1989 1 Andy Campbell	2 Steve Lawson	3 Richard Hellsén
1990 1 Andy Campbell	2 Richard Hellsén	3 Alun Rossiter
1991 1 Andy Campbell	2 Tony Briggs	3 Richard Hellsén
1992 1 Graham Jones	2 Andy Campbell	3 Richard Hellsén

16 *MILTON Keynes reveal their first SIX signings: Ian Barney, Peter Glanz, Richard Hellsén, Gordon Kennett, Lars Munkedal and David Steen.*

17 IN A surprise swoop Exeter sign Reading's Swedish Test star Tony Olsson as a replacement for Middlesbrough-bound Steve Regeling.

18 ***OLD favourites Kevin Hawkins (team manager), Richard Greer (Clerk of the Course) and Ken Matthews (junior team manager)***

are returning to Peterborough.

19 *TOP Scot Kenny McKinna agrees to join Edinburgh, after failing to agree terms with his previous club Glasgow – Coventry complete the signing of Paul Bentley from Middlesbrough.*

20 ANDERS Michanek, 1973 World Champion, will manage Swedish League side Rospiggarna on an early season tour of Britain – Aussie ace Glenn Doyle opts to join Eastbourne, despite talks with several Second Division tracks – Middlesbrough's Steve Regeling is appointed skipper of his new club – Arena Essex win the race to sign sensational American prospect Josh Larsen.

21 *CZECHOSLOVAKIA offer Zdenek Schneiderwind and Jan Holub to any interested Second Division track – Peterborough bring Mick Poole back to the East of England Showground in an £8,000 deal – Leigh Adams, John Davis and Dean Standing all agree to stay with Swindon – Wayne Garratt moves to Newcastle.*

22 GLASGOW are to give former Danish starlet Tim Korneliussen a chance to resurrect his injury-hit career – King's Lynn's popular timekeeper and programme columnist Herbert (H.H.) Howard collapses and dies on a family outing to Bognor Regis.

23 DEON Prinsloo is to link up with Long Eaton, on loan from First Division Eastbourne – Ipswich sign Polish international Jacek Rempala – Belle Vue continue talks with Jason Lyons and Edinburgh's Frede Schøtt – Richard Knight says he will stay at Berwick and race in Division Two – Sheffield are to give a team chance to 20-year-old unknown Australian Steve Johnston.

24 *DAZ Sumner is to return to his old club Middlesbrough after being left out of Belle Vue's team plans.*

25 PETERBOROUGH complete their team building by signing 16-year-old Jason Crump on loan from Poole and Rodney Colquhoun in a full transfer from the same club.

26 NEVILLE Tatum finally accepts Eastbourne's terms – Peter McNamara's name is circulated to all tracks after missing out at Long Eaton – Simon Cross and Gert Handberg sign their Cradley Heath contracts. Mark Robinson is also offered a team place at Dudley Wood.

27 IWADE has been granted a Training Track licence – after operating as a training ground for riders for 22 years.

28 *RICK Miller unveils details of his Testimonial meeting at the Speedway Star Speedway and Grass Track Show. He reveals that Bruce Penhall and Ole Olsen will compete in a series of match races.*

29 THE FIM allocate the 1994 World Final to England in a series of Spring Congress decisions – Jason Lyons will link up with Belle Vue in a £15,000 move from Glasgow – Mildenhall make their first signings, Nigel Leaver and David Smart – Ipswich put David Norris on the transfer list at his own request – Wolverhampton complete their line-up by naming Stephen Morris as number seven – Berwick turn their sights elsewhere after failing to agree financial terms with Bradford's Craig Hodgson– Andy Hackett is ruled out for the season after further tests on his broken leg – Edinburgh are to blood Polish rider Dariusz Fliegert, runner up in the 1990 Polish Under 21 Championship.

WORLD FINAL ROTA

	1993	1994	1995	1996	1997
INDIVIDUAL	Germany	England	Denmark	Sweden	Poland
TEAM	England	Denmark	Poland	Denmark	England
PAIRS	Denmark	Sweden	Czechoslovakia	Germany	Italy
UNDER 21	Czechoslovakia	Norway	Finland	Hungary	Denmark
LONG TRACK	Germany	Czechoslovakia	Denmark	n.a.	n.a.

MARCH

1 RYE House make a double swoop for the Courtney brothers! Mark switches from Berwick and Sean from Glasgow – Marvyn Cox agrees terms for another season with Poole – Newcastle wrap up a deal with Wolverhampton and sign Aussie Scott Norman.

2 ALUN Rossiter, left out of Poole's team plans, has talks with King's Lynn – Mistral Boilers tie up a sponsorship deal with Stoke.

3 *RICHARD GREEN finally agrees to continue his career at Exeter after lengthy negotiations with promoter Colin Hill.*

4 THE DRAW for the opening British rounds of the World Championship is made – and former World Finalists Simon Cross, Les Collins and Neil Evitts must start their title quest on Division Two tracks – Exeter ask the Speedway Control Board to re-asses Australian Frank Smart's average to four points, based on the six meetings he completed in 1991 – Video king Mike Bennett is to sponsor Sheffield's Reserve League team – Martin Goodwin breaks his wrist, playing with his children at his Tonbridge home.

5 ONE of the three Homefire international between England and Australia will be staged at Second Division Peterborough, the first time an English Second Division track has hosted an official senior Test.

6 SCOTT Lamb joins Berwick –Alun Rossiter formally signs for King's Lynn –Steve Camden is given the number seven race-jacket at Swindon.

7 *OIL giants Mobil are to sponsor Arena Essex's Troy Pratt – Eastbourne complete the full transfer of Andy Grahame from Oxford – Local van and truck dealers JT Commercials will back Poole.*

8 JURI Ivanov is crowned 1993 World Ice Speedway Champion after dropping just one point on each of the two-day title race.

9 MELVYN TAYLOR returns to his old club Mildenhall after local hauliers Taylor-Balls Transport agree to sponsor him.

10 *PETER CARR signs on the dotted line for another spell with Sheffield, the fourth Tiger to re-sign. Louis Carr, Neil Evitts and reserve Mark Hepworth have already agreed terms – Jamie Habbin joins Mildenhall.*

11 COAL Products Ltd., speedway biggest sponsors, offer a £50,000 bonus if a British rider wins both the World Under 21 Championship and the World Final – Bradford's Kelvin Tatum resigns as England skipper – Ipswich's David Norris asks to come off the transfer list – Jimmy Nilsen is returning to parent club Swindon after a season on loan to Berwick.

12 *GARY Tagg becomes the fifth rider to join newcomers Mildenhall, from First Division Reading – Ian Barney changes his mind about joining Milton Keynes, who sign Justin Walker as his replacement.*

13 THE Danish Motor Union give approval for 21 of their riders to race in Britain, including Frank Andersen – Glasgow give Sheffield permission to talk with transfer-listed Shane Bowes but insist they won't allow him to join them on loan for the season.

14 *SHEFFIELD tie up a team sponsorship deal with franchise leisure group Entertainment Xpress – Shane Bowes refuses to talk to First Division Belle Vue over a possible move.*

15 THE official opening of the 1993 season...and Rye House's Barron Janitorial Supplies individual meeting is called off because of heavy rain – Carl Stonehewer breaks his collar bone at Belle Vue's practice.

16 *WOLVERHAMPTON have new team sponsors. A local garage are to back the team who will be known as the Don Everall Ford Wolves – Speedway loses a weekly TV slot with the Sportscast Channel when they shut down.*

17 VETERAN Vaclav Verner turns down an offer to ride for Mildenhall, to concentrate on his coaching job at neighbours Peterborough – Frede Schøtt accepts Belle Vue's terms and will join them in a £9,000 move from Edinburgh – Chris Morton and his family are at Buckingham Palace where he receives his M.B.E.

18 IPSWICH teenager Ben Howe is in a 15-strong England squad from which the teams to face Australia will be chosen. Also back in contention is Simon Wigg – Kenny McKinna claims he was pushed out of Glasgow and says he was willing to sign for the Clyde Two Tigers by taking a pay cut – Shawn Moran is axed by Belle Vue after a contract dispute.

19 *KIWI Test star Mitch Shirra joins Swindon and will be the new*

club skipper. German Peter Schroeck is also signed by the ADT Robins – Teenager Mike Hampson gets a surprise late call up for his Belle Vue debut against Oxford as a replacement for Max Schofield who has refused terms. He's poised to join Second Division Newcastle – Peterborough official Richard Greer blacks out 600 homes after slicing through an 11,000 volt electricity cable – Ipswich's Tony Rickardsson wins the first meeting of the season, the Billy Sanders Memorial Trophy at his home track.

20 DANISH star Peter Ravn signs for Arena Essex even though he has been told there is no immediate team place for him – Local newspaper the Evening Telegraph are to sponsor Peterborough.

21 DAVID Wolstenholme completes the Sheffield line-up for the new season – Martin Goodwin is cleared to ride for Rye House, only a fortnight after breaking his wrist.

22 PAUL Fry is joining Exeter – Jens Rasmussen pencils in a May comeback date.

23 EXETER release promising young Aussie Frank Smart to sister track Milton Keynes. They also let teenager Justin Elkins return to parent track Poole. Ian Humphreys, out for a year, completes their squad.

24 ARENA Essex call off their scheduled opener against Kumla after two days of consistent rain.

25 STEPHEN Davies is appointed skipper at Peterborough, by a vote of his team-mates – Jan Stæchmann damages his knee in a first race crash before Long Eaton's match against touring Swedish side Rospiggarna is abandoned because of rain.

26 MICHAEL Lee announces his retirement, saying he will now concentrate solely on tuning engines – Peter Carr is to take over from brother Louis as Sheffield skipper.

27 SHEFFIELD cancel their planned opening fixture (April 2) because work on a new track fence won't be completed in time for the clash with Edinburgh.

28 BRADFORD's Premiership tie with Wolverhampton is postponed because of floodlighting failure at Odsal – Alan Grahame scores a 15-point debut maximum for Stoke – First Division new boys Arena Essex lose by only two points at King's Lynn.

29 OXFORD'S Troy Butler is rushed to hospital with back injuries after crashing on his Polish League debut – Mildenhall open contract talks with impressive Swedish visitor Mikael Teurnberg – Eastbourne's opening meeting is delayed, while the track doctor returns home for a vital piece of medical equipment.

30 DEBUTANT Ian Humphreys didn't complete a lap for new club Exeter as he fell in his opening ride and was ruled out with a badly grazed back – Gary Havelock will captain England in the first Test series of the summer against Australia.

31 ENGLAND name their first Test team of the year: Gary Havelock, Chris Louis, Joe Screen, Martin Dugard, Mark Loram, Marvyn Cox, Dean Barker and David Norris – Rospiggarna complete their British tour with their third successive victory, this time at Long Eaton. They also won at Mildenhall and Exeter.

APRIL

1 DANISH Under 21 international Jesper Olsen is joining Mildenhall.

2 EDINBURGH'S Gold Cup match at Middlesbrough is rained off – their FIFTH successive away postponement – Joe Screen is released by England to ride for his club side Belle Vue in their first Homefire League match of the season.

3 MILDENHALL take Ian Barney on a month's loan from Milton Keynes – Rodney Colquhoun scores his first British maximum in Peterborough's first home Gold Cup match against Stoke. Potters' Ade Hoole breaks his wrist after crashing through the pits fence.

4 BERWICK'S Scott Robson is taken to hospital with a suspected broken wrist after a spill in the shock 18-point Gold Cup home defeat against Newcastle.

5 EXETER team-mates Peter Jeffrey and Paul Fry end up in hospital after crashing at Rye House. Both are released – X-rays reveal that Scott Robson has no fracture.

6 REFEREE David Hughes, in charge at Jan O. Pedersen's first British meeting in 1983, will officiate at the World Champion's Testimonial – Simon Cross suffers an ankle injury at Wolverhampton.

7 SHEFFIELD cancel their second successive home match as work continues on their safety fence – America ask James Easter to become co-manager with long-serving John Scott – Peter Jeffery faces a lay-off after suffering a reaction to his Rye House crash. Doctors say he has delayed concussion and a fractured foot.

8 RYE House's Trevor O'Brien is called up by Australia for his first Test cap after manager Neil Street agrees to release Belle Vue's Jason Lyons to ride for his club – England pull out of a proposed three-Test series in Sweden after failing to agree financial terms.

9 SPARTA Aspro pay a Polish League record fee of £25,630 to Unia Leszno for Adam Labedzki – Bill Rawlinson resigns his Speedway Control Board position. He will be replaced by Colin Sweby who also took over from him as chairman of the Auto-Cycle Union Speedway and Grass Track Committee.

10 ENGLAND thrash Australia 73-35 in the first Homefire Test. Martin Dugard and Gary Havelock are unbeaten for the Homefire Lions – Richard Musson is axed by Belle Vue after failing to turn up for their match against Reading.

11 GARETH Rogers and Mick Powell hope to revive speedway in South Wales at a new venue midway between Cardiff and Newport – Dean Standing wins the World Championship qualifier on his return to former track Stoke.

12 A BUMPER crowd attend Rick Miller's Testimonial meeting where Ole Olsen and Bruce Penhall are the major on-track attractions – Sheffield's Simon Green is taken to hospital after crashing at Newcastle after team-mate Louis Carr pulled out after only two rides with suspected food poisoning.

13 REFEREE Barrie Richardson abandons Exeter's World Championship qualifier after an nasty accident in which Andy Galvin is taken to hospital with neck injuries. Because of the delay while the doctor accompanies him to hospital the meeting overruns the track's curfew. Richardson declares the result as it stood after 16 heats.

14 ANDY Galvin is released from hospital – Neil Evitts pulls out of the World Championship claiming he hasn't got the determination necessary to compete in the title chase.

15 SWINDON sign teenager Justin Elkins on loan from Poole, with Darren Boulton moving in the opposite direction – Coventry agree to let teenager Andy Meredith go on loan to Second Division Stoke.

16 THE Speedway Control Board order the re-staging of the abandoned Exeter World Championship round – Paul Bentley returns to his old track Middlesbrough and wins the World Championship qualifier.

17 KENNY McKinna fractures his cheekbone after crashing during Edinburgh's Gold Cup fixture against Berwick – Paul Smith is back in the Belle Vue side, replacing the sacked Richard Musson – Sheffield finally stage their opening home match and recover from a 10 point deficit to beat Middlesbrough.

18 SWEDISH star Mikael Teurnberg makes his debut for Mildenhall at Stoke. Ian Barney is dropped – Berwick consider an approach for sidelined Australian Nigel Alderton.

19 FIM Track Commission President Gunter Sorber hits out at rumours that the Grand Prix scheme has been shelved.

20 UNLUCKY Simon Cross fractures his knee cap in a tumble against Coventry – Wolverhampton take the Premiership – Jan Pedersen (Rye

DAY BY DAY

House) and ex-Rocket Melvyn Taylor (Mildenhall) have a centre green punch-up after a heat 4 clash. Gary Tagg refuses to ride in the meeting after his mechanic was barred from entering the pits as part of a long standing feud with the Rockets' management.

21 POOLE have talks with both Belle Vue and Shawn Moran over a move to Wimborne Road.

22 DAVID Mullett is a surprise name in the 16-strong England squad for the last two Tests against Australia – Cradley Heath ask the authorities to seed the injured Simon Cross through to the British semi finals of the World Championship – Scott Smith is a shock winner of the British Under 21 crown as favourite Joe Screen stops in his last race when bidding for a 15 point maximum.

23 KENNY McKinna undergoes surgery on his fractured cheek-bone – Cradley Heath's Simon Cross plea is turned down.

24 JOHN Davis breaks his leg at Arena Essex, crashing in heat three – Lars Munkedal is released by Milton Keynes. His team place goes to Ian Barney.

25 SIMON Cross insists he will ride in his World Championship round at Exeter despite his knee injury.

26 NEIL Collins withdraws from the World Championship British semi finals to ride for his club Glasgow – The Reserve League match between Rye House and Milton Keynes was abandoned after a heat two crash in which Mark Jolly wrecked the safety fence beyond on-the-day repair – Alan Mogridge (Arena Essex) suffers facial injuries at Swindon – Gary Tagg is suspended by Mildenhall following his Rye House no show.

27 ALAN Grahame is called up to replace broken leg victim John Davis in the World Championship British semi final at his old track Cradley Heath – Simon Cross rides through the pain barrier to win the re-arranged World Championship round at Exeter with a five-ride maximum – Armando Castagna (Reading) breaks three fingers at Wolverhampton.

28 SWINDON pull out of talks with Peter Nahlin – Sheffield axe reserve David Wolstenholme and bring in teenager Steve Knott as his replacement – Wolverhampton are preparing to call up novice Craig Taylor if Charles Ermolenko (gashed knee) fails a fitness test before their Speedway Star Cup tie with Swindon.

29 BELLE Vue's Kelly Moran is to join Swindon on loan – and elder brother Shawn ends his stand-off and will return to the Aces' line up – Tom Knudsen breaks his collar bone in Poole's clash with Eastbourne.

30 STEVE Masters misses his Swindon debut as he is delayed en route to Blunsdon. But new boy Kelly Moran makes it.

MAY

1 VETERAN John Davis insists he plans to return to track action when he recovers from a broken leg.

2 SHANE Bowes is set to make a dramatic comeback for his old club Glasgow.

3 SIMON Cross is forced to withdraw from the World Championship British semi final, suffering from his damaged knee. Gary Havelock takes the honours with a 15 point maximum while Ipswich's Chris Louis wins the other semi on his home track.

4 KELLY Moran fails to turn up at Reading – Tony Olsson smashes Scott Autrey's 13 year old Exeter track record – Andy Galvin hurts his wrist in a crash at Rye House – Edinburgh's Michael Coles is taken to hospital with ankle injuries after crashing at Newcastle – Simon Cross is told to take three weeks' rest to allow his damaged knee to recover.

5 CHAMPION Scott Smith, runner-up Mark Loram and third-placed Joe Screen are joined by the seeded David Norris as Britain's qualifiers for the World Under 21 Championship round at Belle Vue.

6 KENNY McKinna returns to the Edinburgh line-up in their Gold Cup derby at Glasgow.

7 GLASGOW sack pre-season signing Tim Korneliussen and release Hungarian Robert Csillick as Shane Bowes agrees to race again.

8 PETERBOROUGH unveil plans to turn their East of England Showground stadium into an FIM-rated track – Oxford's Gold Cup match against Cradley Heath is called off by referee Graham Brodie when he ruled conditions too dangerous for racing. Five visiting riders, including World Champion Jan O. Pedersen, had fallen in the first four heats – Shane Bowes Glasgow comeback lasts less than a lap as he crashes with team-mate Robert Nagy in his first race at Edinburgh.

9 ERIC Boothroyd, ex-rider and former Halifax and Bradford promoter, is appointed BSPA Track Commissioner.

10 BO Petersen notifies the Danish Motor Union he will not be competing in the World Championship – Hans Nielsen lops more than a second off the Mildenhall track record. Aussie Troy Butler makes his come-back and only misses out on a maximum because of mechanical problems in his last race – Newcastle's Scott Norman is forced to miss their BSPA Cup tie against Belle Vue after ricking his back while taking his toolbox out of his van.

11 NEWCASTLE'S David Bargh (above) declines nomination for one of New Zealand's two places in the Commonwealth Final. Instead he asked selector Trevor Redmond to seed Debmat Diamonds team-mate Mark Thorpe to the meeting.

12 DAVID Mullett is included in the England team to face Australia at Peterborough, the only new cap in the side – Swindon's Kelly Moran breaks his collar bone at Poole – Ian Barney tells Milton Keynes he doesn't want to ride for them again.

13 SHEFFIELD promoter Cliff Carr reveals the club is in financial difficulty and is running on a week-to-week basis – Wolverhampton's Wayne Carter breaks his leg in a road accident.

14 RYE House are set to recall Danish veteran Jens Rasmussen. To accommodate him both Wayne Baxter and John Wainwright are axed and Chris Young comes into the squad – Glasgow tempt Mark Burrows out of retirement.

15 WORLD Champion Jan O. Pedersen is seriously injured in an individual meeting in Denmark. He is in hospital with a fractured vertebra and definitely out of the 1993 world title chase. Hans Nielsen breaks his collar bone in the same meeting – American Ronnie Correy goes into hospital for a sinus operation.

16 ARENA Essex are to forge a permanent link with struggling Second Division Rye House – Sheffield sign junior Dean Child as a replacement for David Wolstenholme who is made available for transfer at his own request – Andrew Mountain makes his home debut for King's Lynn.

17 GARY Havelock retains his British Championship – Doctors tell Jan O. Pedersen he will not race again this year – Better

DAY BY DAY

news for Hans Nielsen, he is seeded to the Scandinavian Final of the World Championship – America scraps its World Championship qualifying round – Eastbourne ask their riders to take a pay cut and offer them a deal based on crowd figures.

18 *ENGLAND axe Kelvin Tatum from the World Pairs. Gary Havelock, Martin Dugard and Chris Louis will form the three-rider squad – Sixteen-year-old Michael Smith signs for Berwick despite counter offers from several other Northern tracks – Sheffield is put up for sale by promoter Cliff Carr – Jeremy Doncaster breaks his right wrist at Reading.*

19 EDINBURGH, Middlesbrough and Peterborough ask the BSPA to institute a short-term ban on the use of Dunlop tyres because of their unavailability.

20 ***SHEFFIELD hold a public meeting to outline their financial crisis and promoter Cliff Carr tells fans he is losing £1,000 a week – Peterborough rest pre-season signing Paul Whittaker and advise him to have a further operation on his elbow – Gary Havelock suffers a catalogue of injuries during Stal Gorzow's Polish League defeat at Bydgoszcz – Unia Tarnow are awarded a walk over after Motor Lublin refuse to ride because opposition rider Simon Wigg could not produce his international licence.***

21 WOLVERHAMPTON sign Richard Musson on loan from Belle Vue as a replacement for Wayne Carter – Neil Evitts, in financial dispute with promoter Cliff Carr, fails to turn up at Middlesbrough but the official explanation is that he is suffering from an ear infection.

22 **POOLE sign Swedish international Jörgen Johansson, a team-mate of their Australian star Craig Boyce at Vastervik – Henrik Gustafsson (broken hand) is seeded to the Nordic Final of the World Championship.**

23 *PETERBOROUGH complete the signing of Neville Tatum from First Division Eastbourne as a replacement for Paul Whittaker – America seed five rides to the Overseas Final and that means no World Championship chance for in-form Bobby Ott and Greg Hancock.*

24 JOE Screen wins the World Under 21 qualifier at Belle Vue. Scott Smith is the only British entrant to be eliminated – Eastbourne will stay in business after the majority of their riders agree to continue racing under a new pay formula.

25 **IPSWICH make inquiries about the availability of Swedish youngster Niklas Klingberg, third behind Joe Screen and Leigh Adams in the World Under 21 qualifier at Belle Vue.**

26 ***POOLE drop their Polish newcomer Slawomir Drabik and make him available for loan – Milton Keynes' match against Peterborough starts an hour late after referee Frank Ebdon orders watering.***

27 JAN O. Pedersen is released from hospital – Milton Keynes make a move for Peterborough's out-of-favour Paul Whittaker but they have possible opposition from Long Eaton.

28 *SWINDON go down to a heavy home defeat after skipper Mitch Shirra arrives back late from an overseas commitment. He takes only two of his programmed rides and scores only one point – Milton Keynes' Peter Glanz smashes his thigh in a crash in his native Denmark – Glenn Doyle breaks two bones in his foot in a practice session at Eastbourne.*

29 JOHNNY Jørgensen scores his first British maximum in Edinburgh's win over Sheffield – The Homefire Test between England and Australia at Peterborough is postponed because of heavy rain.

30 **MILDENHALL face Berwick without top-scoring Nigel Leaver who breaks down en route to Berrington Lough – Allan Ham threatens changes after Bradford suffer a shock home defeat against King's Lynn.**

31 *MARTIN Dugard overcomes a broken collar bone, sustained in his second race, to qualify for the World Championship Overseas Final. Kelvin Tatum wins the Commonwealth Final at King's Lynn, but the surprise performance comes from Newcastle's Mark Thorpe who claims a rostrum place after losing a run-off against Tatum and his Bradford team-mate Gary Havelock for the title.*

JUNE

1 *IT IS revealed that thieves broke into the Kent home of King's Lynn promoter Bill Barker in the early hours and stole the £26,000 uninsured takings from the Ancit Commonwealth Final – Martin Dugard undergoes an operation on his fractured collar bone but is ruled out of the World Pairs. Paul Thorp is called up as his replacement. Ray Morton gets a dramatic late call to take his place in the scheduled England Test against Australia at Reading but the match is postponed because of the weather – Andy Phillips is dropped by Poole as they sign Alastair Stevens – Exeter clock up a 71-19 win against luckless Mildenhall with four of their riders being unbeaten by an opponent*

2 EASTBOURNE sign Swedish star Stefan Dannö, younger brother of former Belle Vue and Hackney favourite Roland – Rye House will be known as the Sabre Rockets, following a sponsorship tie-up with Sabre Office Cleaning, a Kent based cleaning contractor of which Terry Russell is a director – Referee David Hughes called off the meeting against Long Eaton claiming the Elfield Park track is too dangerous for racing and Milton Keynes promoter Colin Hill admits: "Our future is looking bleak."

3 **IN THE wars Simon Cross is taken to hospital with slight concussion after crashing against a Poole side that includes new signings Jörgen Johansson and Alastair Stevens. The Reserve League match is abandoned when the ambulance takes Cradley's Anthony Boyd to hospital (he is not detained).**

4 REFEREE David Dowling impounds the silencer used by Bohumil Brhel in King's Lynn's Speedway Star KO Cup tie at Ipswich and, after examination, deducts the 10 points he had scored from the result. A 50-40 on-track victory for Ipswich becomes a 50-30 win for the Suffolk club – In Poland, Katarzyna Jancarz is jailed for 11 years for the murder of her husband Edward.

5 ***RACING at Milton Keynes is halted for the second time in a year. The Speedway Control Board suspend both the promoting and track licences – Edinburgh drop only three points (all conceded by Brett Saunders) in the opening round of the H.E.A.T. Team Championship.***

6 TEENAGE sensation Jason Crump (right) is taken to hospital at Stoke after suffering a suspected scaphoid break. The Potters book their place in the Gold Cup Final with a convincing 60-29 win.

7 **ENGLAND qualify for the World Pairs Final by finishing two points ahead of holders Denmark in Norden, Germany. In the other semi final at Pardubice, Czechoslovakia, American take the honours – Belle Vue's Joe Screen breaks his collar bone at Eastbourne – Peterborough teenager Paul Hurry fractures his scaphoid at the British Masters Grass Track meeting – King's Lynn fans pledge £6,000 to keep the club afloat following a crisis meeting at which promoter Bill Barker explains the cash problems following the theft of the Commonwealth Final takings – Peterborough offer a record £20,000 for Newcastle's Mark Thorpe. Newcastle stage the Chris Prime Memorial Trophy, using the proposed FIM Grand Prix knock out formula with 24 riders. Stuart Parnaby wins the Final.**

8 *THE Speedway Control Board amend the amended result of the controversial Ipswich–King's Lynn Speedway Star Knock Out Cup match to a 56-33 home win.*

9 EXETER leave Tony Olsson out of their side for the away visits to Long Eaton and Sheffield because of a cash row with his parent track

1992 Diary
JUN

DAY BY DAY

Reading – Sheffield talk to Ian Barney and Thierry Hilaire as they consider team changes.

10 EXETER recall Australian Frank Smart, previously on loan to beleaguered Milton Keynes – Hans Nielsen scores 16 points for Oxford at Poole on his track return after injury.

11 *NORWEGIAN star Lars Gunnestad is joining Poole – but won't make his debut until 1993. The JTC Pirates agree transfer terms with Sheffield – Middlesbrough score only 19 points to finish last in their home leg of the H.E.A.T. Team Championship – A rift between Mildenhall promoters Dick Partridge and Derek Hewitt is revealed – Tommy Knudsen crashes in Poland and suffers rib injuries.*

12 EASTBOURNE agree to let Andy Grahame join Cradley Heath once they sign a replacement. They hope to sign Swedish international Peter Nahlin – Stoke's Alan Grahame is taken to hospital with a back injury after crashing at Peterborough – American Donny Odom fractures a scaphoid in Middlesbrough's defeat at Edinburgh.

13 AMERICAN favourite Bobby Schwartz is returning to Eastbourne after an eight season absence – Edinburgh junior Grant Blackie fractures a thumb at Berwick – Bradford's Kevin Little breaks his leg in a heat eight crash against Eastbourne.

14 *THREE-TIME World Champion Hans Nielsen goes out of the World Championship as he fails to make the cut in the Nordic Final at Elgane, Norway – Gary Havelock adds the Overseas crown to his British Championship. But Simon Wigg and Billy Hamill (who crashes in his fourth ride) go out in an eventful Coventry meeting – Edinburgh lose three riders in crashes at Newcastle: Johnny Jørgensen (broken elbow), Mike McLuskey (broken elbow and shoulder ligament damage) and Stewart McDonald (shoulder and neck injuries). Home skipper David Bargh is also ruled out of two rides with double vision.*

15 DOCTORS confirm that Cradley Heath's Billy Hamill has fractured his wrist and could be out for six weeks. A further blow to the Heathens is Mark Robinson's decision to retire – England beat Australia 55-53 in the second Homefire Test at Reading but lose the services of Andy Smith and Dean Barker who are taken to hospital. X-rays reveal neither has been as seriously injured as first suspected.

16 ANDY Grahame agrees personal terms to join Cradley Heath.

17 TONY Olsson is made available for loan or transfer after Reading refuse to let him continue at Exeter because of an unpaid loan fee – Poole's Tom Knudsen crashes against Belle Vue and is taken to hospital with leg and ankle injuries – Louis Carr pulls out of Sheffield H.E.A.T. Team Championship qualifier at Long Eaton after only one ride claiming he is suffering from migraine – A poor crowd sees Mildenhall's final home meeting of the season.

18 THE ballot for the World Pairs Final draw is delayed for four days because of Denmark's success in the European soccer championship. It was scheduled to take place live during a Danish sports programme but the football overran – Stoke's Gary Chessell (hand and internal injuries) and Peterborough's Rodney Colquhoun (broken ankle) are taken to hospital after tangling down the home straight at Sheffield.

19 *MILDENHALL close down with promoter Dick Partridge blaming poor crowds. They will race their last match in two days time – Peterborough sign former skipper Ian Barney as emergency cover for injured Rodney Colquhoun and he turns out at 90 minutes notice to score paid eight against Rye House – Belle Vue junior Mike Lewthwaite is offered an Edinburgh contract after finishing third in the Scottish Individual Championship.*

20 ANDY Phillips is re-instated by Poole following the injury to Tom Knudsen – Bobby Schwartz makes his re-appearance for Eastbourne at his old track King's Lynn but scores only one point – Reserve League rider Lee Coleman cracks a vertebra in a training school crash at Peterborough.

21 *BO Brhel is banned for 14 days after being found guilty of illegally altering his silencer – Long Eaton offer Nigel Sparshott a contract after impressive trials at Station Road – Belle Vue completedtheir H.E.A.T. Team Championship at Bradford under protest after a heat one incident in which Bobby Ott slows up to avoid the fallen Charles Ermolenko. He was passed but referee Geoif Dalby refuses to order a re-run claiming he had not stopped the race – Nigel Leaver breaks his collar bone at Rye House, in Mildenhall's final match of the season.*

22 ENGLISHMEN Gary Havelock, Kelvin Tatum and Andy Smith are all drawn at Bradford for their World Championship semi final. Martin Dugard must travel to Austria for his round – Glasgow declare an interest in Mildenhall's Jesper Olsen and Peterborough talk with Nigel Leaver – Uproar at Exeter where angry fans throw a cup of coffee over St. John's Ambulance workers and Rye House team manager Ronnie Russell after a series of controversial decisions by referee John Morgan.

23 *WOLVERHAMPTON name Simon Wolstenholme in their first team squad as a replacement for Richard Musson, released from his loan contract – Nigel Sparshott will replace Paul Blackbird in the Long Eaton line up – Exeter vow to ban the fan responsible for incidents at the track in the Second Division match against Rye House.*

24 MILTON Keynes withdraw from the Homefire League. Their results will be expunged from the records – The BSPA veto any transfer dealings involving Mildenhall riders – Plans to launch speedway in Blackpool are turned down by the council's Estates Committee. The application was made by the bosses at the resort's greyhound track Blackpool Arena.

25 READING call on youngster Gary Sweet to replace missing Per Jonsson (on Swedish League duty) for a re-arranged Gold Cup match at Ipswich – X-rays reveal that Tommy Knudsen fractured a rib in a Polish crash earlier in the month.

26 KELVIN Tatum is recalled to the England squad. He has been named for the first Homefire Test against the United States and is also included in the World Pairs Final trio along with Gary Havelock and Martin Dugard. Chris Louis is stand by reserve – Josh Larsen is named by America for the opening Homefire Test against England for his first Test cap.

27 *TONY Olsson joins Ipswich – Axed Rye House reserve Wayne Baxter says he will return home to Australia at the end of July if he has still not found a team place.*

28 SHEFFIELD make inquiries about the availability of Czechoslovakian Roman Matousek – Henrik Gustafsson and Brian Karger need a run-off to decide the televised Barum Trophy, after they deadheat in the six-lap final.

29 *CRADLEY Heath's Gert Handberg fractures his jaw at Reading – Rye House boss Ronnie Russell hits out at the BSPA over the growing number of tracks being allowed to stage fixtures on a Sunday.*

30 CLIFF Carr is banned as a promoter because of mounting debts at Sheffield. The Speedway Control Board revoke his track licence and take over the riders' contracts – Bradford are to bring back their ex-World Finalist Antal Kocso after plans to use Henrik Christensen fall through because of his Danish commitments.

JULY

1 VETERAN Richard Hellsén, 41, is returning to his old club Long Eaton following Milton Keynes' cash problems – Mildenhall promoter Dick Partridge meets with BSPA Management Committee in a bid to save the Fen Tigers.

2 SHEFFIELD's scheduled match against Peterborough is called off because of the track's insolvency – Middlesbrough team manager Ken Knott and Newcastle's Max Schofield come to blows after Schofield appears to lay down his bike while the Bears were on a heat maximum.

3 SHEFFIELD will re-open next week, following a take-over by businessmen Tim Lucking and Neil Machin – Cradley Heath, suffering an injury crisis, sign Andy Phillips – Edinburgh call off their BSPA Cup tie with Bradford because of heavy rain to become the last club in the country to have a home meeting postponed because of the weather.

4 *SIX RIDER Berwick (they lose in form reserve Chris Readshaw in his first ride) go down by only five points to Wolverhampton in the BSPA Cup – Rodney Colquhoun withdraws from the Australian team to meet England at his home track Peterborough with a broken ankle. Middlesbrough's David*

Cheshire gets a late call from manager Neil Street.

5 **AUSTRALIA win the third and final Homefire Test 59-49 after England lose Martin Dugard with a broken collar bone – Marvyn Cox (Poole) and Andy Smith (Coventry) qualify for the World Long Track Final but sixth-placed Jeremy Doncaster (Reading) is ruled out because of a regulation that only two riders from the same nation can qualify from each of the three semi finals – Simon Wigg is considered as a replacement for Martin Dugard for the opening Test against America. Selectors Eric Boocock and Colin Pratt agree to ignore his claims because of a previously committed Continental contract – Glasgow defeat First Division Cradley Heath in the BSPA Cup.**

6 DAVID Mullett is drafted into the Homefire Lions squad to take on America at Belle Vue as a replacement for injured Martin Dugard – Last-ditch attempts to save Mildenhall from closure have failed. Promoter Dick Partridge officially notifies the Speedway Control Board that there is no chance of the track surviving.

7 ***READING clinch their place in the Gold Cup Final with a two point win at Arena Essex. They will meet Wolverhampton in the Final – David Cheshire shocks Middlesbrough by revealing he is returning home to Australia instead of accepting a pay cut.***

8 *GLASGOW and Jesper Olsen agree personal terms and the Clyde Two Tigers hope to finalise the deal with the BSPA within the next few days*

9 IPSWICH skipper Chris Louis and team manager-father John arrive at Foxhall Heath 40 minutes late after attending a Buckingham Palace Garden party for the sport's English World Champions as part of the celebrations of the Queen's 30 year rein – The re-opening of Sheffield under a new promotion falls victim to the wet weather.

10 **GLASGOW complete the signing of Jesper Olsen – Sheffield offer Frenchman Thierry Hilaire a team place as a replacement for Mark Hepworth.**

11 *PETERBOROUGH's Paul Whittaker agrees to join struggling Middlesbrough on loan until the end of the season – Simon Wigg knocks a tenth of a second off Gary Havelock's Odsal track record.*

12 ***ENGLAND go down heavily (40-68) to America in the opening Homefire Test. Belle Vue's Bobby Ott scores an 18 point maximum in front of his home fans – Joe Screen, Mark Loram, David Norris and Leigh Adams finish in the top eight at Tarnow, Poland, to qualify for the World Under 21 Final –New boy Jesper Olsen recovers from a first race fall to win three races on his long-awaited Glasgow debut – Stoke's Darren Standing suffers concussion and leg injuries in a three-rider crash at Newcastle and is accompanied to hospital by the track doctor – Neil Evitts crashes in the opening race at Rye House and is out for the rest of the meeting. Later Rockets chief Ronnie Russell warns the track could close unless crowds improve.***

13 TREVOR O'Brien breaks his thigh when he crashes during Exeter's Westernapolis and will be out for the remainder of the season – In France, Coventry's Paul Bentley breaks a vertebra in a grass track crash at Marmande.

14 *PROMOTERS are asked to prepare their thoughts on the 1993 season as the BSPA look forward to the future.*

15 SHEFFIELD go down 21-68 at Long Eaton in their first match under new promoters Tim Lucking and Neil Machin.

16 ***TROY Pratt breaks his ankle during Arena Essex's win against Wolverhampton – Coventry fail in a bid to sign Melvyn Taylor – Middlesbrough give debuts to American Doug Nicol and Paul Whittaker but go down by 16 points at home to Rye House.***

17 KING'S Lynn promoter Bill Barker announces the track's closure because of increasing financial difficulties – Rye House ask Swindon if they can take former Mildenhall skipper David Smart on loan. But they can't fit him in until the beginning of August.

18 **AMERICA win the World Pairs Final in Lonigo, Italy, as Greg Hancock defeats England's Gary Havelock in a run-off – Brett Saunders quits as Edinburgh skipper and former World number two Les Collins takes over – Richard Musson fails to score as Coventry gave him a trial in a challenge match against Arena Essex – David Steen makes his debut for Stoke, replacing the injured Darren Standing.**

19 *MORE trouble for Arena Essex as skipper Alan Mogridge breaks a rib at Eastbourne – Carl Stonehewer puts in a written transfer request at Belle Vue.*

20 ***DAVID Smart is offered a new career, with parent club Swindon – Middlesbrough transfer list Australian Mark Lemon after dropping him for American Doug Nicol – Glasgow come from 10 points behind to win at Exeter with Shane Bowes and Robert Nagy scoring 30 points between them.***

21 ***SHEFFIELD consider making a move for King's Lynn's unsettled Alun Rossiter – Bradford are forced to call off their match against Reading on police advice because of a major fire at a nearby chemical firm .***

22 GRAHAM Jones is recalled by the England selectors for the second Homefire Test against America at Wolverhampton.

23 *BERWICK teenage signing Mike Smith drops only one point on his Reserve League debut at Middlesbrough – Stoke's Eric Monaghan beats home star Neil Evitts at Sheffield to end the former British Champion's run of 33 successive Owlerton race wins – Hans Nielsen suffers concussion when he crashes in Poland.*

24 **GIANT-KILLERS Glasgow will meet the winners of the Ipswich-Coventry tie in the BSPA Cup quarter final – Gert Handberg, riding with a still broken jaw, is forced to pull out of Cradley Heath's Speedway Star Knock Out Cup tie at Arena Essex after falling in his opening ride – Hans Nielsen is barred from turning out for Oxford against Swindon on medical advice. ADT Auctions Robins' Dean Standing fractures his collar bone in the first race.**

25 ***SHEFFIELD are to re-open their Training Track – Reading's Ray Morton suffers whiplash in a road accident.***

26 HOME side Peterborough win the H.E.A.T. Team Championship Second Division Final in dramatic style as Mick Poole defeats Edinburgh's Les Collins in the last race. Poole had only returned from a two-week visit to Australia for the birth of his son, the day before the meeting. Belle Vue are easy winners of the Division One Final after Oxford go into the meeting without the injured Hans Nielsen.

27 **THE BSPA formally announce that local businessmen Martin Griffiths and William Broughton have been accepted as the new King's Lynn promoters – Unlucky Graham Jones breaks his wrist and is likely to be out for six weeks after a collision with Cradley Heath guest Sean Wilson – Mitch Shirra records a 15-point maximum as Swindon win at Exeter in the BSPA Cup.**

28 COVENTRY sign Jamie Habbin (ex-Mildenhall) on a month's loan to cover for the injury absence of Paul Bentley – Paul Whittaker enters hospital for a further operation on his injured elbow – Peterborough are told they cannot stage a junior meeting on August 17 because it clashes with the England-America Test at Wolverhampton.

29 *OXFORD are told they cannot sign out-of-work Gordon Kennett because his green sheet average is too high to fit him into their squad – Andy Smith is charged with bringing the sport into disrepute following an incident at Monmore Green on May Bank Holiday Monday evening when he tossed a broken piece of mudguard into the crowd.*

30 ***PETERBOROUGH end Sheffield's 100% home record with a two point win after Thierry Hilaire, who had finished second in heat eight, is excluded for using an illegal tyre – Long Eaton confirm they plan to operate in 1993 despite a Government inquiry into a planning application by stadium owners Northern Sports to develop the stadium for retail purposes and build a new stadium elsewhere in the area.***

31 THE BSPA formally announce that Martin Griffiths and William Broughton have not been able to complete negotiations with the Kings Lynn Stadium owner and will not be promoters there – A crowd collection for Edinburgh reserve Mike McLuskey (out with a broken wrist) raises £610.

1992 Diary AUG

DAY BY DAY

AUGUST

1 **RICK Miller misses Coventry's Homefire League visit to Bradford because he is in hospital with his wife for the birth of their first baby. His replacement is junior Colin Thorpe – Alan Mogridge has a practice at Arena Essex and reports he is fit to return to track action – Newcastle take a 16 point lead at Stoke in the first leg of the Gold Cup Final – Glasgow's Jesper Olsen damages his shoulder in a spill at Berwick during the Scottish Team Championship.**

2 *NEWCASTLE reserves Wayne Garratt and Max Schofield both suffer broken right collar bones in separate crashes in the Gold Cup Final victory over Stoke – Mark Courtney hurts his back during Rye House's win against struggling Middlesbrough.*

3 KEITH Chapman, former second halfer at Oxford, takes over King's Lynn – Poole bring back former skipper Alun Rossiter and drop Aussie Tony Langdon to accommodate him – Ex-World number two Gordon Kennett reveals he is about to sign on the dole having been without a club since Milton Keynes' closure – Wolverhampton fail in a bid to tempt former World Pairs gold medallist Chris Morton out of retirement – Middlesbrough promoter Tim Swales reveals his company has applied for planning permission to run speedway at Hartlepool greyhound stadium.

4 ***AMERICA axe long-serving Rick Miller. He is not included in the squad to face England at Wolverhampton, the first time in a decade he has been overlooked – Manchester businessman Peter Walsh and former World Finalist Chris Morton are behind a move to introduce speedway at The Watersheddings, home of Oldham Rugby League Football Club.***

5 *SHEFFIELD make an official protest against the referee's decision to exclude Thierry Hilaire for a tyre offence in the previous Thursday's defeat against Peterborough – Mitch Shirra takes the £500 first prize in a run-off in Poole's annual Elfords Daihatsu Blue Riband.*

6 **NIGEL Alderton is refused a work permit to return to the Edinburgh side – Exeter make inquiries about signing Gordon Kennett – Wolverhampton are without Peter Karlsson at Ipswich when he is delayed by an air traffic controllers' strike in Scandinavia – Thieves steal Thierry Hilaire's van and bikes from the Owlerton Stadium car park. The van is later recovered at Wakefield but the two machines are missing.**

7 TOMMY Knudsen fractures his collar bone in a spill at Belle Vue – Les Collins knocks .7 of a second off the three-year-old Edinburgh track record.

8 ***ARENA Essex's Allan Johansen decides to return home to Denmark, disappointed with his form – Outline planning permission is given for a new track at Wentloog, South Wales, midway between Cardiff and Newport.***

9 PER Jonsson wins the World Championship semi final at Bradford to head the eight World Final qualifiers. Kelvin Tatum gets through but collapses in the pits complaining of a lack of energy – Tommy Knudsen undergoes a pinning operation to his broken collar bone – Rye House agree to sign Robert Ledwith on loan from First Division Arena Essex – Sheffield talk to Czechoslovakian Roman Matousek after the World Championship semi final at Bradford.

10 **RYE House skipper Martin Goodwin (pictured right with Sheffield's Steve Johnston) is rushed to Newcastle Royal Victoria Infirmary with internal injuries after being involved in a heat 11 three-man pile-up. He is put on a life support machine – Specialists tell Swindon's John Davis he will not be able to race again this season and recommend a cartilage operation – Long Eaton skipper Jan Stæchmann collapses from exhaustion in the pits at Exeter.**

11 *THE SCB uphold an appeal by Glasgow about David Nagel's eligibility to ride for Berwick on June 17. His points are deducted to make the amended score Glasgow 51 Berwick 39. It gives Glasgow the bonus point.*

12 AUSSIE Tony Langdon signs for Sheffield, on loan from Poole – John Wainwright agrees to return to help Edinburgh through an injury crisis. He will replace the inexperienced Stewart McDonald – Martin Goodwin is off the life support machine and making good progress in a Newcastle hospital.

13 ***DUNCAN Chapman is ruled out of Middlesbrough's match against Sheffield after colliding with a track official during a pre-meeting practice lap. He suffers a broken nose.***

14 *COVENTRY make a surprise bid for Carl Stonehewer which is turned down by Belle Vue.*

15 TOMMY Knudsen qualifies for the World Final, after bravely riding in the semi final in Austria with his fractured collar bone – Neil Evitts is refused permission to compete in the Barum-Jawa Division Two Riders' Championship because of his dispute with Sheffield. Peterborough's Stephen Davies will replace him.

16 **CARL Stonehewer asks to come off the transfer list at Belle Vue – Gordon Kennett agrees to join Wolverhampton to replace the injured Graham Jones – Oxford's Dean Barker returns to his former track Eastbourne and sets a new Arlington track record – Richard Juul scores his first British maximum in Newcastle's 40 point win over Exeter – New signing Tony Langdon records a 15 point maximum in his first home match for Sheffield.**

17 KING'S Lynn cancel their scheduled weekend match against Reading because they will be without Henrik Gustafsson (World Long Track semi final) and Mark Loram (World Under 21 Final) – America clinch the Homefire series against England with a 61-47 victory at Wolverhampton.

18 *TEENAGER Joe Screen is short-listed for the World Team Cup squad. He is one of nine riders named by the England selectors.*

19 **OXFORD ask for permission to talk to Middlesbrough's Daz Sumner about a loan move to Sandy Lane – Keith Chapman is fined £1,000 by the BSPA Management Committee for calling off King's Lynn's scheduled weekend fixture against Reading. He says he won't pay.**

20 *CRADLEY Heath claim a draw at Ipswich after Billy Hamill pushes his bike for a complete lap to claim a vital third place after running out of fuel in a three-man re-run of the final heat – Swindon's Reserve League match against Wolverhampton is abandoned after two races because of a fire alarm in the grandstand. The Fire Brigade arrive to investigate and evacuate the area.*

21 ***YOUNGSTER Jason Crump recordshis first British maximum for Peterborough against local rivals Long Eaton – Rick Miller crashes out of Coventry's match at Oxford in a first heat three fall – Daz Sumner has an after-the-meeting practice at Oxford and is offered a contract for the remainder of the season. Sheffield are to revive the Northern Riders' Championship.***

22 JAMIE Habbin is excluded for touching the tapes in heat 12 of Coventry's Homefire League clash with Eastbourne but brought back in as a reserve replacement for Andy Smith when he was unable to take his place in a subsequent rerun of the race.

23 *LEIGH Adams beats Mark Loram in a run-off for the World Under 21 crown at Pfaffenhofen, Germany, and deprives the King's Lynn star of a £10,000 bonus to any Englishman*

winning the title – Rain forces John Whitaker to abandon Glasgow's match against Peterborough before a run-off for the bonus point can be staged – Local fan Nigel Jowett holds a Bring Back Speedway forum at Workington's Lonsdale Park greyhound stadium – Newcastle's Richard Juul fractures his collar bone against Middlesbrough – Referee Lew Stripp fines Reading's David Mullett £50 for protesting after being excluded from the final heat of the Racers' Speedway Star Knock Out Cup tie against Wolverhampton.

24 THE top of the table clash between Wolverhampton and Reading is abandoned after only five races with the Racers three points in front. Referee Geoff Dalby calls it off after steady drizzle turns the track into a quagmire.

25 LONG Eaton complete the signing of Middlesbrough's transfer-listed Mark Lemon and tell Gary O'Hare he is out.

26 THE SCB amend the result of the Coventry-Eastbourne Homefire League match after deducting a point scored by the Bees' Jamie Habbin when he was allowed to replace Andy Smith in heat 12 even though he had previously been excluded from the race. The revised score: Coventry 48 Eastbourne 41 – Arena Essex bring Peter Ravn into their 1-7 as a replacement for Allan Johansen – Long Eaton become the first side to complete their home League programme with a win against Edinburgh despite the absence through injury of skipper Jan Stæchmann.

27 KING'S Lynn sign Robbie Fuller on loan from Ipswich to replace Alun Rossiter.

28 GREG Hancock retains the Scottish Open Championship at Edinburgh – one of only three Division One riders in the field.

29 GARY Havelock is the 1992 World Champion after a brilliant performance ion Poland. A thunderstorm holds up the meeting for an hour but Havvy keeps his cool to become England's first World Champion since Michael Lee triumphed in 1981 – Berwick screen the World Final live by satellite at Berrington Lough, as Mike Smith, 16, wins the Stars of Tomorrow meeting with a maximum.

30 GLASGOW and Peterborough are awarded half a bonus point each by the BSPA Management Committee after the cancellation of a run-off between a nominated rider from each side because of torrential rain – The FIM Track Commission vote 8-7 in favour of introducing the Grand Prix at an informal meeting after the World Final.

31 BERWICK owner Terry Lindon is considering allowing fans to take shares in the club – Arena Essex's Josh Larsen suffers a suspected broken wrist at Coventry and the Bees Rick Miller fractures his collar bone – King's Lynn beat East Anglian rivals Peterborough in a challenge in which the Division One side are off a 20-yard handicap as long as they are 10 points ahead – Angry fans barrack Swindon skipper Mitch Shirra after a fourth successive home defeat against Ipswich – Poole skipper Marvyn Cox (pictured left) fails to arrive at Exeter for the BSPA Cup tie against the Falcons after being stranded in France by storms in the English Channel. Exeter captain Peter Jeffery fractures his scaphoid.

SEPTEMBER

1 COVENTRY sign 16-year-old star Scott Kirton, runner-up in the British Schoolboy Grass Track Championship – Six-time World Champion Ivan Mauger hands out advice to new title-holder Gary Havelock and tells him: "Don't change the way you look." Mauger says that Havelock can be an icon for a new generation of speedway fans – Glasgow's Robert Nagy discharges himself from hospital after doctors want to put a broken wrist in plaster.

2 THE big end of season Division One Riders' Championship is being switched from Belle Vue to Bradford – Eastbourne are barred from staging a challenge match against Second Division leaders Peterborough on September 6 because it clashes with the World Team Cup semi final at King's Lynn.

3 CONTROVERSY at Swindon where referee Mick Barnes orders a run-off to decide the BSPA Cup tie against Poole after the two teams had drawn 45-45. Despite Poole's protest he insists the race-off should take place and a bewildered crowd goes home believing Swindon are through to a semi final at Eastbourne – World Champion Gary Havelock is guest of honour at his first track Middlesbrough – promisiung Polish teenager Grzegorz Kowszewicz, 17, of Apator Torun dies after a training crash.

4 NEWLY-CROWNED World Champion Gary Havelock is installed as England's permanent captain after being on a temporary basis throughout the season. He will lead the World Team Cup semi final challenge. The rest of the squad is: Joe Screen, Mark Loram, Martin Dugard and Kelvin Tatum – Poole lodge an official protest over their BSPA Cup match at Swindon – Arena Essex's Troy Pratt collects his first Division One maximum against Eastbourne.

5 STOKE'S Eric Monaghan crashes out of the match against title hopefuls Peterborough with a broken collar bone.

6 ENGLAND storm to a place in the World Team Cup Final with victory over Australia, Czechoslovakia and Hungary at King's Lynn – World Finalist Brian Karger (above) suffers internal injuries during a Danish SuperLeague match and is taken to hospital – American John Cook wins the Swedish Championship – In Poland, Tomasz Gollob is the new national titleholder.

7 BRIAN Karger is released from hospital – Exeter offer to stage the Division One Reserve League Riders' Championship at the County Ground.

8 PROMOTERS meet to discuss plans for 1993 at a two-day General Council – Berwick's Terry Lindon resigns in writing his role as a promoter.

9 POOLE and Swindon are ordered to replay their BSPA Cup tie after ruling that referee Mick Barnes was wrong to insist on a run-off to decide the initial clash – Eastbourne's Paul Dugard is banned for five years (four of them suspended) after being found guilty by a SCB Tribunal of failing a drugs test. The tribunal is told traces of cannabis were found in the sample he gave at a domestic meeting. The ban is to start immediately – Long Eaton announce they

1992 Diary SEP

DAY BY DAY

are to close their 1992 season on September 23.

10 *KEVIN Brice, without a team place all season, signs for 1991 club King's Lynn – Terry Lindon withdraws his resignation as Berwick promoter after talks with the Speedway Control Board.*

11 SHEFFIELD reveal that top-scoring Neil Evitts is in dispute following a disagreement over financial terms. They are given permission to operate rider replacement in his absence.

12 ***ENGLAND keep faith with the five riders who took them to the World Team Cup Final by naming the same squad – Swindon's Dean Standing aggravates his collar bone injury in a collision with Coventry's Brian Andersen who was taken to hospital for a precautionary x-ray***

13 **NEWCASTLE'S Wayne Garratt is rushed to hospital and placed on a life support machine after crashing heavily during the Debmat Diamonds Phonesport Division Two Knock Out Cup semi final against Peterborough. Promoter Richard Bailey admits: "He is very seriously ill and the next 48 hours will be critical" – Coventry's Andy Smith suffers leg and hand injuries in an horrific crash in the World Long Track Final. Germany's Uwe Gessner, involved in the same incident, is taken by helicopter to a local hospital where he is in intensive care – Reading grab a five-point lead in the first leg of their Gold Cup Final against Wolverhampton.**

14 WOLVERHAMPTON snatch Gold Cup Final victory with a last race 5-1 from Ronnie Correy and Sam Ermolenko – Edinburgh bring in youngster Stewart McDonald at reserve – America spring a selection shock for the third and final Homefire Test against England by naming Middlesbrough duo Donny Odom and Doug Nicol in their squad. Greg Hancock and Billy Hamill are rested.

15 *ANDY Smith is airlifted back to England and transferred to the Coventry and Warwickshire Hospital. In Germany Uwe Gessner is now out of danger and making a rapid recovery.*

16 **BERWICK renegotiate riders' contracts because of a cash crisis at the club – Tommy Knudsen withdraws from Denmark's World Team Cup Final squad after aggravating his broken collar bone. Brian Karger will take his place – Sheffield sign novice Richard Moss, son of former Belle Vue Colt Ken Moss.**

17 STEPHEN Davies' newly-born son Alexander is in intensive care at Northampton General Hospital – Councillors at Hartlepool turn down a planning application for speedway at the town's greyhound stadium.

18 ***ANDY Smith is banned until April, 1993, after being found guilty by an SCB Tribunal of ungentlemanly conduct following an inquiry into an incident at Coventry's match at Wolverhampton on May Bank Holiday Monday – Stephen Davies withdraws from the Barum-Jawa Division Two Riders' Championship to stay at his newly-born son's bedside. His place will be taken by Berwick's David Blackburn – Belle Vue and King's Lynn meet in a Homefire League Division One match despite the absence of Joe Screen, Bobby Ott, Henrik Gustafsson, Mark Loram and Bohumil Brhel – Edinburgh beat Newcastle 66-60 in a 21 heat challenge match which incorporates juniors in 11-man teams!***

19 *AMERICA win the World Team Cup Final ahead of Sweden with England in third place. Denmark are relegated to Group A – Hungarian Robert Nagy wins the Barum-Jawa Division Two Riders' Championship at rain-soaked Coventry, beating Mick Poole in a title run-off.*

20 ROBERT Nagy pledges his 1993 future to Second Division Glasgow – Ipswich co-promoter Mike Western says he will not stand for re-election to the Management Committee at the winter conference – Sheffield say Neil Evitts will never race for the club again after his latest cash dispute – Appropriately Andrew Silver wins the Championship of Sussex, sponsored by his father's travel company Silver-Ski. Paul Woods scores six in his track return.

21 ***SIMON Cross is recalled to the England side after being out for two years with injury. Poole's Steve Schofield is named for his first international cap – Glasgow admit an interest in Hungarian youngster Zsolt Böszörményi, who has been turning in impressive performances on the Continent.***

22 **SWINDON make another team change, giving former Coventry and Stoke rider David Clarke a four-match trial – Newcastle launch a fund for their critically injured rider Wayne Garratt.**

23 SIMON Cross reveals he is considering his speedway future and may retire during the winter – Poole go through to the BSPA Cup semi final with victory over Swindon in the officially-ordered replay – Kelvin Tatum damages his shoulder during Bradford's BSPA Cup quarter final defeat at Reading – Long Eaton bring down the curtain on their season with a challenge match win over First Division Belle Vue.

24 *HENRIK Gustafsson and Dennis Löfqvist claim they won't be returning to King's Lynn in 1993 – David Bargh is taken to hospital with concussion after a heat three crash at Sheffield – Glasgow tell Dane Jesper Olsen (left), who lives at Peterborough, that he must promise to move to Scotland to secure a 1993 team place.*

25 **WOLVERHAMPTON recall the fit again Graham Jones with Gordon Kennett dropping out – Stoke call off their scheduled Division Two match against Exeter because of the decision to run the First Division Riders' Championship at Bradford the same evening.**

26 *RICHARD Hellsén fails to turn up for Long Eaton's match at Stoke – Terry Lindon gives out cheques to pay off all outstanding debts at Berwick, claiming he has had a VAT refund – Bradford's Speedway Star Knock Out Cup semi final against Belle Vue is fogged off.*

27 ***SAM Ermolenko, who only rides for his country because an aircraft malfunction prevented him travelling to Poland, inspires America to a third successive Homefire Test win against England – Edinburgh are to sign Under 21 international Jan Andersen. Fellow Dane Johnny Jørgensen makes way – Jesper Olsen ractures his shoulder blade after falling when his engine seized during Glasgow's BSPA Cup quarter final defeat against Ipswich – Berwick lose four riders in their Phonesport Knock Out Cup semi final defeat at Rye House: Michael Lowrie (ankle), Chris Readshaw (ankle), Scott Lamb (arm) and Scott Robson (foot) are all injured in the first nine races.***

28 WAYNE Garratt dies in hospital from a chest and lung infection. He had spent 16 days on a life support machine – Eastbourne are told they cannot sign Gordon Kennett.

29 *EXPERIENCED Paul Woods is back in League action. He signs for Eastbourne as a replacement for the suspended Paul Dugard – The Speedway Control announce they have awarded Reading a 75-0 victory following the cancellation of their Homefire League match at King's Lynn – Long Eaton fine Richard Hellsén £100 for his non-arrival at Stoke.*

30 **SHEFFIELD transfer-list their former number one Neil Evitts.**

OCTOBER

1 HENRIK Gustafsson and King's Lynn promoter Keith Chapman have a clear the air meeting and announce that the Swedish star will be staying at Saddlebow Road – Ipswich's Tony Olsson is taken to hospital with a badly gashed hand during the home win over Coventry – King's Lynn reserve Darren Spicer breaks his wrist in a Reserve League spill at Swindon

DAY BY DAY

– Jan Andersen makes an impressive debut for Edinburgh.

2 ***MICHAEL Coles weds his sweetheart Michelle in the clubroom at Powderhall Stadium. They originally planned the ceremony on the centre green after his Testimonial but rain put paid to that.***

3 *TEENAGER Joe Screen is the new Dunlop Division One Riders' Champion, three points ahead of five riders who tie on 11 points each – Andy Hackett, out of racing for the whole of 1992, is told he can resume his career in 1993 after the latest medical check on his broken thigh – Exeter Supporters' Club vote Tony Olsson their Rider of the Year even though he spent less than half a season with the club.*

4 EASTBOURNE confirm they will operate in 1993 after months of doubt – Glasgow tell Australian Shane Bowes they will not stand in his way of a move to the First Division in 1993 – Newcastle stage their first home match since Wayne Garratt's death and lose to Peterborough who, ironically, had been the visitors when Garratt had his fatal crash – Teenager Chris Manchester wins the American National Championship at Costa Mesa.

5 *SWINDON axe trialist David Clarke and recall home-grown junior Matthew Cross.*

6 WAYNE Garratt is cremated at Stourbridge after a service at St. Peter's Church, Cradley. A packed congregation includes riders, officials and friends.

7 *BSPA Chairman Maurice Ducker has promising talks with Wembley officials about taking the 1994 World Final to the Empire Stadium – Poole book their place in the BSPA Cup Final with victory over Wolverhampton.*

8 NEWCASTLE and Cradley Heath will meet at Brough Park in the Wayne Garratt Memorial Trophy before the end of the season – A bemused Hans Nielsen is excluded by referee Barrie Richardson in a heat 11 incident at Swindon for which he is excluded after team-mate Mark Carlson and home rider Mitch Shirra come down.

9 ***HANS Nielsen plans to send a video of the Swindon incident to the SCB to protest his innocence claiming: "It was the most peculiar decision I have seen this season."***

10 RYE House qualify for their first Cup Final since 1979 – King's Lynn book in new American titleholder Chris Manchester and Polish Champion Tomasz Gollob for their traditional end of season Pride of the East.

11 RICHARD Knight says he will not return to Berwick in 1993 – Alan Grahame (above) tells Stoke he would like to stay at Loomer Road for at least another season – Long Eaton confirm they will be running in 1993.

12 *THE Swedish League Club Association – representing all clubs – issue a statement confirming they will co-operate with other major nations to persuade the FIM to drop their plan to replace the traditional World Championship with a Grand Prix series from the beginning of 1994 – Reading edge closer to the Division One League title with double-header victories over Bradford and Eastbourne.*

13 RIDERS and promoters meet at a Midlands Hotel to discuss the problems speedway is facing during the recession.

14 GLASGOW promise teenager James Grieves a place in their 1993 first team squad.

15 *MIDLANDS-BASED Sam Ermolenko becomes the new Northern Riders' Champion at Sheffield after accepting a late, late booking as replacement for the injured Jan Stæchmann.*

16 PETERBOROUGH clinch the Homefire League Second Division title with a home win against Edinburgh – Poole's Craig Boyce, an accomplished rock guitarist, joins local group Rex and the Recliners in a charity gig for Cot Death Research at Bournemouth's Showbar on the Pier Approach.

17 ***BERWICK promoter Terry Lindon goes missing amidst claims that cheques paid to riders and other clubs for outstanding debts have bounced – Swindon's defeat at Bradford means they must wait and see if they are relegated. They complete their programme with 14 points, one ahead of both Arena Essex and Eastbourne who have yet to meet. Arena have another match in hand – John Jørgensen joins Coventry's growing injury list, suffering concussion in a crash also involving team-mate Michael Warren.***

FIM AUTUMN CONGRESS

Columbus, Ohio, United States of America
October 21 – October 23

THE FIM, motor-cycling's world governing body, made the most dramatic decision in their post-war history when they voted to end the traditional World Championship.

OUT goes the sudden-death World Final in a decision that angered the three nations – Britain, Denmark and Sweden – who voted against the proposal.

IN (by a 10-3 vote) is a new Grand Prix which will include at least six rounds with events planned for five seeded nations (England, Denmark, Germany, Poland and Sweden) and Austria in 1994.

In 1995 Italy will stage a round instead of Austria, in 1996 it will be Czechoslovakia, in 1997 Hungary, 1998 Norway, 1999 Russia and 2000 Finland.

Another outcome of the decision is that the 1993 World Final at Pocking, Germany, will be the last of the conventional title deciders and the scheduled 1994 World Final, due to be held in England, will no longer take place.

The FIM justify the changes by claiming the present system is half a century old, has no major attraction to TV companies or sponsors, and is losing support with attendances going down on a virtual annual basis.

They believe the Grand Prix series will attract both TV and new financial backers to provide staging nations with a profitable meeting.

Each Grand Prix will be staged over a series of 24 races. The first 20 will be to determine seedings for four final races which will decide finishing positions with the four lowest scorers contesting finishing positions 16, 15, 14 and 13 and so on with the top four scorers contesting heat 24. In each race-off the highest finishing qualifier has gate choice.

Grand Prix points will be scored in relation to finishing position: 1st: 20; 2nd: 17; 3rd: 15; 4th: 13; 5th: 11; 6th: 10; 7th: 9; 8th: 8; 9th: 7; 12th: 6; 11th: 5; 12th: 4; 13th: 3; 14th: 2; 15th: 1; 16th: 0.

The winner of the Grand Prix series, and that season's World Champion, will be the rider with the most GP points from all rounds.

■ ***GUNTER Sorber is re-elected President of the Track Commission. Also voted back are England's Bill Smith, Bill Bates-Brownsword (Australia), Frank Hansen (Denmark) and Hennie Van Den Boomen (Holland)***

■ ***TOP English referee Frank Ebdon will miss out on 1993 World Championship events – he is not nominated by the Auto-Cycle Union.***

■ ***BELLE Vue's FIM track licence is suspended for 12 months following complaints about the circuit and the organisation of the 1992 World Under 21 qualifying round.***

■ ***TO accommodate the Grand Prix there will be no World Pairs or Champions Cup competitions from the end of 1993.***

■ ***FULL details of 1992 World Championship events are given on the final page of this Yearbook.***

1992 Diary
OCT

DAY BY DAY

18 *RESERVE Paul Pickering is the surprise choice as Middlesbrough's Rider of the Year – Cradley Heath's Justin Walker wins the Division One Reserve League Riders' Championship at Poole – Reading keep alive their hopes of a treble by beating Ipswich in the BSPA Cup semi final.*

19 IAN Thomas and Graham Drury announce details of their eighth indoor ice international at Telford on St. Valentine's Day, Sunday, February 14. There will be an afternoon England-Rest of the World International and the British Open Indoor Ice Championship in the evening.

20 CRADLEY Heath's defeat at Bradford confirms Reading as Homefire League First Division champions – Gary Havelock is willing to lose his world title to help Bradford win a Cup Final. He says he wants to ride instead of travelling to Columbus, Ohio, for the official FIM prize-giving awards ceremony – Bradford promoter Allan Ham tells a poor crowd: "This is the last time we will stage a meeting on a Tuesday night"

21 ***THE FIM vote to introduce a Grand Prix in 1994 (see previous page for full details).***

22 THE FIM clear Gary Havelock to miss the awards ceremony to ride for Bradford in the Speedway Star Cup Final – Ipswich admit the crowd for the Star of Anglia is the lowest since the event started in 1979 – Andy Grahame (Cradley Heath) and Ray Morton break collar bones in separate incidents as Reading go through to the Speedway Star Cup Final.

23 ***THE Mayor of Peterborough hosts a Civic reception for the victorious Evening Telegraph Panthers – Arena Essex make sure of First Division safety with victory against Bradford – Poole fans vote Marvyn Cox their Rider of the Year.***

24 GLASGOW'S Steve Lawson confirms that he will be hanging up his leathers at the end of the season

25 *FRAUD squad officers in the North East confirm they are investigating the business affairs of Berwick promoter Terry Lindon – Len Silver is making a promoting comeback at Eastbourne. He severed his financial links with the sport at the end of 1985 to concentrate on building up a travel company specialising in skiing holidays.*

26 READING win the BSPA Cup but fail to make it a treble as Bradford retain the Speedway Star Knock Out Cup by four points on aggregate – Oxford's Mark Carlson says he wants to race in the Second Division in 1993 – Justin Walker is recalled by Cradley Heath as a replacement for broken collar bone victim Andy Grahame – The Wayne Garratt Memorial Trophy is called off 45 minutes before start time because of heavy rain.

27 RYE House switch the second leg of the Phonesport Knock Out Cup Final to Arena Essex because they cannot fit in a re-staging before the official end of the 1992 season – Oxford transfer list Dean Barker – Tetleys Brewery are the latest company to claim they are owed money by missing Berwick boss Terry Lindon.

28 *COVENTRY skipper Tommy Knudsen (seen chasing Gert Handberg above) announces his retirement from British racing. He plans to return home to Denmark but will continue competing on the continent. It ends a 14-season career at Brandon – Reading's young reserve Philip Morris injures his wrist against Ipswich in the first part of a double header, allowing Mark Sayer to make his debut against King's Lynn – The cancellation of Glasgow's Division Two match against Rye House ensures the League programme is not completed.*

29 DETAILS are revealed of plans to build a new £50 million sports complex at Bristol that could include speedway. It is a joint venture between Bristol Rovers Football Club and Bristol City Council and the complex could be open by 1995 – Ipswich co-promoter Mike Western appears on the BBC Radio Five afternoon show talking about the sport.

30 PETERBOROUGH complete the Second Division treble by adding the Knock Out Cup to the League and H.E.A.T. Team Championship trophies.

31 JASON Crump is named Rider of the Year at Peterborough by both members of the Supporters' Club and readers of sponsors the Evening Telegraph – Joe Screen is Belle Vue's Rider of the Year – Coventry round off an injury-hit season with their eighth successive League defeat as they go down in their last match of the season against Bradford as Tommy Knudsen says his farewells to the Brandon crowd.

NOVEMBER

1 *BOBBY Ott says he will not return to Belle Vue unless he is on the same wage scale in 1993 as this year – Henrik Gustafsson is put on the transfer list – Former Peterborough and Sheffield rider Wayne Bridgeford wins the Northern Territory Championship at Tennant Creek, Australia.*

2 THE SCB hold an emergency board meeting to discuss the implications of the FIM decision to introduce the World Championship Grand Prix. They refuse to release details of any decisions. – Eastbourne's Olli Tyrvainen (below) confirms his retirement from British racing.

3 ***STOKE'S riders contracts are taken over as the promoting company's debts outstrip their assets – Len Silver's application to be accepted as Eastbourne promoter is approved by the BSPA Management Committee.***

4 MEMBERS of the BSPA meet in General Council session but all decisions reached are kept secret pending the Annual Conference – Zdenek Tesar is Ipswich's Rider of the Year.

5 PETER Brown resigns as Eastbourne promoter – Peter Ravn says he wants to stay with Arena Essex in 1993 after his loan spell at Purfleet.

6 *WOLVERHAMPTON agree to let their teenage discovery Stephen Morris approach Division Two tracks with a view to winning a 1993 team place – Fraud Squad detectives, probing Terry Lindon's disappearance, interview Berwick manager Dave Younghusband.*

7 ***READERS of the Reading Evening Post vote Per Jonsson***

the Racers' Rider of the Year – Ronnie Russell tells the Rye House Speedway Supporters Club that the Rockets will definitely be operating in 1993 as Martin Goodwin is named Mr. Rocket.

8 A REGIONAL Sunday newspaper reports that a computer firm claim they are owed £30,000 by former Berwick promoter Terry Lindon.

9 AUSSIE Rodney Colquhoun agrees terms to return to Peterborough in 1993.

10 *GREG Hancock is voted Cradley Heath Riders of the Year for the second successive season.*

11 POOLE are given the go-ahead to plan for the 1993 season by the local council who have taken control of the Stadium lease following the liquidation of Derek Block's Poole Stadium Development Corporation, the former lease-holders – Gary Chessell is Stoke's Rider of the Year.

12 *WORK will start in the winter on providing covered accommodation at Middlesbrough's Cleveland Park. Fans have been without a grandstand since a fire seven years ago – Stoke boss Dave Tattum reveals he hopes to form a consortium to run the club.*

13 GLASGOW agree a new lease with Shawfield Park stadium owners – Sean Wilson is to ask parent track Coventry to let him stay at Bradford for at least another season – Belle Vue skipper Joe Screen says he wants to be relieved of the captaincy and wants it to return to team-mate Shawn Moran.

14 ***AUSTRALIA'S newest track, at Gosford, New South Wales, opens under the promotion of Terry Poole, father of Test star Mick.***

15 KING'S Lynn vow to carry out any improvements necessary to ensure their stadium retains its FIM status – Sheffield apply for permission to stage a meeting at Owlerton on Sunday, December 27.

16 *ENGLAND Test star Martin Dugard is considering a year's sabbatical from British racing.*

17 ANDY Smith returns to hospital for an exploratory operation on his injured knees and is told he will need further winter surgery.

18 DEAN Standing has the plaster off his broken wrist – Carl Blackbird pledges his future to Long Eaton – Belle Vue unveil a Gold Card scheme for fans in conjunction with local commercial radio station Piccadilly Gold.

19 ***FORMER World Champion Per Jonsson agrees terms to race in the 1993 Telford Ice spectacular – Neil Collins, who injured his arm in Belle Vue's last meeting of the season, is told he will be out of work until the New Year as the injury fails to respond to treatment The BSPA Annual Conference opens in Tenerife (full details on the next page).***

20 COVENTRY'S Paul Bentley, his season cut short with a bad back injury, is planning a New Year comeback.

21 JUNIOR Team managers react angrily to the axing of the Reserve League. Belle Vue's Gordon Smith calls for a meeting with the BSPA chairman Tim Swales and Reading's Paul King campaigns for a new Third Division for British youngsters.

22 *SWINDON hint that they could rent out their stadium for speedway in 1993.*

23 DIRECTORS of Newcastle company Autocoachworks are exploring the possibility of taking over at Berwick.

24 GLASGOW plan to tune up for the 1993 season with a March training trip to Hungary.

25 *AMERICA is considering staging their 1993 World Championship qualifier at Daytona, during the traditional bike week in March – Sheffield plan to offer a 1993 contract to a Russian rider after initially targeting Poole's Slawomir Drabik as a possible New Year signing as they bid to build up a 1993 squad.*

26 CHRIS Young and Martin Cobbin are earmarked as 1993 Rye House reserves by promoter Ronnie Russell who guarantees them their chance.

27 TEENAGER Darren Spicer tells King's Lynn he wants a reserve slot in 1993 – World Champion Gary Havelock has been invited to appear on the popular BBC TV sports quiz A Question of Sport.

28 *MIDDLESBROUGH will be offering former Cleveland Park favourite Steve Wilcock the 1993 team manager's job. Wilcock spent 15 seasons with the club as a rider.*

29 *COVENTRY manager Bob Tanser urges promoters to think again about the new race formula which brings reserves against each other in three races.*

30 AUTOCOACHWORKS pull out of a deal to take over Berwick leaving the track's future in serious doubt – Polish businessman Zbigniew Morawski, owner of First Division Zielona Gora, is sought by police after being involved in a hit-and-run accident.

DECEMBER

1 MIDDLESBROUGH announce plans for a Training School to start in mid-February under the control of newly-appointed team manager Steve Wilcock.

2 WOLVERHAMPTON'S Ronnie Correy goes into hospital for a sinus operation. He had been admitted during the season but was released without the operation taking place

3 *BRADFORD boss Allan Ham lends his support to a move to launch a new Third Division.*

4 LOCAL businessmen Peter Redfern and Roger Shout join Ronnie Russell on the board of directors at Rye House to guarantee the track's flong-term future.

5 ***WOLVERHAMPTON promoter Chris Van Straaten has talks with four riders who weren't in the club's first team in 1992 – Scott Norman (on loan to Newcastle), Wayne Carter (recovering from a broken leg), Andy Phillips (loaned to Poole and then Cradley Heath) and Ade Hoole (farmed out to Stoke) – Glenn Doyle wins his fifth successive Western Australian Championship at Collie, near Perth, to qualify for the Australian Final.***

6 COVENTRY confirm they are looking for a new number one to replace the retired Tommy Knudsen. Swindon's Leigh Adams is top of their shopping list but they also cast eyes in the direction of Oxford's Martin Dugard.

7 *HANS Nielsen urges riders to revert to a hard compound rear tyre in 1993 claiming it is safer and more conducive to passing – Local policeman Peter Brown (no relation to former promoter) is appointed Eastbourne's Community Relations Officer.*

8 ARENA ESSEX'S Andy Galvin undergoes an operation to remove the pin in his thigh in readiness for the start of the 1993 season –

The draw for the first round of the 1993 Cup competitions is made:

DIVISION ONE	DIVISION TWO
First round	*First round*
Belle Vue v Cradley Heath	Swindon v Rye House
Arena Essex v King's Lynn	Sheffield v Long Eaton
Wolverhampton v Ipswich	Newcastle v Edinburgh
Oxford v Reading	Stoke v Berwick
Byes	*Byes*
Bradford, Coventry, Eastbourne, Poole	Exeter, Glasgow, Middlesbrough, Peterborough

1992 Diary DEC

DAY BY DAY

9 THE BSPA Management Committee discuss amendments to the 1993 race formula and agree to several alterations which will go forward to the next General Copuncil for ratification. The changes are details below in italics:

	Home	Away
Heat 1	1 & 2	1 & 2
Heat 2	3 & 4	3 & 4
Heat 3	5 & 6	5 & 6
Heat 4	7 & 8	7 & 8
Heat 5	1 & 2	3 & 4
Heat 6	*5 & 6*	*1 & 2*
Heat 7	*3 & 4*	*5 & 6*
Heat 8	*2 & 7*	*2 & 7*
Heat 9	*5 & 6*	*3 & 4*
Heat 10	*1 & 2*	*5 & 6*
Heat 11	*3 & 4*	*1 & 2*
Heat 12	*6 & 8*	*6 & 8*
Heat 13	*3 & 5*	*3 & 5*
Heat 14	*1 & 4*	*1 & 4*
Heat 15	7 & 8	7 & 8
	Interval	
Heat 16	5 & 6 highest scorers	
Heat 17	3 & 4 highest scorers	
Heat 18	1 & 2 highest scorers	

– Juniors riders from Belle Vue, Bradford, Cradley Heath, Middlesbrough, Sheffield and Stoke meet at Belle Vue to discuss their future following the axing of the Reserve League.

10 *POOLE promoters meet with their 1992 sponsors JT Commercials to discuss renewing the deal for 1993 but no final decision is taken – Newcastle Reserve team manager Roy Clarke fractures his hip in a road accident on his way to a Berwick Speedway Supporters' Club Video evening. He and Debmat Diamonds programme editor George English, who escaped with cuts and bruises, were travelling on the A1 when they were in collision with a lorry.*

11 **AUSTRALIAN star Stephen Davies, who led the club to victory in three major competitions, tells Peterborough he will not be returning to race in Britain in 1993 under the new pay scales.**

12 GLASGOW declare an interests in Hungarian Jozsef Petrikovics, reserve at the 1989 World Final. They will monitor his form in South Africa before deciding whether to offer him a contract.

13 ***LATE season loan signing Andy Phillips wants to stay with Cradley Heath – Australian Tony Primmer, who returned home at the beginning of the 1991 season, wants to return to Britain and join a Division Two track.***

14 SHEFFIELD withdraw their application to run a Christmas meeting on the advice of the BSPA – Middlesbrough admit that they expect Americans Donny Odom and Doug Nicol to be refused work permits in 1993 as neither came up to a six-point average.

15 *POOLE announce that they are taking over rivals Swindon and will operate in the 1993 Second Division.*

16 **COAL Products Limited are to end their 15-year association with the sport. They will cease to offer sponsorship from the end of the year – Prospective promotions companies meet the newly formed BSPA marketing sub-committee in Rugby for confidential discussions.**

17 A GROUP of businessmen bidding to take over Berwick call a public meeting for December 21 in the hope of setting up a Fighting Fund to keep the Bandits alive – Bradford announce that they have lost their team sponsors Keyline Builders Merchants who have backed the club for the last eight years – Eastbourne deny that Nathan Simpson has asked for a transfer but admit he has told them he will not ride in 1993 for the new pay rates.

18 **A CONSORTIUM, headed by local garage owner Mike Hope and former Newcastle team manager Tom Graham, make an official written bid to take over Berwick Speedway.**

19 *NEIL Collins asks to leave Glasgow to cut down his travelling for home meetings under the new pay code – Rye House are considering switching their traditionmal start time to 6 p.m. – Sheffield make approaches to sign*

1992 BSPA ANNUAL CONFERENCE

MEMBERS of the British Speedway Promoters' Association held their annual conference at the Guayarmina Princess Hotel, Tenerife, from Thursday, November 19 to Sunday, November 22.

The following tracks were represented: Arena Essex, Bradford, Coventry, Cradley Heath, Eastbourne, Ipswich, King's Lynn, Oxford, Poole, Reading, Swindon, Wolverhampton, Edinburgh, Exeter, Glasgow, Long Eaton, Middlesbrough, Newcastle, Peterborough and Sheffield.

ELECTION OF OFFICERS

President
Charles Ochiltree

Chairman
Tim Swales

Vice-chairman
Chris Van Straaten

Management Committee
Neil Macfarlane, Eric Boocock, Colin Pratt

Reserve Management Committee Members
Richard Bailey, Tim Lucking (Division Two), Terry Russell, Mervyn Stewkesbury (Division One).

Technical Committee
John Louis, Len Silver, and Management Committee members.

Marketing Sub Commmittee
James Easter, Tim Lucking, Neil Machin, Bill Reay

England Team Managers
Eric Boocock and Colin Pratt

LEAGUE competition in 1993 will be contested by 8-rider teams with numbers seven and eight being British, under 25, and with a starting average below four points a meeting. The following race formula was approved:

	Home	Away
Heat 1	1 & 2	1 & 2
Heat 2	3 & 4	3 & 4
Heat 3	5 & 6	5 & 6
Heat 4	7 & 8	7 & 8
Heat 5	1 & 2	3 & 4
Heat 6	3 & 4	5 & 6
Heat 7	5 & 6	1 & 2
Heat 8	1 & 2	5 & 6
Heat 9	3 & 4	1 & 2
Heat 10	5 & 6	3 & 4
Heat 11	7 & 8	7 & 8
Heat 12	1 & 2	3 & 4
Heat 13	3 & 5	1 & 5
Heat 14	4 & 6	2 & 6
Heat 15	7 & 8	7 & 8
	Interval	
Heat 16	5 & 6 highest scorers	
Heat 17	3 & 4 highest scorers	
Heat 18	1 & 2 highest scorers	

● Gate positions to be decided by toss of a coin. For nominated races there will be a further toss. The winning side will have choice of starting positions in heats 16 and 18. In reserve rider races the visiting team will have choice of gates.

● Tactical substitutes will be allowed if a team is six points behind after heat five.

DAY BY DAY

1992 Diary '93

Tony Langdon on a permanent basis – Daz Sumner reverts to Middlesbrough after Belle Vue decide not to take up their final option on his services

20 KELVIN Tatum and Simon Wigg have preliminary talks with Bradford – Poole succesfully complete negotiations for JT Commercials to continue as their team sponsors.

21 ***GULF Oil confirm they will continue to sponsor Edinburgh in 1993 – The Berwick consortium appeal for an extra £10,000 to ensure they can keep Division Two racing at Berrington Lough.***

22 *EASTBOURNE continue their bid to sign Peter Nahlin, now that he is a Poole asset following their take-over of Swindon*

23 **EXETER promoter Colin Hill agrees a new four-year lease to stay at the County Ground Stadium.**

24 HANS Nielsen drops the bomshell news that he won't accept the new pay scales and says he will retire from British racing unless their is a dramatic change of heart by promoters

26 *ZDENEK Tesar agrees another season at Ipswich.*

27 **OXFORD receive an approach from a consortium headed by Peter Schroeck's father to take over the spewedway franchise at Sandy Lane and to enter Division Two. Former Swindon manager Ron Byford will be the front man.**

28 MILDENHALL'S preliminary application to join Division One is turned down – Oxford's Troy Butler wins his fifth successive Queensland Championship – Scott Norman is the South Australian Champion.

29 *EXETER tell Cornish youngster Scott Pegler he will get his chance at number eight in 1993.*

30 **PETERBOROUGH make an official approach to the BSPA to sign Kieran McCullagh on a full transfer**

31 ***BERWICK officials apply for Division Two membership.***

JANUARY...IN BRIEF...JANUARY...IN BRIEF...JANUARY...IN BR

THE pay policies agreed by promoters brought howls of protest from riders – many of whom said they would retire rather than accept the new rates.

THE Battle to save Berwick Speedway finally floundered early in the New Year when the Consortium withdrew their application because of a lack of working capital.

THE FUTURE of Stoke Speedway remained in doubt throughout January with separate take-over talks involving Manchester businessman Peter Walsh and Long Eaton owner Tony Mole taking place.

PETERBOROUGH became the first Division Two team to announce a major new signing, snapping up Alan Mogridge on loan from Arena Essex while Edinburgh signed Finnish Champion Vesa Ylinen for his first spell in British Speedway.

THE BRITISH Speedway Promoters' Association appointed a Marketing company to promote the sport. South Coast entrepreneur Grant Rayner won the six-figure contract from two other marketing companies.

PROMOTERS voted to introduce a new Third Division in 1993. Non-league tracks Iwade (Kent) and Linlithgow (Scotland) indicated their interest in any new junior set-up.

1991 WORLD Champion Jan O. Pedersen seems certain to miss the 1993 season with the back injury he sustained in Denmark during the 1992 campaign.

ENGLAND international Dean Barker formally signed for Eastbourne in the middle of January.

RYAN Sullivan won the 1993 Australian Under 21 Championship – and Leigh Adams grabbed his second senior title.

COMPETITIONS

Both Divisions will meet home and away twice and also compete in a Divisional Knock Out Cup. Both Divisions will also hold qualifying rounds of the Four Team Tournament. Teams must include their number one and at least another heat leader in their qualifying teams.

GUESTS

Any team missing its number one will be allowed a guest or the use of rider replacement.

BETTING

The Management Committee to consider discussing the possibility of allowing gambling.

SEASON

It was agreed that permission be granted to operate up to and including November 5 provided no official fixture is held after October 31.

THIRD DIVISION

Further investigation to take place.

TESTIMONIALS

The following riders were granted Testimonials in 1993: Hans Nielsen, Martin Goodwin, Alan Mogridge, John Jørgensen, Sam Ermolenko, David Smart and Paul Whittaker.

RACE DAYS

Eastbourne change their race-day from a Sunday afternoon to a Saturday evening (7 p.m.).

DIVISIONAL CHAMPIONSHIP

A rider must have competed in half of a club's official fixtures to qualify for the respective Divisional Riders' Championship Finals.

LEAGUE MEMBERSHIP

Swindon were confirmed as having been relegated to the 1993 Division Two. 1992 Second Division champions Peterborough remain in Division Two in 1993 to ensure there are equal numbers in each of the two Divisions.

AWARDS

Promoters voted in various categories for the following awards:
Promoter of the Year: John Louis and Richard Bailey.
Rider of the Year: Gary Havelock and Robert Nagy.
Newcomer: Jason Lyons and Robert Nagy.
Best Track: Eastbourne and Sheffield.
Best Stadium: Coventry and Sheffield.
Best Programme: Arena Essex and Edinburgh.
Best Racejacket: Arena Essex and Exeter.
Best Visiting Supporters: Poole and Glasgow.

RESERVE LEAGUE

To accommodate the new 18-heat League formula it was agreed to dispense with the Reserve League although tracks will be allowed to stage a maximum of three junior races if they wish.

ABANDONMENT

The result shall stand if a meeting is called off after Heat 12.

In Memorium

WAYNE MALCOLM GARRATT always wanted to be a speedway rider.
He achieved that ambition but at the cost of his life.
And, if you could ask Bodger now whether the sacrifice was worthwhile then his unequivocal answer would be yes.
Even though his life was relatively short it was overflowing with fulfilment.
He enjoyed himself and brought enjoyment to countless thousands.
Wayne's love for motor-cycles was first evident when, at the age of four, he watched a TV programme featuring American mini-bikes.
He decided he wanted one and his 1974 Christmas present was a 50 c.c. bike which launched him on a schoolboy grass track career.
He was crowned the youngest ever British Youth Division Champion in his first season and when he was nine he became Oxford mascot.
Wolverhampton and Cradley Heath competed for his signature when he was 16 and he chose the Heathens, making his British League debut on September 27, 1986. He had four seasons at Dudley Wood and two on loan to Arena Essex before joining Newcastle.
While his death leaves a sadness and a void that will never be filled for his family, his close friends, his team-mates, his rivals and his admirers from the terraces, let us always cherish his memory with joy and pleasure.
Life can be cruel, death never is....

Wayne Garratt

BRITISH UNDER 21 CHAMPIONSHIP

Long Eaton, Wednesday, April 22

1	Scott Smith	3 2 3 3 3	14
2	Mark Loram	2 3 2 3 3	13
3	Joe Screen	3 3 3 3 R	12
4	Paul Dugard	1 2 3 3 1	10
5	Darren Pearson	3 1 2 F 3	9
6	Carl Stonehewer	0 2 2 2 3	9
7	Chris Readshaw	1 3 2 1 2	9
8	Garry Stead	2 1 3 1 2	9
9	Stephen Morris	3 fx1 2 2	8
10	Colin White	2 fx1 2 1	6
11	Glenn Cunningham	1 0 1 1 2	5
12	Scott Robson	F 1 1 2 1	5
13	Mark Simmonds	0 3 0 0 0	3
14	Richard Musson	2 fnN N N	2
15	Paul Hurry	0 0 0 1 1	2
16	Duncan Chapman	1 X 0 R R	1
Reserve:			
	Jason Reed	*2 0 0 0*	*2*

Roll of Honour

1969 Graham Plant (Leicester)
1970 Barry Thomas (Canterbury) 14
1971 Ian Turner (King's Lynn) 15
1972 Allan Emmett (Rayleigh) 13
1973 Peter Collins (Belle Vue) 14
1974 Chris Morton (Belle Vue) 15
1975 Neil Middleditch (Eastbourne) 13
1976 Michael Lee (King's Lynn) 15
1977 Les Collins (Belle Vue) 15
1978 Phil Collins (Ellesmere Port) 15
1979 Kenny Carter (Halifax) 12
1980 Mark Courtney (Middlesbrough) 14
1981 Rob Lightfoot (Stoke) 14
1982 Peter Carr (Belle Vue) 12
1983 Keith Millard (Exeter) 13
1984 Marvyn Cox (Oxford) 13
1985 Carl Blackbird (Belle Vue) 15
1986 Gary Havelock (Middlesbrough) 15
1987 Darren Sumner (Stoke) 14
1988 Mark Loram (Hackney) 15
1989 Martin Dugard (Oxford) 15
1990 Joe Screen (Belle Vue) 14
1991 *Not staged*
1992 Scott Smith (Cradley Heath) 14

■ *The meeting was held at Wimbledon in 1969 and 1990 Swindon, 1970-71, Canterbury, 1972-85, Stoke, 1986-87, Eastbourne, 1988-89, Long Eaton, 1992.*

■ *The first staging was as a second half event involving only nine riders. Since 1970 it has been staged as a conventional individual meeting over 20 heats with 16 riders.*

DUNLOP DIVISION ONE RIDERS' CHAMPIONSHIP FINAL

Bradford, Saturday, October 3

FOR the first time in the competition's history the British League Riders' Championship moved away from its spiritual home at Belle Vue.

In an attempt to bring back some of the missing glamour of the event – once the biggest domestic meeting of the season – it was switched to Bradford's Odsal Stadium and its former traditional Saturday night staging.

But heavy, incessant rain destroyed any hopes of the meeting re-establishing itself although it did provide yet another Belle Vue victor.

Joe Screen revelled in the wet conditions to become the first teenage champion while behind him five riders had a sudden death shoot-out for the other rostrum placings.

Roll of Honour

1965 Barry Briggs (Swindon) 14
1966 Barry Briggs (Swindon) 15
1967 Barry Briggs (Swindon) 15
1968 Barry Briggs (Swindon) 14
1969 Barry Briggs (Swindon) 14
1970 Barry Briggs (Swindon) 13
1971 Ivan Mauger (Belle Vue) 14
1972 Ole Olsen (Wolverhampton) 15
1973 Ivan Mauger (Exeter) 14
1974 Peter Collins (Belle Vue) 15
1975 Peter Collins (Belle Vue) 15
1976 Ole Olsen (Coventry) 15
1977 Ole Olsen (Coventry) 15
1978 Ole Olsen (Coventry) 13
1979 John Louis (Ipswich) 14
1980 Les Collins (Leicester) 14
1981 Kenny Carter (Halifax) 15
1982 Kenny Carter (Halifax) 15
1983 Erik Gundersen (Cradley Heath) 14
1984 Chris Morton (Belle Vue) 13
1985 Erik Gundersen (Cradley Heath) 14
1986 Hans Nielsen (Oxford) 15
1987 Hans Nielsen (Oxford) 14
1988 Jan O. Pedersen (Cradley Heath) 14
1989 Shawn Moran (Belle Vue) 15
1990 Hans Nielsen (Oxford) 15
1991 Sam Ermolenko (Wolverhampton) 15
1992 Joe Screen (Belle Vue) 14

■ *The meeting was held at Belle Vue (Hyde Road) from 1965-87, Belle Vue (Kirkmanshulme Lane), 1988-91 and Bradford 1992.*

1	Joe Screen	3 3 2 3 3	14	
2	Per Jonsson	2 1 2 3 3	11	+4
3	Gary Havelock	1 2 3 2 3	11	+3
4	Marvyn Cox	3 1 3 2 2	11	+2
5	Leigh Adams	3 2 R 3 3	11	+1
6	Simon Wigg	0 3 3 3 2	11	+0
7	Hans Nielsen	2 3 3 E 2	10	
8	Robert Nagy	1 0 2 2 2	7	
9	Brian Karger	3 2 0 0 1	6	
10	Sam Ermolenko	2 0 1 1 1	5	
11	Greg Hancock	0 3 0 0 1	4	
12	Henrik Gustafsson	2 2 0 0 0	4	
13	John Jørgensen	0 R 1 2 1	4	
14	Peter Nahlin	1 1 1 1 0	4	
15	Tony Rickardsson	0 0 2 1 0	3	
16	Martin Dugard	1 1 1 0 0	3	
Reserves:				
	Darren Pearson	*1*	*1*	
	Stuart Swales	*did not ride*		

BARUM JAWA DIVISION TWO RIDERS' CHAMPIONSHIP

Coventry, Saturday, September 19

ROBERT Nagy, almost sent back home by Glasgow as they sought early season success, repaid the faith the Scottish management had shown in him by becoming the first Hungarian to win the Second Division Riders' Final.

There was a dramatic finale to an otherwise mundane event raced on a treacherously slippery Coventry track.

Exeter's Richard Green won his first three rides and seemed to be heading for the title when he overdid it in his last race to leave an opening for Nagy and chief rival Mick Poole, who won his last three outings to force a title run-off.

Referee Ronnie Allan had three attempts to complete the race – Poole twice coming off as he got the worse of first bend buffeting. Nagy made no mistake at the third time of asking to finish in front.

And to heap irony on the result Peterborough's Poole was later fined £100 – almost half of what he earned – for wearing his own sponsor's cap and logo for a trophy photograph!

1	Robert Nagy	3 2 2 3 3	13	+3
2	Mick Poole	2 2 3 3 3	13	+2
3	Richard Green	3 3 3 2 fx	11	
4	Martin Goodwin	0 3 2 3 2	10	
5	David Blackburn	3 3 R 0 2	8	
6	Jan Stæchmann	fx1 3 1 3	8	
7	David Bargh	2 R 1 2 3	8	
8	Tony Langdon	3 2 0 1 2	8	
9	Shane Bowes	0 1 3 2 2	8	
10	Kenny McKinna	2 0 1 3 1	7	
11	Alan Grahame	1 2 2 1 1	7	
12	Richard Knight	0 3 1 2 fx	6	
13	Les Collins	2 1 0 1 1	5	
14	Mark Thorpe	1 0 2 0 R	3	
15	Steve Regeling	1 0 1 R 0	2	
16	Paul Whittaker	1 1 0 0 0	2	

Roll of Honour

1968 Graham Plant (Middlesbrough) 13
1969 Geoff Ambrose (Crayford) 14
1970 Dave Jessup (Eastbourne) 14
1971 John Louis (Ipswich) 14
1972 Phil Crump (Crewe) 12
1973 Arthur Price (Boston) 12
1974 Carl Glover (Boston) 13
1975 Laurie Etheridge (Crayford) 13
1976 Joe Owen (Newcastle) 14
1977 Colin Richardson (Eastbourne) 15
1978 Steve Koppe (Canterbury) 14
1979 Ian Gledhill (Stoke) 14
1980 Wayne Brown (Berwick) 14
1981 Mike Ferreira (Canterbury) 15
1982 Joe Owen (Newcastle) 14
1983 Steve McDermott (Berwick) 13
1984 Ian Barney (Peterborough) 14
1985 Neil Middleditch (Arena Essex) 14
1986 Paul Thorp (Stoke) 15
1987 Andrew Silver (Arena Essex) 15
1988 Troy Butler (Milton Keynes) 15
1989 Mark Loram (Ipswich) 14
1990 Andy Grahame (Wimbledon) 14
1991 Jan Stæchmann (Long Eaton) 14
1992 Robert Nagy (Glasgow) 13

■ *The meeting was held at Hackney from 1968-71, Wimbledon, 1972-84 and Coventry 1985-92. In 1984 the Final at Wimbledon was abandoned after eight races and re-staged at Peterborough.*

ACES HIGH

A WINNING HAND ... the successful Belle Vue H.E.A.T. Team Champions: Shawn Moran, Jason Lyons, promoter John Perrin, Frede Schøtt, Joe Screen and Bobby Ott

PANTHERS PRIDE

HOME AND DRY ... the first leg of a Second Division treble for Peterborough as their winning Four Team tournament squad parade the trophy: Kevin Hawkins (team manager), Rod Colquhoun, Neville Tatum, Mick Poole, mascot Jason Bunyan, Paul Hurry and skipper Stephen Davies

DIVISION TWO ROLL OF HONOUR

1976 NEWCASTLE
Tom Owen, Joe Owen, Andy Cusworth, Phil Michelides, Ron Henderson
1977 PETERBOROUGH
Ian Clark, Andy Hines, Kevin Hawkins, Brian Clark, Nigel Flatman
1978 PETERBOROUGH
Nigel Couzens, Nigel Flatman, Tim Hunt, Dave Gooderham, Brian Clark
1979 ELLESMERE PORT
John Jackson, Louis Carr, Steve Finch, Pete Ellams, Eric Monaghan
1980 CRAYFORD
Les Rumsey, Paul Woods, Steve Naylor, Alan Sage, Laurie Etheridge
1981 EDINBURGH
Dave Trownson, Neil Collins, Chris Turner, Ivan Blacka, Guy Robson
1982 NEWCASTLE
Joe Owen, Bobby Beaton, Rod Hunter, Alan Emerson, Tom Owen
1983 NEWCASTLE
Alan Emerson, Rod Hunter, Joe Owen, Bobby Beaton, Martin Scarisbrick
1984 MILDENHALL
Ray Bales, Carl Blackbird, Robert Henry, Carl Baldwin, David Jackson
1985 MIDDLESBROUGH
Geoff Pusey, Steve Wilcock, Martin Dixon, Mark Fiora, Gary Havelock
1986 MIDDLESBROUGH
Jim Burdfield, Mark Courtney, Martin Dixon, Steve Wilcock, Glenn Hornby
1987 MILDENHALL
Melvyn Taylor, Eric Monaghan, Dave Jessup, David Jackson, Glen Baxter
1988 PETERBOROUGH
Ian Barney, Kevin Jolly, Mick Poole, Craig Hodgson, Jon Stokes
1989 PETERBOROUGH
Ian Barney, Mick Poole, Kevin Jolly, Craig Hodgson, Scott Norman
1990 STOKE
Louis Carr, Mark Carlson, Nigel Crabtree, Eric Monaghan, Chris Cobby
1991 ARENA ESSEX
Alan Mogridge, Andy Galvin, Bo Petersen, Brian Karger, Troy Pratt
1992 PETERBOROUGH
Mick Poole, Neville Tatum, Stephen Davies, Paul Hurry, Rodney Colquhoun

DIVISION ONE ROLL OF HONOUR

1991 IPSWICH
Chris Louis, David Norris, Shane Parker, Tony Rickardsson, Ben Howe
1992 BELLE VUE
Bobby Ott, Jason Lyons, Joe Screen, Shawn Moran, Frede Schøtt

DIVISION ONE FINAL

BELLE VUE 24		
1 Bobby Ott	2 2 3	7
2 Jason Lyons	2 1 R	3
3 †Joe Screen	3 2 2	7
4 Shawn Moran	3 2 2	7
5 Frede Schøtt	did not ride	
IPSWICH 18		
1 Tony Olsson	0 N N	0
2 Zdenek Tesar	fx fx 3	3
3 Tony Rickardsson	3 3 3	9
4 †Chris Louis	0 3 3	6
5 David Norris	0 0	0
OXFORD 18		
1 Mark Carlson	2 1 1	4
2 Troy Butler	2 1 2	5
3 †Martin Dugard	1 3 E	4
4 Dean Barker	1 2 2	5
5 Wayne Parker	0	0
SWINDON 12		
1 David Smart	R 0 1	1
2 †Mitch Shirra	3 E N	3
3 Kelly Moran	1 1 1	3
4 Jimmy Nilsen	1 3 1	5
5 Justin Elkins	0 0	0

Qualifying Rounds

CRADLEY HEATH (Saturday, June 20)
1 CRADLEY HEATH 27 (Andy Grahame 4, Gert Handberg 7, Simon Cross 7, Greg Hancock 9, Scott Smith, did not ride) 2 WOLVERHAMPTON 24 (Charles Ermolenko 8, Sam Ermolenko 6, Ronnie Correy 6, Peter Karlsson 4, Stephen Morris, did not ride) 3 BELLE VUE 23 (Bobby Ott 7, Frede Schøtt 2, Joe Screen 8, Shawn Moran 6, Jason Lyons 0) 4 BRADFORD 22 (Gary Havelock 5, Paul Thorp 1, Kelvin Tatum 6, Simon Wigg 8, Sean Wilson 2).

BRADFORD (Sunday, June 21)
1 BRADFORD 34 (Havelock 10, Thorp 6, Wilson 9, Tatum 9, Darren Pearson, did not ride) 2 WOLVERHAMPTON 25 (Correy 8, C. Ermolenko 4, Karlsson 7, S. Ermolenko 6, Shane Cooper, did not ride) 3 CRADLEY HEATH 21 (Handberg 5, Cross 6, Hancock 5, Grahame 5, Smith, did not ride) 4 BELLE VUE 16 (Ott 1, Schøtt 3, Screen 7, Moran 2, Lyons 3).

WOLVERHAMPTON (Monday, June 22)
1 BELLE VUE 36 (Ott 10, Schøtt 6, Screen 10, Moran 10, Lyons, did not ride) 2 WOLVERHAMPTON 30 (S. Ermolenko 8, C. Ermolenko 8, Karlsson 5, Correy 9, Morris, did not ride) 3 CRADLEY HEATH 18 (Grahame 4, Hancock 9, Handberg 4, Cross 1, Smith, did not ride) 4 BRADFORD 12 (Havelock 1, Thorp 1, Tatum 6, Wigg 1, Wilson 3).

BELLE VUE (Friday, June 26)
1 BELLE VUE 34 (Ott 8, Schøtt 2, Screen 11, Moran 9, Lyons 4) WOLVERHAMPTON 25 (S. Ermolenko 6, Karlsson 6, C. Ermolenko 6, Correy 7, Morris, did not ride) 3 BRADFORD 23 (Havelock 2, Wigg 8, Tatum 9, Thorp 1, Wilson 3) 4 CRADLEY HEATH 14 (Hancock 3, Smith 3, Grahame 7, Cross 1, Jon Armstrong, did not ride).

Aggregate scores: BELLE VUE 109, Wolverhampton 104, Bradford 91, Cradley Heath 80.

COVENTRY (Saturday, June 20)
1 OXFORD 33 (Hans Nielsen 7, Martin Dugard 10, Mark Carlson 5, Troy Butler 11, Morten Andersen, did not ride) 2 SWINDON 27 (Leigh Adams 3, Jimmy Nilsen 8, Mitch Shirra 9, Kelly Moran 7, Dean Standing, did not ride) 3 COVENTRY 25 (Brian Andersen 3, John Jørgensen 9, Rick Miller 9, Andy Smith 4, Michael Warren, did not ride) 4 READING 11 (Jeremy Doncaster 3, Armando Castagna 6, David Mullett 0, Ray Morton 1, Phillip Morris 1).

READING (Monday, June 22)
1 SWINDON 34 (Shirra 8, Moran 8, Adams 9, Nilsen 9, Standing, did not ride) 2 POOLE 31 (Marvyn Cox 10, Steve Schofield 6, Craig Boyce 12, Tony Langdon 3, Alastair Stevens 0) 3 COVENTRY 16 (Miller 8, Warren 1, Jørgensen 6, Andersen 1, Colin Thorpe, did not ride) 4 READING 15 (Doncaster 3, Castagna 1, Mullett 4, Morton 7, Morris, did not ride).

SWINDON (Thursday, June 25)
1 SWINDON 29 (Shirra 9, Standing 6, Adams 11, Moran 3, Justin Elkins, did not ride) 2 POOLE 27 (Cox 8, Schofield 6, Boyce 9, Langdon 0, Stevens 4) & OXFORD 27 (Nielsen 10, Dugard 8, Carlson 3, Butler 6, Andersen, did not ride) 4 COVENTRY 13 (Jørgensen 4, Andersen 5, Miller 3, Paul Bentley 1, Scott Wormleighton, did not ride).

OXFORD (Friday, June 26)
1 SWINDON 29 (Adams 6, Shirra 7, Nilsen 10, Moran 6, Standing, did not ride) 2 OXFORD 27 (Nielsen 9, Dugard 8, Carlson 4, Butler 6, Andersen, did not ride) 3 POOLE 24 (Cox 9, Schofield 7, Boyce 6, Langdon 0, Stevens 2) 4 READING 16 (Per Jonsson 9, Jan Andersson 3, Castagna 4, Morton 0, Gary Sweet, did not ride).

POOLE (Wednesday, July 1)
1 OXFORD 30 (Nielsen 9, Dugard 8, Dean Barker 6, Butler 7, Carlson, did not ride) 2 POOLE 28 (Cox 9, Schofield 4, Jörgen Johansson 6, Boyce 9, Stevens, did not ride) & READING 28 (Jonsson 10, Andersson 6, Castagna 8, Morton 4, Morris, did not ride) 4 COVENTRY 10 (Warren 4, Miller, did not arrive, Jørgensen 4, Andersen 2, Darren Boulton 0).

Aggregate scores: SWINDON 119, OXFORD 117, Poole 110, Reading 70, Coventry 64.

KING'S LYNN (Saturday, June 20)
1 KING'S LYNN 28 (Dennis Löfqvist 8, Bohumil Brhel 11, Mark Loram 8, Gary Allan 0, Alun Rossiter 1) & IPSWICH 28 (Chris Louis 8, David Norris 4, Zdenek Tesar 5, Tony Rickardsson 9, Ben Howe 2) 3 ARENA ESSEX 25 (Brian Karger 9, Allan Johansen 6, Alan Mogridge 0, Bo Petersen 3, Troy Pratt 7) 4 EASTBOURNE 15 (Andrew Silver 5, Stefan Dannö 4, Bobby Schwartz 1, Nathan Simpson 5, Paul Dugard, did not ride).

EASTBOURNE (Sunday, June 21)
1 IPSWICH 31 (Louis 7, Norris 6, Rickardsson 11, Tesar 7, Howe, did not ride) 2 EASTBOURNE 26 (Silver 8, Dannö 10, Schwartz 5, Olli Tyrvainen 3, Dugard 0) 3 ARENA ESSEX 21 (Andy Galvin 0, Karger 9, Petersen 4, Mogridge 2, Pratt 6) 4 KING'S LYNN 18 (Löfqvist 5, Loram 6, Brhel 2, Allan 5, Darren Spicer, did not ride).

ARENA ESSEX (Friday, June 26)
1 ARENA ESSEX 32 (Galvin 7, Johansen 5, Petersen 9, Karger 11, Pratt, did not ride) 2 IPSWICH 28 (Tesar 6, Rickardsson 8, Norris 4, Louis 10, Howe, did not ride) 3 EASTBOURNE 22 (Silver 9, Tyrvainen 6, Schwartz 6, Dugard 0, Dannö 1) 4 KING'S LYNN 14 (Löfqvist 3, Henrik Gustafsson 0, Loram 7, Allan 3, Rossiter 1).

IPSWICH (Thursday, July 9)
1 IPSWICH 37 (Louis 7, Tesar 11, Rickardsson 9, Parker 7, Norris 3) 2 KING'S LYNN 24 (Löfqvist 4, Brhel 8, Allan 2, Gustafsson 10, Spicer, did not ride) 3 ARENA ESSEX 21 (Petersen 6, Galvin 0, Mogridge 2, Karger 10, Pratt 3) 4 EASTBOURNE 14 (Silver 5, Glenn Doyle 0, Peter Nahlin 5, Dannö 4, Simpson, did not ride).

Aggregate scores: IPSWICH 124, Arena Essex 99, King's Lynn 84, Eastbourne 77.

ABSENT ... Oxford skipper Hans Nielsen, out with concussion

DIVISION TWO FINAL

PETERBOROUGH 24		
1 Mick Poole	3 3 3	9
2 Neville Tatum	0 3 2	5
3 †Stephen Davies	2 2 2	6
4 Paul Hurry	N 0 N	0
5 Rodney Colquhoun	1 3	4
EDINBURGH 23		
1 Brett Saunders	3 0 1	4
2 Michael Coles	0 2 2	4
3 Kenny McKinna	1 3 3	7
4 †Les Collins	3 3 2	8
5 Dariusz Fliegert	did not ride	
RYE HOUSE 17		
1 †Martin Goodwin	3 2 1	6
2 Sean Courtney	N N N	0
3 Jan Pedersen	2 2 1	5
4 Jens Rasmussen	2 F N	2
5 Mark Courtney	R 1 R 3	4
GLASGOW 8		
1 Shane Bowes	fn N N	0
2 †Steve Lawson	0 N E	0
3 Robert Nagy	2 1 0	3
4 Neil Collins	1 1 0	2
5 Mick Powell	1 1 0 1 0	3

Qualifying Rounds

EXETER (Monday, June 8)
1 EXETER 42 (Peter Jeffery 12, Paul Fry 8, Richard Green 12, Colin Cook 10, Mark Simmonds, did not ride) 2 RYE HOUSE 21 (Martin Goodwin 9, Trevor O'Brien 6, Jens Rasmussen 3, Jan Pedersen 3, Chris Young, did not ride) 3 MILTON KEYNES 17 (Richard Hellsén 4, Frank Smart 10, Justin Walker 2, David Steen 1, Kieran McCullagh, did not ride) 4 MILDENHALL 16 (David Smart 6, Nigel Leaver 3, Melvyn Taylor 6, Mikael Teurnberg 0, Gary Tagg 1).

MILDENHALL (Wednesday, June 17)
1 RYE HOUSE 30 (Goodwin 10, Sean Courtney 0, Rasmussen 4, Mark Courtney 9, O'Brien 7) 2 MILDENHALL 26 (Smart 8, Leaver 8, Taylor 5, Jamie Habbin 5, Jesper Olsen 0) 3 MILTON KEYNES 23 (Gordon Kennett 6, Walker 3, Hellsén 5, Steen 9, Tony Kingsbury, did not ride) 4 EXETER 17 (Jeffery 0, Fry 4, Green 9, Cook 3, Ian Humphreys 1).

RYE HOUSE (Sunday, June 21)
1 RYE HOUSE 40 (Rasmussen 12, M. Courtney 12, S. Courtney 5, Goodwin 11, O'Brien, did not ride) 2 MILDENHALL 21 (Smart 8, Leaver 0, Habbin 6, Teurnberg 7, Olsen 0) & MILTON KEYNES 21 (Kennett 4, Steen 4, Hellsén 8, Walker 5, Sean McCullagh, did not ride) 4 EXETER 14 (Simmonds 3, Cook 0, Green 8, Humphreys 2, Tommy Palmer 1).

Aggregate scores: RYE HOUSE 91, Exeter 73, Mildenhall 63, Milton Keynes 61.

● ***The qualifying round at Milton Keynes was scheduled for Tuesday, June 9, but was never staged because of the suspension of the track licence and subsequent closure.***

● ***The qualifying round at Mildenhall on Wednesday, June 17, was the final meeting of the season at the West Row Stadium.***

PETERBOROUGH (Friday, June 12)
1 PETERBOROUGH 35 (Stephen Davies 12, Neville Tatum 11, Rodney Colquhoun 7, Mick Poole 5, Mark Blackbird, did not ride) 2 SHEFFIELD 26 (Neil Evitts 9, Peter Carr 9, Louis Carr 4, Simon Green 4, Steve Johnston, did not ride) 3 STOKE 20 (Alan Grahame 2, Nigel Crabtree 7, Gary Chessell 1, Eric Monaghan 8, Darren Standing 2) 4 LONG EATON 15 (Jan Stæchmann 8, Carl Blackbird 4, Martin Dixon 1, Colin White 2, Deon Prinsloo 0).

STOKE (Saturday, June 13)
1 STOKE 28 (Standing 3, Chessell 10, Crabtree 7, Monaghan 8, Andy Meredith, did not ride) 2 PETERBOROUGH 25 (Poole 9, Colquhoun 6, Tatum 6, Davies 4, Blackbird, did not ride) 3 LONG EATON 24 (Stæchmann 8, Blackbird 7, Dixon 5, Gary O'Hare 2, Prinsloo 2) 4 SHEFFIELD 19 (Evitts 9, P. Carr 7, Johnston 1, Green 2, Rob Goldstone, did not ride).

LONG EATON (Wednesday, June 17)
1 PETERBOROUGH 30 (Davies 5, Poole 5, Tatum 10, Colquhoun 10, Blackbird, did not ride) 2 LONG EATON 27 (Stæchmann 10, Blackbird 4, Dixon 8, White 3, Prinsloo 2) 3 STOKE 22 (Chessell 6, Monaghan 8, Crabtree 5, Standing 3, Ade Hoole, did not ride) 4 SHEFFIELD 17 (Evitts 8, P. Carr 8, L. Carr 0, Johnston 1, Green 0).

SHEFFIELD (Thursday, June 18)
1 PETERBOROUGH 29 (Davies 8, Colquhoun 7, Tatum 1, Poole 9, Blackbird 4) & SHEFFIELD 29 (Evitts 12, P. Carr 11, L. Carr 6, Johnston 0, Green 0) 3 LONG EATON 21 (Stæchmann 11, Dixon 3, Prinsloo 3, White 3, Jason Reed 1) 4 STOKE 17 (Monaghan 4, Chessell 5, Crabtree 6, Standing 2, Meredith, did not ride).

Aggregate scores: PETERBOROUGH 119, Sheffield 91, Stoke 87, Long Eaton 87.

EDINBURGH (Friday, June 5)
1 EDINBURGH 45 (Les Collins 12, Michael Coles 12, Brett Saunders 9, Kenny McKinna 12, Johnny Jørgensen, did not ride) 2 BERWICK 20 (Richard Knight 3, David Blackburn 4, Scott Lamb 4, David Walsh 7, Scott Robson 2) 3 GLASGOW 18 (Neil Collins 6, Shane Bowes 6, Robert Nagy 0, Steve Lawson 4, Mick Powell 2) 4 NEWCASTLE 13 (Richard Juul 3, Scott Norman 7, Wayne Garratt 0, Phil Jeffrey 3, David Nagel, did not ride).

BERWICK (Saturday, June 6)
1 BERWICK 38 (Knight 12, Blackburn 11, Lamb 6, Walsh 9, Robson, did not ride) 2 EDINBURGH 29 (Collins 8, Coles 10, McKinna 6, Saunders 2, Jørgensen 3) 3 MIDDLESBROUGH 18 (Daz Sumner 5, Donny Odom 0, David Cheshire 2, Steve Regeling 9, Mark Lemon 2) 4 NEWCASTLE 11 (Norman 4, Juul 2, Garratt 4, Jeffrey 1, Nagel 0).

GLASGOW (Sunday, June 7)
1 GLASGOW 41 (Nagy 12, Collins 10, Bowes 9, Lawson 10, M. Powell, did not ride) 2 EDINBURGH 23 (Collins 4, McKinna 10, Coles 5, Saunders 4, Jørgensen 0) 3 BERWICK 20 (Knight 8, Blackburn 3, Lamb 3, Walsh 6, Robson, did not ride) 4 MIDDLESBROUGH 12 (Regeling 5, Cheshire 2, Odom 1, Sumner 2, Lemon 2).

MIDDLESBROUGH (Thursday, June 11)
1 EDINBURGH 29 (Collins 11, Coles 9, McKinna 5, Saunders 4, Dariusz Fliegert, did not ride) 2 NEWCASTLE 27 (Bargh 11, Norman 7, Juul 0, Thorpe 9, Max Schofield, did not ride) 3 GLASGOW 21 (Bowes 6, Lawson 7, Nagy 3, Collins 5, M. Powell, did not ride) 4 MIDDLESBROUGH 19 (Sumner 3, Odom 6, Cheshire 3, Regeling 2, Lemon 5).

NEWCASTLE (Sunday, June 21)
1 NEWCASTLE 32 (Bargh 11, Norman 9, Jeffrey 7, Juul 5, Max Schofield, did not ride) 2 GLASGOW 25 (Lawson 7, M. Powell 6, Collins 4, Nagy 8, Geoff Powell, did not ride) 3 BERWICK 24 (Knight 11, Blackburn 5, Walsh 1, Lamb 7, Chris Readshaw, did not ride) 4 MIDDLESBROUGH 15 (Regeling 6, Sumner 7, Cheshire 0, Lemon 2, Duncan Chapman, did not ride).

Aggregate scores: EDINBURGH 126, GLASGOW 105, Berwick 102, Newcastle 83, Middlesbrough 64.

1992 HOMEFIRE LEAGUE DIVISION ONE

Pos	Team	M	W	D	L	PtsF	PtsA	BP	TPts
1	READING	24	19	1	4	1199	944	11	50
2	Bradford	24	15	0	9	1132	1027	8	38
3	Poole	24	15	2	7	1129	1028	6	38
4	Cradley Heath	24	14	2	8	1118.5	1038.5	8	38
5	Wolverhampton	24	14	1	9	1106	1051	9	38
6	Belle Vue	24	14	1	9	1144	1011	8	37
7	Ipswich	24	11	2	11	1090	1065	6	30
8	Coventry	24	10	1	13	1056.5	1097.5	5	26
9	King's Lynn	24	9	0	15	1005	1136	7	25
10	Oxford	24	8	4	12	1053	1103	4	24
11	Arena Essex	24	7	0	17	1008	1149	3	17
12	Eastbourne	24	6	2	16	965	1190	1	15
13	Swindon	24	5	2	17	996	1162	2	14

Roll of Honour

1965	1 WEST HAM	2 Wimbledon	3 Coventry
1966	1 HALIFAX	2 Coventry	3 Swindon
1967	1 SWINDON	2 Coventry	3 West Ham
1968	1 COVENTRY	2 Hackney	3 Exeter
1969	1 POOLE	2 Belle Vue	3 Wimbledon
1970	1 BELLE VUE	2 Wimbledon	3 Coventry
1971	1 BELLE VUE	2 Leicester	3 Coventry
1972	1 BELLE VUE	2 Reading	3 King's Lynn
1973	1 READING	2 Sheffield	3 King's Lynn
1974	1 EXETER	2 Belle Vue	3 Ipswich
1975	1 IPSWICH	2 Belle Vue	3 Newport
1976	1 IPSWICH	2 Belle Vue	3 Exeter
1977	1 WHITE CITY	2 Exeter	3 Reading
1978	1 COVENTRY	2 Belle Vue	3 Hull
1979	1 COVENTRY	2 Hull	3 Cradley Heath
1980	1 READING	2 Hackney	3 Belle Vue
1981	1 CRADLEY HEATH	2 Ipswich	3 Swindon
1982	1 BELLE VUE	2 Cradley Heath	3 Ipswich
1983	1 CRADLEY HEATH	2 Ipswich	3 Coventry
1984	1 IPSWICH	2 Belle Vue	3 Cradley Heath
1985	1 OXFORD	2 Sheffield	3 Coventry
1986	1 OXFORD	2 Cradley Heath	3 Wolverhampton
1987	1 COVENTRY	2 Cradley Heath	3 Swindon
1988	1 COVENTRY	2 Belle Vue	3 Cradley Heath
1989	1 OXFORD	2 Wolverhampton	3 Cradley Heath
1990	1 READING	2 Wolverhampton	3 Belle Vue
1991	1 WOLVERHAMPTON	2 Bradford	3 Cradley Heath
1992	1 READING	2 Bradford	3 Poole

BELLE VUE, Coventry, Cradley Heath and Swindon are the only founder members of the British League in 1965 to have competed in each of the 28 seasons as members of the top flight.

Swindon will lose that status in 1993 having been relegated to Division Two.

King's Lynn applied to join the 1965 British League but were turned down and operated on an open licence that season but joined the top flight in 1966 and have remained members ever since.

A TOTAL of 31 tracks – Arena Essex, Belle Vue, Birmingham, Bradford, Bristol, Coatbridge, Coventry, Cradley Heath, Eastbourne, Edinburgh, Exeter, Glasgow, Hackney, Halifax, Hull, Ipswich, King's Lynn, Leicester, Long Eaton, Newcastle, Newport, Oxford, Poole, Reading, Sheffield, Swindon, Wembley, West Ham, White City (London), Wimbledon and Wolverhampton – have competed in the First Division since its launch in 1965.

Of the 31, only nine tracks, Bradford, Bristol, Coventry, Cradley Heath, Halifax, Leicester, Swindon (until 1993!), Wembley and White City have not also competed in Division Two!

THE First Division was launched as the British League in 1965; was re-named the Sunbrite League Division One in 1991; and the Homefire League Division One in 1992.

NO team has ever failed to complete a Division One season – although there have been several instances of tracks closing down mid-season because of financial problems.

But they have always been rescued by new promoters.

AUTOMATIC promotion and relegation was introduced between the two Divisions in 1991.

Arena Essex, Second Division champions in 1991, were promoted but Swindon, who finished bottom of the First Division, were spared relegation.

At the end of the 1992 season, Swindon, who collected the wooden spoon for the second successive season, were relegated but Peterborough declined promotion for financial reasons.

ALL THE 1992 DIVISION ONE RESULTS

	ARENA ESSEX	BELLE VUE	BRADFORD	COVENTRY	CRADLEY HEATH	EASTBOURNE	IPSWICH	KING'S LYNN	OXFORD	POOLE	READING	SWINDON	WOLVERHAMPTON
ARENA ESSEX		54-36	53-37	49-40	43-47	53-32	38-52	51-39	47-43	43-47	44-46	43-47	49-41
BELLE VUE	63-27		48-41	55-35	55-35	54-36	52-38	56-33	51-39	53-36	43-47	54-36	46-44
BRADFORD	49-41	49-41		53-37	52-38	64-26	49-41	40-50	57-33	54-36	47-43	50-40	56-34
COVENTRY	55-35	40-50	35-55		40-50	43-41	51-39	48-42	38-48	44-46	45-45	50-40	56-34
CRADLEY HEATH	59-31	52-38	40-50	46.5-43.5		43-41	51-39	57-33	50-40	39-51	42-47	51-38	50-40
EASTBOURNE	46-43	46-44	44-46	40-50	35-55		49-41	48-42	49-41	45-45	41-49	49-41	37-53
IPSWICH	58-32	53-36	50-40	55-35	45-45	53-31		50-39	48-42	48-42	41-48	62-28	45-45
KING'S LYNN	49-41	36-54	53-37	49-41	40-50	43-42	51-38		51-39	49-41	0-75	49-40	40-50
QXFORD	49-41	45-45	48-42	49-41	45-45	58-32	48-42	48-42		45-45	46-44	45-45	43-47
POOLE	57-32	51-39	47-43	41-49	49-41	52-38	65-25	47-43	55-35		46-44	57-33	48-42
READING	54-36	46-44	59-31	51-39	53-37	58-32	52-38	46-44	53-37	50-40		51-39	54-36
SWINDON	53-37	43-47	41-49	43-47	46-44	45-45	42-48	46-44	46-44	43-47	40-50		40-50
WOLVERH'PTON	50-40	49-40	49-41	41-49	44-46	49-40	54-36	51-39	47-43	51-38	56-34	49-41	

Bo and Reading caught short as Dukes reign again

WORLD Champion Gary Havelock led his club Bradford to a second successive Speedway Star Knock Out Cup win...but it was team-mate Simon Wigg who was the real star of the show.

For Wigg never dropped a point to an opponent in three Odsal cup-ties as he recaptured the spark that had been missing from his British racing for a few seasons.

He followed up a paid 15 point maximum against Eastbourne in the quarter final (as holders, the Keyline Dukes were given a bye in the first round) with another paid full score against Belle Vue in the semi final and he was again unbeaten by a rival as his club built up a 20 point lead in the first leg of the hastily arranged Final.

Bradford's success was built on home form as they were blessed with the first leg in each of their three ties. Leads of 28 points (against the Eagles), 32 (v Belle Vue) and 20 (in the Final) meant they only needed to defend in depth in their away matches.

Belle Vue complained bitterly about the slickness of the Odsal track for the semi final – "It's the worst track I'd seen in many a long day" claimed promoter John Perrin – and it was no surprise that when the Yorkshire club arrived at Kirkmanshulme Lane for the return they found it deep and heavy.

Bradford suffered three successive 5-1 reversals and then asked referee David Dowling to inspect the circuit after only four races but he ruled the meeting should go on.

And it did, acrimoniously, with riders gesturing not only to each other but also the fans on the terraces.

There were also controversial scenes elsewhere. None more so than in the East Anglian derby tie between Ipswich and King's Lynn which erupted just before the four riders went out for the nominated riders' heat.

King's Lynn named their flying Czechoslovakian Bohumil Brhel to partner team-mate Mark Loram...but before he went out onto track for what would have been his sixth ride of the evening Ipswich lodged an official protest about the silencer he had been using.

It was impounded by the machine examiner, referee David Dowling accepted that it had been tampered with and, according to the rulebook, excluded Brhel from the meeting, deducting the 10 points he had already scored from the final tallies turning what would have been a 50-40 Ipswich win into a rather more convincing 22 point first round, first leg victory.

Barum Stars' promoter Bill Barker hit out: "I was gutted. It was heat 10, when it was noticed that Bob Brhel's silencer was not the usual length.

"But they allowed him to ride in Heat 11. Not until he was nominated in Heat 15 was any protest made."

Barker also claimed that it had not been the Ipswich machine examiner who noticed the silencer but Richard Arbon,

manufacturer of the KNE silencers.

Added a furious Barker: "If anything brings the sport down it's petty things like this and makes me think twice before letting all the sundry hangers on into the pits. They don't even pay to watch, but they do make money out of the sport."

Ipswich co-promoter John Louis retorted: "As soon as the problem was brought to our attention – round about heat 10 – Machine Examiner Fred Cotton and Clerk of the Course Keith Barton went up to the ref's box to inform the referee of our suspicions and he came down to the pits after heat 14 to examine the silencer in person. The silencer was measured and found to be 60 mm short of the statutory length.

"There have been one or two insinuations that we were aware of the problem from the start of the meeting and deliberately waited until Bo had taken a number of rides before protesting. This is absolutely untrue."

Yet again the inability of the sport's controlling authority to convince its members that Cup Finals should not be held in the depths of October produced criticism.

Cradley Heath and Reading didn't complete their semi final tie until October 22nd – and the first leg of the Final took place two nights later with the return staged within 48 hours!

No wonder competition backers Speedway Star were moved to write an editorial: "If speedway is to attract – and keep – significant new sponsorship then it should learn how to look after those writing the cheques!"

They had a point as it took from April 25th to October 26th to complete just 24 matches!

What was quite inexplicable was the time taken to complete individual ties with what must have been a resultant lessening of expectation and anticipation by the fans of the respective clubs.

Poole and Cradley Heath supporters had to wait nearly six weeks for the completion of their first round match and it was 10 weeks between the two legs of that stormy Ipswich-King's Lynn tie because of the mid-season Saddlebow Road closure!

The time has come when clubs must be told that they will forfeit matches if they can't be completed within a reasonable time span of, say (and let's give some leeway), three weeks.

Finally a curious statistical note: the three teams that had most recently graced Division Two (or the 1990 National League as was) all went out in their first ties.

Poole were beaten 95-85 by Cradley Heath; Arena Essex (given a bye in round one) also went down to the Heathens; and Eastbourne were beaten by Bradford.

First Round

Saturday, April 25

CRADLEY HEATH 54

1 Peter McNamara	0 fxN N	0	
2 Greg Hancock	**3 3 3 3**	**12**	
3 Billy Hamill	**3 3 3 3 3**	**15**	
4 Gert Handberg	1 1 2 3	7	
5 †Jan O. Pedersen	**3 3 3 2 2**	**13**	**2**
6 Scott Smith	1 1 1 2 N 2 0	7	2
7 Mark Robinson	0 N 0 0 0	0	

POOLE 36

1 †Marvyn Cox	2 2 2 2 1 1	10	
2 Slawomir Drabik	1 0 N T	1	1
3 Steve Schofield	2 1 1 3 0	7	2
4 Tony Langdon	0 2 0 0	2	
5 Craig Boyce	2 0 1 1 1	5	1
6 Tom Knudsen	2 2 1 T 1 2	8	2
7 Andy Phillips	3 0 0 T	3	

Wednesday, June 3

POOLE 49

1 †Marvyn Cox	1 2 2 3 3	11	
2 Jörgen Johansson	0 1 0 1	2	2
3 Steve Schofield	3 3 2 3 0	11	1
4 Craig Boyce	1 3 1 2	7	1
5 Tony Langdon	0 1 1 1	3	1
6 Tom Knudsen	2 2 0 2	6	1
7 Alastair Stevens	1 2 3 3	9	1

CRADLEY HEATH 41

1 †Simon Cross	2 fxN N	2	1
2 Jan O. Pedersen	*rider replacement*		
3 Billy Hamill	3 1 3 3 0	10	
4 Gert Handberg	3 1 3 3 2 2	14	1
5 Greg Hancock	2 2 2 2 1 1	10	2
6 Scott Smith	3 0 1 0 1 0	5	
7 Anthony Boyd	0 0 N 0 0 0	0	
8 Peter McNamara	*did not ride*		

Aggregate: Cradley Heath 95 Poole 85

Thursday, April 30

SWINDON 43

1 †Mitch Shirra	2 1 2 0	5	1
2 Dean Standing	1 2 3 1	7	2
3 Leigh Adams	3 3 3 1 2	12	
4 Jimmy Nilsen	3 3 2 3 1	12	1
5 Kelly Moran	R 1 2 0	3	
6 Steve Camden	1 N F F	1	
7 Justin Elkins	E 1 2 fxF	3	1

WOLVERHAMPTON 47

1 Ronnie Correy	3 2 2 2	9	1
2 Charles Ermolenko	0 0 0 N	0	
3 †Sam Ermolenko	2 3 3 3 3	14	
4 Graham Jones	2 1 3 3 0	9	1
5 Peter Karlsson	1 2 1 2	6	1
6 Stephen Morris	3 0 0 1 1 N	5	1
7 Wayne Carter	2 N 1 0 1	4	2

Monday, May 11

WOLVERHAMPTON 50

1 Ronnie Correy	3 2 3 3 1	12	
2 Charles Ermolenko	0 1 2 1	4	1
3 †Sam Ermolenko	**3 3 3 3 3**	**15**	
4 Graham Jones	2 2 2 2	8	2
5 Peter Karlsson	1 3 2 2	8	2
6 Wayne Carter	1 1 0 1	3	1
7 Stephen Morris	fx0 0 0	0	

SWINDON 40

1 †Mitch Shirra	1 0 2 0	3	1
2 Dean Standing	2 1 3 1	7	1
3 Leigh Adams	2 3 3 1 3 0	12	
4 Kelly Moran	0 1 2 1	4	1
5 Jimmy Nilsen	3 2 0 1 2	8	
6 Justin Elkins	3 0 N 0 T	3	
7 Steve Masters	2 N 0 1 0	3	1

Aggregate: Wolverhampton 97 Swindon 83

LEGEND

R = retired, engine failure; E = excluded for tapes offence; F = fell; fx = fell, excluded; X = excluded; fn = fell, unable to take part in re-run; T = replaced by tactical substitute; N = excluded under two minutes or replaced by a reserve.

First Round

Thursday June 4

IPSWICH 55

1 †Chris Louis	R 3 1 2 3	9	1
2 Jacek Rempala	3 0 1 3	7	1
3 Tony Rickardsson	3 3 2 3 1	12	
4 Shane Parker	1 2 3 2	8	1
5 Zdenek Tesar	3 3 2 2	10	1
6 Ben Howe	1 1 2 0	4	2
7 David Norris	2 2 R 1	5	1

KING'S LYNN 33

1 Dennis Löfqvist	2 1 1 3 0	7	
2 Bohumil Brhel	*ineligible*	*0*	
3 †Mark Loram	2 2 3 1 1 3 2	14	
4 Gary Allan	2 0 2 1	5	
5 Henrik Gustafsson	*rider replacement*		
6 Alun Rossiter	3 1 3 0 0 0	7	
7 Darren Spicer	0 R N 0	0	

Bohumil Brhel scored 10 points but they were deducted from the final score after he was adjudged to have been using an illegal silencer. Actual scores were: IPSWICH 50 (Louis R-3-1-2-3- 9:1, Rempala 3-0-0-3- 6, Rickardsson 3-3-1-3-1- 11, Parker 1-1-3-2- 7:1, Tesar 3-2-2-2- 9:1, Howe 1-1-2-0- 4:2, Norris 2-1-R-1- 4:1) KING'S LYNN 40 (Löfqvist 1-0-1-3- 5:1, Brhel 2-0-3-3-2-N- 10:1, Loram 2-2-2-1-1-3-2- 13:1, Allan 2-0-2-1- 5, Rossiter 3-1-3-0-0-0- 7:1, Spicer 0-R-N-0- 0).

Sunday, August 16

KING'S LYNN 48

1 Bohumil Brhel	2 1 R F	3	2
2 Gary Allan	3 2 2 3 1	11	
3 Mark Loram	**3 3 3 3 3**	**15**	
4 Henrik Gustafsson	2 3 1 3	9	
5 Dennis Löfqvist	1 0 2 0	3	1
6 Darren Spicer	1 R N N	1	1
7 Kevin Brice	2 2 0 1 1 0	6	2

IPSWICH 40

1 †Chris Louis	1 1 0 2	4	1
2 Tony Olsson	0 2 F 2 2	6	
3 Tony Rickardsson	X 3 3 3	9	
4 David Norris	3 fx1 1	5	2
5 Zdenek Tesar	0 F N N	0	
6 Ben Howe	0 0 1 1 0	2	1
7 Shane Parker	3 2 3 2 2 2	14	1

Aggregate: Ipswich 95 King's Lynn 81

Monday, July 6

READING 56

1 Per Jonsson	2 3 3 3 2	13	1
2 David Mullett	3 1 1 1	6	1
3 Jan Andersson	3 3 2 1	9	1
4 Armando Castagna	2 1 2 3 R	8	3
5 †Jeremy Doncaster	3 2 2 2	9	
6 Phillip Morris	1 2 0 1	4	3
7 Ray Morton	2 2 1 2	7	2

OXFORD 34

1 †Hans Nielsen	1 3 2 3 3 3 3	18	
2 Dean Standing	0 0 0 0 0	0	
3 Martin Dugard	*rider replacement*		
4 Mark Carlson	0 1 2 1 0	4	1
5 Dean Barker	1 2 3 0 0 1 1	8	
6 Morten Andersen	3 1 0 fxT	4	
7 Glenn Cunningham	0 0 T 0 T	0	
8 Spencer Timmo	*did not ride*		

Friday, July 10

OXFORD 45

1 †Hans Nielsen	1 3 3 3 3 2	15	
2 Troy Butler	0 3 1 1 2 1	8	2
3 Martin Dugard	*rider replacement*		
4 Mark Carlson	0 1 2 0 2	5	
5 Dean Barker	1 3 1 1 0	6	
6 Glenn Cunningham	1 1 0 R	2	
7 Morten Andersen	3 3 3 0 0	9	

READING 45

1 Per Jonsson	2 0 3 2 3	10	1
2 David Mullett	3 2 0 1	6	
3 Jan Andersson	2 2 2 1	7	1
4 †Jeremy Doncaster	2 3 1 1	7	2
5 Armando Castagna	3 2 2 3 0	10	1
6 Ray Morton	2 0 2 0 1	5	
7 Phillip Morris	0 0 R 0 R	0	

Aggregate: Reading 101 Oxford 79

First Round

Friday, July 10

BELLE VUE 57

1 Bobby Ott	**3 3 3 3 2**	**14**	**1**
2 Frede Schøtt	2 2 fx2	6	3
3 †Joe Screen	**3 3 3 3 3**	**15**	
4 Jason Lyons	2 2 fx3	7	2
5 Shawn Moran	3 3 3 0	9	
6 Paul Smith	1 0 1 0	2	
7 Carl Stonehewer	0 1 2 1	4	1

COVENTRY 33

1 Andy Smith	0 1 0 1	2	1
2 Paul Bentley	1 0 T T	1	
3 †Tommy Knudsen	1 1 2 1 2 1	8	1
4 Rick Miller	1 0 R N	1	
5 John Jørgensen	0 2 3 1 2 0	8	1
6 Michael Warren	2 0 1 N	3	2
7 Brian Andersen	3 2 2 1 2 0	10	1

Saturday, July 25

COVENTRY 51

1 Andy Smith	2 3 3 3 2	13	1
2 Jamie Habbin	0 1 0 N	1	
3 †Tommy Knudsen	2 3 2 3 3	13	
4 Rick Miller	1 2 0 3	6	1
5 John Jørgensen	0 3 3 1	7	
6 Michael Warren	2 1 0 1	4	2
7 Brian Andersen	3 3 0 0 1	7	

BELLE VUE 39

1 Bobby Ott	3 0 3 2 1	9	
2 Frede Schøtt	1 1 1 T	3	1
3 †Joe Screen	3 2 2 1 1 0	9	1
4 Jason Lyons	2 1 1 0 2	6	3
5 Shawn Moran	3 2 2 2 R	9	
6 Paul Smith	1 0 0 T	1	
7 Carl Stonehewer	0 0 2 T	2	

Aggregate: Belle Vue 96 Coventry 84

Byes: Arena Essex, Bradford and Eastbourne.

Quarter Final

Saturday, June 21

BRADFORD 59

1 †Gary Havelock	**3 3 3 3 2**	**14**	**1**
2 Antal Kocso	2 1 3 1	7	1
3 Kelvin Tatum	1 0 3 3	7	
4 Paul Thorp	3 0 1 1	5	
5 Simon Wigg	**2 3 3 2 3**	**13**	**2**
6 Sean Wilson	3 3 2 2 3	13	1
7 Stuart Parnaby	0 0 0 N	0	

EASTBOURNE 31

1 †Andrew Silver	1 1 2 1 0	5	1
2 Paul Dugard	0 T 1 1	2	2
3 Glenn Doyle	2 2 2 1 X	7	
4 Olli Tyrvainen	R 1 0 2 R	3	
5 Peter Nahlin	1 2 3 2 2 1	11	
6 Nathan Simpson	2 0 T 0	2	
7 Stefan Dannö	1 0 T 0	1	1

Friday, July 24

EASTBOURNE 48

1 Peter Nahlin	2 3 3 1 0	9	1
2 Olli Tyrvainen	3 1 1 2	7	2
3 Glenn Doyle	1 E 1 2	4	2
4 Stefan Dannö	3 3 0 2	8	
5 Paul Dugard	2 0 0 N	2	1
6 †Andrew Silver	3 2 1 2 3 2	13	
7 Nathan Simpson	1 0 N 2 1 1	5	2

BRADFORD 42

1 †Gary Havelock	1 2 3 3 3 3	15	
2 Paul Thorp	0 1 0 E	1	1
3 Kelvin Tatum	3 2 2 1 3 N	11	2
4 Antal Kocso	0 N 0 N	0	
5 Simon Wigg	1 3 3 2 0	9	1
6 Sean Wilson	2 0 0 2 0 1	5	
7 Darren Pearson	0 0 T 1	1	

Aggregate: Bradford 101 Eastbourne 79

Quarter Final

Saturday, July 11

CRADLEY HEATH 56

1 †Simon Cross	1 3 1 3 2 3	13	2
2 Billy Hamill	*rider replacement*		
3 Greg Hancock	3 3 3 2 1	12	1
4 Andy Grahame	2 1 1 0 3 3	10	2
5 Gert Handberg	3 2 3 2 2 2	14	2
6 Andy Phillips	3 0 0 1	4	
7 Scott Smith	F 2 1 0	3	1
8 Anthony Boyd	*did not ride*		

ARENA ESSEX 34

1 Brian Karger	2 3 3 3 3 0	14	
2 †Andy Galvin	0 0 T 0	0	
3 Allan Johansen	2 0 0 2 0	4	
4 Robert Ledwith	0 N T 0	0	
5 Bo Petersen	1 2 1 1 2	7	
6 Josh Larsen	2 2 1 N 0 1 1	7	2
7 Colin White	1 1 T 0 T	2	2

Friday, July 24

ARENA ESSEX 49

1 Brian Karger	**3 3 3 2 2**	**13**	**2**
2 †Andy Galvin	0 1 2 2	5	1
3 Allan Johansen	3 1 3 3 3	13	1
4 Bo Petersen	2 3 3 1	9	
5 Robert Ledwith	1 0 0 N	1	1
6 Josh Larsen	3 0 2 2 fx1	8	
7 Colin White	F 0 N 0	0	

CRADLEY HEATH 41

1 †Simon Cross	1 1 3 2 2 2	11	3
2 Billy Hamill	*rider replacement*		
3 Greg Hancock	2 2 2 3 1 3 0	13	
4 Andy Grahame	3 2 3 1 0 1	10	
5 Gert Handberg	fxN N N	0	
6 Scott Smith	2 0 1 0 N	3	
7 Andy Phillips	1 1 0 1 0 1	4	3
8 Justin Walker	*did not ride*		

Aggregate: Cradley Heath 97 Arena Essex 83

Sunday, August 23

READING 49

1 Per Jonsson	3 1 2 3 3	12	
2 David Mullett	2 3 1 1 fx	7	3
3 †Jeremy Doncaster	2 2 1 1	6	2
4 Ray Morton	1 2 F 2	5	2
5 Armando Castagna	2 1 3 2	8	1
6 Phillip Morris	fxF N 0	0	
7 Jan Andersson	3 1 2 2 3	11	1

WOLVERHAMPTON 40

1 Gordon Kennett	1 0 0 E	1	
2 Ronnie Correy	0 3 3 3 2	11	
3 Peter Karlsson	3 2 2 E	7	
4 †Sam Ermolenko	3 3 3 3 1	13	1
5 Charles Ermolenko	0 fx1 1	2	1
6 Nigel Leaver	2 F 1 0 2 0	5	1
7 Stephen Morris	fx1 0 N E	1	

Monday, September 14

WOLVERHAMPTON 45

1 Ronnie Correy	3 2 2 2 1	10	1
2 Gordon Kennett	0 0 2 0	2	
3 Peter Karlsson	2 3 2 3	10	
4 †Sam Ermolenko	3 2 3 2 R	10	1
5 Charles Ermolenko	2 3 1 1	7	1
6 Stephen Morris	2 1 1 0	4	1
7 Nigel Leaver	F 1 0 1	2	2

READING 45

1 Per Jonsson	2 1 3 2 3	11	
2 David Mullett	1 0 0 1	2	1
3 †Jeremy Doncaster	3 3 3 3 0 2	14	1
4 Armando Castagna	0 2 1 0	3	
5 Ray Morton	1 0 N N	1	
6 Jan Andersson	3 1 2 3 1 3	13	1
7 Phillip Morris	1 0 T N 0	1	

Aggregate: Reading 94 Wolverhampton 85

The original staging on August 24 was abandoned after five races because of heavy rain. Scores at the time were: WOLVERHAMPTON 13 (Ronnie Correy 3- 3, Gordon Kennett 0- 0, Peter Karlsson

Quarter Final

2- 2, †Sam Ermolenko 3-3- 6, Charles Ermolenko 0-fx- 0, Stephen Morris R-N- 0, Nigel Leaver 2-fx- 2) READING 16 (Per Jonsson 1-fn- 1:1, David Mullett 2-2- 4, †Jeremy Doncaster 3- 3, Armando Castagna 1- 1:1, Ray Morton 2- 2, Jan Andersson 3-1- 4:1, Phillip Morris 1-fx- 1:1).

Friday, September 4

BELLE VUE 47

1 Bobby Ott	3 3 3 3 1	13	1
2 Frede Schøtt	0 2 3 0	5	1
3 †Joe Screen	3 3 2 3 2	13	
4 Jason Lyons	R 1 R 1	2	
5 Shawn Moran	**3 3 3 2**	**11**	**1**
6 Carl Stonehewer	1 1 0 1 fx	3	
7 Paul Smith	0 0 0 N	0	

IPSWICH 43

1 †Chris Louis	1 0 2 1 0	4	1
2 Tony Olsson	2 2 2 2 3 3 3	17	
3 Tony Rickardsson	0 1 2 2 2	7	1
4 David Norris	1 1 2 1	5	2
5 Zdenek Tesar	*rider replacement*		
6 Ben Howe	2 0 0 T	2	1
7 Shane Parker	3 2 1 1 1	3	3

Thursday, September 10

IPSWICH 39

1 †Chris Louis	0 3 2 0	5	
2 Tony Olsson	3 X 3 fx2 R	8	
3 Tony Rickardsson	3 1 1 0	5	1
4 David Norris	1 2 3 fx1	7	
5 Zdenek Tesar	0 0 1 N	1	
6 Ben Howe	1 1 0 N	2	
7 Shane Parker	3 2 3 2 1 T	11	1

BELLE VUE 51

1 Bobby Ott	2 3 3 3 3	14	
2 Frede Schøtt	1 1 1 0	3	1
3 †Joe Screen	2 1 2 1	6	2
4 Jason Lyons	3 2 1 2 2	10	3
5 Shawn Moran	2 3 2 3	10	1
6 Carl Stonehewer	2 2 0 3 1	8	
7 Paul Smith	0 0 0 N	0	

Aggregate: Belle Vue 98 Ipswich 82

Semi Final

Wednesday, October 7

READING 55

1 Per Jonsson	2 3 3 2 2	12	
2 David Mullett	1 2 1 0	4	3
3 Jan Andersson	2 2 2 3 0	9	2
4 Armando Castagna	3 2 0 3	8	
5 †Jeremy Doncaster	2 1 3 2	8	3
6 Phillip Morris	fx N N N	0	
7 Ray Morton	3 3 3 2 1 2	14	2

CRADLEY HEATH 35

1 Greg Hancock	3 3 3 3 1 3	16	
2 Andy Grahame	0 0 T 0	0	
3 Billy Hamill	R 1 2 1 3 1	8	1
4 †Simon Cross	R 1 1 2 0	4	1
5 Gert Handberg	1 0 1 R	2	
6 Andy Phillips	1 0 T 1	2	1
7 Scott Smith	2 1 0 T	3	

Thursday, October 22

CRADLEY HEATH 45

1 †Simon Cross	1 1 2 1	5	
2 Andy Grahame	0 3 fnN	3	
3 Billy Hamill	3 3 3 3 2	14	
4 Gert Handberg	1 R 0 3	4	
5 Greg Hancock	3 2 3 2 1	11	2
6 Andy Phillips	fx1 fx1 N	2	
7 Scott Smith	3 fx1 1 R 1	6	1

READING 44

1 Per Jonsson	2 3 2 0 3	10	1
2 David Mullett	3 1 3 1	8	1
3 Jan Andersson	2 2 2 3 0	9	
4 †Jeremy Doncaster	0 1 3 1	5	1
5 Armando Castagna	2 2 2 2	8	1
6 Ray Morton	fnN N N	0	
7 Phillip Morris	2 0 0 2 0 R	4	1

Aggregate: Reading 99 Cradley Heath 80

Semi Final

Saturday, October 17

BRADFORD 61

1 †Gary Havelock	**2 3 3 2 3 3**	**16**	**2**
2 Sean Wilson	3 3 2 3 2 1	14	2
3 Kelvin Tatum	*rider replacement*		
4 Paul Thorp	0 3 3 3 2	11	1
5 Simon Wigg	**3 2 3 3 2**	**13**	**2**
6 Antal Kocso	3 0 N 0 N 1 3	7	
7 Stuart Swales	0 E N 0 N N	0	
8 Stuart Parnaby	*did not ride*		

BELLE VUE 29

1 Bobby Ott	1 1 2 2 1 2	9	
2 Frede Schøtt	0 0 T N	0	
3 †Joe Screen	2 1 2 1 R	6	
4 Jason Lyons	2 2 1 0 1 0	6	
5 Shawn Moran	1 1 1 0 T	3	3
6 Paul Smith	1 0 T 0 T	1	1
7 Carl Stonehewer	2 1 1 0	4	2

Sunday, October 18

BELLE VUE 54

1 Bobby Ott	3 3 3 F 2	11	1
2 Frede Schøtt	2 2 1 0	5	2
3 †Joe Screen	fx3 2 3 3	11	1
4 Jason Lyons	3 1 2 3	9	
5 Shawn Moran	2 F 1 N	3	1
6 Carl Stonehewer	3 fx2 3 3 2	13	2
7 Paul Smith	2 0 N 0 N	2	1

BRADFORD 35

1 †Gary Havelock	1 3 2 0 3 2	11	1
2 Sean Wilson	0 3 2 1 3 1 0	10	1
3 Kelvin Tatum	*rider replacement*		
4 Paul Thorp	1 1 T 2 1 1	6	1
5 Simon Wigg	0 0 2 1 1 1	5	1
6 Antal Kocso	0 fx0 N	0	
7 Stuart Swales	1 2 T T 0	3	1
8 Stuart Parnaby	*did not ride*		

Aggregate: Bradford 96 Belle Vue 83

1991 Speedway Star Division One Knock Out Cup

BRADFORD'S growing status as one of the country's top teams was confirmed – as they won the Speedway Star Knock Out Cup for the first time in their history.

They brushed aside early opponents Berwick and Belle Vue quite ruthlessly and then won both legs of the final.

First Round

Coventry 46 Berwick 44
Berwick 47 Coventry 43
Aggregate: Berwick 91 Coventry 89

King's Lynn 40 Wimbledon 50
Wimbledon 52 King's Lynn 38
Aggregate: Wimbledon 102 King's Lynn 78

Belle Vue 55 Swindon 35
Swindon 46 Belle Vue 44
Aggregate: Belle Vue 99 Swindon 81

Wolverhampton 50 Oxford 40
Oxford 48 Wolverhampton 41
Aggregate: Wolverhampton 91 Oxford 88

Poole 47 Reading 43
Reading 48 Poole 42
Aggregate: Reading 91 Poole 89

Byes: Bradford, Cradley Heath, and Ipswich,

■ ***Wimbledon moved to Eastbourne between the staging of their first and second round matches.***

Second Round

Ipswich 46 Cradley Heath 44
Cradley Heath 50 Ipswich 39
Aggregate: Cradley Heath 94 Ipswich 85

Wolverhampton 42.5 Belle Vue 47.5
Belle Vue 44 Wolverhampton 46
Belle Vue 91.5 Wolverhampton 88.5

Reading 56 Eastbourne 34
Eastbourne 50 Reading 40
Aggregate: Reading 96 Eastbourne 84

Bradford 50 Berwick 40
Berwick 43 Bradford 47
Aggregate: Bradford 97 Berwick 83

Semi Final

Reading 46 Cradley Heath 43
Cradley Heath 50 Reading 39
Aggregate: Cradley Heath 93 Reading 85

Bradford 56 Belle Vue 34
Belle Vue 51 Bradford 39
Aggregate: Bradford 96 Belle Vue 85

Final

Bradford 50 Cradley Heath 40
Cradley Heath 43 Bradford 47
Aggregate: Bradford 97 Cradley Heath 83

FINAL

SIMON WIGG took his personal collection of Speedway Star Knock Out Cup gold medals to five.

But, more important to Bradford, the former England skipper maintained his astonishing First Division Cup Final record as he has never figured on the losing side.

Wigg's won his first medal in Cradley Heath's 1982 winning side, picked up his second a year later also for the Heathens, moved onto Oxford where he figured in their successful squad in 1985, reappeared in the 1986 Cup Final which was never settled on track, and has now ridden in Bradford's two-in-a-row victories.

Wigg played a major part in the success, recording a paid maximum on a heavy Odsal track in the first leg and then being paid for double figures in the return at Smallmead where the Keyline Dukes had a four point overall winning margin even though they conceded a 5-1 in the final race.

Everything had been tied up in the previous race when Wigg and partner Kelvin Tatum pegged back Reading skipper Jeremy Doncaster to ensure the result of the last race was of purely academic interest.

Reading, chasing the treble, could never overcome the absence of their powerful reserve Ray Morton who missed both legs because of a broken collar bone. His replacement Lance Sealey didn't take a point off a Bradford rider.

Saturday, October 24

BRADFORD 55

1 †Gary Havelock	3 2 3 2 3	13	
2 Sean Wilson	1 0 2 2	5	1
3 Kelvin Tatum	3 1 1 3	8	
4 Paul Thorp	3 0 1 0	4	1
5 Simon Wigg	**2 3 3 2 2**	**12**	**3**
6 Antal Kocso	3 1 3 2 2	11	1
7 Stuart Parnaby	2 0 0 N	2	1

READING 35

1 Per Jonsson	0 1 3 3 1 1	9	1
2 David Mullett	2 2 3 1 X	8	
3 Jan Andersson	2 1 1 0	4	
4 †Jeremy Doncaster	0 2 1 0	3	
5 Armando Castagna	1 0 2 3 3 0	9	1
6 Lance Sealey	0 0 T N N 0	0	
7 Phillip Morris	1 N T 0 N 1	2	

Monday, October 26

READING 53

1 Per Jonsson	**2 3 3 3**	**11**	**1**
2 David Mullett	3 1 3 2 3	12	1
3 Jan Andersson	3 1 2 1	7	
4 †Jeremy Doncaster	2 3 2 1	8	2
5 Armando Castagna	3 1 2 3 2	11	1
6 Phillip Morris	F 2 0 F 1	3	2
7 Lance Sealey	1 0 N F	1	

BRADFORD 37

1 †Gary Havelock	1 2 2 3 2	10	
2 Sean Wilson	0 0 1 0	1	1
3 Kelvin Tatum	1 2 1 N 3 1	8	
4 Paul Thorp	1 2 1 0	4	1
5 Simon Wigg	0 3 3 1 2 0	9	1
6 Antal Kocso	2 0 N T 0 T	2	1
7 Stuart Parnaby	3 N 0 T 0	3	

Aggregate: Bradford 92 Reading 88

Roll of Honour

1965 WEST HAM 114 Exeter 78
1966 HALIFAX 113 Wimbledon 79
1967 COVENTRY 104 West Ham 88
1968 WIMBLEDON 119 Wolverhampton 98
1969 WIMBLEDON 94 Sheffield 62
1970 WIMBLEDON 80 Belle Vue 75
1971 HACKNEY 88 Cradley Heath 68
1972 BELLE VUE 82 Hackney 73
1973 BELLE VUE 78 Reading 78†
1974 SHEFFIELD 90 Ipswich 66
1975 BELLE VUE 86 Leicester 70
1976 IPSWICH 92 King's Lynn 63
1977 KING'S LYNN 79 Reading 77
1978 IPSWICH 92 Belle Vue 64
1979 CRADLEY HEATH 120 Hull 96
1980 CRADLEY HEATH 116 Belle Vue 100
1981 IPSWICH 110 Birmingham 92
1982 CRADLEY HEATH 81 Belle Vue 75
1983 CRADLEY HEATH 86 Coventry 70
1984 IPSWICH 92 Belle Vue 64
1985 OXFORD 79 Ipswich 76
1986 CRADLEY HEATH shared with Oxford††
1987 CRADLEY HEATH 94 Coventry 86
1988 CRADLEY HEATH 100 Coventry 80
1989 CRADLEY HEATH 95 Wolverhampton 85
1990 READING 98 Bradford 82
1991 BRADFORD 97 Cradley Heath 83
1992 BRADFORD 92 Reading 88

† Peter Collins (Belle Vue) defeated Anders Michanek (Reading) in a run-off.
† The first leg at Cradley Heath was drawn 39-39 but the second leg was never raced because of adverse weather conditions.

CRADLEY HEATH have seven wins in the Speedway Star Division One Knock Out Cup – and also shared the trophy with Oxford in 1986.

BRADFORD became only the fourth team to successfully defend the Speedway Star Knock Out Cup...in a repeat of the 1990 Final. It was also the Keyline Dukes' third successive Cup Final appearance.

Arena Essex

King's Lynn (A), March 28, L44-46

1 Brian Karger	3 3 3 2 3	14	
2 Andy Galvin	1 2 1 0	4	1
3 Bo Petersen	2 3 3 2 0	10	
4 †Alan Mogridge	2 2 E 1	5	1
5 Allan Johansen	0 1 0 1	2	1
6 Josh Larsen	0 0 2 1 0	3	1
7 Troy Pratt	2 1 3 0	6	1

KING'S LYNN (H), April 3, W56-34

1 Brian Karger	3 3 3 2 2	13	1
2 Andy Galvin	0 2 3 R	5	1
3 Bo Petersen	**3 3 3 3 3**	**15**	
4 †Alan Mogridge	2 2 0 1	5	1
5 Allan Johansen	R 3 3 1	7	
6 Josh Larsen	0 1 0 1	2	
7 Troy Pratt	3 2 1 3	9	1

Eastbourne (A), April 5, L38-52

1 Brian Karger	3 0 1 2 2 1	9	
2 Andy Galvin	0 2 0 T 0	2	
3 Bo Petersen	2 3 3 1 0 3	12	1
4 †Alan Mogridge	1 2 F 2 T	5	
5 Allan Johansen	3 0 T 0	3	
6 Josh Larsen	2 0 T 1	3	
7 Troy Pratt	1 1 1 1	4	2

Poole (A), April 8, L37-53

1 Brian Karger	3 3 3 2 3 0	14	
2 Andy Galvin	0 2 2 1 R	5	3
3 Bo Petersen	2 2 3 1 3 1	12	
4 †Alan Mogridge	2 1 1 0	4	
5 Allan Johansen	1 0 N 0	1	1
6 Josh Larsen	1 0 0 N	1	
7 Troy Pratt	0 0 N 0	0	

EASTBOURNE (H), April 10, W56-34

1 Brian Karger	R 2 3 3	8	
2 Andy Galvin	1 0 1 1	3	1
3 Bo Petersen	**3 3 3 2**	**11**	**1**
4 †Alan Mogridge	2 2 2 2	8	3
5 Allan Johansen	3 3 2 3 3	14	
6 Josh Larsen	2 2 1 1 1	7	3
7 Troy Pratt	3 2 0 0	5	

SWINDON (H), April 24, W53-37

1 Brian Karger	3 2 3 3 2	13	1
2 Allan Johansen	0 R 3 2	5	1
3 Bo Petersen	3 R 2 3 3	11	
4 †Alan Mogridge	2 2 0 3	7	
5 Andy Galvin	1 0 2 1	4	1
6 Troy Pratt	3 1 2 E	6	
7 Josh Larsen	2 2 1 1 1	7	4

Swindon (A), April 26, W46-43

1 Brian Karger	2 3 1 2 2	10	1
2 Allan Johansen	0 2 1 2	5	1
3 Bo Petersen	2 3 3 3 1	12	1
4 †Alan Mogridge	2 1 fxN	3	
5 Andy Galvin	1 0 0 1	2	2
6 Troy Pratt	2 0 2 2	6	2
7 Josh Larsen	3 1 3 fx1	8	2

IPSWICH (H), May 1, W47-43

1 Brian Karger	2 1 3 3	9	1
2 Allan Johansen	3 3 1 2 1	10	1
3 Bo Petersen	3 3 2 2 fx	10	
4 †Alan Mogridge	2 1 1 1	5	
5 Andy Galvin	1 0 0 N	1	1
6 Troy Pratt	3 2 2 1 0	8	2
7 Josh Larsen	0 R 1 3	4	1

Ipswich (A), May 7, L34-56

1 Brian Karger	2 3 3 3 2 0	13	
2 Allan Johansen	1 0 T N	1	1
3 Bo Petersen	fx2 0 3 3 1	9	
4 †Alan Mogridge	2 1 1 1 0	5	2
5 Robert Ledwith	0 T 0 N	0	
6 Troy Pratt	1 0 0 T T	1	
7 Josh Larsen	0 1 2 T 2 0 0	5	

POOLE (H), May 8, W62-28

1 Brian Karger	**3 3 3 3 3**	**15**	
2 Robert Ledwith	1 1 N N	2	
3 Bo Petersen	3 3 2 1 2	11	2
4 †Alan Mogridge	1 1 fxN	2	
5 Allan Johansen	**3 3 3 3**	**12**	
6 Troy Pratt	3 2 1 1 1 3	11	1
7 Josh Larsen	2 R 2 3 2	9	3

Reading (A), May 25, L38-52

1 Brian Karger	3 1 2 2 3 2	13	
2 †Alan Mogridge	0 0 T 1 1	2	2
3 Bo Petersen	3 1 2 3 1 1	11	2
4 Andy Galvin	R 2 1 0 0	3	
5 Allan Johansen	1 1 0 T	2	1
6 Troy Pratt	fxT T N	0	
7 Josh Larsen	1 2 1 1 2	7	2

READING (H), July 7, L44-46

1 Brian Karger	3 3 3 3 2	14	
2 †Alan Mogridge	0 1 R 2	3	1
3 Bo Petersen	3 3 2 3 1	12	1
4 Andy Galvin	1 0 0 2	3	1
5 Allan Johansen	2 1 N N	3	
6 Troy Pratt	3 0 R 2 1	6	
7 Josh Larsen	1 1 X 1 0	3	1

Eastbourne

ARENA ESSEX (H), April 5, W52-38

1 Andrew Silver	2 1 3 3 2	11	1
2 Nathan Simpson	1 2 2 2	7	3
3 †Andy Grahame	0 3 3 1	7	
4 Glenn Doyle	2 3 1 3 0	9	
5 Olli Tyrvainen	0 1 2 3	6	
6 Neville Tatum	3 3 1 0	7	
7 Paul Dugard	0 3 0 2	5	1

Arena Essex (A), April 10, L34-56

1 Andrew Silver	3 0 1 3 2 1 0	10	
2 Nathan Simpson	2 0 0 1 0	3	2
3 †Andy Grahame	F 3 2 3 2 0 2	12	
4 Glenn Doyle	*rider replacement*		
5 Olli Tyrvainen	1 0 1 1	3	
6 Neville Tatum	1 1 0 3	5	
7 Paul Dugard	0 1 T 0	1	
8 Nathan Gaymer	*did not ride*		

POOLE (H), April 12, L44-46

1 Andrew Silver	3 2 3 1 1	10	
2 Nathan Simpson	1 0 fx1	2	
3 †Andy Grahame	3 2 0 3	8	
4 Glenn Doyle	2 1 0 3 3	9	2
5 Olli Tyrvainen	3 2 R 0	5	
6 Neville Tatum	3 2 0 2 0	7	1
7 Paul Dugard	0 2 1 N	3	

Swindon (A), May 7, L41-49

1 Andrew Silver	fx1 1 0	2	1
2 Olli Tyrvainen	1 R 2 2	5	1
3 †Andy Grahame	2 3 2 1 2 2	12	
4 Nathan Simpson	0 1 1 1	3	1
5 Glenn Doyle	3 2 3 1 0	9	1
6 Neville Tatum	2 0 1 T	3	2
7 Paul Dugard	3 1 3 0	7	1

Reading (A), May 18, L39-51

1 Andrew Silver	0 2 1 2 2 1	8	1
2 Olli Tyrvainen	1 0 T 1	2	1
3 †Andy Grahame	2 2 2 2 3	11	
4 Nathan Simpson	1 1 1 1	4	2
5 Glenn Doyle	2 3 2 1 2 0	10	2
6 Neville Tatum	3 1 0 T	4	1
7 Paul Dugard	0 0 T 0	0	

READING (H), April 19, L42-48

1 Andrew Silver	2 1 2 2 1 0	8	1
2 Olli Tyrvainen	0 3 0 3 1	7	
3 †Andy Grahame	3 1 1 3 3 2	13	
4 Glenn Doyle	1 0 0 T	1	
5 Nathan Simpson	3 1 1 T	5	1
6 Paul Dugard	3 1 0 2	6	
7 Neville Tatum	1 1 0 T	2	

King's Lynn (A), April 25, L36-54

1 Andrew Silver	2 1 2 1 1	7	
2 Olli Tyrvainen	fx0 T R	0	
3 †Andy Grahame	1 3 2 2 3	11	1
4 Nathan Simpson	0 1 T fx	1	1
5 Glenn Doyle	2 2 3 1 1	9	
6 Paul Dugard	3 0 0 0	3	
7 Neville Tatum	1 2 0 2 0	5	1

Poole (A), April 29, L32-58

1 Andrew Silver	1 1 2 R	4	1
2 Olli Tyrvainen	2 fx2 0	4	
3 †Andy Grahame	1 2 3 3 0 2	11	
4 Nathan Simpson	0 0 0 N	0	
5 Glenn Doyle	1 1 1 3 1	7	1
6 Paul Dugard	2 0 2 1 1	6	1
7 Neville Tatum	R R R N N	0	

KING'S LYNN (H), May 1, L44-46

1 Andrew Silver	3 2 2 3 2	12	1
2 Olli Tyrvainen	2 0 0 3	5	1
3 †Andy Grahame	3 1 1 3 1	9	1
4 Glenn Doyle	1 3 0 2	6	1
5 Nathan Simpson	2 2 1 1	6	1
6 Paul Dugard	2 1 0 0	3	
7 Neville Tatum	1 2 0 0	3	1

SWINDON (H), May 15, L41-49

1 Andrew Silver	3 2 2 1 1	9	1
2 Olli Tyrvainen	2 1 3 3	9	2
3 †Andy Grahame	2 1 3 1 0	7	
4 Glenn Doyle	0 1 0 1	2	2
5 Nathan Simpson	1 2 1 N	4	1
6 Neville Tatum	R N 0 2	2	
7 Paul Dugard	1 1 2 2 0 2	8	3

Ipswich (A), June 11, L28-62

1 Andrew Silver	2 1 2 X 3 1 1	10	
2 Olli Tyrvainen	1 0 2 0	3	1
3 †Andy Grahame	2 2 1 2 0	7	
4 Glenn Doyle	*rider replacement*		
5 Nathan Simpson	0 1 1 0 0	2	
6 Paul Dugard	2 1 0 1 1	5	2
7 Stefan Dannö	0 1 0 T	1	1

IPSWICH (H), June 28, L41-49

1 †Andrew Silver	2 3 1 2 0	8	1
2 Olli Tyrvainen	3 1 3 0 2	9	
3 Bobby Schwartz	0 1 3 0	4	1
4 Glenn Doyle	1 E R N	1	1
5 Paul Dugard	2 1 1 1	5	2
6 Stefan Dannö	1 2 2 2 0	7	
7 Nathan Simpson	3 2 0 1 1	7	

Ipswich

POOLE (H), April 9, W50-40

1 †Chris Louis	E 3 2 3 2	10	1
2 Jacek Rempala	0 0 F N	0	
3 Tony Rickardsson	3 2 2 1	8	1
4 Shane Parker	2 3 fx1	6	2
5 Zdenek Tesar	3 2 2 2 3	12	1
6 Ben Howe	2 1 1 0	4	2
7 David Norris	2 3 1 1 1 2	10	2

KING'S LYNN (H), April 17, L42-48

1 †Chris Louis	2 3 1 2 1	9	1
2 Jacek Rempala	0 0 N N	0	
3 Tony Rickardsson	3 2 1 R 2	8	1
4 Shane Parker	2 2 1 3	8	1
5 Zdenek Tesar	0 0 3 3 0	6	
6 Ben Howe	2 1 N 0 0	3	1
7 David Norris	3 0 3 2 0 T	8	

Swindon (A), April 20, L43-47

1 †Chris Louis	2 1 2 2 2	9	
2 Jacek Rempala	0 0 T N	0	
3 Tony Rickardsson	2 3 2 1 3 1	12	2
4 Shane Parker	0 2 2 1	5	2
5 Zdenek Tesar	1 0 0 2	3	1
6 Ben Howe	1 0 T 0	1	
7 David Norris	3 1 3 3 3 0	13	1

Poole (A), April 22, L44-46

1 †Chris Louis	3 2 3 3 0	11	
2 Jacek Rempala	0 0 1 2	3	1
3 Tony Rickardsson	3 3 3 2 3	14	
4 Shane Parker	0 2 2 0	4	
5 Zdenek Tesar	3 0 0 1	4	1
6 Ben Howe	1 0 0 N	1	
7 David Norris	fx2 3 0 2	7	1

SWINDON (H), April 23, W51-39

1 †Chris Louis	3 2 2 3 3	13	
2 Jacek Rempala	1 1 1 0	3	2
3 Tony Rickardsson	3 3 1 3 2	12	1
4 Shane Parker	2 0 0 3	5	
5 Zdenek Tesar	fx1 3 1	5	
6 Ben Howe	2 1 0 N	3	1
7 David Norris	3 2 2 3 0	10	1

Arena Essex (A), May 1, L43-47

1 †Chris Louis	1 3 3 3 3 3	16	
2 Savalas Clouting	0 2 T 0	2	1
3 Tony Rickardsson	0 2 2 2 2	8	2
4 Shane Parker	fx1 0 1	2	
5 Zdenek Tesar	3 0 3 fx2	8	
6 Ben Howe	1 0 T 0	1	1
7 David Norris	2 1 2 1	6	1

ARENA ESSEX (H), May 7, W56-34

1 †Chris Louis	3 3 3 1 3	13	1
2 Jacek Rempala	0 1 1 0	2	1
3 Tony Rickardsson	3 3 1 3 2	12	2
4 Shane Parker	3 1 2 2	8	1
5 Zdenek Tesar	1 2 2 1	6	1
6 Ben Howe	2 2 0 3	7	2
7 David Norris	3 2 2 1	8	1

King's Lynn (A), May 10, W48-42

1 †Chris Louis	1 2 3 1	7	
2 Jacek Rempala	0 0 N N	0	
3 Tony Rickardsson	3 1 2 3 1	10	
4 Shane Parker	1 2 3 3 3	12	1
5 Zdenek Tesar	2 1 0 2	5	1
6 Ben Howe	2 0 1 1 0	4	3
7 David N orris	3 2 2 2 1	10	2

Shane Parker lost to Henrik Gustafsson in a run-off for the bonus point.

Reading (A), May 11, L43-47

1 †Chris Louis	2 1 2 2 2	9	1
2 Jacek Rempala	1 2 2 0	5	1
3 Tony Rickardsson	2 1 2 1	6	2
4 Shane Parker	2 2 2 0	6	1
5 Zdenek Tesar	1 3 2 3 1	10	2
6 Ben Howe	1 0 1 N	2	2
7 David Norris	2 3 R 0 R	5	

EASTBOURNE (H), June 11, W62-28

1 †Chris Louis	**3 3 3 3 3**	**15**	
2 Savalas Clouting	fx0 1 0	1	
3 Tony Rickardsson	3 3 2 3	11	
4 Shane Parker	2 1 2 3	8	2
5 Zdenek Tesar	3 3 E 2 2	10	2
6 Ben Howe	3 0 2 2	7	2
7 David Norris	1 3 3 1 2	10	2

READING (H), June 25, W51-39

1 †Chris Louis	3 2 3 3 3	14	
2 Jacek Rempala	1 1 0 0	2	1
3 Zdenek Tesar	2 2 2 1	7	1
4 Savalas Clouting	1 0 1 N	2	1
5 Shane Parker	2 3 3 3 2	13	1
6 Ben Howe	3 1 0 1 0	5	1
7 David Norris	2 2 3 1	8	1

Eastbourne (A), June 28, W49-41

1 †Chris Louis	1 3 2 2 2 1	11	1
2 Jacek Rempala	0 0 T 0	0	
3 Tony Rickardsson	3 2 3 3 3	14	
4 Shane Parker	**3 3 3 3**	**12**	
5 Zdenek Tesar	0 R 1 3	4	
6 Ben Howe	0 0 0 N	0	
7 David Norris	2 1 1 2 2	8	3

King's Lynn

ARENA ESSEX (H), March 28, W46-44

1 Bohumil Brhel	2 2 3 3 2	12	
2 Dennis Löfqvist	0 1 0 T	1	1
3 †Mark Loram	3 3 2 1 0	9	2
4 Gary Allan	1 0 1 3	5	
5 Henrik Gustafsson	3 1 R 3 1	8	1
6 Darren Spicer	1 0 N 1	2	
7 Alun Rossiter	3 0 2 2 2	9	1

Arena Essex (A), April 3, L34-56

1 Bohumil Brhel	2 0 R 2	4	
2 Dennis Löfqvist	1 1 0 2	4	1
3 †Mark Loram	2 1 2 3 1	9	
4 Gary Allan	1 1 2 0	4	1
5 Henrik Gustafsson	3 2 1 1 2 0	9	
6 Alun Rossiter	2 R R 0	2	
7 Darren Spicer	1 F T 1	2	2

Roll of Honour

The Gold Cup was introduced to the national calendar in 1989 and has been contested by the respective winners of South and Northern sections.

1989 Oxford 102 Cradley Heath 78
1990 Bradford 106 Oxford 74
1991 Berwick 93 Oxford 87
1992 Wolverhampton 92 Reading 88

SWINDON (H), April 4, W47-43

1 Bohumil Brhel	0 2 2 3	7	1
2 Dennis Löfqvist	1 1 2 3	7	1
3 †Mark Loram	3 2 3 1 1	10	
4 Gary Allan	0 1 0 0	1	
5 Henrik Gustafsson	2 3 3 3 3	14	
6 Darren Spicer	2 1 0 0	3	1
7 Alun Rossiter	3 0 1 1	5	

Reading (A), April 6, L36-53

1 Bohumil Brhel	1 2 2 1 2	8	
2 Dennis Löfqvist	0 1 0 T	1	1
3 †Mark Loram	fx1 1 1 0	3	1
4 Gary Allan	1 1 1 0	3	
5 Henrik Gustafsson	3 3 3 2 3 0	14	
6 Alun Rossiter	2 0 T 1	3	
7 Darren Spicer	1 2 1 F	4	1

POOLE (H), April 11, W51-39

1 Bohumil Brhel	3 2 2 1	8	1
2 Dennis Löfqvist	1 1 1 3	6	1
3 †Mark Loram	3 3 2 1 0	9	
4 Gary Allan	1 1 0 R	2	
5 Henrik Gustafsson	**3 3 3 3 3**	**15**	
6 Darren Spicer	3 1 1 0	5	
7 Alun Rossiter	2 3 0 1	6	1

Ipswich (A), April 17, W48-42

1 Bohumil Brhel	3 3 3 2 3	14	
2 Dennis Löfqvist	1 1 1 2	5	2
3 †Mark Loram	2 2 2 0	6	
4 Gary Allan	1 1 3 1	6	1
5 Henrik Gustafsson	3 3 3 1 2	12	1
6 Alun Rossiter	1 1 2 1 0	5	2
7 Darren Spicer	0 0 N 0	0	

EASTBOURNE (H), April 25, W54-36

1 Bohumil Brhel	3 2 0 2	7	
2 Dennis Löfqvist	1 1 3 1	6	1
3 †Mark Loram	**3 3 3 3 3**	**15**	
4 Gary Allan	1 2 0 3	6	1
5 Henrik Gustafsson	**3 3 3 2 2**	**13**	**2**
6 Darren Spicer	R 0 0 N	0	
7 Alun Rossiter	2 1 1 1 2	7	1

Eastbourne (A), May 1, W46-44

1 Bohumil Brhel	1 0 2 2	5	
2 Dennis Löfqvist	0 1 1 N	2	
3 †Mark Loram	2 3 2 2 3	12	
4 Gary Allan	0 2 1 0	3	
5 Henrik Gustafsson	3 3 1 3 R	10	
6 Alun Rossiter	3 1 3 3 3 1	14	
7 Darren Spicer	0 0 N 0	0	

Poole (A), May 6, W48-42

1 Bohumil Brhel	3 2 fx1	6	
2 Dennis Löfqvist	1 0 3 2	6	
3 †Mark Loram	3 2 2 1 2	10	2
4 Henrik Gustafsson	1 2 1 2 3	9	2
5 Gary Allan	2 3 2 2	9	
6 Alun Rossiter	2 1 2 1 1	7	4
7 Darren Spicer	0 1 N 0	1	

IPSWICH (H), May 10, L42-48

1 Bohumil Brhel	2 3 1 2 E 0	8	1
2 Dennis Löfqvist	3 2 3 0	8	1
3 †Mark Loram	1 3 2 2	8	
4 Henrik Gustafsson	3 3 1 3 2	12	1
5 Gary Allan	0 1 3 0	4	
6 Darren Spicer	1 0 0 0	1	
7 Alun Rossiter	0 0 R T 1	1	

Henrik Gustafsson defeated Shane Parker in a run-off for the bonus point.

READING (H), May 16, W48-42

1 Bohumil Brhel	1 2 1 2	6	2
2 Dennis Löfqvist	2 3 3 3	11	
3 †Mark Loram	3 3 2 2 1	11	
4 Henrik Gustafsson	3 3 X 3 3	12	
5 Gary Allan	1 1 1 0	3	
6 Darren Spicer	2 1 0 0 1	4	1
7 Andy Mountain	1 0 N 0	1	1

Swindon (A), May 28, W54-36

1 Dennis Löfqvist	1 3 3 2 2 0	11	1
2 Bohumil Brhel	2 2 2 3 1	10	2
3 †Mark Loram	3 3 3 2 3 3	17	
4 Gary Allan	2 0 2 1 1	6	4
5 Henrik Gustafsson	*rider replacement*		
6 Alun Rossiter	3 0 1 3 2	9	2
7 Darren Spicer	0 1 0 N	1	
8 Tom Grinstead	*did not ride*		

Poole

ARENA ESSEX (H), April 8, W53-37

1 †Marvyn Cox	2 3 3 2 3	13	1
2 Slawomir Drabik	1 1 1 2	5	2
3 Steve Schofield	3 3 3 2 2	13	1
4 Craig Boyce	3 1 3 2	9	
5 Tony Langdon	0 0 2 1	3	1
6 Tom Knudsen	3 1 2 1	7	2
7 Andy Phillips	2 0 0 1	3	2

Ipswich (A), April 9, L40-50

1 †Marvyn Cox	3 1 3 3 3 1	14	
2 Slawomir Drabik	1 0 T T	1	
3 Steve Schofield	2 2 3 0 1	8	1
4 Tony Langdon	0 0 0 N	0	
5 Craig Boyce	1 3 3 2 3 0	12	
6 Tom Knudsen	1 1 2 1 0	5	2
7 Andy Phillips	0 0 N T 0	0	

King's Lynn (A), April 11, L39-51

1 †Marvyn Cox	R 2 1 3 2 2	10	
2 Slawomir Drabik	2 0 T T	2	
3 Steve Schofield	2 3 2 2 2 1	12	3
4 Tony Langdon	2 2 0 0 0	4	
5 Craig Boyce	R 0 1 3 3	7	
6 Tom Knudsen	1 N 2 1 T	4	1
7 Andy Phillips	0 0 0 N T	0	

Eastbourne (A), April 12, W46-44

1 †Marvyn Cox	2 3 3 2 0	10	
2 Slawomir Drabik	0 0 T N	0	
3 Steve Schofield	1 3 1 3 3 2	13	
Tony Langdon	1 1 0 1	3	1
5 Craig Boyce	0 3 2 1	6	2
6 Tom Knudsen	2 1 3 1 2 2	11	1
7 Andy Phillips	1 0 T 2	3	1

Reading (A), April 13, L42-48

1 †Marvyn Cox	1 3 3 3 2 1	13	
2 Slawomir Drabik	0 0 T T	0	
3 Steve Schofield	E 1 3 1 1	6	1
4 Tony Langdon	0 1 T 0	1	
5 Craig Boyce	3 3 3 2 3 0	14	
6 Tom Knudsen	2 1 0 0 2	5	1
7 Andy Phillips	0 3 0 0	3	

READING (H), April 17, L43.5-46.5

1 †Marvyn Cox	1 3 3 3 2	12	
2 Slawomir Drabik	0 1 N N	1	
3 Steve Schofield	3 2 1 0	6	1
4 Craig Boyce	3 2 2 2 0	9	1
5 Tony Langdon	0 1 1 2.5	4.5	1
6 Tom Knudsen	1 0 3 1 N 1 1	7	3
7 Andy Phillips	2 2 fn0 N	4	

IPSWICH (H), April 22, W46-44

1 †Marvyn Cox	2 2 3 3 1	11	1
2 Slawomir Drabik	1 1 2 1	5	2
3 Steve Schofield	0 3 1 1	5	1
4 Craig Boyce	2 3 1 3 2	11	
5 Tony Langdon	1 1 2 2	6	1
6 Tom Knudsen	2 1 1 1	5	2
7 Andy Phillips	3 R 0 0	3	

EASTBOURNE (H), April 29, W58-32

1 †Marvyn Cox	3 3 2 2 3	13	1
2 Slawomir Drabik	0 1 3 1	5	1
3 Steve Schofield	**3 3 3 3**	**12**	
4 Craig Boyce	2 3 3 2	10	1
5 Tony Langdon	3 2 fx2 0	7	2
6 Tom Knudsen	3 2 2 fn	7	2
7 Andy Phillips	1 1 1 1 0	4	

KING'S LYNN (H), May 6, L42-48

1 †Marvyn Cox	2 3 3 3 1	12	
2 Slawomir Drabik	0 0 0 N	0	
3 Steve Schofield	2 1 2 3 3 0	11	1
4 Craig Boyce	3 3 3 0 3	12	
5 Tony Langdon	fx1 R 0	1	
6 Steve Leigh	1 R 0 N	1	
7 Andy Phillips	3 1 1 0	5	

Arena Essex (A), May 8, L28-62

1 †Marvyn Cox	2 2 3 1 0 1	9	
2 Slawomir Drabik	0 0 N N	0	
3 Steve Schofield	0 2 2 0 2 0	6	
4 Tony Langdon	0 0 1 2	3	
5 Craig Boyce	2 2 0 1 1	6	1
6 Steve Leigh	0 0 N 0	0	
7 Andy Phillips	1 1 2 0	4	1

SWINDON (H), May 13, W48-42

1 †Marvyn Cox	1 1 3 2	7	2
2 Slawomir Drabik	0 2 3 2 1	8	2
3 Steve Schofield	1 3 1 1	6	2
4 Craig Boyce	2 3 3 1	9	
5 Tony Langdon	1 2 3 2 2	10	2
6 Steve Leigh	0 N 0 2	2	1
7 Andy Phillips	3 2 1 0 0	6	

Swindon (A), June 11, L42-48

1 †Marvyn Cox	1 3 3 2 2 3	14	1
2 Jörgen Johansson	F R 1 T	1	
3 Steve Schofield	2 1 2 2 E 1	8	
4 Tony Langdon	0 1 T 0	1	
5 Craig Boyce	2 3 3 1 1	10	2
6 Tom Knudsen	3 0 1 2 2	8	1
7 Alastair Stevens	R 0 T 0	0	

Reading

KING'S LYNN (H), April 6, W53-36

1 Per Jonsson	E 3 3 3 3	12	
2 David Mullett	3 2 3 2 1	11	2
3 Jan Andersson	3 2 3 2	10	1
4 †Jeremy Doncaster	0 3 1 2	6	
5 Armando Castagna	2 F 2 3	7	
6 Phil Morris	F N 0 0 0	0	
7 Ray Morton	2 3 R 2 0 N	7	2

Swindon (A), April 9, W46-44

1 Per Jonsson	1 3 3 2 2	11	
2 David Mullett	0 1 2 2	5	1
3 Jan Andersson	3 2 2 1	8	1
4 Armando Castagna	fx2 1 0	3	
5 †Jeremy Doncaster	3 1 2 3 1	10	2
6 Ray Morton	R 1 1 2	4	3
7 Phil Morris	3 1 1 0	5	1

POOLE (H), April 13, W48-42

1 Per Jonsson	3 2 2 3 3	13	1
2 David Mullett	2 3 2 1	8	2
3 Jan Andersson	2 2 2 3 2	11	1
4 Armando Castagna	1 1 0 1	3	2
5 †Jeremy Doncaster	2 2 1 1	6	1
6 Phil Morris	1 0 0 N	1	
7 Ray Morton	3 1 2 0 0	6	1

Poole (A), April 17, W46.5-43.5

1 Per Jonsson	2 3 3 1 3	12	1
2 David Mullett	3 0 3 2 1	9	1
3 Jan Andersson	2 0 2 1	5	1
4 Armando Castagna	2 0 2 2.5	6.5	
5 †Jeremy Doncaster	1 1 0 3	5	1
6 Ray Morton	3 1 2 3 0	9	1
7 Phil Morris	0 N 0 0	0	

Eastbourne (A), April 19, W48-42

1 Per Jonsson	3 3 3 2 3	14	
2 David Mullett	1 2 2 2 1	8	3
3 Jan Andersson	2 2 3 3	10	
4 Armando Castagna	2 3 0 0	5	
5 †Jeremy Doncaster	0 2 1 2	5	1
6 Ray Morton	2 0 3 1 0	6	
7 Phil Morris	F 0 N 0	0	

SWINDON (H), May 4, W48-42

1 Per Jonsson	2 3 3 3 R	11	
2 David Mullett	1 1 1 2	5	3
3 Jan Andersson	3 2 3 3 2	13	
4 Lance Sealey	0 0 N N	0	
5 †Jeremy Doncaster	2 2 1 1	6	1
6 Phil Morris	2 0 1 N 1	4	3
7 Ray Morton	3 2 2 0 0 2	9	

IPSWICH (H), May 11, W47-43

1 Per Jonsson	3 3 3 3 F	12	
2 David Mullett	0 2 3 1	6	1
3 Jan Andersson	1 1 3 3	8	
4 Lance Sealey	0 N 0 N	0	
5 †Jeremy Doncaster	3 3 3 1 3	13	
6 Phil Morris	0 0 0 N 1	1	1
7 Ray Morton	3 R 1 F 1 2	7	

King's Lynn (A), May 16, L42-48

1 Per Jonsson	3 2 2 3 3 2	15	
2 Lance Sealey	0 0 T T	0	
3 Jan Andersson	2 1 2 3	8	1
4 †Jeremy Doncaster	2 1 3 0 1 0	7	1
5 David Mullett	0 2 2 1 2	7	
6 Ray Morton	3 0 T 1 1	5	2
7 Phil Morris	0 0 T T 0	0	

EASTBOURNE (H), May 18, W51-39

1 Per Jonsson	**3 3 3 3 3**	**15**	
2 David Mullett	2 F 3 2 2	9	3
3 Jan Andersson	1 2 3 3	9	
4 Lance Sealey	0 N 0 N	0	
5 †Jeremy Doncaster	3 3 3 fx	9	
6 Phil Morris	1 3 0 1 0	5	1
7 Ray Morton	2 1 0 0 1	4	

ARENA ESSEX (H), May 25, W52-38

1 Per Jonsson	2 2 3 3 2 3	15	2
2 David Mullett	1 0 3 2 1	7	3
3 †Jan Andersson	1 3 3 2 0	9	
4 Armando Castagna	3 2 2 3 3	13	1
5 Jeremy Doncaster	*rider replacement*		
6 Phil Morris	3 0 F N 0	3	
7 Ray Morton	2 3 0 R 0 N	5	1
8 Gary Sweet	*did not ride*		

Ipswich (A), June 25, L39-51

1 David Mullett	2 1 0 2	5	1
2 Armando Castagna	0 2 3 1 3	9	
3 Jan Andersson	3 3 1 2 2 1	12	
4 †Jeremy Doncaster	3 3 2 0 2 0	10	1
5 Gary Sweet	0 T 0 T	0	
6 Ray Morton	0 0 1 0 T	1	
7 Phil Morris	1 0 N 1	2	1

Arena Essex (A), July 7, W46-44

1 Per Jonsson	2 3 3 2 3	13	
2 David Mullett	1 2 2 0	5	3
3 Jan Andersson	1 2 3 2 0	8	1
4 Armando Castagna	0 1 0 R	1	1
5 †Jeremy Doncaster	3 2 1 1	7	1
6 Phil Morris	F 0 1 N	1	
7 Ray Morton	2 2 3 1 3	11	

Swindon

King's Lynn (A), April 4, L43-47

1 †Mitch Shirra	3 0 0 2	5	
2 Dean Standing	2 2 3 2	9	1
3 Jimmy Nilsen	2 3 2 1 2	10	2
4 John Davis	1 1 1 0	3	
5 Leigh Adams	3 3 2 3 2	13	
6 Darren Boulton	0 0 0 N 0 T	0	
7 Peter Schroeck	1 N 1 1 N	3	1

READING (H), April 9, L44-46

1 †Mitch Shirra	2 R 3 3	8	1
2 Dean Standing	3 3 3 2 0	11	1
3 Jimmy Nilsen	2 3 1 3	9	
4 John Davis	1 0 0 1	2	1
5 Leigh Adams	2 2 3 1 3	11	
6 Peter Schroeck	1 0 0 N 0	1	1
7 Darren Boulton	2 0 0 0 N	2	

IPSWICH (H), April 20, W47-43

1 †Mitch Shirra	1 2 0 1	4	1
2 Dean Standing	3 1 1 1	6	1
3 Leigh Adams	**3 3 3 3 3**	**15**	
4 Jimmy Nilsen	2 2 2 1	7	2
5 John Davis	3 3 3 0 2	11	1
6 Peter Schroeck	0 0 1 X	1	
7 Justin Elkins	2 0 1 0	3	

Ipswich (A), April 23, L39-51

1 †Mitch Shirra	2 2 2 2	8	1
2 Dean Standing	0 3 3 1 E	7	
3 Leigh Adams	2 3 1 1 2 1	10	1
4 John Davis	3 2 3 0 0	8	
5 Jimmy Nilsen	1 1 2 1	5	2
6 Peter Schroeck	1 0 N 0 0 T	1	
7 Justin Elkins	fx N 0 0 T	0	

Arena Essex (A), April 24, L37-53

1 †Mitch Shirra	2 3 3 0 0	8	
2 Dean Standing	1 1 1 0	3	1
3 Leigh Adams	2 3 3 1 2 1	12	1
4 John Davis	fx N N N	0	
5 Jimmy Nilsen	3 3 2 2 0	10	
6 Peter Schroeck	1 1 0 0 1 N	3	
7 Justin Elkins	0 0 1 E 0	1	

ARENA ESSEX (H), April 26, L43-46

1 †Mitch Shirra	3 1 2 2 1	9	4
2 Dean Standing	1 2 2 3	8	
3 Leigh Adams	**3 3 3 3 3**	**15**	
4 Jimmy Nilsen	3 1 2 3 fx	9	
5 Matthew Cross	0 0 0 0	0	
6 Peter Schroeck	1 0 T 1	2	
7 Justin Elkins	0 0 fx0	0	

Reading (A), May 4, WL42-48

1 †Mitch Shirra	3 3 2 0 R	8	
2 Dean Standing	0 1 3 1	5	1
3 Leigh Adams	2 2 3 1 2 3	13	1
4 Matthew Cross	N fn N T	0	
5 Jimmy Nilsen	3 3 2 3 1	12	
6 Steve Masters	0 0 0 0 1 N	1	
7 Justin Elkins	1 1 1 0 R	3	1

EASTBOURNE (H), May 7, W49-41

1 †Mitch Shirra	2 2 3 2 1	10	1
2 Dean Standing	3 1 0 2	6	2
3 Leigh Adams	**3 3 3 3 3**	**15**	
4 Jimmy Nilsen	2 3 0 3	8	
5 Kelly Moran	1 2 3 2	8	3
6 Steve Masters	0 0 fx 0 F	0	
7 Justin Elkins	1 1 E N	2	

Poole (A), May 13, L42-48

1 †Mitch Shirra	3 1 2 3 R	9	1
2 Kelly Moran	2 N 2 3 fx	7	1
3 Leigh Adams	3 3 R 0 2 3	11	1
4 Dean Standing	0 1 0 N	1	1
5 Jimmy Nilsen	3 2 1 1 3	10	
6 Steve Masters	2 0 N 1 N	3	
7 Justin Elkins	1 0 0 0 N	1	1

Eastbourne (A), May 15, W49-41

1 †Mitch Shirra	1 3 1 3	8	
2 Matthew Cross	0 0 N N	0	
3 Leigh Adams	**3 3 3 3 3**	**15**	
4 Dean Standing	2 2 1 2	7	3
5 Jimmy Nilsen	**3 3 2 3 2**	**13**	**2**
6 Steve Masters	2 0 0 N 0 0	2	1
7 Justin Elkins	3 0 1 0 N 0	4	

KING'S LYNN (H), May 28, L36-54

1 Jimmy Nilsen	3 2 1 1 3 1	11	1
2 Dean Standing	0 1 2 0 0	3	1
3 Leigh Adams	2 3 2 3 3 2	15	
4 †Mitch Shirra	N N R 1	1	
5 Steve Camden	0 1 T N	1	
6 Steve Masters	2 1 N 0 T 0 0	3	
7 Justin Elkins	1 0 1 T 0	2	2

POOLE (H), June 11, W48-42

1 †Mitch Shirra	3 3 3 0 2	11	
2 Dean Standing	2 2 2 1	7	2
3 Leigh Adams	3 2 1 3	9	
4 Jimmy Nilsen	3 1 3 3 0	10	1
5 Kelly Moran	1 2 3 1	7	
6 Steve Masters	2 1 F 0 F	3	
7 Justin Elkins	1 fx 0 N	1	1

Belle Vue

OXFORD (H), March 20, W49-41

1 Bobby Ott	2 R 3 3 3 2	13	1
2 Jason Lyons	1 1 3 1 0	6	1
3 †Joe Screen	3 1 3 2 3 3	15	
4 Shawn Moran	*rider replacement*		
5 Kelly Moran	3 3 3 1 3	13	
6 Richard Musson	1 1 R R R	2	
7 Mike Hampson	0 0 0 N	0	
8 Michael Howe	*did not ride*		

Coventry (A), March 28, L42-48

1 Bobby Ott	2 1 3 1	7	1
2 Jason Lyons	3 0 3 3 2 F	11	1
3 †Joe Screen	2 2 2 2 3 2	13	1
4 Frede Schøtt	1 1 1 0	3	1
5 Kelly Moran	R 2 0 3	5	
6 Richard Musson	2 1 R N	3	1
7 Mike Hampson	R 0 T T 0	0	

CRADLEY HEATH (H), April 3, L39-50

1 Bobby Ott	1 3 F 1	5	1
2 Jason Lyons	2 1 3 3 2 1	12	1
3 †Joe Screen	3 2 2 2 2	11	
4 Frede Schøtt	1 3 0 1	5	2
5 Kelly Moran	2 1 2 0	5	
6 Richard Musson	fx F N fn 0	0	
7 Mike Hampson	R R N 1 0 T	1	

Cradley Heath (A), April 4, L32-58

1 Bobby Ott	0 0 1 1 1	3	2
2 Jason Lyons	3 3 2 2 2 1	13	
3 †Joe Screen	2 2 1 1 0	6	1
4 Frede Schøtt	0 1 0 N 0	1	1
5 Kelly Moran	1 2 1 2	6	
6 Richard Musson	2 0 T 1	3	1
7 Jon Armstrong	0 0 T T N	0	

Bradford (A), April 11, L31-59

1 Bobby Ott	1 2 2 1 0	6	1
2 Jason Lyons	0 1 1 3 2 0	7	2
3 †Joe Screen	2 1 1 2 1 1	8	
4 Frede Schøtt	0 1 1 T 1	3	1
5 Kelly Moran	1 2 1 T	4	1
6 Mike Hampson	F 0 T 0	0	
7 Carl Stonehewer	3 0 T 0	3	

Wolverhampton (A), April 13, D45-45

1 Bobby Ott	2 3 3 2 0	10	1
2 Jason Lyons	3 1 3 2	9	1
3 †Joe Screen	2 3 2 3 2	12	
4 Frede Schøtt	0 2 2 0	4	
5 Kelly Moran	2 1 1 F	4	1
6 Jon Armstrong	1 1 0 N	2	1
7 Carl Stonehewer	2 0 1 0 1	4	

WOLVERHAMPTON (H), April 17, L43-47

1 Bobby Ott	3 1 3 F 3	10	
2 Jason Lyons	1 3 3 2 0	9	1
3 †Joe Screen	2 3 1 R	6	
4 Kelly Moran	2 2 1 3	8	
5 Frede Schøtt	0 1 3 1	5	1
6 Paul Smith	2 1 0 2 0	5	2
7 Carl Stonehewer	fx 0 0 N	0	

COVENTRY (H), April 24, W50-40

1 Bobby Ott	R 3 3 2	8	
2 Frede Schøtt	**3 2 3 2 2**	**12**	**3**
3 †Joe Screen	**3 3 3 3 3**	**15**	
4 Jason Lyons	2 0 1 3	6	1
5 Kelly Moran	0 2 0 2	4	1
6 Paul Smith	2 1 0 1	4	
7 Carl Stonehewer	1 0 0 0	1	1

Oxford (A), April 29, L39-51

1 Bobby Ott	2 1 1 1	5	2
2 Frede Schøtt	0 2 3 2 0	7	
3 †Joe Screen	R 2 2 2 3 2	11	
4 Kelly Moran	0 1 2 0	3	1
5 Jason Lyons	1 2 0 1	4	
6 Paul Smith	3 0 1 N	4	1
7 Carl Stonehewer	0 3 2 0	5	1

BRADFORD (H), May 1, W56-34

1 Bobby Ott	R 3 3 3 2	11	1
2 Frede Schøtt	2 2 2 2	8	2
3 †Joe Screen	3 3 2 3 3	14	
4 Jason Lyons	1 2 2 3	8	1
5 Shawn Moran	3 R 3 1	7	
6 Paul Smith	2 1 1 0	4	1
7 Carl Stonehewer	3 0 1 fx	4	1

Bradford

Oxford (A), April 3, L34-56

1 †Gary Havelock	1 0 2 2 2 1	8	1
2 Sean Wilson	2 1 1 1 F	5	1
3 Paul Thorp	2 R N N	2	
4 Kelvin Tatum	1 2 3 1 0	7	
5 Simon Wigg	0 1 3 2 2 0	8	1
6 Kevin Little	2 1 N 1	4	1
7 Darren Pearson	E 0 N N 0	0	

COVENTRY (H), April 4, W46-44

1 †Gary Havelock	2 3 1 2	8	
2 Sean Wilson	1 2 3 3 1	10	2
3 Paul Thorp	3 3 1 2 0	9	
4 Kelvin Tatum	3 3 1 2	9	1
5 Simon Wigg	2 1 3 1	7	2
6 Kevin Little	2 0 0 0	2	
7 Darren Pearson	1 0 0 0	1	1

BELLE VUE (H), April 11, W59-31

1 †Gary Havelock	**3 3 3 3 3**	**15**	
2 Sean Wilson	**2 2 3 2**	**9**	**3**
3 Kelvin Tatum	**3 3 3 3 2**	**14**	**1**
4 Paul Thorp	2 0 0 3	5	1
5 Simon Wigg	3 3 2 2	10	1
6 Kevin Little	1 1 0 0	2	1
7 Darren Pearson	2 0 0 2	4	1

WOLVERHAMPTON (H), April 25, L41-49

1 †Gary Havelock	1 2 3 2	8	1
2 Sean Wilson	2 1 3 2	8	2
3 Kelvin Tatum	3 3 3 0 1	10	
4 Paul Thorp	1 1 0 2	4	1
5 Simon Wigg	3 2 2 2 0	9	
6 Kevin Little	0 0 0 1	1	1
7 Darren Pearson	1 0 0 0	1	

Belle Vue (A), May 1, L34-56

1 †Gary Havelock	3 3 3 3 2 1	15	
2 Sean Wilson	1 1 1 2 R	5	
3 Kelvin Tatum	2 0 1 F 2	5	1
4 Paul Thorp	E F 0 N	0	
5 Simon Wigg	2 2 1 1 1 0	7	1
6 Kevin Little	1 R 1 N T	2	
7 Darren Pearson	0 F N T T 0	0	

CRADLEY HEATH (H), May 2, W48-42

1 †Gary Havelock	2 3 3 2 2	12	1
2 Sean Wilson	1 2 1 1	5	2
3 Kelvin Tatum	3 2 3 2 3	13	
4 Paul Thorp	2 1 0 2	5	2
5 Simon Wigg	3 2 2 1	8	1
6 Kevin Little	2 1 0 0	3	
7 Darren Pearson	1 0 0 1	2	2

OXFORD (H), May 23, W57-33

1 Gary Havelock	*rider replacement*		
2 Sean Wilson	1 2 2 1 2	8	2
3 †Kelvin Tatum	3 3 3 2 3 3	17	
4 Paul Thorp	1 3 3 3 3	13	1
5 Simon Wigg	2 R 3 3 2 2	12	2
6 Darren Pearson	3 1 1 0	5	
7 Kevin Little	1 0 0 1	2	
8 Stuart Parnaby	*did not ride*		

Coventry (A), May 25, L40-50

1 Gary Havelock	*rider replacement*		
2 Sean Wilson	3 1 3 3 3 0	13	1
3 †Kelvin Tatum	1 2 2 2 0	7	
4 Paul Thorp	0 2 1 0 R	3	1
5 Simon Wigg	1 2 3 2 2 1	11	
6 Darren Pearson	1 X 0 N	1	1
7 Kevin Little	2 1 2 0 0	5	2
8 Stuart Parnaby	*did not ride*		

Wolverhampton (A), June 1, L35-55

1 Gary Havelock	*rider replacement*		
2 Sean Wilson	fx F 3 1 1 2 1	8	2
3 †Kelvin Tatum	1 2 2 2 1 1	9	2
4 Paul Thorp	0 0 2 0	2	
5 Simon Wigg	3 3 2 2 0 3 2	15	
6 Darren Pearson	R 0 T 0 T	0	
7 Kevin Little	1 0 T 0	1	
8 Stuart Parnaby	*did not ride*		

Cradley Heath (A), June 10, L40-50

1 †Gary Havelock	1 2 1 3 2	9	1
2 Sean Wilson	0 1 3 2	6	1
3 Kelvin Tatum	2 3 1 0 0	6	1
4 Paul Thorp	1 3 1 0	5	
5 Simon Wigg	fx 2 2 2 1 1	8	3
6 Darren Pearson	2 T 2 0 T	4	
7 Kevin Little	1 0 1 N	2	1

Coventry

OXFORD (H), March 21, L44-46

1 †Tommy Knudsen	2 2 3 fn	7	
2 Brian Andersen	1 1 3 0	5	2
3 Rick Miller	2 2 R 2 3	9	
4 John Jørgensen	1 1 1 R	3	2
5 Andy Smith	2 2 3 0 3 2	12	1
6 Paul Bentley	3 1 0 0	4	1
7 Michael Warren	1 1 2 0 T	4	

Oxford (A), March 27, L40-49

1 †Tommy Knudsen	2 3 2 1 3 0	11	1
2 Brian Andersen	1 0 F N	1	1
3 Rick Miller	1 2 3 3 2 1	12	1
4 John Jørgensen	1 2 1 1	5	
5 Andy Smith	0 1 1 3	5	2
6 Paul Bentley	3 2 N F N 0	5	
7 Michael Warren	X N 1 N 0	1	1

BELLE VUE (H), March 28, W48-42

1 †Tommy Knudsen	1 3 2 2	8	
2 Brian Andersen	0 0 1 fx	1	
3 Rick Miller	3 3 1 3 3	13	
4 John Jørgensen	2 2 1 2	7	3
5 Andy Smith	3 3 3 2 1	12	1
6 Paul Bentley	1 1 0 1	3	
7 Michael Warren	3 0 0 1	4	1

Bradford (A), April 4, L44-46

1 †Tommy Knudsen	3 2 2 3 3 2	15	1
2 Brian Andersen	R 0 1 T	1	1
3 Rick Miller	2 1 2 0	5	
4 John Jørgensen	0 2 2 2 0	6	1
5 Andy Smith	1 1 3 3 3	11	1
6 Paul Bentley	3 0 1 1	5	1
7 Michael Warren	0 1 T 0	1	1

WOLVERHAMPTON (H), April 11, L42-48

1 †Tommy Knudsen	2 2 0 2 1	7	1
2 Brian Andersen	0 1 3 3	7	1
3 Rick Miller	2 3 2 0	7	
4 John Jørgensen	2 3 3 3 0	11	
5 Andy Smith	1 0 2 1	4	1
6 Paul Bentley	2 0 0 0	2	1
7 Michael Warren	3 F 1 0	4	1

Cradley Heath (A), April 20, W48-42

1 †Tommy Knudsen	1 2 3 2 1	9	2
2 Brian Andersen	2 1 3 1	7	1
3 Rick Miller	0 2 3 R	5	
4 John Jørgensen	1 1 2 3 3	10	
5 Andy Smith	0 3 1 fx	4	
6 Paul Bentley	2 1 1 2	6	2
7 Michael Warren	3 1 2 1	7	2

CRADLEY HEATH (H), April 20, W48-42

1 †Tommy Knudsen	3 3 3 3 2	14	
2 Brian Andersen	2 1 1 0	4	1
3 Rick Miller	2 2 2 0	6	
4 John Jørgensen	0 2 1 3	6	1
5 Andy Smith	3 3 1 3 1	11	1
6 Paul Bentley	3 0 1 0	4	1
7 Michael Warren	2 0 1 0	3	2

Belle Vue (A), April 24, L40-50

1 †Tommy Knudsen	1 3 1 R 1	6	3
2 Brian Andersen	2 1 1 2	6	1
3 Rick Miller	0 0 3 R	3	
4 John Jørgensen	1 1 1 1	4	1
5 Andy Smith	3 2 3 2 0	10	
6 Paul Bentley	3 1 2 2 T 1	9	1
7 Michael Warren	0 2 N 0	2	

Wolverhampton (A), May 4, L31-58

1 Andy Smith	F 0 2 fx 0	2	
2 Brian Andersen	1 1 F 1 2	5	1
3 †Tommy Knudsen	2 2 3 2 fx	9	
4 John Jørgensen	2 1 1 2 1 2	9	1
5 Rick Miller	0 0 1 T	1	
6 Paul Bentley	1 T fx 1	2	2
7 Michael Warren	2 1 T 0	3	1

BRADFORD (H), May 25, W50-40

1 Andy Smith	2 3 3 3 2	13	1
2 Brian Andersen	0 1 R 2	3	1
3 †Tommy Knudsen	3 1 2 2 3	11	
4 Rick Miller	3 3 1 3	10	
5 John Jørgensen	2 0 3 1	6	2
6 Paul Bentley	0 0 0 N 1	1	
7 Michael Warren	3 1 1 1 E	6	1

Cradley Heath

OXFORD (H), March 28, W50-40

1 Greg Hancock	1 1 3 2	7	3
2 †Simon Cross	2 2 3 2 1	10	1
3 Billy Hamill	3 2 2 1	8	
4 Jan O. Pedersen	R 2 3 3 3	11	
5 Gert Handberg	3 1 3 0	7	1
6 Scott Smith	2 1 1 0 1	5	2
7 Mark Robinson	R 0 N 2	2	1

Belle Vue (A), April 3, W50-39

1 Greg Hancock	3 2 3 1	9	
2 †Simon Cross	0 0 2 1	3	
3 Billy Hamill	1 2 3 2 0	8	2
4 Gert Handberg	0 1 2 3	6	
5 Jan O. Pedersen	**3 3 3 3 3**	**15**	
6 Scott Smith	3 0 1 F	4	
7 Mark Robinson	2 2 X 1	5	2

BELLE VUE (H), April 4, W58-32

1 †Simon Cross	2 3 3 2 2	12	2
2 Gert Handberg	1 1 3 2	7	2
3 Jan O. Pedersen	**3 3 3 3 3**	**15**	
4 Greg Hancock	3 1 3 3	10	1
5 Billy Hamill	2 2 3 2	9	2
6 Scott Smith	3 1 0 0	4	
7 Mark Robinson	1 0 0 0	1	

Wolverhampton (A), April 6, L43-47
1 Greg Hancock 3 3 3 2 2 1 14 1
2 †Simon Cross fnN T T 0
3 Billy Hamill 3 3 3 1 3 2 15 1
4 Gert Handberg 0 0 0 1 3 4 1
5 Jan O. Pedersen 3 1 2 0 1 7 1
6 Scott Smith fx1 0 N T 1
7 Mark Robinson 0 0 0 1 1 2

COVENTRY (H), April 20, L42-48
1 Greg Hancock 3 3 3 2 1 2 14 1
2 †Simon Cross 0 fxN N 0
3 Billy Hamill 2 0 2 0 4 1
4 Gert Handberg 3 fx3 3 0 9
5 Jan O. Pedersen 2 3 R 1 6 1
6 Scott Smith 1 3 2 0 N R 6
7 Mark Robinson 0 1 2 F T 3

Coventry (A), April 20, L42-48
1 Greg Hancock 1 1 2 3 2 9 1
2 Anthony Boyd 0 0 T T 0
3 Billy Hamill 3 2 3 3 0 0 11
4 Gert Handberg 1 R 2 1 4 2
5 †Jan O. Pedersen 2 3 2 2 2 3 14
6 Mark Robinson 0 0 T 1 1
7 Scott Smith 1 1 T 1 0 3

Bradford (A), May 2, L42-48
1 Greg Hancock 3 0 2 2 3 0 10
2 †Simon Cross 0 3 3 1 7
3 Billy Hamill R R 3 3 1 7
4 Gert Handberg 0 1 2 0 3
5 Jan O. Pedersen 1 3 1 3 8
6 Scott Smith 3 1 1 0 5
7 Mark Robinson 0 2 T 0 2

WOLVERHAMPTON (H), May 23, L42-47
1 †Simon Cross 1 2 fxR 3 6 1
2 Greg Hancock 2 2 1 3 2 0 10 2
3 Billy Hamill 2 3 3 3 fx2 13
4 Jan O. Pedersen rider replacement
5 Gert Handberg 3 F 2 1 fx 6
6 Scott Smith 3 1 0 F 1 5 1
7 Anthony Boyd 1 1 0 N 2
8 Peter McNamara did not ride

BRADFORD (H), June 10, W50-40
1 †Simon Cross 2 0 2 3 1 8 1
2 Jan O. Pedersen rider replacement
3 Billy Hamill 3 1 fx3 1 8 1
4 Gert Handberg 3 3 2 3 3 2 16 2
5 Greg Hancock 3 2 0 3 2 3 13 1
6 Scott Smith 3 1 1 X F 5
7 Mark Meredith 0 N 0 0 0
8 Peter McNamara did not ride

Cradley Heath (A), June 12, L41-49
1 †Simon Cross 0 0 2 2 1 3 8 1
2 Jan O. Pedersen rider replacement
3 Billy Hamill 2 2 2 3 1 2 3 15
4 Greg Hancock 3 3 2 3 2 3 1 17
5 Peter McNamara 0 0 0 N 0
6 Scott Smith 1 0 N 0 0 1
7 Mark Meredith 0 0 N 0 0

The original staging of the match on May 8 was abandoned after Mark Robinson had fallen at the start of heat four by referee Graham Brodie because of the state of the track. Scores at the time: OXFORD 12 CRADLEY HEATH 5 (Peter McNamara F- 0, Greg Hancock 2- 2, Billy Hamill, had not ridden, Jan O. Pedersen F- 0, Gert Handberg F- 0, Scott Smith F- 0, Mark Robinson 3- 3).

Oxford

Belle Vue (A), March 20, L41-49
1 †Hans Nielsen 3 2 3 2 0 10
2 Spencer Timmo 0 0 1 N 1 1
3 Martin Dugard R 2 2 2 1 7
4 Troy Butler 1 1 2 0 4 2
5 Dean Barker 2 2 1 2 7 1
6 Morten Andersen 2 0 1 1 1 5 3
7 Glenn Cunningham 3 2 2 0 7

Coventry (A), March 21, W46-44
1 †Hans Nielsen 3 3 3 3 0 12
2 Spencer Timmo 0 0 N N 0
3 Martin Dugard 3 3 2 3 11
4 Troy Butler 0 1 2 1 4
5 Dean Barker 3 3 2 1 9 2
6 Morten Andersen 2 0 2 1 1 2 8 1
7 Glenn Cunningham 0 R 0 1 1 2 1

COVENTRY (H), March 27, W49-40
1 †Hans Nielsen 3 3 3 3 2 14 1
2 Spencer Timmo 0 0 2 N 2 1
3 Martin Dugard 3 3 2 2 3 13
4 Troy Butler 3 1 0 2 6 1
5 Dean Barker 2 2 1 0 5 1
6 Glenn Cunningham 1 0 0 0 1 1
7 Morten Andersen 2 3 2 0 1 8 2

Cradley Heath (A), March 28, L40-50
1 †Hans Nielsen 3 3 3 3 3 2 17
2 Spencer Timmo 0 R N N 0
3 Martin Dugard rider replacement
4 Troy Butler 1 R 1 1 2 0 5 3
5 Dean Barker 2 2 3 F R 7
6 Morten Andersen 3 0 1 2 1 1 8 1
7 Glenn Cunningham 1 fx2 0 0 3
8 Wayne Parker did not ride

BRADFORD (H), April 3, W56-34
1 †Hans Nielsen 3 3 3 2 3 3 17
2 Mark Carlson 0 2 2 0 4 1
3 Martin Dugard 3 3 3 3 3 2 17 1
4 Troy Butler rider replacement
5 Dean Barker 2 2 3 1 3 11 2
6 Glenn Cunningham 1 1 0 0 2
7 Morten Andersen 3 0 1 1 F 5

BELLE VUE (H), April 29, W51-39
1 †Hans Nielsen 3 3 3 3 3 3 18
2 Mark Carlson 1 1 1 1 4
3 Martin Dugard 2 3 3 3 2 1 14
4 Troy Butler rider replacement
5 Dean Barker 2 3 3 1 2 11 2
6 Glenn Cunningham 2 1 F 0 3 1
7 Morten Andersen 1 F 0 0 0 1 1

Wolverhampton (A), May 18, L37-52
1 Hans Nielsen rider replacement
2 Mark Carlson 0 0 3 0 0 3
3 †Martin Dugard 3 R 2 fx1 2 8
4 Troy Butler 1 1 2 2 2 2 10 2
5 Dean Barker 2 3 2 0 fx 7
6 Morten Andersen 3 1 2 1 T 7 2
7 Glenn Cunningham 0 1 1 0 2
8 Spencer Timmo did not ride

WOLVERHAMPTON (H), May 22, L39-50
1 †Martin Dugard 3 2 3 2 3 2 15
2 Mark Carlson 1 1 1 N 3 2
3 Hans Nielsen rider replacement
4 Troy Butler 0 2 3 2 0 2 0 9 1
5 Dean Barker 2 F 2 R R 4
6 Glenn Cunningham F 0 0 0 0
7 Morten Andersen 2 2 2 1 1 8 1

Bradford (A), May 23, L33-57
1 †Martin Dugard 2 2 1 3 3 0 0 11
2 Mark Carlson 0 1 T 1 2 1
3 Hans Nielsen rider replacement
4 Troy Butler 0 R 1 2 0 1 4 1
5 Dean Barker 3 2 2 1 2 1 11
6 Morten Andersen E 0 0 T 0 0
7 Glenn Cunningham 2 2 1 0 5
8 Spencer Timmo did not ride

CRADLEY HEATH (H), June 12, W49-41
1 †Hans Nielsen 3 3 3 3 12
2 Mark Carlson 1 1 1 1 0 4
3 Martin Dugard 3 3 3 2 11
4 Troy Butler 1 2 1 2 6 1
5 Dean Barker 2 1 2 0 2 7 1
6 Glenn Cunningham 2 1 1 0 4 1
7 Morten Andersen 3 0 1 1 5 1

The original staging of the match on May 8 was abandoned after Mark Robinson had fallen at the start of heat four by referee Graham Brodie because of the state of the track. Scores at the time: OXFORD 12 (Hans Nielsen 3- 3, Mark Carlson 1- 1, Martin Dugard, had not ridden, Troy Butler 2- 2:1, Dean Barker 3- 3, Glenn Cunningham 2- 2, Morten Andersen 1- 1:1) CRADLEY HEATH 5.

Wolverhampton

CRADLEY HEATH (H), April 6, W47-43
1 §Ronnie Correy 2 2 3 2 0 9
2 Charles Ermolenko 1 1 2 2 6 3
3 †Sam Ermolenko 2 3 3 3 3 14
4 Graham Jones 2 2 1 X 5 1
5 Peter Karlsson 1 1 1 0 3 2
6 Wayne Carter 2 1 2 0 2 7 3
7 Stephen Morris 3 fx0 N 3

Coventry (A), April 11, W48-42
1 Ronnie Correy 3 1 3 2 2 11 3
2 Charles Ermolenko 1 2 1 X 4 1
3 †Sam Ermolenko 3 3 3 1 3 13
4 Graham Jones 0 1 2 3 6 1
5 Peter Karlsson 3 2 0 2 7
6 Wayne Carter 1 0 1 1 3 1
7 Stephen Morris 0 1 2 1 4 1

BELLE VUE (H), April 13, D45-45
1 Ronnie Correy 1 2 3 0 2 8 1
2 Charles Ermolenko F 0 2 1 3
3 †Sam Ermolenko 3 3 3 1 3 3 16
4 Graham Jones 3 2 2 3 1 11
5 Peter Karlsson 1 0 T 1 2
6 Wayne Carter 3 1 0 1 5
7 Stephen Morris fx0 0 T 0

Belle Vue (A), April 17, W47-43
1 Ronnie Correy 2 3 3 2 2 12 1
2 Charles Ermolenko 0 0 1 T 1 1
3 †Sam Ermolenko 3 2 1 2 2 1 11 3
4 Graham Jones 3 2 fx3 8
5 Peter Karlsson 1 1 3 2 7 1
6 Stephen Morris 3 fx0 N 3
7 Wayne Carter 1 0 2 1 1 5 1

Bradford (A), April 25, W49-41
1 Ronnie Correy 3 3 2 3 2 13 1
2 Charles Ermolenko 0 0 2 1 3 1
3 †Sam Ermolenko 1 3 3 3 3 13 1
4 Graham Jones 0 2 1 1 4
5 Peter Karlsson 2 1 1 3 7 1
6 Stephen Morris 2 0 0 N 2 1
7 Wayne Carter 3 2 1 0 1 7 1

COVENTRY (H), May 4, W58-31
1 Ronnie Correy 3 3 3 2 1 12 1
2 Charles Ermolenko 2 0 fx1 3 1
3 †Sam Ermolenko 3 3 3 3 3 15
4 Graham Jones 1 3 3 3 10
5 Peter Karlsson 3 2 3 2 10 2
6 Wayne Carter 3 0 2 1 6 1
7 Stephen Morris fx2 fx0 2

OXFORD (H), May 18, W52-37
1 Ronnie Correy 2 3 3 2 1 11 1
2 Charles Ermolenko 1 0 fx1 2 1
3 †Sam Ermolenko 2 3 3 R 3 11 1
4 Graham Jones 3 1 3 3 10 1
5 Peter Karlsson 0 2 3 3 8
6 Simon Wolstenholme 1 3 0 fx 4 1
7 Stephen Morris 2 2 1 1 6

Oxford (A), May 22, W50-39
1 Ronnie Correy 2 3 3 2 1 11
2 Charles Ermolenko 0 1 3 2 6 1
3 †Sam Ermolenko 3 3 3 1 3 13
4 Graham Jones 1 1 1 1 4 2
5 Peter Karlsson 3 2 3 3 11
6 Stephen Morris R F 1 F 1
7 Richard Musson 3 1 F 0 4

Cradley Heath (A), May 23, W47-42
1 Ronnie Correy 3 1 1 2 3 1 11 1
2 Charles Ermolenko fxT 2 1 3 1
3 †Sam Ermolenko 3 2 3 3 2 3 16 1
4 Graham Jones 1 0 1 3 2 7 2
5 Peter Karlsson 0 2 3 2 7
6 Stephen Morris 2 T 1 0 3
7 Richard Musson fx0 0 T 0

BRADFORD (H), June 1, W55-35
1 Ronnie Correy 3 3 3 2 3 14 1
2 Simon Wolstenholme 2 1 0 1 4 1
3 †Sam Ermolenko 3 3 2 3 R 11 1
4 Graham Jones 2 1 3 X 6 1
5 Peter Karlsson 1 2 3 2 8 2
6 Richard Musson 2 1 1 fx 4 1
7 Stephen Morris 3 1 3 1 8

The Gold Cup Tables

Southern Section

	M	W	D	L	W	D	L	PtsF	PtsA	BP	TPts
READING	12	6	0	0	4	0	2	566.5	512.5	5	25
King's Lynn	12	5	0	1	4	0	2	554	525	4	22
Ipswich	12	5	0	1	2	0	4	582	498	5	19
Arena Essex	12	5	0	1	1	0	5	555	524	4	16
Poole	12	4	0	2	1	0	5	527.5	552.5	1	11
Swindon	12	3	0	3	1	0	5	519	560	2	10
Eastbourne	12	1	0	5	0	0	6	474	606	0	2

Northern Section

	M	W	D	L	W	D	L	PtsF	PtsA	BP	TPts
WOLVERHAMPTON	10	4	1	0	5	0	0	498	398	5	24
Oxford	10	4	0	1	1	0	4	441	456	2	12
Cradley Heath	10	3	0	2	1	0	4	460	438	3	11
Coventry	10	3	0	2	1	0	4	435	463	2	10
Bradford	10	4	0	1	0	0	5	434	466	2	10
Belle Vue	10	3	0	2	0	1	4	426	473	1	8

The Gold Cup Final

First leg, Smallmead, Monday, September 13

READING 47
1 Per Jonsson 3 3 3 3 2 14 1
2 David Mullett 0 1 0 2 3 1
3 †Jeremy Doncaster 3 1 1 R 5 1
4 Ray Morton 1 2 1 R 4
5 Armando Castagna F 1 3 1 5 1
6 Phillip Morris 2 2 0 N 4 2
7 Jan Andersson 3 2 0 2 2 3 12

WOLVERHAMPTON 43
1 Gordon Kennett 1 0 3 T 4 1
2 Ronnie Correy 2 3 3 0 8
3 Peter Karlsson N 2 1 0 3 1
4 Charles Ermolenko 3 2 1 3 1 10 1
5 †Sam Ermolenko 2 3 2 2 3 R 12 2
6 Nigel Leaver 1 fx0 2 1 4
7 Stephen Morris 0 fx1 0 1

Second leg, Monmore Green, Monday, September 14

WOLVERHAMPTON 49
1 Ronnie Correy 3 3 3 3 3 15
2 Gordon Kennett 1 1 0 1 3
3 Peter Karlsson 3 3 2 0 8
4 †Sam Ermolenko 3 2 1 3 2 11 2
5 Charles Ermolenko 2 3 2 1 8 1
6 Stephen Morris 0 1 0 0 1 2
7 Nigel Leaver 1 1 F N 2

READING 41
1 Per Jonsson 2 1 3 3 3 0 12
2 David Mullett 0 F 2 1 3 1
3 †Jeremy Doncaster 2 2 1 2 1 8
4 Armando Castagna 0 2 2 2 6 1
5 Ray Morton 1 1 0 0 2 1
6 Jan Andersson 3 0 3 2 8
7 Phillip Morris 2 0 T F 2 1

WOLVERHAMPTON win 92-88 on aggregate.

Chart Topping Champs

WORLD Champion Jan O. Pedersen was heading for the top of the charts – when his Homefire League Division One season ended prematurely.

For the Cradley Heath skipper headed a trio of title-holders who dominated the three top spots in our exclusive Division One averages table.

The Danish star, ruled out of racing for the season when he crashed in an individual meeting on the eve of the beginning of his World Championship defence, only rode in three League matches for his club and was beaten by an opponent in only one of his 14 races – when he finished last in heat seven of the visit to Arena Essex!

Per Jonsson, World Champion in 1990, was second in the rankings (and arguably the best rider in the Homefire League if you discount Jan O.'s three meetings), fractionally ahead of three-time World Champion Hans Nielsen who, for the tenth successive season, maintained a double figure average to once again confirm his status as the world's most consistent points scorer.

Their principal opposition came from the exciting thrillmaker Sam Ermolenko (left) who, once again, picked up a hatful of bonus points in Wolverhampton's title challenge.

World Under 21 Champion Leigh Adams had a marvellous season in a team that finished bottom of the League for the second year in a row while teenager Joe Screen soared into the Top Ten.

Best Division One newcomer was Belle Vue's Australian Jason Lyons and Arena's American freshman Josh Larsen had a superb first season in British speedway.

Ranking	Rider	Club	Matches	Rides	Points	Bonus Points	Total Points	Average	Maximums Full	Maximums Paid	Maximums Total
1	Jan O. Pedersen	Cradley Heath	3	14	35.0	4.0	39.0	11.143		2	2
2	Per Jonsson	Reading	23	115	284.0	12.0	296.0	10.296	6	1	7
3	Hans Nielsen	Oxford	23	126	315.0	8.0	323.0	10.254	3	1	4
4	Sam Ermolenko	Wolverhampton	24	131	316.0	17.0	333.0	10.168	4	4	8
5	Leigh Adams	Swindon	24	129	298.0	10.0	308.0	9.550	2	2	4
6	Marvyn Cox	Poole	24	125	285.0	9.0	294.0	9.408	2		2
7	Ronnie Correy	Wolverhampton	24	125	271.0	22.0	293.0	9.376	1	1	2
8	Greg Hancock	Cradley Heath	24	126	279.0	16.0	295.0	9.365		1	1
9	Gary Havelock	Bradford	20	100	213.0	20.0	233.0	9.320		3	3
10	Joe Screen	Belle Vue	21	103	228.0	9.0	237.0	9.204	3	1	4
11	Tommy Knudsen	Coventry	13	68	148.0	6.0	154.0	9.059			
12	Shawn Moran	Belle Vue	23	102	207.0	23.0	230.0	9.020	1	1	2
13	Martin Dugard	Oxford	21	102	215.0	13.0	228.0	8.941	1	1	2
14	Kelvin Tatum	Bradford	17	84	180.0	7.0	187.0	8.905	2		2
15	Henrik Gustafsson	King's Lynn	15	80	163.0	14.0	177.0	8.850		1	1
16	Craig Boyce	Poole	23	99	197.0	20.0	217.0	8.768	2		2
17	Mark Loram	King's Lynn	22	120	251.0	12.0	263.0	8.767		1	1
18	Peter Nahlin	Eastbourne	16	90	188.0	9.0	197.0	8.756	1		1
19	Brian Karger	Arena Essex	22	115	240.0	11.0	251.0	8.730	1	1	2
20	Bobby Ott	Belle Vue	23	109	218.0	18.0	236.0	8.661			
21	Rick Miller	Coventry	11	50	99.0	9.0	108.0	8.640		1	1
22	Billy Hamill	Cradley Heath	20	94	183.5	17.0	200.5	8.532			
23	Tony Rickardsson	Ipswich	23	115	226.0	16.0	242.0	8.417	2	1	3
24	Jeremy Doncaster	Reading	23	99	185.0	22.0	207.0	8.364		1	1
25	Bo Petersen	Arena Essex	24	128	244.0	20.0	264.0	8.250		1	1
26	Simon Wigg	Bradford	23	126	231.0	24.0	255.0	8.095		1	1
27	David Mullett	Reading	23	99	162.0	37.0	199.0	8.040		2	2
28	Simon Cross	Cradley Heath	24	114	206.0	23.0	229.0	8.035		1	1
29	Wayne Carter	Wolverhampton	2	8	13.0	3.0	16.0	8.000			
30	Steve Schofield	Poole	24	119	220.0	16.0	236.0	7.933			
31	Dennis Löfqvist	King's Lynn	22	103	174.0	26.0	200.0	7.767		1	1
32	Sean Wilson	Bradford	24	118	199.0	30.0	229.0	7.763			
33	Chris Louis	Ipswich	24	116	201.0	24.0	225.0	7.759			
34	Peter Karlsson	Wolverhampton	23	98	170.0	18.0	188.0	7.673		1	1
35	Andy Smith	Coventry	13	63	114.5	6.0	120.5	7.651			
36	Gert Handberg	Cradley Heath	21	88	151.0	14.0	165.0	7.500		1	1
37	Jan Andersson	Reading	23	110	192.0	14.0	206.0	7.491			
38	Mitch Shirra	Swindon	22	106	184.0	10.0	194.0	7.321			
39	Jimmy Nilsen	Swindon	24	117	192.0	21.0	213.0	7.282			
40	John Jørgensen	Coventry	22	108	175.0	18.0	193.0	7.148		1	1
41	Zdenek Tesar	Ipswich	21	88	138.0	18.0	156.0	7.091			
42	Peter Ravn	Arena Essex	12	61	102.0	6.0	108.0	7.082			
43	Allan Johansen	Arena Essex	9	39	58.0	9.0	67.0	6.872			
44	Paul Thorp	Bradford	24	108	168.0	17.0	185.0	6.852			
45	Jason Lyons	Belle Vue	24	107	158.0	25.0	183.0	6.841	1		1
46	Armando Castagna	Reading	23	95	145.0	16.0	161.0	6.779			
47	Shane Parker	Ipswich	24	113	170.0	21.0	191.0	6.761			
48	David Norris	Ipswich	23	99	142.0	25.0	167.0	6.747			
49	Ray Morton	Reading	19	83	118.0	20.0	138.0	6.651			
50	Andy Grahame	Eastbourne/Cradley H.	23	109	163.0	17.0	180.0	6.606			

Ranking	Rider	Club	Matches	Rides	Points	Bonus Points	Total Points	Average	Maximums Full	Maximums Paid	Maximums Total
51	Tony Olsson	Ipswich	19	80	114.0	18.0	132.0	6.600			
52	Andrew Silver	Eastbourne	24	133	198.0	20.0	218.0	6.556			
53	Graham Jones	Wolverhampton	16	63	94.0	9.0	103.0	6.540			
54	Gary Allan	King's Lynn	23	100	138.0	23.0	161.0	6.440			
55	Bohumil Brhel	King's Lynn	16	71	101.0	13.0	114.0	6.423			
56	Antal Kocso	Bradford	14	65	93.0	11.0	104.0	6.400			
57	Dean Barker	Oxford	24	105	146.0	18.0	164.0	6.248			
58	Brian Andersen	Coventry	24	114	148.0	29.0	177.0	6.211			
59	Tom Knudsen	Poole	22	87	102.0	33.0	135.0	6.207			
60	Frede Schøtt	Belle Vue	24	98	123.0	29.0	152.0	6.204			
61	Kelly Moran	Belle Vue/Swindon	24	109	148.0	19.0	167.0	6.128			
62	Troy Pratt	Arena Essex	17	78	104.0	15.0	119.0	6.103		1	1
63	Carl Stonehewer	Belle Vue	23	100	120.0	30.0	150.0	6.000			
64	Olli Tyrvainen	Eastbourne	20	76	92.0	20.0	112.0	5.895		1	1
65	Glenn Doyle	Eastbourne	17	75	101.0	8.0	109.0	5.813			
66	Alun Rossiter	King's Lynn/Poole	22	87	97.0	29.0	126.0	5.793			
67	Stefan Dannö	Eastbourne	19	84	102.0	18.0	120.0	5.714			
68	Jörgen Johansson	Poole	21	87	109.0	15.0	124.0	5.701			
69	Paul Bentley	Coventry	8	33	36.0	11.0	47.0	5.697			
70	Nathan Simpson	Eastbourne	24	112	128.0	30.0	158.0	5.643			
71	Gordon Kennett	Wolverhampton	5	16	17.0	5.0	22.0	5.500			
72	Josh Larsen	Arena Essex	20	92	109.0	17.0	126.0	5.478			
73	Alastair Stevens	Poole	21	93	101.0	23.0	124.0	5.333			
74	Mark Carlson	Oxford	24	106	121.0	20.0	141.0	5.321			
75	Charles Ermolenko	Wolverhampton	24	94	111.0	14.0	125.0	5.319		1	1
76	Dean Standing	Swindon	13	47	51.0	11.0	62.0	5.277			
77	Kevin Brice	King's Lynn	11	49	55.0	9.0	64.0	5.224			
78	Andy Galvin	Arena Essex	19	71	78.0	13.0	91.0	5.127			
79	Morten Andersen	Oxford	20	84	90.0	17.0	107.0	5.095			
80	Ben Howe	Ipswich	24	92	87.0	29.0	116.0	5.043			
81	Troy Butler	Oxford	22	109	117.0	20.0	137.0	5.028			
82	Bobby Schwartz	Eastbourne	1	4	5.0	0.0	5.0	5.000			
83	Paul Dugard	Eastbourne	18	69	64.0	18.0	82.0	4.754			
84	Michael Warren	Coventry	24	99	96.0	20.0	116.0	4.687			
85	Tony Langdon	Poole	12	48	50.0	6.0	56.0	4.667			
86	Slawomir Drabik	Poole	2	6	5.0	2.0	7.0	4.667			
87	Neville Tatum	Eastbourne	3	11	12.0	0.0	12.0	4.364			
88	Andy Phillips	Poole/Cradley Heath	20	89	85.0	11.0	96.0	4.315			
89	Paul Smith	Belle Vue	23	83	69.0	18.0	87.0	4.193			
90	Nigel Leaver	Wolverhampton	16	68	58.0	10.0	68.0	4.000			
	Jamie Habbin	Coventry	16	57	49.0	8.0	57.0	4.000			
	Jacek Rempala	Ipswich	3	8	8.0	0.0	8.0	4.000			
	Jon Armstrong	Belle Vue	2	7	7.0	0.0	7.0	4.000			
	Spencer Timmo	Oxford	2	6	6.0	0.0	6.0	4.000			
95	David Smart	Swindon	17	73	56.0	11.0	67.0	3.671			
96	Scott Smith	Cradley Heath	23	88	66.0	14.0	80.0	3.636			
97	Savalas Clouting	Ipswich	3	6	4.0	1.0	5.0	3.333			
98	Paul Woods	Eastbourne	5	16	10.0	3.0	13.0	3.250			
99	Alan Mogridge	Arena Essex	21	76	46.0	13.0	59.0	3.105			
100	Colin White	Arena Essex	11	39	22.0	8.0	30.0	3.077			

BEST OF BRITISH

MARK Loram (left) stormed into the British Top Twenty – to challenge World Finalist Henrik Gustafsson for the top spot at King's Lynn.

But it was Poole's Marvyn Cox who was the top Englishman in the 1992 Homefire League First Division averages.

He overhauled World Champion Gary Havelock at the top of the score charts.

LEGEND

THE 1992 Homefire League averages listed are taken from the referee's official programme for all matches and may differ from unofficial figures listed in other publications.

Reading from left to right the figures list the following: overall ranking, rider, track or tracks, matches, rides, points, bonus points, total points, calculated match average, paid maximums, full maximums, total maximums.

The calculated match average s is taken by dividing the total number scored by the number of rides and then multiplied by four to give a calculated match average out of a maximum of 12.000.

■ *Guest appearances are NOT included in the figures but a list of guest rider scores is given overleaf.*

Ranking	Rider	Club	Matches	Rides	Points	Bonus Points	Total Points	Average	Maximums Full	Maximums Paid	Maximums Total
101	Michael Graves	Bradford	1	4	3.0	0.0	3.0	3.000			
102	Phillip Morris	Reading	20	66	33.0	15.0	48.0	2.909			
103	Steve Masters	Swindon	13	45	23.0	9.0	32.0	2.844			
104	Steve Leigh	Poole	2	6	3.0	1.0	4.0	2.667			
	Mark Meredith	Cradley Heath	1	3	1.0	1.0	2.0	2.667			
106	Justin Elkins	Swindon	23	80	43.0	10.0	53.0	2.650			
107	Glenn Cunningham	Oxford	15	50	28.0	4.0	32.0	2.560			
108	Justin Walker	Cradley Heath	4	16	8.0	2.0	10.0	2.500			
109	Kevin Little	Bradford	6	18	10.0	1.0	11.0	2.444			
110	Darren Spicer	King's Lynn	18	60	29.0	7.0	36.0	2.400			
111	Darren Sumner	Oxford	11	34	15.0	5.0	20.0	2.353			
112	Stephen Morris	Wolverhampton	24	88	43.0	8.0	51.0	2.318			
113	Simon Wolstenholme	Wolverhampton	5	16	7.0	1.0	8.0	2.000			
	Ricky Sandford	Arena Essex	1	2	1.0	0.0	1.0	2.000			
115	Richard Musson	Wolverhampton	4	15	6.0	1.0	7.0	1.867			
116	Darren Pearson	Bradford	17	64	26.0	3.0	29.0	1.813			
117	Emmerson Fairweather	King's Lynn	8	24	7.0	3.0	10.0	1.667			
	Andrew Mountain	King's Lynn	4	12	3.0	2.0	5.0	1.667			
119	Stuart Parnaby	Bradford	3	10	4.0	0.0	4.0	1.600			
	Tom Grinstead	King's Lynn	2	5	2.0	0.0	2.0	1.600			
121	Matthew Cross	Swindon	3	6	2.0	0.0	2.0	1.333			
	Scott Swain	Poole	1	3	1.0	0.0	1.0	1.333			
123	Lance Sealey	Reading	3	16	5.0	0.0	5.0	1.250			
	Darren Grayling	Eastbourne	6	16	4.0	1.0	5.0	1.250			
125	Stuart Swales	Bradford	6	20	5.0	0.0	5.0	1.000			
126	Mark Robinson	Cradley Heath	3	12	2.0	1.0	3.0	1.000			
	Chris Clarence	Coventry	2	4	1.0	0.0	1.0	1.000			
128	David Clarke	Swindon	4	13	2.0	1.0	3.0	0.923			
129	Colin Thorp	Coventry	3	5	1.0	0.0	1.0	0.800			
130	Gary Sweet	Reading	1	2	0.0	0.0	0.0	0.000			
	Richard Smith	Bradford	1	2	0.0	0.0	0.0	0.000			
	Roland Pollard	Arena Essex	1	2	0.0	0.0	0.0	0.000			
	Scott Kirton	Coventry	1	2	0.0	0.0	0.0	0.000			
	Shaun Tacey	Ipswich	1	2	0.0	0.0	0.0	0.000			
	Steve Camden	Swindon	1	2	0.0	0.0	0.0	0.000			
136	Jason Gage	King's Lynn	1	3	0.0	0.0	0.0	0.000			
	Mark Sayer	Reading	1	3	0.0	0.0	0.0	0.000			
	Mike Hampson	Belle Vue	1	3	0.0	0.0	0.0	0.000			
139	Anthony Boyd	Cradley Heath	2	6	0.0	0.0	0.0	0.000			
	Mick Tomlin	Reading	2	6	0.0	0.0	0.0	0.000			
141	Robert Ledwith	Arena Essex	6	13	0.0	0.0	0.0	0.000			

Listed below are the individual club averages of those who rode for more than one team in 1992.

Rider	Club	Matches	Rides	Points	Bonus Points	Total Points	Average
Andy Grahame	Eastbourne	6	34	60.0	1.0	61.0	7.176
	Cradley Heath	17	75	103.0	16.0	119.0	6.347
Alun Rossiter	Poole	12	40	45.0	19.0	64.0	6.400
	King's Lynn	10	47	52.0	10.0	62.0	5.277
Kelly Moran	Swindon	23	105	145.0	19.0	164.0	6.248
	Belle Vue	1	4	3.0	0.0	3.0	3.000
Andy Phillips	Poole	3	11	11.0	2.0	13.0	4.727
	Cradley Heath	17	78	74.0	9.0	83.0	4.256

GUESTS '92

IN RECENT years there has been a conscious effort to cut down on the number of guest riders used in Homefire League racing.

In 1992 there were only four teams – Arena Essex (1), Belle Vue (1), Coventry (19), Cradley Heath (2) and King's Lynn (3) – who used any guest riders in League competition.

Coventry's considerable use of guest riders was understandable as they lost the services of all three heat leaders for the last nine matches of the season and went into their two final meetings without their top four, Tommy Knudsen, Rick Miller, Andy Smith and John Jørgensen!

Listed alongside are the guests' averages.

Rider	Matches	Rides	Points	Bonus Points	Total Points	Average
Jeremy Doncaster	2	13	33.0	2.0	35.0	10.769
Rick Miller	1	6	13.0	2.0	15.0	10.000
Tony Olsson	1	7	16.0	1.0	17.0	9.714
Kelly Moran	2	11	24.0	2.0	26.0	9.455
Simon Cross	1	6	10.0	2.0	12.0	8.000
Sean Wilson	2	13	23.0	1.0	24.0	7.385
Jan Andersson	2	11	20.0	0.0	20.0	7.273
Gert Handberg	1	7	12.0	0.0	12.0	6.857
Glenn Doyle	1	5	6.0	2.0	8.0	6.400
Mitch Shirra	2	12	19.0	0.0	19.0	6.333
Peter Ravn	2	12	15.0	4.0	19.0	6.333
Jimmy Nilsen	2	10	13.0	2.0	15.0	6.000
Jason Lyons	2	11	13.0	3.0	16.0	5.818
Dean Barker	2	10	10.0	4.0	14.0	5.600
Peter Karlsson	1	6	6.0	1.0	7.0	4.667
Steve Schofield	1	7	7.0	0.0	7.0	4.000
Zdenek Tesar	1	5	4.0	0.0	4.0	3.200

Survival at last gasp...

HAVING totally dominated the Second Division in 1991, the Kent Sweepers Hammers had already made history by becoming the first team to earn promotion to the top flight. 1992 was all about staying there and they achieved that aim – just!

Co-promoters Terry Russell and Ivan Henry largely kept faith with the side that had earned them the right to be in the First Division merely loaning out young reserves Colin White and Paul Hurry to Long Eaton and Peterborough respectively.

Replacing them were talented young American Josh Larsen, signed despite interest from several other clubs, and Dane Allan Johansen returning for another crack at the British League. Peter Ravn was also signed as cover although the points limit debarred him from being in the side. Nevertheless his capture was to prove significant later in the season.

If anyone thought that the Essex side would be the First Division whipping boys they were soon in for a shock.

After the scheduled opener against Swedish tourists Kumla was washed out, Kings Lynn were thrashed by 22 points in the opening Gold Cup fixture with Brian Karger and Bo Petersen showing that the First Division held no fears for them. After five matches they topped their section of the competition thanks to that victory over Kings Lynn and the same margin of victory over Eastbourne.

Not that anyone was deceived though and an injury to Andy Galvin in the world championship round at Exeter coupled with a home defeat to Cradley Heath in the League, emphasised that life wouldn't be easy.

So it proved – especially away from home with Allan Johansen not showing anything like the form he was demonstrating around the Purfleet track. Alan Mogridge was struggling, too, but the encouraging signs were the performances of the two reserves – Troy Pratt and Larsen who was proving to be an astute acquisition. They reaped a paid 20 points between them as the Kent Sweepers Hammers routed Milton Keynes in the BSPA Cup and a further 20 in the narrow defeat at Oxford.

Fourth place in the Southern section of the Gold Cup was a reasonable enough start to their First Division career but injuries were to take their toll in the league campaign and keep them in the relegation zone all season.

Andy Galvin tore ankle ligaments at Ipswich, Troy Pratt suffered a similar injury at home against Wolverhampton and skipper Moggo broke a rib at Eastbourne. It was a triple blow to the side who had to soldier on by promoting juniors in view of the 'three Englishmen a side rule'.

"Replacing a foreigner is no problem," said co-promoter Terry Russell, "but there just isn't an English rider about at the moment who we could sign."

Johansen's away form was a major worry and it was no real surprise when he decided to return home to Denmark at the beginning of August. That probably saved the club axing him anyway for they were now able to bring in Peter Ravn to replace him with the publication of new averages.

By the time he arrived the Kent Sweepers Hammers were rooted to the bottom of the League but with Pratt returning after a seven week absence, at least they were back to full strength.

They began to pick up points at home again and with Eastbourne and Swindon both struggling a victory over Bradford in their final home league match was more than enough for them to avoid relegation.

They had survived their opening season in the First Division, learnt a great deal in the process and will be looking to build on that in the years to come.

1992 RIDER ROSTER

	Club Record								Career Record							
	M	R	Pts	BP	TPts	Ave	F	P	M	R	Pts	BP	TPts	Ave	F	P
Andy Galvin	21	78	83.0	14.0	97.0	4.974	0	0	91	348	402.0	67.0	469.0	5.391	0	0
Allan Johansen	11	49	75.0	10.0	85.0	6.939	0	0	125	540	741.0	104.0	845.0	6.259	0	1
Brian Karger	24	126	267.0	13.0	280.0	8.889	1	2	174	791	1341.0	127.0	1468.0	7.424	1	4
Josh Larsen	22	104	124.0	19.0	143.0	5.500	0	1	22	104	124.0	19.0	143.0	5.500	0	1
Robert Ledwith	8	18	1.0	1.0	2.0	0.444	0	0	8	18	1.0	1.0	2.0	0.444	0	0
Alan Mogridge	21	76	46.0	13.0	59.0	3.105	0	0	120	378	283.0	62.0	345.0	3.651	0	0
Bo Petersen	26	137	260.0	20.0	280.0	8.175	0	1	357	1606	3209.0	195.0	3404.0	8.478	23	12
Troy Pratt	17	78	104.0	15.0	119.0	6.103	0	1	17	78	104.0	15.0	119.0	6.103	0	1
Roland Pollard	1	2	0.0	0.0	0.0	0.000	0	0	1	2	0.0	0.0	0.0	0.000	0	0
Peter Ravn	12	61	102.0	6.0	108.0	7.082	0	0	409	1639	2544.5	305.0	2849.5	6.954	5	5
Ricky Sandford	1	2	1.0	0.0	1.0	2.000	0	0	1	2	1.0	0.0	1.0	2.000	0	0
Colin White	13	45	24.0	10.0	34.0	3.022	0	0	14	46	24.0	10.0	34.0	2.957	0	0

ARENA ESSEX

Arena Essex became the first club in speedway history to be automatically promoted after being crowned Division Two champions. They faced their first season in Division One in 1992.

Promoters: Terry Russell and Ivan Henry.
Address: Arena Essex Sports Complex, A1306 Arterial Road, Purfleet, Essex, RM16 1NX.
Telephone: 0708-863443.
Hotline: 0891 800 694.
Track Length: 252.5 metres.
Track Record: 56.0 secs, Brian Karger (Arena Essex), August 15, 1991, Heat 1, Arena Essex v Newcastle (Sunbrite League Division Two).
Seasons in Division One: 1 (1992).
Best Division One Season: Eleventh, 1992.
World Finalists: Brian Karger (1992).
Division One Riders' Championship Finalists: Brian Karger (1992).

Seasons in Division Two: 8 (1984-1991).
Division Two Record: Champions (1), 1991.
Division Two Cup Record: Winners (1), 1991.
Division Two Team Championship: Winners (1), 1991. Runners-up (2), 1986, 1987. Qualified (5), 1985, 1986, 1987, 1989, 1991.
Appearances: Martin Goodwin, 235 (1984-1990).
Points: Martin Goodwin, 2363.5 (1984-1990).
Division Two Riders' Championship Finalists: Alan Sage (1984), Neil Middleditch (1985), Andrew Silver (1986-87), Martin Goodwin (1988-89-90), Bo Petersen (1991).

1992

ARENA ESSEX

Back row: Ivan Henry (co-promoter), Bo Petersen, Andy Galvin, Alan Mogridge, Peter Thorogood (team manager), Troy Pratt, Brian Karger, Terry Russell (co-promoter). Front: Josh Larsen, mascot Wayne Russell and Allan Johansen.

CRADLEY HEATH (H), April 17, L43-47

1 §Brian Karger	3 2 3 1 0	9	
2 §Allan Johansen	2 1 3 2	8	3
3 §Bo Petersen	3 1 3 2 1	10	1
4 †§Alan Mogridge	1 1 0 1	3	1
5 §§Robert Ledwith	0 0 N N	0	
6 §§Troy Pratt	3 1 2 2 0	8	
7 §§Josh Larsen	R 1 1 2 1	5	1

Oxford (A), May 13, L41-49

1 Brian Karger	2 1 1 1	5	1
2 Robert Ledwith	0 0 N N	0	
3 Bo Petersen	1 1 3 2 1	8	2
4 †Alan Mogridge	0 2 2 0	4	
5 Allan Johansen	3 1 1 0	5	2
6 Troy Pratt	3 2 3 0 3	11	
7 Josh Larsen	1 2 2 1 2 0	8	2

BELLE VUE (H), May 22, W54-36

1 Brian Karger	**3 3 2 3 3**	**14**	1
2 †Alan Mogridge	0 1 fxN	1	
3 Bo Petersen	1 1 3 3	8	
4 §Andy Galvin	1 1 2 3	7	2
5 Allan Johansen	0 2 3 2	7	
6 Troy Pratt	2 3 0 F	5	
7 Josh Larsen	3 3 3 0 2 1	12	

SWINDON (H), July 10, L43-47

1 Brian Karger	3 2 3 2 1	11	
2 †Alan Mogridge	1 1 1 1	4	2
3 Bo Petersen	2 3 F 2 2	9	
4 Robert Ledwith	0 0 N N	0	
5 Allan Johansen	1 2 2 1	6	
6 Troy Pratt	3 1 0 1 1	6	3
7 Josh Larsen	2 2 1 0 2	7	

WOLVERHAMPTON (H), July 16, W49-41

1 Brian Karger	3 3 2 3 2	13	
2 Andy Galvin	1 F 3 1	5	
3 Allan Johansen	1 3 3 3 3	13	
4 Bo Petersen	3 2 1 2	8	
5 †Alan Mogridge	1 1 0 0	2	
6 Troy Pratt	3 2 fnN	5	
7 Josh Larsen	1 0 1 1 0 0	3	

Swindon (A), July 23, L37-53

1 Brian Karger	2 3 2 2 1 3	13	
2 †Andy Galvin	0 1 2 N	3	
3 Allan Johansen	0 1 T 1 0	2	
4 Robert Ledwith	0 0 T T	0	
5 Bo Petersen	2 3 2 3 2 1	13	
6 Josh Larsen	1 fx0 1 1	3	3
7 §Colin White	2 1 fx0	3	

Belle Vue (A), July 31, L27-63

1 Brian Karger	3 2 3 2 2 3	15	
2 †Andy Galvin	0 0 N N	0	
3 Allan Johansen	1 1 1 0 0	3	
4 Robert Ledwith	F fxN 0	0	
5 Bo Petersen	1 1 1 0	3	
6 Josh Larsen	1 0 0 N 2 1 2	6	1
7 Colin White	0 0 T 0 0	0	

IPSWICH (H), August 1, L38-52

1 Brian Karger	3 1 1 R 1	6	2
2 †Andy Galvin	0 2 0 3 0	5	
3 Allan Johansen	1 2 2 3 0	8	
4 Bo Petersen	3 3 1 2 3 1	13	
5 Robert Ledwith	0 T N 0	0	
6 Josh Larsen	1 0 1 2	4	1
7 Colin White	0 T 1 T 1	2	1

POOLE (H), August 7, L43-47

1 Brian Karger	**3 3 3 3 3**	**15**	
2 Andy Galvin	0 1 3 1	5	
3 Allan Johansen	3 1 2 0 fn	6	1
4 Bo Petersen	1 3 1 1	6	
5 †Alan Mogridge	F 0 0 N	0	
6 Josh Larsen	R 0 2 3 0 1	6	
7 Colin White	2 2 1 0	5	2

Wolverhampton (A), August 10, L40-50

1 Brian Karger	2 2 2 1 3 2	12	1
2 Andy Galvin	1 1 1 0 T	3	2
3 Allan Johansen	*rider replacement*		
4 †Alan Mogridge	1 1 1 0	3	2
5 Bo Petersen	2 2 2 2 1 1 1	11	2
6 Josh Larsen	3 1 3 2 0 2	11	1
7 Colin White	0 0 N 0	0	
8 Roland Pollard	*did not ride*		

OXFORD (H), August 14, W47-43

1 Zdenek Tesar	*2 1 1 R F*	*4*	
2 Andy Galvin	1 3 0 3 3 0	10	1
3 Allan Johansen	*rider replacement*		
4 Bo Petersen	2 2 3 3 2 3	15	1
5 †Alan Mogridge	0 fxN N	0	
6 Josh Larsen	2 2 3 2 2 3	14	1
7 Colin White	1 1 1 0 1 N	4	3
8 Roland Pollard	*did not ride*		

KING'S LYNN (H), August 21, W51-39

1 Brian Karger	3 3 3 2 3 3	17	
2 Allan Johansen	*rider replacement*		
3 Andy Galvin	2 2 1 0 2	7	2
4 Bo Petersen	3 3 2 0 3 2	13	2
5 †Alan Mogridge	1 0 0 0	1	
6 Josh Larsen	2 fx2 3	7	1
7 Colin White	3 0 1 1 1	6	1
8 Roland Pollard	*did not ride*		

Coventry (A), August 31, L35-55

1 Brian Karger	R 2 2 2 2 3	11	
2 Andy Galvin	1 0 1 1	3	2
3 §Peter Ravn	2 3 1 fxN	6	1
4 †Alan Mogridge	0 0 T T 1	1	1
5 Bo Petersen	1 1 2 1 2 2	9	2
6 Josh Larsen	R fxT T	0	
7 Troy Pratt	1 1 2 1 0	5	1

EASTBOURNE (H), September 4, W58-32

1 Brian Karger	1 2 1 1	5	1
2 Andy Galvin	3 0 3 2	8	
3 §Peter Ravn	3 3 0 3 3	12	
4 Bo Petersen	**3 3 3 3 2**	**14**	**1**
5 Josh Larsen	0 1 1 N	2	
6 †Alan Mogridge	fx1 1 N	2	
7 Troy Pratt	**3 2 3 3 2 2**	**15**	**3**

Bradford (A), September 5, L41-49

1 Brian Karger	1 3 2 0	6	
2 Andy Galvin	0 0 2 N	2	
3 Peter Ravn	3 3 0 2 3 2	13	
4 Colin White	0 2 0 T	2	1
5 Bo Petersen	2 3 1 3 0	9	1
6 Troy Pratt	2 0 2 1 0	5	1
7 †Alan Mogridge	3 1 0 N 0	4	

Poole (A), September 9, L32-57

1 Brian Karger	*rider replacement*		
2 Andy Galvin	R 0 fxN	0	
3 Peter Ravn	2 3 1 2 2 0 0	10	2
4 Colin White	0 T 0 0	0	
5 Bo Petersen	2 2 3 3 1 1 3	15	
6 †Alan Mogridge	0 0 0 1 N	1	
7 Troy Pratt	1 2 fx1 2 0	6	1
8 Roland Pollard	*did not ride*		

READING (H), September 11, L44-46

1 Brian Karger	3 2 2 3 3 0	13	1
2 Colin White	0 0 N fx	0	
3 Peter Ravn	2 3 3 2 1	11	1
4 Bo Petersen	fx1 2 3 2	8	1
5 §§Ricky Sandford	1 0 N N	1	
6 †Alan Mogridge	F F N 0	0	
7 Troy Pratt	3 2 3 F 2 1	11	1

Cradley Heath (A), September 12, L31-59

1 Brian Karger	2 1 3 2 2 0	10	
2 Colin White	0 0 N N	0	
3 Peter Ravn	0 1 2 1 0	4	
4 §§Roland Pollard	0 N N 0	0	
5 Bo Petersen	2 1 2 1 3 1	10	
6 †Alan Mogridge	1 0 N 0 1	2	1
7 Troy Pratt	2 1 1 0 N 1	5	2

Reading (A), October 5, L36-54

1 Brian Karger	1 3 2 3 2 2	13	1
2 Troy Pratt	0 0 0 2 1	3	2
3 Peter Ravn	3 1 1 3 F	8	
4 Josh Larsen	R 0 T T	0	
5 Bo Petersen	2 3 2 1 2 1	11	1
6 †Alan Mogridge	fx0 T F	0	
7 Andy Galvin	1 0 T 0	1	

Ipswich (A), October 8, L32-58

1 Brian Karger	fx1 2 1	4	
2 Troy Pratt	1 0 T 3 0	4	
3 Peter Ravn	3 3 1 2 1 0	10	1
4 Josh Larsen	0 1 2 0 3	6	1
5 Bo Petersen	1 0 2 2 1	6	1
6 Andy Galvin	2 0 0 T	2	
7 †Alan Mogridge	0 0 0 T	0	

COVENTRY (H), October 9, W49-40

1 Brian Karger	3 3 3 0 3	12	
2 Troy Pratt	1 1 1 1	4	
3 Peter Ravn	3 0 3 2	8	
4 Bo Petersen	1 3 3 3 2	12	2
5 Josh Larsen	2 1 2 R	5	
6 †Alan Mogridge	R 1 2 1 1	5	1
7 Andy Galvin	3 R R N	3	

King's Lynn (A), October 17, L41-49

1 Brian Karger	2 3 2 3 3 1	14	
2 Troy Pratt	0 0 2 T	2	
3 Peter Ravn	0 2 1 2 0	5	1
4 Josh Larsen	0 0 T 0	0	
5 Bo Petersen	3 3 1 2 2 0	11	1
6 †Alan Mogridge	1 0 E 1	2	1
7 Andy Galvin	3 3 1 0 T	7	1

BRADFORD (H), October 23, W53-37

1 Brian Karger	3 F 2 3	8	
2 Troy Pratt	1 2 2 0	5	
3 Peter Ravn	2 3 fx3 1	9	
4 Bo Petersen	2 3 1 3 3	12	1
5 Josh Larsen	3 2 2 2	9	2
6 †Alan Mogridge	3 1 2 0	6	2
7 Andy Galvin	1 1 2 0	4	1

Eastbourne (A), October 25, L43-46

1 Brian Karger	3 2 1 2 3 3	14	1
2 Troy Pratt	1 3 0 0	4	
3 Peter Ravn	0 3 3 0	6	
4 Josh Larsen	0 1 0 0	1	1
5 Bo Petersen	3 2 3 2 0	10	1
6 †Alan Mogridge	2 2 0 1 T	5	1
7 Andy Galvin	1 1 1 N	3	1

At-a-Glance Results

Belle Vue	W54-36	L27-63	81-99
Bradford	W53-37	L41-49	94-86
Coventry	W49-40	L35-55	84-95
Cradley Heath	L43-47	L31-59	74-106
Eastbourne	W58-32	L43-46	101-78
Ipswich	L38-52	L32-58	70-110
King's Lynn	W51-39	L41-49	92-88
Oxford	W47-43	L41-49	88-92
Poole	L43-47	L32-57	75-104
Reading	L44-46	L36-54	80-100
Swindon	L43-47	L37-53	80-100
Wolverhampton	W49-41	L40-50	89-91

WHO WAS WHO IN '92

Andrew Simon (Andy) GALVIN
Born: November 13, 1965, Whitstable, Kent.
Still not back to his old form after recovering from a broken thigh sustained towards the end of 1990 but established himself as a regular first teamer.

Allan JOHANSEN
Born: December 2, 1966, Odense, Denmark.
Returned to British racing after a two season absence but quit during the season.

Brian KARGER
Born: February 9, 1967, Horsens, Denmark.
Joined the Hammers at the beginning of the season on a full transfer from Swindon after helping them win the 1991 Division Two championship while on loan.

Josh Randall LARSEN
Born: May 12, 1972, Anaheim, California, United States of America.
American newcomer making his British debut.

Robert Tience LEDWITH
Born: November 10, 1971, Forest Gate, London.
Regular member of the club's Reserve League team until he joined Second Division Rye House on loan.
See also Rye House – Division Two.

Alan John MOGRIDGE
Born: November 6, 1963, London.
Captained the club in their first season in the top flight.

Bo PETERSEN
Born: February 21, 1958, Bolbro, Denmark.
High-scoring survivor from the 1991 title winning squad.

Roland Clive POLLARD
Born: August 23, 1971, Lewisham, London.
Local junior pressed into service during an injury crisis.

Troy Gavin PRATT
Born: January 21, 1968, Harlow, Essex.
Made an impressive First Division debut season, scoring his first maximum against Eastbourne at the beginning of September.

Peter RAVN
Born: March 16, 1962, Bogense, Denmark.
Surplus to Coventry's requirements at the beginning of the season. He sat out the first half of the year before making his debut for the Hammers in September.

Ricky SANDFORD
Born: July 7, 1972, Maidstone, Kent.
Reserve League member, called up when the first team hit injury problems.

Colin Peter WHITE
Born: August 12, 1972, Ilford, Essex.
Began the season on loan to Second Division Long Eaton but recalled to fill in for injured riders after being dropped by the Invaders.
See also Long Eaton – Division Two

Our track's just Ace...

CRITICISM of Belle Vue's circuit from various quarters cut no ice with their outspoken promoter John Perrin. "This sport used to be called dirt track racing," he said, "so why people moan because we put dirt down is beyond me!"

Most teams struggled on their visits to Kirkmanshulme Lane with only champions Reading returning home with the league points.

Success came to the Lookers Piccadilly Gold Aces in the H.E.A.T. Fours but, in general, it was a disappointing year for the famous Manchester club, at least as far as the end of season silverware collection was concerned!.

That disappointment stemmed from as early as their pre-season Press and Practice day, intended to introduce the media to a new-look squad.

Perrin had splashed out a five figure fee during the winter to purchase Jason Lyons from Glasgow; Bobby Ott had returned after a year's sabbatical at Wimbledon-Eastbourne; Shawn Moran was set to end his premature retirement and with both younger brother Kelly and Joe Screen re-signing the Aces had a top five that brought envious glances from around the country.

Carl Stonehewer and Max Schofield were earmarked for the two reserve berths and there was every cause to believe that 1992 might just be Belle Vue's year and allow Perrin to achieve his ambition of bringing the League title back to Manchester. That is until that press day.

Schofield decided he wanted Second Division racing and was allowed to move to Newcastle. Stonehewer broke a collarbone during practice but the biggest blow was when Shawn Moran decided that the terms offered to him were unacceptable.

Perrin went on record as saying: "Shawn's a great rider and I've stuck by him through thick and thin but now I've been made a fool of."

With Shooey ruling himself out of action interest was quickly renewed in Edinburgh's Dane Frede Schøtt, a deal was struck and despite one or two scares during the week before the opening of the Aces' latest season he made his debut in a home challenge match against Bradford.

After such a catalogue of early disasters it was no surprise that the Aces finished bottom of their Gold Cup section especially with youngsters Richie Musson and Mike Hampson drafted in at reserve.

Something had to be done and, in a surprise move, Shawn Moran ended his self-imposed exile to return to the fold replacing younger brother Kelly who moved on loan to Swindon.

There was an immediate upturn in the clubs' fortunes particularly at home but four successive away defeats in May were to prove costly.

However such was their home form that the Aces still topped the league table going into October with Jason Lyons having a superb first season in the top flight.

And the Aces had triumphed in the H.E.A.T. Four Team Championship Division One Final at Peterborough.

Perrin wasn't deceived though. He candidly admitted: "We're only on top because we've ridden more matches than everyone else."

He was proved correct as his side were gradually overtaken by others as they completed their valuable matches in hand.

There was disappointment, too, in the Speedway Star Knock Out Cup as they lost out to Bradford in the semi-final – a 32 point deficit at Odsal proving far too much to pull back.

It was Perrin who hit the headlines more often than his riders during the season – over the Shawn Moran affair, blasting the condition of Bradford's track, defending his own, slamming the decision to switch the Dunlop Division One Riders' Championship to Odsal and taking various other verbal swipes at officialdom.

His blunt and outspoken style of management may not win him many allies within the BSPA but there's no denying he loves the sport and Belle Vue in particular. He admitted at the end of the season that it had been a struggle financially throughout 1992 but he was still in there fighting!

1992 RIDER ROSTER

	Club Record								Career Record							
	M	R	Pts	BP	TPts	Ave	F	P	M	R	Pts	BP	TPts	Ave	F	P
Jon Armstrong	2	7	7.0	0.0	7.0	4.000	0	0	2	7	7.0	0.0	7.0	4.000	0	0
Michael Hampson	1	3	0.0	0.0	0.0	0.000	0	0	1	3	0.0	0.0	0.0	0.000	0	0
Jason Lyons	30	135	198.0	33.0	231.0	6.844	1	0	30	135	198.0	33.0	231.0	6.844	1	0
Kelly Moran	80	380	726.0	62.0	788.0	8.295	3	2	368	1651	3230.0	265.0	3495.0	8.468	32	21
Shawn Moran	107	501	971.0	110.0	1081.0	8.631	5	11	327	1975	4143.0	329.0	4472.0	9.057	35	43
Frede Schøtt	30	119	145.0	37.0	182.0	6.118	0	0	33	133	171.0	40.0	211.0	6.346	0	1
Joe Screen	120	563	950.5	87.0	1037.5	7.371	4	2	120	563	950.5	87.0	1037.5	7.371	4	2
Paul Smith	72	254	217.0	51.0	268.0	4.220	0	1	108	384	318.0	68.0	386.0	4.021	0	1
Carl Stonehewer	90	389	461.0	108.0	569.0	5.851	0	0	113	496	586.0	128.0	714.0	5.758	0	0

BELLE VUE

Promoters: Don Bowes and John Perrin.
Address: The Greyhound Stadium, Kirkmanshulme Lane, Gorton, Manchester M18 7BA.
Telephone: 061-223-7720.
Hotline: 0891 800 672
Track Length: 285 metres.
Track Record: 59.3 secs, Erik Gundersen (Cradley Heath), October 9, 1988, Heat 1, Division One Riders' Championship Final.
Seasons in Division One: 28 (1965-1987 [Hyde Road], 1988-1992 [Kirkmanshulme Lane]).
Division One Record: Champions (4), 1970, 1971, 1972, 1982. Runners-up (7), 1969, 1974, 1975, 1976, 1978, 1984, 1988. Third (2), 1980, 1990.
Speedway Star Cup Record: Winners (3), 1972, 1973, 1975. Runners-up (5), 1970, 1978, 1980, 1982, 1984.
Best League Cup Record: Winners (1), 1983. Runners-up (2), 1984, 1987.
Inter League Cup Record: Winners (1), 1975.
Premiership: Winners (1), 1979. Runners-up (1), 1984.
Division One Team Championship: Winners (1), 1992.
Appearances: Chris Morton, 703 (1973-1990).
Points: Chris Morton, 7041 (1973-1990).
World Finalists: Joe Abbott (1937), Peter Collins (1973-74-75-76-77, 1979-80, 1982), Peter Craven (1954-55-56-57-58-59-60-61-62-63), Dick Fisher (1956-57, 1963-64), Ove Fundin (1967), Bob Harrison (1936), Ron Johnston (1955, 1958, 1960), Bill Kitchen (1937-38), Eric Langton (1936-37-38), Louis Lawson (1949, 1951), Henry Long (1952), Cyril Maidment (1964), Ivan Mauger (1969-70-71-72), Shawn Moran (1990), Chris Morton (1976, 1980-81, 1983, 1986-87-88), Dent Oliver (1949-50), Jack Parker (1949-50-51), Peter Ravn (1987), Larry Ross (1981), Sören Sjösten (1962, 1969-70-71, 1974), Frank Varey (1937-38).
Division One Riders' Championship Finalists: Cyril Maidment (1965-66), Ove Fundin (1967), Sören Sjösten (1968, 1973), Ivan Mauger (1969-70-71-72), Peter Collins (1974-75-76-77-78-79-80, 1985), Chris Morton (1981-82-83-84-85-86-87-88), Shawn Moran (1989-90), Peter Ravn (1989), Kelly Moran (1990), Joe Screen (1991-92).
Other Honours: Division One Champions, 1933, 1934, 1935, 1936, 1963. Division Two Champions, 1968, 1969. National Trophy Winners, 1933, 1934, 1935, 1936, 1937, 1946, 1947, 1949, 1958. Division Two Cup Winners, 1969.

1992

BELLE VUE

Back row: Jason Lyons, Paul Smith, Frede Schøtt, Carl Stonehewer. Front: Bobby Ott, Joe Screen and Shawn Moran.

READING (H), April 10, L43-47

1 Bobby Ott	2 2 3 3 3 2	15	1
2 §§Jason Lyons	1 F 1 E 0	2	1
3 †Joe Screen	**3 3 2 3 3 3**	**17**	**1**
4 Kelly Moran	1 0 1 1	3	
5 §Frede Schøtt	0 2 3 0	5	
6 §§Jon Armstrong	1 0 0 T	1	
7 §§Mike Hampson	0 T fxT 0	0	

SWINDON (H), May 8, W54-36

1 Bobby Ott	3 2 2 3 1	11	1
2 Frede Schøtt	2 1 3 1	7	3
3 †Joe Screen	3 3 3 3 2	14	
4 Jason Lyons	1 2 2 3	8	2
5 Shawn Moran	2 1 1 2	6	2
6 Paul Smith	3 1 2 0	6	1
7 Carl Stonehewer	0 1 0 1	2	

Ipswich (A), May 14, L36-53

1 Bobby Ott	R 2 2 3 2 N	9	1
2 Frede Schøtt	2 1 3 1 2	9	3
3 †Joe Screen	R 2 2 R	4	
4 Jason Lyons	0 2 2 0 1	5	
5 Shawn Moran	2 0 1 R N	3	1
6 Paul Smith	2 1 T 0	3	1
7 Carl Stonehewer	1 1 T T 1	3	1

Bradford (A), May 16, L41-49

1 Bobby Ott	1 2 2 1	6	
2 Frede Schøtt	0 1 2 1	4	2
3 †Joe Screen	2 3 3 2 0	10	
4 Jason Lyons	0 2 2 0 1	5	1
5 Shawn Moran	3 3 1 2	9	1
6 Paul Smith	2 0 0 1	3	2
7 Carl Stonehewer	3 1 R R	4	1

Arena Essex (A), May 22, L36-54

1 Bobby Ott	2 fx 1 1	4	1
2 Frede Schøtt	1 3 2 2 1	9	1
3 †Joe Screen	2 2 2 1	7	
4 Jason Lyons	2 2 1 0 R	5	2
5 Shawn Moran	3 3 0 0 2	8	
6 Paul Smith	1 0 1 N	2	1
7 Carl Stonehewer	0 0 1 0	1	1

Eastbourne (A), June 7, L44-46

1 Bobby Ott	1 3 3 3 1 3	14	1
2 Frede Schøtt	0 1 2 0	3	
3 †Joe Screen	3 fx 3 0	6	
4 Jason Lyons	0 2 2 2	6	1
5 Shawn Moran	**3 3 3 3 2**	**14**	**1**
6 Paul Smith	0 T 0 0	0	
7 Carl Stonehewer	1 0 R 0	1	

BRADFORD (H), June 12, W48-41

1 Bobby Ott	R 2 2 3 0 3	10	
2 Frede Schøtt	X R 1 2 0	3	2
3 Joe Screen	*rider replacement*		
4 Jason Lyons	2 2 3 1 1	9	3
5 †Shawn Moran	3 3 R 3 1 2	12	1
6 Paul Smith	1 1 2 1	5	1
7 Carl Stonehewer	3 2 2 2	9	1

King's Lynn (A), June 13, W54-36

1 Bobby Ott	2 3 1 3 3 3	15	1
2 Frede Schøtt	fx 1 3 0 1	5	
3 Joe Screen	*rider replacement*		
4 Jason Lyons	2 3 1 3 1	10	1
5 †Shawn Moran	**3 3 3 3 3**	**15**	
6 Paul Smith	1 0 2 2	5	1
7 Carl Stonehewer	0 1 2 1 R	4	1

Poole (A), June 17, L39-51

1 Bobby Ott	3 1 2 fx	6	
2 Frede Schøtt	1 0 2 1	4	1
3 †Joe Screen	3 2 3 1 1 1	11	1
4 Jason Lyons	0 1 2 N 3 2	8	1
5 Shawn Moran	1 2 0 0	3	
6 Paul Smith	3 1 0 N	4	1
7 Carl Stonehewer	1 2 0 0	3	1

WOLVERHAMPTON (H), June 19, W46-44

1 Bobby Ott	2 1 2 2 1	8	2
2 Frede Schøtt	1 2 1 3	7	1
3 †Joe Screen	2 3 2 2 R	9	
4 Jason Lyons	1 0 1 3	5	1
5 Shawn Moran	3 3 2 1	9	1
6 Paul Smith	3 1 2 1 1	8	3
7 Carl Stonehewer	R 0 0 N	0	

Reading (A), July 13, L44-46

1 Bobby Ott	1 0 1 T	2	
2 Frede Schøtt	0 2 0 0	2	
3 †Joe Screen	3 3 3 1 2 2	14	
4 Jason Lyons	1 2 2 0	5	
5 Shawn Moran	3 3 3 3 3 1	16	
6 Paul Smith	2 0 0 T	2	
7 Carl Stonehewer	0 2 1 0	3	

POOLE (H), July 24, W53-36

1 Bobby Ott	2 2 3 2 3	12	
2 Frede Schøtt	1 3 2 2	8	
3 †Joe Screen	3 3 2 2 1	11	
4 Jason Lyons	2 1 3 3	9	
5 Shawn Moran	3 3 fx 1	7	
6 Paul Smith	0 0 0 2	2	
7 Carl Stonehewer	2 1 1 R	4	

Swindon (A), July 30, W47-43

1 Bobby Ott	3 2 3 3 2	13	
2 Frede Schøtt	1 1 2 2	6	
3 †Joe Screen	F 1 2 2	5	
4 Jason Lyons	0 1 2 2 0	5	
5 Shawn Moran	3 3 3 2	11	
6 Paul Smith	2 2 1 0	5	
7 Carl Stonehewer	0 1 1 0	2	

The original staging of the match on July 9 was abandoned because of rain after four heats. Scorers were: SWINDON 11 BELLE VUE 13 (Bobby Ott 3- 3, Frede Schøtt 0- 0, †Joe Screen 3- 3, Jason Lyons R- 0, Shawn Moran 3- 3, Carl Stonehewer 3- 3, Paul Smith 1-0- 1).

ARENA ESSEX (H), July 31, W63-27

1 Bobby Ott	2 2 3 2	9	
2 Frede Schøtt	1 3 2 1 1	8	
3 †Joe Screen	**3 3 3 3**	**12**	
4 Jason Lyons	**3 3 3 3**	**12**	
5 Shawn Moran	2 1 2 1	6	
6 Carl Stonehewer	3 2 2 3 2	12	
7 Paul Smith	2 1 0 1	4	

COVENTRY (H), August 7, W55-35

1 Bobby Ott	3 1 2 3 2	11	
2 Frede Schøtt	1 2 2 1	6	1
3 †Joe Screen	**3 3 3 3 3**	**15**	
4 Jason Lyons	2 3 1 2	8	1
5 Shawn Moran	3 R 2 1	6	1
6 Carl Stonehewer	3 2 R 3 0	8	1
7 Paul Smith	1 0 0 N	1	

EASTBOURNE (H), August 14, W54-36

1 Bobby Ott	3 3 3 0	9	
2 Frede Schøtt	fnN N N	0	
3 †Joe Screen	**3 3 3 3 3**	**15**	
4 Jason Lyons	2 3 3 3 1	12	1
5 Shawn Moran	3 2 2 1	8	2
6 Carl Stonehewer	F 2 2 R 2 3	9	2
7 Paul Smith	0 1 0 0 E 0	1	

CRADLEY HEATH (H), September 11, W55-35

1 Bobby Ott	3 3 F 3 2	11	1
2 Frede Schøtt	1 2 2 3	8	1
3 †Joe Screen	**3 3 3 3 3**	**15**	
4 Jason Lyons	1 fx 1 1	3	1
5 Shawn Moran	3 2 2 2	9	1
6 Carl Stonehewer	3 2 1 1 2	9	2
7 Paul Smith	0 0 0 N	0	

Oxford (A), September 16, D45-45

1 Bobby Ott	2 2 3 2 2	11	
2 Frede Schøtt	1 1 1 2	5	3
3 †Joe Screen	3 2 3 2 1	11	1
4 Jason Lyons	3 F 2 1	6	1
5 Shawn Moran	1 3 1 3	8	1
6 Paul Smith	2 0 0 N	2	
7 Carl Stonehewer	1 0 0 1 F	2	2

KING'S LYNN (H), September 18, W56-33

1 Frede Schøtt	0 0 1 1	2	1
2 Kelly Moran	*3 3 3 2*	*11*	
3 Jason Lyons	0 3 3 3	9	
4 Jon Armstrong	1 3 0 2	6	
5 †Shawn Moran	**3 2 2 2 3**	**12**	**3**
6 Carl Stonehewer	3 3 2 3 1	12	1
7 Paul Smith	2 1 0 1	4	2

OXFORD (H), September 25, W51-39

1 Bobby Ott	3 1 2 3 1	10	2
2 Frede Schøtt	1 2 1 1	5	1
3 †Joe Screen	2 2 2 2 2	10	1
4 Jason Lyons	2 0 1 3	6	1
5 Shawn Moran	3 3 1 1	8	2
6 Carl Stonehewer	3 3 1 2 2	11	2
7 Paul Smith	1 0 0 N	1	

IPSWICH (H), October 9, W52-38

1 Bobby Ott	F 3 3 3 2	11	1
2 Frede Schøtt	2 2 2 R	6	1
3 †Joe Screen	3 3 2 3 3	14	
4 Jason Lyons	0 2 0 3	5	1
5 Shawn Moran	3 3 2 2	10	1
6 Carl Stonehewer	3 fx0 1 1	5	1
7 Paul Smith	0 1 0 N	1	1

Coventry (A), October 10, W50-40

1 Bobby Ott	3 2 3 3	11	
2 Frede Schøtt	0 0 1 1 1	3	1
3 †Joe Screen	3 2 3 3	11	
4 Jason Lyons	0 2 1 2	5	2
5 Shawn Moran	3 3 1 3 F	10	
6 Paul Smith	3 1 0 0	4	1
7 Carl Stonehewer	2 2 2 0	6	2

Wolverhampton (A), October 12, L40-49

1 Bobby Ott	2 X 3 1	6	
2 Frede Schøtt	0 X 1 T	1	1
3 †Joe Screen	2 3 2 1 0 2	10	
4 Jason Lyons	3 1 1 T 1 1	7	1
5 Shawn Moran	1 3 2 0 3	9	1
6 Paul Smith	2 0 N 0 T	2	
7 Carl Stonehewer	1 1 2 1 N	5	3

Cradley Heath (A), October 24, L38-52

1 Bobby Ott	2 1 R 1	4	
2 Frede Schøtt	0 3 2 2 0	7	
3 †Joe Screen	2 1 1 2 1	7	2
4 Jason Lyons	0 1 2 fx0	3	
5 Shawn Moran	2 3 0 3	8	
6 Paul Smith	0 2 2 T	4	
7 Carl Stonehewer	3 fx 1 1	5	2

At-a-Glance Results

Arena Essex	W63-27	L36-54	99-81
Bradford	W48-41	L41-49	89-90
Coventry	W55-35	W50-40	105-75
Cradley Heath	W55-35	L38-52	93-87
Eastbourne	W54-36	L44-46	98-82
Ipswich	W52-38	L36-53	88-91
King's Lynn	W56-33	W54-36	110-69
Oxford	W51-39	D45-45	96-84
Poole	W53-36	L39-51	92-87
Reading	L43-47	L44-46	87-93
Swindon	W54-36	W47-43	101-79
Wolverhampton	W46-44	L40-49	86-93

WHO WAS WHO IN '92

Jon Thomas ARMSTRONG
Born: August 1, 1974, Manchester.
Diminutive local discovery who made his first team debut in 1992. Regular member of the Colts Reserve League side since 1991.

Michael John HAMPSON
Born: July 26, 1973, Ashton-under-Lyne, Gt. Manchester
Made his first senior appearance because early in the season.

Jason Rodney LYONS
Born: June 15, 1970, Mildura, Victoria, Australia.
Signed from Glasgow at the beginning of the season. Reached the Overseas Final of the 1992 World Championship.

Kelly MORAN – See Swindon

Shawn MORAN
Born: November 19, 1961, Lakewood, California, United States of America.
In dispute with the club at the beginning of the season over financial terms. He made his comeback and replaced brother Kelly who was loaned to Swindon.

Robert Wiliam (Bobby) OTT
Born: November 17, 1962, Inglewood, California, United States of America.
Returned to the Aces after a season on loan to Eastbourne in 1991. Impressive in the Homefire Tests against England and a member of the USA gold medal winning World Team Cup side.

Frede SCHØTT
Born: December 28, 1970, Kolding, Denmark.
An eve of season signing from Homefire League Second Division Edinburgh. Had an impressive debut season in the top flight.

Joseph SCREEN
Born: November 27, 1972, Chesterfield, Derbyshire.
Maintained his progress and took over as the Aces' number one, winning the Dunlop Division One Riders' Championship at Bradford. Third in the World Under 21 Final. Became an automatic choice for his country.

Paul SMITH
Born: July 17, 1970, York, Cleveland.
Back at Kirkmanshulme Lane after finishing the 1991 season on loan to wooden spoonists Swindon. Missed the first few weeks of the season but reinstated and retained his team place for the remainder of the campaign.

Carl Bryan STONEHEWER
Born: May 16, 1972, Manchester.
Fractured his collar bone in the pre-season practice day and missed the first few matches. Struggled to recapture his end of 1991 form and asked for a transfer in the middle of the summer but subsequently withdrew that request as his form improved dramatically. Won his first England cap as a late replacement in the Homefire Test against America on his home track.

Silver's not good enough

ALLAN and Bobby Ham's abiding and unfulfilled dream of winning the league with an all-British team didn't quite materialise but what a season it turned out to be for the Keyline Dukes.

Pride of place goes to skipper Gary Havelock's achievement in becoming the first English World Champion since Michael Lee way back in 1980 (winning the British and Overseas titles along the way). Kelvin Tatum won the Commonwealth Final and qualified for the World Final while Simon Wigg took his customary place in the World Long Track Final.

The team didn't do too badly either, retaining the Speedway Star Knock Out Cup, and, for the second year running, claiming the runners–up spot in the League.

It would, perhaps, be churlish to suggest that a record such as that was disappointing in any way but the firm belief before the season even got underway was that the Keyline Dukes would storm to a clean sweep.

That belief was borne out of the winter activity at the club that saw Havelock signed on a two year deal, Simon Wigg purchased outright from Oxford after being on loan in 1991, Paul Thorp re-signing along with Sean Wilson and a hefty £near £20,000 fee being splashed out to buy England skipper Kelvin Tatum to complete a powerhouse top five.

That left little room for manoeuvre as far as the reserve berths were concerned but Kevin Little was signed on loan from Berwick to join local lad Darren Pearson.

The side just failed to click in the opening weeks of the season with Thorp and Wilson struggling to find form. The first shock was a home defeat against Wolverhampton in the first leg of the Premiership and the Wolves were back at Odsal seven days later and winning, this time in the Gold Cup.

Individually the riders were doing well – Havelock, Tatum, Wilson, Thorp and Wigg all reaching the British Final although Wilson dipped out at that stage. Riding as a team though they didn't manage to hit the same heights although a win at Eastbourne seemed to have got the club back onto an even keel especially as they were without the injured Havelock.

Without him they slumped to a shock home defeat against King's Lynn and Allan Ham started thinking seriously of making a change to the side which eventually was forced upon him anyway. Kevin Little fractured a leg in the home match against Eastbourne, ruling him out for the season.

Ham firstly turned to former Duke Henrik Kristensen but found he wouldn't be available for all matches so turned to his former team-mate Antal Kocso who readily agreed to return to Britain. He added some much needed bite to the lower end of the side and they hit a purple patch towards the end of July, winning six matches on the trot before losing at Reading in the BSPA Cup.

In August Gary Havelock made everyone proud to be British by taking the World title in Poland. A remarkable achievement after all his past hassles but, nevertheless, a well-deserved reward for all his efforts in putting the past behind him.

Back on the domestic front, from the day the Keyline Dukes re-signed Kocso they didn't lose again at home but their difficulty in winning away cost them any hopes of taking the league.

They remained in contention throughout the campaign but it was obvious that Reading would overtake them – which they eventually did as they made up their backlog of outstanding fixtures in hand.

They got revenge though in the K.O. Cup producing a masterful first leg display at Odsal, inspired by a five ride paid maximum from Simon Wigg, which produced a 20 point lead to take to Smallmead which they defended admirably to take the silverware.

A fitting end to the season which promised so much and, in many respects delivered – except for that elusive League title. But you can guarantee that Bradford have set their sights on finishing one place higher in the table in 1993 to end what would be a disappointing hat-trick.

1992 RIDER ROSTER

	Club Record								Career Record							
	M	R	Pts	BP	TPts	Ave	F	P	M	R	Pts	BP	TPts	Ave	F	P
Michael Graves	187	645	588.0	131.0	719.0	4.459	0	2	187	645	588.0	131.0	719.0	4.459	0	2
Gary Havelock	183	897	1761.5	152.0	1913.5	8.533	12	11	187	909	1766.5	152.0	1918.5	8.442	12	11
Antal Kocso	49	200	231.0	33.0	264.0	5.280	0	0	49	200	231.0	33.0	264.0	5.280	0	0
Kevin Little	6	18	10.0	1.0	11.0	2.444	0	0	34	128	76.0	18.0	94.0	2.938	0	0
Stuart Parnaby	16	50	21.0	2.0	23.0	1.840	0	0	16	50	21.0	2.0	23.0	1.840	0	0
Darren Pearson	21	75	28.0	3.0	31.0	1.653	0	0	21	75	28.0	3.0	31.0	1.653	0	0
Richard Smith	1	2	0.0	0.0	0.0	0.000	0	0	1	2	0.0	0.0	0.0	0.000	0	0
Stuart Swales	8	26	8.0	1.0	9.0	1.385	0	0	8	26	8.0	1.0	9.0	1.385	0	0
Kelvin Tatum	21	102	214.0	9.0	223.0	8.745	2	0	374	1658	3558.0	157.0	3715.0	8.963	39	16
Paul Thorp	102	484	854.0	67.0	921.0	7.612	2	2	260	1081	1708.0	139.0	1847.0	6.834	5	5
Simon Wigg	58	289	538.0	64.0	602.0	8.332	0	5	397	1775	3645.0	252.0	3897.0	8.782	25	25
Sean Wilson	60	282	440.0	77.0	517.0	7.333	0	1	223	968	1312.0	183.0	1495.0	6.178	0	1

BRADFORD

Promoters: Northern Speedways Limited (Allan and Bobby Ham).
Address: Odsal Stadium, Rooley Avenue, Bradford, West Yorkshire, BO6 1BS.
Telephone: 0274 729443.
Hotline: 0891 800 673.
Track Length: 338 metres.
Track Record: 58.3 secs, Per Jonsson (Reading), August 9, 1992, Heat 6, World Championship Phurnacite Semi Final.
Seasons in Division One: 7 (1986-1992).
Division One Record: Runners-up (2), 1991, 1992.
Speedway Star Cup Record: Winners (2), 1991, 1992. Runners-up (1), 1990.
Best League Cup Record: Seventh, 1986.
Inter League Cup Record: Winners (1), 1991.
Premiership: Runners-up (1), 1992.
Gold Cup: Winners (1), 1990.
Appearances: Michael Graves, 187 (1986-89, 1991-92).
Points: Gary Havelock, 1761.5 (1986-88, 1990-92).
World Finalists: Jack Biggs (1950), Ron Clarke (1949-50), Neil Evitts (1986), Arthur Forrest (1952-53-54-55-56), Oliver Hart (1949), Gary Havelock (1992), Dent Oliver (1953), Eddie Rigg (1951, 1954), Andy Smith (1989), Kelvin Tatum (1992), Paul Thorpe (1991), Arthur Wright (1955).
Division One Riders' Championship Finalists: Neil Evitts (1986), Sean Willmott (1987), Gary Havelock (1988, 1990-91-92), Paul Thorpe (1989), Marvyn Cox (1990), Simon Wigg (1991).

1992

BRADFORD

Back row: Simon Wigg, Kelvin Tatum, Kevin Little, Paul Thorp, Allan Ham (co-promoter). Front: Darren Pearson, Gary Havelock and Sean Wilson.

King's Lynn (A), May 4, L37-53

1 †Gary Havelock	3 3 1 2 F 1	10	1
2 Sean Wilson	0 1 0 1	2	1
3 §Kelvin Tatum	2 3 2 1 2	10	
4 Paul Thorp	R R 1 N	1	
5 Simon Wigg	1 2 3 0 3 2	11	
6 §Kevin Little	2 T T 0 0	2	
7 Darren Pearson	0 0 T N 1	1	

BELLE VUE (H), May 16, W49-41

1 †Gary Havelock	2 2 3 3 2	12	2
2 Sean Wilson	3 1 3 1	8	1
3 Kelvin Tatum	3 1 3 3	10	
4 Paul Thorp	1 R 0 3	4	1
5 Simon Wigg	2 3 2 2 3	12	1
6 Darren Pearson	1 0 0 N	1	
7 Kevin Little	X 1 1 R 0	2	1

Eastbourne (A), May 24, W46-44

1 †Gary Havelock	*rider replacement*		
2 Sean Wilson	0 2 F 2 3	7	1
3 †Kelvin Tatum	1 2 3 3 0 3	12	
4 Paul Thorp	0 3 3 1 1	8	1
5 Simon Wigg	3 3 1 2 3 2 2	16	2
6 Darren Pearson	0 F T 1 fx	1	
7 Kevin Little	1 0 1 N	2	

Poole (A), May 27, L43-47

1 Gary Havelock	*rider replacement*		
2 Sean Wilson	0 2 3 2 0	7	1
3 †Kelvin Tatum	2 1 2 2 3 3	13	
4 Paul Thorp	0 2 2 2	6	1
5 Simon Wigg	2 3 3 1 2 3 0	14	2
6 Darren Pearson	3 0 0 N 0 0	3	
7 Kevin Little	0 0 N 0 N	0	
8 Stuart Parnaby	*did not rid*		

KING'S LYNN (H), May 30, L40-50

1 Gary Havelock	*rider replacement*		
2 Sean Wilson	0 0 2 0 0 R	2	1
3 †Kelvin Tatum	1 1 0 3 3	8	
4 Paul Thorp	3 3 3 3 2 3 1	18	
5 Simon Wigg	2 R 3 3 2 0	10	1
6 Darren Pearson	1 X T 0	-	
7 Kevin Little	0 T 1 0	-	

Belle Vue (A), June 12, L41-48

1† Gary Havelock	2 1 1 T	4	1
2 Paul Thorp	3 0 3 R	6	
3 Kelvin Tatum	3 3 2 3 3 0	14	
4 Sean Wilson	0 1 1 T	2	
5 Simon Wigg	1 3 2 2 3 1	12	2
6 Stuart Parnaby	0 1 0 N	1	
7 Darren Pearson	2 0 0 0 F	2	

EASTBOURNE (H), June 13, W64-26

1 †Gary Havelock	**3 3 3 2**	**11**	**1**
2 Sean Wilson	**2 2 3 2**	**9**	**3**
3 Kelvin Tatum	**3 3 3 3 3**	**15**	
4 Paul Thorp	1 2 3 2	8	1
5 Simon Wigg	**3 3 3 2 2**	**13**	**2**
6 Darren Pearson	2 1 0 1 1 0	5	1
7 Kevin Little	3 N N N	3	

Ipswich (A), July 23, L40-50

1 †Gary Havelock	1 1 3 1	6	1
2 Paul Thorp	0 T 0 T	0	
3 Kelvin Tatum	1 3 3 1 3 0	11	
4 Antal Kocso	1 3 0 0 N	4	1
5 Simon Wigg	2 2 2 2 X 1	9	2
6 Sean Wilson	3 0 1 T 3 3	10	
7 Darren Pearson	0 0 N 0	0	

Cradley Heath (A), July 25, W50-40

1 †Gary Havelock	1 3 3 3 2	12	1
2 Paul Thorp	0 2 1 1	4	1
3 Kelvin Tatum	2 0 2 3	7	1
4 Antal Kocso	0 1 3 N	4	
5 Simon Wigg	2 3 3 1 2 3	14	
6 Sean Wilson	2 2 3 2 R	9	1
7 Darren Pearson	0 0 N N 0	0	

COVENTRY (H), August 1, W53-37

1 Gary Havelock	*rider replacement*		
2 Paul Thorp	3 2 2 2 2	11	1
3 †Kelvin Tatum	0 2 3 3 3	11	1
4 Antal Kocso	2 2 F R 0	4	2
5 Simon Wigg	3 3 2 3 1 2	14	1
6 Sean Wilson	1 3 1 3 2 1	11	2
7 Darren Pearson	2 0 0 N	2	
8 Stuart Parnaby	*did not ride*		

POOLE (H), August 15, W54-36

1 †Gary Havelock	**2 3 3 3**	**11**	**1**
2 Paul Thorp	3 2 2 2 0	9	2
3 Kelvin Tatum	2 2 3 3 1	11	2
4 §§Richard Smith	fx 0 N N	0	
5 Simon Wigg	3 3 3 1	10	
6 Sean Wilson	3 3 3 2 0 1	12	1
7 Darren Pearson	1 0 0 0	1	

ARENA ESSEX (H), September 5, W49-41

1 †Gary Havelock	3 2 3 3 3	14	
2 Sean Wilson	2 1 3 2	8	3
3 Kelvin Tatum	2 0 3 1	6	1
4 Paul Thorp	3 2 R 1	6	1
5 Simon Wigg	1 1 3 2 1	8	1
6 Antal Kocso	1 0 1 1	3	
7 Darren Pearson	0 1 1 2	4	

Swindon (A), September 10, W49-41

1 †Gary Havelock	2 0 3 2 2	9	2
2 Sean Wilson	3 3 3 1	10	
3 Kelvin Tatum	**3 3 3 3 3**	**15**	
4 Paul Thorp	R 1 1 0	2	
5 Simon Wigg	2 3 0 3	8	
6 Antal Kocso	3 0 0 1	4	
7 Darren Pearson	0 1 0 0	1	

WOLVERHAMPTON (H), September 12, W56-34

1 Simon Wigg	*rider replacement*		
2 Sean Wilson	3 2 2 3 3 3	16	1
3 Kelvin Tatum	2 3 2 3 1	11	1
4 †Gary Havelock	1 3 2 2 2	10	2
5 Paul Thorp	0 3 3 2 3 1	12	
6 Michael Graves	3 0 0 0	3	
7 Darren Pearson	2 1 1 0	4	2

OXFORD (H), September 29, W57-33

1 †Gary Havelock	3 3 3 2 1	12	1
2 Sean Wilson	1 2 2 2 2 3	12	3
3 Kelvin Tatum	*rider replacement*		
4 Paul Thorp	3 1 R 3 3	10	1
5 Simon Wigg	2 2 0 3 3 2	12	2
6 Antal Kocso	2 3 1 3 2	11	1
7 Darren Pearson	0 R 0 N	0	

IPSWICH (H), October 6, W49-41

1 †Gary Havelock	1 3 0 2 3 3	12	
2 Sean Wilson	3 3 2 3 3 0	14	1
3 Kelvin Tatum	*rider replacement*		
4 Paul Thorp	1 2 2 0 3	8	1
5 Simon Wigg	3 R 1 3 1	8	
6 Antal Kocso	3 0 3 0 1	7	
7 Darren Pearson	0 0 0 N	0	
8 Stuart Swales	*did not ride*		

READING (H), October 10, W47-43

1 †Gary Havelock	1 3 3 3 2 3	15	
2 Sean Wilson	0 3 2 3 2	10	2
3 Kelvin Tatum	*rider replacement*		
4 Paul Thorp	1 1 3 0 1	6	1
5 Simon Wigg	3 2 3 3 1 1	13	1
6 Stuart Parnaby	2 0 1 0	3	
7 Darren Pearson	0 0 0 0	0	
8 Stuart Swales	*did not ride*		

Reading (A), October 12, L31-59

1 †Gary Havelock	0 2 2 3 2 2	11	
2 Kelvin Tatum	*rider replacement*		
3 Sean Wilson	1 1 0 1 0	3	2
4 Paul Thorp	2 0 0 1 0	3	
5 Simon Wigg	1 1 1 1 2 0	6	1
6 Antal Kocso	2 2 1 2 1	8	1
7 §§Stuart Swales	0 N 0 0	0	

Oxford (A), October 16, L42-48

1 †Gary Havelock	2 1 3 3 1	10	1
2 Kelvin Tatum	*rider replacement*		
3 Sean Wilson	0 3 2 2 1 1 3	12	3
4 Paul Thorp	3 2 1 1 0	7	
5 Simon Wigg	1 0 2 2 3 0	8	1
6 Antal Kocso	2 1 2 0	5	1
7 Stuart Swales	0 0 N 0	0	

SWINDON (H), October 17, W50-40

1 †Gary Havelock	2 3 R 3 1	9	1
2 Sean Wilson	1 3 2 3 2	11	2
3 Kelvin Tatum	*rider replacement*		
4 Paul Thorp	2 2 3 2 3	12	2
5 Simon Wigg	3 1 1 2 2 1	10	1
6 Antal Kocso	3 2 N 1 N 1 1 0	8	2
7 Stuart Swales	0 0 N 0 N N	0	
8 Stuart Parnaby	*did not ride*		

Wolverhampton (A), October 19, L41-49

1 †Gary Havelock	3 2 1 3 2 3	14	1
2 Kelvin Tatum	*rider replacement*		
3 Sean Wilson	0 3 3 1 0 2	9	
4 Paul Thorp	2 1 0 1 0 N	4	1
5 Simon Wigg	1 1 1 3 0	6	2
6 Antal Kocso	3 0 0 2	5	
7 Stuart Swales	1 0 2 T 0	3	
8 Stuart Parnaby	*did not ride*		

CRADLEY HEATH (H), October 20, W52-38

1 †Gary Havelock	2 3 1 0	6	2
2 Sean Wilson	3 2 2 2	9	1
3 Kelvin Tatum	1 0 3 3	7	
4 Paul Thorp	3 3 3 3 2	14	
5 Simon Wigg	2 2 2 0	6	2
6 Antal Kocso	3 3 1 1 1	9	2
7 Stuart Swales	0 0 0 1	1	

Arena Essex (A), October 23, L37-53

1 †Gary Havelock	2 1 3 3 1 2	12	
2 Sean Wilson	0 0 0 N	0	
3 Kelvin Tatum	3 3 3 3 2	14	
4 Paul Thorp	N 1 1 0	2	
5 Simon Wigg	1 1 0 0 2	4	
6 Antal Kocso	2 0 N 1 1 0	4	1
7 Stuart Swales	0 0 N N 1	1	

Coventry (A), October 31, W55-35

1 †Gary Havelock	**3 3 3 2 2**	**13**	**2**
2 Sean Wilson	1 1 3 1	6	
3 Kelvin Tatum	3 2 R 0	5	1
4 Paul Thorp	1 1 2 3	7	2
5 Simon Wigg	3 2 1 1	7	
6 Antal Kocso	2 3 3 3 3 3	17	
7 Stuart Parnaby	0 0 0 N	0	

At-a-Glance Results

Arena Essex	**W49-41**	**L37-53**	**86-94**
Belle Vue	**W49-41**	**L41-48**	**90-89**
Coventry	**W53-37**	**W55-35**	**108-72**
Cradley Heath	**W52-38**	**W50-40**	**102-78**
Eastbourne	**W64-26**	**W46-44**	**110-70**
Ipswich	**W49-41**	**L40-50**	**89-91**
King's Lynn	**L40-50**	**L37-53**	**77-103**
Oxford	**W57-33**	**L42-48**	**99-81**
Poole	**W54-36**	**L43-47**	**97-83**
Reading	**W47-43**	**L31-59**	**78-102**
Swindon	**W50-40**	**W49-41**	**99-81**
Wolverhampton	**W56-34**	**L41-49**	**97-83**

WHO WAS WHO IN '92

Michael GRAVES
Born: January 26, 1970, Wyke, near Bradford, West Yorkshire.
Sat out most of the season and turned down several approaches from Second Division tracks.

Robert Gary HAVELOCK
Born: November 4, 1968, Eaglescliffe, Cleveland.
Became England's first World Champion since 1980 and took over from Keyline Dukes' team-mate Kelvin Tatum as the Homefire Lions captain.

Antal KOCSO
Born: December 22, 1962, Szeged, Hungary.
Returned to Odsal after missing out on the 1990 and 1991 seasons. Rejoined the club when Kevin Little was injured.

Kevin LITTLE
Born: September 24, 1972, Edinburgh, Scotland.
Joined the Keyline Dukes on loan from Second Division Berwick on the recommendation of former Bandit Kelvin Tatum. Broke his leg in a crash against Eastbourne on June 13 and ruled out for the remainder of the season.

Stuart Graham PARNABY
Born: May 2, 1970, Bradford, West Yorkshire.
Regular member of the Reserve League team who had occasional outings with the first team.

Darren PEARSON
Born: July 26, 1975, Huddersfield, West Yorkshire.
Completed his first full season of League racing after making his debut shortly after his 16th birthday in 1991.

Richard Stephen SMITH
Born: February 11, 1974, Stone, Staffordshire.
Made his senior debut at home to Poole and was a regular member of the Reserve League team.

Stuart John SWALES
Born: May 8, 1975, Northallerton, North Yorkshire.
Nephew of Middlesbrough promoter Tim Swales. Unable to break into the Bears squad he joined Bradford on loan towards the end of the season.

Kelvin Martin TATUM
Born: February 8, 1964, Epsom, Surrey.
Moved to Odsal in a pre-season transfer from Berwick and reached his seventh World Final. Asked to be relieved of the England captaincy at the beginning of the season.

Paul THORP
Born: September 9, 1964, Macclesfield, Cheshire.
Had another inconsistent season and failed to repeat the 1991 form which saw him finish sixth on his World Final debut.

Simon Antony WIGG
Born: October 15, 1960, Aylesbury, Buckinghamshire.
Bounced back after a poor start to the season to finish on a high with his best First Division average since 1987.

Sean WILSON
Born: November 7, 1969, York, North Yorkshire.
Established himself in the England squad as he upped his average by more than a point in a meeting in his best ever season.

1992

COVENTRY

Left to right: John Jørgensen, Brian Andersen, Tommy Knudsen, Michael Warren, Jamie Habbin and Andy Smith.

Sting in tail for Bees

IF THE BBC wanted a new storyline for their 'Casualty' series, they should have been pointed in the direction of Bees promoter Charles Ochiltree. He most certainly would have provided them with a multitude of ideas following a season that saw his side decimated by injury.

It was a season that promised so much but delivered so little after blow upon blow hit the Midlanders. Manager Bob Tanser summed it all up by saying: "I like to have a team talk before each meeting but there was little point towards the end of the season as we didn't have a team left!"

With the introduction of three British riders per team rule for 1992, Roman Matousek and Peter Ravn found themselves discarded from the previous year's squad.

World Under 21 Champion Brian Andersen got the nod for one of four available places for foreigners alongside skipper Tommy Knudsen, Rick Miller and John Jørgensen with Michael Warren also retained from 1991.

Bees splashed out to purchase Paul Bentley from Middlesbrough and the team was completed by the loan signing of Andy Smith from Bradford.

Bentley was the first to succumb to injury when he broke a vertebra in his back in a grass track accident in France. That brought his racing year to an abrupt end in mid-July after he'd earlier shown that the £10,000 spent to purchase him was proving to be a shrewd investment.

At the time of Paul's crash, the Bees were sitting proudly on top of the league table despite having suffered a shock home defeat against Oxford which was quickly forgotten as they romped to victory in their first three away matches at Poole, Wolverhampton and Eastbourne.

The Bees snapped up Jamie Habbin, who'd been left on the sidelines following Mildenhall's closure, to fill the gap after being turned down by Fen Tigers' experienced Melvyn Taylor.

Following three successive away defeats – at Ipswich, Bradford and Belle Vue – Tommy Knudsen broke his collarbone a week before his World Championship semi-final in Austria. Bravely the Bees number one rode in that meeting and made it through to the World Final but he missed the Bees' away match at Oxford which ended in yet another defeat.

He was soon back in action though, having undergone surgery to pin the broken bone but two days after Knudsen had finished fifth in Wroclaw, team-mate Rick Miller broke his collarbone in a challenge match against Arena-Essex and his season was at an end. One week later he was joined on the sick list by Andy Smith who sustained multiple injuries in the World Long Track Final.

Surely nothing else could go wrong! It could, and DID. In the same week that Smith received the news of a long term SCB suspension, Knudsen dropped the bombshell that he was out for the rest of the season too! X-rays on his damaged collarbone revealed that the plate inserted to fill the gap in his fractured bone had cracked and further immediate surgery was needed.

The Bees had to face the last six weeks of the season without all three of their heat leaders and if they could have ended their season there and then they would have jumped at the chance.

Surprisingly they pulled off a victory at Swindon, bolstered by the inclusion of guests Peter Ravn and Jeremy Doncaster but that was to be their last success and the season ended miserably for them, the final eight League fixtures spelling defeat.

Jørgensen, who somehow had escaped the injury nightmare, finally succumbed when he crashed heavily with team-mate Michael Warren against Poole, sustaining severe bruising.

The final hammer blow was when Knudsen announced that he would not be returning to Britain for the 1993 season. Bright spots? Well Knudsen, Miller and Jørgensen made it through to the World Final and fellow countryman Andersen can feel satisfied with his debut season in Britain. Not least for the fact that he managed to avoid injury!

1992 RIDER ROSTER

	Club Record								Career Record							
	M	R	Pts	BP	TPts	Ave	F	P	M	R	Pts	BP	TPts	Ave	F	P
Brian Andersen	26	125	165.0	30.0	195.0	6.240	0	0	26	125	165.0	30.0	195.0	6.240	0	0
Paul Bentley	9	35	37.0	11.0	48.0	5.486	0	0	9	35	37.0	11.0	48.0	5.486	0	0
Chris Clarence	3	6	1.0	0.0	1.0	0.667	0	0	3	6	1.0	0.0	1.0	0.667	0	0
Andy Hackett	142	540	555.0	103.0	658.0	4.874	0	0	142	540	555.0	103.0	658.0	4.874	0	0
Jamie Habbin	17	60	50.0	8.0	58.0	3.867	0	0	17	60	50.0	8.0	58.0	3.867	0	0
John Jørgensen	339	1446	2327.0	325.0	2652.0	7.336	3	12	381	1602	2496.0	356.0	2852.0	7.121	3	13
Scott Kirton	1	2	0.0	0.0	0.0	0.000	0	0	1	2	0.0	0.0	0.0	0.000	0	0
Tommy Knudsen	418	1892	4067.5	272.0	4339.5	9.174	41	28	418	1892	4067.5	272.0	4339.5	9.174	41	28
Rick Miller	375	1536	2298.0	327.0	2625.0	6.836	4	11	375	1536	2298.0	327.0	2625.0	6.836	4	11
Andy Smith	15	72	129.5	8.0	137.5	7.639	0	0	319	1260	1897.5	248.0	2145.5	6.811	8	10
Colin Thorpe	3	5	1.0	0.0	1.0	0.800	0	0	3	5	1.0	0.0	1.0	0.800	0	0
Michael Warren	40	168	169.0	33.0	202.0	4.810	0	0	43	173	171.0	33.0	204.0	4.717	0	0

COVENTRY

Promoter: Charles Ochiltree (in Association with Midland Sports Stadiums Limited).
Address: Coventry Stadium, Rugby Road, Brandon, Near Coventry, CV8 3GJ.
Telephone: 0203-542395.
Clubcall: 0898 12 18 90.
Track Length: 335 metres.
Track Record: 61.3 secs, Peter Ravn (Denmark), June 29, 1983, heat 1, England v Denmark.
Seasons in Division One: 28 (1965-1992).
Division One Record: Champions (5), 1968, 1978, 1979, 1987, 1988. Runners-up (2), 1966, 1967. Third (5), 1965, 1970, 1971, 1983, 1985.
Speedway Star Cup Record: Winners (1), 1967. Runners-up (3), 1983, 1987, 1988.
League Cup Record: Winners (3), 1981, 1985, 1987. Runners-up (1), 1983.
Inter League Cup Record: Second round, 1991.
Premiership: Winners (1), 1986. Runners-up (2), 1988, 1989.
Division One Team Championship: Finalists (1), 1991.
Appearances: Nigel Boocock, 415 (1965-1976).
Points: Nigel Boocock, 4495.5 (1965-1976).
World Finalists: Nigel Boocock (1963-64-65, 1968-69, 1971-72), Rick France (1967), John Jørgensen (1988, 1992), Tommy Knudsen (1981, 1985-86, 1991-92), Jim Lightfoot (1963), Roman Matousek (1990-91), Ken McKinlay (1962, 1964), Rick Miller (1990, 1992), Ron Mountford (1962), Ole Olsen (1977-78-79, 1981, 1983), Jan Simensen (1972), Peo Söderman (1956), Jiri Stancl (1976), Kelvin Tatum (1985-86, 1988-89-90), Jack Young (1960), Henryk Zyto (1960).
Division One Riders' Championship Finalists: Nigel Boocock (1965-66-67-68, 1970-71-72, 1974), Garry Middleton (1973), Bob Valentine (1975), Ole Olsen (1976-77-78-79-80-81-82-83), Tommy Knudsen (1984-85-86-87-88, 1991), Kelvin Tatum (1985, 1987-88-89-90), John Jørgensen (1986, 1990, 1992), Rick Miller (1989).
Other Honours: Division Two Champions, 1953.

READING (H), April 18, D45-45

1 †Tommy Knudsen	1 3 3 3 2	12	
2 §§Brian Andersen	0 T **1** 1	2	1
3 Rick Miller	3 **2** 2 2 0	9	1
4 John Jørgensen	0 0 1 3	4	
5 §Andy Smith	1 3 3 3 **1**	11	1
6 §§Paul Bentley	2 1 E 0	3	
7 Michael Warren	**1** 0 2 R 1	4	1

OXFORD (H), April 25, L38-48

1 †Tommy Knudsen	2 2 3 3 2 1	13	
2 Brian Andersen	**1** 0 3 0	4	1
3 Rick Miller	2 **1** 2 1 3 0	9	2
4 John Jørgensen	**1** 0 fx1	2	1
5 Andy Smith	2 1 0 0	3	
6 Paul Bentley	3 **1** 2 fx1 N	7	1
7 Michael Warren	fnN N T	0	

Poole (A), May 20, W49-41

1 Andy Smith	3 fx3 1 1	8	
2 Brian Andersen	0 2 2 1	5	
3 †Tommy Knudsen	3 3 3 fx	9	
4 Rick Miller	3 **1** 3 3 0	10	1
5 John Jørgensen	**2** 2 1 3	8	1
6 Paul Bentley	3 **2** 1 0 **2**	8	2
7 Michael Warren	1 0 0 N	1	

Wolverhampton (A), June 8, W49-41

1 Andy Smith	2 **1** 2 1	6	1
2 Brian Andersen	0 2 2 **1**	5	1
3 †Tommy Knudsen	**1** 2 3 3 3	12	1
4 Rick Miller	**2** 1 3 3	9	2
5 John Jørgensen	3 2 0 2 1	8	
6 Paul Bentley	3 **1** 0 **1**	5	2
7 Michael Warren	1 2 **1** 0	4	1

IPSWICH (H), May 23, W51-39

1 Andy Smith	2 3 3 2	10	
2 Brian Andersen	**1 2** 1 0	4	2
3 †Tommy Knudsen	3 3 2 3 3	14	
4 Rick Miller	**2** 1 0 3	6	1
5 John Jørgensen	**3 3 3 2 2**	**13**	**2**
6 Paul Bentley	0 0 fxN	0	
7 Michael Warren	2 R 1 **1** 0	4	1

KING'S LYNN (H), June 27, W48-42

1 Andy Smith	2 2 1 2 3	10	
2 Brian Andersen	0 3 3 0 0	6	
3 Tommy Knudsen	*rider replacement*		
4 Rick Miller	3 3 2 1 3 1	13	
5 John Jørgensen	R **2** 1 3 2 3	11	1
6 Paul Bentley	3 0 **1** 0	4	1
7 Michael Warren	1 **2** 0 1	4	1
8 Chris Clarence	*did not ride*		

Eastbourne (A), July 5, W50-40

1 Rick Miller	3 3 3 2 3	14	
2 Chris Clarence	1 0 N N	1	
3 †Tommy Knudsen	3 2 1 0	6	
4 Paul Bentley	1 2 **2 1**	6	2
5 John Jørgensen	3 **1** 2 3 **2**	11	2
6 Michael Warren	**1 1** R 3 0	5	2
7 Brian Andersen	2 1 1 3 0	7	

WOLVERHAMPTON (H), July 11, W56-34

1 Andy Smith	2 2 3 3	10	
2 Paul Bentley	**1 1 1** 0	3	3
3 †Tommy Knudsen	3 3 1 3 **1**	11	1
4 Rick Miller	1 3 **2** 2	8	1
5 John Jørgensen	3 0 3 **2**	8	1
6 Michael Warren	**2** 1 1 1	5	1
7 Brian Andersen	3 2 3 **1** 2	11	1

Bradford (A), August 1, L37-53

1 Andy Smith	2 1 2 2 2 X	9	
2 Brian Andersen	**1** 0 **1** 1	3	2
3 †Tommy Knudsen	1 1 3 1 3 3	12	
4 §§Colin Thorpe	0 T N 0	0	
5 John Jørgensen	1 0 1 1	3	
6 Michael Warren	fx3 R 1 3	7	
7 §§Jamie Habbin	3 0 T R	3	

Belle Vue (A), August 7, L35-55

1 Andy Smith	2 **1 1** 0	4	2
2 Brian Andersen	0 2 1 T	3	
3 †Tommy Knudsen	0 3 3 1 fx	7	
4 Rick Miller	0 2 3 2 2 1	10	
5 John Jørgensen	**1** 1 2 3 0	7	1
6 Michael Warren	2 0 0 1	3	
7 Jamie Habbin	0 1 T 0	1	

Oxford (A), August 21, L41-49

1 Andy Smith	3 3 1 2 3 2 1	15	
2 Brian Andersen	1 0 2 1 1 **2**	7	1
3 Tommy Knudsen	*rider replacement*		
4 Rick Miller	F N N N	0	
5 John Jørgensen	2 2 2 2 0 3 0	11	
6 Michael Warren	0 **1** 0 N	1	1
7 Jamie Habbin	3 **2** 0 **1 1** 0	7	3

EASTBOURNE (H), August 22, W48-41

1 Andy Smith	3 2 2 3 fn	10	
2 Brian Andersen	1 **1** 0 1 **1**	4	2
3 †Tommy Knudsen	3 **2 1** 0 3	9	2
4 Rick Miller	*rider replacement*		
5 John Jørgensen	**1** 3 **1** 1 3 2	11	2
6 Michael Warren	**2** 0 2 2 X	6	-
7 Jamie Habbin	3 3 2 E 0	8	
8 Chris Clarence	*did not ride*		

Coventry's Jamie Habbin was re-introduced in heat 12 as a reserve replacement for Andy Smith who was unable to take part in a re-run after falling. Habbin had originally been excluded from the race for touching the tapes and his replacement Michael Warren was excluded for being the cause of Smith's fall. Habbin scored one point as the only Coventry rider in the re-run but that point was later deducted from the final score by the Speedway Control Board. The on-track score was Coventry 49 Eastbourne 41.

ARENA ESSEX (H), August 31, W55-35

1 Andy Smith	3 **1** 3 1	8	1
2 Brian Andersen	**2** 2 F **2**	6	2
3 †Tommy Knudsen	0 **2** 3 3 1	9	1
4 Rick Miller	**2** 3 3 3 fn	11	1
5 John Jørgensen	3 1 3 0	7	
6 Michael Warren	**2** 3 3 0 0	8	1
7 Jamie Habbin	3 3 0 R	6	

Cradley Heath (A), September 5, L43.5-46.5

1 Andy Smith	**2** 0 3 1 1.5 2 1	10.5	1
2 Rick Miller	*rider replacement*		
3 †Tommy Knudsen	3 3 1 **1** 3 3 3	17	1
4 Jamie Habbin	0 0 N N	0	
5 John Jørgensen	1 1 3 2 0 3	10	
6 Brian Andersen	1 N 2 **1** 1	5	1
7 Michael Warren	0 1 0 N 0	1	

SWINDON (H), September 12, W50-40

1 Dean Barker	**2 1** 2 **1** 1	7	3
2 Rick Miller	*rider replacement*		
3 †Tommy Knudsen	3 2 3 3 3 3	17	
4 Jamie Habbin	**1** 3 0 0	4	1
5 John Jørgensen	2 **2** 2 2 **2** 1	11	2
6 Michael Warren	3 **1 1 1** 2 N 1	9	2
7 Brian Andersen	1 **1** fnN	2	1
8 Chris Clarence	*did not ride*		

Swindon (A), September 17, W47-43

1 Peter Ravn	***1** 0 **1** 3 0*	*5*	*2*
2 Jeremy Doncaster	*2 3 3 3 **2** 2*	*15*	*1*
3 Tommy Knudsen	*rider replacement*		
4 Jamie Habbin	0 0 N N	0	
5 †John Jørgensen	1 1 2 2 3 **1**	10	1
6 Michael Warren	3 2 **1** 0 1 N	7	1
7 Brian Andersen	**2 2 2** 2 F **2**	10	4
8 Colin Thorpe	*did not ride*		

CRADLEY HEATH (H), September 26, L40-50

1 Jan Andersson	*3 2 1 2 1 3*	*12*	
2 Peter Ravn	*0 3 **2 1** 3 1 0*	*10*	*2*
3 Tommy Knudsen	*rider replacement*		
4 Jamie Habbin	0 0 N T	0	
5 †John Jørgensen	1 1 1 **1** 1	5	1
6 Michael Warren	3 **1** 0 N fx	4	1
7 Brian Andersen	**2** 3 2 1 0 T 1	9	1
8 Chris Clarence	*did not ride*		

Ipswich (A), October 1, L35-55

1 †John Jørgensen	**1** 0 **1** 0 **1**	3	2
2 Brian Andersen	2 2 0 E 3 **1** 1	9	1
3 Tommy Knudsen	*rider replacement*		
4 Jason Lyons	0 2 **2** 1 0 2	7	2
5 Sean Wilson	2 2 3 3 2 R 0	12	
6 Michael Warren	0 T 2 N 1	3	
7 Jamie Habbin	1 0 T 0 T	1	
8 Chris Clarence	*did not ride*		

King's Lynn (A), October 4, L41-49

1 †John Jørgensen	0 **1** 2 3	6	1
2 Brian Andersen	2 2 2 **1**	7	1
3 Simon Cross	***2** 3 3 0 **2** 0*	*10*	*2*
4 Chris Clarence	0 0 N T	0	
5 Jan Andersson	*2 2 1 2 1*	*8*	
6 Michael Warren	**1** 0 **2** 1 fx	4	2
7 Jamie Habbin	2 3 **1** 0	6	1

Arena Essex (A), October 9, L40-49

1 †John Jørgensen	2 2 1 2 1	8	
2 Brian Andersen	0 3 0 3 **1** 1	8	1
3 Kelly Moran	*2 2 **2** 3 1 3 0*	*13*	*2*
4 Tommy Knudsen	*rider replacement*		
5 Mitch Shirra	*0 3 2 2 2*	*9*	
6 Michael Warren	fx0 0 N	0	
7 Jamie Habbin	2 0 N 0 0	2	
8 Chris Clarence	*did not ride*		

BELLE VUE (H), October 10, L40-50

1 †John Jørgensen	2 0 3 3 3 2 3	16	
2 Brian Andersen	**1** 0 0 T 1	2	1
3 Tommy Knudsen	*rider replacement*		
4 Jimmy Nilsen	***1** 3 **1** 2 0 2*	*9*	*2*
5 Peter Karlsson	*2 1 0 1 2 R*	*6*	*1*
6 Michael Warren	1 1 T 2 **2**	6	1
7 Jamie Habbin	0 N 0 **1**	1	1
8 Colin Thorpe	*did not ride*		

POOLE (H), October 17, L44-46

1 †John Jørgensen	2 fnN T N	2	
2 Brian Andersen	**1** 2 3 **2** 3 1 **2**	14	3
3 Tommy Knudsen	*rider replacement*		
4 Jeremy Doncaster	*3 2 3 3 2 **2** 3*	*18*	*1*
5 Dean Barker	*0 **1** 0 2 0*	*3*	*1*
6 Michael Warren	**2** fxN N	2	1
7 Jamie Habbin	3 0 0 0 1 0	4	
8 Colin Thorpe	1	1	

Reading (A), October 25, L39-51

1 §§Scott Kirton	0 0 T N	0	
2 Brian Andersen	1 0 N 0 2 **1**	4	1
3 Gert Handberg	*2 2 3 3 0 2 0*	*12*	
4 Tommy Knudsen	*rider replacement*		
5 Tony Olsson	***3** 2 2 2 2 3 2*	*16*	*1*
6 Michael Warren	1 1 T 0 0 0 1	3	
7 Jamie Habbin	3 **1** R N	4	1
8 Colin Thorpe	*did not ride*		

BRADFORD (H), October 31, L35-55

1 Brian Andersen	2 2 1 2 1 **2** 1	11	1
2 Colin Thorp	0 0 fxT	0	
3 Tommy Knudsen	*rider replacement*		
4 Mitch Shirra	*2 2 3 0 3 F 0*	*10*	
5 Steve Schofield	*0 0 2 2 1 2*	*7*	
6 Michael Warren	3 **1** 0 **1** 0	5	2
7 Jamie Habbin	1 **1** 0 T	2	1
8 Scott Kirton	*did not ride*		

WHO WAS WHO IN '92

Brian ANDERSEN
Born: March 13, 1971, Horsens, Denmark.
Joined Coventry during the winter after spending the last month of 1991 with Second Division Newcastle. Won the 1991 World Under 21 Final at Brandon. Younger brother of Edinburgh's Jan Andersen.

Paul BENTLEY
Born: January 18, 1968, Newcastle-upon-Tyne, Tyne & Wear.
Transferred from Middlesbrough during the winter. His season was curtailed when he fractured a bone in his spine in a grass track crash in France.

Christopher CLARENCE
Born: April 16, 1973, Marston Green, West Midlands.
Had the occasional match for the first team, mainly as number eight.

James William (Jamie) HABBIN
Born: May 5, 1966, Welwyn Garden City, Hertfordshire.
Began the season with Second Division Mildenhall and moved to Brandon as a replacement for the injured Paul Bentley after the Fen Tigers' enforced closure.

Andrew Justin (Andy) HACKETT
Born: March 6, 1970, Halesowen, West Midlands.
Missed the full season because of a broken thigh sustained towards the end of 1991. Plans a comeback in 1993.

John JØRGENSEN
Born: July 18, 1962, Middelfart, Denmark.
Reached his second World Final in his ninth successive season at Brandon.

Scott KIRTON
Born: August 6, 1976, Coventry, Warwickshire.
Delayed his speedway debut until after the British Schoolboy Grass Track Championships where he failed to follow up his 1991 victory in the Youth Division Senior A1 class, losing out to Lee Lanham in the Senior A category. Made his debut for the Bees at Reading – riding at number one!

Tommy KNUDSEN
Born: November 9, 1961, Roager, Denmark.
Qualified for his sixth World Final but fractured his collar bone the week before and had to ride with a steel plate holding together the bones. Announced his retirement from British racing at the end of the season – his 13th with the Bees.

Richard Leonard (Rick) MILLER
Born: January 12, 1961, Reseda, California, United States of America.
Celebrated a successful Testimonial and reached his second World Final. Missed the last few weeks of the season with a badly broken collar bone.

Andrew (Andy) SMITH
Born: May 25, 1966, York, North Yorkshire.
Joined the Bees on loan from Bradford. Seriously injured in the World Long Track Final which forced him to miss the last two months of the season. Banned until April, 1993, by the Speedway Control Board after being found guilty throwing a piece of mudguard into the crowd at Wolverhampton on May Bank Holiday.

Colin Simon THORPE
Born: March 23, 1972, Birmingham, West Midlands.
Joined the club on loan from Wolverhampton and made a couple of appearances during the injury crisis.

Michael James (Mick) WARREN
Born: November 17, 1966, Enfield, Middlesex.
Completed his first full season at Brandon after his move there on Hackney's 1991 closure.

At-a-Glance Results

Arena Essex	**W55-35**	**L40-49**	**95-84**
Belle Vue	**L40-50**	**L35-55**	**75-105**
Bradford	**L35-55**	**L37-53**	**72-108**
Cradley Heath	**L40-50**	**L43.5-46.5**	**83.5-96.5**
Eastbourne	**W48-41**	**W50-40**	**98-81**
Ipswich	**W51-39**	**L35-55**	**86-94**
King's Lynn	**W48-42**	**L41-49**	**89-91**
Oxford	**L38-48**	**L41-49**	**79-97**
Poole	**L44-46**	**W49-41**	**93-87**
Reading	**D45-45**	**L39-51**	**84-96**
Swindon	**W50-40**	**W47-43**	**97-83**
Wolverhampton	**W56-34**	**W49-41**	**105-75**

Fate proves a winner

Judging by most pre-season predictions, the Heathens were going to be THE side of 1992. Fate conspired to prove otherwise...as it has so often done so in Colin Pratt's spell at Dudley Wood.

Having assembled a side that had an invincible look about it, they were cruelly robbed of the services of World Champion Jan O. Pedersen as early in the season as May 15.

Peter Ravn crashed and Jan O. came down heavily trying to avoid him and was rushed to hospital where two broken vertebra at the base of his spine which were pinned and plated.

It was a cruel blow to both club and rider. The popular Heathen had climbed to the pinnacle in 1991 by taking the World title and was beginning to enjoy the fruits of that success and his testimonial season. The sport had to face up to the rest of the season without him.

The season had started so brightly for the Heathens who, after shaking off the cobwebs in three challenge matches, topped their section of the Gold Cup and had won their first three league matches.

There had been a hiccup on Easter Monday though when Coventry plundered the Gold Cup points at Dudley Wood after Simon Cross had crashed sustaining a fractured kneecap. Against doctors' advice Crossi rode in the re-staging of the British quarter Final of the World Championship at Exeter, and romped to an amazing 15 point maximum. His individual success was repeated by teenage reserve Scott Smith who took the British Under 21 title at Long Eaton.

Cross couldn't repeat the heroics in the British semi-final on his home track crashing in his opening ride aggravating his knee injury. Then came Jan O's tragic accident and the tide had turned against the Heathens, Greg Hancock was the next to suffer – not through injury – but from an incredible about turn from the A.M.A. that denied Greg progress in the World Championship by stripping him of a seeded place to the Overseas Final.

As if to show his country's Federation how wrong they were he made up for that bitter disappointment by leading the Yanks to the World Pairs title defeating Gary Havelock in a run-off. Billy Hamill, who was seeded through to that Overseas Final, was the next Heathen to suffer a serious injury, breaking his wrist in the Coventry title meeting.

By now Colin Pratt was having to perform miracles to marshal his depleted resources and eased the situation by signing Andy Grahame from Eastbourne. The respite lasted exactly two meetings before the Heathens lost another rider through injury. This time it was Gert Handberg with a broken jaw sustained at Reading.

A much depleted Cradley side then travelled to Glasgow and, perhaps not surprisingly, went down to defeat in the BSPA Cup. Andy Phillips had been signed on loan from Wolverhampton and the gloom lifted as Handberg returned from injury to win his World Championship semi-final as well as helping the Heathens to dispose of Arena-Essex in the Speedway Star K.O. Cup.

Although still mathematically in with a chance of the league title the cup represented the more realistic prospect of honours, However, semi-final opponents Reading had run into a rich vein of form and the Heathens went into the tie reeling from the shock news of Wayne Garratt's death.

A dismal 20 point defeat in the first leg at Smallmead left manager Pratt fuming particularly with the performance of Gert Handberg who failed to live up to his 'third in the world' billing.

Whether Jan O. will ever be fit to return remains to be seen and Simon Cross, another so unlucky with injuries in recent years, spent the winter considering his future, a sure sign that he doesn't see a long term career within the sport.

Colin Pratt, entering his tenth season as co-promoter of the club, will be keeping his fingers crossed that the dreadful jinx which has stalked him during most of his years at Dudley Wood has finally been exorcised measure!

1992 RIDER ROSTER

	Club Record								Career Record							
	M	R	Pts	BP	TPts	Ave	F	P	M	R	Pts	BP	TPts	Ave	F	P
Anthony Boyd	4	13	0.0	0.0	0.0	0.000	0	0	4	13	0.0	0.0	0.0	0.000	0	0
Simon Cross	327	1367	2402.0	276.0	2678.0	7.836	9	7	327	1367	2402.0	276.0	2678.0	7.836	9	7
Andy Grahame	21	92	126.0	18.0	144.0	6.261	0	0	498	2130	3656.0	272.0	3928.0	7.377	20	9
Billy Hamill	77	367	684.5	51.0	735.5	8.016	1	0	77	367	684.5	51.0	735.5	8.016	1	0
Greg Hancock	113	555	977.5	68.0	1045.5	7.535	2	2	113	555	977.5	68.0	1045.5	7.535	2	2
Gert Handberg	160	687	973.0	138.0	1111.0	6.469	0	1	160	687	973.0	138.0	1111.0	6.469	0	1
Peter McNamara	1	2	0.0	0.0	0.0	0.000	0	0	29	90	60.0	12.0	72.0	3.200	0	0
Mark Meredith	3	8	1.0	1.0	2.0	1.000	0	0	3	8	1.0	1.0	2.0	1.000	0	0
Jan O. Pedersen	280	1221	2516.0	239.0	2755.0	9.025	12	24	305	1317	2646.0	253.0	2899.0	8.805	12	24
Andy Phillips	21	95	86.0	13.0	99.0	4.168	0	0	216	795	782.0	141.0	923.0	4.644	0	0
Mark Robinson	51	181	104.0	23.0	127.0	2.807	0	0	51	181	104.0	23.0	127.0	2.807	0	0
Scott Smith	60	242	169.0	38.0	207.0	3.421	0	0	60	242	169.0	38.0	207.0	3.421	0	0
Justin Walker	10	32	18.0	5.0	23.0	2.875	0	0	10	32	18.0	5.0	23.0	2.875	0	0

CRADLEY HEATH

Promoters: Derek Pugh and Colin Pratt.
Address: Cradley Heath Stadium Limited, Dudley Wood Road, Dudley, West Midlands, DY2 0DH.
Telephone: 0384-69008/66604.
Clubcall: 0898 12 18 78.
Track Length: 338 metres.
Track Record: 60.7 secs, Hans Nielsen (Oxford), July 18, 1990, Heat 2, SpeedwayCall Golden Hammer.
Seasons in Division One: 28 (1965-1992).
Division One Record: Champions (2), 1981, 1983. Runners-up (3), 1982, 1986, 1987. Third (4), 1979, 1984, 1988, 1989, 1991.
Speedway Star Cup Record: Winners (7*), 1979, 1980, 1982, 1983, 1987, 1988, 1989. Joint Winners (1), 1986. Runners-up (2), 1971, 1991.
League Cup Record: Winners (2*), 1982, 1984. Joint winners (1), 1986.
Inter League Cup Record: Winners (1), 1979. Runners-up (1), 1977.
Gold Cup: Runners-up (1), 1989.
Premiership: Winners (6), 1982, 1984, 1985, 1988, 1989, 1990. Losers (1), 1983.
Division One Team Championship: Runners-up (1), 1991. Finalists (1), 1991.
Appearances: Alan Grahame, 534 (1978-1985, 1987-1991).
Points: Erik Gundersen, 4858.5 (1979-1989).
World Finalists: Phil Collins (1983), Simon Cross (1987), Alan Grahame (1984), Erik Gundersen (1981, 1983-84-85-86-87-88-89), Billy Hamill (1991), Gert Handberg (1992), Lance King (1983-84), Anders Michanek (1977), Jan O. Pedersen (1985-86-87-88, 1991), Bruce Penhall (1980-81-82), Bernt Persson (1971-72-73, 1975, 1977).
Division One Riders' Championship Finalists: George Major (1965), Brian Brett (1967), Roy Trigg (1968-69), Bernt Persson (1970, 1972), Howard Cole (1973), John Boulger (1974-75-76), Steve Bastable (1978), Bruce Penhall (1979-80-81), Erik Gundersen (1982-83-84-85-86-87-88), Phil Collins (1985), Jan O. Pedersen (1986-87-88, 1991), Alan Grahame (1989), Greg Hancock (1990, 1992).
Other Honours: Provincial League Cup Winners, 1961, 1963.

1992

CRADLEY HEATH

Left to right: Gert Handberg, Andy Grahame, Billy Hamill, Simon Cross, Scott Smith, Andy Phillips and Greg Hancock

EASTBOURNE (H), April 11, W48-41

1 Greg Hancock	3 3 3 0 2	11	1
2 †Simon Cross	2 2 3 0	7	2
3 Billy Hamill	R 1 3 fx	4	
4 Gert Handberg	3 2 1 2	8	1
5 Jan O. Pedersen	2 3 3 3 3	14	1
6 Scott Smith	2 1 R 1	4	
7 Mark Robinson	fx0 0 0	0	

Arena Essex (A), April 17, W47-43

1 Greg Hancock	1 2 2 1	6	1
2 †Simon Cross	0 3 2 E	5	
3 Billy Hamill	2 3 3 2 3	13	1
4 Gert Handberg	3 3 fx3	9	
5 Jan O. Pedersen	2 0 3 3 2	10	2
6 Scott Smith	2 R 0 0 F	2	
7 Mark Robinson	1 0 0 1	2	1

KING'S LYNN (H), April 18, W57-33

1 Greg Hancock	2 1 3 1	7	1
2 †Simon Cross	3 3 3 2 2	13	2
3 Billy Hamill	3 2 1 0	6	
4 Gert Handberg	3 2 3 3 3	14	1
5 Jan O. Pedersen	2 3 3 3	11	1
6 Scott Smith	3 1 1 1	6	1
7 Mark Robinson	F 0 0 0	0	

SWINDON (H), May 25, W51-38

1 †Simon Cross	3 3 3 1 3 0	13	
2 Greg Hancock	2 3 1 3 2 3	14	2
3 Billy Hamill	R 2 2 3 3	10	1
4 Jan O. Pedersen	*rider replacement*		
5 Gert Handberg	2 3 3 0 0	8	1
6 Scott Smith	2 2 1 1 0	6	1
7 Anthony Boyd	R 0 0 N	0	
8 Peter McNamara	*did not ride*		

Swindon (A), May 25, L44-46

1 †Simon Cross	1 3 0 2 1	7	1
2 Greg Hancock	2 2 2 3 1 1	11	2
3 Billy Hamill	2 2 3 2 2 0	11	1
4 Gert Handberg	0 2 1 3 3	9	
5 Jan O. Pedersen	*rider replacement*		
6 Scott Smith	3 0 2 R 1	6	2
7 Anthony Boyd	0 0 N 0	0	
8 Mark Meredith	*did not ride*		

READING (H), June 27, L42-47

1 †Simon Cross	1 0 1 3 2 3 0	10	2
2 Jan O. Pedersen	*rider replacement*		
3 §Andy Grahame	0 1 1 2 2 0	6	1
4 Gert Handberg	3 0 0 2 3 1	9	1
5 Greg Hancock	2 2 2 2 3 1 3	15	1
6 Scott Smith	fnN T T	0	
7 Justin Walker	2 0 T 0	2	
8 Mark Meredith	*did not ride*		

Reading (A), June 29, L37-53

1 †Simon Cross	1 2 1 3 2 1	10	1
2 Billy Hamill	*rider replacement*		
3 Andy Grahame	3 1 1 2 1 0	8	1
4 Greg Hancock	2 3 3 3 1 0 2	14	
5 Gert Handberg	2 fxN N T	2	1
6 Mark Meredith	1 0 0 T T	1	1
7 Justin Walker	2 0 0 N 0 0 0	2	
8 Shaun Naylor	*did not ride*		

OXFORD (H), July 4, W50-40

1 †Simon Cross	1 2 3 3 2 3	14	1
2 Billy Hamill	*rider replacement*		
3 Greg Hancock	3 2 3 3 3 2	16	1
4 Andy Grahame	2 0 2 3 1	8	1
5 Jason Lyons	*0 2 1 3 0*	*6*	*1*
6 Scott Smith	2 0 N 0	2	1
7 §Andy Phillips	3 0 1 0 0	4	
8 Justin Walker	*did not ride*		

BRADFORD (H), July 25, L40-50

1 †Simon Cross	2 3 2 0 0 E	7	1
2 Billy Hamill	*rider replacement*		
3 Greg Hancock	3 3 2 2 2 1 0	13	1
4 Jimmy Nilsen	*1 1 1 N 1*	*4*	
5 Andy Grahame	3 0 1 1 2 1	8	
6 Scott Smith	1 1 0 N	2	
7 Andy Phillips	3 0 0 0 N 3	6	
8 Justin Walker	*did not ride*		

Ipswich (A), August 20, D45-45

1 †Simon Cross	2 3 1 3	9	1
2 Andy Grahame	3 2 1 0	6	1
3 Greg Hancock	3 2 3 3 3	14	
4 Billy Hamill	3 2 1 2 1 1	10	1
5 Gert Handberg	1 0 T 2	3	
6 Andy Phillips	0 0 0 1	1	1
7 Scott Smith	1 1 0 0	2	

Poole (A), September 2, L41-49

1 †Simon Cross	3 3 2 3 0	11	
2 Andy Grahame	0 0 3 1	4	1
3 Greg Hancock	1 1 2 0	4	
4 Billy Hamill	1 1 N 2	4	1
5 Gert Handberg	3 3 3 fx1	10	
6 Andy Phillips	0 3 0 0 2 2	7	
7 Scott Smith	1 R N 0	1	

COVENTRY (H), September 5, W46.5-43.5

1 †Simon Cross	1 R 0 1	2	1
2 Andy Grahame	0 2 3 3	8	
3 Billy Hamill	2 1 1.5 3	7.5	1
4 Gert Handberg	2 2 2 2 2	10	2
5 Greg Hancock	3 3 3 1 0	10	
6 Andy Phillips	3 0 2 0	5	
7 Scott Smith	2 2 0 0	4	2

Belle Vue (A), September 11, L35-55

1 Greg Hancock	2 3 3 2 1	11	
2 Gert Handberg	fxN T N	0	
3 †Simon Cross	1 1 R N	2	
4 Andy Grahame	0 0 2 0	2	
5 Billy Hamill	2 2 3 2 3 1	13	
6 Andy Phillips	1 1 0 T 0 0	2	1
7 Scott Smith	2 0 1 1 1 0	5	2

ARENA ESSEX (H), September 12, W59-31

†Simon Cross	3 1 2 2 2	10	3
2 Andy Grahame	1 3 3 3 2	12	
3 Billy Hamill	3 2 2 3 1 2	13	2
4 Gert Handberg	*rider replacement*		
5 Greg Hancock	3 3 1 3 3	13	
6 Andy Phillips	3 2 0 3 3	11	1
7 Scott Smith	0 0 0 0	0	
8 Justin Walker	*did not ride*		

WOLVERHAMPTON (H), September 23, W50-40

1 †Simon Cross	1 3 3 0	7	1
2 Andy Grahame	2 0 1 1	4	
3 Billy Hamill	2 2 3 2	9	1
4 Gert Handberg	0 1 2 3 2	8	1
5 Greg Hancock	2 3 E 1 3	9	1
6 Andy Phillips	3 3 1 3 1 0	11	1
7 Scott Smith	1 0 1 N N	2	

Coventry (A), September 26, W50-40

1 †Simon Cross	2 3 2 2	9	1
2 Andy Grahame	1 2 1 0	4	2
3 Billy Hamill	3 2 3 2	10	1
4 Greg Hancock	2 2 3 3 2	12	3
5 Gert Handberg	3 3 3 2 3	14	
6 Andy Phillips	1 0 0 0 0	1	
7 Scott Smith	0 0 0 N	0	

Wolverhampton (A), September 30, W46-44

1 Greg Hancock	3 2 2 3 3	13	
2 Andy Grahame	2 1 2 fn	5	2
3 Billy Hamill	2 3 3 3 1	12	
4 †Simon Cross	fx1 3 2	6	1
5 Gert Handberg	2 0 0 R	2	
6 Andy Phillips	3 2 0 0 0 1	6	1
7 Scott Smith	2 0 N 0	2	1

Oxford (A), October 9, D45-45

1 Greg Hancock	3 3 2 3 1	12	1
2 Andy Grahame	2 0 3 1	6	2
3 Billy Hamill	3 2 3 2 2	12	
4 †Simon Cross	3 0 2 1	6	
5 Gert Handberg	2 2 0 3	7	1
6 Andy Phillips	0 0 0 0	0	
7 Scott Smith	1 0 1 0	2	

POOLE (H), October 10, L39-51

1 †Simon Cross	0 1 3 2 2	8	2
2 Andy Grahame	1 2 3 0	6	
3 Billy Hamill	2 0 2 0 0	4	1
4 Gert Handberg	1 1 3 2	7	1
5 Greg Hancock	2 3 3 2 2 fx	12	
6 Andy Phillips	1 0 T 0	1	
7 Scott Smith	0 T 1 0	1	

At-a-Glance Results

Arena Essex	W59-31	L36-54	95-85
Belle Vue	W52-38	L35-55	87-93
Bradford	L40-50	L38-52	78-102
Coventry	W46.5-43.5	W50-40	96.5-83.5
Eastbourne	W48-41	W55-35	103-76
Ipswich	W51-39	D45-45	96-84
King's Lynn	W57-33	W50-40	107-73
Oxford	W50-40	D45-45	95-85
Poole	L39-51	L41-49	80-100
Reading	L42-47	L37-53	79-100
Swindon	W51-38	L44-46	95-84
Wolverhampton	W50-40	W46-44	96-84

IPSWICH (H), October 17, W51-39

1 †Simon Cross	1 3 1 1	6	
2 Andy Grahame	E 2 1 3 0	6	1
3 Billy Hamill	3 2 2 1	8	1
4 Gert Handberg	2 2 3 3	10	1
5 Greg Hancock	3 1 3 3 3	13	1
6 Andy Phillips	0 1 0 3 1	5	1
7 Scott Smith	2 0 1 0	3	1

Bradford (A), October 20, L38-52

1 †Simon Cross	1 1 2 1	5	1
2 Andy Grahame	0 0 T 1	1	1
3 Billy Hamill	0 1 3 1	5	1
4 Greg Hancock	0 3 3 3 2 3	14	
5 Gert Handberg	1 2 2 2 0	7	1
6 Andy Phillips	2 0 0 0	2	
7 Scott Smith	1 2 1 0	4	1

Eastbourne (A), October 18, W55-35

1 Greg Hancock	3 3 3 3	12	
2 Andy Grahame	2 2 3 2	9	3
3 Billy Hamill	2 3 3 3 1	12	1
4 †Simon Cross	2 3 3 2 2	12	1
5 Gert Handberg	1 fx2 0	3	2
6 Andy Phillips	3 2 1 1	7	1
7 Scott Smith	0 0 R 0	0	

BELLE VUE (H), October 24, W52-38

1 Greg Hancock	3 3 3 1 3	13	
2 Justin Walker	1 0 0 N	1	
3 †Simon Cross	3 2 3 3 2	13	1
4 Gert Handberg	1 2 3 2	8	
5 Billy Hamill	3 fx3 2	8	1
6 Andy Phillips	1 1 0 N 1	3	1
7 Scott Smith	2 3 R 0 N 1	6	1

King's Lynn (A), October 27, W50-40

1 Greg Hancock	3 2 3 2	10	
2 Justin Walker	1 1 1 0	3	2
3 †Simon Cross	3 3 2 3 3	14	
4 Billy Hamill	3 3 3 1 2	12	2
5 Gert Handberg	0 0 1 2	3	
6 Andy Phillips	1 0 N 1	2	1
7 Scott Smith	3 0 2 1 0	6	1

WHO WAS WHO IN '92

Anthony Phillip BOYD
Born: May 23, 1971, Ashton-under-Lyne, Lancashire.
Made three first team appearances during an injury crisis.

Simon James CROSS
Born: May 31, 1965, Hereford, Hereford & Worcester.
Took over as the Heathens skipper in his full-time track return after breaking a bone in his back in the 1990 World Pairs Final.

Andrew George (Andy) GRAHAME
Born: September 10, 1957, Birmingham.
Began the season at Eastbourne but moved to Dudley Wood as a replacement for the injured Jan O. Pedersen.

William Gordon (Billy) HAMILL
Born: May 23, 1970, San Marino, California, United States of America.
Continued his improvement in his third season as a Heathen. Overcame a broken wrist which ended his World Championship challenge.

Gregory Alan (Greg) HANCOCK
Born: June 3, 1970, Whittier, California, United States of America.
Spent his fourth season at Dudley Wood.

Gert HANDBERG
Born: May 30, 1969, Brastrup, Denmark.
Qualified for his first World Final, finishing third in his debut. Also won the Champions Cup but often disappointed in domestic racing.

Peter Lee McNAMARA
Born: March 23, 1968, Halifax, West Yorkshire.
Signed for the Heathens on loan from Second Division Long Eaton but only had the occasional first team opportunity. Rode in a Knock Out Cup match only.

Mark Stephen MEREDITH
Born: February 11, 1974, Krefeld, Germany.
Recovered from a broken leg to re-established himself with the Reserve League side.

Shaun Alan NAYLOR
Born: December 20, 1971, Leicester, Leicestershire.
Made a stand-in appearance as number eight on loan from Second Division Long Eaton.

Jan Osvald PEDERSEN
Born: November 9, 1962, Middlefart, Denmark.
Fractured a bone in his spine in an individual meeting in his native Denmark which ruled him out of defending his World title.

Andrew David (Andy) PHILLIPS
Born: October 10, 1968, Worcester, Hereford & Worcester.
Signed for Poole at the beginning of the season but lost his team place with the JTC Pirates before moving back to the Midlands.

Mark ROBINSON
Born: February 7, 1968, Cradley Heath, West Midlands.
Began the season as the Heathens reserve but announced his retirement because of financial problems.

Scott Anthony SMITH
Born: September 29, 1972, Sheffield, South Yorkshire.
Became the 1992 British Under 21 Champion with a fine performance at Long Eaton.

Justin Lee WALKER
Born: February 16, 1971, Wordsley, West Midlands.
Returned to Dudley Wood on a full-time basis on the closure of Second Division Milton Keynes.

Last gasp saviour

EVERY cloud has a silver lining goes the sating and there was plenty of cloud at Arlington over the year but there was also that Silver lining when Len Silver was revealed as the new promoter after a seven year absence from running his own track.

The news was revealed to the fans immediately after the Eagles final home match of the season and gave them cause for a double celebration. Not only was the club's future secure but so too was their First Division status as their side had just defeated Arena-Essex in a nail-biting finish.

Eastbourne simply had to win that match as any other result would have consigned them to the Second Division and it was Len's own son Andrew and Peter Nahlin who grabbed a share of the points in a dramatic last heat that secured the Eagles those vital two league points.

That the Eagles were in business at all in 1992 was due only due to the intervention of the late John Cearns, for decades a champion of the sport at Wimbledon, who helped to resolve a board-room battle that threatened the club's existence.

Co-promoters Peter Brown and Trevor Geer set about assembling their side looking to improve on their twelfth position in the League in 1991. Bobby Ott had returned to parent club Belle Vue, similarly Armando Castagna went back to Reading. A further blow was the rejection of a work permit for Deon Prinsloo to ride in the First Division and with both Gordon Kennett and Jesper Olsen signing for Second Division clubs, a major re-building task was on hand.

The first move was hardly a surprise as they bought Andrew Silver from Swindon convinced that he could re-capture the form that had once made him England's hottest prospect. Neville Tatum returned after a loan spell at Ipswich and Bob Dugard's influence had much to do with Finn Olli Tyrvainen returning for another crack at making the grade. Bob's own son Paul was pencilled in at reserve and, finally, Glenn Doyle was signed on loan from Bradford. Skipper Andy Grahame and Nathan Simpson were the only two retained from the 1991 side.

A 14 point victory over Arena-Essex in the opening Gold Cup fixture flattered to deceive. The Eagles then lost nine consecutive matches including a home defeat at the hands of Wolverhampton and only a last ditch effort prevented an embarrassing BSPA Cup defeat at Long Eaton.

Attendances had dipped alarmingly and a crisis meeting was held which resulted in a new pay structure being implemented – gearing riders' earnings to crowd levels at home matches. Changes to the team were imperative to halt the slump and attention was turned to Scandinavia. They swooped for Swede Stefan Dannö who replaced Tatum.

A paid 10 return on his debut was encouraging but clearly not the sole answer to the Eagles' problems. Travelling from the Midlands was taking its toll on skipper Andy Grahame who was transferred to Cradley Heath. That paved the way for a brief return to Arlington for former favourite Bobby Schwartz but, behind the scenes, a deal had been struck to take Peter Nahlin on loan from Swindon. When his work permit arrived Schwartz returned to the States and Nahlin soon settled in.

Continuity of fixtures proved an added obstacle to overcome: Friday night racing drew abysmal attendances and with preference having to be given to shared events on several Sundays it hardly helped the team establish any measure of consistency.

Despite improved performances with Nahlin in the side the Eagles hovered in the bottom three all summer although another victory over Arena-Essex – this time in the BSPA Cup – boosted morale.

Poole ended the Eagles' interest in that competition at the quarter-final stage and while a home victory over fellow strugglers Swindon seemed to have eased relegation fears they soon re-appeared. A dismal defeat against Cradley Heath left the Eagles having to win that last match against Arena-Essex. It all came down to the last heat and the rest is history!

1992 RIDER ROSTER

	Club Record								Career Record							
	M	R	Pts	BP	TPts	Ave	F	P	M	R	Pts	BP	TPts	Ave	F	P
Stefan Dannö	21	91	111.0	19.0	130.0	5.714	0	0	**21**	**91**	**111.0**	**19.0**	**130.0**	**5.714**	**0**	**0**
Glenn Doyle	19	84	112.0	10.0	122.0	5.810	0	0	**119**	**513**	**680.0**	**83.0**	**763.0**	**5.949**	**0**	**1**
Paul Dugard	20	75	68.0	21.0	89.0	4.747	0	0	**73**	**262**	**192.0**	**46.0**	**238.0**	**3.634**	**0**	**0**
Andy Grahame	33	178	390	11	401	9.011	3	0	**498**	**2130**	**3656.0**	**272.0**	**3928.0**	**7.377**	**20**	**9**
Darren Grayling	6	16	4.0	1.0	5.0	1.250	0	0	**19**	**60**	**22.0**	**4.0**	**26.0**	**1.733**	**0**	**0**
Peter Nahlin	18	101	208.0	10.0	218.0	8.634	1	0	**114**	**534**	**856.5**	**114.0**	**970.5**	**7.270**	**2**	**1**
Bobby Schwartz	41	183	417.5	9.0	426.5	9.322	10	1	**310**	**1382**	**3028.5**	**163.0**	**3191.5**	**9.237**	**32**	**14**
Andrew Silver	26	144	216.0	21.0	237.0	6.583	0	0	**175**	**828**	**1286.0**	**139.0**	**1425.0**	**6.884**	**1**	**3**
Nathan Simpson	50	239	282.0	60.0	342.0	5.724	0	0	**50**	**239**	**282.0**	**60.0**	**342.0**	**5.724**	**0**	**0**
Neville Tatum	13	52	49.0	7.0	56.0	4.308	0	0	**78**	**315**	**368.0**	**54.0**	**422.0**	**5.359**	**1**	**0**
Olli Tyrvainen	103	387	387.5	65.0	452.5	4.677	0	2	**139**	**518**	**519.5**	**88.0**	**607.5**	**4.691**	**0**	**2**
Paul Woods	213	947	1568.0	140.0	1708.0	7.214	6	7	**268**	**1141**	**1739.0**	**183.0**	**1922.0**	**6.738**	**6**	**7**

EASTBOURNE

Promoters: Len Silver and Jon Cook.
Addresses: Arlington Stadium, Arlington Road West, Hailsham, East Sussex, BN27 3RE. **Telephone:** 0323-841642.
Hotline: 0891 800 694.
Track Length: 302 metres.
Track Record: 56.3 secs, Dean Barker (Oxford), August 16, 1992, Heat 6, Eastbourne v Oxford (Division One).
Seasons in Division One: 8 (1979-84, 1991-92).
Division One Record: Eleventh, 1984.
Speedway Star Cup Record: Semi Finalists, 1982.
League Cup Record: Runners-up, Southern Section, 1982.
Inter League Cup Record: Round Two, 1979 and 1980.
Appearances: Paul Woods, 213 (1979-84, 1992).
Points: Gordon Kennett, 1815.5 (1979-82, 1991).
World Finalists: Kelly Moran (1982), Kai Niemi (1980).
Division One Riders' Championship Finalists: Andy Grahame (1991), Gordon Kennett (1979-80-81-82), Bobby Schwartz (1984), Paul Woods (1983), Peter Nahlin (1992).
Other Honours: Division Two Champions, 1971, 1977, 1986, 1987. Division Three Champions, 1947. Division Two Cup Winners, 1975, 1977, 1978, 1985, 1986, 1987.

■ *Gordon Kennett holds the all-time Division Two appearance record for Eastbourne and, in total, has made 477 appearances for the club, scoring a record 5339 points.*

WIMBLEDON began the 1991 season at Plough Lane but moved to Eastbourne after their last meeting on Wednesday, June 5.
The first 1991 meeting at Eastbourne was on Friday, June 30.
At the end of the 1992 season Peter Brown and Trevor Geer resigned as co-promoters with Len Silver returning to promoting.

1992

EASTBOURNE

Back row: Glenn Doyle, Olli Tyrvainen, Darren Grayling, Paul Dugard, Stefan Dannö, Peter Brown (co-promoter). Front: Andrew Silver, Andy Grahame and Nathan Simpson.

Cradley Heath (A), April 11, L41-48

1 §Andrew Silver	1 1 1 1	4	2
2 Nathan Simpson	0 0 2 T	2	
3 †Andy Grahame	3 0 2 2 3 1	11	
4 Olli Tyrvainen	0 2 2 2	6	1
5 §Glenn Doyle	1 3 1 2 3 0	10	2
6 Neville Tatum	3 1 R 1	5	
7 §Paul Dugard	fx 2 1 T	3	2

WOLVERHAMPTON (H), May 10, L37-53

1 Andrew Silver	2 1 1 2 1	7	1
2 Olli Tyrvainen	1 2 X 0	3	1
3 †Andy Grahame	1 2 2 3 2	10	
4 Glenn Doyle	1 2 0 3 0	6	
5 Nathan Simpson	0 0 1 1	2	2
6 Neville Tatum	3 F 0 T	3	
7 Paul Dugard	2 3 0 1	6	1

BRADFORD (H), May 24, L44-46

1 Andrew Silver	3 2 2 1 0	8	1
2 Olli Tyrvainen	2 1 3 R	6	2
3 †Andy Grahame	3 2 3 2 1	11	
4 Nathan Simpson	1 1 2 3	7	1
5 Glenn Doyle	2 0 1 0	3	
6 Neville Tatum	3 1 0 0	4	
7 Paul Dugard	2 2 0 1	5	2

BELLE VUE (H), June 7, W46-44

1 Andrew Silver	2 2 2 3 1 1	11	2
2 Olli Tyrvainen	3 1 1 1 1	7	2
3 †Andy Grahame	2 2 0 2 3	9	
4 Glenn Doyle	*rider replacement*		
5 Nathan Simpson	1 0 1 0	2	2
6 §§Stefan Dannö	2 1 1 2 2	8	2
7 Paul Dugard	3 3 1 2 0	9	1
8 Darren Grayling	*did not ride*		

Bradford (A), June 13, L26-64

1 Andrew Silver	1 0 0 1 1 1 1	5	1
2 Olli Tyrvainen	0 1 2 2 0	5	
3 †Andy Grahame	2 1 2 2 1 3 0	11	
4 Nathan Simpson	2 1 0 0 1	4	1
5 Glenn Doyle	*rider replacement*		
6 Stefan Dannö	R 0 0 T	0	
7 Paul Dugard	1 0 X T	1	

Wolverhampton (A), June 15, L40-49

1 Andrew Silver	2 1 1 3 1 1	9	1
2 Olli Tyrvainen	1 2 1 2	6	2
3 †Andy Grahame	2 2 2 2 0 0	8	1
4 Glenn Doyle	*rider replacement*		
5 Nathan Simpson	0 3 1 2	6	
6 Paul Dugard	1 1 3 1 0 1	7	3
7 Stefan Dannö	0 1 N 3 0	4	1
8 Paul Mitchell	*did not ride*		

COVENTRY (H), July 5, L40-50

1 †Andrew Silver	fx3 fx3 3 1	10	
2 Olli Tyrvainen	2 0 3 1	6	
3 Bobby Schwartz	0 3 2 0	5	
4 Glenn Doyle	2 2 2 1 2 0	9	1
5 Paul Dugard	0 1 0 T	1	1
6 Stefan Dannö	3 2 0 2	7	
7 Nathan Simpson	0 T 1 1	2	2

POOLE (H), July 12, D45-45

1 †Andrew Silver	2 3 3 3 R	11	
2 Paul Dugard	0 1 0 N	1	
3 Glenn Doyle	3 3 X 2 1	9	
4 §§Peter Nahlin	3 1 fx2	6	1
5 Olli Tyrvainen	1 2 1 1	5	2
6 Nathan Simpson	0 1 1 2	4	
7 Stefan Dannö	3 2 2 1 1	9	2

Swindon (A), July 16, D45-45

1 †Andrew Silver	3 1 2 3 0	9	1
2 Paul Dugard	0 0 3 3	6	
3 Glenn Doyle	2 1 2 0	5	1
4 Olli Tyrvainen	0 1 0 N	1	
5 Peter Nahlin	2 3 3 3 2	13	
6 Nathan Simpson	0 2 1 F	3	1
7 Stefan Dannö	3 1 1 3 0	8	1

Poole (A), July 22, L38-52

1 †Andrew Silver	2 2 1 1 3	9	1
2 Paul Dugard	1 0 N 0	1	1
3 Glenn Doyle	3 1 2 0 R	6	1
4 Olli Tyrvainen	1 0 0 N	1	1
5 Peter Nahlin	2 3 2 2 1	10	
6 Nathan Simpson	1 2 1 1 0	5	2
7 Stefan Dannö	2 2 0 2	6	1

KING'S LYNN (H), August 2, W48-42

1 †Andrew Silver	2 2 2 2 1	9	2
2 Olli Tyrvainen	1 1 0 1	3	3
3 Glenn Doyle	3 1 1 F	5	1
4 Peter Nahlin	E 3 3 2 2	10	
5 Stefan Dannö	0 2 2 2	6	1
6 Paul Dugard	2 0 0 N	2	1
7 Nathan Simpson	3 3 3 1 2 1	13	2

King's Lynn (A), August 8, L42-48

1 †Andrew Silver	2 1 2 1 0	6	
2 Olli Tyrvainen	0 0 T T	0	
3 Glenn Doyle	3 2 2 3 1 0	11	1
4 Stefan Dannö	1 2 3 2	8	
5 Peter Nahlin	fx0 1 2 3 3	9	1
6 Paul Dugard	2 F T 1	3	
7 Nathan Simpson	1 1 1 2	5	3

In a race-off for the bonus point Peter Nahlin lost to Henrik Gustafsson.

Belle Vue (A), August 14, L36-54

1 †Andrew Silver	2 0 1 3 2 2 2	12	
2 Peter Nahlin	*rider replacement*		
3 Glenn Doyle	fnN T N	0	
4 Olli Tyrvainen	1 2 2 1 0	6	1
5 Stefan Dannö	0 1 1 0 1 2	5	2
6 Paul Dugard	2 0 0 1 1 0	4	2
7 Nathan Simpson	1 3 1 1 1 2	9	2
8 Nathan Gaymer	*did not ride*		

OXFORD (H), August 16, W49-41

1 †Andrew Silver	2 3 0 3 2 3	13	1
2 Olli Tyrvainen	fnN N N	0	
3 Glenn Doyle	*rider replacement*		
4 Peter Nahlin	1 2 2 3 3	11	2
5 Stefan Dannö	2 3 3 2 2 1	13	
6 Paul Dugard	1 2 0 1 0 2	6	3
7 Nathan Simpson	fx1 2 2 1 0	6	2
8 Paul Mitchell	*did not ride*		

Coventry (A), August 22, L41-48

1 †Andrew Silver	N 1 1 2 3 0 0	7	1
2 §Darren Grayling	0 0 T N	0	
3 Glenn Doyle	*rider replacement*		
4 Stefan Dannö	R 0 0 3 2 1	6	1
5 Peter Nahlin	3 3 3 3 2 2 3	19	1
6 Paul Dugard	2 R 0 0 T	2	
7 Nathan Simpson	1 2 1 2 1	7	1
8 Nathan Gaymer	*did not ride*		

Coventry's Jamie Habbin was re-introduced in heat 12 as a reserve replacement for Andy Smith who was unable to take part in a re-run after falling. Habbin had originally been excluded from the race for touching the tapes and his replacement Michael Warren was excluded for being the cause of Smith's fall. Habbin scored one point as the only Coventry rider in the re-run but that point was later deducted from the final score by the Speedway Control Board. The on-track score was Coventry 49 Eastbourne 41.

IPSWICH (H), August 23, W49-41

1 †Andrew Silver	3 1 2 1 0	7	
2 Darren Grayling	F 0 3 0	3	
3 Glenn Doyle	*rider replacement*		
4 Peter Nahlin	**3 3 3 3 3 3**	**18**	
5 Stefan Dannö	2 2 R 2 3 0	9	3
6 Paul Dugard	2 0 1 N	3	
7 Nathan Simpson	R 2 2 3 0 2	9	2
8 Nathan Gaymer	*did not ride*		

Ipswich (A), September 3, L31-58

1 †Andrew Silver	1 R 0 1 1	3	1
2 Nathan Simpson	0 1 0 T	1	
3 Glenn Doyle	2 1 2 3 3	11	
4 Stefan Dannö	0 1 3 0 2 fx	6	1
5 Peter Nahlin	3 2 1 1 1	8	
6 Paul Dugard	1 0 1 N	2	1
7 Darren Grayling	0 R T T 0	0	

Arena Essex (A), September 4, L32-58

1 †Andrew Silver	2 2 1 1 1 1	8	1
2 Nathan Simpson	fx0 1 2	3	
3 Glenn Doyle	2 3 0 2 2 0	9	
4 Stefan Dannö	1 0 N F	1	1
5 Peter Nahlin	2 2 3 0 1	8	
6 Paul Dugard	2 N 0 0	2	
7 Darren Grayling	1 0 N 0	1	1

At-a-Glance Results

Arena Essex	W46-43	L32-58	78-101
Belle Vue	W46-44	L36-54	82-98
Bradford	L44-46	L26-64	70-110
Coventry	L40-50	L41-48	81-98
Cradley Heath	L35-55	L41-48	76-103
Ipswich	W49-41	L31-58	80-99
King's Lynn	W48-42	L42-48	†90-90
Oxford	W49-41	L32-58	81-99
Poole	D45-45	L38-52	83-97
Reading	L41-49	L32-58	73-107
Swindon	W49-41	D45-45	94-86
Wolverhampton	L37-53	L40-49	77-102

† Lost the bonus point when Peter Nahlin lost to Henrik Gustafsson.

SWINDON (H), September 26, W49-41

1 †Andrew Silver	2 1 3 1 2	9	
2 Stefan Dannö	*rider replacement*		
3 Glenn Doyle	3 0 2 0 2	7	
4 Peter Nahlin	2 1 3 F 2 0	8	2
5 Nathan Simpson	1 3 3 1 1 1	10	2
6 Darren Grayling	0 1 0 N	1	
7 Olli Tyrvainen	3 2 3 3 3	14	1
8 Nathan Gaymer	*did not ride*		

Oxford (A), September 30, L32-58

1 †Andrew Silver	2 2 2 3 1 1 0	11	
2 Nathan Simpson	1 1 0 0 0	2	2
3 Glenn Doyle	1 1 3 F N	5	
4 Stefan Dannö	*rider replacement*		
5 Peter Nahlin	1 2 0 2 2 3 3	13	1
6 Paul Woods	1 0 N 0	1	
7 Olli Tyrvainen	0 0 N N R	0	
8 Darren Grayling	0	0	

READING (H), October 11, L41-49

1 †Andrew Silver	1 3 1 1 1	7	
2 Glenn Doyle	0 1 0 0	1	
3 Peter Nahlin	3 3 3 3 3 2	17	
4 Stefan Dannö	0 2 0 T	2	
5 Nathan Simpson	3 0 1 1 3 1	9	1
6 Paul Woods	1 1 0 T	2	1
7 Olli Tyrvainen	2 1 T 0	3	

Reading (A), October 12, L32-58

1 †Andrew Silver	1 1 R 3 0 1	6	1
2 Nathan Simpson	0 0 T 2 2	4	1
3 Peter Nahlin	1 1 1 3 2 2	10	1
4 Stefan Dannö	1 0 0 T	1	
5 Glenn Doyle	0 2 0 N	2	
6 Paul Woods	1 0 T 0	1	
7 Olli Tyrvainen	0 3 2 2 1	8	

CRADLEY HEATH (H), October 18, L35-55

1 †Andrew Silver	0 1 2 1 2	6	1
2 Glenn Doyle	1 0 T 1	2	1
3 Peter Nahlin	3 2 2 1 0 3	11	
4 Stefan Dannö	0 1 0 T	1	
5 Nathan Simpson	3 0 2 1 3 0	9	
6 Paul Woods	2 1 1 0	4	1
7 Olli Tyrvainen	1 1 0 T	2	2

ARENA ESSEX (H), October 25, W46-43

1 †Andrew Silver	2 1 3 2 2 1	11	2
2 Glenn Doyle	*rider replacement*		
3 Peter Nahlin	3 3 3 3 3 2	17	
4 Stefan Dannö	1 fx1 fx	2	2
5 Nathan Simpson	2 fx0 1 1	4	1
6 Paul Woods	0 2 0 N	2	1
7 Olli Tyrvainen	fx3 2 2 2 1	10	2
8 Darren Grayling	*did not ride*		

WHO WAS WHO IN '92

Mark BRUTON
Born: December 17, 1973, Brighton, Sussex.
Reserve team member awaiting his first team debut.

Stefan DANNÖ
Born: February 10, 1969, Ostersund, Sweden.
Younger brother of former Hackney and Belle Vue rider Roland. Joined the Eagles early in the season making an immediate impact although his form tailed off towards the end of the season.

Glenn DOYLE
Born: March 4, 1965, Sydney, New South Wales, Australia.
Moved to Eastbourne after being left out of Bradford's team plans. Suffered a broken foot which forced him to miss a handful of meetings.

Paul Charles DUGARD
Born: October 17, 1972, Shoreham, Sussex.
Ended his retirement to race for the family club but missed the final weeks of the season after being banned for five years (four of them suspended) by the Speedway Control Board after failing a drugs test.

Nathan GAYMER
Born: January 9, 1972, Margate, Kent.
Local discovery who made several appearances as number eight.

Andy GRAHAME – see Cradley Heath

Darren GRAYLING
Born: March 3, 1972, Eastbourne, Sussex.
Skipper of the Eastbourne Reserve League side, he was given a number of outings during the season.

Paul MITCHELL
Born: April 19, 1972, Shoreham-by-Sea, Sussex.
Another of the Eastbourne juniors who was named as number eight.

Peter Jan Erik NAHLIN
Born: May 1, 1968, Eskilstuna, Sweden.
Left out of Swindon's team plans, he agreed to join Eastbourne in the middle of the summer and subsequently had his best ever British season.

Michael RANDALL
Born: May 25, 1971, Epsom, Surrey.
Local discovery.

Robert Benjamin (Bobby) SCHWARTZ
Born: August 10, 1956, Santa Barbara, California, United States of America.
Made a fleeting mid-summer comeback after missing four complete seasons.

Andrew George SILVER
Born: January 13, 1967, North London.
Signed from Swindon during the winter. Took over as the Eagles skipper on Andy Grahame's departure. His father Len announced he was joining the club as promoter at the end of the season.

Nathan Vincent SIMPSON
Born: March 15, 1969, Slough, Berkshire.
Reliable middle order scorer in his second First Division season.

Neville TATUM – see Peterborough

Olli TYRVAINEN
Born: January 11, 1960, Varkaus, Finland.
Given an unexpected chance to resume his British career after a three season absence. His form fluctuated wildly and he announced his retirement from British racing at the end of the year.

Paul WOODS
Born: January 17, 1959, Canterbury, Kent.
Popular veteran who returned to track action as a stand-in reserve after Paul Dugard had been banned.

Brewing up a hot-lot!

VERY much a case of 'as you were' for the Connells Witches who went into the new season with just one change from 1991, a season when their performances exceeded all expectation.

That was an enforced one, too, with Neville Tatum being recalled by parent club Eastbourne. John Louis used his Polish connections as he sought a replacement and signed one of their hottest young prospects, Jacek Rempala, who had been reserve at the previous season's World Under 21 Final.

World number two Tony Rickardsson and John's son Chris were again expected to lead the assault on honours with the hope that the rest of young squad would maintain the progress from the previous season.

It turned out to be a season of consolidation rather than real progress although the signs for the future prosperity of the club are very good indeed.

Their reserve side, the Sorcerer's Apprentices, literally swept all before them demonstrating that there's a wealth of talent coming through the ranks with Savalas Clouting particularly catching the eye. He's rated very highly indeed by the Suffolk club and could well be the latest in a growing stream on home-produced riders to make the grade.

An early season shock saw Kings Lynn plunder the Gold Cup points at Foxhall Heath but Ipswich recovered to do reasonably well in their group. Narrow away defeats at Poole, Reading, Swindon and Arena-Essex were the main disappointment but, nevertheless, it had been an encouraging start.

Rempala was having difficulty coming to terms with the rigours of British racing and was clearly unhappy. With Tony Olsson being released by Exeter the Ipswich management moved quietly and quickly to sign him which allowed the Pole to return home. Olsson made an immediate impact and proved to be a shrewd signing.

As reigning H.E.A.T. Team Division One champions the Connells Witches were eager to regain their title and came out on top in the tough Southern qualifying group.

In the final, at Peterborough, they made a calamitous start scoring just three points from the first six heats. They staged a remarkable fight back in the second half but had left themselves far too much to do to catch eventual winners Belle Vue.

The Manchester side also proved to be too big an obstacle for them to overcome in the Speedway Star Knock Out Cup. Having defeated them by 17 points in the League in May, Ipswich were confident of pulling back a four point deficit when the two teams met in the second leg at Foxhall.

However, nothing went right for them and Belle Vue progressed to the semi-finals. That's the stage reached by the Connells' Witches in the BSPA Cup before going down narrowly to eventual winners Reading.

The League campaign was only so-so with points hard to come by on their travels. They were never really in with a shout of the title even though the only blemish on their home record was inflicted by champions-elect Reading. A mid-table position at the end of the year was a fair reflection on their efforts.

There were a considerable number of bright spots on the individual front though. Rickardsson and Sam Tesar both made it through to the World Final although the Swede couldn't match his success of 1991. Shane Parker reached the World Long Track Final at his first attempt and David Norris battled through to the World Under 21 Final.

Chris Louis, still one of England's brightest prospects, had an up and down year with his exit from the World Championship in the Commonwealth Final being his biggest disappointment.

Providing Ipswich can hold onto both Louis and Rickardsson along with their improving youngsters they could well emerge as the club that dominates British speedway in the years to come.

1992 RIDER ROSTER

	Club Record								Career Record							
	M	R	Pts	BP	TPts	Ave	F	P	M	R	Pts	BP	TPts	Ave	F	P
Savalas Clouting	3	6	4.0	1.0	5.0	3.333	0	0	3	6	4.0	1.0	5.0	3.333	0	0
Ben Howe	54	199	164.0	52.0	216.0	4.342	0	0	54	199	164.0	52.0	216.0	4.342	0	0
Chris Louis	53	257	451.0	49.0	500.0	7.782	1	0	55	263	457.0	51.0	508.0	7.726	1	0
David Norris	53	233	326.0	55.0	381.0	6.541	0	0	53	233	326.0	55.0	381.0	6.541	0	0
Tony Olsson	22	98	145.0	18.0	163.0	6.653	0	0	181	796	1132.0	181.0	1313.0	6.598	0	2
Shane Parker	52	245	361.0	52.0	413.0	6.743	0	0	52	245	361.0	52.0	413.0	6.743	0	0
Jacek Rempala	4	12	15.0	1.0	16.0	5.333	0	0	4	12	15.0	1.0	16.0	5.333	0	0
Tony Rickardsson	49	242	468.0	31.0	499.0	8.248	3	1	49	242	468.0	31.0	499.0	8.248	3	1
Shaun Tacey	1	2	0.0	0.0	0.0	0.000	0	0	1	2	0.0	0.0	0.0	0.000	0	0
Zdenek Tesar	49	211	328.5	38.0	366.5	6.948	0	0	49	211	328.5	38.0	366.5	6.948	0	0

IPSWICH

Promoters: John Louis and Mike Western.
Address: Foxhall Stadium, Foxhall Road, Ipswich,. Suffolk, IP4 5TL.
Telephone: 0473-623640.
Hotline: 0891 800 674.
Track Length: 300 metres.
Track Record: 58.8 secs, Tony Rickardsson (Ipswich), May 23, 1991, Heat 5, Ipswich v Bradford (Sunbrite League Division One).
Seasons in Division One: 19 (1972-1988, 1991-92).
Division One Record: Champions (3), 1975, 1976, 1984. Runners-up (2), 1981, 1983. Third (2), 1974, 1982.
Speedway Star Cup Record: Winners (4), 1976, 1978, 1981, 1984. Runners-up (2), 1974, 1985.
League Cup Record: Runners-up (1), 1982.
Inter League Cup Record: Winners (1), 1977.
Division One Team Championship: Winners (1), 1991. Joint Runners-up (1), 1992. Finalists (2), 1991, 1992.
Appearances: Billy Sanders, 403 (1972-78, 1979-80, 1983-85).
Points: Billy Sanders, 3745 (1972-78, 1979-80, 1983-85).
World Finalists: John Cook (1985), Ray Cresp (1961), Jeremy Doncaster (1987), John Louis (1972, 1974-75-76), Peter Moore (1958, 1960), Kai Niemi (1984-85), Tony Rickardsson (1991-92), Gerd Riss (1987), Billy Sanders (1977, 1980, 1983-84), Dennis Sigalos (1982-83), Zdenek Tesar (1992).
Division One Riders' Championship Finalists: John Louis (1972-73-74-75-76, 1979-80), Billy Sanders (1977-78, 1983-84), Dennis Sigalos (1981-82), Jeremy Doncaster (1985-86, 1988), John Cook (1985), Kai Niemi (1986), Louis Carr (1987), Shane Parker (1991), Tony Rickardsson (1992).

Seasons in Division Two: 5 (1969-1971; 1989-1990).
Division Two Record: Third (2), 1971, 1990.
Division Two Cup Record: Winners (2), 1970, 1971.
Division Two Team Championship: Fourth (1), 1990. Qualified (1), 1990.
Appearances: The late Peter Bailey, 100 (1969-1971).
Points: Chris Louis, 973 (1989-1990).
Division Two Riders' Championship Finalists: Ted Spittles (1969), John Harrhy (1970), John Louis (1971), Mark Loram (1989), Chris Louis (1990).

1992
IPSWICH

Left to right: Shane Parker, Tony Rickardsson, Zdenek Tesar, Chris Louis, Ben Howe, Jacek Rempala and David Norris.

BELLE VUE (H), May 14, W53-36

1 †Chris Louis	3 3 0 2 2	10	2
2 §§Jacek Rempala	1 0 N 3	4	
3 Tony Rickardsson	3 1 1 3	8	
4 Shane Parker	1 0 3 3	7	
6 Zdenek Tesar	3 3 3 1 3	13	
6 Ben Howe	3 2 3 0 0 2	10	2
7 David Norris	R 1 R N	1	

Coventry (A), May 23, L39-51

1 †Chris Louis	3 2 3 3 1 1	13	
2 Savalas Clouting	0 0 T T	0	
3 Tony Rickardsson	1 1 2 3 2	9	1
4 Jacek Rempala	1 2 T 0 N	3	
5 Shane Parker	0 1 1 1 1	4	3
6 Ben Howe	1 0 0 T	1	
7 David Norris	3 2 2 2 0 0	9	1

Wolverhampton (A), May 25, L36-54

1 †Chris Louis	3 2 1 1 2	9	1
2 Jacek Rempala	1 0 N T	1	
3 Tony Rickardsson	3 2 2 2 2 0	11	
4 Shane Parker	1 2 2 0 1	6	
5 Zdenek Tesar	R fx0 N	0	
6 Ben Howe	2 1 1 0 T	4	2
7 David Norris	3 1 R 1 0	5	1

OXFORD (H), July 16, W48-42

1 †Chris Louis	2 3 3 3 2	13	
2 §Tony Olsson	1 2 0 2	5	3
3 Tony Rickardsson	3 3 2 2 1	11	1
4 Shane Parker	3 0 1 R	4	
5 Zdenek Tesar	2 3 2 1	8	2
6 Ben Howe	0 1 1 0	2	
7 David Norris	2 2 0 1	5	

BRADFORD (H), July 23, W50-40

1 †Chris Louis	2 2 2 1	7	1
2 Tony Olsson	3 1 3 1	8	2
3 Tony Rickardsson	3 fx2 3 3	11	
4 Shane Parker	0 0 0 2	2	
5 Zdenek Tesar	3 3 2 2 2	12	2
6 Ben Howe	1 2 1 N	4	2
7 David Norris	2 2 1 0 1	6	3

Arena Essex (A), August 1, W52-38

1 †Chris Louis	2 2 1 2	7	
2 Tony Olsson	1 0 2 3	6	2
3 Tony Rickardsson	2 3 3 0 2	10	2
4 Shane Parker	1 F 1 1	3	3
5 Zdenek Tesar	2 3 3 2 3	13	
6 Ben Howe	2 0 fx0	2	1
7 David Norris	3 3 3 2	11	

WOLVERHAMPTON (H), August 6, D45-45

1 †Chris Louis	3 2 1 3 2	11	
2 Tony Olsson	1 1 3 0	5	1
3 Tony Rickardsson	2 2 2 2 0	8	
4 Shane Parker	1 1 1 1	4	3
5 Zdenek Tesar	2 2 2 1	7	1
6 Ben Howe	2 0 0 N	2	1
7 David Norris	3 2 1 R 2	8	2

CRADLEY HEATH (H), August 20, D45-45

1 †Chris Louis	1 3 2 1 N	7	1
2 Tony Olsson	0 1 3 3	7	
3 Tony Rickardsson	2 3 2 0 fx	7	1
4 David Norris	2 1 0 F	3	
5 Zdenek Tesar	F R 1 N	1	1
6 Ben Howe	2 F N 2 2	6	1
7 Shane Parker	3 1 2 3 2 3	14	1

Eastbourne (A), August 23, L41-49

1 †Chris Louis	1 0 1 1 1	4	2
2 Tony Olsson	2 1 0 fx	3	
3 Tony Rickardsson	2 3 3 1 2	11	2
4 §§Savalas Clouting	0 2 N N	2	
5 Zdenek Tesar	1 fx2 0 1	4	1
6 Ben Howe	1 1 T 2 N	4	1
7 Shane Parker	3 3 1 3 2 1	13	

KING'S LYNN (H), August 27, W50-39

1 †Chris Louis	2 3 3 1 2	11	1
2 Savalas Clouting	0 2 N N	2	1
3 David Norris	2 1 3 1	7	1
4 §§Shaun Tacey	F 0 N N	0	
5 Tony Olsson	3 1 2 3 3	12	
6 Ben Howe	3 1 2 0 1 0	7	2
7 Shane Parker	2 3 2 2 0 2	11	3

Swindon (A), August 31, W48-42

1 †Chris Louis	3 3 2 1 3	12	
2 Tony Olsson	1 2 2 1	6	2
3 Tony Rickardsson	3 3 0 3 1	10	
4 David Norris	2 1 1 0	4	1
5 Zdenek Tesar	3 0 F N	3	
6 Ben Howe	2 1 1 0	4	1
7 Shane Parker	3 0 1 3 2	9	1

EASTBOURNE (H), September 3, W58-31

1 †Chris Louis	2 2 3 1 0	8	2
2 Tony Olsson	3 3 2 3 2	13	1
3 Tony Rickardsson	**3 3 3 3 3**	**15**	
4 David Norris	1 2 2 2 2	9	3
5 Zdenek Tesar	*rider replacement*		
6 Ben Howe	2 1 0 F	3	1
7 Shane Parker	3 2 2 3 fx	10	2
8 Savalas Clouting	*did not ride*		

Oxford (A), September 11, L42-48

1 †Chris Louis	1 2 0 2	5	1
2 Tony Olsson	2 F 0 N	2	
3 Tony Rickardsson	3 2 2 1 3 2	13	1
4 David Norris	3 2 2 0	7	
5 Zdenek Tesar	F 0 2 N 1	3	1
6 Ben Howe	1 1 1 N	3	3
7 Shane Parker	2 1 3 0 2 1	9	

In a race-off for the bonus point Tony Rickardsson lost to Hans Nielsen.

Poole (A), September 16, L25-65

1 †Chris Louis	1 1 0 0	2	
2 Tony Olsson	0 0 0 1	1	
3 Tony Rickardsson	2 1 1 0 2	6	1
4 David Norris	0 0 0 N	0	
5 Zdenek Tesar	1 1 3 2 3	10	
6 Ben Howe	1 0 0 1	2	1
7 Shane Parker	0 0 1 2 1	4	

POOLE (H), September 17, W48-42

1 †Chris Louis	3 2 1 0 2	8	1
2 Tony Olsson	2 0 0 0	2	1
3 Tony Rickardsson	**3 3 3 3 3**	**15**	
4 David Norris	3 2 1 1	7	
5 Zdenek Tesar	1 1 3 0	5	1
6 Ben Howe	0 1 1 N	2	
7 Shane Parker	3 3 1 2 0	9	1

SWINDON (H), September 24, W62-28

1 †Chris Louis	3 3 3 2 1	12	1
2 Tony Olsson	2 1 3 2	8	2
3 Tony Rickardsson	**3 3 2 3**	**11**	**1**
4 Zdenek Tesar	2 2 3 1	8	2
5 David Norris	3 3 2 1	9	
6 Ben Howe	2 0 0 1	3	2
7 Shane Parker	3 2 3 3 0	11	1

COVENTRY (H), October 1, W55-35

1 †Chris Louis	3 3 2 0	8	
2 Tony Olsson	0 1 N N	1	
3 Tony Rickardsson	3 1 2 3 2	11	1
4 Zdenek Tesar	1 3 3 3 3	13	
5 Shane Parker	3 1 3 0	7	
6 Ben Howe	2 1 0 0 N 1	4	2
7 David Norris	3 3 2 1 2	11	3

Bradford (A), October 6, L41-49

1 †Chris Louis	2 3 2 1 2 1	11	2
2 Tony Olsson	*rider replacement*		
3 Tony Rickardsson	0 2 0 2 2 3 2	11	1
4 Shane Parker	0 0 1 0	1	1
5 Zdenek Tesar	2 1 1 3 1 2	10	
6 Ben Howe	1 1 T 0	2	1
7 David Norris	2 1 1 2	6	2

ARENA ESSEX (H), October 8, W58-32

1 †Chris Louis	2 1 1 3 2	9	3
2 Tony Olsson	3 2 2 0	7	1
3 Tony Rickardsson	1 3 3 2	9	2
4 Zdenek Tesar	3 2 0 F 3	8	1
5 Shane Parker	**2 3 3 3**	**11**	**1**
6 Ben Howe	1 2 2 1	6	1
7 David Norris	3 3 1 1	8	

Belle Vue (A), October 9, L38-52

1 †Chris Louis	1 1 3 1 0	6	
2 Tony Olsson	*rider replacement*		
3 Tony Rickardsson	3 1 1 3 3 2 1	14	1
4 Shane Parker	2 R 2 2 1 0	7	
5 Zdenek Tesar	1 1 1 0	3	3
6 Ben Howe	2 0 0 N	2	
7 David Norris	1 2 0 1 2	6	2
8 Savalas Clouting	*did not ride*		

READING (H), October 15, L41-48

1 †Chris Louis	1 2 1 2	6	3
2 Tony Olsson	0 3 2 2 3 1	11	
3 Tony Rickardsson	3 fx1 N	4	
4 Zdenek Tesar	1 3 3 2 0	9	1
5 Shane Parker	0 1 3 1	5	
6 Ben Howe	2 2 fx0	4	1
7 David Norris	1 1 0 0 T	2	2

Cradley Heath (A), October 17, L39-51

1 †Chris Louis	2 3 2 0 R 2	9	2
2 Tony Olsson	3 0 3 3 0 1	10	1
3 Tony Rickardsson	1 0 2 2 2	7	1
4 Shane Parker	1 1 2 2	6	
5 Zdenek Tesar	fx N N N	0	
6 Ben Howe	0 1 0 N	1	
7 David Norris	3 2 0 N 0 1	6	1

King's Lynn (A), October 27, L38-51

1 †Chris Louis	2 1 1 3 2 1	10	1
2 Tony Olsson	0 0 1 0	1	1
3 Tony Rickardsson	3 3 2 0 0	8	
4 Shane Parker	1 1 3 0	5	1
5 Zdenek Tesar	0 2 1 2	5	
6 Ben Howe	1 0 T 1	2	2
7 David Norris	2 1 2 2	7	1

Reading (A), October 28, L38-52

1 †Chris Louis	0 0 2 1	3	
2 Tony Olsson	1 2 2 1 0	6	1
3 Tony Rickardsson	2 1 2 1	6	
4 Shane Parker	N 3 1 3 1	8	
5 Zdenek Tesar	1 1 R 1	3	2
6 Ben Howe	2 2 0 1 2	7	2
7 David Norris	3 1 1 R	5	2

At-a-Glance Results

Arena Essex	W58-32	W52-38	110-70
Belle Vue	W53-36	L38-52	91-88
Bradford	W50-40	L41-49	91-89
Coventry	W55-35	L39-51	94-86
Cradley Heath	D45-45	L39-51	84-96
Eastbourne	W58-31	L41-49	99-80
King's Lynn	W50-39	L38-51	88-90
Oxford	W48-42	L42-49	†90-90
Poole	W48-42	L25-65	73-107
Reading	L41-48	L38-52	79-100
Swindon	W62-28	W48-42	110-70
Wolverhampton	D45-45	L36-54	81-99

† Lost the bonus point when Tony Rickardsson lost to Hans Nielsen.

WHO WAS WHO IN '92

Savalas CLOUTING
Born: September 8, 1975, Ipswich, Suffolk.
Began the season on loan to Second Division Mildenhall but had to be released by the Fen Tigers to allow them to come up to the minimum points average. Returned to Foxhall Heath and made some impressive stand-in performances for the club in official competition.

Lawrence Charlton HARE
Born: December 23, 1969, Elmsett, Near Ipswich, Suffolk.
Helped Ipswich Reserve team complete the League and Cup double but was not given any further opportunities in the Homefire League.

Benjamin George HOWE
Born: December 6, 1974, Crawley, Sussex.
Brought into the England squad in his second season of Division One activity although he was never actually named in the Homefire Lions side.

Christopher LOUIS
Born: July 9, 1969, Ipswich, Suffolk.
Established himself as an England regular although his form suffered towards the end of the season.

David Michael NORRIS
Born: August 20, 1972, Eastbourne, Sussex.
A potent reserve for much of a season which saw him add to his England appearances. Qualified for the World Under 21 Final.

John Tony OLSSON
Born: March 13, 1965, Visby, Sweden.
Signed for Ipswich after being released by Second Division Exeter when they were unable to meet the loan fee demanded by parent track Reading.

Shane Andrew PARKER
Born: April 29, 1970, Semaphore Park, South Australia.
Reached the World Under 21 Final and enjoyed a golden spell of points-piling when programmed at reserve by the Connells' Witches.

Jacek REMPALA
Born: February 16, 1971, Tarnow, Poland.
Made his Homefire League debut for Ipswich but released by the club and replaced by Tony Olsson.

Jan Tony Sören RICKARDSSON
Born: August 17, 1970, Grytas, Sweden.
Took over as Ipswich number one and reached his second successive World Final.

Shaun TACEY
Born: November 27, 1974, Norwich, Norfolk.
Regular member of the Ipswich Reserve League side who made his first team debut against King's Lynn in August.

Zdenek TESAR
Born: July 30, 1964, Ostrava, Czechoslovakia.
Qualified for his second World Final and established himself as a permanent – and popular – fixture in the Ipswich side.

It's all Stars and strife

STARS' promoter Bill Barker saw everything turn sour on him in his fifth season in charge of the Norfolk club...and the season ended with a new promoter at the Norfolk track and a new job for the club's former owner!

Confidence was high at the beginning of the year with the belief that Barker had put together the best team seen at Saddlebow Road in years. He had retained Henrik Gustafsson, Mark Loram, Bo Brhel and Dennis Löfqvist from the previous year's side and brought in both Alun Rossiter and New Zealand Champion Gary Allan from Poole. Darren Spicer, a product of the junior side, was handed the number seven race jacket to complete the line up.

Rossiter made an immediate impact scoring 11 points in the opening meeting, a challenge against deadly local rivals Ipswich and the Barum Stars maintained their early season form by winning at Foxhall Heath in the Gold Cup.

Ipswich avenged that defeat by winning the return at Saddlebow Road but victories at Eastbourne and Poole saw Kings Lynn move to the top of the table. Reading had matches in hand though and eventually overtook them. Nevertheless the signs were encouraging and even more so as they won three out of their first four League matches to set the pace. No problems so far except for a wrist injury for Gustafsson but they were soon to rear up – and how!

The Commonwealth Final at the end of May attracted a 4,000 crowd but disaster struck when the takings of around £26,000 were stolen from Barker's Kent home. Barker called a crisis meeting with supporters at the stadium and revealed that this latest blow added considerably to the clubs' precarious state. Crowds were down 18% on the previous year and a fighting fund had to be set up to keep King's Lynn in business. Nearly £6,000 was raised as the fans rallied to the cause. It wasn't enough though. After a home defeat against Beile Vue and two successive rain-offs, Barker announced in mid-July that his company had ceased to trade.

The speedway world was in a state of shock – surely Kings Lynn wouldn't go the same way as Second Division Mildenhall and Milton Keynes who had already gone out of business.

Frantic efforts were made to save the club. Local businessmen Willie Broughton and Martin Griffiths looked set to assume control at one stage but it was former Oxford junior Keith Chapman who stepped into the breach. He met with the league's management committee together with the riders in a cloak-and-dagger operation at Arena-Essex and he was installed as the new promoter.

Rossiter was the only rider not to remain with the club. He moved back to Poole and ultimately was replaced by Kevin Brice. The re-opening fixture on August 8 was a league match against Eastbourne, Chapman himself taking to the track dressed in a Mickey Mouse outfit!

The Barum Stars took the points and looked set to pick up from where they left off but more problems were soon to arise.

In the main they were caused by the considerable overseas commitments of both Gustafsson and Loram and those commitments caused Chapman to postpone the home League match against Reading rather than stage the fixture without his top two riders. It was a decision that landed him in hot water as he was fined £1,000 (later suspended) by the BSPA and the SCB subsequently awarded the Racers a 75-0 victory.

Chapman was unrepentant saying that he took the decision with the supporters in mind whom he felt sure would not want to watch a Kings Lynn side bereft of its top two. It was a painful early lesson for him in the perils of being a speedway promoter.

The off-track events had its effect on the side who slid down the table eventually finishing ninth in the league and finishing the season with Spicer sidelined with a broken wrist.

A rocky year for the Barum Stars but Chapman is determined, along with stadium owner-cum team manager Alan Littlechild, to bring the good times back to Norfolk and few would bet against them achieving that target.

1992 RIDER ROSTER

	Club Record								Career Record							
	M	R	Pts	BP	TPts	Ave	F	P	M	R	Pts	BP	TPts	Ave	F	P
Gary Allan	25	109	154.0	23.0	177.0	6.495	0	0	51	224	327.0	35.0	362.0	6.464	1	0
Bohumil Brhel	71	312	433.0	44.0	477.0	6.115	0	0	71	312	433.0	44.0	477.0	6.115	0	0
Kevin Brice	38	158	155.0	26.0	181.0	4.582	0	0	38	158	155.0	26.0	181.0	4.582	0	0
Emmerson Fairweather	8	24	7.0	3.0	10.0	1.667	0	0	8	24	7.0	3.0	10.0	1.667	0	0
Jason Gage	2	5	0.0	0.0	0.0	0.000	0	0	2	5	0.0	0.0	0.0	0.000	0	0
Tom Grinstead	6	15	5.0	1.0	6.0	1.600	0	0	6	15	5.0	1.0	6.0	1.600	0	0
Henrik Gustafsson	42	199	454.0	27.0	481.0	9.668	1	2	42	199	454.0	27.0	481.0	9.668	1	2
Dennis Löfqvist	100	451	579.0	91.0	670.0	5.942	0	1	100	451	579.0	91.0	670.0	5.942	0	1
Mark Loram	81	446	863.5	50.0	913.5	8.193	1	1	131	594	1019.0	83.0	1102.0	7.421	1	1
Andrew Mountain	4	12	3.0	2.0	5.0	1.667	0	0	4	12	3.0	2.0	5.0	1.667	0	0
Alun Rossiter	11	53	59.0	11.0	70.0	5.283	0	0	235	845	926.0	210.0	1136.0	5.378	0	0
Darren Spicer	23	72	34.0	10.0	44.0	2.444	0	0	23	72	34.0	10.0	44.0	2.444	0	0

KING'S LYNN

Promoter: Keith Chapman.
Address: The Stadium, Saddlebow Road, King's Lynn, Norfolk, PE34 3AG.
Telephone: 0553-771111.
Hotline: 0891 800 644.
Track Length: 342 metres.
Track Record: 60.8 secs, Hans Nielsen (Oxford), July 1, 1989, Heat 5, Barum Individual Trophy.
Seasons in Division One: 27 (1966-1992).
Division One Record: Third (2), 1972, 1973.
Speedway Star Cup Record: Winners (1), 1977. Runners-up (1), 1976.
League Cup Record: Runners-up (1), 1981.
Inter League Cup Record: Winners (2), 1978, 1980. Runners-up (1), 1979.
Appearances: Terry Betts, 471 (1966-1978).
Points: Terry Betts, 5017.5 (1966-1978).
World Finalists: Terry Betts (1974), Armando Castagna (1985), Howard Cole (1969), John Cook (1987), John Davis (1988), Henrik Gustafsson (1992), Dave Jessup (1979-80-81), Richard Knight (1990), Michael Lee (1977-78-79-80-81).
Division One Riders' Championship Finalists: Terry Betts (1966-67-68-69-70-71-72, 1974-75-76), Malcolm Simmons (1973), Michael Lee (1977-78-79-80), Dave Jessup (1981, 1985), Billy Sanders (1982), John Louis (1983-84), Andy Campbell (1986), Richard Knight (1987-88-89), Lance King (1989), Mark Loram (1990), Henrik Gustafsson (1991-92).

Bill Barker announced the closure of the track at the end of June but after negotiations former second half rider Keith Chapman took over as promoter on August 2 and racing resumed.

1992

KING'S LYNN

Back row: Alan Littlechild (team manager), Darren Spicer, Gary Allan, Henrik Gustafsson, Bohumil Brhel, Bill Barker (co-promoter). Front: Dennis Löfqvist, Mark Loram and Alun Rossiter.

Cradley Heath (A), April 18, L33-57

1 Bohumil Brhel	1 0 2 2	5	1
2 Dennis Löfqvist	0 1 1 0 3	5	1
3 †Mark Loram	2 2 2 2 0 1	9	
4 §Gary Allan	0 0 T 1	1	1
5 Henrik Gustafsson	1 3 1 2 2 0	9	
6 Alun Rossiter	2 0 R N	2	
7 Darren Spicer	1 fx T T 1	2	2

OXFORD (H), May 2, W51-39

1 Bohumil Brhel	2 F 3 3 1	9	1
2 Dennis Löfqvist	1 2 3 2	8	2
3 †Mark Loram	3 2 1 1	7	1
4 Henrik Gustafsson	3 3 2 3 2	13	1
5 Gary Allan	2 1 2 0	5	1
6 Darren Spicer	1 1 0 N	2	1
7 Alun Rossiter	2 2 0 2 1	7	1

BRADFORD (H), May 4, W53-37

1 Bohumil Brhel	2 0 2 1	5	1
2 Dennis Löfqvist	1 2 3 3	9	1
3 †Mark Loram	3 3 3 3 0	12	
4 Henrik Gustafsson	2 2 3 2 3	12	1
5 Gary Allan	3 0 2 2	7	1
6 Darren Spicer	1 1 1 fx	3	
7 Alun Rossiter	3 1 0 1	5	1

SWINDON (H), May 23, W49-40

1 Dennis Löfqvist	1 3 1 2 E 0	7	2
2 Glenn Doyle	*2 1 2 fx 1*	*6*	*2*
3 †Mark Loram	3 3 3 2 3 3	17	
4 Henrik Gustafsson	*rider replacement*		
5 Gary Allan	2 2 1 2 2	9	3
6 Darren Spicer	1 1 0 N 0	2	
7 Alun Rossiter	3 2 2 0 1	8	1
8 Emmerson Fairweather	*did not ride*		

Bradford (A), May 30, W50-40

1 Dennis Löfqvist	3 0 2 2 2 2	11	1
2 Bohumil Brhel	2 1 1 1 0	5	3
3 †Mark Loram	3 2 3 3 2	13	
4 Gary Allan	1 2 2 1 1 3	10	1
5 Henrik Gustafsson	*rider replacement*		
6 Alun Rossiter	3 2 1 1 1 1	9	4
7 Darren Spicer	2 fn N N	2	1

POOLE (H), June 6, W49-41

1 Dennis Löfqvist	1 2 3 1 2	9	2
2 Rick Miller	*2 1 2 3 3 2*	*13*	*2*
3 †Mark Loram	3 2 2 2 3	12	
4 Henrik Gustafsson	*rider replacement*		
5 Gary Allan	2 1 3 3 1 1	11	3
6 Darren Spicer	1 0 0 N 0	1	
7 Alun Rossiter	0 1 0 N 2	3	1

BELLE VUE (H), June 13, L36-54

1 Dennis Löfqvist	3 E 2 2 2 0 2	11	
2 Andy Mountain	1 1 0 N	2	1
3 †Mark Loram	2 2 3 1 2 1 1	12	2
4 Henrik Gustafsson	*rider replacement*		
5 Gary Allan	1 2 R 2 0	5	
6 Darren Spicer	2 0 0 0 T	2	1
7 Alun Rossiter	3 fx 1 0 T 0	4	

Poole (A), June 24, L43-47

1 Dennis Löfqvist	3 1 2 1	7	1
2 Gary Allan	1 2 3 1	7	1
3 †Mark Loram	3 2 3 1 2	11	
4 Henrik Gustafsson	2 3 2 3 0	10	
5 §§Emmerson Fairweather	1 fx N 0	1	1
6 Alun Rossiter	3 0 1 1 0 2	7	
7 Darren Spicer	0 0 N 0	0	

Coventry (A), June 27, L42-48

1 Dennis Löfqvist	3 0 2 1	6	
2 Gary Allan	1 1 1 1	4	1
3 †Mark Loram	3 2 2 2 0	9	1
4 Henrik Gustafsson	2 3 3 3 3 2	16	
5 Andy Mountain	1 0 N N	1	1
6 Alun Rossiter	2 0 T 1 0 2	5	
7 Darren Spicer	0 1 0 N 0	1	

Eastbourne (A), August 2, L42-48

1 Bohumil Brhel	*rider replacement*		
2 Dennis Löfqvist	0 0 2 3 1	6	
3 †Mark Loram	3 2 3 3 1 0 3	15	
4 Henrik Gustafsson	1 1 3 3 3 3 0	14	1
5 Gary Allan	2 2 0 0 T	4	1
6 Darren Spicer	1 0 N 0 T	1	
7 Alun Rossiter	0 1 1 0 N	2	2
8 Emmerson Fairweather	*did not ride*		

Oxford (A), August 7, L42-48

1 Bohumil Brhel	1 3 1 1	6	2
2 Gary Allan	2 0 2 2 1	7	1
3 †Mark Loram	3 3 2 3 2	13	
4 Dennis Löfqvist	3 0 1 0	4	
5 Henrik Gustafsson	2 1 2 2	7	2
6 Darren Spicer	3 0 0 0 0	3	
7 Tom Grinstead	1 1 N 0	2	

EASTBOURNE (H), August 8, W48-42

1 Bohumil Brhel	3 3 fx N	6	
2 Gary Allan	1 1 3 1	6	
3 Mark Loram	2 3 2 3 2	12	
4 Henrik Gustafsson	2 2 3 2 1	10	3
5 Dennis Löfqvist	3 3 3 1	10	
6 Darren Spicer	3 F 1 0 0	4	
7 Andy Mountain	0 0 0 0	0	

In a race-off for the bonus point Henrik Gustafsson defeated Peter Nahlin.

Arena Essex (A), August 21, L39-51

1 Bohumil Brhel	1 2 3 3 1 F	10	
2 Gary Allan	0 1 0 2 2	5	2
3 †Mark Loram	3 R 2 2 3 1	11	
4 Tom Grinstead	0 T 0 T	0	
5 Dennis Löfqvist	2 3 1 1 2	9	2
6 Darren Spicer	F 1 T 0	1	
7 Kevin Brice	1 1 1 T	3	1

Ipswich (A), August 27, L39-50

1 Bohumil Brhel	3 2 F R 1	6	1
2 Gary Allan	1 3 2 1	7	
3 †Mark Loram	3 fx 3 3 2 0	11	
4 Emmerson Fairweather	1 0 0 T	1	1
5 Dennis Löfqvist	2 3 2 3 1	11	1
6 Darren Spicer	F R N T	0	
7 Kevin Brice	1 0 1 0 1	3	1

Wolverhampton (A), September 7, L39-51

1 Bohumil Brhel	1 1 1 1	4	
2 Gary Allan	0 0 F T	0	
3 †Mark Loram	3 3 2 fx 0 3	11	
4 Dennis Löfqvist	1 1 1 3 F	6	3
5 Henrik Gustafsson	2 2 3 1 3 0	11	
6 Darren Spicer	2 F T 0	2	1
7 Kevin Brice	3 0 2 T	5	

Belle Vue (A), September 18, L33-56

1 Dennis Löfqvist	2 R 3 1 1	7	1
2 Emmerson Fairweather	1 fx T T 0	1	1
3 Sean Wilson	*2 2 2 1 2 2*	*11*	*1*
4 §§Andrew Mountain	0 0 T 0	0	
5 Gary Allan	2 1 2 3 3	11	
6 Darren Spicer	0 1 0 N	1	1
7 Kevin Brice	1 1 0 0 0	2	1

WOLVERHAMPTON (H), September 26, L40-50

1 Dennis Löfqvist	1 2 1 0	4	2
2 Gary Allan	2 0 1 2	5	
3 †Mark Loram	3 2 2 1 0	8	1
4 Henrik Gustafsson	2 3 1 1 1	8	1
5 Bohumil Brhel	1 2 3 2 2	10	2
6 Darren Spicer	1 0 0 N	1	
7 Kevin Brice	3 0 1 0 T	4	

Swindon (A), October 1, L44-46

1 †Mark Loram	2 3 2 3 3 2	15	1
2 Gary Allan	1 0 F 1	2	1
3 Bohumil Brhel	0 1 0 0	1	1
4 Dennis Löfqvist	0 3 3 2	8	1
5 Henrik Gustafsson	3 2 2 2 3 1	13	2
6 Darren Spicer	0 T 1 0	1	
7 Kevin Brice	1 1 2 T	4	

COVENTRY (H), October 4, W49-41

1 †Mark Loram	3 2 3 3 2	13	1
2 Gary Allan	1 1 3 2	7	2
3 Bohumil Brhel	1 3 3 X	7	
4 Dennis Löfqvist	**3 3 2 3 3**	**14**	**1**
5 Emmerson Fairweather	1 0 0 N	1	
6 Kevin Brice	3 0 1 1 1 1	7	
7 Jason Gage	F 0 0 N	0	

ARENA ESSEX (H), October 17, W49-41

1 †Mark Loram	**3 3 3 3 2**	**14**	**1**
2 Gary Allan	1 1 3 0	5	
3 Bohumil Brhel	1 2 1 2	6	1
4 Henrik Gustafsson	2 2 1 3 3	11	
5 Dennis Löfqvist	1 1 2 1	5	4
6 Kevin Brice	2 2 1 0 3	8	1
7 Emmerson Fairweather	0 N 0 0	0	

CRADLEY HEATH (H), October 27, L40-50

1 †Mark Loram	fx 2 2 2 1	7	
2 Gary Allan	2 1 3 1	7	2
3 Bohumil Brhel	2 2 2 3 0	9	
4 Henrik Gustafsson	2 0 0 3	5	
5 Dennis Löfqvist	1 3 3 0	7	1
6 Kevin Brice	R 1 1 0 1	3	3
7 Emmerson Fairweather	2 0 N 0	2	

IPSWICH (H), October 27, W51-38

1 †Mark Loram	3 2 X 2 2	9	2
2 Gary Allan	1 1 3 fx	5	1
3 Bohumil Brhel	0 0 2 3	5	
4 Henrik Gustafsson	**2 2 3 3 3**	**13**	**2**
5 Dennis Löfqvist	3 3 3 1	10	
6 Kevin Brice	3 2 3 F 1	9	1
7 Emmerson Fairweather	0 0 N 0	0	

Reading (A), October 28, L44-46

1 †Mark Loram	2 F 1 3 2 2	10	2
2 Gary Allan	1 2 2 2 1	8	1
3 Bohumil Brhel	3 1 3 0 R	7	
4 Dennis Löfqvist	*rider replacement*		
5 Henrik Gustafsson	2 1 1 1 3 3	11	1
6 Emmerson Fairweather	1 0 N 0 N	1	
7 Kevin Brice	3 1 1 1 N 1	7	1
8 Sid Cooper	*did not ride*		

The scheduled match at home to Reading was never staged although the Speedway Control Board subsequently awarded the match to Reading 75-0.

At-a-Glance Results

Arena Essex	W49-41	L39-51	88-92
Belle Vue	L36-54	L33-56	69-110
Bradford	W53-37	W50-40	103-77
Coventry	W49-41	L42-48	91-89
Cradley Heath	L40-50	L33-57	73-107
Eastbourne	W48-42	L42-48	†90-90
Ipswich	W51-38	L39-50	90-88
Oxford	W51-39	L42-48	93-87
Poole	W49-41	L43-47	92-88
Reading	††L0-75	L44-46	44-121
Swindon	W49-40	L44-46	93-86
Wolverhampton	L40-50	L39-51	79-101

†† King's Lynn refused to stage their Homefire League match against Reading because they were missing both Henrik Gustafsson and Mark Loram on World Championship duty. The BSPA ruled the match should go ahead and as a result the Speedway Control Board ruled the result should be awarded 75-0 to Reading.
† Won the bonus point when Henrik Gustafsson defeated Peter Nahlin.

WHO WAS WHO IN '92

Gary Karl ALLAN
Born: June 21, 1967, Manchester.
Moved to East Anglia at the beginning of the season after spending all his British career with Poole.

Bohumil BRHEL
Born: June 10, 1965, Gottwaldov, Czechoslovakia.
Spent his third season at King's Lynn, reaching the 1992 World Final.

Kevin Neil BRICE
Born: August 23, 1958, Canterbury, Kent.
Expected to return to Second Division Rye House but was replaced after his machinery was stolen prior to the start of the season. Eventually became new promoter Keith Chapman's first signing on taking over the club.

Sidney Christopher (Sid) COOPER
Born: May 6, 1971, Greenwich, London.
Named as number eight in the final League match of the season but has yet to make his official senior debut.

Emmerson John FAIRWEATHER
Born: August 18, 1973, Ipswich, Suffolk.
Made his First Division debut for the Barum Stars after some impressive Reserve League performances.

Jason GAGE
Born: July 9, 1969, Wisbech, Cambridgeshire.
Went on loan to Second Division Mildenhall but returned to Saddlebow Road on their closure and rode in several late season matches before being ruled out with leg ligament damage.

Thomas Andrew GRINSTEAD
Born: September 14, 1972, Maldon, Essex.
Unable to break into the team although he had two League outings during the season to take his appearances over four seasons to only six.

Henrik Anders (Henka) GUSTAFSSON
Born: August 14, 1970, Kumla, Sweden.
Completed his third season with King's Lynn, qualifying for the 1992 World Final.

Dennis Fritz LÖFQVIST
Born: January 5, 1967, Visby, Gotland, Sweden.
A regular member of the Barum Stars' line-up in his fourth season in the British League.

Mark Royston Gregory LORAM
Born: January 12, 1971, Malta.
Finished runner up in the 1992 World Under 21 Final and rode for England in the World Team Cup Final.

Andrew Thomas (Andy) MOUNTAIN
Born: March 3, 1973, King's Lynn, Norfolk.
Local discovery who made his only senior appearance at Belle Vue when the Barum Stars were without three of their top riders because of World Championship commitments.

Alun John ROSSITER – see Poole

Darren William SPICER
Born: March 28, 1974, London.
Given a team place after impressive form at winter training sessions. Missed the last month of the season through injury.

When two's too few

THE LACK of a genuine third heat leader had much to do with the Cheetahs having a mediocre season by the high standards they themselves set. Hans Nielsen and Martin Dugard hardly put a foot wrong throughout the season but failed to get the support they needed, and expected, to enable Oxford to land any major trophies.

Dean Barker had confidently been expected to fill the other heat leader role but struggled to attain any measure of consistency.

He, in the main, blamed the state of the Cowley circuit for his shortcomings (as did many of the teams who visited Oxford) and it was no surprise when he signed for his former club Eastbourne at the beginning of 1993.

Certainly there were track problems at one stage, more often than not aggravated by the weather, and things came to a head when Cradley Heath were the visitors early in May. The three heats that were run saw at least one Heathen fall in each of them and, after an abortive attempt to run heat four, the match was abandoned. Oxford maintained that the track was rideable and landed themselves in trouble by running a practice session after the abandonment.

They accepted though that their racing strip was not all it might be and, somewhat ironically, it was Cradley Heath co-promoter Colin Pratt whose help was enlisted to try and rectify the situation.

His efforts were successful and the track did improve but the Cheetahs suffered an on-track blow when Nielsen broke his collarbone whilst riding in an open meeting in Denmark in the middle of May. Without him they suffered a home defeat at the hands of Wolverhampton in the Gold Cup which ended any slim hopes they had of reaching the Final.

Nielsen's injury had much to do with his shock exit from the World championship at the Scandinavian Final stage. Martin Dugard, too, was a victim of the sports' most common injury during the Commonwealth Final at Kings Lynn but bravely defied the pain to qualify for the next stage.

Back in harness for the club the duo continued to dominate the Cheetahs' scorechart week in and week out but must have felt frustrated that their efforts on away circuits went unrewarded in terms of League points.

Barker, Troy Butler, Mark Carlson, Glen Cunningham and young Dane Morten Andersen were, on paper at least, a strong back up to the top two but more often than not failed to click at the same time.

Efforts were made to strengthen the side but the Oxford management were constantly thwarted by the vagaries of the rule-book. They wanted to sign Gordon Kennett but found that the dreaded regulations decreed that if they did, then they would have to release one of their heat leaders!

Spencer Timmo made a brief return to replace Cunningham but, in turn, he lost his place in the side to Daz Sumner, signed late on in the season from Middlesbrough. Even that signing couldn't prevent another home defeat against Wolverhampton – this time in the league – but that was the only time the Cheetahs lost on their own track in the Homefire League although they were held to a draw on no less that four occasions. It may have been heart-stopping stuff but no-one could complain about the entertainment value!

Tenth place in the league is not the position the Oxford management or indeed supporters envisaged at the start of the season but, by and large, the constraints of the points limit prevented them from strengthening the side when they most wanted and needed to.

What the future holds remains to be seen for, at the beginning of February, both Nielsen and Dugard were adamant that they would not ride for the new Division one pay rates being implemented for the 1993 season.

Furthermore, the Oxford management had received offers from interested parties to take the club back into the Second Division but vowed to resist the overtures if at all possible.

It seems almost unthinkable that Nielsen might not be seen in a Cheetahs' racejacket again as he has had a truly remarkable record since joining them from Birmingham back in 1984.

1992 RIDER ROSTER

	Club Record								Career Record							
	M	R	Pts	BP	TPts	Ave	F	P	M	R	Pts	BP	TPts	Ave	F	P
Morten Andersen	22	93	103.0	17.0	120.0	5.161	0	0	28	117	135.0	19.0	154.0	5.265	0	0
Dean Barker	84	371	506.0	80.0	586.0	6.318	0	1	109	453	571.0	93.0	664.0	5.863	0	1
Troy Butler	135	530	492.0	85.0	577.0	4.355	0	0	138	538	498.0	87.0	585.0	4.349	0	0
Mark Carlson	53	231	224.0	42.0	266.0	4.606	0	1	53	231	224.0	42.0	266.0	4.606	0	1
Glenn Cunningham	27	95	53.0	9.0	62.0	2.611	0	0	27	95	53.0	9.0	62.0	2.611	0	0
Martin Dugard	156	749	1404.0	103.0	1507.0	8.048	5	5	158	758	1416.0	104.0	1520.0	8.021	5	5
Hans Nielsen	321	1535	4075.0	154.0	4229.0	11.020	99	52	575	2704	6805.0	265.0	7070.0	10.459	151	64
Darren Sumner	11	34	15.0	5.0	20.0	2.353	0	0	41	146	124.5	25.0	149.5	4.096	0	0
Spencer Timmo	18	63	38.0	6.0	44.0	2.794	0	0	18	63	38.0	6.0	44.0	2.794	0	0

OXFORD

Promoters: Bernard Crapper and K Hedderley.
Address: Oxford Sports & Leisure Centre, Sandy Lane, Cowley, Oxford, OX4 5LJ.
Telephone: 0865-778222.
Hotline: 0891 800 693.
Track Length: 297 metres.
Track Record: 56.2 secs, Hans Nielsen (Oxford), October 13, 1988, Heat 1, Oxford v Coventry (Speedway Star KO Cup).
Seasons in Division One: 20 (1965-1975, 1984-1992).
Division One Record: Champions (3), 1985, 1986, 1989.
Speedway Star Cup Record: Winners (1*), 1985. Joint Winners (1), 1986.
League Cup Record: Joint winners (1), 1986. Runners-up (1), 1985.
Inter League Cup Record: Semi-finalists, 1975.
Gold Cup: Winners (1), 1989. Runners-up (2), 1990-91.
Premiership: Winners (1), 1987. Runners-up (2), 1986, 1990.
Division One Team Championship: Joint Runners-up (1), 1992. Finalists (1), 1992.
Appearances: Hans Nielsen 421 (1984-1991).
Points: Hans Nielsen, 4229 (1984-1991).
World Finalists: Troy Butler (1989), Marvyn Cox (1986), Martin Dugard (1990), Ronnie Genz (1961), Jimmy Gooch (1965), Ron How (1964), Hans Nielsen (1984-85-86-87-88-89-90-91), Simon Wigg (1984, 1988-89).
Division One Riders' Championship Finalists: Jimmy Gooch (1965-66), Roy Trigg (1967), Colin Gooddy (1969), Hasse Holmkvist (1970), Garry Middleton (1972), Gordon Kennett (1973), Bob Kilby (1974), Dag Lovaas (1975), Hans Nielsen (1984-85-86-87-88-89-90-91-92), Simon Wigg (1985-86, 1988-89), Martin Dugard (1989-90, 1992).
Other Honours: Division One Champions, 1964. Division Three Champions, 1950. Division Two Cup Winners, 1964.

1992

OXFORD

Back row: John Tremblin (team manager), Dean Barker, Morten Andersen, Troy Butler, Mark Carlson, Bernard Crapper (co-promoter). Front: Martin Dugard, Hans Nielsen and Glenn Cunningham.

Coventry (A), April 25, W48-38

1 †Hans Nielsen	3 3 3 1 2 3	15	1
2 Mark Carlson	0 2 0 R 0	2	1
3 Martin Dugard	3 3 2 3 3 2	16	2
4 Troy Butler	*rider replacement*		
5 Dean Barker	0 3 2 1 2	8	
6 §Morten Andersen	X 1 3 0	4	
7 Glenn Cunningham	N 0 2 1	3	1
8 Spencer Timmo	*did not ride*		

King's Lynn (A), May 2, L39-51

1 †Hans Nielsen	3 N 2 3 3 3 3	17	
2 Mark Carlson	0 0 1 0	1	
3 Martin Dugard	2 3 3 0 1 2 0	11	1
4 Troy Butler	*rider replacement*		
5 Dean Barker	1 1 1 1 0 2	6	
6 Spencer Timmo	0 1 T 0	1	
7 Glenn Cunningham	3 0 0 0 T	3	
8 Wayne Parker	*did not ride*		

ARENA ESSEX (H), May 13, W49-41

1 †Hans Nielsen	3 3 3 3 2	14	1
2 Mark Carlson	1 0 0 0	1	
3 Martin Dugard	3 3 3 3 3	15	
4 Troy Butler	1 2 0 2	5	2
5 Dean Barker	2 3 2 2	9	1
6 Glenn Cunningham	0 0 0 N	0	
7 Morten Andersen	2 1 1 0 1	5	2

Poole (A), June 10, L35-55

1 †Hans Nielsen	2 0 3 3 2 3 3	16	
2 Mark Carlson	R 2 1 0 0	3	
3 Martin Dugard	*rider replacement*		
4 Troy Butler	0 1 3 2 1 0	7	
5 Dean Barker	1 2 R 2 1	6	
6 Morten Andersen	2 1 0 0	3	1
7 Glenn Cunningham	0 0 N R	0	
8 Spencer Timmo	*did not ride*		

Cradley Heath (A), July 4, L40-50

1 †Hans Nielsen	2 3 2 2 2	11	1
2 Troy Butler	R 1 2 1 1 0	5	2
3 Martin Dugard	3 3 2 1 3 1	13	
4 Mark Carlson	3 1 0 T	4	1
5 Dean Barker	1 2 0 T	3	
6 Morten Andersen	1 0 1 1 T	3	1
7 Glenn Cunningham	0 1 0 N	1	

Ipswich (A), July 16, L42-48

1 †Hans Nielsen	3 2 3 1 3 3 3	18	
2 Troy Butler	fx2 1 1 1 2 0	7	2
3 Martin Dugard	*rider replacement*		
4 Mark Carlson	E 2 1 E	3	
5 Dean Barker	1 1 R R	2	
6 Morten Andersen	3 0 0 3 2 3	11	
7 Glenn Cunningham	1 0 0 0	1	

SWINDON (H), July 24, D45-45

1 Hans Nielsen	*rider replacement*		
2 Troy Butler	1 1 2 1	5	1
3 †Martin Dugard	3 3 3 3 3 1	16	
4 Morten Andersen	2 2 2 1 2	9	1
5 Dean Barker	3 1 1 0 2 0	7	3
6 Glenn Cunningham	0 1 0 N	1	
7 Mark Carlson	2 0 1 2 1 1	7	2

POOLE (H), July 31, D45-45

1 †Hans Nielsen	3 1 3 3 3	13	
2 Troy Butler	0 0 0 2	2	1
3 Martin Dugard	3 3 2 2 1 1	12	2
4 Morten Andersen	1 1 N 3	5	1
5 Dean Barker	3 2 1 2	8	
6 Glenn Cunningham	1 1 0 N	2	1
7 Mark Carlson	2 1 0 0 0	3	

Wolverhampton (A), August 3, L43-47

1 †Hans Nielsen	1 2 3 3 1	10	1
2 Troy Butler	2 1 3 0 0	6	1
3 Martin Dugard	2 2 3 1	8	
4 Morten Andersen	2 1 2 0	5	1
5 Dean Barker	1 2 0 2	5	1
6 Mark Carlson	3 1 2 N 1 1	8	4
7 Glenn Cunningham	1 0 N 0 N	1	

KING'S LYNN (H), August 7, W48-42

1 †Hans Nielsen	3 2 3 3 1 3	15	
2 Troy Butler	F 1 1 2	4	2
3 Martin Dugard	R 2 3 3	8	1
4 Morten Andersen	0 1 0 1	2	1
5 Dean Barker	1 2 3 2 0	8	1
6 Spencer Timmo	2 2 N 1	5	
7 Mark Carlson	F 3 0 3	6	

Arena Essex (A), August 14, L43-47

1 †Hans Nielsen	3 3 3 2 3 1	15	1
2 Troy Butler	0 1 F 1 1	3	1
3 Dean Barker	1 2 2 3 1 2	11	2
4 Morten Andersen	1 fx2 2 X	5	
5 Martin Dugard	*rider replacement*		
6 Mark Carlson	3 3 0 1 0	7	1
7 Glenn Cunningham	0 0 2 N	2	
8 Wayne Parker	*did not ride*		

Eastbourne (A), August 16, L41-49

1 †Hans Nielsen	3 1 3 3 2 2	14	
2 Troy Butler	fx0 1 0	1	
3 Dean Barker	2 3 F 0	5	
4 Morten Andersen	F F fxT	0	
5 Martin Dugard	3 3 1 1 1	9	1
6 Mark Carlson	3 2 1 0	6	1
7 Glenn Cunningham	1 1 3 1	6	1

COVENTRY (H), August 21, W49-41

1 †Hans Nielsen	2 3 3 3 2	13	1
2 Morten Andersen	0 fxN N	0	
3 Dean Barker	1 3 2 1	7	
4 Troy Butler	3 2 1 0	6	1
5 Martin Dugard	1 3 3 3 3	13	
6 Glenn Cunningham	1 0 1 0 0	2	1
7 Mark Carlson	2 3 2 0 1	8	1

READING (H), August 31, W46-44

1 †Hans Nielsen	F 3 2 2 2	9	1
2 §Darren Sumner	1 0 0 0	1	
3 Dean Barker	2 3 1 2 3	11	2
4 Troy Butler	1 0 0 3	4	
5 Martin Dugard	3 1 2 1	7	2
6 Mark Carlson	3 3 0 3 2	11	
7 Glenn Cunningham	1 1 N 1	3	

Reading (A), August 31, L37-53

1 †Hans Nielsen	3 3 3 2 3 3	17	
2 Darren Sumner	0 0 1 T	1	
3 Dean Barker	3 2 1 0 0 0	6	
4 Troy Butler	2 0 1 0	3	
5 Martin Dugard	1 1 1 2	5	1
6 Mark Carlson	3 0 T 0 0	3	
7 Glenn Cunningham	1 1 0 N	2	

WOLVERHAMPTON (H), September 2, L43-47

1 †Hans Nielsen	3 2 3 3 0	11	
2 Darren Sumner	0 1 1 1	3	1
3 Dean Barker	1 N N N	1	1
4 Glenn Cunningham	0 0 1 N	1	
5 Martin Dugard	3 1 3 2 1	10	
6 Mark Carlson	3 2 0 2 0 1	8	2
7 Troy Butler	2 3 F 2 0 2	9	1

IPSWICH (H), September 11, W48-42

1 †Hans Nielsen	3 3 3 3 3	15	
2 Darren Sumner	0 0 N N	0	
3 Dean Barker	0 3 1 1	5	
4 Morten Andersen	2 1 0 N	3	
5 Martin Dugard	1 3 3 3 0	10	1
6 Mark Carlson	3 2 1 2 1 0	9	
7 Troy Butler	0 1 0 3 2	6	1

In a race-off for the bonus point Hans Nielsen defeated Tony Rickardsson.

BELLE VUE (H), September 16, D45-45

1 †Hans Nielsen	3 3 3 3 3	15	
2 Darren Sumner	0 1 2 0	3	1
3 Dean Barker	1 1 1 0	3	2
4 Morten Andersen	0 fx0 N	0	
5 Martin Dugard	2 3 2 3 0	10	
6 Mark Carlson	3 2 2 1 1	9	2
7 Troy Butler	F 3 0 2	5	

Belle Vue (A), September 25, L39-51

1 †Hans Nielsen	2 1 3 3 3 3	15	1
2 Morten Andersen	0 2 3 1 E 0	6	
3 Martin Dugard	1 3 3 3 2	12	
4 Darren Sumner	0 T 0 T	0	
5 Dean Barker	1 0 0 N	1	
6 Troy Butler	0 0 0 0 1	1	
7 Mark Carlson	2 0 2 T 0	4	1

Bradford (A), September 29, L33-57

1 †Hans Nielsen	2 3 3 2 2 1	13	
2 Morten Andersen	fnR T T	0	
3 Martin Dugard	0 1 1 T T	2	1
4 Darren Sumner	0 2 0 0	2	1
5 Dean Barker	1 3 1 0 1 0	6	1
6 Troy Butler	0 3 0 2 1 0	6	
7 Mark Carlson	1 1 1 1	4	

EASTBOURNE (H), September 30, W58-32

1 †Hans Nielsen	3 3 3 3	12	
2 Morten Andersen	0 2 1 1 2	6	2
3 Martin Dugard	3 3 3 3	12	
4 Darren Sumner	0 0 1 1	2	1
5 Dean Barker	3 3 1 2	9	2
6 Mark Carlson	2 2 1 2	7	2
7 Troy Butler	3 2 2 2 1	10	2

Swindon (A), October 8, L44-46

1 †Hans Nielsen	2 3 X 2 3	10	
2 Mark Carlson	1 2 2 fn	5	2
3 Martin Dugard	3 2 2 R	7	
4 Darren Sumner	0 1 0 N	1	1
5 Dean Barker	3 2 2 1	8	
6 Troy Butler	3 1 0 2 3 F	9	1
7 Morten Andersen	0 1 1 2 0	4	1

CRADLEY HEATH (H), October 9, D45-45

1 †Hans Nielsen	1 3 3 3 3	13	
2 Mark Carlson	0 1 0 N	1	
3 Martin Dugard	2 3 3 2	10	
4 Darren Sumner	0 2 N N	2	
5 Dean Barker	1 1 2 0	4	1
6 Morten Andersen	2 1 1 1 1 2	8	3
7 Troy Butler	3 2 1 0 1 0	7	1

BRADFORD (H), October 16, W48-42

1 †Hans Nielsen	3 3 3 3 2	14	
2 Mark Carlson	1 0 0 N	1	
3 Martin Dugard	2 3 0 3 1	9	1
4 Darren Sumner	0 0 N N	0	
5 Dean Barker	2 3 0 2	7	1
6 Morten Andersen	1 1 2 3 2 2	11	3
7 Troy Butler	3 1 1 0 1	6	1

At-a-Glance Results

Arena Essex	W49-41	L43-47	92-88
Belle Vue	D45-45	L39-51	84-96
Bradford	W48-42	L33-57	81-99
Coventry	W49-41	W48-38	97-79
Cradley Heath	D45-45	L40-50	85-95
Eastbourne	W58-32	L41-49	99-81
Ipswich	W48-42	L42-48	†90-90
King's Lynn	W48-42	L39-51	87-93
Poole	D45-45	L35-55	80-100
Reading	W46-44	L37-53	83-97
Swindon	D45-45	L44-46	89-91
Wolverhampton	L43-47	L43-47	86-94

† Won the bonus point when Hans Nielsen defeated Tony Rickardsson.

WHO WAS WHO IN '92

Morten ANDERSEN
Born: April 11, 1970, Middelfart, Denmark.
Returned to parent track Oxford after a short spell on loan to Swindon at the end of the 1991 season. Struggled at first but was still an impressive newcomer.

Dean BARKER
Born: August 2, 1970, Isleworth, Middlesex.
Came off the transfer list at the beginning of the season but his form fluctuated wildly throughout the year. Returned to his old club Eastbourne at the beginning of 1993.

Troy Steve BUTLER
Born: September 22, 1967, Melbourne, Victoria, Australia.
Missed early matches through injury and failed to live up to his previous promise but still scored consistently as a second string.

Mark Gary CARLSON
Born: October 24, 1965, Sydney, New South Wales, Australia.
Had a fine conclusion to his second season in the top flight although he has indicated he wants to return to Division Two racing in 1993.

Glenn Arthur CUNNINGHAM
Born: June 10, 1975, Bristol, Avon.
Began the season in the Cheetahs line-up but was replaced by new signing Daz Sumner towards the end of the season.

Martin Robert DUGARD
Born: May 18, 1969, Worthing, West Sussex.
Had his best ever season in the First Division, establishing himself as an automatic England choice despite missing out on the World Championship at the semi final stage.

Hans Hollen NIELSEN
Born: December 26, 1959, Arrentsminde, near Brovst, Denmark.
Ended the season without an FIM gold medal for the first time since 1982 but still could claim to be the most consistent rider in the world as he topped the Homefire League averages. Failed to reach the World Final for the first time since 1979.

Wayne Martin PARKER
Born: March 26, 1971, Swindon, Wiltshire.
Member of the Oxford Reserve League side who is still awaiting his League debut.

Darren SUMNER – see Middlesbrough

Spencer TIMMO – see Newcastle

Poole make a splash

THIRD place in the league and beaten finalists in the BSPA Cup is a record that Poole can look back on with a great deal of pride and satisfaction in only their second season back in the top flight.

It seemed highly unlikely that such a record would be possible six weeks into the season with co-promoter Mervyn Stewkesbury warning that performances at that stage were simply not good enough and threatening changes to the side he had assembled during the winter.

Having struggled for much of 1991 to avoid relegation, team changes were inevitable and the most significant signing was that of Craig Boyce who returned to Dorset after just one season with Oxford. He joined Marvyn Cox and Steve Schofield to form a powerful heat leader trio and with Polish Champion Slawomir Drabik on board, too, there were great expectations as the season got under way.

Mediocre performances in the Gold Cup Southern section, an 18 point drubbing in the first leg of their Speedway Star Knock Out Cup tie at Cradley Heath and defeat at the hands of Coventry in their opening home league fixture convinced Stewkesbury that further surgery was necessary.

OUT went Drabik who returned home to Poland. **OUT** went Andy Phillips, who had been a surprise loan signing during the winter.

Their replacements were talented Swedish newcomer Jörgen Johansson and another 'old boy', Ali Stevens.

The changes had the desired effect for the JTC Pirates remained unbeaten at home from that point and began to pick up momentum on their travels, starting with a draw at Eastbourne which was followed by another draw, this time at Oxford.

Despite that result another change was made immediately with Tony Langdon, who had been struggling for points, being loaned to Second Division Sheffield paving the way for a return of another 'prodigal son' Alun Rossiter who had begun the season on loan to King's Lynn.

The chirpy former skipper made his re-appearance in the away match at Arena-Essex which saw the JTC Pirates romp to their first away League victory of the season and gave credence to the growing belief that the Dorset side could mount a championship charge although few believed that the title was realistically within their grasp and so it was proved.

Having been dumped out of the Speedway Star K.O. Cup at the first hurdle and having failed to qualify for the H.E.A.T. Team Championship Final, their most realistic chance of winning a major trophy was in the BSPA Cup. They safely negotiated the tricky first tie away at Second Division Rye House for which their reward was another away draw which saw them travel to local rivals Swindon in the second round.

What controversy that produced as the two sides battled to a 45-all draw at the end of the regulation 15 heats. Confusion reigned as Swindon demanded a run off to decide the outcome and Poole insisted that they had earned the right to a replay at Wimborne Road.

Referee Mick Barnes ordered a decider which Leigh Adams won but Poole's protest was subsequently upheld and the JTC Pirates duly won the replay with some comfort, but again were denied a home draw in the quarter final.

This time they travelled to Eastbourne and reserve Ali Stevens produced a memorable paid 17 tally from his six rides to lead his side into the final against Reading.

Three successive away league victories at Cradley Heath, Swindon and Coventry had clinched third place in the League for the JTC Pirates and boosted their confidence for the clash with the Racers.

A 10-point home victory in the first leg gave them a realistic chance of taking the trophy and they fought tigerishly at Smallmead to protect that advantage but were edged out in a thrilling last heat decider that saw Reading take the silverware.

1992 RIDER ROSTER

	Club Record								Career Record							
	M	R	Pts	BP	TPts	Ave	F	P	M	R	Pts	BP	TPts	Ave	F	P
Craig Boyce	25	108	209.0	22.0	231.0	8.556	2	0	37	166	301.0	34.0	335.0	8.072	2	0
Marvyn Cox	51	267	586.0	13.0	599.0	8.974	5	0	356	1557	2748.0	222.0	2970.0	7.630	12	9
Slawomir Drabik	3	8	6.0	3.0	9.0	4.500	0	0	3	8	6.0	3.0	9.0	4.500	0	0
Jörgen Johansson	22	91	111.0	17.0	128.0	5.626	0	0	22	91	111.0	17.0	128.0	5.626	0	0
Tom Knudsen	39	142	163.0	44.0	207.0	5.831	0	0	41	148	168.0	45.0	213.0	5.757	0	0
Tony Langdon	40	181	219.0	37.0	256.0	5.657	0	1	40	181	219.0	37.0	256.0	5.657	0	1
Steve Leigh	13	41	15.0	7.0	22.0	2.146	0	0	13	41	15.0	7.0	22.0	2.146	0	0
Andy Phillips	5	18	23.0	3.0	26.0	5.778	0	0	216	795	782.0	141.0	923.0	4.644	0	0
Alun Rossiter	27	92	92.0	25.0	117.0	5.087	0	0	235	845	926.0	210.0	1136.0	5.378	0	0
Steve Schofield	52	260	478.0	41.0	519.0	7.985	1	0	113	466	671.0	74.0	745.0	6.395	1	0
Alastair Stevens	21	93	101.0	23.0	124.0	5.333	0	0	119	481	482.0	87.0	569.0	4.732	0	0
Scott Swain	1	3	1.0	0.0	1.0	1.333	0	0	2	5	2.0	1.0	3.0	2.400	0	0

POOLE

Promoters: Mervyn Stewkesbury and Peter Ansell.
Address: Poole Stadium, Wimborne Road, Poole, Dorset, BH15 2BP.
Telephone: 0202-681145.
Information Line: 0891 31 21 48.
Track Length: 371 metres.
Track Record: 63.9 secs, Sam Ermolenko (Wolverhampton), October 1, 1991. Heat 6, Poole v Wolverhampton (Sunbrite League Division One).
Seasons in Division One: 22 (1965-1984, 1991-1992).
Division One Record: Champions (1), 1969. Runners-up (1), 1992.
Speedway Star Cup Record: Semi Finalists (1), 1974.
League Cup Record: Third, Southern Section, 1983.
Inter League Cup Record: Runners-up (2), 1991, 1992.
Premiership: Runners-up (1), 1991.
Appearances: Pete Smith, 452 (1965-77).
Points: Pete Smith, 3135.5 (1965-77).
World Finalists: Brian Crutcher (1952), Slawomir Drabik (1992), Michael Lee (1983), Christer Löfqvist (1972), Malcolm Simmons (1975-76, 1978), Vaclav Verner (1982).
Division One Riders' Championship Finalists: Ronnie Genz (1965), Bill Andrew (1966), Göte Nordin (1967), Pete Smith (1969, 1973), Reidar Eide (1971), Christer Löfqvist (1972), Malcolm Simmons (1975-76-78-79-80), Scott Autrey (1981), John Davis (1982), Michael Lee (1983), Sam Ermolenko (1984), Marvyn Cox (1991-92).

Seasons in Division Two: 6 (1985-1990).
Division Two Record: Champions (2), 1989, 1990. Runners-up (3), 1985, 1986, 1988.
Division Two Cup Record: Winners (1), 1990. Runners-up (1), 1989.
Division Two Team Championship: Runners-up (1), 1990. Fourth (1), 1988. Qualified (5), 1985, 1986, 1987, 1988, 1990.
Appearances: David Biles, 140 (1985-1988).
Points: Craig Boyce, 1341 (1988-1990).
Division Two Riders' Championship Finalists: Stan Bear (1985), Steve Schofield (1986, 1988), David Biles (1987), Leigh Adams (1989), Craig Boyce (1990).
Other Honours: Division Two Champions, 1952, 1955. Division Three Champions, 1957. Provincial League Champions, 1961, 1962.

1992

POOLE

Left to right: Steve Schofield, Tony Langdon, Andy Phillips, Marvyn Cox, Neil Street (team manager), Craig Boyce, Tom Knudsen and Slawomir Drabik.

COVENTRY (H), May 20, L41-49

1 †Marvyn Cox	2 E 0 2 2 3	9	1
2 §§Slawomir Drabik	1 fx N N	1	1
3 Steve Schofield	2 3 2 2 0 2	11	1
4 §Craig Boyce	1 3 1 3 0	8	
5 Tony Langdon	0 1 N 0 2	3	
6 Tom Knudsen	2 1 N 3 N 1 1	8	2
7 §Andy Phillips	0 1 N 0 N N	1	

BRADFORD (H), May 27, W47-43

1 †Marvyn Cox	3 3 3 0 1	10	1
2 Slawomir Drabik	1 1 1 1	4	1
3 Steve Schofield	3 1 3 1 2	10	
4 Craig Boyce	3 1 1 1	6	1
5 Tony Langdon	1 0 3 3	7	
6 Tom Knudsen	1 2 0 1	4	2
7 Andy Phillips	2 2 0 2	6	

King's Lynn (A), June 6, L41-49

1 †Marvyn Cox	**3 3 3 3 3 3**	**18**	
2 Tony Langdon	0 F R N 1	1	
3 §§Jörgen Johansson	E 0 1 N 0	1	1
4 Craig Boyce	*rider replacement*		
5 Steve Schofield	3 1 2 1 1	8	
6 Tom Knudsen	2 1 1 0 2 0 N	6	2
7 §Alastair Stevens	3 2 2 0 0 R	7	

OXFORD (H), June 10, W55-35

1 †Marvyn Cox	3 3 3 3 2	14	
2 Jörgen Johansson	1 0 2 1	4	
3 Steve Schofield	3 2 3 2 1	11	1
4 Craig Boyce	2 3 1 3	9	1
5 Tony Langdon	3 1 2 0	6	
6 Tom Knudsen	1 2 1 1	5	3
7 Alastair Stevens	3 0 1 2	6	1

BELLE VUE (H), June 17, W51-39

1 †Marvyn Cox	2 3 3 3 X	11	
2 Jörgen Johansson	0 0 1 N	1	
3 Steve Schofield	R 3 3 2	8	1
4 Craig Boyce	3 3 2 1	9	2
5 Tony Langdon	2 2 2 3 N	9	2
6 Tom Knudsen	2 1 0 1 fn	4	1
7 Alastair Stevens	0 3 1 0 2 3	9	

KING'S LYNN (H), June 24, W47-43

1 †Marvyn Cox	2 3 3 2 1	11	1
2 Jörgen Johansson	0 1 2 1	4	
3 Steve Schofield	2 1 3 0	6	1
4 Craig Boyce	**3 3 3 3 3**	**15**	
5 Tony Langdon	0 0 2 2	4	
6 Andy Phillips	1 1 2 0	4	2
7 Alastair Stevens	2 0 0 1	3	

WOLVERHAMPTON (H), July 8, W48-42

1 †Marvyn Cox	2 2 3 1 0	8	1
2 Alastair Stevens	1 0 0 N	1	1
3 Steve Schofield	3 2 2 3 2	12	1
4 Craig Boyce	3 3 2 2	10	
5 Jörgen Johansson	0 0 1 2	3	2
6 Tony Langdon	3 1 3 2 1 1	11	1
7 Steve Leigh	2 1 0 N	3	1

Eastbourne (A), July 12, D45-45

1 †Marvyn Cox	**3 3 3 3 3 3**	**18**	
2 Alastair Stevens	1 R T T	1	
3 Steve Schofield	2 2 3 2 2 2	13	2
4 Jörgen Johansson	0 2 1 0	3	
5 Craig Boyce	2 0 1 3	6	1
6 Tony Langdon	2 0 1 R 0	3	
7 Tom Knudsen	1 0 N 0	1	1

EASTBOURNE (H), July 22, W52-38

1 †Marvyn Cox	3 3 3 1	10	
2 Alastair Stevens	R 0 E 1	1	
3 Steve Schofield	0 2 2 3	7	1
4 Craig Boyce	3 3 3 2 2	13	1
5 Tony Langdon	0 1 0 N	1	
6 Jörgen Johansson	R 1 1 3 3 0	8	1
7 Tom Knudsen	3 2 3 3 1	12	2

Belle Vue (A), July 24, L36-53

1 †Marvyn Cox	3 2 3 3 3 2	16	
2 Alastair Stevens	0 0 T T	0	
3 Steve Schofield	1 1 3 0 1 0	6	1
4 Tony Langdon	0 1 1 0	2	1
5 Craig Boyce	1 2 0 1	4	1
6 Tom Knudsen	1 0 fx2	3	
7 Jörgen Johansson	3 2 0 0	5	

Reading (A), July 27, L40-50

1 †Marvyn Cox	3 3 3 3 3 2	17	
2 Alastair Stevens	1 1 1 0	3	
3 Steve Schofield	F 1 1 0 3	5	1
4 Tony Langdon	1 R N 0	1	1
5 Craig Boyce	2 3 2 1 1 1	10	1
6 Tom Knudsen	1 0 T 0 T	1	1
7 Jörgen Johansson	2 1 0 T	3	

Oxford (A), July 31, D45-45

1 †Marvyn Cox	2 3 1 3 2	11	
2 Alastair Stevens	1 0 2 3	6	2
3 Steve Schofield	2 2 3 0 F	7	1
4 Tony Langdon	0 1 1 N	2	1
5 Craig Boyce	2 2 1 2	7	
6 Tom Knudsen	3 3 3 2 0 1	12	2
7 Jörgen Johansson	0 0 N 0	0	

Arena Essex (A), August 7, W47-43

1 †Marvyn Cox	1 2 3 2 2	10	2
2 Alun Rossiter	2 1 1 0	4	1
3 Steve Schofield	1 2 2 0	5	1
4 Tom Knudsen	2 0 2 3	7	1
5 Craig Boyce	3 3 2 3 1	12	1
6 Alastair Stevens	3 2 N E 1 0 2	8	2
7 §Scott Swain	1 N 0 0	1	

Bradford (A), August 15, L36-54

1 †Marvyn Cox	1 2 3 2 2 3	13	
2 Alun Rossiter	0 1 T 1	2	2
3 Steve Schofield	0 1 1 2 3 2	9	1
4 Tom Knudsen	1 0 1 0	2	1
5 Craig Boyce	2 1 1 2	6	2
6 Steve Leigh	fx0 0 T	0	
7 Jörgen Johansson	2 1 1 0	4	

READING (H), August 19, W46-44

1 †Marvyn Cox	3 2 2 3 R	10	
2 Alun Rossiter	0 1 1 N	2	2
3 Steve Schofield	2 2 3 2 2	11	
4 Craig Boyce	3 1 0 3	7	
5 Tom Knudsen	1 0 1 N	2	1
6 Alastair Stevens	1 1 1 2 1	6	4
7 Jörgen Johansson	2 2 1 1 2	8	2

CRADLEY HEATH (H), September 2, W49-41

1 †Marvyn Cox	2 2 3 2 3	12	
2 Alun Rossiter	1 0 1 1	3	2
3 Steve Schofield	3 2 3 1 2	11	1
4 Craig Boyce	0 N 1 3	4	1
5 Tom Knudsen	2 1 3 0	6	1
6 Alastair Stevens	2 2 0 1	5	2
7 Jörgen Johansson	3 2 2 0 1	8	

ARENA ESSEX (H), September 9, W57-32

1 †Marvyn Cox	3 3 3 2 2	13	1
2 Alun Rossiter	1 2 2 2	7	3
3 Steve Schofield	0 1 3 3	7	
4 Craig Boyce	**3 3 3 3**	**12**	
5 Tom Knudsen	1 1 0 2	4	1
6 Alastair Stevens	2 1 R 1	4	1
7 Jörgen Johansson	3 3 1 2 1	10	2

IPSWICH (H), September 16, W65-25

1 †Marvyn Cox	3 3 3 2	11	
2 Alun Rossiter	2 2 2 1	7	3
3 Steve Schofield	3 3 3 3 1	13	
4 Craig Boyce	2 3 1 3	9	2
5 Tom Knudsen	3 2 2 2 0	9	3
6 Alastair Stevens	2 1 2 3	8	2
7 Jörgen Johansson	3 3 2 0	8	1

Ipswich (A), September 17, L42-48

1 †Marvyn Cox	0 3 2 1 2	8	
2 Alun Rossiter	1 0 T T	1	
3 Steve Schofield	2 3 2 0 3 1	11	
4 Tom Knudsen	0 0 T N	0	
5 Craig Boyce	2 2 3 2 2 0	11	2
6 Alastair Stevens	1 1 0 2 1 3	8	3
7 Jörgen Johansson	2 0 1 N	3	1

SWINDON (H), September 30, W57-33

1 †Marvyn Cox	2 3 3 3 2	13	1
2 Alun Rossiter	1 0 3 2	6	2
3 Steve Schofield	1 2 3 N	6	1
4 Craig Boyce	3 2 2 2 3	12	2
5 Tom Knudsen	2 1 1 1	5	4
6 Alastair Stevens	2 2 R N 1 2	7	1
7 Jörgen Johansson	3 0 2 N 3	8	

Wolverhampton (A), October 5, L38-51

1 †Marvyn Cox	X 2 0 X 1 0	3	1
2 Alun Rossiter	F N N N	0	
3 Steve Schofield	1 3 3 1 2 1	11	1
4 Tom Knudsen	1 1 0 T	2	2
5 Craig Boyce	2 2 fxT	4	
6 Alastair Stevens	1 0 2 1 2 2	8	1
7 Jörgen Johansson	3 2 3 1 1	10	

Cradley Heath (A), October 10, W51-39

1 †Marvyn Cox	3 2 3 3 3	14	
2 Alun Rossiter	2 0 1 2	5	2
3 Steve Schofield	3 3 3 0 1	10	
4 Tom Knudsen	0 1 2 1	4	1
5 Craig Boyce	3 2 1 3	9	
6 Alastair Stevens	3 0 1 1 1	6	1
7 Jörgen Johansson	2 1 0 N	3	1

Swindon (A), October 15, W47-43

1 †Marvyn Cox	2 3 3 3 2	13	
2 Alun Rossiter	1 2 3 1	7	2
3 Steve Schofield	3 2 2 2 F	9	
4 Tom Knudsen	1 0 0 N	1	1
5 Craig Boyce	2 3 1 3	9	1
6 Alastair Stevens	0 1 0 1	2	1
7 Jörgen Johansson	3 0 2 1 0	6	1

Coventry (A), October 17, W46-44

1 †Marvyn Cox	3 3 3 3 0	12	
2 Alun Rossiter	0 0 N 1	1	
3 Steve Schofield	3 3 3 3 1	13	
4 Tom Knudsen	1 2 1 N	4	1
5 Craig Boyce	2 1 1 1	5	1
6 Alastair Stevens	R 1 1 N R 0	2	1
7 Jörgen Johansson	1 2 2 N 2 2	9	3

At-a-Glance Results

Arena Essex	W57-32	W47-43	104-75
Belle Vue	W51-39	L36-53	87-92
Bradford	W47-43	L36-54	83-97
Coventry	L41-49	W46-44	87-93
Cradley Heath	W49-41	W51-39	100-80
Eastbourne	W52-38	D45-45	97-83
Ipswich	W65-25	L42-48	107-73
King's Lynn	W47-43	L41-49	88-92
Oxford	W55-35	D45-45	100-80
Reading	W46-44	L40-50	86-94
Swindon	W57-33	W47-43	104-76
Wolverhampton	W48-42	L38-51	86-93

WHO WAS WHO IN '92

Darren John BOULTON
Born: October 9, 1970, Dorchester, Dorset.
Rejoined his old club Poole in a loan exchange which saw Justin Elkins move to Swindon. His season was interrupted by a knee injury.

Craig BOYCE
Born: August 2, 1967, Sydney, New South Wales, Australia.
Rejoined his old club Poole in a full transfer after only one season with Oxford.

Marvyn COX
Born: July 11, 1964, Whitstable, Kent.
Topped the Poole averages for the second successive season and also reached the World Long Track Final.

Jason CRUMP – see Peterborough

Slawomir DRABIK
Born: June 2, 1966, Czestochowa, Poland.
The 1991 Polish Champion who made his British debut for the JTC Pirates. Released midway through the season but went on to turn in an impressive World Final debut.

Justin ELKINS – see Swindon

Jörgen JOHANSSON
Born: April 24, 1967, Vastervik, Sweden.
Surprise mid-season signing who came to Britain as a dark horse but who showed considerable improvement by the end of the season.

Tom KNUDSEN
Born: September 14, 1968, Gørding, Denmark.
A survivor from Poole's National League double winning side who proved a potent reserve for part of the season and a reliable team member when promoted.

Tony LANGDON – see Sheffield

Steven LEIGH
Born: July 26, 1967, Romsey, Hampshire.
Continued in the Poole second half even though he was made available for loan or free transfer to a Second Division club.

Andy PHILLIPS – see Cradley Heath

Alun John ROSSITER
Born: July 23, 1965, Swindon, Wiltshire.
Loaned out to King's Lynn at the beginning of the season but sought a move on Bill Barker's withdrawal as promoted and returned to parent track Poole for the remainder of the season.

Steven SCHOFIELD
Born: February 27, 1958, Mitcham, Surrey.
Capped by England for the first time in his career.

Alastair STEVENS
Born: October 15, 1968, Aylesbury, Buckinghamshire.
Ended a brief retirement by rejoining his old National League club Poole as the JTC Pirates looked to strengthen up after a disappointing Gold Cup season.

Scott SWAIN
Born: October 29, 1971, Eastbourne, East Sussex.
Made his Homefire League debut for Poole at Arena Essex early in August. Rode one match for Eastbourne in 1991.

Sheer bliss for Pat's boys

VERY much of question of going backwards in order to move forward for the Reading Racers and that retrograde step paid handsome dividends. Not only did they regain the League title but they also won the BSPA Cup and were just edged out by Wolverhampton in the Gold Cup final and a treble!

Having been forced to break up their 1990 championship winning side to keep within the points limit, they struggled in 1991 to finish in eleventh spot but that was to work to their advantage.

It enabled promoter Pat Bliss to consider a multitude of options as she planned her 1992 side although those options were reduced when Todd Wiltshire was seriously injured in the Australian Final. She turned to Per Jonsson, the man who had led the Racers to success two years earlier, and he agreed to return after a year's sabbatical.

"We just couldn't agree a business deal last year," was how he explained his year's break from the British League, "but I'm glad to be back."

Back too came Italian Armando Castagna and the two Old Boys joined testimonial man David Mullett, Jan Andersson, Jeremy Doncaster, Ray Morton and Welsh teenager Phil Morris.

The return of Jonsson was to prove the key factor in Reading's success. He soon formed a formidable opening partnership with Mullett and the Racers began the season in scintillating style. A double over Cradley Heath in a two-legged challenge was followed by a fine unbeaten run in the Gold Cup. A league victory at Belle Vue and a draw at Coventry demonstrated that the Berkshire outfit were real championship material.

However, they were brought down to earth with a bump in the league match at Wolverhampton being thumped 54-36 and finishing the match with Castagna out of action with three broken fingers.

"I'm sure we'll give a better account of ourselves next time," said team manager Tim Sugar... and how prophetic those words were!

Bouncing back from that defeat they continued on their winning streak in the Gold Cup before losing their unbeaten record in that competition at Kings Lynn although, by that stage, they were virtually assured of their place in the Final.

June produced very little action with few fixtures but when the league matches re-started they soon got back in the groove completing a double over Cradley, then defeated Stoke in the BSPA Cup, Oxford in the Speedway Star KO Cup and won at Arena-Essex to confirm their place in the Gold Cup Final.

With Jan Andersson having dropped to reserve they were proving formidable opposition for anyone but a 10 match unbeaten run finally ended at Poole where they went down by just two points. The first major disappointment came when they could only eke out a slender five point advantage over Wolverhampton in the home leg of the Gold Cup Final.

It was too slender a lead to hang onto at Monmore Green but they extracted revenge in the second half of a double-header battling a draw to progress to the KO Cup semis where they easily overcame Cradley.

Success in the cup competitions and the inactive period in June meant that the Racers were falling drastically behind with fixtures although it didn't seem to have any effect on them and when they beat both Bradford and Eastbourne on the same night at Smallmead, they climbed to the top of the table.

Only fatigue could stand in the way of the league title but six of their last nine fixtures were to be raced at home and an 'awarded' 75-0 victory from the cancelled match at Kings Lynn was gratefully accepted.

A home victory over Coventry clinched the League crown, they overcame a 10 point deficit to defeat Poole in the BSPA Cup Final but found a 20 point disadvantage too much to claw back in the second half of a unique Cup Final double header against Bradford.

Whichever way you look, the Racers were THE team of the year in the First Division.

1992 RIDER ROSTER

	Club Record								Career Record							
	M	R	Pts	BP	TPts	Ave	F	P	M	R	Pts	BP	TPts	Ave	F	P
Jan Andersson	504	2254	4864.0	276.0	5140.0	9.122	46	20	599	2667	5525.0	339.0	5864.0	8.795	48	22
Armando Castagna	48	203	299.0	40.0	339.0	6.680	0	0	130	572	915.0	94.0	1009.0	7.056	1	1
Jeremy Doncaster	133	644	1303.0	88.0	1391.0	8.640	2	3	453	2047	4075.0	325.0	4400.0	8.598	29	18
Per Jonsson	271	1194	2246.0	189.0	2435.0	8.157	17	8	271	1194	2246.0	189.0	2435.0	8.157	17	8
Phillip Morris	34	118	53.0	23.0	76.0	2.576	0	0	34	118	53.0	23.0	76.0	2.576	0	0
Ray Morton	55	240	333.0	64.0	397.0	6.617	0	0	118	429	500.0	98.0	598.0	5.576	0	0
David Mullett	188	779	996.0	197.0	1193.0	6.126	0	2	190	783	999.0	197.0	1196.0	6.110	0	2
Mark Sayer	1	3	0.0	0.0	0.0	0.000	0	0	1	3	0.0	0.0	0.0	0.000	0	0
Lance Sealey	5	22	6.0	0.0	6.0	1.091	0	0	6	26	6.0	0.0	6.0	0.923	0	0
Gary Sweet	1	2	0.0	0.0	0.0	0.000	0	0	1	2	0.0	0.0	0.0	0.000	0	0
Mick Tomlin	3	9	0.0	0.0	0.0	0.000	0	0	3	9	0.0	0.0	0.0	0.000	0	0

READING

Promoters: Pat Bliss and Bill Dore.
Address: Smallmead Stadium, Bennet Road, Reading, Berkshire.
Telephone: 0734-863161.
Clubcall: 0898 12 18 75.
Track Length: 307 metres.
Track Record: 58.1 secs, Per Jonsson (Reading), October 12, 1987, heat 1, Reading v Coventry (Division One).
Seasons in Division One: 21 (1971-1973 [Tilehurst]; 1975-1992).
Division One Record: Champions (4), 1973, 1980, 1990, 1992. Runners-up (1), 1972. Third (1), 1977.
Speedway Star Cup Record: Winners (1), 1990. Runners-up (3), 1973, 1977, 1992.
Best League Cup Season: Semi-finalists (Group winners), 1984.
Inter League Cup Record: Winners (1), 1992.
Gold Cup: Runners-up (1), 1992.
Premiership: Winners (1), 1991.
Division One Team Championship: Third (1), 1991.
Appearances: Jan Andersson, 443 plus 1991 (1980-1988, 1990-91).
Points: Jan Andersson, 4582.5 plus 1991 (1980-1988, 1990-91).
World Finalists: Jan Andersson (1980-81-82, 1984-85), John Davis (1980), Jeremy Doncaster (1989, 1991), Bengt Jansson (1977), Dave Jessup (1978), Per Jonsson (1987-88, 1990, 1992), Anders Michanek (1971-72-73, 1975), Tony Olsson (1989), Mitch Shirra (1983-84, 1986, 1989), Jiri Stancl (1980, 1982), Alois Wiesböck (1979), Todd Wiltshire (1990).
Division One Riders' Championship Finalists: Anders Michanek (1971-72-73, 1975), Dave Jessup (1976-77-78), John Davis (1979), Jan Andersson (1980-81-82-83-84-85-86-87-88), Bobby Schwartz (1982), Mitch Shirra (1983, 1989), John Davis (1986), Per Jonsson (1988, 1992), Jeremy Doncaster (1989-90), Todd Wiltshire (1990).

1992

READING

Left to right: Per Jonsson, David Mullett, Jan Andersson, Tim Sugar (team manager), Jeremy Doncaster, Ray Morton, Phillip Morris and Armando Castagna.

Belle Vue (A), April 10, W47-43

1 Per Jonsson	3 3 2 X 0	8	
2 David Mullett	0 1 fx1	2	1
3 Jan Andersson	2 1 1 0	4	
4 †Jeremy Doncaster	3 2 2 2 1	10	
5 Armando Castagna	2 1 2 3	8	2
6 Ray Morton	3 3 2 0 1 2	11	2
7 Phillip Morris	2 1 N 1	4	3

Coventry (A), April 18, D45-45

1 Per Jonsson	3 2 3 2 3	13	
2 David Mullett	2 1 3 1	7	2
3 Jan Andersson	2 1 2 0	5	
4 †Jeremy Doncaster	2 1 2 1	6	2
5 Armando Castagna	3 3 2 2 0	10	
6 Ray Morton	3 0 N 0 N 0 0	3	
7 Phillip Morris	0 N 0 N 1 N	1	1

Wolverhampton (A), April 27, L34-56

1 Per Jonsson	0 3 2 2 2 1	10	1
2 David Mullett	1 0 3 0	4	
3 Jan Andersson	1 0 3 1 0	5	
4 †Jeremy Doncaster	2 1 3 1 1	8	2
5 Armando Castagna	0 2 fxT	2	
6 Ray Morton	2 2 0 0	4	
7 Phillip Morris	1 0 T T 0	1	1

Cradley Heath (A), June 27, W47-42

1 Per Jonsson	2 3 3 2 2	12	2
2 David Mullett	3 1 3 1 1	9	1
3 Jan Andersson	2 3 1 0	6	1
4 †Jeremy Doncaster	0 2 1 3	6	1
5 Armando Castagna	1 3 1 E	5	
6 Ray Morton	3 3 1 N 0 2	9	
7 Phillip Morris	fxN 0 0 N 0	0	

CRADLEY HEATH (H), June 29, W53-37

1 Per Jonsson	**3 3 3 3 3**	**15**	
2 David Mullett	0 2 3 2 1	8	2
3 Jan Andersson	2 2 0 1	5	
4 Armando Castagna	0 3 2 3	8	1
5 †Jeremy Doncaster	1 1 2 3	7	
6 Phillip Morris	fx1 N 0 1	2	1
7 Ray Morton	3 1 2 N 2	8	3

BELLE VUE (H), July 13, W46-44

1 Per Jonsson	3 2 3 2 3	13	
2 David Mullett	2 1 3 1	7	2
3 Jan Andersson	0 1 3 2 0	6	
4 †Jeremy Doncaster	2 3 0 1	6	
5 Armando Castagna	0 1 2 1	4	1
6 Phillip Morris	1 1 N 1	3	1
7 Ray Morton	3 0 2 2 0	7	2

POOLE (H), July 27, W50-40

1 Per Jonsson	R 3 2 3 3	11	
2 David Mullett	2 2 3 1 0	8	2
3 †Jeremy Doncaster	3 1 1 2	7	2
4 §§Gary Sweet	0 0 N N	0	
5 Armando Castagna	3 2 3 1	9	1
6 Phillip Morris	0 2 N 0 0	2	1
7 Jan Andersson	3 2 2 2 2 2	13	2

Swindon (A), August 6, W50-40

1 Per Jonsson	**3 3 3 3 3**	**15**	
2 David Mullett	2 1 1 1	5	1
3 †Jeremy Doncaster	2 1 2 0	5	2
4 Armando Castagna	0 2 3 1 0	6	
5 Ray Morton	1 1 N 2	4	2
6 Jan Andersson	2 2 3 3 2 3	15	
7 Mick Tomlin	0 F N F	0	

Poole (A), August 19, L44-46

1 Per Jonsson	2 3 2 3 3	13	
2 David Mullett	1 2 3 0 1	7	2
3 †Jeremy Doncaster	3 0 0 2	5	
4 Armando Castagna	2 3 0 0	5	
5 Ray Morton	0 fxN 0	0	
6 Jan Andersson	3 3 3 3 1 1	14	1
7 Phillip Morris	0 0 0 N	0	

Oxford (A), August 31, L44-46

1 Per Jonsson	2 2 3 3 1	11	2
2 David Mullett	3 3 2 fx	8	1
3 †Jeremy Doncaster	1 2 1 3 0	7	
4 Armando Castagna	2 1 1 0	4	1
5 Ray Morton	0 2 1 0	3	
6 Jan Andersson	2 0 1 3 3 2	11	1
7 Phillip Morris	F N N N	0	

OXFORD (H), August 31, W53-37

1 Per Jonsson	2 3 3 3	11	
2 David Mullett	1 1 3 2	7	2
3 †Jeremy Doncaster	2 2 1 2 2	9	1
4 Ray Morton	3 2 2 1 1	9	2
5 Armando Castagna	0 1 2 1	4	2
6 Mick Tomlin	0 0 N 0	0	
7 Jan Andersson	2 3 2 3 3	13	1

SWINDON (H), September 7, W51-39

1 Per Jonsson	1 2 3 3 3	12	1
2 David Mullett	2 1 2 1	6	2
3 †Jeremy Doncaster	2 1 3 3 1	10	1
4 Ray Morton	1 1 1 0	3	1
5 Armando Castagna	0 2 3 2	7	1
6 Phillip Morris	1 0 N F	1	
7 Jan Andersson	3 2 3 1 3	12	

Arena Essex (A), September 11, W46-44

1 Per Jonsson	2 3 3 3 3	14	
2 David Mullett	1 2 1 1	5	2
3 †Jeremy Doncaster	3 3 2 1 1	10	
4 Armando Castagna	E 1 2 0	3	
5 Ray Morton	3 0 0 0	3	
6 Jan Andersson	2 1 1 1 1 2	8	2
7 Phillip Morris	1 2 0 N	3	2

WOLVERHAMPTON (H), September 28, W54-36

1 Per Jonsson	2 3 3 2 2	12	1
2 David Mullett	3 1 3 2 0	9	1
3 †Jeremy Doncaster	3 2 N N	5	
4 Ray Morton	2 2 0 1	5	2
5 Armando Castagna	1 3 3 0	7	1
6 Phillip Morris	1 0 N 1 F	2	
7 Jan Andersson	3 1 2 3 3 2	14	2

ARENA ESSEX (H), October 5, W54-36

1 Per Jonsson	**3 3 3 3 3**	**15**	
2 David Mullett	2 2 3 1 0	8	2
3 Jan Andersson	2 2 1 0	5	
4 †Jeremy Doncaster	3 1 2 3	9	2
5 Armando Castagna	1 2 1 3	7	
6 Phillip Morris	2 1 1 0	4	3
7 Ray Morton	3 2 0 1	6	1

Bradford (A), October 10, L43-47

1 Per Jonsson	3 3 2 2 3 X	13	
2 David Mullett	2 0 2 1	5	2
3 Jan Andersson	1 0 2 T 2	5	2
4 †Jeremy Doncaster	0 2 1 0	3	
5 Armando Castagna	2 X 1 3 2	8	1
6 Ray Morton	3 1 1 N 1 T	6	2
7 Phillip Morris	1 2 N E 0	3	

Eastbourne (A), October 11, W49-41

1 Per Jonsson	2 1 fx2 0	5	1
2 David Mullett	3 3 2 2 3	13	1
3 Jan Andersson	2 2 2 2	8	1
4 Armando Castagna	1 2 2 0	5	2
5 †Jeremy Doncaster	2 1 3 2	8	1
6 Ray Morton	3 0 3 N 3 1	10	1
7 Phillip Morris	0 fxN F N	0	

BRADFORD (H), October 12, W59-31

1 Per Jonsson	**2 3 3 2 3**	**13**	**2**
2 David Mullett	**3 2 3 2**	**10**	**2**
3 Jan Andersson	3 2 X 1	6	1
4 Armando Castagna	0 1 3 3	7	
5 †Jeremy Doncaster	3 3 3 3 1	13	
6 Phillip Morris	1 0 N F	1	
7 Ray Morton	3 3 1 2 0	9	

EASTBOURNE (H), October 12, W58-32

1 Per Jonsson	3 2 3 2 3	13	1
2 David Mullett	2 3 1 1	7	1
3 Jan Andersson	2 3 R 3 E	8	
4 †Jeremy Doncaster	2 2 1 3	8	3
5 Armando Castagna	3 3 3 1	10	
6 Phillip Morris	2 0 1 0 0	3	1
7 Ray Morton	3 3 1 2	9	1

Ipswich (A), October 15, W48-41

1 Per Jonsson	3 2 3 2 3	13	1
2 David Mullett	2 0 0 2	4	2
3 Jan Andersson	1 0 2 0	3	
4 †Jeremy Doncaster	**3 3 3 3 2**	**14**	**1**
5 Armando Castagna	2 2 1 fx	5	2
6 Ray Morton	3 1 3 1 1	9	1
7 Phillip Morris	0 0 N 0	0	

COVENTRY (H), October 25, W51-39

1 Per Jonsson	**3 3 3 3 3**	**15**	
2 David Mullett	2 1 3 1	7	1
3 Jan Andersson	3 fx3 1	7	
4 †Jeremy Doncaster	1 2 1 2	6	2
5 Armando Castagna	2 3 2 3 1	11	
6 Phillip Morris	R 0 1 1	2	1
7 §Lance Sealey	2 1 0 0	3	

IPSWICH (H), October 28, W52-38

1 Per Jonsson	**3 3 3 3 3**	**15**	
2 David Mullett	**2 2 3 2**	**9**	**3**
3 Jan Andersson	3 2 3 R	8	
4 Armando Castagna	R 1 2 3	6	1
5 †Jeremy Doncaster	3 3 3 2 2	13	1
6 Phillip Morris	1 fxN N	1	
7 Lance Sealey	fx0 0 0 0 0	0	

KING'S LYNN (H), October 28, W46-44

1 Per Jonsson	**3 3 3 3**	**12**	
2 David Mullett	F 2 3 2	7	2
3 Jan Andersson	2 3 2 3 1	11	
4 †Jeremy Doncaster	3 3 2 2	10	1
5 Armando Castagna	1 R 2 1	4	
6 §§Mark Sayer	0 fx0 N	0	
7 Lance Sealey	2 0 0 0 0 0	2	

The match at King's Lynn was never staged but the Speedway Control Board subsequently awarded the match to Reading 75-0.

At-a-Glance Results

Arena Essex	W54-36	W46-44	100-80
Belle Vue	W46-44	W47-43	93-87
Bradford	W59-31	L43-47	102-78
Coventry	W51-39	D45-45	96-84
Cradley Heath	W53-37	W47-42	100-79
Eastbourne	W58-32	W49-41	107-73
Ipswich	W52-38	W48-41	100-79
King's Lynn	W46-44	†W75-0	121-44
Oxford	W53-37	L44-46	97-83
Poole	W50-40	L44-46	94-86
Swindon	W51-39	W50-40	101-79
Wolverhampton	W54-36	L34-56	88-92

† King's Lynn refused to stage their Homefire League match against Reading because they were missing both Henrik Gustafsson and Mark Loram on World Championship duty. The BSPA ruled the match should go ahead and as a result the Speedway Control Board ruled the result should be awarded 75-0 to Reading.

WHO WAS WHO IN '92

Jan Håkan ANDERSSON
Born: May 7, 1955, Alingsas, Sweden.
Completed his 13th season with the Racers, winning his third Division One championship medal, having been a member of the title-winning side in both 1980 and 1990.

Armando CASTAGNA
Born: September 22, 1963, Arzignano, Italy.
Spent his first full season in Britain since 1988 although he had helped out Eastbourne at the end of 1991.

Jeremy DONCASTER
Born: June 16, 1961, Grimsby, Humberside.
Won his third Division One championship – having been a member of Ipswich's successful squad in 1984 and the Racers in 1990.

Per JONSSON
Born: March 21, 1966, Stockholm, Sweden.
Took second place in the World Final and topped the Reading averages in his most successful British season as he ended a year long absence from the Smallmead.

Phillip William MORRIS
Born: September 10, 1975, Newport, Gwent, South Wales.
After riding in the final half dozen League matches in 1991 he held down a regular team berth throughout the year until being injured in the final week of the season.

Raymond Paul MORTON
Born: June 19, 1968, London.
Spent his second successful season at Smallmead although he ended the year on the sidelines with a fractured collar bone.

David John MULLETT
Born: June 27, 1965, Folkestone, Kent.
Enjoyed a highly successful Testimonial season, being capped by his country in the summer Test series.

Mark Leslie SAYER
Born: May 13, 1975, Reading, Berkshire.
Made his debut in the final match of the season after Phillip Morris had been injured in the first part of a double header.

Lance SEALEY
Born: March 8, 1970, Swindon, Wiltshire.
Stood in for injured Ray Morton in the final matches of the campaign.

Gary Kenneth SWEET
Born: December 3, 1967, Clapham, London.
Made his debut for the Racers in their early season Gold Cup programme.

Michael Ross (Mick) TOMLIN
Born: February 4, 1972, Poole, Dorset.
Reserve League rider who had made just two official League appearances in 1992 to add to the one he made in 1991.

1992

SWINDON

Left to right: Kelly Moran, Justin Elkins, David Smart, Mitch Shirra, John Davis, Leigh Adams, Jimmy Nilsen, Steve Masters and Ron Byford (co-promoter).

No escaping this time!

WHEN someone is thrown a lifeline they normally grab it with both hands – Swin don didn't! Having finished bottom of Division One in 1991, they suffered the ignominy of becoming the first team to suffer boardroom relegation but escaped.

It seemed inconceivable that a club with their tradition should then allow them selves to be left in exactly the same position a year later!

Throughout the winter they had argued and pleaded to be allowed to remain in the top flight and were eventually reprieved under the Constitution which decreed that the Second Division should always have at least an equal number of tracks as in Division One.

Swindon were granted their reprieve and seemed determined to learn from the previous year's mistakes. The management set about making wholesale changes to their squad. Only Leigh Adams, John Davis and Dean Standing were retained and the first move was to welcome back Jimmy Nilsen after his unhappy year away at Berwick.

His return meant no place in the line up for fellow Swede Peter Nahlin who, many felt, should have been retained at all costs. Mitch Shirra, surplus to requirements at Reading, returned to Blunsdon and with such a powerful looking top five signed up it left precious few points to play with for the two reserve berths. Shirra recommended that German Peter Schroeck be given another chance to prove his mettle in Britain and the last place went to junior Steve Camden.

The theory was that the top five should be strong enough to combat any shortcomings at reserve and, in the first few weeks it worked in practice but the first blow to hit home was when John Davis broke a leg in the Gold Cup fixture at Arena-Essex. Despite initial optimism that he would be back in the saddle within six weeks, it was an injury that would sideline him for the rest of the year.

Kelly Moran was signed from Belle Vue as a replacement but couldn't prevent Wolverhampton winning at Blunsdon in the first leg of the Speedway Star Knock Out Cup. A Gold Cup double over Eastbourne boosted morale only for the ADT Robins to lose their first four away league fixtures, that despite Adams being in quite brilliant form.

Both Schroeck and Camden fell by the wayside, being replaced by youngsters Justin Elkins and Steve Masters.

The ADT Robins lost six home league matches on the trot to plunge deep into relegation trouble once again, and team manager Ron Byford bore the brunt of the criticism from the terraces. The club appeared to be in disarray but Byford remained defiant convinced that his riders would pull them out of trouble.

Their BSPA Cup aspirations ended in controversy when they were held to a draw by Poole at Blunsdon. Adams beat Steve Schofield in a run off but a subsequent appeal by the visitors was upheld, a replay was ordered and Swindon went out of the competition.

At last they managed to win a match, at home to Kings Lynn, and with a further victory over Oxford seven days later it looked as if they might avoid relegation. However, a disastrous home defeat at the hands of Poole virtually sealed their fate.

With Eastbourne defeating Arena-Essex in their last match of the season the ADT Robins were confirmed as wooden spoonists and relegated – again!

This time there was no escape but how ironic that it was the Poole promotion, whose side had all but ended Swindon's hopes of remaining in Division One, who stepped in to buy the franchise at the Abbey Stadium.

Undoubtedly it was the injury to Standing that upset the applecart more than anything else as he was a vital cog in the side. The remaining team members, though, should have provided better backing to the outstanding Adams and if they had, then the ADT Robins might still be in Division One...and Ron Byford in a job!

1992 RIDER ROSTER

	Club Record								Career Record							
	M	R	Pts	BP	TPts	Ave	F	P	M	R	Pts	BP	TPts	Ave	F	P
Leigh Adams	82	430	839.0	54.0	893.0	8.307	2	3	82	430	839.0	54.0	893.0	8.307	2	3
Steve Camden	3	5	1.0	0.0	1.0	0.800	0	0	3	5	1.0	0.0	1.0	0.800	0	0
David Clarke	4	13	2.0	1.0	3.0	0.923	0	0	139	506	419.0	73.0	492.0	3.889	0	0
Matthew Cross	33	74	28.0	7.0	35.0	1.892	0	0	33	74	28.0	7.0	35.0	1.892	0	0
John Davis	53	200	323.0	38.0	361.0	7.220	2	1	654	2686	5294.0	258.0	5552.0	8.268	47	15
Justin Elkins	25	88	49.0	11.0	60.0	2.727	0	0	25	88	49.0	11.0	60.0	2.727	0	0
Steve Masters	14	49	26.0	10.0	36.0	2.939	0	0	19	58	28.0	10.0	38.0	2.621	0	0
Kelly Moran	25	113	152.0	20.0	172.0	6.088	0	0	368	1651	3230.0	265.0	3495.0	8.468	32	21
Jimmy Nilsen	205	951	1888.0	121.0	2009.0	8.450	5	11	229	1076	2177.0	133.0	2310.0	8.587	5	12
Peter Schroeck	0	0	0.0	0.0	0.0	n.a.	0	0	19	41	11.0	3.0	14.0	1.366	0	0
Mitch Shirra	66	293	601.0	22.0	623.0	8.505	4	1	588	2528	5033.0	243.0	5276.0	8.348	46	19
David Smart	101	374	297.0	76.0	373.0	3.989	0	0	101	374	297.0	76.0	373.0	3.989	0	0
Dean Standing	37	166	213.0	38.0	251.0	6.048	0	0	47	204	250.0	44.0	294.0	5.765	0	0

SWINDON

Swindon became the first club to be officially relegated after finishing bottom of the 1991 Sunbrite League First Division. They were subsequently re-elected to Division One when Mildenhall's application to return to League racing took the number of competing clubs to 26. Under the constitution each Division has to be of equal number of tracks and after all other Division Two clubs turned down the late chance of elevation to Division One Swindon were unanimously elected to return to the First Division.

Promoters: Ted Nelson, Bill Chandler and Ron Byford.
Address: Abbey Stadium, Blunsdon, Swindon, Wiltshire, SN2 4ND.
Telephone: 0793-721253.
Hotline: 0898 800 671.
Track Length: 359.6 metres.
Track Record: 64.8 secs, Hans Nielsen (Oxford), September 8, 1990, heat 1, Swindon v Oxford (Sunbrite League).
Seasons in Division One: 28 (1965-1992).
Division One Record: Champions (1), 1967. Third (3), 1966, 1981, 1987.
Best Speedway Star Cup Seasons: Semi-finalists (5), 1968, 1970, 1980, 1981, 1990.
Best League Cup Season: Fifth, 1986.
Inter League Cup Record: Runners-up (1), 1980.
Division One Team Championship: Finalists (1), 1992.
Appearances: Martin Ashby, 425 (1965-1967, 1971-1979).
Points: Martin Ashby, 4288.5 (1965-1967, 1971-1979).
World Finalists: Jan Andersson (1978), Barry Briggs (1964-65-66-67-68-69-70, 1972), Mike Broadbank (1958, 1961-62, 1964, 1966), Arne Carlsson (1962), Phil Crump (1982), Peter Moore (1963), Jimmy Nilsen (1986-87, 1990, 1992), Bo Petersen (1984), Bob Roger (1957), Mitch Shirra (1987, 1992), George White (1957, 1959), Ian Williams (1957).
Division One Riders' Championship Finalists: Barry Briggs (1965-66-67-68-69-70-71), Martin Ashby (1972-73-74-75-76), Bob Kilby (1977), Phil Crump (1979, 1981, 1983-84), Scott Autrey (1980), Steve Bastable (1982), Bo Petersen (1985), Alan Grahame (1986), Jimmy Nilsen (1987, 1989-90), Mitch Shirra (1987), Brian Karger (1988-89), Andrew Silver (1990), Leigh Adams (1991-92).
Other Honours: Division One Champions, 1957. Division Two Champions, 1956.

Belle Vue (A), May 8, L36-54

1 †Mitch Shirra	0 0 2 0	2	
2 §Kelly Moran	1 3 2 2 1 0	9	2
3 Leigh Adams	2 3 3 3 1 3	15	
4 Dean Standing	0 1 0 1	2	
5 Jimmy Nilsen	3 0 0 2	5	
6 §Steve Masters	1 0 T 0	1	1
7 §§Justin Elkins	2 0 0 T	2	

King's Lynn (A), May 23, L40-49

1 †Mitch Shirra	3 R 3 2 R	8	
2 Steve Camden	F T T T 0	0	
3 Leigh Adams	2 3 3 1 3 1	13	2
4 Dean Standing	0 3 1 0 R	4	1
5 Jimmy Nilsen	1 2 3 1 3 2	12	
6 Justin Elkins	2 0 0 T	2	
7 Steve Masters	0 0 1 T	1	

Cradley Heath (A), May 25, L38-51

1 †Mitch Shirra	1 1 2 2 2	8	
2 Kelly Moran	R E T N	0	
3 Leigh Adams	3 2 2 2 1 2	12	2
4 Dean Standing	F R R 1 1	2	2
5 Jimmy Nilsen	1 3 1 3 2	10	
6 Steve Masters	1 0 0 T	1	
7 Justin Elkins	3 F 1 T 1	5	2

CRADLEY HEATH (H), May 25, W46-44

1 †Mitch Shirra	R 3 3 1	7	
2 Dean Standing	3 1 1 2	7	1
3 Leigh Adams	3 3 3 2 2	13	1
4 Jimmy Nilsen	3 1 fn3 3	10	
5 Kelly Moran	1 0 N N	1	
6 Steve Masters	2 1 1 1 F	5	1
7 Justin Elkins	1 0 2 0 0 0	3	1

Wolverhampton (A), June 29, L41-49

1 †Mitch Shirra	3 0 2 0	5	
2 Dean Standing	2 2 2 1	7	2
3 Leigh Adams	2 2 2 0 1 2	9	
4 Kelly Moran	fxR 2 1	3	1
5 Jimmy Nilsen	3 2 3 2 3 1	14	1
6 Steve Masters	1 1 1 T	3	2
7 Justin Elkins	0 0 fxT	0	

Arena Essex (A), July 10, W47-43

1 †Mitch Shirra	F 3 3 3 0	9	
2 Dean Standing	2 1 3 2	8	1
3 Leigh Adams	**3 3 3 3 3**	**15**	
4 Kelly Moran	2 2 2 0	6	1
5 Jimmy Nilsen	3 1 1 3	8	1
6 Steve Masters	F 0 0 0	0	
7 Justin Elkins	1 0 F 0	1	

EASTBOURNE (H), July 16, D45-45

1 †Mitch Shirra	1 3 2 1 1	8	2
2 Dean Standing	2 0 2 1	5	1
3 Leigh Adams	3 2 fx1	6	1
4 Jimmy Nilsen	1 2 2 2	7	1
5 Kelly Moran	3 3 3 2 3	14	
6 Justin Elkins	2 0 0 0	2	
7 Steve Masters	1 0 1 1	3	2

ARENA ESSEX (H), July 23, W53-37

1 †Mitch Shirra	1 3 3 2	9	
2 Dean Standing	3 2 3 1	9	1
3 Leigh Adams	3 2 3 3 2	13	
4 David Smart	1 R R 0	1	
5 Jimmy Nilsen	3 2 3 2 0	10	1
6 Kelly Moran	3 2 1 1 3	10	2
7 Justin Elkins	0 1 R N	1	

Oxford (A), July 24, D45-45

1 †Mitch Shirra	2 0 2 1	5	
2 Dean Standing	F N N N	0	
3 Leigh Adams	2 2 3 3 3	13	1
4 David Smart	0 2 0 0	2	
5 Jimmy Nilsen	1 3 1 2 3 2	12	3
6 Justin Elkins	1 0 N 0 0 N	1	
7 Kelly Moran	3 3 3 3 R X	12	

BELLE VUE (H), July 30, L43-47

1 †Mitch Shirra	R 3 3 0 1	7	
2 Steve Masters	2 0 E 1	3	
3 Leigh Adams	3 2 0 1 3	9	
4 Jimmy Nilsen	2 3 1 1	7	
5 David Smart	1 0 0 0	1	1
6 Kelly Moran	3 2 N 3 3 1 3	15	1
7 Justin Elkins	1 0 N 0 N N	1	

The original staging of the match on July 9 was abandoned because of rain after four heats. Scorers were: SWINDON 11 (†Mitch Shirra 2- 2, Dean Standing 1-1:1, Leigh Adams 2- 2, Jimmy Nilsen 2-2, Kelly Moran 1- 1:1, Justin Elkins 2-1-3:1, Steve Masters F- 0) BELLE VUE 13

READING (H), August 6, L40-50

1 Jimmy Nilsen	1 3 2 3 1	10	1
2 Steve Masters	0 F 2 1	3	1
3 Leigh Adams	3 3 2 2 2	12	
4 †Mitch Shirra	3 2 1 1	7	
5 David Smart	2 0 0 N	2	1
6 Kelly Moran	3 1 N R 1 0 R	5	
7 Justin Elkins	1 fxN N 0	1	

WOLVERHAMPTON (H), August 20, L40-50

1 Leigh Adams	3 3 2 2 1 R	11	
2 Steve Masters	0 R 1 1	2	1
3 Mitch Shirra	*rider replacement*		
4 †Jimmy Nilsen	1 E 0 1 2	4	1
5 David Smart	0 2 2 2 0 1	7	
6 Kelly Moran	3 1 1 1 2 1	9	3
7 Justin Elkins	2 1 3 1 N	7	3

IPSWICH (H), August 31, L42-48

1 †Mitch Shirra	2 2 2 2 2	10	1
2 Dean Standing	0 0 T T	0	
3 Leigh Adams	1 3 3 3 3 2	15	1
4 David Smart	E 0 N 1	1	
5 Jimmy Nilsen	1 1 3 0 2 0	7	1
6 Justin Elkins	0 0 N N T 0	0	
7 Kelly Moran	1 2 2 0 1 3	9	2

Reading (A), September 7, L39-51

1 †Mitch Shirra	3 3 2 0 2	10	
2 Dean Standing	0 0 1 N	1	
3 Leigh Adams	3 3 2 0 0	8	
4 Kelly Moran	2 3 2 1 2	10	1
5 Jimmy Nilsen	3 0 2 1	6	1
6 Justin Elkins	0 0 N 0 T	0	
7 David Smart	2 1 0 1 N 0	4	1

BRADFORD (H), September 10, L41-49

1 †Mitch Shirra	1 2 3 1 1	8	1
2 Dean Standing	0 1 2 2	5	2
3 Leigh Adams	2 2 2 3 0	9	
4 Kelly Moran	1 2 2 2 2	9	
5 Jimmy Nilsen	3 1 1 1	6	2
6 Steve Masters	1 0 0 T	1	1
7 David Smart	2 1 0 0	3	1

Coventry (A), September 12, L40-50

1 Kelly Moran	0 1 3 2 0	6	
2 Dean Standing	1 0 0 fn	1	
3 Leigh Adams	3 3 3 3 3 0	15	
4 Justin Elkins	0 N T 1	1	
5 †Jimmy Nilsen	3 0 2 2 3 2	12	1
6 David Smart	2 T 0 N 0 1 2	5	2
7 Steve Masters	fx0 T 0 N	0	

COVENTRY (H), September 17, L43-47

1 Leigh Adams	**3 3 3 3 3**	**15**	
2 Justin Elkins	0 0 0 N	0	
3 †Mitch Shirra	1 2 1 3	7	1
4 Kelly Moran	3 1 1 1	6	1
5 Jimmy Nilsen	2 2 3 2 0	9	2
6 Steve Masters	F 0 N 0	0	
7 David Smart	1 3 1 1 0 R	6	

Ipswich (A), September 24, L28-62

1 †Leigh Adams	1 1 E 2	4	
2 David Smart	0 0 1 1	2	
3 Mitch Shirra	2 2 3 1 3	11	
4 Kelly Moran	R 1 1 0	2	1
5 Jimmy Nilsen	1 2 0 2 2	7	1
6 §David Clarke	0 0 0 R	0	
7 Justin Elkins	1 1 0 0 0	2	1

Eastbourne (A), September 26, L41-49

1 Leigh Adams	3 2 3 2 3 3	16	
2 David Smart	0 F 1 T 0	1	
3 †Mitch Shirra	2 2 2 1 1	8	2
4 Kelly Moran	0 1 0 T	1	
5 Jimmy Nilsen	1 3 2 3 1 2	12	1
6 David Clarke	1 T 0 0	1	1
7 Justin Elkins	2 0 0 T	2	

Poole (A), September 30, L33-57

1 Leigh Adams	3 3 2 2 3 1	14	
2 David Smart	0 0 2 0	2	
3 †Mitch Shirra	3 1 3 3 R 0	10	1
4 Kelly Moran	0 N 1 0	1	
5 Jimmy Nilsen	1 1 1 1 1	5	1
6 David Clarke	1 T 0 0	1	
7 Justin Elkins	F 0 T R	0	

KING'S LYNN (H), October 1, W46-44

1 Leigh Adams	3 3 1 3 3	13	
2 David Clarke	0 F N 0	0	
3 †Mitch Shirra	3 1 2 1	7	
4 Kelly Moran	2 1 1 1	5	2
5 Jimmy Nilsen	1 2 3 0 0	6	1
6 David Smart	2 2 0 3 N 2	9	2
7 Justin Elkins	3 1 2 0 N	6	1

OXFORD (H), October 8, W46-44

1 Leigh Adams	3 3 3 3 2	14	
2 Matthew Cross	0 0 T N	0	
3 †Mitch Shirra	2 3 3 3 3 1	15	1
4 Kelly Moran	1 0 3 1 2	7	1
5 Jimmy Nilsen	2 1 1 1	5	
6 David Smart	2 0 0 T 1	3	
7 Justin Elkins	1 0 1 0	2	1

POOLE (H), October 15, L43-47

1 Leigh Adams	**3 3 3 2 3 3**	**17**	**1**
2 Matthew Cross	0 0 N T	0	
3 †Mitch Shirra	2 2 3 2 2 1	12	
4 Kelly Moran	R 1 0 2	3	
5 Jimmy Nilsen	3 R 1 1	5	1
6 David Smart	2 1 1 R T 0	4	2
7 Justin Elkins	1 1 0 N	2	1

Bradford (A), October 17, L40-50

1 Leigh Adams	**3 3 2 3 3 3**	**17**	**1**
2 Matthew Cross	0 T 2 T	2	
3 †Mitch Shirra	1 1 3 3 1 2	11	1
4 Kelly Moran	0 1 1 0 0	2	1
5 Jimmy Nilsen	1 0 2 0 0	3	
6 David Smart	1 0 T 2	3	1
7 Justin Elkins	2 0 0 T	2	

At-a-Glance Results

Arena Essex	**W53-37**	**W47-43**	**100-80**
Belle Vue	**L43-47**	**L36-54**	**879-101**
Bradford	**L41-49**	**L40-50**	**81-99**
Coventry	**L43-47**	**L40-50**	**83-97**
Cradley Heath	**W46-44**	**L38-51**	**84-96**
Eastbourne	**D45-45**	**L41-49**	**86-94**
Ipswich	**L42-48**	**L28-62**	**70-110**
King's Lynn	**W46-44**	**L40-49**	**86-93**
Oxford	**W46-44**	**D45-45**	**91-89**
Poole	**L43-47**	**L33-57**	**76-104**
Reading	**L40-50**	**L39-51**	**79-101**
Wolverhampton	**L40-50**	**L41-49**	**81-99**

WHO WAS WHO IN '92

Leigh Scott ADAMS
Born: April 28, 1971, Mildura, Victoria, Australia.
Became his country's first-ever World Under 21 Champion and took over at the top of the Swindon averages.

Steven CAMDEN
Born: June 19, 1973, Oxford, Oxfordshire.
Began the season at reserve but a string of poor scores destroyed his confidence.

David CLARKE
Born: March 25, 1969, Rugby, Warwickshire.
Came out of retirement for a four match trial for Swindon after impressing in after the meeting rides at Blunsdon. Failed to take his chance and was released in October.

Matthew John CROSS
Born: August 26, 1968, Taunton, Somerset.
Still searching for a regular team place, five years after making his debut for Swindon. Brought back into the line-up as a replacement for David Clarke at the end of the season.

John Harry DAVIS
Born: October 10, 1954, Oxford, Oxfordshire.
Broke his leg in a crash at Arena Essex in an April Gold Cup fixture and was ruled out for the remainder of the season.

Justin Mark ELKINS
Born: August 27, 1974, Salisbury, Wiltshire.
Expected to spend the season with Second Division Exeter but was dropped from their team plans on the eve of the new season. Moved to Blunsdon in a loan exchange deal that took Darren Boulton to Poole.

Steve MASTERS
Born: December 6, 1970, Eastbourne, East Sussex.
Signed on loan from Eastbourne and had a long but unproductive spell at reserve.

Kelly Michael MORAN
Born: September 21, 1960, Huntingdon Beach, California, United States of America.
A surprise early season loan signing from Belle Vue who was frustratingly inconsistent throughout the season.

Jimmy Øivind NILSEN
Born: November 19, 1966, Stockholm, Sweden.
Returned to the ADT Auctions Robins after spending 1991 on loan to Berwick. Reached the World Final but was too often a disappointment in League racing.

Peter Engnaz SCHROECK
Born: September 18, 1966, Aschaffenburg, Germany.
Given an unexpected chance by Swindon but was released after only a few Gold Cup matches at reserve.

Mitchell Owen SHIRRA
Born: September 27, 1959, Auckland, New Zealand.
Signed from neighbours Reading for his second spell with the Robins. He qualified for his seventh World Final.

David John SMART
Born: December 28, 1965, Swindon, Wiltshire.
Resumed his Swindon career after starting the season on loan to Second Division Mildenhall.

Dean STANDING
Born: June 20, 1969, Southampton, Hampshire.
Continued his fairly impressive First Division form until he suffered a collar bone injury which affected his performances.

Cracks show at Monmore

ALTHOUGH they failed to retain their League championship, Wolverhampton still had two trophies and plenty of satisfaction to show from a hard season in whey took the Premiership, overcame team of the year Reading in the Gold Cup, reached the last four of the BSPA Cup and finished fifth in the League!

"I prefer to believe that we finished joint second!" quipped promoter Chris Van Straaten after his side were only denied that position on race points difference.

"Despite the fact that we didn't retain the League title," he added, "we have to feel satisfied with the team's efforts taking two major trophies and always being there or thereabouts in the League."

Yes, quite a year for the Don Everall Wolves who were forced to make changes to their squad during the winter in order to come within the points limit.

Scott Norman and Andy Phillips were the unlucky two who had to leave but, if anything, their replacements Swedish international Peter Karlsson and local youngster Stephen Morris made the side look even stronger on paper.

It certainly looked as if that were true as they started the season as they had left off the previous year by winning every match in sight, the only slight hiccup seeing them held to a draw at home in the Gold Cup by Belle Vue.

That was soon forgotten as they won the return at Kirkmanshulme Lane and then people really began to sit up and take notice as they went to Bradford in the Premiership and won there to make the home leg a formality.

One trophy on the shelf already and every sign of more to come as they went through the remainder of April and the whole of May unbeaten – despite losing the services of in-form reserve Wayne Carter with a broken leg sustained in a motor-cycle road accident.

That injury was to prove a significant factor as initially it was envisaged that he'd only be out of action for a couple of months but in fact it ruled him out for the rest of the season.

The first chink in the armour appeared in June when Coventry stunned the Monmore Green camp by taking the league points on a wet and miserable evening.

"That demonstrated to other teams that we weren't invincible after all," said Van Straaten. Although Andy Phillips had been released by Poole, Wolves couldn't bring him in to replace Carter and so he was loaned out to local rivals Cradley Heath.

Successive away defeats at Belle Vue, Poole, Coventry and Arena-Essex saw their title challenge falter but they brought in Nigel Leaver from now-defunct Mildenhall in order to solve their problem at reserve.

One problem solved but another appeared straight away as Graham Jones crashed heavily during the home challenge match against Cradley.

With Peter Karlsson occupying the third heat leader berth behind Sam Ermolenko and Ronnie Correy, the loss of Jones with a broken wrist for what turned out to be nine weeks was a body blow as no facility was available to cover for his absence.

Showing great character, a draw was achieved at Ipswich with 'Rocket Ronnie' and 'Sudden Sam' scoring a mammoth 35 points between them, and a win at Swindon, with veteran Gordon Kennett having been signed on a short term contract.

The League title wasn't going to be lost without a fight but Reading were looking likely winners of that competition and stood in the way of the Don Everall Wolves in both the Gold Cup and Knock Out Cups. Honours finished even with Wolverhampton taking the Gold Cup and Reading progressing to the final of the national competition.

The injuries to Carter and Jones in all probability prevented Wolverhampton effecting a clean sweep in Division One but two major trophies were a just reward for the effort put in over the season.

1992 RIDER ROSTER

	Club Record								Career Record							
	M	R	Pts	BP	TPts	Ave	F	P	M	R	Pts	BP	TPts	Ave	F	P
Wayne Carter	44	154	133.0	30.0	163.0	4.234	0	0	44	154	133.0	30.0	163.0	4.234	0	0
Ronnie Correy	194	957	1802.0	143.0	1945.0	8.130	9	7	194	957	1802.0	143.0	1945.0	8.130	9	7
Charles Ermolenko	56	229	297.0	41.0	338.0	5.904	0	3	56	229	297.0	41.0	338.0	5.904	0	3
Sam Ermolenko	202	1044	2483.0	171.0	2654.0	10.169	18	31	247	1237	2766.0	202.0	2968.0	9.597	18	31
Graham Jones	99	428	667.5	54.0	721.5	6.743	0	2	106	459	708.5	59.0	767.5	6.688	0	2
Peter Karlsson	41	169	259.0	23.0	287.0	6.793	0	1	41	169	259.0	28.0	287.0	6.793	0	1
Gordon Kennett	10	35	36.0	6.0	42.0	4.800	0	0	529	2308	4590.0	364.0	4954.0	8.586	58	12
Nigel Leaver	18	78	65.0	13.0	78.0	4.000	0	0	113	397	306.0	57.0	363.0	3.657	0	0
Stephen Morris	29	107	53.0	10.0	63.0	2.355	0	0	29	107	53.0	10.0	63.0	2.355	0	0
Richard Musson	4	15	6.0	1.0	7.0	1.867	0	0	37	141	124.0	32.0	156.0	4.426	0	0
Simon Wolstenholme	5	16	7.0	1.0	8.0	2.000	0	0	5	16	7.0	1.0	8.0	2.000	0	0

WOLVERHAMPTON

Promoter: Chris Van Straaten on behalf of Powar Limited.
Address: Ladbroke Stadium, Sutherland Avenue, Monmore Green, Wolverhampton WV2 2JJ.
Telephone: 0902-870400.
Clubcall: 0898 12 18 79.
Track Length: 280 metres.
Track Record: 57.73 secs, Ronnie Correy (Wolverhampton), August 27, 1990, Heat 1, Wolverhampton v Belle Vue (Sunbrite League).
Seasons in Division One: 25 (1965-1980, 1984-1992).
Division One Record: Champions (1), 1991. Runners-up (2), 1989, 1990. Third (1), 1986.
Speedway Star Cup Record: Runners-up (2), 1968, 1989.
League Cup Record: Fifth, 1985.
Inter League Cup Record: Runners-up (1), 1976.
Gold Cup: Winners (1), 1992.
Premiership: Winners (1), 1992.
Appearances: George Hunter, 195 (1972-1980).
Points: Ole Olsen, 2248 (1970-1975).
World Finalists: Ronnie Correy (1989-90-91-92), Sam Ermolenko (1986-87-88, 1991-92), Hasse Holmkvist (1968), Hans Nielsen (1980), Ole Olsen (1970-71-72-73-74-75), Petr Ondrasik (1980), Finn Thomsen (1977).
Division One Riders' Championship Finalists: Peter Jarman (1965), Peter Vandenberg (1966), Jim Airey (1967), Hasse Holmkvist (1968), James Bond (1969), Ole Olsen (1970-71-72-73, 1975), George Hunter (1974), Jim McMillan (1976-77), Hans Nielsen (1978-79-80), Peter Ravn (1984-85), Preben Eriksen (1986-87), Ronnie Correy (1988-89-90-91), Sam Ermolenko (1990-91-92).
Other Honours: Provincial League Champions, 1963.

READING (H), April 27, W56-34

1 Ronnie Correy	2 3 2 2 2	11	3
2 Charles Ermolenko	3 1 1 1	6	1
3 †Sam Ermolenko	3 3 3 3 3	15	
4 Graham Jones	1 2 3 2	8	1
5 Peter Karlsson	3 1 1 0	5	2
6 Wayne Carter	3 2 0 2	7	1
7 Stephen Morris	0 0 1 3	4	

Eastbourne (A), May 10, W53-37

1 Ronnie Correy	3 1 1 3 2	10	2
2 Charles Ermolenko	R 3 2 1	6	1
3 †Sam Ermolenko	3 3 3 3 3	15	
4 Graham Jones	2 3 3 0	8	1
5 Peter Karlsson	3 1 1 2	7	
6 Stephen Morris	1 0 0 0	1	
7 Wayne Carter	0 2 2 2	6	2

IPSWICH (H), May 25, W54-36

1 Ronnie Correy	2 3 3 3 3	14	
2 Charles Ermolenko	R 0 3 0	3	
3 †Sam Ermolenko	2 3 3 2 2	12	2
4 Graham Jones	3 3 1 3	10	
5 Peter Karlsson	2 1 3 3	9	1
6 §Richard Musson	0 R 1 N	1	
7 Stephen Morris	1 2 1 0 1	5	1

COVENTRY (H), June 8, L41-49

1 Ronnie Correy	3 3 2 1 2	11	1
2 Charles Ermolenko	1 0 3 1	5	1
3 †Sam Ermolenko	3 3 3 R 3 X	12	
4 Graham Jones	0 0 2 fx	2	
5 Peter Karlsson	1 3 2 2	8	
6 Richard Musson	0 0 0 N	0	
7 Stephen Morris	2 0 1 0 T	3	1

EASTBOURNE (H), June 15, W49-40

1 Ronnie Correy	3 3 2 3 2	13	1
2 Charles Ermolenko	E 0 2 1	3	1
3 †Sam Ermolenko	3 fxfx3 3	9	
4 Graham Jones	2 0 2 3	7	2
4 Peter Karlsson	**3 3 3 2**	**11**	**1**
6 Richard Musson	0 2 0 1 F	3	1
7 Stephen Morris	3 0 fx0	3	

Belle Vue (A), June 19, L44-46

1 Ronnie Correy	3 2 2 3 3 3	16	1
2 Charles Ermolenko	0 1 3 1	5	1
3 †Sam Ermolenko	3 3 3 3 2	14	1
4 Graham Jones	fx0 N N	0	
5 Peter Karlsson	2 1 0 0	3	
6 Richard Musson	2 0 0 0 N	2	
7 Stephen Morris	1 0 T 1 0 2	4	1

SWINDON (H), June 29, W49-41

1 Ronnie Correy	1 3 0 1	5	
2 Charles Ermolenko	0 fx3 1	4	
3 †Sam Ermolenko	3 3 3 3 3	15	
4 Graham Jones	2 1 3 2	8	
5 Peter Karlsson	1 3 3 2 R	9	2
6 §§Simon Wolstenholme	2 1 1 0	4	1
7 Stephen Morris	3 1 0 0	4	

Poole (A), July 8, L42-48

1 Ronnie Correy	3 1 2 3 1 1	11	2
2 Charles Ermolenko	0 2 3 1 0	6	
3 †Sam Ermolenko	2 3 3 3 3 3	17	
4 Graham Jones	2 0 2 0	4	
5 Peter Karlsson	1 1 0 N	2	1
6 Simon Wolstenholme	1 1 0 N	2	
7 Stephen Morris	0 0 N 0	0	

Coventry (A), July 11, L34-56

1 Ronnie Correy	3 2 3 0 1	9	
2 Charles Ermolenko	0 T 0 T	0	
3 †Sam Ermolenko	2 3 2 1 R 3	11	1
4 Graham Jones	fx0 2 2 R	4	
5 Peter Karlsson	2 1 2 1 3 0	9	1
6 §Nigel Leaver	1 0 0 N	1	
7 Stephen Morris	0 0 T T 0	0	

Arena Essex (A), July 16, L41-49

1 Ronnie Correy	2 3 2 1 2 1	11	2
2 Charles Ermolenko	fx0 N 2	2	
3 †Sam Ermolenko	3 2 3 2 3 X	13	
4 Graham Jones	2 2 2 3 1	10	1
5 Peter Karlsson	0 1 0 0 N	1	1
6 Stephen Morris	2 1 N 1	4	1
7 Nigel Leaver	0 0 N 0	0	

OXFORD (H), August 3, W47-43

1 Ronnie Correy	**3 3 3 3 2**	**14**	**1**
2 Simon Wolstenholme	0 0 0 N	0	
3 Peter Karlsson	3 3 1 2	9	1
4 †Sam Ermolenko	**3 3 2 3 3**	**14**	**1**
5 Charles Ermolenko	fx0 2 1	3	1
6 Stephen Morris	2 1 0 1 0	4	1
7 Nigel Leaver	0 1 2 fx	3	

Ipswich (A), August 6, D45-45

1 Ronnie Correy	2 3 3 3 3 3 3	20	
2 Simon Wolstenholme	0 0 N 1	1	
3 Peter Karlsson	*rider replacement*		
4 Charles Ermolenko	fx1 3 2 0	6	
5 †Sam Ermolenko	3 3 3 2 0 3 1	15	1
6 Stephen Morris	1 0 0 N	1	
7 Nigel Leaver	0 1 1 0 R	2	

ARENA ESSEX (H), August 10, W50-40

1 Ronnie Correy	**3 3 3 3 3**	**15**	
2 Simon Wolstenholme	0 0 0 N	0	
3 Peter Karlsson	3 3 3 1	10	1
4 †Sam Ermolenko	3 3 2 3 F	11	1
5 Charles Ermolenko	0 F 3 2	5	
6 Stephen Morris	2 1 0 1	4	
7 Nigel Leaver	1 2 2 0 0	5	2

Swindon (A), August 20, W50-40

1 Ronnie Correy	2 3 3 3 2	13	1
2 Gordon Kennett	1 0 2 0	3	1
3 Peter Karlsson	3 2 3 0	8	
4 Charles Ermolenko	**3 2 3 2**	**10**	**2**
5 †Sam Ermolenko	**2 3 3 3 3**	**14**	**1**
6 Stephen Morris	1 1 0 N	2	1
7 Nigel Leaver	N 0 0 R 0	0	

Oxford (A), September 2, W47-43

1 Ronnie Correy	2 2 3 3 2	12	2
2 Gordon Kennett	1 3 3 1	8	1
3 Peter Karlsson	3 3 1 2	9	
4 Charles Ermolenko	2 1 2 1	6	1
5 †Sam Ermolenko	1 2 F 3 3	9	1
6 Stephen Morris	0 0 2 0 0 0	2	1
7 Nigel Leaver	1 F N N	1	

KING'S LYNN (H), September 7, W51-39

1 Ronnie Correy	3 2 2 3 2	12	
2 Gordon Kennett	2 1 1 1	5	3
3 Peter Karlsson	2 3 2 2	9	1
4 †Sam Ermolenko	3 2 2 2 1	10	3
5 Charles Ermolenko	F 3 3 3	9	
6 Stephen Morris	F 1 F 0	1	1
7 Nigel Leaver	1 3 0 1	5	1

Bradford (A), September 12, L34-56

1 Ronnie Correy	2 0 3 2 2	9	
2 Gordon Kennett	0 1 N N	1	
3 Peter Karlsson	3 1 1 1 0	6	
4 Charles Ermolenko	2 1 0 0	3	1
5 †Sam Ermolenko	1 2 3 1 3 2	12	1
6 Stephen Morris	R N 0 T 0 N	0	
7 Nigel Leaver	1 1 0 T T 1 F	3	

Cradley Heath (A), September 23, L40-50

1 Ronnie Correy	3 2 2 0 3 0	10	1
2 Gordon Kennett	0 0 T T	0	
3 Peter Karlsson	1 1 2 1 1	6	2
4 Charles Ermolenko	1 fx2 0	3	
5 †Sam Ermolenko	3 3 2 3 2 1	14	
6 Stephen Morris	0 0 N 0 T	0	
7 Nigel Leaver	2 N 2 3 0	7	

King's Lynn (A), September 26, W50-40

1 Ronnie Correy	3 1 3 3 2	12	1
2 Graham Jones	0 0 3 1	4	
3 Peter Karlsson	2 1 2 2	7	1
4 Charles Ermolenko	0 1 3 0	4	
5 †Sam Ermolenko	**3 3 3 3 3 3**	**18**	
6 Stephen Morris	0 T 0 0	0	
7 Nigel Leaver	2 1 2 0	5	2

Reading (A), September 28, L36-54

1 Ronnie Correy	R 1 1 2 2 1	7	
2 Graham Jones	1 0 T 1	2	1
3 Peter Karlsson	1 0 2 1 1	5	1
4 Charles Ermolenko	F 0 T 1	1	1
5 †Sam Ermolenko	3 2 3 3 3 3	17	
6 Stephen Morris	0 T 0 0	0	
7 Nigel Leaver	2 2 0 0	4	

CRADLEY HEATH (H), September 30, L44-46

1 Ronnie Correy	E E 1 2 2	5	1
2 Graham Jones	1 1 3 2	7	
3 Peter Karlsson	3 2 3 0	8	1
4 †Sam Ermolenko	3 3 3 1 3 R	13	1
5 Charles Ermolenko	1 0 2 1	4	
6 Nigel Leaver	R 1 T 1 1 1 2	6	2
7 Stephen Morris	0 1 fxN N	1	

POOLE (H), October 5, W51-38

1 Ronnie Correy	3 0 3 3 3	12	
2 Graham Jones	2 1 2 1	6	1
3 Peter Karlsson	3 3 3 1	10	
4 †Sam Ermolenko	**3 3 2 3 2**	**13**	**2**
5 Charles Ermolenko	0 1 2 3	6	
6 Nigel Leaver	2 0 R 2 0	4	1
7 Stephen Morris	F 0 0 N	0	

BELLE VUE (H), October 12, W49-40

1 Ronnie Correy	3 1 2 3 3	12	2
2 Graham Jones	1 2 3 3	9	
3 Peter Karlsson	3 2 1 3	9	
4 †Sam Ermolenko	2 3 2 2 0	9	1
5 Charles Ermolenko	0 2 3 2	7	2
6 Nigel Leaver	3 0 0 0 0	3	
7 Stephen Morris	0 0 0 N	0	

BRADFORD (H), October 19, W49-41

1 Ronnie Correy	2 2 2 1	7	1
2 Graham Jones	1 1 3 0	5	2
3 Peter Karlsson	1 3 3 2 1	10	1
4 †Sam Ermolenko	3 3 2 3 3	14	
5 Charles Ermolenko	0 fx3 1	4	1
6 Nigel Leaver	2 2 2 2 1	9	2
7 Stephen Morris	0 0 0 N	0	

At-a-Glance Results

Arena Essex	W50-40	L41-49	91-89
Belle Vue	W49-40	L44-46	93-86
Bradford	W49-41	L34-56	83-97
Coventry	L41-49	L34-56	75-105
Cradley Heath	L44-46	L40-50	84-96
Eastbourne	W49-40	W53-37	102-77
Ipswich	W54-36	D45-45	99-81
King's Lynn	W51-39	W50-40	101-79
Oxford	W47-43	W47-43	94-86
Poole	W51-38	L42-48	93-86
Reading	W56-34	L36-54	92-88
Swindon	W49-41	W50-40	99-81

WHO WAS WHO IN '92

Wayne CARTER
Born: December 19, 1970, Halifax, West Yorkshire.
Broke his leg in an off-track motor-cycle accident in May and sidelined for the remainder of the season.

Ronnie Dean CORREY
Born: November 8, 1966, Bellflower, California, United States of America.
Qualified for his third successive World Final and helped his country to victory in both the World Pairs and World Team Cup Finals.

Charles Anthony (Duke) ERMOLENKO
Born: November 9, 1968, Artesia, California, United States of America.
Younger brother of team skipper Sam Ermolenko. Had a successful second season in Britain.

Guy Allen (Sam) ERMOLENKO
Born: November 23, 1960, Maywood, California, United States of America.
Had another superb season, save for a disappointing World Final where he had been among the pre-meeting favourites.

Graham Tudor JONES
Born: May 5, 1963, Oswestry, Shropshire.
Missed a chunk of the season with a broken wrist.

Peter Gunnar KARLSSON
Born: December 17, 1969, Gullspång, Sweden.
Returned to Monmore Green after missing the 1991 season and developed into a sound scoring third heat leader.

Gordon William KENNETT
Born: September 2, 1953, Bromley, Kent.
Brought in as a stop-gap replacement for the injured Graham Jones after being sidelined following the closure of Second Division Milton Keynes.

Nigel Paul LEAVER
Born: September 28, 1965, Walsall, West Midlands.
Signed by Wolverhampton after the closure of Mildenhall where he had taken over the number one spot.

Stephen MORRIS
Born: December 22, 1972, Wolverhampton, West Midlands.
Regular choice throughout his debut first team season, having ridden in only one official fixture in 1991.

Richard Neil MUSSON
Born: July 14, 1973, Leeds, West Yorkshire.
Signed on loan from Belle Vue as a replacement for the injured Wayne Carter but released after only a handful of matches.

Simon WOLSTENHOLME
Born: January 25, 1971, Sheffield, South Yorkshire.
Signed from Second Division Sheffield and given a few team opportunities due to injuries.

1992

WOLVERHAMPTON

Back row: Peter Adams (team manager), Ronnie Correy, Charles Ermolenko, Sam Ermolenko, Graham Jones, Peter Karlsson. Kneeling: Stephen Morris and Richard Musson.

1992 HOMEFIRE LEAGUE DIVISION TWO

Pos	Team	M	W	D	L	PtsF	PtsA	BP	TPts
1	PETERBOROUGH	20	14	0	6	946	852	7.5	35.5
2	Berwick	20	12	1	7	964	832	7	32
3	†Glasgow	19	11	0	8	905	803	7.5	30.5
4	Newcastle	20	11	0	9	932	861	7	29
5	†Rye House	19	12	0	7	858	845	4	29
6	Exeter	20	9	0	11	870	925	4	22
7	Edinburgh	20	8	0	12	897	899	5	21
8	Stoke	20	8	0	12	879	913	5	21
9	Long Eaton	20	7	2	11	878	915	4	20
10	Sheffield	20	9	1	10	837	958	1	20
11	Middlesbrough	20	6	0	14	813	976	2	14

† The Glasgow-Rye House match was never staged but each side was awarded one point by the Speedway Control Board.

Roll of Honour

1968	1 BELLE VUE	2 Nelson	3 Middlesbrough
1969	1 BELLE VUE	2 Reading	3 Romford
1970	1 CANTERBURY	2 Eastbourne	3 Rochdale
1971	1 EASTBOURNE	2 Bradford	3 Ipswich
1972	1 CREWE	2 Boston	3 Peterborough
1973	1 BOSTON	2 Workington	3 Eastbourne
1974	1 BIRMINGHAM	2 Eastbourne	3 Boston
1975	1 BIRMINGHAM	2 Newcastle	3 Stoke
1976	1 NEWCASTLE	2 Ellesmere Port	3 Workington
1977	1 EASTBOURNE	2 Rye House	3 Ellesmere Port
1978	1 CANTERBURY	2 Newcastle	3 Rye House
1979	1 MILDENHALL	2 Rye House	3 Oxford
1980	1 RYE HOUSE	2 Newcastle	3 Middlesbrough
1981	1 MIDDLESBROUGH	2 Weymouth	3 Newcastle
1982	1 NEWCASTLE	2 Mildenhall	3 Ellesmere Port
1983	1 NEWCASTLE	2 Mildenhall	3 Crayford
1984	1 LONG EATON	2 Mildenhall	3 Stoke
1985	1 ELLESMERE PORT	2 Poole	3 Middlesbrough
1986	1 EASTBOURNE	2 Poole	3 Middlesbrough
1987	1 EASTBOURNE	2 Mildenhall	3 Milton Keynes
1988	1 HACKNEY	2 Poole	3 Eastbourne
1989	1 POOLE	2 Wimbledon	3 Berwick
1990	1 POOLE	2 Middlesbrough	3 Ipswich
1991	1 ARENA ESSEX	2 Glasgow	3 Newcastle
1992	1 PETERBOROUGH	2 Berwick	3 Glasgow

PETERBOROUGH became only the second team in Division Two history to finish top of the table – after collecting the wooden spoon the previous season.

The feat had been first accomplished by Long Eaton when they jumped from bottom of the 1983 National League to 1984 League champions.

MIDDLESBROUGH remain the only club to have figures in each of the Second Division's 25 seasons.

THE Second Division was launched in 1968 as the British League Division Two; was renamed the New National League in 1975; dropped the prefix new to become the National League in 1976; was re-launched as the Sunbrite League Second Division in 1991 with promotion and relegation; and became the Homefire League Second Division in 1992.

SUPERNATIONAL

THE Supernational was an end of season tournament run on a knock-out basis involving the top eight tracks in the National League.
It was abandoned after two seasons because of the problems of determining the top eight tracks when fixtures were postponed.

1982 NEWCASTLE 121 Ellesmere Port 71
1983 NEWCASTLE 100 Crayford 91

NATIONAL SERIES

THE competition embraced the top nine tracks as of September 23, 1990. They were split into three groups, with each team having a home round.
The Final was also run over three rounds although the first round at Wimbledon was abandoned and the score after 12 of the scheduled 18 heats was allowed to stand.

1990 1 GLASGOW 107
2 Wimbledon 104
3 Stoke 75

ALL THE 1992 DIVISION TWO RESULTS

	BERWICK	EDINBURGH	EXETER	GLASGOW	LONG EATON	MIDDLESBROUGH	NEWCASTLE	PETERBOROUGH	RYE HOUSE	SHEFFIELD	STOKE	MILDENHALL	MILTON KEYNES
BERWICK		49-40	60-30	50-40	54-36	58-32	46-43	55-35	52-38	66-24	60-30	*68-22*	
EDINBURGH	38-52		55-34	47-43	54-36	57-33	48-42	60-30	43-46	60-30	46-44		
EXETER	47-43	58-32		43-47	59-30	54-36	62-28	41-49	56-33	63-27	61-29		
GLASGOW	51-39	48-42	65-25		56-34	54-36	50-40	54-36	Not Staged	58-32	51-38		*55-35*
LONG EATON	45-45	47-43	44-46	50-40		55-35	49-41	36-54	63-27	68-21	59-31		
MIDDLESBROUGH	43-46	48-41	55-34	55-35	50-39		45-44	43-47	37-53	43-46	48-41		
NEWCASTLE	51-38	47-43	65-25	47-43	56-33	49-41		56-34	57-33	58-32	50-39		
PETERBOROUGH	60-30	56-34	56-34	54-36	54-36	55-34	57-32		50-40	49-41	62-28		
RYE HOUSE	46-44	53-37	55-35	47-43	50-39	52-35	48-41	62-28		59-31	51-39		
SHEFFIELD	56-34	53-37	51-38	46-44	45-45	63-27	52-38	44-46	58-32		51-37		
STOKE	47-43	50-40	65-25	42-47	54-34	53-37	43-47	56-34	57-33	56-34			
MILDENHALL				*45-45*	*48-39*					*52-37*			
MILTON KEYNES						*48-42*							

Tragedy strikes as ET Panthers make their mark

THERE was one face missing from the Peterborough side that paraded their third major trophy of the season at the conclusion of the Phonesport Division Two Knock Out Cup.

Mark Blackbird disappeared into the Purfleet dressing rooms as soon as he had completed his third ride...deeply disappointed at failing to score a point in the second leg.

And, perhaps, his reaction summed up one of the major reasons that Peterborough were able to win the Knock Out Cup for the first time in their history.

As a team they WANTED to win...on and off the track!

Their most daunting hurdle on their way to a first success in 23 seasons came in the match that was to turn into the most tragic of the season.

Newcastle – and virtually every Peterborough supporter – thought the semi final tie was as good as over when they held the powerful Evening Telegraph Pirates to a mere eight points in the first leg at the East of England Showground.

Peterborough's riders were locked into their dressing room at the end of the meeting – as co-promoter James Easter hit out at their performance.

The team responded magnificently with a backs-to-the-wall performance of the highest calibre at Brough Park which left the Debmat Diamonds needed to split the Mick Poole-Jason Crump pairing in the penultimate heat if they were to force a replay!

Crump and Poole made the start and going into the third turn Wayne Garratt, striving to split the opposing partnership, misjudged his line, touched Poole's rear wheel and tumbled off, rolling towards the fence.

From the pits it looked a relatively harmless crash but as Garratt lay groaning on the track it quickly became obvious that he had been seriously injured.

The meeting was held up for around 40 minutes as the Newcastle doctor accompanied Garratt to the local hospital.

When the race was re-run Peterborough claimed their expected maximum and it needed a 5-1 in the final heat from the unbeaten Mark Thorpe and David Bargh to win Newcastle a replay.

Tragically the first leg of that replay was to be Newcastle's next match and this time both teams stood in silence to mourn the death, in hospital, of Bodger who had died from the brain injuries he had received in the first staging.

Both teams were under considerable stress but it was Peterborough who were the more aggressive as they booked their place in their first Cup Final since 1972 by winning at Brough Park.

Earlier the ET Panthers had comfortably accounted for Long Eaton in the first round and overhauled a 10 point deficit against an Edinburgh side convinced the Alwalton track had been deliberately doctored to their disadvantage.

An ill-at-ease Les Collins, who took seven rides to reach a dozen points, complained of its slickness but that didn't prevent home youngster Jason Crump recording what is certain to be the first of many Cup maximums.

Track conditions were also blamed by Berwick when they went out of the competition at the semi final stage.

Already troubled by cash problems they hoped for a Cup Final to help their financial predicament but Rye House coped far better with the sticky conditions.

Berwick were reduced to a three man team by the start of heat eight – Scott Robson, Scott Lamb, Chris Readshaw and Michael Lowrie were all ruled out of the meeting with a variety of injuries – and had no real hope of overturning a 28-62 defeat in the second leg although, by then, only Michael Lowrie was missing.

Strangely the Rockets qualified for the final by racing only four matches. They slaughtered a Sheffield side missing their former British Champion Neil Evitts, and were then given a walk-over in round two following Milton Keynes' closure!

Newcastle's progress to the last four was similarly blessed with an easier than expected route (they should have met Mildenhall in the quarter final) after they had beaten their North East rivals Middlesbrough.

That had been one of several derby ties – produced to much surprise by a straight draw rather than judicial seeding - in the opening rounds where Edinburgh thrashed Glasgow by 12 points at Shawfield.

Exeter, fancying their chances of a good cup run, held a 26 point lead from victory at the County Ground in June, had plenty of time to think about their defensive strategy at Loomer Road as they didn't complete the second leg until seven weeks later.

Stoke pulled back a dozen points in the first five races but the real turning point of the tie was heat seven when Richard Green lifted on the first bend, took the other three riders into the fence and was rightly excluded by referee John Rhodes.

But the more damaging blow was that Green had written off his helmet and suffered a neck injury which sidelined him for the rest of the meeting.

Eventually Stoke won the right to face Berwick in the quarter final with a last race 4-2 from Nigel Crabtree and Eric Monaghan after the two sides had been locked 87-87 after 29 of the 30 heats!

Falcons manager Colin Hill claimed: "It was a terrible blow for us and, without it, I think we might have won overall."

First Round

Friday, May 8

EDINBURGH 58

1 Les Collins	3 3 3 3 2 3	17	
2 Michael Coles	*rider replacement*		
3 Kenny McKinna	1 3 3 3 3 2	15	1
4 †Brett Saunders	3 3 1 1 2	10	2
5 Dariusz Fliegert	2 1 fx 1 1	5	1
6 Mike McLuskey	3 F F N	3	
7 Johnny Jørgensen	2 0 1 2 3	8	2
8 Stewart McDonald	*did not ride*		

GLASGOW 32

1 †Steve Lawson	2 2 2 1 2	9	1
2 Mick Powell	0 F 1 1 0 0	2	2
3 Neil Collins	2 2 2 3 3 1	13	
4 Shane Bowes	N T T N	0	
5 Robert Nagy	fx 2 2 0 fx	4	
6 Tim Korneliussen	0 1 0 T N	1	
7 Jason Straughan	1 1 T 0 0 1	3	1

Sunday, June 28

GLASGOW 39

1 †Steve Lawson	2 3 1 0	6	1
2 Mick Powell	0 1 2 2	5	
3 Neil Collins	3 3 0 1 2 1	10	1
4 Robert Nagy	3 2 1 3 0	9	
5 Shane Bowes	1 0 2 0	3	
6 Geoff Powell	0 1 0 N	1	
7 James Grieves	1 1 1 2 T	5	2

EDINBURGH 51

1 Les Collins	3 3 1 3 3	13	
2 Dariusz Fliegert	1 1 3 3	8	
3 Michael Coles	2 2 3 2 2	11	2
4 †Brett Saunders	0 2 3 2	7	1
5 Kenny McKinna	2 1 3 fx	6	1
6 John Wainwright	2 0 0 1	3	1
7 Mike Lewthwaite	3 0 0 0	3	

Aggregate: Edinburgh 109 Glasgow 71

Sunday, May 24

SHEFFIELD 50

1 †Peter Carr	**3 3 3 3 3 3**	**18**	
2 Simon Green	1 0 0 1 3	5	
3 Neil Evitts	*rider replacement*		
4 Louis Carr	2 1 3 2 2 2	12	3
5 Steve Johnston	F 0 2 1 0	3	1
6 Mark Hepworth	2 1 1 1 2	7	1
8 Steve Knott	1 1 E 3	5	1
8 Rob Homer	*did not ride*		

RYE HOUSE 40

1 †Martin Goodwin	2 3 3 2 1	11	
2 Sean Courtney	0 2 3 0	5	1
3 Jens Rasmussen	2 2 3 1	8	
4 Jan Pedersen	3 2 2 1 X	8	1
5 Mark Courtney	1 0 0 R	1	
6 Trevor O'Brien	3 1 2 0 1 0	7	2
7 Chris Young	0 R N E	0	

Monday, May 25

RYE HOUSE 63

1 †Martin Goodwin	**3 3 3 3 3**	**15**	
2 Sean Courtney	2 1 3 2 1	9	2
3 Jens Rasmussen	3 3 3 1	10	
4 Jan Pedersen	2 1 2 2	7	2
5 Mark Courtney	1 3 3 3	10	1
6 Trevor O'Brien	3 1 2 2 N	8	2
7 Chris Young	1 N 0 0 3	4	

SHEFFIELD 26

1 †Peter Carr	R 2 2 2 2 2	10	
2 Simon Green	fx fx 0 1	1	1
3 Neil Evitts	*rider replacement*		
4 Louis Carr	3 2 1 2 1 0	9	
5 Steve Johnston	0 0 1 0 R	1	
6 Mark Hepworth	2 0 1 1	4	1
7 Steve Knott	0 0 1 0 fx	1	
8 Martin Cobbin	*did not ride*		

Aggregate: Rye House 103 Sheffield 76

First Round

Monday, May 25

PETERBOROUGH 57

1 Mick Poole	1 3 3 3 3	13	
2 Mark Blackbird	0 2 1 E	3	2
3 †Stephen Davies	1 3 2 2 2	10	3
4 Rodney Colquhoun	0 1 1 3	5	1
5 Neville Tatum	3 2 3 3	11	
6 Paul Hurry	2 3 0 1 0	6	1
7 Jason Crump	3 2 3 1	9	

LONG EATON 33

1 †Jan Stæchmann	3 3 0 1	7	
2 Colin White	2 0 3 0 1 0	6	1
3 Martin Dixon	2 F 2 0 E	4	
4 Gary O'Hare	1 1 1 R	3	3
5 Carl Blackbird	2 2 2 2 2	10	
6 Jason Reed	0 1 T 0	1	
7 Paul Blackbird	1 0 0 T 1	2	

Wednesday, May 27

LONG EATON 49

1 †Jan Stæchmann	3 3 3 3 1	13	1
2 Colin White	0 2 3 0	5	1
3 Carl Blackbird	3 3 3 3 2	14	
4 Martin Dixon	3 3 1 2	9	
5 Gary O'Hare	1 0 0 0	1	
6 Paul Blackbird	0 0 0 N	0	
7 Deon Prinsloo	2 2 2 1 0	7	1

PETERBOROUGH 41

1 Mick Poole	1 2 2 2 3	10	1
2 Mark Blackbird	2 1 1 0	4	1
3 †Stephen Davies	1 1 3 2 1	8	2
4 Rodney Colquhoun	0 1 1 T	2	2
5 Neville Tatum	2 2 0 3 0	7	
6 Paul Hurry	1 0 1 N	2	
7 Jason Crump	3 2 0 2 1	8	

Aggregate: Peterborough 98 Long Eaton 82

Thursday May 28

MIDDLESBROUGH 46

1 †Steve Regeling	3 3 3 1 2	12	
2 Donny Odom	0 2 R 2	4	2
3 David Cheshire	3 2 fx 3 0	8	
4 Mark Lemon	1 3 0 2	6	1
5 Darren Sumner	2 2 2 1	7	1
6 Duncan Chapman	3 1 1 fx	5	1
7 Paul Pickering	1 1 2 0	4	

NEWCASTLE 43

1 Mark Thorpe	2 0 3 3 2	10	
2 Phil Jeffrey	1 1 T 1	3	1
3 Scott Norman	E 1 3 fx 2 1	7	1
4 Wayne Garratt	R R 1 fx	1	
5 †David Bargh	**3 3 2 3 3 3**	**17**	**1**
6 Richard Juul	2 2 N T 0 1	5	
7 David Nagel	0 0 0 T N	0	

Sunday, May 31

NEWCASTLE 53

1 Phil Jeffrey	2 0 0 0	2	
2 Mark Thorpe	*rider replacement*		
3 Scott Norman	3 3 3 3 1 3	16	
4 Wayne Garratt	R fx 2 2 2	6	
5 †David Bargh	1 3 3 3 3 2	15	2
6 Richard Juul	2 2 2 2 2 1	11	5
7 David Nagel	3 0 fx N	3	
8 Andrew Howe	*did not ride*		

MIDDLESBROUGH 36

1 †Steve Regeling	3 2 2 2 1	10	
2 Donny Odom	0 1 0 1	2	2
3 David Cheshire	0 3 1 1 3	8	
4 Mark Lemon	1 2 1 0	4	1
5 Darren Sumner	2 1 3 1 3 0	10	1
6 Duncan Chapman	F 1 0 N	1	
7 Paul Pickering	R 1 T T 0	1	

Aggregate: Newcastle 96 Middlesbrough 82

First Round

Monday, June 28

EXETER 58

1 †Peter Jeffery	2 3 3 1 1	10	1
2 Paul Fry	1 1 3 1	6	1
3 Frank Smart	2 1 2 2	7	3
4 Colin Cook	1 1 2 1	5	1
5 Richard Green	**3 3 3 3 3**	**15**	
6 Mark Simmonds	3 3 2 2	10	1
7 Ian Humphreys	2 fx 1 2	5	2

STOKE 32

1 Alan Grahame	*rider replacement*		
2 Ade Hoole	0 0 N 0	0	
3 †Nigel Crabtree	3 1 2 1 3 3 2	15	
4 Eric Monaghan	2 2 3 2 3 1 0	13	
5 Darren Standing	0 fx 0 0 0 T	0	
6 Garry Stead	1 0 2 0 0	3	
7 Andy Meredith	0 0 1 T	1	1
8 Anthony Barlow	*did not ride*		

Saturday, August 15

STOKE 59

1 Alan Grahame	2 0 1 3	6	1
2 Gary Chessell	3 2 3 3	11	
3 †Nigel Crabtree	**3 3 3 3 3**	**15**	
4 Eric Monaghan	3 3 1 3 1	11	
5 Garry Stead	2 2 0 2	6	3
6 David Steen	2 0 2 2 2	8	2
7 Darren Standing	1 1 N 0	2	1

EXETER 31

1 †Peter Jeffery	1 1 2 1 fx 0	5	
2 Mark Simmonds	0 0 T 0	0	
3 Frank Smart	2 1 1 2 2 2	10	
4 Colin Cook	0 E 0 fx 1	1	
5 Richard Green	1 fx N T	1	
6 Paul Fry	3 1 3 2 3 1	13	2
7 Ian Humphreys	0 N 1 T T 0	1	

Aggregate: Stoke 91 Exeter 89

Byes:
Berwick, Mildenhall and Milton Keynes.

EDINBURGH – at neighbours Glasgow in the first round – and eventual winners Peterborough – at Newcastle in the semi final replay – were the only teams to win a Cup match on their travels.

IN THEIR semi final against Peterborough, Newcastle had three riders who were unbeaten by an opponent.

DAVID BARGH (twice), Peter Carr, Les Collins, Nigel Crabtree, Jason Crump, Martin Goodwin, Richard Green, Phil Jeffrey, Richard Knight, Scott Lamb, Kenny McKinna, Eric Monaghan, Mick Poole (twice), Mark Thorpe (twice) and David Walsh were all unbeaten by an opponent in Phonesport Knock Out Cup matches.

GEOFF POWELL and Tim Korneliussen both rode in the Knock Out Cup for Glasgow – but never made a single League appearances for the Clyde Two Tigers.

SIXTEEN–YEAR–OLD Mike Smith made his first team debut for Berwick in the semi final of the Knock Out Cup against Rye House – his only official appearance of the season.

Quarter Final

Friday, August 14

EDINBURGH 50

1 †Les Collins	**3 3 3 2 2**	**13**	**2**
2 Brett Saunders	2 1 1 1	5	2
3 Michael Coles	1 2 2 2	7	
4 Kenny McKinna	**3 2 3 3 3**	**14**	**1**
5 Dariusz Fliegert	0 3 2 1	6	1
6 John Wainwright	0 0 N 1	1	1
7 Johnny Jørgensen	2 0 2 0 0	4	

PETERBOROUGH 40

1 Mick Poole	1 1 1 3	6	
2 Rodney Colquhoun	0 R 0 N	0	
3 †Stephen Davies	3 2 fx 0	5	
4 Paul Hurry	1 1 0 0	2	1
5 Neville Tatum	2 3 1 2 0	8	
6 Mark Blackbird	3 0 3 1	7	1
7 Jason Crump	1 2 3 2 3 1	12	1

Monday, August 31

PETERBOROUGH 58

1 Mick Poole	**3 2 3 3**	**11**	**1**
2 Rodney Colquhoun	2 3 3 1 0	9	1
3 †Stephen Davies	1 3 3 1	8	1
4 Neville Tatum	2 3 1 1	7	1
5 Paul Hurry	1 0 1 2 1	5	1
6 Jason Crump	**3 3 2 3**	**11**	**1**
7 Mark Blackbird	2 1 2 2	7	2

EDINBURGH 32

1 †Les Collins	1 3 2 0 0 3 3	12	
2 Brett Saunders	0 1 2 2 1 0	6	1
3 Michael Coles	2 1 1 2 2 3 2	13	1
4 Dariusz Fliegert	0 0 0 0	0	
5 Kenny McKinna	*rider replacement*		
6 John Wainwright	1 0 0 T	1	
7 Johnny Jørgensen	0 0 T 0	0	
8 Stewart McDonald	*did not ride*		

Aggregate: Peterborough 98 Edinburgh 82

Saturday, August 29

STOKE 49

1 Alan Grahame	2 0 1 1	4	2
2 Gary Chessell	3 2 3 2	10	
3 †Nigel Crabtree	3 3 1 2 1	10	1
4 Eric Monaghan	**3 3 3 3 3**	**15**	
5 Garry Stead	0 0 1 1	2	2
6 David Steen	1 1 0 2 2	6	1
7 Andy Meredith	2 fx N 0	2	

BERWICK 41

1 †Richard Knight	1 2 3 3 0	9	
2 Chris Readshaw	0 1 1 N	2	2
3 David Blackburn	2 3 3 0 2	10	
4 David Walsh	2 2 3 0 2	9	
5 Scott Robson	1 1 2 1	5	3
6 Scott Lamb	3 1 2 0 0 T	6	
7 Michael Lowrie	0 0 N 0	0	

Monday, August 31

BERWICK 52

1 †Richard Knight	**3 3 3 3 3**	**15**	
2 Chris Readshaw	0 1 1 R	2	
3 David Blackburn	3 1 1 3	8	
4 Scott Robson	0 0 2 2	4	1
5 David Walsh	3 2 3 2 2	12	2
6 Michael Lowrie	R 0 0 N	0	
7 Scott Lamb	3 3 2 3 0	11	1

STOKE 38

1 Alan Grahame	1 1 2 1 3 1	9	1
2 Gary Chessell	2 3 2 0	7	
3 †Nigel Crabtree	1 2 R 0	3	1
4 Eric Monaghan	1 3 1 0	5	2
5 Garry Stead	2 2 1 1 0	6	1
6 David Steen	2 0 1 2 T	5	
7 Andy Meredith	1 2 0 N	3	1

Aggregate: Berwick 93 Stoke 87

***Rye House** go through on default after Milton Keynes' closure.*

***Newcastle** go through on default after Mildenhall's closure.*

LEGEND

THROUGHOUT the 1993 Speedway Yearbook the following abbreviations are used in the ride-by-ride match details: E = excluded for tapes offence; R = retired, engine failure; F = fell; fx = fell, excluded; fn = fell, unable to take part in re-run; T = replaced by a tactical substitute; N = excluded under two minutes or replaced by a reserve; X = excluded.

Semi Final

Friday, September 11

PETERBOROUGH 49

1 Mick Poole	**3 3 3 3 3**	15	
2 Rodney Colquhoun	0 0 1 N	1	
3 †Stephen Davies	2 3 2 **2** 0	9	1
4 Neville Tatum	R R 0 N	0	
5 Jason Crump	2 2 3 3	10	
6 Paul Hurry	**2 1** 1 1 **2** 0	7	3
7 Mark Blackbird	3 3 0 1	7	

NEWCASTLE 41

1 Mark Thorpe	**1** 3 1 1 3 2	11	1
2 Phil Jeffrey	2 1 2 1 T	6	
3 Scott Norman	3 2 2 **1** 0	8	1
4 Richard Juul	1 0 0 T	1	
5 †David Bargh	3 2 3 2 **2 1**	13	2
6 Spencer Timmo	1 N 0 0 T	1	
7 Wayne Garratt	0 R **1** N T	1	1

Sunday, September 13

NEWCASTLE 49

1 Mark Thorpe	**3 3 3 3 3**	15	
2 Phil Jeffrey	**2 2 2 2**	8	4
3 Scott Norman	0 1 1 0	2	
4 Richard Juul	0 0 0 N	0	
5 †David Bargh	**3 3 3 3 2**	14	1
6 Max Schofield	3 3 3 0 1	10	
7 Wayne Garratt	0 0 0 fx	0	

PETERBOROUGH 41

1 Mick Poole	1 **1** 3 2 3 R	10	1
2 Rodney Colquhoun	fx N N T	0	
3 †Stephen Davies	**1** 0 2 2	5	1
4 Neville Tatum	**1** 3 1 **1**	6	2
5 Jason Crump	2 **2 2 1 2** 1	10	4
6 Mark Blackbird	2 1 1 **1**	5	1
7 Paul Hurry	**1** 2 2 N 0	5	1

Aggregate: Peterborough 90 Newcastle 90

THE closely fought semi final was marred by the tragic heat 14 accident which was to lead to Wayne Garratt's death. He crashed going into the third turn on the opening lap after clipping Mick Poole's rear wheel. The meeting continued after a near 40 minute delay.

Sunday, September 27

RYE HOUSE 60

1 †Martin Goodwin	**1** 3 **2** 2	8	2
2 Mikael Teurnberg	2 **2** 3 3 0	10	1
3 Jens Rasmussen	**2** 3 0 2	7	1
4 Jan Pedersen	**2** 3 **1** 3 2	11	2
5 Mark Courtney	3 1 **1 1**	6	2
6 Robert Ledwith	3 3 **2** 2	10	1
7 Sean Courtney	**2 2** 2 **2**	8	3

BERWICK 28

1 †Richard Knight	3 2 3 3 3 3	17	
2 Scott Robson	fx fx fx T	0	
3 David Blackburn	fx 1 0 1 0	2	
4 Chris Readshaw	0 fx N N	0	
5 David Walsh	1 1 1 3 1 1	8	
6 Michael Lowrie	0 fx T N	0	
7 Scott Lamb	1 fx fn T	1	

Saturday, October 10

BERWICK 53

1 †Richard Knight	2 3 3 **2**	10	1
2 Scott Robson	0 1 3 0	4	
3 David Blackburn	3 2 0 **2**	7	1
4 David Walsh	**2 2 3 3 2**	12	3
5 Scott Lamb	**3 3 3 3 3**	15	
6 Mike Smith	1 1 0 N	2	
7 Chris Readshaw	R **2** 0 1 0	3	1

RYE HOUSE 37

1 †Martin Goodwin	3 F 3 1	7	
2 Sean Courtney	1 1 1 2 2 1	8	
3 Jens Rasmussen	2 2 2 1	7	
4 Jan Pedersen	0 1 2 0	3	
5 Mark Courtney	1 3 R T	4	
6 Mikael Teurnberg	**2** 0 **1 1**	4	3
7 Robert Ledwith	3 0 0 **1** 0	4	1

Aggregate: Rye House 97 Berwick 81

Semi Final Replay

Sunday, October 4

NEWCASTLE 44

1 Mark Thorpe	**3 3 3 3 3**	15	
2 Phil Jeffrey	0 **2 1 2**	5	3
3 Scott Norman	3 1 **2** 3 0	9	1
4 Richard Juul	0 0 0 N	0	
5 †David Bargh	1 3 2 3 2 **2**	13	1
6 Max Schofield	1 0 T 0 1	2	
7 David Nagel	0 T 0 R	0	

PETERBOROUGH 46

1 Mick Poole	**1 1** 2 3	7	2
2 Rodney Colquhoun	2 2 R **1**	5	1
3 †Stephen Davies	**1** 0 0 N	1	1
4 Neville Tatum	**2** 3 1 1	7	1
5 Jason Crump	3 **2 2** 2 1	10	2
6 Mark Blackbird	3 1 1 **1** 3	9	1
7 Paul Hurry	**2** 2 3 0 0	7	1

Friday, October 9

PETERBOROUGH 51

1 Mick Poole	2 3 3 2 3	13	
2 Rodney Colquhoun	**1 2 1 2**	6	3
3 †Stephen Davies	3 2 2 3 1	11	
4 Jason Crump	2 2 0 3	7	
5 Neville Tatum	0 **1 2** 0	3	2
6 Paul Hurry	**2** 1 **1** 3	7	2
7 Mark Blackbird	3 R 0 1	4	

NEWCASTLE 39

1 Mark Thorpe	3 3 3 1 2 2	14	
2 Phil Jeffrey	0 0 T T	0	
3 Scott Norman	2 1 R 3 1	7	
4 Richard Juul	1 0 1 **1** 0 0	3	1
5 David Bargh	3 3 **2** 3 2	13	1
6 Max Schofield	1 0 1 T	2	
7 David Nagel	0 0 T 0	0	

Aggregate: Peterborough 97 Newcastle 83

1991 Phonesport Division Two Knock Out Cup

FOR the first time in the competition's history the Knock Out Cup Final went to a replay as Glasgow defied the odds and held favourites and already crowned League Champions Arena Essex.

And the Scottish club could count themselves unlucky at not pulling off a shock as they had led by 16 points when their home leg was called off because of heavy rain!

First Round

Long Eaton 54 Edinburgh 36
Edinburgh 45 Long Eaton 45
Aggregate: Long Eaton 99 Edinburgh 81

Stoke 54 Rye House 36
Rye House 54 Stoke 35
Aggregate: Rye House 90 Stoke 89

Middlesbrough 51 Arena Essex 39
Arena Essex 53 Middlesbrough 36
Aggregate: Arena Essex 92 Middlesbrough 87

Exeter 49 Newcastle 40
Newcastle 54 Exeter 35
Aggregate: Newcastle 94 Exeter 84

Byes: Glasgow, Hackney, Milton Keynes and Peterborough.

Second Round

Glasgow 61 Milton Keynes 28
Milton Keynes 44 Glasgow 45
Aggregate: Glasgow 106 Milton Keynes 72

Peterborough 50 Arena Essex 40
Arena Essex 61 Peterborough 29
Aggregate: Arena Essex 101 Peterborough 79

Newcastle 52 Hackney 38
Hackney 46 Newcastle 44
Aggregate: Newcastle 96 Hackney 84

Rye House 46 Long Eaton 43
Long Eaton 50 Rye House 40
Aggregate: Long Eaton 93 Rye House 86

Semi Finals

Arena Essex 65 Long Eaton 25
Long Eaton 43 Arena Essex 47
Aggregate: Arena Essex 112 Long Eaton 68

Glasgow 48 Newcastle 42
Newcastle 46 Glasgow 43
Aggregate: Glasgow 91 Newcastle 88

Final

Arena Essex 46 Glasgow 44
†Glasgow 46 Arena Essex 44
Aggregate: Glasgow 90 Arena Essex 90
†The originally scheduled first leg was abandoned after eight races with Glasgow leading 32-16.

Final Replay

Arena Essex 60 Glasgow 30
Glasgow 50 Arena Essex 40
Aggregate: Arena Essex 100 Glasgow 80

FINAL

PETERBOROUGH completed a remarkable treble on the penultimate day of the season...by adding the Phonesport Knock Out Cup to their collection of Homefire League Division Two and H.E.A.T. Team Championship trophies.

Remarkable that it was also the first time in their 23 year history that the Alwalton club had won either the League or the Cup!

Victory was virtually assured after a one-sided first leg at the East of England Showground in which the Evening Telegraph Panthers overcame a couple of vital mechanical problems to build up a 30 points lead.

And when they led the second leg – staged at Arena Essex – by six points after only five races it was all over bar the vociferous shouting!

By the end of heat seven Peterborough needed only one finisher in each of the remaining races to be certain of overall success and that signalled terrace celebrations by their fans and a far less committed on track effort by their jubilant riders!

Rye House, who switched their home tie to Purfleet because they didn't have floodlights at Hoddesdon and the ET Panthers refused to race out of season, became the second Division Two club to stage a home Cup Final meeting on a neutral track...Berwick raced their home leg at Newcastle's Brough Park in both 1980 (when they beat Middlesbrough) and 1981 (when they lost to Edinburgh).

Friday, October 23

PETERBOROUGH 60

1 Mick Poole	3 **2** 3 0 **2**	10	2
2 Rodney Colquhoun	1 3 3 1	8	
3 †Stephen Davies	F 3 3 **2**	8	1
4 Jason Crump	1 3 3 3 3	13	
5 Neville Tatum	3 1 **1** 3	8	1
6 Paul Hurry	3 2 **2** 2	9	1
7 Mark Blackbird	1 1 0 **2**	4	1

RYE HOUSE 30

1 †Martin Goodwin	2 2 2 1 1 0	8	1
2 Sean Courtney	0 0 T T	0	
3 Jens Rasmussen	3 1 3 2 2 1	12	
4 Jan Pedersen	0 1 0 0	1	
5 Mark Courtney	2 0 R **1** 1	4	1
6 Mikael Teurnberg	R 0 T 2 0	2	
7 Robert Ledwith	2 1 0 N	3	

Friday, October 30, at Arena Essex

RYE HOUSE 51

1 †Martin Goodwin	0 3 3 3 **2**	11	1
2 Sean Courtney	2 1 **2** 1	6	1
3 Jens Rasmussen	3 2 **2** 1	8	1
4 Jan Pedersen	2 1 **2** 1	6	1
5 Mark Courtney	0 0 3 0	3	
6 Robert Ledwith	1 0 N 0	1	
7 Mikael Teurnberg	3 **1** 3 3 3 3	16	1

PETERBOROUGH 39

1 Mick Poole	3 3 1 **2**	9	1
2 Rodney Colquhoun	**1** 2 0 0	3	1
3 †Stephen Davies	2 2 2 1	7	
4 Neville Tatum	3 R 2 3 1	9	
5 Jason Crump	1 3 0 2	6	
6 Paul Hurry	2 **1** N **1 1** fx0	5	2
7 Mark Blackbird	0 N 0 0	0	

Aggregate: Peterborough 99 Rye House 81

Roll of Honour

1968 CANTERBURY 112 Reading 80
1969 BELLE VUE 91 Crewe 45
1970 IPSWICH 80 Berwick 76
1971 IPSWICH 92 Crewe 64
1972 CREWE 89 Peterborough 67
1973 BOSTON 89 Workington 66
1974 BIRMINGHAM 81 Eastbourne 74
1975 EASTBOURNE 83 Workington 72
1976 NEWCASTLE 83 Berwick 72
1977 EASTBOURNE 98 Berwick 57
1978 EASTBOURNE 83 Rye House 73
1979 RYE HOUSE 92 Berwick 64
1980 BERWICK 79 Middlesbrough 76
1981 EDINBURGH 101 Berwick 89
1982 NEWCASTLE 118 Ellesmere Port 74
1983 EXETER 96 Weymouth 95
1984 HACKNEY 83 Berwick 72
1985 EASTBOURNE 83 Ellesmere Port 73
1986 EASTBOURNE 90 Mildenhall 64
1987 EASTBOURNE 100 Mildenhall 91
1988 HACKNEY 110 Wimbledon 82
1989 BERWICK 109 Poole 83
1990 POOLE 107 Middlesbrough 85
1991 ARENA ESSEX 100 Glasgow 80†
1992 PETERBOROUGH 99 Rye House 81

†In a replay after the two teams had drawn 90-90.

EASTBOURNE lead the way in Division Two Knock Out Cup wins...having taken the trophy on six separate occasions including three in a row from 1985 to 1987.

BERWICK have appeared in a record eight Cup Finals – but have won only twice, in 1980 and again in 1989.

GLASGOW, Long Eaton, Middlesbrough, Milton Keynes, Sheffield and Stoke are the only teams who started the 1992 Homefire League Division Two season who have never won the KO Cup. Glasgow and Milton Keynes have been beaten finalists.

Exeter

Stoke (A), April 4, L37-53

1 †Peter Jeffery	2 0 0 1 1	4	1
2 Paul Fry	3 2 2 1 3	11	
3 Tony Olsson	0 E 3 2 3 2	10	
4 Colin Cook	2 0 0 0	2	
5 Richard Green	F 1 1 1	3	1
6 Mark Simmonds	1 1 F T 0	2	
7 Ian Humphreys	3 2 N T T	5	

Rye House (A), April 5, L39-51

1 †Peter Jeffery	1 0 fnT T	1	
2 Paul Fry	0 3 fnT	3	
3 Tony Olsson	2 3 3 0 3 3	14	
4 Colin Cook	0 1 0 1	2	1
5 Richard Green	1 2 3 2 3 0	11	
6 Mark Simmonds	2 0 0 2 1 0	5	1
7 Ian Humphreys	R 0 T 2 1	3	

RYE HOUSE (H), April 6, W53-37

1 Peter Jeffery	*rider replacement*		
2 Richard Knight	1 1 1 0	3	2
3 Tony Olsson	3 3 1 3 1 3	14	1
4 Colin Cook	2 3 3 3 3 0	14	1
5 Richard Green	2 3 0 3 2	10	
6 Mark Simmonds	3 1 3 2 N 1 2	12	1
7 Ian Humphreys	R N fx	0	
8 Dean Garton	0	0	

MILTON KEYNES (H), April 20, W63-27

1 Peter Jeffery	*rider replacement*		
2 Paul Fry	**2 3 3 3 3**	**14**	**1**
3 Tony Olsson	**3 3 3 2 3**	**14**	**1**
4 †Colin Cook	**2 2 2 3 2**	**11**	**4**
5 Richard Green	**3 3 3 3 3**	**15**	
6 Mark Simmonds	3 1 1 1	6	
7 Ian Humphreys	2 1 R R	3	1
8 Richard Knight	*did not ride*		

Milton Keynes (A), April 21, L43-46

1 Peter Jeffery	*rider replacement*		
2 Paul Fry	0 E 2 2 2	6	
3 Tony Olsson	2 3 3 3 3 2	16	1
4 †Colin Cook	F 0 3 0 0	3	
5 Richard Green	3 3 3 1 2 3	15	
6 Mark Simmonds	2 0 0 0 0	2	
7 Ian Humphreys	1 0 0 N 0	1	1

Peterborough (A), April 24, L38-52

1 Peter Jeffery	*rider replacement*		
2 Paul Fry	1 0 3 1 3 0	8	1
3 Tony Olsson	2 2 2 3 0 1	10	
4 †Colin Cook	1 3 1 0 0	5	
5 Richard Green	3 3 2 1 3 1	13	1
6 Mark Simmonds	1 0 1 T	2	
7 Ian Humphreys	R 0 fx0	0	
8 Tommy Palmer	*did not ride*		

Mildenhall (A), April 26, L42-48

1 Peter Jeffery	*rider replacement*		
2 Paul Fry	1 2 1 2 3 1	10	1
3 Tony Olsson	1 2 2 1 3 3 0	12	
4 †Colin Cook	0 2 0 N 0	2	1
5 Richard Green	3 3 2 3 2 2 2	17	2
6 Mark Simmonds	1 0 0 T	1	
7 Ian Humphreys	0 0 T 0	0	
8 Scott Pegler	*did not ride*		

LONG EATON (H), May 11, W62-28

1 †Peter Jeffery	1 1 3 3 1	9	1
2 Paul Fry	3 2 3 2	10	1
3 Tony Olsson	1 1 3 3	8	
4 Colin Cook	3 2 1 1	7	2
5 Richard Green	**2 3 3 2 3**	**13**	**2**
6 Mark Simmonds	3 3 3 R	9	
7 Ian Humphreys	2 R 2 2	6	2

PETERBOROUGH (H), May 18, W54-36

1 †Peter Jeffery	1 0 1 1	3	2
2 Paul Fry	2 2 3 2	9	
3 Tony Olsson	2 3 3 2	10	1
4 Colin Cook	3 1 3 2	9	1
5 Richard Green	2 3 2 1 2	10	2
6 Mark Simmonds	3 3 1 1 3	11	1
7 Ian Humphreys	1 1 0 N R	2	

Long Eaton (A), May 20, W48-42

1 †Peter Jeffery	2 1 2 2 3	10	1
2 Tony Olsson	*rider replacement*		
3 Paul Fry	3 3 3 3 1 2	15	1
4 Colin Cook	0 0 F 0 0	0	
5 Richard Green	**3 3 3 3 3 3**	**18**	
6 Mark Simmonds	2 0 0 1	3	
7 Ian Humphreys	1 fxR 1	2	1
8 Scott Pegler	*did not ride*		

STOKE (H), May 25, W66-23

1 †Peter Jeffery	3 2 3 2	10	
2 Paul Fry	2 1 3 X 2	8	3
3 Tony Olsson	**3 3 3 2**	**11**	**1**
4 Colin Cook	1 2 1 2	6	3
5 Richard Green	**3 3 2 3**	**11**	**1**
6 Mark Simmonds	2 1 2 3 3	11	2
7 Ian Humphreys	3 2 1 3	9	1

MILDENHALL (H), June 1, W71-19

1 †Peter Jeffery	**3 3 3 2 3**	**14**	**1**
2 Paul Fry	2 2 1 2	7	4
3 Tony Olsson	**2 2 3 3**	**10**	**2**
4 Colin Cook	2 1 3 3	9	1
5 Richard Green	**3 3 3 2**	**11**	**1**
6 Mark Simmonds	**3 3 3 2 2**	**13**	**2**
7 Ian Humphreys	2 2 1 2	7	2

Long Eaton

STOKE (A), March 28, L36-54

1 †Jan Stæchmann	2 1 3 1	7	1
2 Colin White	1 0 0 1 1 0	3	2
3 Martin Dixon	3 2 3 0	8	
4 Gary O'Hare	0 0 T 2 0	2	
5 Carl Blackbird	3 1 2 1 3	10	
6 Paul Blackbird	0 0 0 T	0	
7 Deon Prinsloo	2 1 1 N 2	6	

MILTON KEYNES (H), April 1, W51-39

1 †Jan Stæchmann	3 3 3 3 2	14	
2 Colin White	1 0 1 1	3	-
3 Martin Dixon	3 1 0 2	6	
4 Carl Blackbird	2 3 2 3 1	11	3
5 Gary O'Hare	3 0 2 0	5	
6 Paul Blackbird	3 2 0 R	5	1
7 Deon Prinsloo	2 2 1 2	7	2

STOKE (H), April 8, W49-41

1 †Jan Stæchmann	0 2 3 3 3	11	
2 Gary O'Hare	3 0 1 N	4	
3 Carl Blackbird	2 3 1 3 2	11	2
4 Martin Dixon	3 1 1 3	8	
5 Colin White	1 0 0 R	1	
6 Deon Prinsloo	2 3 2 3 0	10	2
7 Paul Blackbird	3 0 1 N 0	4	

Mildenhall (A), April 12, L43-47

1 †Jan Stæchmann	3 2 3 2 2 1	13	1
2 Gary O'Hare	1 0 T 0	1	
3 Carl Blackbird	2 2 3 1 2	10	
4 Colin White	1 1 1 0	3	2
5 Martin Dixon	2 0 3 3	8	
6 Paul Blackbird	2 fx2 0	4	1
7 Deon Prinsloo	1 1 0 2	4	2

PETERBOROUGH (H), April 15, W51-39

1 †Jan Stæchmann	R 3 3 3 1	10	
2 Gary O'Hare	2 2 3 0	7	1
3 Carl Blackbird	1 3 3 2 3	12	
4 Martin Dixon	3 2 fnN	5	
5 Colin White	2 1 1 1	5	4
6 Deon Prinsloo	3 3 0 2 1 1	10	1
7 Paul Blackbird	0 0 0 2	2	

Peterborough (A), April 20, L37-53

1 †Jan Stæchmann	3 2 3 0 N 1	9	
2 Gary O'Hare	0 0 T N 2	2	
3 Carl Blackbird	3 1 R 3 0	7	
4 Colin White	2 0 T 0	2	
5 Martin Dixon	1 2 3 2 3 0	11	1
6 Paul Blackbird	0 0 T 0	0	
7 Deon Prinsloo	1 1 2 1 1	6	1

RYE HOUSE (H), April 29, W48-42

1 †Jan Stæchmann	2 3 fx3 0	8	1
2 Gary O'Hare	3 2 2 2	9	1
3 Martin Dixon	2 2 1 fx	5	
4 Colin White	0 1 0 3	4	1
5 Carl Blackbird	3 2 fx3 3	11	
6 Paul Blackbird	3 0 0 1	4	
7 Deon Prinsloo	1 1 3 2	7	2

MILDENHALL (H), May 6, W51-39

1 †Jan Stæchmann	3 fx3 2 2	10	2
2 Gary O'Hare	0 2 1 1	4	
3 Martin Dixon	2 1 0 0	3	
4 Colin White	2 0 3 2	7	1
5 Carl Blackbird	**3 3 3 3 3**	**15**	
6 Paul Blackbird	1 1 3 1	6	1
7 Deon Prinsloo	3 0 3 0	6	

Rye House (A), May 10, L44-46

1 Jan Stæchmann	*rider replacement*		
2 Gary O'Hare	0 2 1 2 2	7	1
3 Martin Dixon	2 2 2 fxN	6	
4 Colin White	1 3 0 1 1	6	2
5 †Carl Blackbird	3 3 X 1 3 2	12	1
6 Deon Prinsloo	3 N 3 2 2 2 fx	12	1
7 Paul Blackbird	0 0 0 N 1	1	
8 Jason Reed	*did not ride*		

Exeter (A), May 11, L28-62

1 Jan Stæchmann	*rider replacement*		
2 Gary O'Hare	0 0 1 0 1	2	1
3 Martin Dixon	2 2 0 2 0	6	
4 Colin White	0 2 0 1 0	3	
5 †Carl Blackbird	1 1 0 2 R	4	
6 Deon Prinsloo	1 3 2 N 1 3 2	12	
7 Paul Blackbird	0 0 T 1 N fx	1	1
8 Jason Reed	*did not ride*		

EXETER (H), May 20, L42-48

1 Martin Dixon	3 2 2 0	7	1
2 Gary O'Hare	1 1 3 3 1	9	1
3 Carl Blackbird	2 2 1 1	6	1
4 †Jan Stæchmann	1 2 2 2	7	1
5 Colin White	2 0 1 2 0	5	1
6 Paul Blackbird	3 1 1 2 0	7	2
7 Jason Reed	0 1 0 N	1	

Long Eaton did not race at Milton Keynes. Two attempts to stage the match were thwarted by the weather and poor track preparation.

Mildenhall

PETERBOROUGH (H), April 5, L42-48

1 †David Smart	1 1 2 2	6	1
2 Nigel Leaver	3 2 3 1 1	10	1
3 Melvyn Taylor	3 3 1 2 0	9	
4 Gary Tagg	F 2 1 2	5	1
5 Ian Barney	1 0 2 1	4	1
6 Jamie Habbin	3 2 0 N 1	6	2
7 Jesper Olsen	0 2 R 0	2	1

Peterborough (A), April 10, W47-43

1 †David Smart	2 3 2 2 0	9	2
2 Nigel Leaver	3 2 2 3 1	11	2
3 Melvyn Taylor	2 1 3 1	7	
4 Gary Tagg	2 1 1 0	4	
5 Ian Barney	1 0 0 3	4	1
6 Jesper Olsen	2 0 2 1	5	2
7 Jamie Habbin	3 1 3 0	7	1

LONG EATON (H), April 12, W47-43

1 †David Smart	0 1 0 2	3	
2 Nigel Leaver	2 3 2 3 3	13	
3 Melvyn Taylor	0 2 N N	2	1
4 Gary Tagg	fxN N 1	1	1
5 Ian Barney	3 3 F 3 0	9	
6 Jamie Habbin	3 3 3 1 3 2	15	
7 Jesper Olsen	fx1 1 1 0 1 N	4	1

RYE HOUSE (H), April 19, W49-41

1 †David Smart	2 1 1 1	5	1
2 Nigel Leaver	**3 3 3 3 2**	**14**	**1**
3 Melvyn Taylor	1 0 1 N	2	
4 Gary Tagg	0 0 R N	0	
5 Mikael Teurnberg	2 3 1 3 3	12	
6 Jamie Habbin	2 3 3 3 R 1	12	
7 Jesper Olsen	1 0 3 R	4	1

Stoke (A), April 18, L42-48

1 †David Smart	0 1 1 T	2	
2 Nigel Leaver	1 0 0 3 3 N	7	
3 Melvyn Taylor	1 1 2 T	4	2
4 Gary Tagg	1 1 0 N	2	1
5 Mikael Teurnberg	2 3 1 1	7	1
6 Jamie Habbin	2 0 3 0 2 2	9	1
7 Jesper Olsen	3 2 2 3 F 1	11	1

Rye House (A), April 20, W53-35

1 †David Smart	3 3 1 1 2	10	1
2 Nigel Leaver	F X 3 3	6	
3 Melvyn Taylor	2 3 3 1	9	1
4 Adrian Mountain	1 N N 0	1	1
5 Mikael Teurnberg	2 3 3 3 3	14	
6 Jamie Habbin	3 0 0 0 3 1	7	
7 Jesper Olsen	2 3 1 0	6	1

EXETER (H), April 26, W48-42

1 †David Smart	3 1 1 1	6	
2 Nigel Leaver	2 3 2 3 1	11	1
3 Melvyn Taylor	2 3 0 2 3	10	2
4 Jason Gage	fx0 N N	0	
5 Mikael Teurnberg	1 1 1 3	6	
6 Jamie Habbin	3 3 1 3 0 1	11	
7 Jesper Olsen	2 0 2 0	4	1

MILTON KEYNES (H), May 3, W49-41

1 †David Smart	3 1 1 3	8	
2 Nigel Leaver	1 3 2 3 3	12	
3 Melvyn Taylor	2 0 3 2 0	7	
4 Jason Gage	0 1 1 1	3	1
5 Mikael Teurnberg	2 0 3 1	6	1
6 Jamie Habbin	3 R 2 2	7	1
7 Jesper Olsen	2 0 2 2	6	2

Long Eaton (A), May 6, L39-51

1 †David Smart	1 2 3 1 2 1	10	2
2 Nigel Leaver	2 1 3 2 3 0	11	1
3 Melvyn Taylor	3 1 2 0	6	
4 Jason Gage	0 N 0 T	0	
5 Mikael Teurnberg	1 0 1 1	3	
6 Jamie Habbin	2 R T 2 0 T	4	
7 Jesper Olsen	R N 2 2 1	5	2

STOKE (H), May 18, L39-51

1 †David Smart	1 2 2 0 3 1	9	
2 Nigel Leaver	0 0 T T	0	
3 Melvyn Taylor	1 2 3 0	6	1
4 Gary Tagg	1 2 1 1	5	1
5 Mikael Teurnberg	2 0 3 2 2 3	12	
6 Jamie Habbin	3 2 1 0 0	6	1
7 Jason Gage	0 1 T 0	1	1

Exeter (A), June 1, L19-71

1 †David Smart	1 0 0 2 0 1	4	
2 Nigel Leaver	0 2 3 1 0 0	6	
3 Melvyn Taylor	fxN T N	0	
4 Gary Tagg	1 1 1 1 1	5	
5 Mikael Teurnberg	0 0 0 1 R	1	
6 Jamie Habbin	1 1 T T	2	
7 Jason Gage	0 1 0 T 0 T 0	1	

Mildenhall did not race at Milton Keynes.

Milton Keynes

Long Eaton (A), April 1, L39-51

1 Gordon Kennett	2 2 3 2 3 3	15	1
2 Frank Smart	0 1 0 T	1	1
3 †Richard Hellsén	1 2 3 3 1	10	
4 Peter Glanz	0 2 2 1 1	6	1
5 Lars Munkedal	1 3 R 0 T	4	
6 David Steen	0 1 1 N 0	2	1
7 Justin Walker	1 R T T 0	1	

Exeter (A), April 20, L27-63

1 Gordon Kennett	0 1 1 2 1	5	1
2 Frank Smart	1 R R 1 2 1	5	1
3 †Richard Hellsén	2 2 0 1	5	
4 Peter Glanz	1 0 T 0	1	
5 Lars Munkedal	0 2 0 T	2	
6 Justin Walker	1 0 N 2 1	4	1
7 David Steen	R N 1 2 2 0	5	1

EXETER (H), April 21, W46-43

1 Gordon Kennett	3 2 2 0	7	
2 Frank Smart	1 1 1 1 0	4	2
3 †Richard Hellsén	2 1 3 3	9	1
4 Peter Glanz	fx2 2 3	7	
5 Lars Munkedal	2 1 1 N	4	2
6 David Steen	3 1 2 3 1 1	11	1
7 Justin Walker	0 2 1 1	4	

Rye House (A), April 26, L35-53

1 Gordon Kennett	3 fxT T	3	
2 Frank Smart	1 1 3 fx	5	
3 †Richard Hellsén	fx1 2 1 2	6	
4 Peter Glanz	3 2 X 3 3 1	12	2
5 Ian Barney	0 3 0 0	3	
6 Justin Walker	1 0 N 0 N	1	
7 David Steen	0 3 0 1 fx1	5	1

Mildenhall (A), May 3, L41-49

1 Gordon Kennett	*rider replacement*		
2 Frank Smart	0 2 1 0 0	3	1
3 †Richard Hellsén	3 2 0 1 T 3 2	11	
4 Peter Glanz	3 3 3 2 2 3 1	17	1
5 Ian Barney	2 1 1 0 T	4	
6 Justin Walker	0 N 1 0	1	
7 David Steen	1 1 0 3 0	5	
8 Kieran McCullagh	*did not ride*		

Peterborough (A), May 8, L30-60

1 Gordon Kennett	*rider replacement*		
2 Frank Smart	1 1 T 1 1 2	6	3
3 †Richard Hellsén	1 2 0 0 R T	3	
4 Peter Glanz	0 0 1 1	2	
5 Ian Barney	2 1 2 3 2 1 3	14	
6 Justin Walker	2 0 3 fxR	5	
7 David Steen	0 0 T 0	0	
8 Kieran McCullagh	0	0	

Stoke (A), May 9, L34-56

1 Gordon Kennett	2 1 R T	3	
2 Frank Smart	0 R T 1	1	
3 †Richard Hellsén	1 2 3 1 2	9	
4 Peter Glanz	2 3 3 0 1 0	9	1
5 Kieran McCullagh	0 0 0 T	0	
6 Justin Walker	2 0 2 0	4	1
7 David Steen	1 0 1 2 2 2	8	1

STOKE (H), May 19, L40-49

1 Gordon Kennett	2 fxfxN	2	
2 Frank Smart	0 2 2 1	5	
3 †Richard Hellsén	3 3 1 1 1	9	1
4 Peter Glanz	2 1 2 3 0	8	
5 Kieran McCullagh	1 0 fxN	1	1
6 David Steen	3 1 1 3 1 fx	9	1
7 Justin Walker	1 1 2 2	6	2

PETERBOROUGH (H), May 26, L41-49

1 Gordon Kennett	2 3 3 1 2 2	13	
2 Frank Smart	R 0 2 1	3	
3 †Richard Hellsén	3 3 2 2 1	11	1
4 Peter Glanz	3 0 0 T	3	
5 Kieran McCullagh	1 2 3 0	6	
6 David Steen	3 0 R 0	3	
7 Justin Walker	0 1 1 0	2	2

The original staging of the match against Rye House on April 7 was abandoned by referee Graham Reeve after heat four because of a waterlogged track. Scorers at the time were: MILTON KEYNES 16 (Gordon Kennett 3- 3, Frank Smart fx- 0, †Richard Hellsén 2- 2, Peter Glanz 3- 3, Lars Munkedal 2- 2:1, David Steen 2-1- 3:2, Justin Walker 3- 3) RYE HOUSE 8. The meeting was never re-staged.

Milton Keynes did not race home meetings against Long Eaton, Mildenhall or Rye House.

Peterborough

STOKE (H), April 3, W49-41

1 Mick Poole	1 3 2 2 1	9	2
2 Mark Blackbird	0 1 0 1	2	1
3 †Stephen Davies	3 2 1 3 2	11	1
4 Rod Colquhoun	**3 3 3 3**	**12**	
5 Paul Whittaker	1 0 1 0	2	1
6 Jason Crump	3 fnN 2 N	5	
7 Paul Hurry	2 0 0 N 2 2 2	8	2

Mildenhall (A), April 5, W48-42

1 Mick Poole	fx3 3 3 3	12	
2 Mark Blackbird	2 1 1 2	6	1
3 †Stephen Davies	1 3 3 3 2	12	1
4 Rod Colquhoun	2 1 3 F	6	2
5 Paul Whittaker	3 2 0 3	8	
6 Jason Crump	1 0 1 0	2	1
7 Paul Hurry	2 0 0 0	2	

MILDENHALL (H), April 10, L43-47

1 Mick Poole	R 3 3 3 3 2	14	1
2 Mark Blackbird	1 T 0 2	3	1
3 †Stephen Davies	3 2 2 0 3 3	13	2
4 Rod Colquhoun	0 1 2 2	5	1
5 Paul Whittaker	3 R 0 1 1	5	
6 Jason Crump	1 0 T 1	2	
7 Paul Hurry	0 1 T 0	1	

Rye House (A), April 12, L41-49

1 Mick Poole	2 R 1 1 F	4	
2 Mark Blackbird	0 1 T N	1	
3 †Stephen Davies	1 2 2 3 0 fx	8	1
4 Paul Whittaker	1 1 3 2 1	8	1
5 Rod Colquhoun	0 2 1 N	3	
6 Jason Crump	2 0 T 1	3	1
7 Paul Hurry	1 3 3 2 3 2	14	2

Long Eaton (A), April 15, L39-51

1 Mick Poole	3 3 2 1 F	9	1
2 Mark Blackbird	1 0 1 2 3 2	9	1
3 †Stephen Davies	2 0 3 2 2	9	
4 Rod Colquhoun	fx1 1 fxT	2	2
5 Paul Whittaker	1 T T 0	1	
6 Jason Crump	1 1 0 3 0	5	1
7 Paul Hurry	2 0 2 N	4	

RYE HOUSE (H), April 17, W59-31

1 Mick Poole	**3 3 3 2**	**11**	**1**
2 Mark Blackbird	1 2 1 1 1	6	2
3 †Stephen Davies	**3 3 3 3**	**12**	
4 Rod Colquhoun	2 3 3 3	11	
5 Paul Whittaker	1 0 3 0	4	1
6 Paul Hurry	2 1 1 1	5	1
7 Jason Crump	3 2 1 1 3	10	

LONG EATON (H), April 20, W53-37

1 Mick Poole	2 3 2 3 2	12	1
2 Mark Blackbird	1 2 1 0	4	2
3 †Stephen Davies	2 3 3 3 3	14	
4 Rod Colquhoun	3 3 1 2	9	
5 Paul Whittaker	0 1 2 1	4	
6 Paul Hurry	2 0 1 1	4	2
7 Jason Crump	3 0 2 1	6	2

EXETER (H), April 24, W52-38

1 Mick Poole	**3 3 3 2 2**	**13**	**2**
2 Mark Blackbird	0 1 1 2	4	2
3 †Stephen Davies	3 1 3 2 3	12	
4 Rod Colquhoun	R 2 3 2	7	
5 Paul Whittaker	2 1 2 N	5	1
6 Paul Hurry	2 1 0 0	3	1
7 Jason Crump	3 2 2 1 0	8	2

MILTON KEYNES (H), May 8, W60-30

1 Mick Poole	**3 3 3 3**	**12**	
2 Mark Blackbird	R 1 1 2 0	4	2
3 †Stephen Davies	**3 3 3 3**	**12**	
4 Rod Colquhoun	2 2 F 3	7	2
5 Paul Whittaker	3 3 2 2 1	11	1
6 Paul Hurry	1 2 1 1	5	2
7 Jason Crump	3 2 2 2	9	2

Exeter (A), May 18, L36-54

1 Mick Poole	3 2 2 1 3 3	14	1
2 Mark Blackbird	0 0 T T	0	
3 †Stephen Davies	0 3 3 2 0 1	9	
4 Paul Whittaker	0 0 T T	0	
5 Rod Colquhoun	1 2 3 2 1	9	
6 Paul Hurry	0 1 0 0	1	
7 Jason Crump	2 1 0 0 0	3	

Milton Keynes (A), May 26, W49-41

1 Mick Poole	**3 3 3 3**	**12**	
2 Mark Blackbird	1 1 3 0	5	
3 †Stephen Davies	1 2 1 3	7	2
4 Neville Tatum	X 2 0 N	2	
5 Rod Colquhoun	2 1 2 1	6	2
6 Paul Hurry	1 1 2 3 3	10	2
7 Jason Crump	2 2 0 2 1 fx	7	

Stoke (A), June 6, L29-60

1 Mick Poole	1 2 0 3 fx2	8	
2 Mark Blackbird	R 0 2 0	2	
3 †Stephen Davies	R 0 3 1	4	
4 Rod Colquhoun	0 1 0 3 0	4	1
5 Neville Tatum	1 2 2 0 2	7	
6 Paul Hurry	1 1 1 1	4	1
7 Jason Crump	F F T T	0	

Rye House

EXETER (H), April 5, W51-39

1 †Martin Goodwin	3 2 3 3 2	13	
2 Sean Courtney	2 1 3 2 1	9	4
3 Jan Pedersen	1 3 2 2	8	
4 Trevor O'Brien	2 2 1 2	7	1
5 Mark Courtney	3 1 fxR	4	1
6 John Wainwright	1 3 0 1	5	
7 Wayne Baxter	3 1 F 1	5	1

Exeter (A), April 6, L37-53

1 †Martin Goodwin	3 2 3 2 3 2	15	
2 Sean Courtney	0 1 0 T	1	1
3 Jan Pedersen	2 2 2 0 1	7	1
4 Trevor O'Brien	1 2 1 2 0 1	7	2
5 Mark Courtney	R R 2 1	3	
6 John Wainwright	2 0 T fx	2	
7 Wayne Baxter	1 0 T 1	2	2

PETERBOROUGH (H), April 12, W49-41

1 †Martin Goodwin	3 3 fx2	8	1
2 Sean Courtney	1 1 1 1	4	
3 Jan Pedersen	2 3 2 1	8	
4 Trevor O'Brien	**2 2 3 3 2**	**12**	**3**
5 Mark Courtney	3 3 2 3 3	14	
6 John Wainwright	3 0 F 0 0	3	
7 Wayne Baxter	0 0 N 0	0	

Peterborough (A), April 17, L31-59

1 †Martin Goodwin	2 2 3 2 2	11	
2 Sean Courtney	0 1 0 0	1	1
3 Jan Pedersen	2 1 0 0	3	
4 Trevor O'Brien	3 2 2 2 1 2	12	1
5 Mark Courtney	0 0 1 2	3	
6 John Wainwright	E 0 T 0 R	0	
7 Wayne Baxter	1 0 T 0	1	

Mildenhall (A), April 19, L41-49

1 †Martin Goodwin	1 2 2 fx2	7	
2 Sean Courtney	0 1 1 2	4	2
3 Jan Pedersen	2 2 0 T	4	
4 Trevor O'Brien	1 2 2 2 1 0	8	2
5 Mark Courtney	3 1 2 3 3 1	13	1
6 John Wainwright	3 0 T 2	5	1
7 Wayne Baxter	0 0 T 0	0	

MILDENHALL (H), April 20, L35-53

1 †Martin Goodwin	1 1 2 1 2	7	3
2 Sean Courtney	2 2 0 2 1	7	
3 Jan Pedersen	X 2 2 2 0	6	1
4 Trevor O'Brien	F R F 2 0	2	
5 Mark Courtney	3 2 1 1 3	10	2
6 John Wainwright	1 R T 2	3	
7 Wayne Baxter	X T 0 0	0	

MILTON KEYNES (H), April 26, W53-35

1 †Martin Goodwin	2 2 3 3 3	13	1
2 Sean Courtney	0 3 1 2	6	2
3 Jan Pedersen	fx1 2 1	4	1
4 Trevor O'Brien	2 3 2 2 0	9	2
5 Mark Courtney	1 2 3 2	8	2
6 John Wainwright	3 2 0 fx	5	
7 Wayne Baxter	2 2 1 3	8	2

Long Eaton (A), April 29, L42-48

1 †Martin Goodwin	fx3 3 2 2 1	11	1
2 Sean Courtney	1 0 T 0	1	
3 Jan Pedersen	1 1 3 2 2	9	
4 Trevor O'Brien	1 1 3 1	6	2
5 Mark Courtney	2 3 2 1 1	9	2
6 John Wainwright	0 R T fx	0	
7 Wayne Baxter	2 3 0 1	6	

Stoke (A), May 2, L42-48

1 †Martin Goodwin	3 3 3 3 1 2	15	1
2 Sean Courtney	0 1 2 0 0	3	
3 Jan Pedersen	*rider replacement*		
4 Trevor O'Brien	2 1 1 1 2	7	2
5 Mark Courtney	3 3 3 1 0 1	11	1
6 John Wainwright	1 0 1 2	4	
7 Wayne Baxter	0 0 0 2	2	
8 Martin Cobbin	*did not ride*		

BOTH MILTON Keynes and Mildenhall failed to finish their Gold Cup programmes. Milton Keynes had their licence suspended immediately after their Gold Cup match against Long Eaton on Tuesday, June 2, was called off by referee David Hughes because of the condition of the track. The promoters (Colin Hill and Roger Jones) and Stadium landlord Terry Cheney were given a month to comply with Speedway Control Board regulations but before the time was up the promoters withdrew from the Homefire League Second Division. Mildenhall also withdrew because of financial problems although they did complete all their home Gold Cup matches and only had their match at Milton Keynes outstanding. All completed Gold Cup fixtures involving the two clubs were allowed to stand in the final, but uncompleted, table.

LONG EATON (H), May 10, W46-44

1 †Martin Goodwin	**3 3 3 3 3 3**	**18**	
2 Sean Courtney	1 1 2 2 2	8	1
3 Jan Pedersen	*rider replacement*		
4 Trevor O'Brien	0 N N N	0	
5 Mark Courtney	2 1 3 3 3 1	13	
6 John Wainwright	2 1 0 1 1 0	5	1
7 Wayne Baxter	1 0 0 0 1	2	1
8 Chris Young	*did not ride*		

STOKE (H), May 31, W46-42

1 †Martin Goodwin	2 2 3 1 X	8	1
2 Sean Courtney	1 3 2 2 2	10	2
3 Jens Rasmussen	2 1 3 0	6	1
4 Jan Pedersen	2 1 0 2	5	1
5 Mark Courtney	3 R 3 1	7	
6 Trevor O'Brien	X 1 2 2 1	6	3
7 Chris Young	2 N 1 1	4	1

The original staging of the match at Milton Keynes on April 7 was abandoned by referee Graham Reeve after heat four because of a waterlogged track. Scorers at the time were: MILTON KEYNES 16 RYE HOUSE 8 (†Martin Goodwin 2- 2, Sean Courtney 1- 1:1, Jan Pedersen 3- 3, Trevor O'Brien 1- 1, Mark Courtney 0- 0, John Wainwright fx- 0, Wayne Baxter 1- 0- 1). The meeting was never re-staged.

Rye House did not race at Milton Keynes.

Stoke

LONG EATON (H), March 28, W54-36

1 Alan Grahame	**3 3 3 3 3**	**15**	
2 Gary Chessell	0 1 3 0	4	
3 †Nigel Crabtree	0 3 2 3	8	
4 Eric Monaghan	2 3 2 2 1	10	1
5 Darren Standing	1 2 1 0	4	3
6 Garry Stead	1 2 2 2 1	8	2
7 Ade Hoole	3 2 0 N	5	1

Peterborough (A), April 3, L41-49

1 Alan Grahame	3 1 3 2 3	12	1
2 Gary Chessell	2 2 3 0	7	1
3 †Nigel Crabtree	1 2 3 1	7	1
4 Eric Monaghan	2 3 3 1 0	9	1
5 Darren Standing	F 1 fx0	1	
6 Garry Stead	1 2 R 1 N 0 1	5	
7 Ade Hoole	0 fnN N	0	

EXETER (H), April 4, W53-37

1 Alan Grahame	0 3 2 3 1	9	1
2 Gary Chessell	1 2 1 3	7	1
3 †Nigel Crabtree	1 3 2 3 3	12	
4 Eric Monaghan	3 3 F 2	8	
5 Darren Standing	1 1 1 2	5	2
6 Garry Stead	2 3 2 3 2	12	1
7 Mark Walsh	X N 0 0	0	

Long Eaton (A), April 8, L41-49

1 Alan Grahame	1 3 2 2 1	9	4
2 Gary Chessell	2 2 3 3 1	11	1
3 †Nigel Crabtree	1 3 2 2 0	8	
4 Eric Monaghan	2 1 2 2	7	
5 Darren Standing	0 0 N 1	1	1
6 Garry Stead	1 1 1 R 2	5	1
7 Andy Meredith	0 0 T 0	0	

MILDENHALL (H), April 18, W48-42

1 Alan Grahame	3 2 2 2 0	9	2
2 Gary Chessell	2 3 3 1	9	2
3 †Nigel Crabtree	3 2 2 2	9	
4 Eric Monaghan	**3 3 3 3 3**	**15**	
5 Darren Standing	0 2 1 1	4	2
6 Garry Stead	1 0 0 fx0	1	
7 Andy Meredith	fx1 N 0	1	

RYE HOUSE (H), May 2, W48-42

1 Alan Grahame	1 3 0 3 3	10	1
2 Gary Chessell	2 2 3 3 0	10	1
3 †Nigel Crabtree	2 2 1 3	8	1
4 Eric Monaghan	1 2 2 3	8	1
5 Darren Standing	0 fx0 N	0	
6 Garry Stead	3 1 0 2 0	6	1
7 Andy Meredith	2 1 2 1	6	1

MILTON KEYNES (H), May 9, W56-34

1 Alan Grahame	3 1 1 3	8	
2 Gary Chessell	1 3 2 3 1	10	
3 †Nigel Crabtree	3 2 3 3 3	14	
4 Eric Monaghan	**3 3 2 3**	**11**	**1**
5 Darren Standing	1 2 R 0	3	1
6 Andy Meredith	3 2 1 1	7	2
7 Ade Hoole	0 0 2 1	3	1

Mildenhall (A), May 18, W51-39

1 Alan Grahame	3 3 2 3 2	13	
2 Gary Chessell	2 1 3 1	7	2
3 †Nigel Crabtree	3 3 2 0	8	
4 Eric Monaghan	3 3 3 1	10	
5 Darren Standing	0 0 2 2 0	4	1
6 Garry Stead	2 1 1 1 3	8	1
7 Andy Meredith	1 0 0 N	1	1

Milton Keynes (A), May 19, W49-40

1 Alan Grahame	**3 2 3 2 3**	**13**	**2**
2 Gary Chessell	1 3 3 0	7	
3 †Nigel Crabtree	2 3 2 3 2	12	1
4 Eric Monaghan	3 fx 3 3	9	
5 Darren Standing	0 2 0 1	3	
6 Garry Stead	2 fx 1 2 0	5	2
7 Andy Meredith	0 0 0 N	0	

Exeter (A), May 25, L23-66

1 Alan Grahame	1 0 0 2 0 0	3	
2 Gary Chessell	0 1 1 0 1	3	
3 †Nigel Crabtree	2 3 1 2 3 1	12	
4 Eric Monaghan	2 1 fx 0 1	4	
5 Darren Standing	0 0 T T	0	
6 Ade Hoole	1 0 N 0	1	
7 Andy Meredith	R 0 T 0 T	0	

Rye House (A), May 31, L42-46

1 Alan Grahame	3 3 1 X 2 X	9	1
2 Gary Chessell	R 2 3 2	7	1
3 †Nigel Crabtree	3 F 1 2	6	1
4 Eric Monaghan	0 3 0 3 3 3	12	
5 Darren Standing	1 0 T 3	4	
6 Ade Hoole	3 0 1 0 0	4	
7 Andy Meredith	X N T	0	

PETERBOROUGH (H), June 6, W60-29

1 Alan Grahame	2 3 1 2	8	2
2 Gary Chessell	**3 2 3 3**	**11**	**1**
3 †Nigel Crabtree	3 3 2 2	10	
4 Eric Monaghan	**3 3 3 3 3**	**15**	
5 Darren Standing	2 1 2 1 1	7	2
6 Ade Hoole	2 2 0 0	4	2
7 Andy Meredith	3 1 1 0	5	1

Berwick

NEWCASTLE (H), April 4, L36-54

1 †Richard Knight	2 2 2 1 2 1	10	
2 Scott Robson	1 fx 2 1 fx	4	2
3 David Walsh	3 3 2 0 0 3	11	
4 Scott Lamb	0 2 0 T	2	
5 David Blackburn	2 1 0 1	4	1
6 Chris Readshaw	2 R 0 T	2	
7 Michael Lowrie	1 0 N 2	3	1

Glasgow (A), April 5, W46-44

1 †Richard Knight	3 3 3 3 2	14	
2 David Nagel	0 N 2 0	2	
3 David Walsh	2 1 3 2 1	9	1
4 Scott Lamb	1 1 2 1	5	1
5 David Blackburn	3 2 0 3	8	
6 Chris Readshaw	3 1 R 0 1	5	
7 Michael Lowrie	1 1 1 0	3	2

Middlesbrough (A), April 9, L40-50

1 †Richard Knight	1 2 3 3 3 3	15	
2 David Nagel	0 0 T T	0	
3 David Walsh	R 3 1 fx 0	4	1
4 Scott Lamb	0 fn 1 1	2	
5 David Blackburn	3 2 2 1 3 0	11	1
6 Chris Readshaw	2 fx 0 2 2	6	1
7 Michael Lowrie	0 1 1 T T	2	1

SHEFFIELD (H), April 11, W59-31

1 †Richard Knight	3 2 3 2 2	12	2
2 Scott Lamb	2 1 1 2	6	4
3 David Walsh	**3 3 3 3 3**	**15**	
4 David Nagel	1 0 N N	1	
5 David Blackburn	3 3 1 1	8	
6 Michael Lowrie	2 1 1 0 2	6	2
7 Chris Readshaw	3 2 0 3 3	11	

Edinburgh (A), April 17, W48-42

1 †Richard Knight	1 3 3 3 3	13	
2 Scott Lamb	0 2 2 1	5	1
3 David Walsh	3 2 1 fx	6	
4 Scott Robson	3 3 2 1 0	9	
5 David Blackburn	1 1 2 1	5	
6 Chris Readshaw	1 0 3 0 3	7	
7 Michael Lowrie	3 0 0 N	3	

GLASGOW (H), April 18, W64-26

1 †Richard Knight	**3 3 3 3**	**12**	
2 Scott Lamb	0 1 2 1 2	6	1
3 David Walsh	2 3 1 fx	6	1
4 Scott Robson	**2 2 2 3**	**9**	**3**
5 David Blackburn	3 3 3 2	11	
6 Michael Lowrie	2 3 2 1 1	9	3
7 Chris Readshaw	**3 3 3 2**	**11**	**1**

MIDDLESBROUGH (H), April 25, W59-31

1 †Richard Knight	3 2 3 3 3	14	
2 Scott Lamb	1 F 3 2	6	1
3 David Walsh	**3 3 2 3 2**	**13**	**2**
4 Scott Robson	2 2 1 3	8	1
5 David Blackburn	3 1 3 2	9	2
6 Michael Lowrie	2 1 1 0 N	4	
7 Chris Readshaw	R E 0 3 2	5	1

EDINBURGH (H), May 2, W58-32

1 †Richard Knight	**3 3 3 3 3**	**15**	
2 Scott Lamb	1 2 1 2	6	2
3 David Walsh	3 2 3 3	11	
4 Scott Robson	R 2 2 2 1	7	2
5 David Blackburn	3 3 3 1	10	
6 Michael Lowrie	2 0 0 1 0	3	1
7 Chris Readshaw	3 3 N 0	6	

Sheffield (A), May 7, L39-51

1 †Richard Knight	1 2 3 2 2 3	13	
2 Scott Lamb	0 1 1 T 2	4	1
3 David Walsh	1 2 1 T	4	
4 Scott Robson	3 2 1 0 1	7	1
5 David Blackburn	2 1 1 2 1 1	8	4
6 Chris Readshaw	3 0 0 T	3	
7 Michael Lowrie	0 0 T 0	0	

Newcastle (A), May 24, L43-46

1 †Richard Knight	3 2 2 3 1	11	1
2 Scott Lamb	0 3 3 1	7	1
3 David Blackburn	3 3 2 0	8	
4 Scott Robson	0 3 3 fx	6	
5 David Walsh	3 1 3 1 0	8	1
6 Chris Readshaw	E 0 R 0 0 2	2	
7 Michael Lowrie	1 R N N	1	

Edinburgh

MIDDLESBROUGH (H), April 3, W55-35

1 Les Collins	3 3 3 3 1	13	1
2 †Brett Saunders	1 2 2 2	7	2
3 Michael Coles	3 2 3 2 2	12	1
4 Kenny McKinna	1 2 1 3	7	1
5 Dariusz Fliegert	2 fx 1 1	4	2
6 Johnny Jørgensen	2 2 3 2	9	1
7 Stewart McDonald	1 1 0 1	3	2

NEWCASTLE (H), April 10, D45-45

1 Les Collins	3 2 2 2 2	11	1
2 †Brett Saunders	1 0 3 1	5	1
3 Michael Coles	1 3 2 2 3	11	1
4 Kenny McKinna	1 2 1 3	7	1
5 Dariusz Fliegert	0 1 1 N	2	2
6 Johnny Jørgensen	3 2 1 2 1 0	9	1
7 Stewart McDonald	0 0 N 0	0	

BERWICK (H), April 17, L42-48

1 Les Collins	3 3 3 3 2	14	
2 †Brett Saunders	2 1 3 1	7	1
3 Michael Coles	2 2 2 2 1	9	1
4 Kenny McKinna	2 N N N	2	
5 Dariusz Fliegert	0 fx 0 0	0	
6 Johnny Jørgensen	2 1 1 1 2 2	9	1
7 Stewart McDonald	F 0 0 1 0	1	

Middlesbrough (A), April 19, L33-57

1 Les Collins	1 2 0 2 2 1 2	10	2
2 †Brett Saunders	0 1 3 1 1 0	6	1
3 Michael Coles	2 2 2 1 3 2 0	12	
4 Kenny McKinna	*rider replacement*		
5 Dariusz Fliegert	0 1 1 1	3	1
6 Johnny Jørgensen	2 0 0 T	2	
7 Stewart McDonald	F 0 T 0	0	
8 Mike McLuskey	*did not ride*		

GLASGOW (H), April 24, W56-33

1 Les Collins	**3 3 3 3 3 3**	**18**	
2 Kenny McKinna	*rider replacement*		
3 Michael Coles	2 fx 3 3 3 2	13	2
4 †Brett Saunders	2 2 2 1 3	10	2
5 Dariusz Fliegert	1 3 2 1 2	9	3
6 Mike McLuskey	fn N 1 0	1	
7 Johnny Jørgensen	fx 2 2 0 1	5	1
8 Stewart McDonald	*did not ride*		

SHEFFIELD (H), May 1, W62-28

1 Les Collins	**3 3 3 3 2**	**14**	**1**
2 Stewart McDonald	0 1 1 N	2	
3 Michael Coles	**3 3 3 3 3**	**15**	
4 †Brett Saunders	2 2 2 3	9	2
5 Dariusz Fliegert	1 3 1 2	7	2
6 Mike McLuskey	2 1 1 0	4	1
7 Johnny Jørgensen	3 3 1 2 2	11	2

Berwick (A), May 2, L32-58

1 Les Collins	0 1 2 1 2 3 2	11	1
2 Kenny McKinna	*rider replacement*		
3 Michael Coles	2 2 1 2 1 R	8	
4 Dariusz Fliegert	1 1 0 N	2	1
5 †Brett Saunders	2 0 3 2 1 1 0	9	
6 Mike McLuskey	1 N 0 fx T	1	
7 Johnny Jørgensen	fx 1 0 0 T	1	1
8 Stewart McDonald	*did not ride*		

Newcastle (A), May 3, L40-50

1 Les Collins	2 3 3 3 2 3 1	17	1
2 Kenny McKinna	*rider replacement*		
3 Michael Coles	3 2 2 3 2 1 F	13	1
4 Dariusz Fliegert	2 0 1 0 T	3	1
5 †Brett Saunders	1 2 0 0 0	3	1
6 Mike McLuskey	fx 0 0 T	0	
7 Johnny Jørgensen	2 1 0 1	4	1
8 Stewart McDonald	*did not ride*		

Glasgow (A), May 6, L43-46

1 Les Collins	2 3 3 2 3 2	15	1
2 Michael Coles	*rider replacement*		
3 Kenny McKinna	3 2 3 2 2 1	13	1
4 Dariusz Fliegert	0 1 fx 1 0	2	2
5 †Brett Saunders	2 1 2 0 1	6	1
6 Mike McLuskey	F 0 0 N	0	
7 Johnny Jørgensen	3 1 0 1 2	7	1
8 Stewart McDonald	*did not ride*		

Sheffield (A), May 28, L38-52

1 Les Collins	1 3 2 2 2 0	10	1
2 Michael Coles	0 2 2 1	5	2
3 Kenny McKinna	2 2 3 1 2 2	12	
4 Dariusz Fliegert	0 2 1 1	4	1
5 †Brett Saunders	2 1 0 0	3	1
6 Mike McLuskey	1 1 T 0 T	2	2
7 Johnny Jørgensen	2 0 0 N	2	

Glasgow

BERWICK (H), April 5, L44-46

1 †Steve Lawson	2 3 3 3 0	11	
2 Mick Powell	1 2 3 1	7	2
3 Neil Collins	3 3 2 2 3	13	
4 Robert Nagy	2 2 1 2	7	
5 Robert Csillik	0 0 1 0	1	1
6 Tim Korneliussen	2 0 0 2 1	5	1
7 James Grieves	0 0 N 0	0	

MIDDLESBROUGH (H), April 12, W51-39

1 †Steve Lawson	3 3 1 3 0	10	1
2 Mick Powell	2 1 3 2	8	1
3 Neil Collins	3 3 2 2 3	13	
4 Robert Nagy	3 0 2 2	7	1
5 Robert Csillik	1 2 1 0	4	1
6 Tim Korneliussen	2 2 2 2 1	9	3
7 James Grieves	F 0 0 N	0	

Berwick (A), April 18, L26-64

1 †Steve Lawson	2 1 0 0 3	6	
2 Mick Powell	1 0 1 2 0	4	1
3 Neil Collins	1 2 2 2 R	7	
4 Robert Csillik	0 1 T 1	2	
5 Robert Nagy	1 0 1 1 3	6	
6 Tim Korneliussen	1 0 0 0	1	
7 Stuart Coleman	F 0 T 0	0	

NEWCASTLE (H), April 19, L42-48

1 †Steve Lawson	2 2 3 2 0	9	
2 Mick Powell	1 1 3 0	5	2
3 Neil Collins	3 3 R 3 1	10	
4 Robert Nagy	2 3 1 3	9	1
5 Robert Csillik	1 0 1 0	2	1
6 Tim Korneliussen	3 1 0 0 0	4	
7 Stuart Coleman	1 1 1 N	3	

Newcastle (A), April 20, L36-54

1 †Steve Lawson	2 2 3 3 0	10	
2 Mick Powell	1 0 1 1 1	4	1
3 Neil Collins	2 3 3 2 fx	10	1
4 Robert Csillik	1 0 F 2 2	5	
5 Robert Nagy	0 1 2 2 0	5	
6 Tim Korneliussen	1 1 T 0	2	
7 Stuart Coleman	fx fx T T	0	

Middlesbrough (A), April 23, L38-52

1 †Steve Lawson	3 2 3 1	9	
2 Mick Powell	0 0 2 2 2 0	6	2
3 Neil Collins	3 2 3 3 2 1	14	
4 Robert Csillik	1 fx 1 0	2	1
5 Robert Nagy	2 2 0 0	4	
6 Tim Korneliussen	2 0 0 T	2	
7 Jason Straughan	0 1 T 0	1	

Edinburgh (A), April 24, L33-56

1 †Steve Lawson	1 1 2 T	4	
2 Mick Powell	0 0 T 1 1	2	1
3 Neil Collins	3 1 1 2 2 1	10	1
4 Robert Csillik	3 2 3 E 1 0	9	
5 Robert Nagy	0 R 0 R	0	
6 Tim Korneliussen	2 0 0 2	4	1
7 Jason Straughan	3 1 0 T 0	4	

SHEFFIELD (H), May 3, W48-42

1 †Steve Lawson	3 2 2 3 3	13	
2 Mick Powell	1 1 3 1	6	2
3 Neil Collins	2 2 2 3 2	11	1
4 Robert Nagy	2 1 2 3	8	2
5 Robert Csillik	0 2 2 1	5	
6 Tim Korneliussen	3 0 0 0	3	
7 Jason Straughan	1 0 1 0	2	1

EDINBURGH (H), May 6, W46-43

1 †Steve Lawson	0 2 3 3 0	8	
2 Robert Csillik	1 1 2 2	6	2
3 Neil Collins	3 3 3 2 3	14	
4 Robert Nagy	1 2 1 3	7	
5 Mick Powell	3 0 3 1	7	1
6 Tom Korneliussen	2 0 0 N	2	
7 Jason Straughan	F 1 1 0 0	2	1

Sheffield (A), June 4, L41-48

1 †Steve Lawson	2 0 0 N	2	
2 Mick Powell	0 1 1 2 2	6	1
3 Neil Collins	2 R 3 3 2 3	13	
4 Robert Nagy	1 2 2 1 2	8	3
5 Shane Bowes	2 1 2 1 3 2	11	3
6 Mark Burrows	1 fx T T	1	
7 James Grieves	0 0 T T 0	0	

The original staging of the match on April 30 was abandoned, after Simon Green had fallen and been excluded at the start of heat 10, because of heavy rain. Scores at the time: SHEFFIELD 36 GLASGOW 18 (Robert Csillik 0-1- 1:1, rider replacement for Steve Lawson, †Neil Collins 1-2-E-3-3- 9, Mick Powell 0-1-0- 1:1, Robert Nagy 1-2-2- 5, Tim Korneliussen 0-1-0- 1, Jason Straughan 1-0-0-T- 1, James Grieves did not ride).

Middlesbrough

Edinburgh (A), April 3, L35-55

1 †Steve Regeling	2 3 3 2 3 3	16	
2 Mark Lemon	0 1 0 1	2	1
3 Darren Sumner	1 0 3 2 0	6	
4 Donny Odom	F fx 1 N	1	
5 David Cheshire	3 1 R R	4	
6 Duncan Chapman	3 1 F 0 2	6	
7 Paul Pickering	0 0 T 0	0	

Roll of Honour

1990 Newcastle 91 Peterborough 89
1991 Newcastle 104 Stoke 75

BERWICK (H), April 9, W50-40

1 †Steve Regeling	2 2 2 3 2	11	2
2 Mark Lemon	3 1 2 3 1	10	2
3 Darren Sumner	3 3 1 0	7	
4 Donny Odom	2 1 2 1	6	1
5 David Cheshire	1 3 3 2	9	1
6 Duncan Chapman	3 2 fx N 0	5	1
7 Paul Pickering	1 1 0 0 N	2	

Glasgow (A), April 12, L39-51

1 †Steve Regeling	1 3 2 3 3 2	14	
2 Mark Lemon	F 1 1 1 1	4	1
3 Darren Sumner	1 2 3 1 3 1	11	1
4 Donny Odom	fx 0 T T	0	
5 David Cheshire	2 1 3 0 0	6	
6 Duncan Chapman	3 F 0 T	3	
7 Paul Pickering	1 fx T 0	1	

Sheffield (A), April 17, L44-46

1 †Steve Regeling	1 3 2 2 0	8	
2 Mark Lemon	3 2 2 1	8	2
3 Darren Sumner	2 2 2 0	6	
4 Donny Odom	2 1 2 1	6	3
5 David Cheshire	3 2 1 3 1	10	
6 Duncan Chapman	1 0 0 2	3	2
7 Paul Pickering	2 1 F 0	3	1

EDINBURGH (H), April 19, W57-33

1 †Steve Regeling	3 3 3 2	11	
2 Mark Lemon	2 1 1 2	6	2
3 Darren Sumner	**3 3 3 3 3**	**15**	
4 Donny Odom	1 2 fx 3	6	1
5 David Cheshire	3 3 2 0 1	9	1
6 Duncan Chapman	3 1 F 3 2	9	1
7 Paul Pickering	1 0 F N	1	

GLASGOW (H), April 23, W52-38

1 †Steve Regeling	1 3 3 3 3	13	1
2 Mark Lemon	2 1 1 2	6	1
3 Darren Sumner	2 3 1 2	8	1
4 Donny Odom	X 3 1 3	7	
5 David Cheshire	3 1 2 3 2	11	1
6 Duncan Chapman	3 fx 1 1 1	6	1
7 Paul Pickering	1 fx R N	1	

Berwick (A), April 25, L31-59

1 †Steve Regeling	0 3 1 0 1	5	1
2 Mark Lemon	2 E 2 F 1 0	5	
3 Darren Sumner	2 3 1 2 1	9	1
4 Donny Odom	0 2 2 1 0 1	6	
5 David Cheshire	1 0 0 T	1	
6 Duncan Chapman	3 0 N T F	3	
7 Paul Pickering	1 0 1 T T	2	

Newcastle (A), April 26, L32-58

1 †Steve Regeling	2 0 1 1	4	2
2 Mark Lemon	1 1 3 1 2	8	2
3 Darren Sumner	1 fx 2 2 1	6	
4 Donny Odom	3 X 1 2 2	8	
5 David Cheshire	2 1 0 1	4	1
6 Duncan Chapman	1 1 0 0	2	
7 Paul Pickering	0 0 T T 0	0	

SHEFFIELD (H), May 21, W55-35

1 †Steve Regeling	2 N 3 0	5	
2 Donny Odom	1 3 2 2 1	9	3
3 David Cheshire	fx 3 3 3	9	
4 Mark Lemon	3 2 2 0	7	
5 Darren Sumner	2 1 3 2	8	3
6 Duncan Chapman	3 3 1 2 2	11	1
7 Paul Pickering	2 0 1 1 2	6	2

NEWCASTLE (H), July 2, L43-47

1 †Steve Regeling	2 3 3 1 1 2	12	1
2 Duncan Chapman	0 fx 3 2 3	8	1
3 David Cheshire	2 1 0 T	3	1
4 Mark Lemon	1 0 F T	1	1
5 Darren Sumner	2 1 R 3 2	8	
6 Donny Odom	2 fx N F N	2	1
7 Paul Pickering	3 2 N 2 2 0	9	

Newcastle

Berwick (A), April 4, W54-36

1 Mark Thorpe	3 3 3 2 2	13	1
2 Wayne Garratt	0 F 3 2 0	5	1
3 †David Bargh	2 3 3 3	11	
4 Scott Norman	3 2 3 3	11	
5 Phil Jeffrey	1 1 1 1	4	1
6 Richard Juul	3 1 N 1 3	8	1
7 Max Schofield	R N 1 1 0	2	

Edinburgh (A), April 10, D45-45

1 Mark Thorpe	2 3 3 3 1	12	
2 Wayne Garratt	0 0 1 fx	1	1
3 †David Bargh	3 3 3 3 F	12	
4 Scott Norman	3 0 3 1	7	
5 Phil Jeffrey	2 2 0 1	5	2
6 Richard Juul	2 1 F 2	5	
7 Max Schofield	1 F 2 0	3	1

SHEFFIELD (H), April 12, W54-36

1 Mark Thorpe	3 1 3 2	9	2
2 Wayne Garratt	1 2 0 2	5	1
3 †David Bargh	2 3 3 2 fx	10	
4 Scott Norman	**3 3 3 3 3**	**15**	
5 Phil Jeffrey	2 X 1 1	4	2
6 Richard Juul	3 1 1 0 2	7	2
7 Max Schofield	2 2 0 N	4	1

Glasgow (A), April 19, W48-42

1 Mark Thorpe	3 2 3 3 2 3	16	
2 Wayne Garratt	0 1 N 2	3	2
3 †David Bargh	2 3 2 3 2	12	2
4 Scott Norman	3 2 2 1	8	1
5 Phil Jeffrey	0 1 0 2	3	1
6 Richard Juul	2 0 2 T 1 1	6	2
7 Max Schofield	0 fx 0 N	0	

GLASGOW (H), April 20, W54-36

1 Mark Thorpe	**3 2 3 3**	**11**	**1**
2 Wayne Garratt	0 R 2 2	4	1
3 †David Bargh	3 2 2 3	10	1
4 Scott Norman	3 3 1 3 3	13	
5 Phil Jeffrey	2 1 0 1	4	1
6 Richard Juul	3 1 3 1 1	9	
7 Max Schofield	2 0 0 1	3	1

Sheffield (A), April 23, L42-48

1 Mark Thorpe	3 3 2 F	8	
2 Wayne Garratt	0 1 2 1	4	1
3 †David Bargh	2 2 3 3 2	12	
4 Scott Norman	3 R 2 2 0	7	
5 Phil Jeffrey	1 1 0 N	2	
6 Richard Juul	1 1 1 2	5	1
7 Max Schofield	3 0 1 0 0	4	1

MIDDLESBROUGH (H), April 26, W58-32

1 Mark Thorpe	**3 3 3 3 3**	**15**	
2 Wayne Garratt	0 2 2 0	4	1
3 †David Bargh	**3 3 3 3 2**	**14**	**1**
4 Scott Norman	1 3 1 3	8	
5 Phil Jeffrey	0 2 1 N	3	1
6 Richard Juul	3 2 2 3 fx	10	2
7 Max Schofield	2 0 0 2	4	2

EDINBURGH (H), May 3, W50-40

1 Mark Thorpe	F 3 3 3 2	11	1
2 Phil Jeffrey	1 1 2 2	6	1
3 †David Bargh	3 3 2 3 3	14	
4 Scott Norman	3 2 1 1	7	1
5 Wayne Garratt	0 1 2 0	3	1
6 Richard Juul	3 fx 0 1	4	1
7 Max Schofield	1 1 1 2	5	2

BERWICK (H), May 24, W46-43

1 Mark Thorpe	2 2 2 2 3	11	
2 Phil Jeffrey	1 1 2 1	5	3
3 Scott Norman	1 2 3 2	8	1
4 Wayne Garratt	2 1 1 3	7	1
5 †David Bargh	1 R 3 X 2	6	2
6 David Nagel	2 2 F N	4	
7 Max Schofield	3 1 1 0 F	5	1

Middlesbrough (A), July 2, W47-43

1 Mark Thorpe	3 3 3 2	11	
2 Phil Jeffrey	1 2 2 1 0	6	1
3 Scott Norman	3 2 3 2 1	11	1
4 Wayne Garratt	0 0 N 0	0	
5 †David Bargh	**3 3 3 3**	**12**	
6 Max Schofield	1 1 1 F 1	4	1
7 Richard Juul	0 1 1 1	3	1

Sheffield

Berwick (A), April 11, L31-59

1 †Peter Carr	1 1 2 2 2 F	8	2
2 Simon Green	0 2 0 1 0	3	1
3 Neil Evitts	2 3 3 3 1	12	
4 Steve Johnston	E F E T 0 1	1	
5 Louis Carr	2 2 R T N	4	
6 Mark Hepworth	1 0 T fx T 1	2	
7 David Wolstenholme	R R T 1 0	1	

Newcastle (A), April 12, L36-54

1 †Peter Carr	2 2 2 2 3 2	13	1
2 Simon Green	fx 1 1 1 1 1	5	3
3 Neil Evitts	3 3 3 3 1	13	
4 Louis Carr	1 2 N T	3	
5 Steve Johnston	0 0 0 T	0	
6 Mark Hepworth	1 R T F 0	1	
7 Steve Knott	0 0 T 1 0	1	

MIDDLESBROUGH (H), April 17, W46-44

1 †Peter Carr	2 3 3 3 2	13	1
2 Simon Green	0 1 3 1	5	
3 Neil Evitts	**3 3 3 3 3 3**	**18**	
4 Louis Carr	1 1 2 X	4	1
5 Steve Johnston	0 0 T 0	0	
6 Mark Hepworth	3 R 0 1 1	5	
7 David Wolstenholme	R 1 0 N	1	

NEWCASTLE (H), April 23, W48-42

1 †Peter Carr	2 3 3 2 1	11	
2 Simon Green	1 0 3 1	5	1
3 Neil Evitts	**3 3 3 3 3**	**15**	
4 Louis Carr	R 2 1 3	6	1
5 Steve Johnston	2 0 0 1	3	
6 Mark Hepworth	2 1 2 2 1	8	1
7 David Wolstenholme	0 0 0 N	0	

Edinburgh (A), May 1, L28-62

1 David Wolstenholme	1 0 1 N	2	1
2 Simon Green	2 1 F fx	3	
3 †Neil Evitts	2 2 3 2 1	10	
4 Steve Johnston	0 0 T 0	0	
5 Louis Carr	3 2 2 0 1 1	9	1
6 Mark Hepworth	R R T R	0	
7 Steve Knott	1 0 2 0 1 0	4	

Glasgow (A), May 3, L42-48

1 Peter Carr	*rider replacement*		
2 Simon Green	0 0 1 0	1	1
3 †Neil Evitts	2 3 3 3 1 fx	12	
4 Louis Carr	3 3 3 3 2 1	15	
5 Steve Johnston	1 1 3 0 2	7	
6 Mark Hepworth	2 0 1 1	4	1
7 Steve Knott	0 1 2 0 0	3	
8 David Wolstenholme	*did not ride*		

BERWICK (H), May 7, W51-39

1 †Peter Carr	**3 3 3 3**	**12**	
2 Simon Green	2 1 2 2	7	2
3 Neil Evitts	**3 3 3 3**	**12**	
4 Louis Carr	1 3 1 3 2	10	
5 Steve Johnston	0 0 2 0	2	1
6 Mark Hepworth	2 2 0 3 0	7	1
7 Steve Knott	1 0 0 0	1	1

Middlesbrough (A), May 21, L35-55

1 †Peter Carr	3 3 3 2 3 1 3	18	
2 Simon Green	R 2 0 0 0	2	
3 Neil Evitts	*rider replacement*		
4 Steve Johnston	0 R 1 1 0	2	
5 Louis Carr	1 2 2 1 3 0	9	
6 Mark Hepworth	R 1 0 N	1	1
7 Steve Knott	1 1 T 0 1	3	1
8 Dean Child	*did not ride*		

EDINBURGH (H), May 28, W52-38

1 †Peter Carr	**3 3 3 3 3**	**15**	
2 Simon Green	2 0 3 2 1	8	2
3 Neil Evitts	**3 3 3 3**	**12**	
4 Louis Carr	3 1 2 3	9	1
5 Steve Johnston	1 0 0 N	1	
6 Mark Hepworth	3 1 0 1 0	5	
7 Steve Knott	0 1 0 1	2	

GLASGOW (H), June 4, W48-41

1 †Peter Carr	**3 3 3 3**	**12**	
2 Simon Green	1 2 2 0 1	6	1
3 Neil Evitts	**3 3 3 3**	**12**	
4 Louis Carr	3 3 N N	6	
5 Steve Johnston	0 2 1 1 0	4	1
6 Mark Hepworth	2 1 0 0 0	3	1
7 Steve Knott	3 0 1 0 1	5	

The original staging of the match on April 30 was abandoned because of heavy rain after Simon Green had fallen and been excluded at the start of heat 10. Scorers at the time were: SHEFFIELD 36 (†Peter Carr 3-3-3- 6, Simon Green 2-2-2-fx- 6:1, Neil Evitts 3-3- 6, Louis Carr 2-R- 2:1, Steve Johnston 3-3-2- 8, Mark Hepworth 2-1-0-1- 4:2, Steve Knott 3-1-3:1) GLASGOW 18.

The Gold Cup Tables

Southern Section

	M	W	D	L	W	D	L	PtsF	PtsA	BP	TPts
STOKE	12	6	0	0	2	0	4	566	509	5	21
Exeter	12	6	0	0	1	0	5	616	462	6	20
Peterborough	12	5	0	1	2	0	4	558	521	4	18
Mildenhall	11	4	0	2	2	0	3	474	514	1	13
Long Eaton	11	5	0	1	0	0	5	480	510	2	12
Rye House	11	5	0	1	0	0	5	473	511	0	10
Milton Keynes	9	1	0	2	0	0	6	333	473	0	2

Northern Section

	M	W	D	L	W	D	L	PtsF	PtsA	BP	TPts
NEWCASTLE	10	5	0	0	3	1	1	498	401	5	22
Berwick	10	4	0	1	2	0	3	492	407	4	16
Middlesbrough	10	4	0	1	0	0	5	438	462	3	11
Sheffield	10	5	0	0	0	0	5	417	482	1	11
Edinburgh	10	3	1	1	0	0	5	446	452	2	9
Glasgow	10	3	0	2	0	0	5	405	492	0	6

The Gold Cup Final

First leg, Loomer Road, Saturday, August 1

STOKE 37

1 Alan Grahame	0 3 2 2 3	10	1
2 Gary Chessell	2 1 0 3 0	6	
3 †Nigel Crabtree	1 0 3 1	5	
4 Eric Monaghan	0 1 3 0 2 1	7	1
5 Garry Stead	1 2 2 2 N	7	
6 David Steen	1 0 T N 1	2	1
7 Andy Meredith	F T fx T 0 N	0	

NEWCASTLE 53

1 Mark Thorpe	3 3 2 3	11	
2 Phil Jeffrey	1 0 2 1	4	1
3 Scott Norman	3 2 3 1 0	9	
4 Richard Juul	3 1 1 2 2	9	1
5 †David Bargh	**2 3 3 3**	**11**	**1**
6 Max Schofield	2 0 1 0	3	1
7 Wayne Garratt	3 2 1 0	6	2

Second leg, Brough Park, Sunday, August 2

NEWCASTLE 51

1 Mark Thorpe	R 3 3 3 3	12	
2 Phil Jeffrey	2 fx 2 1	5	
3 Scott Norman	3 1 3 0	7	1
4 Richard Juul	1 1 0 3	5	
5 †David Bargh	3 3 2 3 1	12	
6 Max Schofield	3 F 2 1 2 F	8	2
7 Wayne Garratt	2 fx N N	2	1

STOKE 38

1 Alan Grahame	3 0 0 1	4	1
2 Gary Chessell	1 2 1 1 1	6	1
3 †Nigel Crabtree	2 2 3 3 1 2	13	1
4 Eric Monaghan	2 0 2 2	6	
5 Garry Stead	0 3 2 2 0	7	
6 Andy Meredith	fx T R fx	0	
7 David Steen	1 1 T 0	2	1

NEWCASTLE win 104-75 on aggregate.

A hard year's Knight

RICHARD KNIGHT survived what he readily admitted was the most torturous season of his career...at the top of the Second Division charts.

The former World Finalist made his surprise decision to stay at Berwick despite their drop back into Division Two but long before the end of the summer must have regretted that decision as club owner Terry Lindon ran into such severe financial problems that, for the second year in a row, the riders weren't paid.

But Knight brushed aside all the off track problems to dominate the Second Division and until the late weeks of the season was still averaging more than 11 points a meeting.

Understandably his form dropped off in the closing two months of the campaign but he still maintained his status as the undisputed kingpin of the Division.

He was unbeaten in seven out of 20 Homefire League matches and only twice failed to record double figure scores.

Martin Goodwin and 1991 National League Riders' Champion Jan Stæchmann were his major challengers once Tony Olsson had left Exeter to return to the First Division.

New boys Robert Nagy (see next page) and teenager Jason Crump – who celebrated his 17th birthday in August – both featured prominently among the tall scorers with Crump reaching double figures in 10 out of his last 11 League matches!

Ranking	Rider	Club	Matches	Rides	Points	Bonus Points	Total Points	Average	Maximums Full	Maximums Paid	Maximums Total
1	Richard Knight	Berwick	20	97	239.0	11.0	250.0	10.309	5	2	7
2	Tony Olsson	Exeter	1	6	14.0	1.0	15.0	10.000			
3	Martin Goodwin	Rye House	17	79	185.0	12.0	197.0	9.975	1	1	2
4	Jan Stæchmann	Long Eaton	17	83	196.0	10.0	206.0	9.928	2	3	5
5	Neil Evitts	Sheffield	15	68	164.0	1.0	165.0	9.706	6		6
6	David Bargh	Newcastle	20	97	218.0	13.0	231.0	9.526	1	2	3
7	Peter Carr	Sheffield	20	105	235.0	14.0	249.0	9.486	2	4	6
8	Tony Langdon	Sheffield	8	43	92.0	7.0	99.0	9.209	1	1	2
9	Shane Bowes	Glasgow	19	96	198.0	23.0	221.0	9.208		2	2
10	Mark Thorpe	Newcastle	19	93	202.0	11.0	213.0	9.161		1	1
11	Steve Regeling	Middlesbrough	20	111	247.0	7.0	254.0	9.153	1		1
12	Robert Nagy	Glasgow	19	101	197.0	29.0	226.0	8.950		3	3
13	Richard Green	Exeter	19	98	197.0	18.0	215.0	8.776		2	2
14	Alan Grahame	Stoke	13	64	131.0	9.0	140.0	8.750	1	1	2
15	Nigel Crabtree	Stoke	20	112	230.0	13.0	243.0	8.679	2	1	3
16	Les Collins	Edinburgh	20	101	204.5	13.5	218.0	8.634	1	2	3
17	Stephen Davies	Peterborough	19	83	158.0	17.0	175.0	8.434	1	1	2
18	David Blackburn	Berwick	20	93	186.0	10.0	196.0	8.430		2	2
19	Neil Collins	Glasgow	18	86	166.0	15.0	181.0	8.419	1		1
20	David Walsh	Berwick	20	87	164.0	19.0	183.0	8.414	1	3	4
21	Mick Poole	Peterborough	20	94	185.0	12.0	197.0	8.383	1	2	3
22	Kenny McKinna	Edinburgh	20	103	195.0	16.0	211.0	8.194			
23	Jason Crump	Peterborough	19	93	172.0	18.0	190.0	8.172		3	3
24	Scott Norman	Newcastle	20	92	174.0	10.0	184.0	8.000	1	1	2
25	Trevor O'Brien	Rye House	4	16	25.0	7.0	32.0	8.000			
26	Michael Coles	Edinburgh	18	92	173.5	9.5	183.0	7.957		1	1
27	Steve Lawson	Glasgow	18	73	135.0	10.0	145.0	7.945		1	1
28	Carl Blackbird	Long Eaton	20	105	202.0	5.0	207.0	7.886	1		1
29	Darren Sumner	Middlesbrough	18	90	167.0	7.0	174.0	7.733			
30	Johnny Jørgensen	Edinburgh	13	58	96.0	13.0	109.0	7.517		1	1
31	Paul Fry	Exeter	17	82	137.0	14.0	151.0	7.366			
32	Eric Monaghan	Stoke	17	91	160.0	7.0	167.0	7.341		1	1
33	Jens Rasmussen	Rye House	19	83	145.0	6.0	151.0	7.277	1		1
34	Jan Pedersen	Rye House	19	91	147.0	18.0	165.0	7.253			
35	Richard Hellsén	Long Eaton	13	56	85.0	14.0	99.0	7.071		1	1
36	Rodney Colquhoun	Peterborough	17	74	108.0	20.0	128.0	6.919			
37	Scott Robson	Berwick	20	82	116.0	25.0	141.0	6.878			
38	Colin Cook	Exeter	17	69	98.0	19.0	117.0	6.783			
39	Peter Jeffery	Exeter	14	66	99.0	12.0	111.0	6.727	1	1	2
40	Brett Saunders	Edinburgh	20	72	92.0	26.0	118.0	6.556		1	1
41	Phil Jeffrey	Newcastle	20	80	102.0	28.0	130.0	6.500			
42	David Cheshire	Middlesbrough	6	26	39.0	3.0	42.0	6.462			
43	Scott Lamb	Berwick	19	83	117.0	16.0	133.0	6.410			
44	Frank Smart	Exeter	19	88	122.0	19.0	141.0	6.409		1	1
45	Ian Barney	Peterborough	3	10	12.0	4.0	16.0	6.400			
46	Mark Simmonds	Exeter	19	83	115.0	15.0	130.0	6.265	1		1
47	Gary Chessell	Stoke	17	78	105.0	17.0	122.0	6.256		1	1
48	Mikael Teurnberg	Rye House	15	67	92.0	11.0	103.0	6.149			
49	Neville Tatum	Peterborough	17	71	99.0	10.0	109.0	6.141			

Ranking	Rider	Club	Matches	Rides	Points	Bonus Points	Total Points	Average	Maximums Full	Maximums Paid	Maximums Total
50	Mark Courtney	Rye House	16	65	87.0	12.0	99.0	6.092			
51	Richard Juul	Newcastle	17	66	82.0	17.0	99.0	6.000	1		1
52	Deon Prinsloo	Long Eaton	20	89	114.0	19.0	133.0	5.978			
53	Mark Blackbird	Peterborough	20	80	105.0	14.0	119.0	5.950			
54	Mick Powell	Glasgow	19	74	89.0	20.0	109.0	5.892		1	1
55	Sean Courtney	Rye House	18	83	101.0	21.0	122.0	5.880			
56	Martin Dixon	Long Eaton	20	89	110.0	20.0	130.0	5.843			
57	Garry Stead	Stoke	19	96	125.0	14.0	139.0	5.792			
58	Gary O'Hare	Long Eaton	16	63	79.0	10.0	89.0	5.651			
59	David Steen	Stoke	13	55	64.0	12.0	76.0	5.527			
60	Paul Hurry	Peterborough	20	83	94.0	20.0	114.0	5.494			
61	Paul Whittaker	Peterboro'/Middlesbro'	10	43	51.0	8.0	59.0	5.488			
62	Wayne Garratt	Newcastle	11	47	56.0	8.0	64.0	5.447			
63	Louis Carr	Sheffield	20	95	114.0	13.0	127.0	5.347			
64	Chris Readshaw	Berwick	20	86	99.0	14.0	113.0	5.256			
65	Doug Nicol	Middlesbrough	11	49	58.0	6.0	64.0	5.224			
66	Duncan Chapman	Middlesbrough	18	85	99.0	11.0	110.0	5.176			
67	Mark Lemon	Middlesbro'/Long Eaton	12	54	58.0	9.0	67.0	4.963			
68	Dariusz Fliegert	Edinburgh	20	81	84.0	15.0	99.0	4.889			
69	Nigel Sparshott	Long Eaton	16	61	57.0	17.0	74.0	4.852		2	2
70	Ian Humphreys	Exeter	16	62	57.0	18.0	75.0	4.839			
71	Jesper Olsen	Glasgow	11	51	54.0	7.0	61.0	4.784			
72	Robert Ledwith	Rye House	12	48	47.0	9.0	56.0	4.667			
73	Max Schofield	Newcastle	17	60	58.0	11.0	69.0	4.600			
74	Simon Green	Sheffield	20	80	79.0	12.0	91.0	4.550			
75	Donny Odom	Middlesbrough	18	70	64.0	12.0	76.0	4.343			
76	Steve Johnston	Sheffield	20	89	80.0	13.0	93.0	4.180			
77	James Grieves	Glasgow	7	23	20.0	4.0	24.0	4.174			
	Mark Burrows	Glasgow/Middlesbro'	7	23	22.0	2.0	24.0	4.174			
79	Colin White	Long Eaton	4	15	14.0	1.0	15.0	4.000			
80	Steve Knott	Sheffield	15	61	50.0	8.0	58.0	3.803			
81	David Nagel	Newcastle	7	33	26.0	4.0	30.0	3.636			
82	Jan Andersen	Edinburgh	5	19	15.0	2.0	17.0	3.579			
83	Chris Young	Rye House	12	39	29.0	5.0	34.0	3.487			
84	Andy Meredith	Stoke	19	65	45.0	11.0	56.0	3.446			
85	Mike Lewthwaite	Edinburgh	7	23	16.0	3.0	19.0	3.304			
86	Spencer Timmo	Newcastle	4	17	11.0	3.0	14.0	3.294		1	1
87	Mike McLuskey	Edinburgh	6	22	13.0	5.0	18.0	3.273			
88	Paul Pickering	Middlesbrough	20	70	42.0	10.0	52.0	2.971			
89	Jason Straughan	Glasgow	14	47	26.0	8.0	34.0	2.894			
90	Tommy Palmer	Exeter	9	32	19.0	4.0	23.0	2.875			
91	Mark Hepworth	Sheffield	6	21	12.0	3.0	15.0	2.857			
92	Michael Lowrie	Berwick	20	71	43.0	7.0	50.0	2.817			
93	Stuart Swales	Middlesbrough	8	22	11.0	4.0	15.0	2.727			
94	David Wolstenholme ■	Sheffield	1	3	2.0	0.0	2.0	2.667			
95	John Wainwright	Edinburgh	4	13	6.0	2.0	8.0	2.462			
	Paul Blackbird	Long Eaton	4	13	7.0	1.0	8.0	2.462			

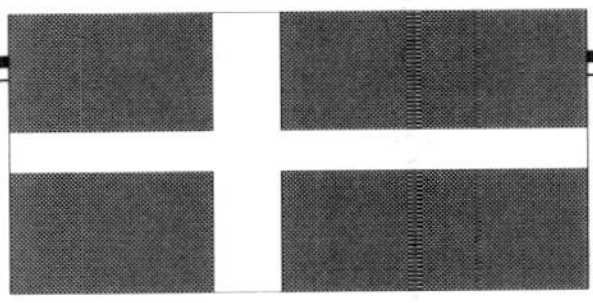

JAN'S THE TOPS...

EVEN though he lost his Division Two Riders' Championship crown Long Eaton's Jan Stæchmann remained one of the biggest attractions in the League.

He suffered all season with a troublesome knee injury – sustained in practice on the eve of the new campaign – but still scored more than 200 points in League matches alone, finishing a healthy fourth in the national charts with a near 10 point average.

LEGEND

THE 1992 Homefire League averages listed are taken from the referee's official programme for all matches and may differ from unofficial figures listed in other publications.

Reading from left to right the figures list the following: overall ranking, rider, track or tracks, matches, rides, points, bonus points, total points, calculated match average, paid maximums, full maximums, total maximums.

The calculated match average is taken by dividing the total number of points scored by the number of rides and then multiplied by four to give a calculated match average out of a maximum of 12.000.

■ Guest appearances are NOT included in the figures but a list of guest rider scores is given overleaf.

Ranking	Rider	Club	Matches	Rides	Points	Bonus Points	Total Points	Average	Maximums Full	Maximums Paid	Maximums Total
97	Darren Standing	Stoke	8	25	13.0	2.0	15.0	2.400			
98	Andrew Howe	Newcastle	4	11	3.0	3.0	6.0	2.182			
99	Ade Hoole	Stoke	5	13	6.0	1.0	7.0	2.154			
100	Rob Homer	Sheffield	5	18	6.0	2.0	8.0	1.778			
101	Michael Howe	Peterborough	2	5	1.0	1.0	2.0	1.600			
102	Stewart McDonald	Edinburgh	4	12	2.0	2.0	4.0	1.333			
103	Scott Pegler	Exeter	1	4	1.0	0.0	1.0	1.000			
104	Thierry Hilaire	Sheffield	6	20	3.0	0.0	3.0	0.600			
105	Jason Reed	Long Eaton	3	7	1.0	0.0	1.0	0.571			
106	Stuart Coleman	Glasgow	1	3	0.0	0.0	0.0	0.000			
	Wayne Park	Edinburgh	1	3	0.0	0.0	0.0	0.000			

Listed below are the individual averages of those who rode for more than one team in 1992.

Rider	Club	Matches	Rides	Points	Bonus Points	Total Points	Average
Mark Burrows	Glasgow	5	16	20.0	2.0	22.0	5.500
Mark Burrows	Middlesbrough	2	7	2.0	0.0	2.0	1.143
Mark Lemon	Middlesbrough	8	37	45.0	8.0	53.0	5.730
Mark Lemon	Long Eaton	4	17	13.0	1.0	14.0	3.294
Paul Whittaker	Peterborough	2	8	12.0	1.0	13.0	6.500
Paul Whittaker	Middlesbrough	8	35	39.0	7.0	46.0	5.257

GUESTS '92

ONLY two teams – Exeter and Sheffield – used guest riders in the 1992 Homefire League Division Two.

Listed alongside are the guests' averages.

Rider	Matches	Rides	Points	Bonus Points	Total Points	Average
Gary Chessell	1	6	11.0	0.0	11.0	7.333
Rob Price	1	1	0.0	0.0	0.0	0.000
Craig Rathbone	1	2	0.0	0.0	0.0	0.000
William Beveridge	1	3	0.0	0.0	0.0	0.000

FLYING SCOT ... the move to Edinburgh saw Kenny McKinna maintain his ranking as Scotland's number one

VETERANS ... Nigel Crabtree (above) and Mark Courtney (below) have both been around for sometime but are still potent points-pilers

❑ THE closure of Milton Keynes and Mildenhall had a major effect on the 1992 careers of some of the best known Second Division riders. David Smart and Nigel Leaver (seen above battling with Rye House's Jan Pedersen in one of Mildenhall's last meetings of the season) both moved onto Division One clubs – Smart recalled by his parent track Swindon and Leaver signed by title-chasing Wolverhampton.

❑ RICHARD Hellsén (below) was able to return to one of his former clubs Long Eaton where he recaptured some of the sparkle that seemed missing during his time with Milton Keynes.

❑ WHEN Reading recalled Swedish international Tony Olsson early in the season it gave Richard Green (left) the opportunity to establish himself as Exeter's undisputed number one and he came close to a major upset when only a fall prevented him winning the Barum-Jawa Division Two Riders' Championship.

1992

BERWICK

Back row: Alan Liddell (joint team manager), David Walsh, Chris Readshaw, David Blackburn, Scott Robson, Dave Younghusband (joint team manager). Front: Michael Lowrie, Richard Knight and Scott Lamb.

Bandit goes missing

THE FUTURE of the sport at Berrington Lough was, once again, thrown into total confusion when, only a week before the scheduled end of the 1992 season, promoter Terry Lindon mysteriously disappeared!

He failed to turn up for the last meeting of the season – a junior event – and within a matter of days it was revealed that the North East Fraud squad were investigating a series of complaints about the way he had run his private company Pi Computers.

And just as quickly the full extent of the problems at Berwick came to light as riders complained that they had received cheques which bounced.

It had been an open secret within the sport that the Bandits were experiencing financial problems for the second successive season and not even the drop back down into the Second Division was sufficient to produce a turn-around in the club's fortunes.

Lindon, the first black promoter the sport has known, started his third season in charge at the Border Country track without his big 1991 signing Kelvin Tatum and Jimmy Nilsen, but retained the services of former World Finalist Richard Knight who, perhaps surprisingly, opted to remain with the club even though it meant a weekly rail trip to Berwick from his Cambridgeshire home.

David Blackburn, who had walked out on the Bandits during their brief flirtation with the First Division, returned and David Walsh, Scott Robson and Michael Lowrie were also retained from Division One days.

They provided a firm backbone and the Bandits were among the pre-season favourites to lift the Division Two League title for what would have been the first time in their history.

What effect the financial worries had on the team no-one can accurately say and for a team with such a solid look about it they missed out on all four major trophies – finishing runners-up to Peterborough in the League, losing to Rye House in the semi final of the Phonesport Knock Out Cup, and failing to reach either the Gold Cup or the H.E.A.T. Team Championship Finals.

Knight, not unexpectedly, was a class act in the lower level and finished top of the national rankings, but he didn't always have the necessary support to turn close away results into victories.

Chris Readshaw, on loan from Middlesbrough, began in brilliant form but couldn't maintain his high scoring as the season progressed, but Scott Lamb, on loan from Edinburgh, again provided consistent middle order performances.

Consistency was a key factor in the Bandits season and they only used seven riders in their entire League campaign, 16-year-old prospect Michael Smith making his debut in the Knock Out Cup semi final against Rye House.

David Nagel, on short-term loan from Newcastle, actually rode at Glasgow in the middle of June but his four points were subsequently expunged from the final scoreline after a protest by the Clyde Two Tigers that he was ineligible was upheld.

Ironically that Speedway Control Board decision also cost the Bandits the bonus point although, in the final analysis, it didn't affect their end of season placing.

As 1992 came towards its close there were frantic efforts being made to keep Berwick in the Second Division. One prospective purchaser – directors of Newcastle sponsors Autocoachworks – pulled out of a possible deal and then a five-man consortium was involved inabortive negotiations in the hope of beating the December 31 Declaration of Intent deadline as the Berwick riders were offered for transfer by the BSPA.

1992 RIDER ROSTER

	Club Record								Career Record							
	M	R	Pts	BP	TPts	Ave	F	P	M	R	Pts	BP	TPts	Ave	F	P
David Blackburn	99	510	1074.0	54.0	1128.0	8.847	5	8	371	1745	2784.0	286.0	3070.0	7.037	8	14
Richard Knight	24	117	290.0	12.0	302.0	10.325	6	2	238	1025	1720.5	235.0	1955.5	7.631	8	11
Scott Lamb	24	103	150.0	17.0	167.0	6.485	1	0	244	1018	1623.0	210.0	1833.0	7.202	1	2
Michael Lowrie	23	79	43.0	7.0	50.0	2.532	0	0	23	79	43.0	7.0	50.0	2.532	0	0
Chris Readshaw	24	100	106.0	17.0	123.0	4.920	0	0	44	167	149.0	22.0	171.0	4.096	0	0
Scott Robson	101	354	425.0	74.0	499.0	5.638	0	0	101	354	425.0	74.0	499.0	5.638	0	0
Michael Smith	1	3	2.0	0.0	2.0	2.667	0	0	1	3	2.0	0.0	2.0	2.667	0	0
David Walsh	130	625	993.0	159.0	1152.0	7.373	2	10	193	884	1286.0	229.0	1515.0	6.855	3	11

BERWICK

Promoters: Terry Lindon and Dave Younghusband.
Address: Berrington Lough, Near Ancroft, Berwick-upon-Tweed, Northumberland.
Telephone: 0289-87345.
Information Line: 0891 31 21 40.
Track Length: 253 metres.
Track Record: 54.1 secs, Jimmy Nilsen (Berwick), May 10, 1991, Heat 4, Berwick v Swindon (Sunbrite League Division One).
Seasons in Division Two: 23 (1968-1980 [Shielfield Park]; 1982-1990, 1992 [Berrington Lough]).
Division Two Record: Runners-up (1), 1992, Third (1), 1989.
Division Two Cup Record: Winners (2), 1980, 1989. Runners-up (6), 1970, 1976, 1977, 1979, 1981, 1984.
Division Two Team Championship: Fourth (1), 1979. Qualified (7), 1979, 1980, 1984, 1985, 1987, 1989, 1990.
Appearances: ■Rob Grant, 377 (1978-1990).
Points: Steve McDermott, 3006 (1979-1988).
World Finalists: None.
Division Two Riders' Championship Finalists: Roy Williams (1968), Maury Robinson (1969-70), Doug Wyer (1971), Doug Templeton (1972), Willie Templeton (1973-74), Graham Jones (1978-79), Wayne Brown (1980-81), Steve McDermott (1982-83, 1985-86), Bruce Cribb (1984), Rob Woffinden (1987), Mark Courtney (1988), David Blackburn (1989, 1992), David Walsh (1990), Richard Knight (1992).

Seasons in Division One: *1 (1991).*
Division One Record: *Highest placing, fifth, 1991.*
Speedway Star Cup Record: *Second rounds, 1991.*
League Cup Record: *Never competed in the competition.*
Inter League Cup Record: *Semi Finalists, 1991.*
Gold Cup: *Winners (1), 1991. Northern Section Winners (1), 1991.*
Appearances: *Kevin Little and Richard Knight, 28 (1991).*
Points: *Kelvin Tatum, 310 (1991).*
World Finalists: *Mikael Blixt (1991), Jimmy Nilsen (1991), Kelvin Tatum (1991).*
DIivision One Riders' Championship Finalists: *Kelvin Tatum (1991).*
■ Rob Grant has made a record number of appearances for Berwick and the figure stood at 385 at the end of the 1991 season, including eight in the Sunbrite League First Division.

Berwick officially withdrew from the First Division at the end of the 1991 season because of financial problems and were subsequently readmitted to the 1992 Homefire League Division Two.

SHEFFIELD (H), May 9, W66-24

1 §†Richard Knight	**3 3 3 3**	**12**	
2 §Scott Lamb	0 2 1 2	5	2
3 David Walsh	**2 3 3 3 3**	**14**	**1**
4 Scott Robson	2 2 2 1	7	3
5 David Blackburn	**3 3 3 2 2**	**13**	**2**
6 §§Michael Lowrie	3 3 1 1	8	
7 §Chris Readshaw	F 3 1 3	7	

NEWCASTLE (H), May 23, W46-43

1 †Richard Knight	3 2 3 3 3	14	
2 Scott Lamb	1 R 2 T	3	
3 David Blackburn	3 1 1 fx1	6	
4 Scott Robson	F 1 1 3	5	1
5 David Walsh	3 2 2 3 0	10	
6 Michael Lowrie	1 0 N 0	1	
7 Chris Readshaw	3 0 0 2 2	7	1

Long Eaton (A), June 3, D45-45

1 †Richard Knight	3 3 3 2 3	14	
2 Scott Lamb	2 0 0 0	2	1
3 David Blackburn	2 2 3 1	8	1
4 Scott Robson	F 3 2 1 1	7	1
5 David Walsh	2 1 2 2	7	
6 Chris Readshaw	3 1 2 1 0	7	1
7 Michael Lowrie	0 0 N 0	0	

Rye House (A), June 14, L44-46

1 †Richard Knight	**3 3 3 2 3 3**	**17**	**1**
2 Scott Lamb	2 1 2 3 3 0	11	1
3 David Blackburn	3 2 0 0	5	
4 David Walsh	1 1 X 0	2	
5 Scott Robson	R F 3 2	5	1
6 Chris Readshaw	3 0 fxT T 0	3	
7 Michael Lowrie	0 fxN 1	1	

Glasgow (A), June 17, L39-51

1 †Richard Knight	3 3 3 3 2	14	
2 David Nagel	*ineligible to ride*		
3 David Blackburn	3 3 2 0	8	
4 Scott Robson	0 1 2 0	3	
5 David Walsh	3 0 2 2 0	7	
6 Chris Readshaw	3 0 1 0 1	5	2
7 Michael Lowrie	1 0 1 N	2	

The match originally finished 42-48 but Glasgow's protest against Berwick's use of David Nagel was upheld by the Speedway Control Board who ruled that Nagel's points should be deducted from the final score. The original scores of riders affected by the decision were: Nagel 2-0-2-0- 4:1, Lowrie 1-0-0-N- 1.

GLASGOW (H), June 20, W50-40

1 †Richard Knight	3 2 3 3 3	14	
2 Scott Lamb	2 0 1 1	4	1
3 David Blackburn	3 X 2 R	5	
4 Scott Robson	1 3 F N	4	
5 David Walsh	3 2 3 1 2	11	2
6 Michael Lowrie	3 0 1 0 0	4	
7 Chris Readshaw	2 3 1 2	8	2

STOKE (H), June 27, W60-30

1 †Richard Knight	**3 3 3 3 3**	**15**	
2 Scott Lamb	1 1 fx1	3	
3 David Blackburn	2 2 3 1 1	9	
4 Scott Robson	**3 3 2 3**	**11**	**1**
5 David Walsh	2 1 3 3	9	1
6 Michael Lowrie	0 1 1 N	2	2
7 Chris Readshaw	3 3 2 2 1	11	2

Stoke (A), June 28, L43-47

1 †Richard Knight	1 2 2 2 2	9	1
2 Scott Lamb	2 1 3 1	7	2
3 David Blackburn	3 3 1 2 0	9	
4 Scott Robson	3 0 2 0	5	
5 David Walsh	2 1 1 1	5	2
6 Chris Readshaw	2 1 2 3 0	8	1
7 Michael Lowrie	0 0 N R	0	

Edinburgh (A), July 17, W52-38

1 †Richard Knight	**3 3 3 3**	**12**	
2 Scott Lamb	1 0 1 1 0	3	1
3 David Blackburn	3 2 2 3	10	
4 Scott Robson	2 1 3 2 1	9	3
5 David Walsh	3 2 2 2	9	1
6 Chris Readshaw	3 1 2 1 0	7	2
7 Michael Lowrie	1 1 N 0	2	

EDINBURGH (H), July 18, W49-40

1 †Richard Knight	**3 3 3 3 3**	**15**	
2 Scott Lamb	1 1 1 1	4	
3 David Blackburn	2 3 3 2	10	
4 Scott Robson	3 2 1 fx	6	1
5 David Walsh	0 3 3 1 2	9	2
6 Michael Lowrie	3 1 0 1	5	1
7 Chris Readshaw	E 0 0 fx	0	

Newcastle (A), July 19, L38-51

1 †Richard Knight	2 1 3 2 3 1	12	2
2 Scott Lamb	0 2 1 3	6	
3 David Blackburn	3 3 1 2 0	9	1
4 Scott Robson	fx0 1 N	1	
5 David Walsh	2 2 1 1	6	1
6 Chris Readshaw	2 F 2 0 0	4	
7 Michael Lowrie	0 0 T 0	0	

Middlesbrough (A), July 23, W46-43

1 †Richard Knight	3 1 2 3 2	11	2
2 Scott Lamb	0 2 3 0	5	
3 David Blackburn	3 1 2 2 3	11	1
4 Scott Robson	2 2 2 0	6	
5 David Walsh	1 fxN N	1	1
6 Chris Readshaw	3 0 3 fx1 3	10	1
7 Michael Lowrie	0 1 1 N 0	2	

EXETER (H), July 25, W60-30

1 †Richard Knight	**3 3 3 3 3**	**15**	
2 Scott Lamb	1 2 3 1	7	1
3 David Blackburn	**3 3 3 3 2**	**14**	**1**
4 Scott Robson	3 3 0 1	7	1
5 David Walsh	1 2 3 2	8	2
6 Michael Lowrie	2 0 0 0	2	1
7 Chris Readshaw	3 0 2 2	7	1

Exeter (A), August 24, L43-47

1 †Richard Knight	2 3 2 R 1	8	2
2 David Walsh	3 2 3 1 2	11	2
3 David Blackburn	3 3 R 3	9	
4 Chris Readshaw	0 0 0 N	0	
5 Scott Robson	1 1 2 1	5	2
6 Scott Lamb	3 2 N 1 1 2	9	1
7 Michael Lowrie	0 0 F 1	1	

RYE HOUSE (H), September 5, W52-38

1 †Richard Knight	2 3 3 3	11	
2 Scott Robson	1 2 3 2 1	9	3
3 David Blackburn	F 3 2 3 3	11	
4 David Walsh	**3 3 2 3**	**11**	**1**
5 Chris Readshaw	0 0 0 0	0	
6 Michael Lowrie	3 1 0 N	4	
7 Scott Lamb	1 2 2 0 1	6	1

Sheffield (A), September 10, L34-56

1 †Richard Knight	1 0 3 2 T	6	1
2 Scott Robson	2 1 1 1 2	7	1
3 David Blackburn	1 0 1 R 3 1	6	1
4 David Walsh	1 2 2 0 0	5	
5 Chris Readshaw	0 0 T N	0	
6 Scott Lamb	3 2 2 1 2	10	1
7 Michael Lowrie	0 0 T 0	0	

LONG EATON (H), September 12, W54-36

1 †Richard Knight	3 3 3 R	9	
2 Scott Robson	2 2 fx2 1	7	3
3 David Blackburn	3 3 1 3	10	1
4 David Walsh	**3 3 3 3 3**	**15**	
5 Chris Readshaw	R 1 1 F	2	
6 Michael Lowrie	2 1 2 0	5	2
7 Scott Lamb	3 1 2 0	6	

Peterborough (A), September 18, L30-60

1 †Richard Knight	2 0 2 3 2 1	10	
2 Scott Robson	F 1 0 N	1	
3 David Blackburn	1 1 3 2 2 0	9	1
4 Chris Readshaw	0 1 R T	1	1
5 David Walsh	1 2 2 0 0	5	1
6 Michael Lowrie	0 0 T 0 T	0	
7 Scott Lamb	2 0 1 1	4	

MIDDLESBROUGH (H), September 20, W58-32

1 †Richard Knight	**3 3 3 2**	**11**	**1**
2 Scott Robson	F 2 3 2	7	2
3 David Blackburn	3 3 1 3	10	1
4 David Walsh	**2 2 3 3**	**10**	**2**
5 Chris Readshaw	3 3 fx1 2	9	
6 Michael Lowrie	1 0 R 1 1	3	1
7 Scott Lamb	3 1 2 2	8	1

PETERBOROUGH (H), September 26, W55-35

1 †Richard Knight	3 2 3 2 E	10	1
2 Scott Robson	2 1 1 E	4	2
3 David Blackburn	3 3 2 3 3	14	
4 David Walsh	0 3 3 3	9	
5 Chris Readshaw	1 0 1 1	3	
6 Michael Lowrie	0 0 0 N 1	1	
7 Scott Lamb	3 3 3 2 1 2	14	3

The original staging of the match against Peterborough on August 22, was abandoned after four races because of heavy rain. The scorers at the time were: BERWICK 17 (†Richard Knight 3- 3, Chris Readshaw 2- 2:1, David Blackburn 3- 3, Scott Robson 3- 3, David Walsh 2- 2:1, Michael Lowrie 1-0- 1, Scott Lamb 3- 3) PETERBOROUGH 7.

MILDENHALL (H), May 30, W68-22

1 †Richard Knight	**3 3 3 2 3**	**14**	**1**
2 Scott Lamb	2 1 3 1	7	1
3 David Blackburn	**3 3 2 3 2**	**13**	**2**
4 Scott Robson	2 1 3 3	9	1
5 David Walsh	**3 3 3 2**	**11**	**1**
6 Michael Lowrie	3 1 1 1	6	
7 Chris Readshaw	2 1 3 2	8	2

At-a-Glance Results

Edinburgh	**W49-40**	**W52-36**	**101-76**
Exeter	**W60-30**	**L43-47**	**103-77**
Glasgow	**W50-40**	**L39-51**	**89-91**
Long Eaton	**W54-36**	**D45-45**	**99-91**
Middlesbrough	**W58-32**	**W46-43**	**104-75**
Newcastle	**W46-43**	**L38-51**	**84-94**
Peterborough	**W55-35**	**L30-60**	**85-95**
Rye House	**W52-38**	**L44-46**	**96-84**
Sheffield	**W66-24**	**L34-56**	**100-80**
Stoke	**W60-30**	**L43-47**	**103-77**
Mildenhall	***W68-22***		

WHO WAS WHO IN '92

David Martin BLACKBURN
Born: January 7, 1962, Coventry, West Midlands.
Rejoined the Bandits after a temporary retirement during the 1991 season after struggling in the top flight. An everpresent.

Richard John KNIGHT
Born: May 26, 1959, Cambridge, Cambridgeshire.
Agreed to remain at Berrington Lough following their return to Division Two racing and finished top of the national averages. He finished out of double figures ion only two of his 20 League matches.

Robert Scott LAMB
Born: October 28, 1966, Edinburgh, Scotland.
Returned to the Bandits after a six season absence, this time on loan from Edinburgh. Finished the season in splendid form with a paid 17 return against champions Peterborough. The only member of the first team squad to miss a meeting.

Michael LOWRIE
Born: January 8, 1971, Hawick, Scotland.
Another survivor from the club's Division One days. He was an everpresent at reserve.

David NAGEL – see Newcastle

Craig Michael RATHBONE
Born: August 21, 1969, Middlesbrough, Cleveland.
Regular member of the Northumbria Raiders Reserve League side who made his Second Division debut for short-handed Exeter at Berrington Lough in July.

Christopher READSHAW
Born: January 14, 1974, Middlesbrough, Cleveland.
One of the most promising teenagers in Division Two. He joined Berwick on loan from Middlesbrough but hit a rocky spell in August and September after a flying start to the season.

Scott ROBSON
Born: August 15, 1971, Sunderland, Tyne & Wear.
Continued his steady progress in his sixth season with the Bandits. One of six everpresents in the 1992 squad.

Michael SMITH
Born: July 20, 1976, Billingham, Cleveland.
Much sought after youngster who signed for Berwick on his 16th birthday and made his debut in their Reserve League side on August 15. Also won the track's traditional Stars of Tomorrow meeting with a 15 point maximum. Turned out for the Bandits senior squad in their Phonesport Division Two Knock Out Cup semi final against Rye House.

David WALSH
Born: August 29, 1963, Sowerby Bridge, West Yorkshire.
Another of the Division One Bandits to stay with the club following their drop back into the Second Division. He was another everpresent.

The rain-ing champions

THE GULF Oil Monarchs approached the new season confident of improving on their fourth spot in the league in 1991. That they weren't able to do so stemmed from two factors – their inability to win away from home and good old Jupiter Pluvius!

The rain Gods ensured that no less than 13 away matches were postponed throughout the season including each and everyone of their scheduled Gold Cup fixtures.

At home it wasn't quite so bad although it did cause the postponement of Michael Coles' Testimonial meeting if not his marriage to fiancee Michelle which was switched from the centre green to a room under the main grandstand!

During the winter Frede Schøtt made it clear that he wanted a move to Division One and that influenced the club's team building plans. The Dane eventually got his wish moving to Belle Vue albeit after the season had begun.

Dave Steen went to Milton Keynes via parent track Reading, and there was no return, either, for Aussie Nigel Alderton. With Les Collins, Brett Saunders, Michael Coles and Johnny Jørgensen retained, rumours soon became rife that Kenny McKinna would be making the short journey across from Glasgow and those rumours turned into reality.

Edinburgh then cast their net a little wider for the next signing bringing in Rybnik-based Pole Dariusz Fliegert leaving Stewart McDonald to be handed the number seven racejacket on press day to complete the side.

The good old British weather then stepped in. Wherever Edinburgh were due to ride it rained and matches were postponed left, right and centre. It hardly allowed the team to gain any impetus or consistency. Losing at home to Berwick is never easy to swallow for Monarchs' fans but even worse was the fact that they lost McKinna with a compound fracture of a cheekbone.

Surprisingly he made a quicker-than-expected return to the saddle but that only made up for Michael Coles being sidelined, having broken his right foot at Newcastle. Yes, injuries were now beginning to play their part in Edinburgh's season.

At least the smiles returned as they dumped Glasgow out of the Phonesport Knock Out Cup, easily winning both legs. Winning at Shawfield was no problem as they returned to win in the Spring Trophy – but at other away venues it just wasn't happening.

June started off in sparkling fashion with the Monarchs rattling up 45 points in their home leg of the H.E.A.T. Team Championship making qualification for the final a virtual certainty.

However Saunders, by this time, had picked up a niggly leg injury and the League match at Newcastle pushed the whole injury situation into crisis. Jørgensen broke an elbow and teenage reserves McDonald and Mike McCluskey both broke collarbones.

"I really don't know what we've done to deserve such luck," said a perplexed Alex Harkness co-promoter of the Monarchs.

Taking a break from League racing, Kenny McKinna won the Scottish Championship but even more interesting was the performance of a certain 'Roy McGregor' who nobody had ever heard of! Not surprising really for it was Mike Lewthwaite riding under an assumed name and he was quickly signed, along with John Wainwright, to alleviate the injury problems.

They were soundly beaten by Bradford in the BSPA Cup and, seven days later, Berwick took the League points with a resounding 52-38 victory which effectively ruled out any lingering championship hopes the Monarchs may have had.

They performed admirably in the H.E.A.T. Team Championship Final, just being pipped by Peterborough but couldn't transfer that sort of form away from home in League matches.

With a further home loss suffered, this time against Rye House, it was decided to replace Jørgensen with fellow Dane Jan Andersen, the elder brother of Coventry's Brian. He was brought in not so much with 1992 in mind but with a view to the future and the disconsolate Jørgensen returned home.

1992 RIDER ROSTER

	Club Record								Career Record							
	M	R	Pts	BP	TPts	Ave	F	P	M	R	Pts	BP	TPts	Ave	F	P
Jan Andersen	5	19	15.0	2.0	17.0	3.579	0	0	5	19	15.0	2.0	17.0	3.579	0	0
Michael Coles	117	608	957.5	109.5	1067.0	7.020	0	1	269	1218	1658.0	229.5	1887.5	6.199	0	2
Les Collins	231	1203	2681.0	160.5	2841.5	9.448	31	12	302	1499	3188.0	160.5	3348.5	8.935	35	17
Dariusz Fliegert	24	98	103.0	17.0	120.0	4.898	0	0	24	98	103.0	17.0	120.0	4.898	0	0
Johnny Jørgensen	40	157	193.0	32.0	225.0	5.732	0	1	40	157	193.0	32.0	225.0	5.732	0	1
Mike Lewthwaite	8	27	19.0	3.0	22.0	3.259	0	3	15	46	39.0	6.0	45.0	3.913	0	0
Stewart McDonald	4	12	2.0	2.0	4.0	1.333	0	0	4	12	2.0	2.0	4.0	1.333	0	0
Kenny McKinna	23	118	230.0	19.0	249.0	8.441	0	1	268	1315	2637.0	121.0	2758.0	8.389	34	9
Mike McLuskey	12	41	18.0	6.0	24.0	2.341	0	0	12	41	18.0	6.0	24.0	2.341	0	0
Wayne Park	1	3	0.0	0.0	0.0	0.000	0	0	1	3	0.0	0.0	0.0	0.000	0	0
Brett Saunders	348	1635	2561.0	335.0	2896.0	7.085	9	10	376	1729	2666.0	356.0	3022.0	6.991	9	10
John Wainwright	7	23	11.0	4.0	15.0	2.609	0	0	73	237	135.0	37.0	172.0	2.903	0	0

EDINBURGH

Promoters: John Campbell and Alex Harkess.
Address: Powderhall Stadium, Beaverhall Road, Edinburgh, EH7 4JE.
Telephone: 031-556-3979.
Hotline: 0891 312 152.
Track Length: 312 metres.
Track Record: 60.9 secs, Les Collins (Edinburgh), August 7, 1992, Heat 1, Edinburgh v Long Eaton (Division Two).
Seasons in Division Two: 16 (1977-1992).
Best Division Two Season: Fourth, 1981, 1991.
Division Two Cup Record: Winners (1), 1981.
Division Two Team Championship: Winners (1), 1981. Runners-up (2), 1991, 1992. Qualified (7), 1978, 1981, 1983, 1986, 1989, 1991, 1992.
Appearances: Dave Trownson, 374 (1977-1987).
Points: Dave Trownson, 3045.5 (1977-1987).
World Finalists: Jack Young (1950-51), Bernt Persson (1967).
Division Two Riders' Championship Finalists: Bert Harkins (1977), Rob Hollingworth (1978), Neil Collins (1981), Dave Trownson (1982-83), Mark Fiora (1984), Les Collins (1986-87, 1989-90-91-92), Jamie Luckhurst (1988), Kenny McKinna (1992).
Other Honours: Provincial League Knock-out Cup Winners, 1961.

1992

EDINBURGH

Back row: Michael Coles, Stewart McDonald, Kenny McKinna, Dariusz Fliegert. Front: Brett Saunders, Les Collins and Jan Andersen.

STOKE (H), May 15, W46-44

1 Les Collins	2 2 2 2 2 F	10	1
2 Michael Coles	*rider replacement*		
3 §Kenny McKinna	1 3 2 2 1 2	11	1
4 †Brett Saunders	3 3 1 1 1	9	3
5 §§Dariusz Fliegert	1 1 R 1 0	3	1
6 Mike McLuskey	2 0 0 N	2	1
7 Johnny Jørgensen	3 3 3 0 2	11	
8 Stewart McDonald	*did not ride*		

PETERBOROUGH (H), May 22, W60-30

1 Les Collins	**2 3 3 2 3 3**	**16**	**2**
2 Michael Coles	*rider replacement*		
3 Kenny McKinna	3 3 1 3 3 2	15	1
4 †Brett Saunders	0 1 2 2	5	2
5 Dariusz Fliegert	3 3 1 1 1	9	
6 Mike McLuskey	0 1 N 0	1	
7 Johnny Jørgensen	1 3 2 3 2 3	14	2

SHEFFIELD (H), May 29, W60-30

1 Les Collins	2 3 3 3 3	14	
2 Michael Coles	1 1 3 R	5	1
3 Kenny McKinna	1 3 2 2 2	**10**	**2**
4 †Brett Saunders	**3 2 2 2**	**9**	**3**
5 Dariusz Fliegert	1 3 1 1	6	1
6 Mike McLuskey	fx N N N	0	
7 Johnny Jørgensen	**3 3 2 2 3 3**	**16**	**2**

MIDDLESBROUGH (H), June 12, W57-33

1 Les Collins	**3 3 3 3 3**	**15**	
2 Dariusz Fliegert	1 2 1 2	6	3
3 Michael Coles	3 3 1 2	9	
4 Kenny McKinna	3 2 2 3 1	11	1
5 †Brett Saunders	N N N N	0	
6 Mike McLuskey	2 2 1 0 0 0	5	3
7 Johnny Jørgensen	3 1 2 3 0 2	11	1

Newcastle (A), June 14, L43-47

1 Les Collins	3 1 1 1 2 1	9	3
2 Dariusz Fliegert	0 3 1 0	4	
3 Michael Coles	1 3 3 0	7	
4 †Brett Saunders	1 2 1 T	4	1
5 Kenny McKinna	2 0 3 2 3 2	12	
6 Mike McLuskey	0 0 1 T	1	
7 Johnny Jørgensen	2 1 3 N R	6	

Middlesbrough (A), June 18, L41-48

1 Les Collins	3 1 3 1 2 0	10	
2 Dariusz Fliegert	0 0 1 2 3	6	
3 Michael Coles	2 2 R 2 1	7	1
4 †Brett Saunders	0 T T N	0	
5 Kenny McKinna	1 3 3 3 2 3	15	
6 §§Wayne Park	F T 0 0 N	0	
7 §John Wainwright	2 R T 0 1	3	1

Exeter (A), July 6, L32-58

1 Les Collins	2 0 0 0	2	
2 Dariusz Fliegert	1 1 2 1 1	6	2
3 Michael Coles	F 2 3 3 R 1	9	
4 †Brett Saunders	0 0 1 N	1	
5 Kenny McKinna	1 1 2 2 3 0	9	1
6 §§Mike Lewthwaite	2 T 0 1 T	3	
7 John Wainwright	1 1 T 0	2	1

BERWICK (H), July 17, L38-52

1 Les Collins	2 3 3 2 1 2	13	1
2 Dariusz Fliegert	N 0 T 1 0	1	1
3 Michael Coles	2 0 3 2 1	8	
4 Kenny McKinna	1 2 3 0 3 3	12	
5 †Brett Saunders	0 1 fx T	1	1
6 Mike Lewthwaite	R F T T 0	0	
7 Johnny Jørgensen	0 2 0 N 1	3	

Berwick (A), July 18, L40-49

1 Les Collins	2 1 3 1 3 1	11	1
2 Dariusz Fliegert	0 0 T T	0	
3 Michael Coles	3 2 2 2 fx	9	
4 †Brett Saunders	1 2 2 0 2	7	2
5 Kenny McKinna	2 1 0 2 3 0	8	1
6 Mike Lewthwaite	2 fx N T	2	
7 Johnny Jørgensen	1 fx 2 0 T	3	2

EXETER (H), July 24, W55-34

1 Les Collins	**3 3 3 3 2.5**	**14.5**	**.5**
2 †Brett Saunders	2 2 fx R	4	2
3 Michael Coles	**3 3 3 3 2.5**	**14.5**	**.5**
4 Kenny McKinna	3 1 2 3	9	1
5 Dariusz Fliegert	0 0 N 1	1	
6 Mike McLuskey	2 1 1 0 0 0	4	1
7 Johnny Jørgensen	3 3 2 N N	8	

LONG EATON (H), August 7, W54-36

1 Les Collins	3 3 3 3 2	14	
2 Brett Saunders	**2 2 3 2**	**9**	**3**
3 Michael Coles	3 3 3 2 1	12	1
4 Kenny McKinna	2 3 1 2	8	1
5 Dariusz Fliegert	3 1 R 1	5	1
6 §§Stewart McDonald	1 F 0 N	1	1
7 Johnny Jørgensen	2 0 1 1 1	5	1

NEWCASTLE (H), August 21, W48-42

1 †Les Collins	3 3 3 2 2	13	1
2 Brett Saunders	0 2 2 1	5	2
3 Michael Coles	3 1 0 0	4	
4 Kenny McKinna	1 3 0 2 3	9	1
5 Dariusz Fliegert	2 1 1 2	6	1
6 John Wainwright	1 F F N	1	
7 Johnny Jørgensen	3 3 2 1 1	10	1

Long Eaton (A), August 26, L43-47

1 †Les Collins	0 0 3 3 3 2	11	
2 Brett Saunders	1 2 2 1	6	
3 Michael Coles	2 3 1 3 2 1	12	2
4 Dariusz Fliegert	2 3 2 0	7	1
5 Kenny McKinna	3 1 0 1	5	1
6 Johnny Jørgensen	1 0 T 1	2	
7 John Wainwright	0 0 T 0	0	

RYE HOUSE (H), September 4, L43-46

1 †Les Collins	2 2 3 3 0	10	1
2 Brett Saunders	3 R F 1	4	
3 Michael Coles	3 3 3 2 1	12	
4 Kenny McKinna	2 2 2 3	9	1
5 Johnny Jørgensen	1 1 2 R	4	2
6 Stewart McDonald	F 0 0 N	0	
7 Dariusz Fliegert	3 fx 1 0 0	4	1

GLASGOW (H), September 25, W47-43

1 †Les Collins	2 2 3 2	9	
2 Brett Saunders	0 1 3 2	6	2
3 Michael Coles	3 3 2 3 0	11	
5 Kenny McKinna	3 2 1 3 2	11	1
5 Johnny Jørgensen	2 1 0 N	3	2
6 Stewart McDonald	0 0 0 N	0	
7 Dariusz Fliegert	3 1 2 1 0 0	7	1

Sheffield (A), October 1, L37-53

1 †Les Collins	2 2 3 3 2 1	13	1
2 Brett Saunders	1 1 1 0	3	2
3 Michael Coles	1 2 2 0 0	5	1
4 §§Jan Andersen	R 2 1 3 0	6	
5 Kenny McKinna	2 0 1 2	5	
6 Dariusz Fliegert	2 2 N 0 N	4	
7 Stewart McDonald	1 N 0 T T 0	1	1

Rye House (A), October 4, L37-53

1 †Les Collins	1 fx T N	1	1
2 Brett Saunders	2 2 1 1 1	7	2
3 Michael Coles	2 2 2 2 3 2	13	
4 Jan Andersen	0 0 2 1	3	
5 Keny McKinna	3 2 0 fx 3 1	9	1
6 Mike Lewthwaite	0 1 T 0	1	1
7 Dariusz Fliegert	2 1 T 0 0	3	1

Peterborough (A), October 16, L34-56

1 †Les Collins	2 1 2 0	5	
2 Brett Saunders	F 0 0 N	0	
3 Michael Coles	3 1 3 3 1 3	14	
4 Jan Andersen	0 fx T 1	1	
5 Kenny McKinna	1 2 3 0 2 2	10	1
6 Dariusz Fliegert	2 1 N 1 0 0	4	
7 Mike Lewthwaite	0 N 0 T 0	0	

Stoke (A), October 17, L40-50

1 †Les Collins	0 2 2 2 0	6	
2 Brett Saunders	3 1 1 0	5	1
3 Michael Coles	1 3 3 3 0 1	11	1
4 Jan Andersen	1 0 1 N	2	1
5 Kenny McKinna	2 2 1 2	7	
6 Dariusz Fliegert	1 0 N 1	2	1
7 Mike Lewthwaite	0 2 T 1 3 1	7	1

Glasgow (A), October 18, L42-48

1 †Les Collins	3 1 3 1	8	1
2 Brett Saunders	1 2 3 1	7	
3 Michael Coles	2 3 2 1 1 2	11	2
4 Jan Andersen	0 2 1 0	3	1
5 Kenny McKinna	2 3 2 2 1	10	1
6 Dariusz Fliegert	R 0 0 T	0	
7 Mike Lewthwaite	2 1 0 0	3	1

At-a-Glance Results

Berwick	L38-52	L40-49	78-101
Exeter	W55-34	L32-56	87-90
Glasgow	W47-43	L42-48	89-91
Long Eaton	W54-36	L43-47	97-83
Middlesbrough	W57-33	L41-48	98-81
Newcastle	W48-42	L43-47	91-89
Peterborough	W60-30	L34-56	94-86
Rye House	L43-46	L37-53	80-99
Sheffield	W60-30	L37-53	87-83
Stoke	W46-44	L40-50	86-94

WHO WAS WHO IN '92

Jan ANDERSEN
Born: August 1, 1969, Sonderborg, Denmark.
Elder brother of 1991 World Under 21 Champion Brian Andersen. He joined Edinburgh towards the end of the season showing considerable style in his five Division Two matches.

Michael Timothy COLES
Born: August 11, 1965, Exeter, Devon.
Ended the season in splendid style with a string of double figure scores as he enjoyed a well-earned Testimonial meeting after 10 seasons as an Exeter contracted rider although he has spent the last four years on loan to the Gulf Oil Monarchs.

Leslie COLLINS
Born: May 24, 1958, Partington, Greater Manchester.
Topped the Edinburgh averages for the sixth successive season although his overall average dropped as he was less proficient on away tracks than in the past.

Dariusz (Darek) FLIEGERT
Born: March 15, 1969, Rybnik, Poland.
One of two racing brothers who was better known by Edinburgh fans by his nickname Darek. He became the first Polish rider to compete in the Second Division and had a satisfactory debut campaign at Powderhall without ever pulling up any trees.

Johnny JØRGENSEN
Born: June 9, 1971, Esbjerg, Denmark.
His end of season sacking prompted terrace demonstrations from his Powderhall backers but he had lived on a knife edge in the last couple of months of the campaign as he never showed his home form on his travels. Surprisingly enough still finished with a seven point plus average.

Michael Grant LEWTHWAITE
Born: December 1, 1967, Rochdale, Greater Manchester.
Made a racing comeback after missing the 1991 season with a serious shoulder injury. Impressed the Edinburgh management in the Scottish Riders' Championship in June when he scored 13 points. He subsequently joined the Gulf Oil Monarchs on loan from First Division Belle Vue.

Stewart McDONALD
Born: June 19, 1975, Bellshill, Strathclyde, Scotland.
Began the season at reserve but was replaced by Mike McLuskey after only four matches. He had the occasional outings later in the season but could never hold onto the reserve's race jacket.

Kenneth Archibald (Kenny) McKINNA
Born: October 21, 1962, Glasgow, Scotland.
The last of the McKinna clan to be racing regularly, he moved from Glasgow to Powderhall at the beginning of the season.

Michael McLUSKEY
Born: November 25, 1964, Perth, Scotland.
His season ended prematurely when he suffered a badly broken right wrist in a second half crash at Powderhall in July.

Wayne PARK
Born: August 16, 1968, Galashiels, Borders, Scotland.
Made a June first team debut at Middlesbrough when both Johnny Jørgensen and Mike McLuskey were unavailable for selection.

Brett Gavin SAUNDERS
Born: November 9, 1961, Sydney, New South Wales, Australia.
Asked to be relieved of the captaincy in August because he felt it was affecting his form. Completed his 11th successive season at Powderhall.

John WAINWRIGHT
Born: November 3, 1969, Harlow, Essex.
Continued his roving after starting the season in the Rye House squad. He was released by the Rockets and spent a few matches on loan to Edinburgh.

Vesa YLINEN
Born: July 23, 1965, Seinajoki, Finland.
Impressive early season visitor to Britain with Swedish touring side Rospiggarna who agreed to join Edinburgh early in 1993. The Finnish National Champion in both 1991 and 1992, he rode in both the Swedish League and the Danish League (for Fredericia) in 1992.

Green's the Devon cream

THE EXETER supporters summed up their club's season when they voted Tony Olsson as their Rider of the Year – after the Swede had been released mid-season by promoter Colin Hill as an economy measure!

It was not so much Exeter's financial position that led to the parting of the ways but more the strain placed on Hill's resources by his brave, but abortive, attempt to run speedway at Milton Keynes as well as the County Ground.

That certainly drained away the money but at least by releasing Olsson, Exeter continued in business even if the move greatly upset some fans.

Olsson had been captured during the winter after Steve Regeling had asked for, and been granted, a transfer moving North to Middlesbrough.

The Swede was the second newcomer to the club joining Paul Fry who'd been signed from Cradley Heath.

Peter Jeffery and Frank Smart (who'd waited patiently in the wings the previous season for his chance) were guaranteed places by Hill who then re-signed veteran Colin Cook and Cornishman Mark Simmonds. As usual the popular Richard Green delayed putting pen to paper until the last minute but did so.

All seemed in place but then Exeter were dealt the body blow that Smart would have to ride with an assessed 7.00 average which put them over the points limit.

Reluctantly they had to switch him to the Milton Keynes operation and with Justin Elkins failing to impress on practice day, Hill signed the experienced Ian Humphreys from Arena-Essex to complete his side.

Although the race-rusty Falcons were well beaten by Swedish visitors Rospiggarna on their opening night and lost their first two away Gold Cup matches the signs were there that the side would come good.

Olsson soon established himself as a favourite with the Devon fans and Green began to hit top form in a big way. Away performances had been pretty dreadful in previous years but a win at Long Eaton, with Green storming to an 18 point maximum, suggested that 1992 could be different.

Stoke ended the Falcons' dream of reaching the Gold Cup Final by taking three points from their final home match against Peterborough but the League campaign got off to a fabulous start –a 54-36 Bank Holiday thumping of Middlesbrough and Olsson smashing Scott Autrey's 13-year -old County Ground track record.

Ironically, it was the only League match that the Swede would ride in for the Falcons as Hill announced his shock decision to part with him after Reading had given him an ultimatum over the late payment of the statutory loan fee.

While the demise of Milton Keynes undoubtedly had much to do with that decision it did allow Smart to slot back into the Exeter set-up but the loss of Olsson was a factor from which the Falcons never recovered.

They failed to qualify for the H.E.A.T. Team Championship Final, surrendered a 26 point lead at Stoke to crash out of the Phonesport Knock Out Cup and lost home League matches to both Glasgow and Peterborough.

Jeffery's season came to a premature end through a broken scaphoid but Richard Green almost brought some glory to the club by going oh-so-close to winning the Jawa-Barum NLRC at Coventry.

Revelling in the muddy conditions he amassed 11 points from his first four rides and needed to win his last to take the title. Whether the pressure got to him no one will ever know but he made a hash of the start and, having forced his way through to second place, slid off whilst trying to pass Long Eaton's Jan Stæchmann.

1992 RIDER ROSTER

	Club Record								Career Record							
	M	R	Pts	BP	TPts	Ave	F	P	M	R	Pts	BP	TPts	Ave	F	P
Colin Cook	241	1067	1679.0	191.0	1870.0	7.010	6	8	**366**	**1587**	**2451.0**	**287.0**	**2738.0**	**6.901**	**7**	**13**
Richard Green	146	747	1280.0	139.0	1419.0	7.598	4	6	**260**	**1154**	**1712.0**	**230.0**	**1942.0**	**6.731**	**4**	**7**
Paul Fry	19	92	156.0	17.0	173.0	7.522	0	0	**118**	**580**	**785.0**	**90.0**	**875.0**	**6.034**	**0**	**1**
Ian Humphreys	18	69	63.0	20.0	83.0	4.812	0	0	**156**	**550**	**451.0**	**101.0**	**552.0**	**4.015**	**0**	**0**
Peter Jeffery	142	680	1037.0	127.0	1164.0	6.847	4	6	**142**	**680**	**1037.0**	**127.0**	**1164.0**	**6.847**	**4**	**6**
Richard Knight	10	34	37.0	8.0	45.0	5.294	0	0	**10**	**34**	**37.0**	**8.0**	**45.0**	**5.294**	**0**	**0**
Tony Olsson	1	6	14.0	1.0	15.0	10.000	0	0	**3**	**17**	**36.0**	**2.0**	**38.0**	**8.941**	**0**	**0**
Tommy Palmer	9	32	19.0	4.0	23.0	2.875	0	0	**13**	**45**	**23.0**	**5.0**	**28.0**	**2.489**	**0**	**0**
Scott Pegler	4	14	7.0	1.0	8.0	2.286	0	0	**4**	**14**	**7.0**	**1.0**	**8.0**	**2.286**	**0**	**0**
Mark Simmonds	85	325	360.0	61.0	421.0	5.182	1	0	**85**	**325**	**360.0**	**61.0**	**421.0**	**5.182**	**1**	**0**
Frank Smart	29	128	158.0	26.0	184.0	5.750	0	1	**29**	**128**	**158.0**	**26.0**	**184.0**	**5.750**	**0**	**1**

EXETER

Promoter: Colin Hill.
Address: County Ground Stadium, Cowick Street, St. Thomas', Exeter, Devon.
Telephone: 0392-51478.
Hotline: 0898 800 625.
Track Length: 396 metres.
Track Record: 66.1 secs, Tony Olsson (Exeter), May 4, 1992, heat 4, Exeter v Middlesbrough (Division Two).
Seasons in Division Two: 12 (1980-1983; 1985-1992).
Best Division Two Season: Fifth, 1989.
Division Two Cup Record: Winners (1), 1983.
Division Two Team Championship: Third (1), 1989. Qualified (2), 1982, 1989.
Appearances: Colin Cook, 241 (1985-1992).
Points: Colin Cook, 1870 (1985, 1986-1992)).
World Finalists: Martin Ashby (1968), Scott Autrey (1976, 1978), Zdenek Kudrna (1979), Ivan Mauger (1973-74-75-76-77), Jan Verner (1978).
Division Two Riders' Championship Finalists: Robert Maxfield (1980-81), Andy Campbell (1982), Keith Millard (1983), Steve Regeling (1988-89-90-91), Richard Green (1992).
Other Honours: Division One Champions, 1974. Division Three Champions, 1948. Provincial League Knock-out Cup Winners, 1962.

1992

EXETER

Left to right: Colin Hill (promoter), Ian Humphreys, Paul Fry, Peter Jeffery, Tony Olsson, Richard Green, Mark Simmonds and Colin Cook.

MIDDLESBROUGH (H), May 4, W54-36

1 Peter Jeffery	*rider replacement*		
2 §Paul Fry	2 3 2 3 2 0	12	
3 §†Tony Olsson	1 3 3 3 3 1	14	1
4 Colin Cook	1 1 fx 2 3	7	3
5 Richard Green	2 2 3 3 2	12	2
6 Mark Simmonds	3 1 1 1	6	
7 §Ian Humphreys	2 1 0 0	3	2
8 Scott Pegler	*did not ride*		

Long Eaton (A), June 10, W46-44

1 †Peter Jeffery	1 1 1 2	5	1
2 Paul Fry	2 3 1 3 1	10	
3 Frank Smart	1 2 2 1	6	2
4 Colin Cook	2 0 2 1	5	2
5 Richard Green	3 2 2 3 3	13	
6 Mark Simmonds	2 0 F 0	2	1
7 Ian Humphreys	3 2 0 F	5	

Sheffield (A), June 11, L38-51

1 †Peter Jeffery	F 2 2 1	5	1
2 Paul Fry	R R 3 0	3	
3 Frank Smart	fx 2 0 0	2	
4 Colin Cook	2 1 1 2 2	8	2
5 Richard Green	3 2 1 3 0	9	
6 Mark Simmonds	3 1 3 0 0	7	1
7 Ian Humphreys	2 1 1 N	4	1

RYE HOUSE (H), June 22, W56-33

1 †Peter Jeffery	1 3 3 3	10	1
2 Tommy Palmer	2 0 1 1	4	
3 Frank Smart	2 3 3 2 2	12	1
4 Colin Cook	3 0 1 N	4	
5 Richard Green	2 3 3 fx	8	1
6 Mark Simmonds	3 3 2 1 3 0	12	1
7 Ian Humphreys	2 X 2 2	6	3

EDINBURGH (H), July 6, W58-32

1 †Peter Jeffery	**3 3 3 3 3**	**15**	
2 Paul Fry	F R 0 2	2	1
3 Frank Smart	**3 3 3 3 2**	**14**	**1**
4 Colin Cook	3 2 1 2	8	1
5 Richard Green	2 3 2 2	9	2
6 Mark Simmonds	3 2 1 1	7	2
7 Ian Humphreys	F 1 2 0	3	1

GLASGOW (H), July 20, L43-47

1 †Peter Jeffery	2 1 1 0	4	1
2 Paul Fry	1 3 3 2 0	9	1
3 Frank Smart	2 F fx 1	3	
4 Colin Cook	2 3 1 X	6	
5 Richard Green	0 2 3 3 1	9	1
6 Mark Simmonds	3 1 1 1	6	1
7 Ian Humphreys	2 2 1 1	6	2

Edinburgh (A), July 24, L34-55

1 †Peter Jeffery	F 3 1 1 2 0	7	2
2 Paul Fry	1 2 N 1	4	1
3 Frank Smart	2 1 3 2 1 1	10	
4 Colin Cook	1 fx 1 0 1	3	3
5 Richard Green	2 2 2 0 2	8	
6 Mark Simmonds	R R 2 T N	2	
7 Ian Humphreys	fx F T T	0	

Berwick (A), July 25, L30-60

1 †Peter Jeffrey	2 1 2 0 1	6	
2 §§Craig Rathbone	*0 0 T T*	*0*	
3 Frank Smart	1 1 1 1 2 0	6	2
4 Colin Cook	fx 1 2 0	3	1
5 Richard Green	2 2 2 1 3 1	11	1
6 Mark Simmonds	1 0 T 0	1	
7 §Tommy Palmer	0 2 1 0	3	1

Middlesbrough (A), July 30, L34-55

1 †Peter Jeffery	0 0 1 2 0	3	1
2 Mark Simmonds	1 3 1 1	6	1
3 Frank Smart	1 R 3 1	5	1
4 Paul Fry	1 1 2 1 1	6	1
5 Richard Green	3 2 R 2 3 3	13	
6 §§William Beveridge	*R R T 0*	*0*	
7 Tommy Palmer	1 0 F T	1	

Peterborough (A), July 31, L34-56

1 †Peter Jeffery	1 1 0 1 3 1	7	2
2 Mark Simmonds	0 2 0 0 0	2	
3 Frank Smart	2 fn 0 1 0	3	1
4 Colin Cook	*rider replacement*		
5 Richard Green	2 2 1 2 2 2	11	1
6 Paul Fry	1 1 2 1 3 2	10	1
7 Tommy Palmer	0 1 0 T T	1	1
8 Scott Pegler	*did not ride*		

PETERBOROUGH (H), August 3, L41-49

1 †Peter Jeffery	2 0 2 3 3 2	12	
2 Mark Simmonds	1 2 3 1 0	7	2
3 Frank Smart	2 1 1 N	4	
4 Colin Cook	1 1 1 1	4	1
5 Richard Green	3 2 2 1	8	
6 Paul Fry	2 1 3 R 0	6	1
7 Tommy Palmer	0 0 0 T	0	

LONG EATON (H), August 10, W59-30

1 †Peter Jeffery	1 X 3 1	5	2
2 Mark Simmonds	2 3 3 2 2	12	2
3 Frank Smart	1 2 2 2	7	3
4 Colin Cook	3 1 2 3	9	
5 Richard Green	1 3 3 3	10	
6 Paul Fry	3 2 3 2 3	13	1
7 Ian Humphreys	1 R 1 1	3	1

Newcastle (A), August 16, L25-65

1 †Peter Jeffery	1 0 0 2 1 2	6	
2 Mark Simmonds	0 1 0 1 1 0	3	2
3 Frank Smart	0 0 0 0	0	
4 Colin Cook	1 1 0 0	2	
5 Richard Green	*rider replacement*		
6 Paul Fry	3 1 3 2 1 2	12	
7 Ian Humphreys	0 1 N 1	2	
8 Tommy Palmer	0	0	

STOKE (H), August 17, W61-29

1 †Peter Jeffery	**2 3 3 3 3**	**14**	**1**
2 Mark Simmonds	3 1 3 2	9	1
3 Frank Smart	2 3 2 1	8	
4 Colin Cook	2 3 0 3	8	1
5 Richard Green	**3 2 3 3 2**	**13**	**2**
6 Paul Fry	1 1 1 2 1	6	2
7 Ian Humphreys	3 0 F N	3	

BERWICK (H), August 24, W47-43

1 †Peter Jeffery	fx R N N	0	
2 Mark Simmonds	1 1 2 2	6	1
3 Frank Smart	1 2 E 3 fx	6	2
4 Colin Cook	2 0 0 3	5	1
5 Richard Green	3 1 3 2 3	12	1
6 Paul Fry	2 2 3 2 3 3	15	1
7 Ian Humphreys	1 1 0 1 0	3	2

NEWCASTLE (H), September 7, W62-28

1 Peter Jeffery	*rider replacement*		
2 Paul Fry	1 2 3 2 2	10	3
3 Frank Smart	1 3 2 2 3 1	12	2
4 †Colin Cook	2 2 3 3 2	12	2
5 Richard Green	3 3 3 2 2 R	13	2
6 Mark Simmonds	3 2 3 3	11	
7 Ian Humphreys	1 1 1 1	4	2
8 Tommy Palmer	*did not ride*		

SHEFFIELD (H), September 14, W63-27

1 Peter Jeffery	*rider replacement*		
2 Paul Fry	3 2 2 2 2	11	1
3 Frank Smart	2 3 2 2 1	10	2
4 †Colin Cook	1 3 1 1 3	9	2
5 Richard Green	**2 3 2 2 3 2**	**14**	**4**
6 Mark Simmonds	**3 3 3 3 3**	**15**	
7 Ian Humphreys	1 0 1 2	4	2
8 Tommy Palmer	*did not ride*		

Glasgow (A), October 4, L25-65

1 †Colin Cook	0 0 3 2	5	
2 Paul Fry	1 1 fn T	2	
3 Frank Smart	2 fx 2 1 1 1	7	1
4 Mark Simmonds	0 0 0 T	0	
5 Richard Green	1 2 R N 2 fx	5	
6 Tommy Palmer	0 1 1 0 0 N	2	
7 Ian Humphreys	1 1 fx 1 1	4	2

Stoke (A), October 10, L25-65

1 †Colin Cook	fx T T T	0	
2 Paul Fry	1 1 2 N 2 R	6	
3 Frank Smart	0 0 fx N	0	
4 Mark Simmonds	0 0 0 1 0	1	
5 Richard Green	1 2 1 3 3 1	11	
6 Tommy Palmer	0 1 2 0 0	3	
7 Ian Humphreys	1 2 F F 1	4	

Rye House (A), October 18, L35-55

1 Gary Chessell	*2 1 3 2 2 1*	*11*	
2 Paul Fry	*rider replacement*		
3 Frank Smart	1 2 2 2 0 0	7	1
4 Ian Humphreys	F 2 1 0	3	
5 Richard Green	3 3 fx 1 1 fx	8	1
6 Tommy Palmer	2 1 1 1	5	2
7 Scott Pegler	0 0 1 0	1	
8 Rob Price	*did not ride*		

At-a-Glance Results

Berwick	**W47-43**	**L30-60**	**77-103**
Edinburgh	**W58-32**	**L34-55**	**92-87**
Glasgow	**L43-47**	**L25-65**	**68-112**
Long Eaton	**W59-30**	**W46-44**	**105-74**
Middlesbrough	**W54-36**	**L34-55**	**88-91**
Newcastle	**W62-28**	**L25-65**	**87-93**
Peterborough	**L41-49**	**L34-56**	**75-105**
Rye House	**W56-33**	**L35-55**	**91-88**
Sheffield	**W63-27**	**L38-51**	**101-78**
Stoke	**W61-29**	**L25-65**	**86-94**

WHO WAS WHO IN '92

William BEVERIDGE – see Middlesbrough

Colin COOK
Born: August 29, 1954, Southwold, Suffolk.
Was granted a Benefit meeting to mark his service to speedway as he completed his eighth successive season at the County Ground.

Paul FRY
Born: October 25, 1964, Ledbury, Hereford & Worcester.
A surprise eve of season signing by the Falcons who swooped when he was made available by Cradley Heath after spending 1991 on loan to King's Lynn. He became a popular addition to the ranks.

Richard GREEN
Born: August 16, 1965, Wreningham, Norfolk.
Took over the mantle of number one following the departure of Tony Olsson. Unlucky not to win – or at least figure on the rostrum – the Second Division Riders' Final when he fell in his last ride.

Ian HUMPHREYS
Born: July 29, 1963, Isleworth, Middlesex.
Made a track comeback after missing the 1991 season. Stayed at reserve all season.

Peter Adrian JEFFERY
Born: November 3, 1966, Bideford, Devon.
Appointed captain in succession to Steve Regeling but had a poor season, mainly because of injuries which saw him sidelined for two separate spells.

Richard KNIGHT
Born: March 22, 1966, Bath, Avon.
Recovered from a serious accident which curtailed his 1991 season but quit the sport after failing to be given a team place with the Falcons.

Tony OLSSON – see Ipswich

Tommy Steven PALMER
Born: January 27, 1971, Maidstone, Kent.
Signed on loan from First Division Arena Essex, he looked impressive in Reserve League competition and showed signs of ability in his occasional first team outings.

Scott PEGLER
Born: August 3, 1973, Exeter, Devon.
Ended a short-lived 1991 retirement and helped the Exeter Reserve League title to the Divisional title.

Craig Michael RATHBONE
Born: August 21, 1969, Middlesbrough, Cleveland.
Helped out a short-handed Falcons line-up at Berwick to make his National League debut.

Mark Douglas SIMMONDS
Born: May 10, 1971, Truro, Cornwall.
Impressive around his home track but still looking for the consistency away from home to make the step from second string to heat leader. Scored his first ever maximum against Sheffield in September.

Frank Dean SMART
Born: October 27, 1969, Perth, Western Australia.
Finally ended up in the Exeter team after a shock switch to sister track Milton Keynes at the beginning of the season. He was brought back when the Knights' closed down and had an impressive first full season of League activity.

Robbie wears the crown

BY THE end of the season Glasgow had lost one hero but welcomed another – and from an unlikely source too. Steve Lawson, for so many years Mr. Glasgow finally decided to hang up his leathers.

Emerging as the man to possibly take his place was Hungarian Robert Nagy who brought glory to Shawfield by storming to victory in the Jawa-Barum Division Two Riders' Championship at Coventry.

That marvellous performance in the mud at Brandon erased all memories of the astonishment shown by the Glasgow fans when co-promoter Neil Macfarlane revealed the signings of Nagy and fellow countryman Robert Csillik during the close season.

Having finished runners up in both the League and Knock Out Cup in 1991 the Glasgow management knew that they had a hard act to follow. Even more so when both Jason Lyons and Shane Bowes indicated during the winter that they were looking to move to First Division racing.

Lyons got his wish switching to Belle Vue but Bowes, recovering from a broken thigh, found that there were no takers for his services from the top flight.

The Courtney brothers, Mark and Sean, were also non-starters from the previous year's squad as was Brian Nixon who failed to get his work permit renewed.

So co-promoter Neil Macfarlane started assembling his side with only Lawson and Mick Powell remaining from the previous year's successes.

The signing of the two Hungarians had many fans calling for Macfarlane's head but even those doubters were delighted when he persuaded Neil Collins to sign on a full transfer from Wolverhampton.

Another controversial signing followed Danish youngster Tim Korneliussen. He'd struggled the previous year at both Reading and Peterborough as he endeavoured to overcome the effects of a broken thigh in his debut season for Hackney sustained, somewhat ironically, at Shawfield. The assessed averages of the Magyars left little scope manoeuvre for the final spot in the team and it was local youngster James Grieves who got the nod.

Macfarlane was confident in the side's ability even if the fans weren't but that confidence hardly seemed justified as the toothless Tigers lost six of their first seven Gold Cup matches. At this point in stepped Douglas Hopes, a long time supporter and sponsor, who not only assumed control at the club but also paved the way for Shane Bowes' return.

Csillik was axed along with Korneliussen with Mark 'Buzz' Burrows making a brief return to racing before being replaced by another Dane, Jesper Olsen, who found himself out of work after Mildenhall's closure.

Suddenly Glasgow's fortunes improved and Nagy was making a name for himself not only with good performances for the Tigers but in making progress in the World Championship. Cradley, albeit weakened by injuries, were sent packing in the BSPA Cup which gave Glasgow the springboard they needed to move up the League.

Wins at Stoke and Exeter had many pundits thinking that favourites Peterborough might not get things all their own way in the title chase but successive defeats at Sheffield, Long Eaton and Middlesbrough ultimately proved costly with the Tigers eventually finishing third.

The usual tartan hoard travelled down to Coventry to support their man in the Division Two Riders' Championship Final and were rewarded when 'Robbie the Racer' defeated Mick Poole in dramatic style in a controversial run-off to take the title.

Yes, Nagy had suddenly become a folk hero but Lawson was The King to most and there were a few tears shed as he announced that he was finally retiring...although, ironically it had to be done at a social event as the Clyde Two Tigers were beaten by the weather in all their attempts to stage their final meeting of the season against Rye House.

Lawson is going to be a hard man to replace...but Nagy could just be the man to do it.

1992 RIDER ROSTER

	Club Record								Career Record							
	M	R	Pts	BF	TPts	Ave	F	P	M	R	Pts	BP	TPts	Ave	F	P
Shane Bowes	137	661	1084.0	130.0	1214.0	7.346	3	3	166	782	1205.0	151.0	1356.0	6.936	3	3
Mark Burrows	5	16	20.0	2.0	22.0	5.500	0	0	115	386	347.0	90.0	437.0	4.528	0	0
Stuart Coleman	2	7	1.0	0.0	1.0	0.571	0	0	2	7	1.0	0.0	1.0	0.571	0	0
Neil Collins	20	98	189.0	16.0	205.0	8.367	1	0	145	621	1101.0	114.0	1215.0	7.826	12	3
James Grieves	10	32	27.0	7.0	34.0	4.250	0	0	10	32	27.0	7.0	34.0	4.250	0	0
Tim Korneliussen	1	3	1.0	0.0	1.0	1.333	0	0	30	107	90.0	11.0	101.0	3.776	0	0
Steve Lawson	486	2297	5253.0	108.0	5361.0	9.336	91	13	595	2744	5974.0	147.0	6121.0	8.923	98	20
Robert Nagy	21	111	210.0	29.0	239.0	8.613	0	3	21	111	210.0	29.0	239.0	8.613	0	3
Jesper Olsen	11	51	54.0	7.0	61.0	4.784	0	0	11	51	54.0	7.0	61.0	4.784	0	0
Geoff Powell	159	530	425.0	82.0	507.0	3.826	0	1	165	542	432.0	82.0	514.0	3.793	0	1
Mick Powell	46	196	233.0	59.0	292.0	5.959	0	1	104	430	503.5	113.0	616.5	5.735	0	2
Jason Straughan	18	61	35.0	9.0	44.0	2.885	0	0	22	69	38.0	11.0	49.0	2.841	0	0

GLASGOW

Promoters: Douglas Hopes and Neil Macfarlane.
Address: Shawfield Stadium, Rutherglow Road, Glasgow, G73 1SZ.
Telephone: 041-613-1552.
Information Line: 0891 31 21 41.
Track Length: 332 metres.
Track Record: 65.4 secs, Chris Louis (Ipswich), 3.6.1990, Heat 1, Glasgow v Ipswich, Division Two Knock Out Cup; Andy Galvin (Hackney), 17.6.1990, Heat 1, Speedway Star Division Two Pairs Championship; Mark Blackbird (Long Eaton), 26.5.1991, Heat 1, Glasgow v Long Eaton, Gold Cup; Steve Regeling (Exeter), 30.6.1991, Heat 5, Glasgow v Exeter, Sunbrite League Division Two; Steve Lawson (Glasgow), 18.8.1991, Heat 1, Glasgow v Peterborough, Sunbrite League Division Two; Jason Lyons (Glasgow), 25.8.1991, Heat 3, Glasgow v Long Eaton, Sunbrite League Division Two.
Seasons in Division Two: 15 (1977-1981 [Blantyre]; 1982-1986 [Craighead Park]; 1988-1992 [Shawfield Park]).
Best Division Two Season: Runners-up (1), 1991. Third (1), 1992.
Division Two Cup Record: Runners-up (1), 1991.
Division Two Team Championship: Qualified (4), 1980, 1988, 1990, 1992.
National Series: Winners (1), 1990.
Appearances: Steve Lawson, 486 (1978-1986, 1988-1992).
Points: Steve Lawson, 5361 (1978-1986, 1988-1992).
World Finalists: Jim McMillan (1972).
Division Two Riders' Championship Finalists: Brian Collins (1977), Steve Lawson (1978-79, 1981-82, 1984-85-86, 1991), Jim McMillan (1983), Kenny McKinna (1988-89), Shane Bowes (1990, 1992), Robert Nagy (1992).
Division One Riders' Championship Finalists: Robert Nagy (1992).

1992

GLASGOW

Left to right: Stuart Coleman, James Grieves, Robert Nagy, Steve Lawson, Shane Bowes, Mick Powell and Neil Collins.

MIDDLESBROUGH (H), May 17, W54-36

1 †Steve Lawson	1 2 3 3	9	2
2 Mick Powell	2 3 3 1 2	11	1
3 §Neil Collins	2 3 1 2	8	1
4 §§Robert Nagy	3 2 2 2 3	12	2
5 Shane Bowes	2 3 2 1	8	2
6 §Mark Burrows	1 3 F R	4	1
7 Jason Straughan	2 0 0 0	2	

STOKE (H), May 27, W51-38

1 †Steve Lawson	2 2 3 1	8	
2 Mick Powell	1 1 3 0	5	2
3 Neil Collins	3 3 X 1	7	1
4 Robert Nagy	2 2 3 3 2	12	2
5 Shane Bowes	3 0 3 2 3	11	
6 Mark Burrows	3 0 N N	3	
7 Jason Straughan	2 0 1 1 fn1	5	1

BERWICK (H), June 17, W51-39

1 †Steve Lawson	1 2 3 3	9	1
2 Mick Powell	2 1 3 1	7	1
3 Neil Collins	2 2 2 2	8	1
4 Robert Nagy	2 1 1 3 3	10	1
5 Shane Bowes	1 2 3 3 1 1	11	2
6 Mark Burrows	2 NT 2 0	4	1
7 Jason Straughan	0 1 N 1 0	2	2

The match originally finished 48-42 but Glasgow's protest against Berwick's use of David Nagel was upheld by the Speedway Control Board who ruled that Nagel's points should be deducted from the final score. The original scores of riders affected by the decision were: Lawson 0-2-3-3- 8:1, Powell 1-1-3-1- 7:1, Burrows 2-N-T-1-0- 3.

Berwick (A), June 20, L40-50

1 †Steve Lawson	1 0 3 3 3	10	
2 Mick Powell	0 1 T 0	1	
3 Neil Collins	2 3 2 1 2 1	11	1
4 Robert Nagy	0 2 0 2 2	6	2
5 Shane Bowes	2 3 2 1 1 fx	9	1
6 Mark Burrows	1 1 T 0 N	2	
7 Jason Straughan	0 1 fnN T	1	1

SHEFFIELD (H), June 24, W58-32

1 †Steve Lawson	3 1 3 0	7	1
2 Mick Powell	2 2 1 2	7	2
3 Neil Collins	R 3 2 2	7	1
4 Robert Nagy	**2 2 3 3 3**	**13**	2
5 Shane Bowes	**3 3 3 3 2**	**14**	1
6 Mark Burrows	3 2 1 1	7	
7 James Grieves	1 0 1 1	3	1

Peterborough (A), June 26, L36-54

1 †Steve Lawson	1 R T T	1	
2 Mick Powell	0 3 3 0 2 1	9	
3 Neil Collins	1 2 1 1 2	7	1
4 Robert Nagy	1 2 1 1 2	7	3
5 Shane Bowes	2 3 2 2 1	10	2
6 Stuart Coleman	R F N 0 T	0	
7 James Grieves	2 0 T 0 T	2	

LONG EATON (H), July 12, W56-34

1 †Steve Lawson	2 2 3 2	9	1
2 Mick Powell	1 fx 2 2	5	2
3 Neil Collins	2 2 1 3 fx	8	2
4 Robert Nagy	**3 3 3 2 3**	**14**	1
5 Shane Bowes	2 1 3 2	8	2
6 §§Jesper Olsen	R 3 3 1 3	10	
7 Jason Straughan	2 0 0 N	2	

Stoke (A), July 18, W47-42

1 †Steve Lawson	2 3 2 R	7	
2 Mick Powell	0 fx1 N	1	
3 Neil Collins	**3 3 3 3**	**12**	
4 Robert Nagy	2 2 2 2 1	9	2
5 Shane Bowes	3 3 2 3 N	11	1
6 Jesper Olsen	2 F 2 1 fx1	6	2
7 Jason Straughan	0 1 0 N 0	1	

Rye House (A), July 19, L43-47

1 †Steve Lawson	1 1 2 2 T	6	
2 Mick Powell	0 0 0 N 0	0	
3 Neil Collins	*rider replacement*		
4 Robert Nagy	3 1 1 3 3 1 3	15	2
5 Shane Bowes	2 3 2 1 0 0	8	1
6 Jesper Olsen	3 2 2 1 fx3	11	1
7 Jason Straughan	2 1 N E	3	1
8 James Grieves	*did not ride*		

Exeter (A), July 20, W47-43

1 †Steve Lawson	3 1 2 0	6	1
2 Mick Powell	R 0 1 T	1	
3 Neil Collins	3 2 0 2	7	1
4 Robert Nagy	3 3 2 3 2 2	15	1
5 Shane Bowes	1 2 3 3 3 3	15	1
6 Jesper Olsen	R 0 fxT 2	2	1
7 Jason Straughan	1 0 N 0	1	

Sheffield (A), August 6, L44-46

1 Steve Lawson	*rider replacement*		
2 Mick Powell	1 2 2 R	5	2
3 Neil Collins	2 2 3 2 3 2 2	16	
4 Robert Nagy	3 3 X 2 0 3 1	12	1
5 Shane Bowes	2 1 2 2 2	9	2
6 James Grieves	2 0 0 N	2	
7 Jason Straughan	fx0 0 0	0	
8 Stuart Coleman	*did not ride*		

Long Eaton (A), August 19, L40-50

1 †Steve Lawson	1 1 0 N	2	
2 Mick Powell	0 0 T T 0	0	
3 Neil Collins	3 1 2 2 0	8	1
4 Robert Nagy	3 1 2 3 3 3	15	1
5 Shane Bowes	2 2 3 1 3	11	1
6 Jesper Olsen	3 0 0 0 F	3	
7 Jason Straughan	1 0 T 0	1	

Middlesbrough (A), August 20, L35-55

1 †Steve Lawson	0 1 1 0	2	1
2 Mick Powell	2 0 2 1 2	7	2
3 Neil Collins	X 2 2 2 2 2	10	
4 Robert Nagy	0 0 0 1 1	2	
5 Shane Bowes	2 3 3 1 3 0	12	1
6 Jesper Olsen	fx1 fxT T	1	
7 Jason Straughan	1 N T T	1	

PETERBOROUGH (H), August 23, W54-36

1 †Steve Lawson	1 3 3 2	9	2
2 Mick Powell	2 1 3 2	8	1
3 Neil Collins	3 3 1 1	8	
4 Robert Nagy	2 1 3 3 3	12	2
5 Shane Bowes	3 2 2 3 2	12	1
6 Jesper Olsen	1 1 0 1 F	3	2
7 Jason Straughan	2 0 0 NN	2	

The race-off for the bonus points was abandoned because of heavy rain. Subsequently the British Speedway Promoters' Association ruled that the two clubs should share the bonus point.

Newcastle (A), August 30, L43-47

1 †Steve Lawson	1 2 3 1	7	
2 Mick Powell	0 1 0 T	1	1
3 Neil Collins	2 3 1 2 1	9	3
4 Robert Nagy	3 fx3 3 3 1	13	1
5 Shane Bowes	1 2 2 2 3 2	12	
6 Jesper Olsen	1 0 T 0 N	1	
7 Jason Straughan	0 0 T E 0	0	

NEWCASTLE (H), September 20, W50-40

1 †Steve Lawson	0 3 3 0	6	
2 Shane Bowes	1 2 3 2 3	11	2
3 Neil Collins	2 1 2 2	7	2
4 Robert Nagy	1 3 3 2 2	11	2
5 Mick Powell	2 0 2 0	4	1
6 Jesper Olsen	fx3 2 3 1	9	1
7 James Grieves	2 0 0 N	2	

Edinburgh (A), September 25, L43-47

1 †Steve Lawson	3 3 0 2 2 3	13	
2 Mick Powell	1 0 2 T	3	
3 Neil Collins	2 3 3 3 3 1	15	
4 Robert Nagy	fx1 0 1	2	2
5 Shane Bowes	1 2 0 1	4	1
6 Jesper Olsen	2 0 1 1 T	4	
7 James Grieves	1 1 0 N	2	2

EXETER (H), October 4, W65-25

1 †Steve Lawson	**3 3 3 2 3**	**14**	1
2 Mick Powell	**2 2 3 2**	**9**	3
3 Neil Collins	3 3 2 3	11	
4 Robert Nagy	**3 2 3 3 2**	**13**	2
5 Shane Bowes	2 3 3 F	8	1
6 James Grieves	3 0 1 1	5	
7 Jason Straughan	2 2 1 0	5	3

EDINBURGH (H), October 18, W48-42

1 †Steve Lawson	2 2 3 3	10	
2 Mick Powell	0 1 2 2	5	2
3 Neil Collins	3 1 R 3 0	7	
4 Robert Nagy	1 0 F 3	4	
5 Shane Bowes	**3 3 3 2 3**	**14**	1
6 Jesper Olsen	3 0 R 1 R	4	
7 James Grieves	1 1 2 N	4	1

The home match against Rye House was never held because of bad weather. The original staging on July 17 was abandoned after 11 heats because of heavy rain. The scorers were: GLASGOW 39.5 (†Steve Lawson 3-3-3- 9, Mick Powell 0-1-3-1- 5, Neil Collins 2-2-3- 7:1, Robert Nagy 3-2-fx- 5, Shane Bowes 0-1-1.5- 2.5:1, Jesper Olsen 3-3-1-fx- 7:1, Jason Straughan 2-1-1- 4:1) RYE HOUSE 26.5.

MILTON KEYNES (H), May 10, W55-35

1 †Steve Lawson	3 3 3 1	10	
2 Mick Powell	2 2 3 1 2	10	3
3 Neil Collins	3 3 3 2 3	14	
4 Robert Nagy	3 R 3 3	9	
5 Shane Bowes	2 3 2 0	7	1
6 Tim Korneliussen	0 0 0 N	0	
7 Jason Straughan	3 0 1 1 0	5	1

Mildenhall (A), May 31, D45-45

1 †Steve Lawson	R 3 3 3 3 3	15	
2 Mick Powell	1 2 3 2 0	8	1
3 Neil Collins	E 2 1 T 3	6	
4 Robert Nagy	2 0 1 0	3	2
5 Shane Bowes	3 3 1 fx2 2	11	2
6 James Grieves	0 0 0 T T	0	
7 Jason Straughan	1 1 T 0 T	2	

At-a-Glance Results

Berwick	W51-39	L40-50	91-89
Edinburgh	W48-42	L43-47	91-89
Exeter	W65-25	W47-43	112-68
Long Eaton	W56-34	L40-50	96-84
Middlesbrough	W54-36	L35-55	89-91
Newcastle	W50-40	L43-47	93-87
Peterborough	W54-36	L36-54	†90-90
Rye House	*not raced*	L43-47	–
Sheffield	W58-32	L44-46	102-78
Stoke	W51-38	W47-42	98-80
Mildenhall		*D45-45*	
Milton Keynes	*W55-35*		

†The BSPA awarded one half of a bonus point to each club when the scheduled race-off was abandoned because of heavy rain.

■ The home match against Rye House was never staged and the Speedway Control Board ordered one point to each team but the bonus point was not awarded.

WHO WAS WHO IN '92

Shane Leonard BOWES
Born: March 4, 1969, Adelaide, South Australia.
Sat out the early weeks of the season after looking for a move to Division One during a winter marred by a fractured thigh in a crash in his native Australia. He finally agreed to return to Shawfield after the Clyde Two Tigers' disappointing start to the new season.

Mark BURROWS – see Middlesbrough

Stuart COLEMAN
Born: May 23, 1970, Glasgow, Scotland.
Spent most of the summer in second half competition.

Neil Jeffrey COLLINS
Born: October 15, 1961, Partington, Greater Manchester.
A £12,000 winter signing from First Division Wolverhampton who never quite lived up to his potential in his first season in Division Two since he was at Edinburgh in 1981.

Robert CSILLICK
Born: June 6, 1966, Eger, Hungary.
A promising newcomer who was the victim of Glasgow's poor start to the season, being released despite scoring 42 points in nine Gold Cup matches.

James Robert GRIEVES
Born: September 28, 1974, Paisley, Scotland.
Started and finished the season at reserve but had to be content with Reserve League action for most of the summer.

Tim KORNELIUSSEN
Born: January 28, 1968, Aalborg, Denmark.
Made an impressive start to the season with a paid 12 points in his second Gold Cup match for the Clyde Two Tigers but could not maintain that form and was axed before the opening of the League campaign.

Stephen Faulder LAWSON
Born: December 11, 1957, Workington, Cumbria.
Announced his retirement at the end of his 19th season in the sport and his 15th as a Glasgow contracted rider. Missed his first League matches since 1989 with a troublesome groin strain.

Robert NAGY
Born: September 20, 1967, Szeged, Hungary.
A sensational newcomer who crowned his season by winning the Division Two Riders' Final at Coventry. Also reached the World Championship semi final as he came close to being the first Second Division rider to qualify for the World Final.

Jesper Ege OLSEN
Born: February 10, 1967, Valby, Denmark.
Moved to Glasgow on the closure on Mildenhall where he had made his Second Division debut at the beginning of the season. He added colour and points at reserve although he suffered a couple of troublesome injuries which restricted his performances.

Geoffrey POWELL
Born: March 22, 1962, Workington, Cumbria.
Didn't make an official appearance for the Clyde Two Tigers but rode for them in a challenge match.

Michael George POWELL
Born: September 24, 1969, Brisbane, Queensland, Australia.
Scored his first maximum for the club against Exeter at the beginning of October.

Jason STRAUGHAN
Born: July 11, 1970, Tweedmouth, Northumberland.
A fairly regular choice at reserve although he was dropped on three occasions during the season.

1992

LONG EATON

Back row: Eric Boocock (co-promoter), Deon Prinsloo, Jan Stæchmann, Martin Dixon, Jason Reed. Front: Colin White, Paul Blackbird, Carl Blackbird and Gary O'Hare.

Booey's still in profit

LONG Eaton have long been regarded as the 'Cinderella' club of the sport and it's doubtful that they will ever shake off that tag no matter what the team or their management may achieve.

But you won't find that tag worrying co-promoters Tony Mole and Eric Boocock...for the fact remains that Long Eaton are a success.

Not in terms of trophies maybe, but they do run at a profit and the fans are provided with great racing week in, week out.

The only threat to their existence is the ongoing attempts by landlord Northern Sports to gain planning permission for the stadium to be redeveloped. So far those efforts have been unsuccessful, but who knows what the future holds and the track (and team) are living on a year to year basis at their Station Road home.

Changes were inevitable as far as the team was concerned for 1992 with Kai Niemi having retired, Mark Blackbird going out on loan to Peterborough and Peter McNamara not returning either.

Skipper Jan Stæchmann was back after a superb first season for the Invaders in Division Two, along with the always dependable Gary O'Hare and the remaining two Blackbird brothers Carl and Paul.

Colin White was signed on loan from Arena-Essex and Boocock chased after veteran Alan Grahame who was surplus to Cradley Heath's requirements.

In the end Big Al opted to join rivals Stoke – much to Boocock's chagrin – so Martin Dixon was quickly snapped up and the jigsaw was completed when the highly promising Deon Prinsloo was signed on loan from First Division Eastbourne.

Maybe not the strongest looking septet in the League, but one which Booey knew would entertain the fans and, more importantly, one which the club knew it could afford even if attendance didn't rise.

"We have to work within a budget if the club is to survive," said Boocock. "Within that budget I think we've put together a good side."

As things turned out results didn't really substantiate Booey's faith in his side though injuries hardly helped their cause. Stæchmann, Dixon, White and Prinsloo were all sidelined at various stages.

Fifth place (out of seven) in their Gold Cup group was hardly an inspirational start but what heroics the team produced when, without both Stæchmann and Dixon, they gave First Division Eastbourne an almighty scare before going down by 12 points – a scoreline that greatly flattered the visitors.

A fortnight later they exited from the Phonesport Knock Out Cup, losing in the first round to Peterborough and with Exeter then taking the League points off the Invaders in the clash at Station Road (repeating their earlier feat in the Gold Cup) it was obvious that changes were in the offing.

White had been injured in a grass track accident and was allowed to return to Arena-Essex. Paul Blackbird was dropped and in came Richard Hellsén following the closure of Milton Keynes together with Nigel Sparshott who, despite being out of the sport for two years, impressed in after-meeting outings.

Their arrival signalled the start of the Invaders' most productive spell of the season which included an away draw at Sheffield as well as five consecutive home league victories.

One further change was made to the side in mid-August when O'Hare was dropped to make way for Australian Mark Lemon.

The point gained at Sheffield was to prove to be the Invaders' only success on their travels which, in essence, was the reason for them finishing ninth in the final League table, three places lower than the previous year.

1992 RIDER ROSTER

	Club Record								Career Record							
	M	R	Pts	BP	TPts	Ave	F	P	M	R	Pts	BP	TPts	Ave	FP	Carl
Blackbird	50	268	535.0	30.0	565.0	8.433	3	2	195	882	1513.0	136.0	1649.0	7.478	10	5
Paul Blackbird	9	33	18.0	3.0	21.0	2.545	0	0	42	129	72.0	11.0	83.0	2.574	0	0
Martin Dixon	22	98	123.0	20.0	143.0	5.837	0	0	450	1989	3448.0	345.0	3793.0	7.628	18	24
Richard Hellsén	79	413	831.0	39.0	870.0	8.426	1	2	101	516	1014.0	46.0	1060.0	8.217	2	2
Mark Lemon	4	17	13.0	[illegible].0	14.0	3.294	0	0	39	182	222.0	28.0	250.0	5.495	0	0
Gary O'Hare	140	673	808.0	104.0	912.0	5.421	0	0	278	1206	1454.0	181.0	1635.0	5.423	0	0
Deon Prinsloo	21	94	121.0	29.0	150.0	6.383	0	0	44	177	180.0	33.0	213.0	4.814	0	0
Jason Reed	9	25	5.0	[illegible].0	6.0	0.960	0	0	9	25	5.0	1.0	6.0	0.960	0	0
Nigel Sparshott	35	147	215.0	23.0	238.0	6.476	1	2	267	1235	1756.0	211.0	1967.0	6.371	3	7
Jan Stæchmann	46	250	566.0	32.0	598.0	9.568	4	5	46	250	566.0	32.0	598.0	9.568	4	5
Colin White	6	25	25.0	3.0	28.0	4.480	0	0	57	203	195.0	26.0	221.0	4.355	0	0

LONG EATON

Promoters: Eric Boocock and Tony Mole.
Address: Long Eaton Stadium, Station Road, Long Eaton, Nottinghamshire.
Telephone: 0602-731112.
Information Line: 0891 31 21 42.
Track Length: 336 metres.
Track Record: 61.7 secs, Jan Stæchmann (Long Eaton), September 9, 1992, Heat 6, Long Eaton v Ex-Leicester Lions (Challenge).
Seasons in Division Two: 19 (1969-1974, 1979-1980, 1982-1992).
Division Two Record: Champions (1), 1984.
Division Two Cup Record: Semi-finalists, 1969, 1991.
Division Two Team Championship: Third (1), 1991. Qualified (2), 1983, 1991.
Appearances: Dave Perks, 190 (1979, 1983-1985, 1989).
Points: Dave Perks, 1831 (1979, 1983-1985, 1989).
World Finalists: Anders Michanek (1967), Ray Wilson (1967).
Division Two Riders' Championship Finalists: Peter Wrathall (1969), Ken Vale (1970), Malcolm Shakespeare (1971), Roger Mills (1971-72), Geoff Bouchard (1973-74), Dave Perks (1979, 1983-84-85), Mike Sampson (1980), Alan Molyneux (1982), Mark Fiora (1986), Nigel Sparshott (1987), Keith White (1988), Richard Hellsén (1989-90), Jan Stæchmann (1991-92).

Newcastle (A), May 18, L33-56

1 Jan Stæchmann	*rider replacement*		
2 Gary O'Hare	1 0 1 0	2	2
3 §Martin Dixon	2 3 1 1 1 2	10	
4 §Colin White	2 0 3 0	5	
5 †Carl Blackbird	X 2 2 2 3 2 E	11	
6 §Deon Prinsloo	1 0 2 T 1 fn	4	
7 Paul Blackbird	0 0 T 0	0	
8 Jason Reed	1	1	

BERWICK (H), June 3, D45-45

1 †Jan Stæchmann	R 3 3 3 2	11	
2 Colin White	1 0 3 1	5	
3 Carl Blackbird	3 2 2 3 R	10	
4 Martin Dixon	1 1 0 1	3	1
5 Gary O'Hare	3 2 0 0	5	
6 Paul Blackbird	1 1 0 2	4	1
7 Deon Prinsloo	2 1 1 3	7	1

Middlesbrough (A), June 4, L39-50

1 †Jan Stæchmann	3 2 3 2 3 fx	13	1
2 Colin White	fx 0 0 T	0	
3 Martin Dixon	2 2 1 3 1	9	
4 Gary O'Hare	0 1 1 1	3	1
5 Carl Blackbird	1 2 3 3 2 2	13	
6 Deon Prinsloo	fx 0 T 0	0	
7 Paul Blackbird	1 0 T 0	1	

EXETER (H), June 10, L44-46

1 †Jan Stæchmann	3 3 3 3 3 2	17	
2 Colin White	0 1 2 1	4	1
3 Carl Blackbird	3 1 2 3 0	9	
4 Martin Dixon	0 2 fx 2	4	
5 Gary O'Hare	1 0 3 0	4	
6 Paul Blackbird	1 0 T 1	2	
7 Deon Prinsloo	0 3 fx 1	4	1

MIDDLESBROUGH (H), July 1, W55-35

1 †Jan Stæchmann	**3 3 3 2**	**11**	**1**
2 Martin Dixon	1 2 2 1	6	1
3 Carl Blackbird	**3 3 3 3**	**12**	
4 Richard Hellsén	1 2 3 2 1	9	
5 Gary O'Hare	3 0 0 1	4	
6 Deon Prinsloo	2 1 2 2	7	2
7 Nigel Sparshott	3 1 1 1 0	6	2

Glasgow (A), July 12, L34-56

1 †Jan Stæchmann	3 2 3 3 1 1	13	1
2 Jason Reed	0 0 T T	0	
3 Carl Blackbird	E 1 2 2 1 2	8	1
4 Gary O'Hare	0 0 T 0	0	
5 Martin Dixon	1 1 R 0 N	2	
6 Deon Prinsloo	3 1 3 1 0 1	9	
7 Nigel Sparshott	1 0 T 1 0	2	

SHEFFIELD (H), July 15, W68-21

1 Jan Stæchmann	**3 3 3 2**	**11**	**1**
2 Deon Prinsloo	1 2 1 1	5	2
3 Carl Blackbird	3 3 3 2 3	14	
4 Richard Hellsén	**3 2 3 2**	**10**	**2**
5 Martin Dixon	2 3 3 1	9	2
6 Nigel Sparshott	**2 2 2 2**	**8**	**4**
7 Gary O'Hare	3 2 1 3 2	11	1

Sheffield (A), July 16, D45-45

1 †Jan Stæchmann	2 3 3 2 1	11	1
2 Martin Dixon	1 0 3 1	5	1
3 Richard Hellsén	2 2 2 0	6	1
4 Deon Prinsloo	2 3 2 3 0	10	
5 Carl Blackbird	0 2 1 3	6	1
6 Nigel Sparshott	0 0 1 0	1	1
7 Gary O'Hare	1 3 1 1	6	1

NEWCASTLE (H), July 22, W49-41

1 †Jan Stæchmann	**3 3 3 3 3**	**15**	
2 Deon Prinsloo	1 1 2 R	4	1
3 Carl Blackbird	3 3 1 2 0	9	
4 Richard Hellsén	0 3 0 2	5	
5 Martin Dixon	3 2 R 1	6	2
6 Nigel Sparshott	1 1 0 1	3	
7 Gary O'Hare	3 3 0 1	7	1

STOKE (H), July 29, W59-31

1 †Jan Stæchmann	**3 3 3 3 3**	**15**	
2 Martin Dixon	1 1 1 0	3	1
3 Carl Blackbird	2 3 3 2 2	12	2
4 Richard Hellsén	R 3 1 3	7	
5 Deon Prinsloo	3 2 2 1	8	2
6 Nigel Sparshott	1 N 1 0	2	
7 Gary O'Hare	3 3 2 2 2	12	2

RYE HOUSE (H), August 5, W63-27

1 †Jan Stæchmann	**3 2 3 3**	**11**	**1**
2 Martin Dixon	1 3 1 1 2	8	1
3 Carl Blackbird	3 3 1 2 3	12	
4 Richard Hellsén	2 R 2 2	6	3
5 Deon Prinsloo	3 2 2 1	8	2
6 Nigel Sparshott	**2 2 2 3**	**9**	**3**
7 Gary O'Hare	3 3 0 3	9	

Edinburgh (A), August 7, L36-54

1 †Jan Stæchmann	1 R 2 2 3	8	1
2 Martin Dixon	0 2 1 0	3	1
3 Carl Blackbird	1 1 3 0 3	8	1
4 Richard Hellsén	0 2 1 0	3	
5 Deon Prinsloo	1 1 2 3 0	7	1
6 Nigel Sparshott	R R T 0	0	
7 Gary O'Hare	3 2 2 0	7	

Exeter (A), August 10, L30-59

1 †Jan Stæchmann	3 2 T T	5	
2 Martin Dixon	0 0 1 3	4	-
3 Carl Blackbird	3 2 1 R	6	
4 Deon Prinsloo	2 1 0 3 0 1	7	
5 Jason Reed	0 0 F T 0	0	
6 Gary O'Hare	0 R 0 2	2	
7 Nigel Sparshott	2 0 2 1 1 0	6	

PETERBOROUGH (H), August 12, L36-54

1 †Jan Stæchmann	2 1 2 3 3	11	
2 Martin Dixon	1 0 1 1 1	4	3
3 Carl Blackbird	1 2 2 3 2 2	12	
4 Richard Hellsén	1 1 2 2	6	-
5 Deon Prinsloo	0 0 0 T 0	0	
6 Nigel Sparshott	2 0 0 T	2	
7 Gary O'Hare	0 1 0 T	1	1

GLASGOW (H), August 19, W50-40

1 †Jan Stæchmann	3 3 3 3 1	13	1
2 Richard Hellsén	2 2 1 1	6	2
3 Carl Blackbird	2 3 2 2 2	11	
4 Martin Dixon	1 2 2 1	6	3
5 Deon Prinsloo	0 3 3 1	7	1
6 Nigel Sparshott	2 1 0 1	4	1
7 Gary O'Hare	R 0 1 2	3	1

Peterborough (A), August 21, L36-54

1 †Jan Stæchmann	1 3 2 2 fn	8	1
2 Richard Hellsén	0 2 3 1 1	7	2
3 Carl Blackbird	fx 2 2 1 R	5	
4 Martin Dixon	3 1 fx N 0	4	
5 Deon Prinsloo	1 0 1 2 3 0	7	1
6 Gary O'Hare	1 0 T 2	3	
7 Nigel Sparshott	0 1 T T 1	2	1

EDINBURGH (H), August 26, W47-43

1 Jan Stæchmann	*rider replacement*		
2 Richard Hellsén	2 1 3 3 3 0	12	2
3 †Carl Blackbird	3 3 R 2 2 3	13	
4 Martin Dixon	1 1 2 0 2	6	
5 Deon Prinsloo	0 3 2 1 1	7	1
6 Nigel Sparshott	2 1 2 1	6	2
7 §Mark Lemon	3 0 0 0	3	
8 Jason Reed	*did not ride*		

Berwick (A), September 12, L36-54

1†Jan Stæchmann	1 fx 2 3 2 2	10	1
2 Richard Hellsén	0 2 3 0	5	
3 Carl Blackbird	2 1 3 2 0	8	
4 Martin Dixon	1 R 1 1	3	2
5 Deon Prinsloo	2 1 1 2	6	1
6 Nigel Sparshott	1 0 T 1	2	1
7 Mark Lemon	0 F 2 0	2	1

Rye House (A), September 20, L39-50

1 Jan Stæchmann	*rider replacement*		
2 Richard Hellsén	0 2 0 T 1	3	1
3 †Carl Blackbird	2 3 2 3 2 2 2	16	
4 Martin Dixon	3 2 2 F 2 0	9	
5 Deon Prinsloo	fx 0 1 1 3	5	2
6 Mark Lemon	1 0 0 1	2	
7 Nigel Sparshott	0 2 1 1	4	2
8 Jason Reed	*did not ride*		

Stoke (A), September 26, L34-54

1 †Jan Stæchmann	3 3 3 X 2 2	13	
2 Richard Hellsen	*did not arrive*		
3 Carl Blackbird	2 R 2 1 2	7	
4 Deon Prinsloo	1 1 0 0	2	1
5 Martin Dixon	0 2 1 3 0	6	1
6 Mark Lemon	1 2 1 T 1 1	6	
7 Nigel Sparshott	0 0 0 N	0	

Mildenhall (A), May 24, L39-48

1 †Jan Stæchmann	3 3 2 2 2 2	14	1
2 Colin White	1 0 1 1	3	1
3 Martin Dixon	1 3 1 0	5	1
4 Gary O'Hare	1 0 2 0	3	
5 Carl Blackbird	3 2 E 3 3 3	14	
6 Paul Blackbird	fx 0 T 0 T 0	0	
7 Jason Reed	fx N 0 N 0	0	

At-a-Glance Results

Berwick	**D45-45**	**L36-54**	**81-99**
Edinburgh	**W47-43**	**L36-54**	**83-97**
Exeter	**L44-46**	**L30-59**	**74-105**
Glasgow	**W50-40**	**L34-56**	**84-96**
Middlesbrough	**W55-35**	**L39-50**	**94-85**
Newcastle	**W49-41**	**L33-56**	**82-97**
Peterborough	**L36-54**	**L36-54**	**72-108**
Rye House	**W63-27**	**L39-50**	**102-77**
Sheffield	**W68-21**	**D45-45**	**113-66**
Stoke	**W59-31**	**L34-54**	**93-85**
Mildenhall		***L39-48***	

WHO WAS WHO IN '92

Carl Ivan BLACKBIRD
Born: March 26, 1965, Peterborough, Cambridgeshire.
Everpresent for the second successive season with the Invaders.

Paul Barry BLACKBIRD
Born: December 17, 1970, Peterborough, Cambridgeshire.
Twin brother of Peterborough's Mark. He was dropped in June and drifted out of the sport.

Martin DIXON
Born: May 30, 1961, Hartlepool, Cleveland.
Moved to Station Road after two seasons at Newcastle and rode in all the club's League matches.

John Richard HELLSÉN
Born: June 1, 1951, Stockholm, Sweden.
Returned to Long Eaton – where he had ridden in 1989 and 1990 – after the closure of Milton Keynes.

Mark Ian John LEMON
Born: February 12, 1973, Brainsdale, Victoria, Australia.
Checked into Station Road in August after spending more than a month on the sidelines after being axed by Middlesbrough. He had rejoined the Bears on loan from First Division Poole for his third season in Britain.

Patrick Gary O'HARE
Born: September 14, 1963, Manchester.
The last remaining survivor from the 1990 Long Eaton side he was axed towards the end of August to accommodate the arrival of Australian Mark Lemon from Middlesbrough.

Deon PRINSLOO
Born: April 24, 1972, Gwelo, Zimbabwe.
Signed on loan from First Division Eastbourne, he made rapid progress with his third Division Two club and graduated from reserve to a top five place.

Jason Scott REED
Born: October 10, 1969, Sydney, New South Wales, Australia.
Australian-born youngster whose family moved to England when he was only two. Made only two League appearances for the Invaders, having made his debut in 1991.

Nigel SPARSHOTT
Born: September 2, 1961, Swanley, Kent.
Came out of an enforced retirement after being axed by Rye-House in 1990. Impressed sufficiently in after-the meeting trials to be offered a reserve berth at the beginning of July.

Jan STÆCHMANN
Born: June 5, 1966, Kolding, Denmark.
Hampered by a troublesome knee injury – sustained in pre-season practice – which affected some of his performances although he had one golden spell in which he was unbeaten in five our of six successive League matches.

Colin WHITE – see Arena Essex.

Boro bear-ly survive crisis

HAVING finished in the nether regions of the Second Division the year before, Middlesbrough had every reason to believe that 1992 would be better – in fact it was worse!

They finished the season bottom of the pile, closing down early in view of dwindling crowds and admitting to losses in the region of £10,000.

If co-promoter Tim Swales had had his way it would quite probably have been the Boro Bears' last season at Cleveland Park, too, as he looked to switch the operation to nearby Hartlepool only for planning permission to be denied.

Re-building the side in the winter, Middlesbrough signed Aussie Steve Regeling, strangely out of favour at Exeter, to lead the anticipated revival in the club's fortunes. That was a popular move but less so was the loan deal that took emerging prospect Chris Readshaw to Berwick.

No complaints though over Paul Bentley opting to move up to Division One with Coventry and the monies received for his transfer helped finance the Regeling deal.

American international Donny Odom opted to join Middlesbrough despite offers from several other tracks whilst the loss of Readshaw resulted in local lad Paul Pickering getting his chance in the side.

A surprise was the return of Daz Sumner who had left the club for Belle Vue only a few months earlier and with Mark Lemon and David Cheshire retained from the previous year, the team was in place. Not the strongest team in the League granted, but one that should have done infinitely better than it did.

So where did it all go wrong? Well, from the outset Lemon was plagued with all sorts of mechanical and personal problems and hefty repair bills from various crashes. Odom found life tough but at least endeared himself to the fans with his all-action style.

Cheshire, meanwhile, was having problems of his own (mainly financial) which culminated in him quitting the club and returning home to his native Australia.

By then Middlesbrough's season was virtually over in terms of opportunities to win honours. They had lost their first League matches, been dumped out of the Phonesport Knock Out Cup by neighbours Newcastle and had lost to Coventry in the BSPA Cup.

Not that troubles were confined to riders for co-promoter and team manager Ken Knott nearly landed himself in the soup after dragging Newcastle's Max Schofield from the track in a spur-of-the-moment incident.

Nothing was going right for the club and with Lemon being dropped on top of Cheshire's retirement, remedial work was imperative. In came Paul Whittaker, dropped mid-term by Peterborough, and Donny Odom's uncle Doug Nicol, who'd impressed in a series of after-meeting spins. No sooner had Whittaker signed than he was in hospital having a further operation on the elbow he had fractured at Newcastle the previous year.

A humiliating 37-53 defeat at home to Rye House brought the club to its lowest ebb and with attendances on the decline there was no surprise at the announcement that the Bears would be the first to bring their season to an end.

Not that it was total gloom. Pickering soon silenced his many critics on the terraces by putting in some gutsy performances and Regeling proved to be an astute buy. However, he expressed his displeasure over the management's cost-cutting exercises and was a vociferous opponent of the economical sanctions.

With Tim Swales assuming the mantle of Chairman of the British Speedway Promoters'' Association at the annual winter conference, Knott will be more heavily involved in the day to day running of the club and one of the first moves was to announce the appointment of Steve Wilcock as new team manager.

The latter was involved in the successes of the past and will be eager to turn the clock back to recapture those glory days.

1992 RIDER ROSTER

	Club Record								Career Record							
	M	R	Pts	EP	TPts	Ave	F	P	M	R	Pts	BP	TPts	Ave	F	P
Mark Burrows	25	80	67.0	15.0	82.0	4.100	0	0	115	386	347.0	90.0	437.0	4.528	0	0
Duncan Chapman	60	228	214.0	30.0	244.0	4.281	0	1	64	243	226.0	32.0	258.0	4.247	0	1
David Cheshire	50	246	404.0	42.0	446.0	7.252	0	0	120	523	834.0	90.0	924.0	7.067	0	4
Mark Lemon	30	149	201.0	21.0	222.0	5.960	0	0	39	182	222.0	28.0	250.0	5.495	0	0
Doug Nicol	11	49	58.0	6.0	64.0	5.224	0	0	11	49	58.0	6.0	64.0	5.224	0	0
Donny Odom	20	78	70.0	16.0	86.0	4.410	0	0	20	78	70.0	16.0	86.0	4.410	0	0
Paul Pickering	22	77	47.0	10.0	57.0	2.961	0	0	22	77	47.0	10.0	57.0	2.961	0	0
Steve Regeling	21	97	199.0	13.0	212.0	8.742	2	1	165	799	1687.0	119.0	1806.0	9.041	11	11
Darren Sumner	132	704	1358.0	78.0	1436.0	8.159	4	3	237	1111	1927.0	181.0	2108.0	7.590	7	9
Stuart Swales	10	25	13.0	4.0	17.0	2.720	0	0	10	25	13.0	4.0	17.0	2.720	0	0
Paul Whittaker	8	35	39.0	7.0	46.0	5.257	0	0	265	1145	1771.0	229.0	2000.0	6.987	6	7

MIDDLESBROUGH

Promoters: Tim Swales and Ken Knott.
Address: Cleveland Park Stadium, Stockton Road, Middlesbrough, Cleveland.
Telephone: 0642-211411.
Information Line: 0891 31 21 43.
Track Length: 302 metres.
Track Record: 61.1 secs, Darren Sumner (Middlesbrough), July 5, 1990, Heat 1, Middlesbrough v Stoke (Division Two).
Seasons in Division Two: 25 (1968-1992).
Division Two Record: Champions (1), 1981. Runners-up (1), 1990. Third (4), 1968, 1980, 1985, 1986.
Division Two Cup Record: Runners-up (2), 1980, 1990.
Division Two Team Championship: Winners (2), 1985, 1986. Third (2), 1981, 1982. Qualified (9), 1981, 1982, 1983, 1984, 1985, 1986, 1987, 1988, 1990.
Appearances: Steve Wilcock, 556 (1976-1987, 1989-1991).
Points: Steve Wilcock, 5200 (1976-1987, 1989-1991).
World Finalists: None.
Division Two Riders' Championship Finalists: Allan Brown (1968), Graham Plant (1968), Terry Lee (1969), Tom Leadbitter (1970, 1975), Bruce Forrester (1971, 1973-74), Dave Durham (1972), Alan Emerson (1976-77), Steve Wilcock (1978-79-80-81-82-83-84-85), Mark Courtney (1986), Martin Dixon (1987-88), Rod Hunter (1990), Kenny McKinna (1991), Steve Regeling (1992), Paul Whittaker (1992).
Other Honours: Division Two (Division Two) Champions, 1947.

Exeter (A), May 4, L36-54

1 §†Steve Regeling	3 2 3 2 1 2	13	1
2 Darren Sumner	0 1 T 1	2	2
3 Mark Lemon	2 1 2 1 1	7	1
4 §§Donny Odom	0 2 0 0 N	2	
5 David Cheshire	3 R 3 fx 2 3	11	
6 Duncan Chapman	1 0 N 0 T	1	
7 §§Paul Pickering	fx N 0 N T 0	0	

PETERBOROUGH (H), May 7, L43-47

1 †Steve Regeling	0 1 2 1	4	2
2 Mark Lemon	2 2 0 3 F	7	
3 Darren Sumner	3 3 3 3 2	14	
4 Donny Odom	3 1 3 R	7	
5 David Cheshire	R 3 1 0	4	1
6 Duncan Chapman	3 0 0 2 1	6	
7 Paul Pickering	0 1 0 N	1	

Glasgow (A), May 17, L36-54

1 †Steve Regeling	3 1 1 3 3 1	12	
2 Mark Lemon	0 F 1 T	1	1
3 Darren Sumner	1 1 3 2 1	8	1
4 Donny Odom	0 1 2 0 0	3	1
5 David Cheshire	1 2 0 3	6	
6 Duncan Chapman	3 N 2 T 0 1	6	
7 Paul Pickering	fx F 0 N T	0	

LONG EATON (H), June 4, W50-39

1 †Steve Regeling	2 3 3 2 3	13	
2 Donny Odom	1 1 2 2	6	2
3 David Cheshire	3 3 1 2	9	
4 Mark Lemon	2 3 0 3 fx	8	1
5 Darren Sumner	3 1 2 0	6	
6 Duncan Chapman	3 1 0 0	4	
7 Paul Pickering	2 1 0 1	4	2

Edinburgh (A), June 12, L33-57

1 Steve Regeling	2 3 3 3 3 2	16	
2 Donny Odom	R F T N	0	
3 David Cheshire	1 F 1 R	2	1
4 Mark Lemon	fx 1 0 N	1	1
5 Darren Sumner	2 2 1 1 N	6	
6 Duncan Chapman	1 1 2 2 1 0	7	1
7 Paul Pickering	0 fx 0 T 1 0	1	

EDINBURGH (H), June 18, W48-41

1 †Steve Regeling	2 1 3 2	8	
2 Stuart Swales	1 0 N 1	2	1
3 David Cheshire	3 1 2 1	7	1
4 Mark Lemon	2 2 F 3 1	8	3
5 Darren Sumner	3 3 3 3 2	14	
6 Duncan Chapman	fx 1 2 2 N F	5	
7 Paul Pickering	3 0 1 N 0	4	

Long Eaton (A), July 1, L35-55

1 †Steve Regeling	2 2 3 3 2 2 3	17	
2 Duncan Chapman	0 1 0 0 2	3	1
3 David Cheshire	*rider replacement*		
4 Mark Lemon	0 1 0 0 N	1	
5 Darren Sumner	2 1 1 1 3	8	
6 Donny Odom	R 0 3 2 0	5	
7 Paul Pickering	1 0 T N 0	1	
8 Stuart Swales	0	0	

Peterborough (A), July 10, L34-55

1 †Steve Regeling	3 2 2 2 3 3	15	
2 Duncan Chapman	0 0 F 0 R	0	
3 David Cheshire	*rider replacement*		
4 Mark Lemon	2 3 2 3 1 0 1	12	1
5 Darren Sumner	1 1 3 0 1 1	7	1
6 Paul Pickering	F N T N	0	
7 Donny Odom	F F R T R	0	
8 Stuart Swales	0	0	

RYE HOUSE (H), July 16, L37-53

1 †Steve Regeling	2 0 1 2	5	
2 Duncan Chapman	F 1 3 3 3 1	11	
3 §Paul Whittaker	2 0 1 0	3	
4 §§Doug Nicol	1 0 E 1	2	
5 Darren Sumner	R 1 2 2 3	8	
6 Donny Odom	2 1 1 1	5	2
7 Paul Pickering	1 1 0 1 T	3	2

BERWICK (H), July 23, L43-46

1 †Steve Regeling	2 3 2 3 3 1	14	1
2 Duncan Chapman	1 3 fx fx 1	5	2
3 Darren Sumner	2 0 3 3 2 0	10	
4 Doug Nicol	0 3 0 0 2	5	
5 Paul Whittaker	*rider replacement*		
6 Donny Odom	1 R 1 1 1	4	2
7 Paul Pickering	2 2 1 E	5	
8 Stuart Swales	*did not ride*		

EXETER (H), July 30, W55-34

1 †Steve Regeling	**3 2 3 3**	**11**	**1**
2 Duncan Chapman	2 3 3 F 2	10	1
3 Darren Sumner	**3 3 3 3**	**12**	
4 Stuart Swales	2 2 0 1	5	1
5 Doug Nicol	R 1 2 2 F	5	2
6 Donny Odom	3 2 0 1	6	2
7 Paul Pickering	2 2 0 2	6	2

Rye House (A), August 2, L35-52

1 †Steve Regeling	2 3 3 3 3 3 0	17	
2 Donny Odom	fx N T T	0	
3 Darren Sumner	2 3 2 2 1 1	11	1
4 Doug Nicol	0 2 R 2 2	6	1
5 Paul Whittaker	*rider replacement*		
6 Paul Pickering	fx 0 F 0 0	0	
7 Duncan Chapman	fx 0 T 1 0	1	
8 Stuart Swales	0 0	0	

STOKE (H), August 6, W48-41

1 †Steve Regeling	3 3 3 3 R 1	13	
2 Donny Odom	X 3 2 0 1	6	1
3 Darren Sumner	2 3 3 fx 2 3	13	
4 Paul Whittaker	*rider replacement*		
5 Doug Nicol	1 2 1 0	4	1
6 Duncan Chapman	3 1 N 2 N 2 1	9	1
7 Paul Pickering	2 0 N 0 N 1	3	1
8 Stuart Swales	*did not ride*		

SHEFFIELD (H), August 13, L43-46

1 †Steve Regeling	3 1 3 3 2	12	
2 Donny Odom	1 3 2 1 0	7	1
3 Darren Sumner	3 3 1 1	8	
4 Doug Nicol	2 1 fx 3	6	1
5 Paul Whittaker	1 2 1 0	4	1
6 Stuart Swales	0 2 0 N	2	1
7 Paul Pickering	1 3 fx 0 0	4	

Sheffield (A), August 16, L27-63

1 †Steve Regeling	2 1 3 2 2 2	12	
2 Donny Odom	0 0 R N	0	
3 Darren Sumner	1 2 3 0 0 1	7	1
4 Doug Nicol	0 2 1 0	3	
5 Paul Whittaker	1 1 1 1	4	1
6 Stuart Swales	1 0 0 0	1	
7 Paul Pickering	0 0 N F	0	

GLASGOW (H), August 20, W55-35

1 †Steve Regeling	3 3 3 0 3	12	
2 Donny Odom	1 1 1 1	4	
3 Darren Sumner	3 2 3 3 1	12	
4 Doug Nicol	1 3 3 2	9	
5 Paul Whittaker	3 2 0 2	7	2
6 Duncan Chapman	3 2 1 3 0	9	2
7 Paul Pickering	2 R R N	2	1

Newcastle (A), August 23, L41-49

1 †Steve Regeling	0 1 3 3 3 3	13	1
2 Donny Odom	1 2 0 1	4	
3 Darren Sumner	1 2 2 3 2 1	11	1
4 Doug Nicol	2 0 1 1	4	
5 Paul Whittaker	0 2 1 2	5	2
6 Duncan Chapman	2 0 0 T	2	
7 Paul Pickering	0 2 T 0	2	

NEWCASTLE (H), August 27, W45-44

1 †Steve Regeling	3 fx 3 3 0	9	
2 Donny Odom	0 1 2 2	5	1
3 Darren Sumner	1 3 3 1 2	10	
4 Doug Nicol	1 3 0 2	6	1
5 Paul Whittaker	2 0 2 0	4	
6 Duncan Chapman	3 3 2 1 X	9	2
7 Paul Pickering	2 0 F N	2	1

Stoke (A), September 12, L37-53

1 †Steve Regeling	3 2 1 3 3 3	15	1
2 Donny Odom	fx 0 T 0	0	
3 Paul Whittaker	1 1 2 1 3	8	
4 Mark Burrows	0 F F T	0	
5 Doug Nicol	1 1 1 1 3 1	8	
6 Duncan Chapman	3 0 0 1	4	
7 Paul Pickering	1 0 T 1	2	

Berwick (A), September 20, L32-58

1 †Steve Regeling	2 1 2 3 3 2 3	16	
2 Stuart Swales	1 0 0 0	1	1
3 Doug Nicol	*rider replacement*		
4 Mark Burrows	fx 2 fx 0	2	
5 Paul Whittaker	1 0 1 1 1 F	4	1
6 Duncan Chapman	2 2 1 2 0 0	7	1
7 Paul Pickering	0 1 T 1	2	1
8 William Beveridge	*did not ride*		

Milton Keynes (A), May 5, L42-48

1 †Steve Regeling	2 1 2 1 3 2	11	2
2 Mark Lemon	R 2 3 3 0	8	
3 Darren Sumner	2 1 2 1	6	1
4 Donny Odom	R 1 3 fx	4	1
5 David Cheshire	2 2 1 2 2	9	
6 Duncan Chapman	3 0 1 N	4	1
7 Paul Pickering	0 F T T 0	0	

At-a-Glance Results

Berwick	L43-46	L32-58	75-104
Edinburgh	W48-41	L33-57	81-98
Exeter	W55-34	L36-54	91-88
Glasgow	W55-35	L36-54	91-90
Long Eaton	W50-39	L35-55	85-94
Newcastle	W45-44	L41-49	86-93
Peterborough	L43-47	L34-44	77-91
Rye House	L37-53	L35-52	72-105
Sheffield	L43-46	L27-63	70-109
Stoke	W48-41	L37-53	85-94
Milton Keynes		*L42-48*	

WHO WAS WHO IN '92

William BEVERIDGE
Born: September 9, 1975, Hexham, Northumberland.
Named as number eight in the final match of the season, his first in the sport. Also made a guest appearance for short handed Exeter at Cleveland Park.

Mark BURROWS
Born: June 10, 1964, Sheffield, South Yorkshire.
After missing four seasons made a comeback at Glasgow but his comeback was hampered by a knee injury. He moved on loan to Middlesbrough when Daz Sumner signed for Oxford.

Duncan Raymond CHAPMAN
Born: November 16, 1971, Scarborough, North Yorkshire.
Established himself in the line-up after three seasons when he could never be certain of a full team place.

David CHESHIRE
Born: May 17, 1966, Perth, Western Australia.
Returned home to Australia in June after being asked to take a pay cut by the financially-strapped management.

Mark LEMON – see Long Eaton

Douglas Dwight NICOL
September 24, 1959, Santa Monica, California, United States of America.
Former moto-cross and road racer who first tired speedway in 1985 before quitting when his father and brother died. He originally came to England to help his nephew Donny Odom but was tempted to have after the meeting rides at several venues and caught the eye at Cleveland Park. An ex-World Mini Cycle Moto Cross Champion he made his debut for the Bears against Rye House and settled into a team role.

Don Wesley (Donny) ODOM
Born: November 22, 1967, Santa Monica, California, United States of America.
Reputedly the tallest rider in speedway at 6 foot 2 inches. He joined Middlesbrough at the beginning of the year having been seemingly set to sign for Rye House towards the end of 1991.

Paul PICKERING
Born: February 15, 1966, Hartlepool, Co. Durham.
A former East Yorkshire Centre Moto Cross Champion he won a team place with some impressive training school performances during the winter and was eventually voted Rider of the Year by Middlesbrough fans.

Steven Grae REGELING
Born: October 2, 1959, Mount Isa, Queensland, Australia.
Asked Exeter for a transfer in the winter and after talking to several clubs opted to join Middlesbrough. Maintained his reputation as one of the most consistent top scorers in the Second Division.

Darren Keith (Daz) SUMNER
Born: March 14, 1968, Stockport, Greater Manchester.
Returned to Cleveland Park after being overlooked in Belle Vue's Division One plans following his 1991 move to his local club. Joined First Division Oxford in September but continued to make a series of guest appearances for the Bears.

Paul Joffre WHITTAKER
Born: March 22, 1968, Folkestone, Kent.
Signed for Peterborough in a £9,000 deal but struggled to get over a badly broken arm sustained in a crash at Newcastle midway through 1991. He was left out of the side, underwent a further operation and joined Middlesbrough on loan for the last three months of the season.

1992

MIDDLESBROUGH

Back row: David Cheshire, Duncan Chapman, Donny Odom, Daz Sumner. Front: Paul Pickering, Steve Regeling and Mark Lemon.

1992

NEWCASTLE

Back row: Mark Thorpe, Scott Norman, Brian Havelock (team manager), Phil Jeffrey, Max Schofield. Front: the late Wayne Garratt, David Bargh and Richard Juul.

Tragedy dulls the sparkle

THE TRAGIC death of Wayne 'Bodger' Garratt cast a huge black shadow over Newcastle's season and took the shine off any of their achievements as well as sending the sport into mourning.

Wayne crashed during the Debmat Diamonds' home leg of the Phonesport Knock Out Cup semi-final against Peterborough on Sunday, September 13 and subsequently succumbed to his injuries.

In a year that promised so much for the Tynesiders, the inherent dangers of the sport were brought home to everyone and the end of the season couldn't come too soon.

There had been much optimism at the start of the year and for good reason.

Kiwis David Bargh and Mark Thorpe returned to lead what should have been a serious assault on the League Championship.

Scott Norman was snapped up on loan from Wolverhampton after attempts to sign Dane Brian Andersen were thwarted. And another Dane, Richard Juul, was given a second chance to prove his worth.

Phil Jeffrey was back and with Garratt being taken on loan from Cradley Heath the team was completed when Max Schofield put pen to paper after turning down the opportunity of First Division racing at Belle Vue.

A win at Berwick followed swiftly by a draw at Edinburgh immediately installed Newcastle as favourites in the northern section of the Gold Cup.

Another away victory, this time at Glasgow, confirmed that status and they took the title by squeezing out a narrow home victory in the return against the Bandits despite being without the injured Richard Juul.

So far so good except for a mauling at Peterborough which was quickly forgotten as local rivals Middlesbrough were despatched in the K.O. Cup.

International demands on Bargh and Thorpe wrecked any chance of success in the H.E.A.T. Team Championship rounds as they missed two of the four legs making the competition something of a mockery.

Thorpe made his mark at World Championship level finishing second in the Commonwealth Final and combining with Mitch Shirra to earn New Zealand a place in the World Pairs Final.

He crashed out of the World Championship trail in a bruising Overseas Final but, on the domestic front, it was still going to plan for the Debmat Diamonds. A League double over Stoke saw them climb to the top of the table and those two victories provided a psychological boost as the Potters were to provide the opposition in the Gold Cup final.

A storming victory for the Debmat Diamonds in the first leg at Loomer Road made overall victory a formality and what joyous scenes there were on the Brough Park terraces as the trophy was paraded.

Success had a price though for both Wayne Garratt and Max Schofield sustained collarbone injuries and when Richard Juul completed an unwanted hat-trick – breaking his collarbone towards the end of August – it left Newcastle far too vulnerable at the bottom end and their title hopes began to fade.

There was still the question of the Phonesport Knock Out Cup and a semi-final tie against Peterborough. The eventual League and Cup champions were held to a mere eight point lead at the East of England Showground and there was eager anticipation as the sides met two days later at Brough Park.

With Garratt being rushed to hospital after his fateful crash it mattered little that Bargh and Thorpe heroically battled to a maximum in the last heat to force a replay – Newcastle's season had ended there and then to all intent and purpose.

Wayne fought bravely for his life in a local hospital but his death cast a depressing pall over Brough Park and his remaining team-mates found it hard to motivate themselves.

1992 RIDER ROSTER

	Club Record								Career Record							
	M	R	Pts	BP	TPts	Ave	F	P	M	R	Pts	BP	TPts	Ave	F	P
David Bargh	207	957	1926.5	139.0	2065.5	8.633	16	7	207	957	1926.5	139.0	2065.5	8.633	16	7
Wayne Garratt	15	63	64.0	8.0	72.0	4.571	0	0	81	392	479.0	70.0	549.0	5.602	0	0
Andrew Howe	5	13	3.0	3.0	6.0	1.846	0	0	5	13	3.0	3.0	6.0	1.846	0	0
Phil Jeffrey	50	194	220.0	59.0	279.0	5.753	0	2	265	1040	1086.5	258.0	1344.5	5.171	0	3
Richard Juul	51	219	210.0	44.0	254.0	4.639	1	0	51	219	210.0	44.0	254.0	4.639	1	0
David Nagel	14	54	31.0	4.0	35.0	2.593	0	0	14	54	31.0	4.0	35.0	2.593	0	0
Scott Norman	26	123	223.0	13.0	236.0	7.675	1	1	102	520	833.0	85.0	918.0	7.062	2	3
Max Schofield	28	101	90.0	13.0	103.0	4.079	0	0	52	168	131.0	20.0	151.0	3.595	0	0
Mark Thorpe	121	589	982.0	76.0	1058.0	7.185	4	2	121	589	982.0	76.0	1058.0	7.185	4	2
Spencer Timmo	20	68	36.0	7.0	43.0	2.529	0	0	32	114	93.0	10.0	103.0	3.614	0	0

NEWCASTLE

Promoter: Richard Bailey and Bill Reay on behalf of Visiongood Limited.
Address: Brough Park Stadium, The Fossway, Byker, Newcastle-upon-Tyne, NE6 2XJ.
Telephone: 091-276-0262.
Information Line: 0891 31 21 46.
Track Length: 330 metres.
Track Record: 63.2 secs, Brian Karger (Arena Essex), August 18, 1991, Heat 1, Newcastle v Arena Essex, Sunbrite League Division Two.
Seasons in Division Two: 15 (1975-1983; 1986-1987; 1989-1992).
Division Two Record: Champions (3), 1976, 1982, 1983. Runners-up (3), 1975, 1978, 1980. Third (2), 1981, 1991.
Division Two Cup Record: Winners (2), 1976, 1982. Semi Finalists (1), 1991.
Division Two Team Championship: Winners (3), 1976, 1982, 1983. Runners-up (1), 1981. Qualified (7), 1976, 1977, 1978, 1979, 1981, 1982, 1983.
Division Two Gold Cup Record: Winners (2), 1991-92.
Appearances: Rod Hunter, 273 (1978-1983, 1989).
Points: Tom Owen, 2950 (1975-1982, 1987).
World Finalists: Brian Brett (1965), Ivan Mauger (1966-67-68), Anders Michanek (1970).
Division Two Riders' Championship Finalists: Joe Owen (1975-76, 1982-83), Tom Owen (1977-78), Rod Hunter (1980, 1989), David Bargh (1981, 1990-91-92), David Blackburn (1987), Paul Thorp (1991-92).
Other Honours: Provincial League Champions, 1964. English Cup Winners, 1939. Division Two Supernational Winners, 1982, 1983.

Peterborough (A), May 1, L32-57

1 Mark Thorpe	2 0 3 3 2 0	10	
2 §Wayne Garratt	0 2 1 0 1 1	5	
3 †David Bargh	2 2 2 R R	6	1
4 §Scott Norman	2 2 3 2 R	9	
5 Phil Jeffrey	0 0 N T	0	
6 Richard Juul	2 0 N 0	2	
7 Max Schofield	0 0 T N fx	0	

LONG EATON (H), May 18, W56-33

1 Mark Thorpe	3 3 0 2	8	
2 Phil Jeffrey	fx2 0 2	4	1
3 †David Bargh	2 3 3 3 2	13	1
4 Scott Norman	3 1 0 3 3	10	
5 Wayne Garratt	1 3 3 1	8	
6 Richard Juul	2 1 1 2	6	3
7 Max Schofield	3 3 1 X	7	

Berwick (A), May 23, L43-46

1 Mark Thorpe	2 3 3 2 2	12	
2 Phil Jeffrey	0 0 N N	0	
3 †David Bargh	2 3 3 2 1	11	1
4 Scott Norman	2 2 2 0	6	1
5 Wayne Garratt	1 3 0 fx	4	1
6 Richard Juul	2 1 1 1 X fn	5	
7 Max Schofield	0 1 3 0 1	5	1

EDINBURGH (H), June 14, W47-43

1 Phil Jeffrey	2 2 0 2 1	7	2
2 Mark Thorpe	*rider replacement*		
3 Scott Norman	1 3 3 3 3 3	16	1
4 Wayne Garratt	0 2 3 2 1 0	8	
5 †David Bargh	3 R X N	3	
6 Richard Juul	3 2 0 1 2 0	8	1
7 Max Schofield	1 2 2 fnR	5	1
8 David Nagel	*did not ride*		

Stoke (A), June 20, W47-43

1 Mark Thorpe	3 0 2 fx	5	
2 Phil Jeffrey	2 2 1 0	5	1
3 Scott Norman	3 2 3 2 1	11	2
4 Wayne Garratt	1 0 2 2	5	
5 †David Bargh	3 3 3 3 2	14	
6 Richard Juul	2 1 2 1	6	2
7 Max Schofield	0 0 X 1	1	1

PETERBOROUGH (H), June 28, W56-34

1 Mark Thorpe	**3 3 3 3 2**	**14**	**1**
2 Phil Jeffrey	1 1 2 2	6	1
3 Scott Norman	fx1 R 2	3	2
4 Wayne Garratt	1 1 1 N	3	
5 †David Bargh	**3 3 3 3 3**	**15**	
6 Max Schofield	2 2 2 0 3	9	1
7 Richard Juul	3 0 3 0	6	

SHEFFIELD (H), July 5, W58-32

1 Mark Thorpe	1 2 3 2 2	10	2
2 Phil Jeffrey	2 1 1 2	6	2
3 Scott Norman	2 3 2 1	8	
4 Richard Juul	2 2 1 3	8	3
5 †David Bargh	3 3 2 3 3	14	
6 Max Schofield	3 1 2 1	7	3
7 Wayne Garratt	2 0 1 2	5	3

STOKE (H), July 12, W50-39

1 Mark Thorpe	3 2 2 3 3	13	
2 Phil Jeffrey	2 1 1 1	5	3
3 Scott Norman	2 3 3 1	9	
4 Richard Juul	2 0 0 2	4	1
5 †David Bargh	3 2 3 3 2	13	1
6 Max Schofield	fnN - N	0	
7 Wayne Garratt	3 1 0 E 2 0	6	2

BERWICK (H), July 19, W51-38

1 Mark Thorpe	3 1 3 3	10	1
2 Phil Jeffrey	1 2 2 2	7	1
3 Scott Norman	2 3 1 2 2	10	1
4 Richard Juul	fx0 0 3	3	
5 †David Bargh	3 3 3 1 3	13	1
6 Max Schofield	1 1 1 0	3	1
7 Wayne Garratt	3 0 0 2	5	1

Long Eaton (A), July 22, L41-49

1 Mark Thorpe	2 0 0 3 3	8	
2 Phil Jeffrey	0 1 1 2	4	1
3 Scott Norman	2 2 3 2 X 2	11	
4 Richard Juul	1 1 1 N	3	3
5 †David Bargh	2 2 2 1 3 1	11	2
6 Max Schofield	0 0 N 0 T	0	
7 Wayne Garratt	2 R T 2 T	4	1

RYE HOUSE (H), August 10, W57-33

1 Mark Thorpe	1 3 3 3	10	1
2 Phil Jeffrey	2 1 3 2	8	1
3 Scott Norman	**3 3 3 2 3**	**14**	**1**
4 Richard Juul	1 2 2 3	8	2
5 †David Bargh	**3 3 3 3 2**	**14**	**1**
6 Max Schofield	1 N N N	1	
7 David Nagel	X 1 0 N 1 fx0	2	

EXETER (H), August 16, W65-25

1 Mark Thorpe	**3 2 2 2**	**9**	**3**
2 Phil Jeffrey	2 3 2 3 1	11	1
3 Scott Norman	**3 3 3 3**	**12**	
4 Richard Juul	**3 3 3 3 3**	**15**	
5 †David Bargh	**2 2 3 2**	**9**	**3**
6 Max Schofield	2 2 2 1	7	2
7 §§Andrew Howe	1 1 0 0	2	2

Edinburgh (A), August 21, L42-48

1 Mark Thorpe	2 0 3 3 0	8	
2 Phil Jeffrey	1 2 1 2	6	2
3 Scott Norman	2 1 fx2 1	6	
4 Richard Juul	0 2 0 1	3	1
5 †David Bargh	3 3 3 3 3 1	16	
6 Max Schofield	2 0 T 0	2	
7 Andy Howe	0 1 0 T	1	1

MIDDLESBROUGH (H), August 23, W49-41

1 Mark Thorpe	3 3 3 3 2	14	
2 Phil Jeffrey	2 1 3 2	8	2
3 Scott Norman	3 3 0 2	8	
4 Richard Juul	1 fxN N	1	
5 †David Bargh	3 3 2 0 N	8	
6 Max Schofield	3 0 1 1 0 0	5	1
7 David Nagel	1 1 2 1 0	5	

Middlesbrough (A), August 27, L44-45

1 Mark Thorpe	2 2 3 2 2 1	12	1
2 Phil Jeffrey	1 1 1 1	4	3
3 Scott Norman	2 3 3 1	9	1
4 David Nagel	0 1 0 T	1	
5 †David Bargh	3 R 2 3 3 3	14	
6 Max Schofield	fxN N N	0	
7 Spencer Timmo	X 0 2 T 0 1 1	4	1

GLASGOW (H), August 30, W47-43

1 Mark Thorpe	3 2 1 3 3	12	1
2 Phil Jeffrey	2 1 2 2	7	2
3 Scott Norman	3 3 1 0	7	
4 Andrew Howe	fxN 0 N	0	
5 †David Bargh	2 3 3 2 R	10	
6 Spencer Timmo	2 1 N 0 1	4	2
7 David Nagel	3 0 1 1 0 2	7	1

Rye House (A), August 31, L41-48

1 Mark Thorpe	2 2 2 T	6	
2 Phil Jeffrey	fx1 R 0	1	1
3 Scott Norman	3 3 3 0 3 0	12	
4 Andrew Howe	0 0 N T	0	
5 David Bargh	3 3 2 2 2 3	15	1
6 Spencer Timmo	3 R 0 0 N	3	
7 David Nagel	2 fx1 1 0	4	1

Exeter (A), September 7, L28-62

1 Mark Thorpe	2 1 2 3 1 2	11	1
2 Phil Jeffrey	fx0 T 0	0	
3 Scott Norman	3 T 0 0 1	4	
4 Richard Juul	0 0 1 N 0	1	
5 †David Bargh	1 1 1 0 3 3	9	
6 Spencer Timmo	N 0 0 N 0 T	0	
7 Wayne Garratt	2 N T 1 R	3	

Glasgow (A), September 20, L40-50

1 Mark Thorpe	3 2 3 2 3 1	14	
2 Phil Jeffrey	2 1 2 1 1	7	2
3 Scott Norman	0 1 0 T	1	
4 Richard Juul	0 0 T T	0	
5 †David Bargh	3 3 X 1 3 0	10	1
6 Max Schofield	1 0 1 0	2	
7 David Nagel	3 1 1 1	6	1

The original staging of the match on August 30 was abandoned after two racesof heavy rain. Scorers were: GLASGOW 4 NEWCASTLE 8 (Mark Thorpe 3- 3, Phil Jeffrey 2- 2:1, Spencer Timmo 3- 3, David Nagel 0- 0, Scott Norman, Andrew Howe, †David Bargh, did not ride).

Sheffield (A), September 24, L38-52

1 Mark Thorpe	3 2 3 3 3 2	16	
2 Phil Jeffrey	1 1 2 1 1 0	6	2
3 Scott Norman	2 2 2 1 1	8	1
4 Richard Juul	N 1 2 fx0	3	1
5 David Bargh	fnT N T	0	
6 Max Schofield	2 1 0 N 1 0	4	
7 David Nagel	1 0 0 N N 0	1	1

At-a-Glance Results

Berwick	W51-38	L43-46	94-84
Edinburgh	W47-43	L42-46	89-88
Exeter	W65-25	L28-62	93-87
Glasgow	W47-43	L40-50	87-93
Long Eaton	W56-33	L41-49	97-82
Middlesbrough	W49-41	L44-45	93-86
Peterborough	W56-34	L32-57	88-91
Rye House	W57-33	L41-48	98-81
Sheffield	W58-32	L38-52	96-84
Stoke	W50-39	W47-43	97-82

WHO WAS WHO IN '92

David Andrew BARGH
Born: March 14, 1962, Martinborough, New Zealand.
Opted to remain at Brough Park despite offers from Division One and was again the Debmat Diamonds mainstay along with fellow Kiwi Mark Thorpe.

Andrew Peter HOWE
Born: August 15, 1969, Northallerton, North Yorkshire.
Rode in four League matches for the Debmat Diamonds as a replacement for the injured Wayne Garratt.

Philip Spencer JEFFREY
Born: February 1, 1965, Berwick-upon-Tweed, Northumberland.
A consistent second string who experienced his best ever season in his 11th campaign.

David Andrew NAGEL
Born: March 1, 1973, Hexham, Northumberland.
Bright Brough Park prospect who scored well when he was finally given an extended run at reserve. He also had one League match for Berwick which was scrubbed from the records when opponents Glasgow successfully objected to his inclusion in the Bandits' line-up.

Scott NORMAN
Born: July 21, 1970, Adelaide, South Australia.
Signed on loan from First Division Wolverhampton who had bought him from Peterborough in 1991.

Max SCHOFIELD
Born: March 10, 1970, Leeds, South Yorkshire.
Returned to Brough Park after making a favourable impression during a loan spell from Belle Vue in 1991. Held down a regular team place for the first time in his colourful career.

Richard Christian Juul SØRENSEN (Richard Juul)
Born: October 30, 1970, Copenhagen, Denmark.
Looked capable of developing into heat leader material early in the season but struggled after a collar bone injury in his second season in Britain.

Mark Andrew THORPE
Born: March 26, 1969, Christchurch, New Zealand.
Had a successful World Championship season, losing a run-off for the Commonwealth crown at King's Lynn before going out at the Overseas Final.

Spencer TIMMO
Born: January 3, 1966, Oxford, Oxfordshire.
Signed on a short term loan from First Division Oxford in August to fill in when the Debmat Diamonds were without injured reserves Wayne Garratt and Max Schofield. The son of former British League rider Rick Timmo, he had actually ridden for Newcastle in 1990.

---

†

Wayne Malcolm GARRATT
Born: October 30, 1968, Halesowen, West Midlands.
Died: September 28, 1992, Newcastle General Hospital.
Suffered brain damage when he crashed at Brough Park during the Phonesport Knock Out Cup semi final against Peterborough on September 13 and died in hospital after two weeks on a life support machine. Had started his speedway career at his local track Cradley Heath and had spells with the Heathens in Division One and with Arena Essex and Newcastle in Division Two. Moved to Brough Park on loan at the beginning of the season.

All change – bottom to top

PETERBOROUGH ARE back on the speedway map again and heaven help the other clubs! Those prophetic words were uttered by James Easter as he and partner Peter Oakes addressed a packed public meeting early in January, announcing their takeover of the club.

After the traumas of 1991, which culminated with then-promoter David Hawkins having his licence suspended, the new promoting duo were bound to succeed. Few envisaged though that their side would emulate Arena-Essex from the year before by winning the League, the H.E.A.T. Team Championship and the Phonesport Knock Out Cup.

Having to build a side from scratch they started by taking Ade Hoole on loan from Wolverhampton although he never made it to the tapes in the club's colours.

Off track an impressive 'backroom team' was put together. Sarah Gudgeon, as commercial manager, immediately gained the team sponsorship from the local Evening Telegraph newspaper and she was joined by three old favourites Kevin Hawkins (team manager), Richard Greer (Clerk of the Course) and Ken Matthews (junior team manager). In, too, came Ivan Mauger as Overseas Scout and, subsequently Vaclav Verner as coach – yes the club meant business!

That was shown as they continued their team building process. Mark Blackbird came on loan from Long Eaton, Paul Whittaker was snapped up in a £9,000 deal from the BSPA eager to prove his fitness after his terrible crash at Newcastle the previous year. Stephen Davies put pen to paper becoming the only rider to return from the previous year and the team was taking shape.

Mick Poole, such a folk hero at Alwalton over the years, was re-signed after a year with Poole in the top flight and then came what proved to be THE capture of the season: 16-year-old Jason Crump, son of the legendary Phil. Rod Colquhoun was the last to sign and that meant no place in the side for Hoole – the ET Panthers first signing!

A formidable looking side and the crowds flocked to see their opening match in which Swedish tourists Rospiggarna were beaten 49-41. Poole led the way with 14 points and young Crumpie made a sensational debut scoring 8 (paid 11) from four rides.

Wins over Stoke and away at Mildenhall followed and it all looked too easy but then the form book was turned upside down when the Fen Tigers won the return match at the East of England Showground!

Team manager Kevin Hawkins was not amused: "You don't win races by being told and reading you're a good team," he said. "You've got to go out onto the track and do it."

The massive jolt to the system was absorbed, Hawkins' words were heeded by the team and little went wrong for them from that point except in a drubbing at Stoke in the Gold Cup.

They lost to Ipswich in the BSPA Cup but totally dominated the remaining three competitions. There were some hiccups on the way (not too many mind!) - including that thumping at Stoke in the final Gold Cup qualifying round, a 30 point defeat at Edinburgh in the League and an even bigger end of season defeat at Rye House. Those apart there was little to stand in the way of the ET Panthers and success.

Sentiment went out of the window in the search for success with Paul Whittaker, who struggled to recapture his previous form, being axed in favour of Neville Tatum.

Victory over Middlesbrough early in July saw the ET Panthers top the table for the first time and, while they were overtaken for a spell, they always had matches in hand and it was merely a question of when, rather than would, they would win the league.

Their Fours success was hard earned. Edinburgh pushed them hard in the final but Poole's last heat victory over Les Collins clinched the title .The Knock Out Cup came a little easier with a 30 point victory in the home leg of the final against Rye House virtually ensuring the final piece of silverware for Messrs Oakes and Easter to clean.

What an amazing transformation in Peterborough's fortunes in such an incredibly short space of time.

1992 RIDER ROSTER

	Club Record								Career Record							
	M	R	Pts	BP	TPts	Ave	F	P	M	R	Pts	BP	TPts	Ave	F	P
Ian Barney	348	1520	2351.0	206.0	2557.0	6.729	16	9	382	1665	2520.0	229.0	2749.0	6.604	16	10
Mark Blackbird	30	120	155.0	23.0	178.0	5.933	0	0	112	483	552.0	74.0	626.0	5.184	0	0
Rodney Colquhoun	36	140	172.0	36.0	208.0	5.943	0	0	75	292	338.0	81.0	419.0	5.740	0	0
Jason Crump	29	140	268.0	26.0	294.0	8.400	0	3	29	140	268.0	26.0	294.0	8.400	0	3
Stephen Davies	52	241	450.0	41.0	491.0	8.149	1	2	52	241	450.0	41.0	491.0	8.149	1	2
Michael Howe	3	11	6.0	2.0	8.0	2.909	0	0	13	32	13.0	3.0	16.0	2.000	0	0
Paul Hurry	30	129	149.0	33.0	182.0	5.643	0	0	58	245	284.0	60.0	344.0	5.616	0	0
Kieran McCullagh	-	-	-	-	-	-	-	-	9	26	14.0	4.0	18.0	2.769	0	0
Mick Poole	135	667	1353.0	117.0	1470.0	8.816	6	13	135	667	1353.0	117.0	1470.0	8.816	6	13
Neville Tatum	27	113	165.0	17.0	182.0	6.442	0	0	222	994	1599.0	158.0	1757.0	7.070	6	6
Paul Whittaker	2	8	12.0	1.0	13.0	6.500	0	0	265	1145	1771.0	229.0	2000.0	6.987	6	7

PETERBOROUGH

Promoters: James Easter and Peter Oakes.
Address: East of England Showground, Alwalton, Peterborough, PE2 0XE.
Telephone: 0733 394494.
Information Line: 0891 31 21 47.
Track Length: 347 metres.
Track Record: 61.5 secs, Martin Goodwin (Rye House), July, 26, 1992. Heat 3, H.E.A.T. Second Division Team Finals.
Seasons in Division Two: 23 (1970-1992).
Division Two Record: Champions (1), 1992. Third (1), 1972.
Division Two Cup Record: Winners (1), 1992. Runners-up (1), 1972.
Division Two Team Championship: Winners (5), 1977, 1978, 1988, 1989, 1992. Runners-up (1), 1985. Third (1), 1979. Qualified (11), 1976, 1977, 1978, 1979, 1981, 1982, 1985, 1987, 1988, 1989, 1992.
Division Two Gold Cup Record: Runners-up (1), 1991.
Appearances: Ian Barney, 348 (1980-1992).
Points: Ian Barney, 2557 (1980-1992).
World Finalists: None.
Division Two Riders' Championship Finalists: Andy Ross (1970), Richard Greer (1971-72-73), Mike Lanham (1974), Brian Clark (1975-76), Dave Gooderham (1978), Nigel Flatman (1979), Andy Hines (1980, 1982), Ian Barney (1984, 1987-88), Kevin Hawkins (1985-86), Mick Poole (1989-90, 1992), Stephen Davies (1991).

**A new promoting company, Ramsden Sports Promotions Limited took over at Peterborough early in 1992.
The former promoting company Eastclub Limited, run by David Hawkins, went into receivership in October, 1991.
He was barred from holding a promoter's licence by the Speedway Control Board because of his trading debts incurred throughout the 1991 season.**

1992
PETERBOROUGH

Left to right: Neville Tatum, mascot Jason Bunyan, Mick Poole, Paul Hurry, Kevin Hawkins (team manager), Stephen Davies, Mark Blackbird and Jason Crump.

NEWCASTLE (H), May 1, W57-32

1 Mick Poole	3 3 3 3 3	15	
2 §Mark Blackbird	1 1 0 1	3	
3 †Stephen Davies	3 3 1 3 2	12	2
4 Rodney Colquhoun	1 3 2 3	9	1
5 §Paul Whittaker	3 1 1 1	6	
6 §Paul Hurry	1 1 1 0	3	
7 §§Jason Crump	3 2 2 2	9	1

Middlesbrough (A), May 7, W47-43

1 Mick Poole	3 0 2 2	7	
2 Mark Blackbird	1 2 3 1	7	1
3 †Stephen Davies	2 3 3 0 3	11	
4 Paul Whittaker	2 2 1 1	6	1
5 Rodney Colquhoun	1 1 2 3 1	8	2
6 Jason Crump	2 0 0 2	4	1
7 Paul Hurry	1 1 2 0	4	3

Edinburgh (A), May 22, L30-60

1 Mick Poole	1 fx0 T R	1	
2 Mark Blackbird	0 2 1 1 1	5	
3 †Stephen Davies	F fxN N	0	
4 Rodney Colquhoun	1 2 0 T 2 0	5	1
5 Michael Howe	N 0 R T T	0	
6 Paul Hurry	3 2 2 3 1 0	11	
7 Jason Crump	2 2 T 2 1 0 1	8	2

RYE HOUSE (H), June 19, W50-40

1 Mick Poole	2 3 3 3 3	14	
2 Ian Barney	1 2 1 1	5	3
3 †Stephen Davies	3 2 2 2	9	1
4 §Neville Tatum	1 2 2 1	6	3
5 Mark Blackbird	2 0 1 N 0	3	
6 Paul Hurry	3 2 3 2 0 2	12	1
7 Michael Howe	0 N 0 1 N	1	1

GLASGOW (H), June 26, W54-36

1 Mick Poole	2 3 3 3 3	14	1
2 Ian Barney	3 1 1 2	7	1
3 †Stephen Davies	3 1 3 3 2	12	1
4 Mark Blackbird	0 1 N 3	4	1
5 Neville Tatum	3 2 3 1	9	
6 Paul Hurry	1 2 0 2 0	5	2
7 Jason Crump	3 0 0 0	3	

Newcastle (A), June 28, L34-56

1 Mick Poole	2 2 1 1 0	6	1
2 Ian Barney	R 0 T T	0	
3 †Stephen Davies	3 2 1 2 1	9	2
4 Neville Tatum	2 0 3 0 1	6	
5 Mark Blackbird	0 3 2 X E	5	
6 Paul Hurry	1 0 2 2 1 T	6	
7 Jason Crump	0 1 T 1 0	2	

MIDDLESBROUGH (H), July 10, W55-34

1 Mick Poole	2 3 3 2	10	1
2 Paul Hurry	1 2 1 2	6	4
3 †Stephen Davies	1 R 3 1	5	2
4 Neville Tatum	3 3 3 3 0	12	
5 Rodney Colquhoun	0 1 3 2 2	8	
6 Mark Blackbird	2 2 1 1	6	1
7 Jason Crump	3 2 1 2	8	1

Sheffield (A), July 30, W46-44

1 Mick Poole	3 0 2 1 2	8	
2 Rodney Colquhoun	1 1 3 1	6	1
3 †Stephen Davies	2 2 3 0 1	8	1
4 Neville Tatum	3 2 1 0	6	1
5 Paul Hurry	2 0 N 1	3	1
6 Mark Blackbird	3 1 2 3	9	2
7 Jason Crump	R 1 2 2 1	6	2

EXETER (H), July 31, W56-34

1 Mick Poole	2 3 0 3 3	11	1
2 Rodney Colquhoun	3 2 2 3 0	10	2
3 †Stephen Davies	fx3 3 1	7	1
4 Neville Tatum	3 3 0 1	7	
5 Paul Hurry	0 1 1 2	4	
6 Jason Crump	2 3 1 3	9	1
7 Mark Blackbird	3 3 2 0	8	1

Exeter (A), August 3, W49-41

1 Mick Poole	0 0 2 3	5	1
2 Rodney Colquhoun	3 3 2 3 3	14	
3 †Stephen Davies	3 1 3 2 1	10	
4 Paul Hurry	2 F 0 N	2	
5 Neville Tatum	0 2 0 0	2	
6 Jason Crump	3 3 1 3 2 2	14	2
7 Mark Blackbird	1 R N 1	2	

Long Eaton (A), August 12, W54-36

1 Mick Poole	3 3 2 3 3	14	
2 Rodney Colquhoun	0 2 F 1	3	2
3 †Stephen Davies	2 2 3 1	8	2
4 Paul Hurry	2 1 0 0	3	1
5 Neville Tatum	3 3 0 3	9	
6 Mark Blackbird	1 3 1 1	6	
7 Jason Crump	3 3 3 2 0	11	

LONG EATON (H), August 21, W54-36

1 Mick Poole	3 3 2 3 3	14	1
2 Rodney Colquhoun	2 1 0 3 2	8	2
3 †Stephen Davies	3 3 3 3	12	
4 Neville Tatum	0 0 1 2	3	
5 Paul Hurry	2 1 0 0	3	
6 Jason Crump	3 2 2 3	10	2
7 Mark Blackbird	2 1 0 1	4	2

Glasgow (A), August 23, L36-54

1 Mick Poole	3 3 3 2 0 fx	11	1
2 Rodney Colquhoun	0 0 2 T 1	3	
3 Stephen Davies	0 R T T	0	
4 Paul Hurry	0 1 0 T	1	1
5 Neville Tatum	1 2 3 0 2	8	
6 Mark Blackbird	X 2 0 1	3	1
7 Jason Crump	3 2 1 1 2 1	10	1

The race-off for the bonus points was abandoned because of heavy rain. Subsequently the British Speedway Promoters' Association ruled that the two clubs should share the bonus point.

SHEFFIELD (H), August 28, W49-41

1 Mick Poole	2 2 3 3	10	
2 Rodney Colquhoun	1 1 2 1	5	3
3 †Stephen Davies	1 2 2 2 3	10	1
4 Neville Tatum	R 2 0 0	2	
5 Paul Hurry	1 1 1 R	3	2
6 Jason Crump	3 3 3 2 1	12	1
7 Mark Blackbird	1 3 N 2 1	7	

Stoke (A), September 5, L34-56

1 Mick Poole	0 1 X 0 2	3	1
2 Rodney Colquhoun	1 2 F T 0	3	
3 †Stephen Davies	3 1 3 3 1 1	12	1
4 Neville Tatum	0 2 1 T	3	
5 Jason Crump	3 fx2 2 R 0	7	
6 Mark Blackbird	3 0 0 N	3	
7 Paul Hurry	2 0 T T 1	3	1

BERWICK (H), September 18, W60-30

1 †Mick Poole	3 3 3 3 1 2	15	1
2 Rodney Colquhoun	1 2 3 2 1	9	2
3 Stephen Davies	*rider replacement*		
4 Jason Crump	2 3 3 3 3 3	17	1
5 Neville Tatum	3 2 1 1 0	7	1
6 Paul Hurry	3 2 0 0	5	1
7 Mark Blackbird	1 2 3 1	7	1
8 Kieran McCullagh	*did not ride*		

Berwick (A), September 26, L35-55

1 Mick Poole	1 2 0 2	5	
2 Rodney Colquhoun	0 1 0 T F	1	1
3 †Stephen Davies	1 3 fx0	4	1
4 Neville Tatum	2 1 fx0	3	2
5 Jason Crump	3 2 3 1 1	10	
6 Paul Hurry	2 0 2 0	4	
7 Mark Blackbird	1 2 2 1 2	8	1

The original staging of the match at Berwick on August 22, was abandoned after four races because of heavy rain. The scorers at the time were: BERWICK 17 PETERBOROUGH 7 (Mick Poole 1-1, Rodney Colquhoun 0-0, †Stephen Davies 2-2, Paul Hurry 0-0, Neville Tatum 1-1, Mark Blackbird X-0, Jason Crump 2-1-3:1).

STOKE (H), October 3, W62-28

1 Mick Poole	2 2 3 3	10	1
2 Rodney Colquhoun	1 3 2 1	7	2
3 †Stephen Davies	3 3 2 2	10	2
4 Jason Crump	2 3 2 3	10	2
5 Neville Tatum	3 0 R 3 2	8	
6 Paul Hurry	2 2 0 3 1	8	2
7 Mark Blackbird	1 3 3 2	9	2

Rye House (A), October 11, L28-62

1 Mick Poole	0 2 0 1	3	
2 Rodney Colquhoun	1 0 T 1	2	
3 †Stephen Davies	3 2 1 1 0 1	8	
4 Neville Tatum	0 1 T 0	1	1
5 Jason Crump	2 2 3 1 2 0	10	
6 Mark Blackbird	2 0 0 0	2	
7 Paul Hurry	1 1 fx0	2	1

EDINBURGH (H), October 16, W56-34

1 Mick Poole	3 3 1 2 0	9	2
2 Rodney Colquhoun	1 2 2 2	7	1
3 †Stephen Davies	2 3 3 3	11	
4 Jason Crump	2 3 3 3 1	12	1
5 Neville Tatum	3 2 0 2	7	2
6 Paul Hurry	3 0 1 2	6	
7 Mark Blackbird	1 1 1 1	4	1

At-a-Glance Results

Berwick	W60-30	L35-55	95-85
Edinburgh	W56-34	L30-60	86-94
Exeter	W56-34	W49-41	105-75
Glasgow	W54-36	L36-54	†90-90
Long Eaton	W54-36	W54-36	108-72
Middlesbrough	W55-34	W47-43	102-77
Newcastle	W57-32	L34-56	91-88
Rye House	W50-40	L28-62	78-102
Sheffield	W49-41	W46-44	95-85
Stoke	W62-28	L34-56	96-84

†The BSPA awarded one half of a bonus point to each club.

WHO WAS WHO IN '92

Ian John BARNEY
Born: February 15, 1961, Stamford, Lincolnshire.
Signed on a short-term loan contract from parent club Exeter in June as a temporary stand-in for the injured Rodney Colquhoun and rode in three matches for his local club. He had started the season with Mildenhall and also rode for Milton Keynes before both tracks closed down.

Mark David BLACKBIRD
Born: December 17, 1970, Peterborough, Cambridgeshire.
Signed for his hometown club on loan from Long Eaton and was an everpresent in their trophy-winning squad without showing the form he had displayed in previous seasons.

Lee John COLEMAN
Born: December 6, 1971, Leicester, Leicestershire.
Fractured a vertebra in his spine in a training school crash in June when he was challenging for the number eight slot with the club.

Rodney Bryce COLQUHOUN
Born: February 28, 1967, Mount Warrigal, New South Wales, Australia.
Turned down team offers from Middlesbrough and Rye House to join the Evening Telegraph Panthers – his club on his first visit to Britain in 1988. Had his best-ever season.

Jason Phillip CRUMP
Born: August 16, 1975, Bristol, Avon.
Son of former World Finalist and Aussie legend Phil Crump. Made a sensational impact as he soared from reserve to heat leader. On loan from First Division Poole, he was voted Peterborough's Rider of the Year by supporters and scored four maximums in official competitions in a sizzling debut season.

Stephen Mark DAVIES
Born: January 31, 1965, Newcastle, New South Wales, Australia.
The only survivor from the 1991 team, he was appointed team captain and led the club to success on three fronts. Missed his only match when his newly-born son Alexander was in intensive care at Northampton General Hospital.

Michael David HOWE
Born: May 5, 1973, Nottingham, Nottinghamshire.
Announced his retirement midway through the season because of financial problems after making just two senior appearances.

PAUL HURRY
Born: April 9, 1975, Canterbury, Kent.
On loan from First Division Arena Essex, he was an everpresent despite suffering from a mid-season virus.

Kieran James McCULLAGH
Born: October 14, 1972, Abingdon, Oxfordshire.
Joined the ET Panthers on loan when Milton Keynes closed down but was denied his team chance other than as number eight.

Michael Garth POOLE
Born: November 27, 1966, Sydney, New South Wales, Australia.
Rejoined his former club in a £6,000 deal and proved a shrewd signing after a year in the First Division with Poole.

Neville John TATUM
Born: July 21, 1965, Epsom, Surrey.
Made a surprise early season move from First Division Eastbourne to the East of England Showground as a replacement for the axed Paul Whittaker.

Paul WHITTAKER – see Middlesbrough

1992

RYE HOUSE

Back row: Norman Kingsbury (team manager), Mark Courtney, Jan Pedersen, Sean Courtney, Wayne Baxter, Ronnie Russell (promoter). Front: Trevor O'Brien, Martin Goodwin and John Wainwright.

End is like a damp squib

SURVIVAL was the name of the game for Rye House in 1992. In a year that was the most successful in terms of results since Ronnie Russell took control way back in 1975, the biggest battle faced and won was to keep the club in existence.

After the home league win against Sheffield in July, Russell took to the microphone and told the fans that the club was in grave danger of closing if attendances did not improve.

Earlier in the season younger brother Terry and his partner at Arena-Essex Ivan Henry had stepped in to bale out the ailing Hertfordshire club's finances. However, Ronnie now admitted, as he stood before his faithful hard-core of supporters, that the point of no return was imminent.

Crowds did improve and the club survived much to everybody's relief, not least that of Russell himself who has put his heart and soul, not to mention all of his money, into the club since buying it from Len Silver.

"I would never wish to see this track close," he said, "as I and others put in too much effort over the years to let that happen."

The season began with everybody full of confidence with Ronnie having assembled the strongest-looking Rockets' side for many a year, including a surprise double swoop in the winter that saw him sign the Courtney brothers, Mark and Sean, from Berwick and Glasgow respectively.

They joined another impressive signing, Jan Pedersen from Arena-Essex, as Mel Taylor finally got his wish of a move from Hoddesdon and Roger Johns confirmed his retirement.

Jens Rasmussen was still recovering from the broken leg sustained the previous season but felt that he might be fit enough to return towards the end of the year. Effectively, he was discounted from the plans and hence the need for those three major signings.

For some reason the side didn't gel for the Gold Cup campaign and an 18-point home defeat at the hands of local rivals Mildenhall left everyone shattered. To their credit the riders accepted total blame, knuckled down to business, and then came an unexpected bonus. Rasmussen phoned Russell in mid-May and told him that he was ready to return to action months ahead of schedule.

It was too good an opportunity to be missed but it meant that reserves John Wainwright and Wayne Baxter had to be discarded even though they hadn't really done anything wrong.

Rasmussen's return produced instantaneous results with Sheffield demolished in the Phonesport Knock Out Cup and the side taking on an invincible look around their own circuit.

Rain-offs and not being able to stage meetings on the same day as BSPA shared events hardly helped to establish continuity as far as fixtures were concerned and, as a result, the Rockets occupied a falsely low position in the League for most of the year.

Trevor O'Brien's season came to an end in July when he broke a thigh at Exeter but, despite the club's precarious financial position, Swede Mikael Teurnberg was snapped up after Mildenhall's closure. What an inspired signing that turned out to be with him scoring a sensational 11 points on his debut at Middlesbrough as the Sabre Rockets romped to a 17 point victory.

Although another victory came at Edinburgh, defeats at Long Eaton, Newcastle, Sheffield and Berwick saw their title challenge fade leaving them to concentrate their efforts on the Cup.

Berwick stood in the way of the Sabre Rockets reaching their first final since 1982 but they were easily brushed aside as the 60-28 scoreline in the first leg at Hoddesdon effectively killed off any chance the Bandits had of stopping them.

The excitement and anticipation built as final opponents Peterborough were despatched with consummate ease -62-28 in the League match a fortnight before the K.O. Cup Final.

Disappointingly they lost the away leg by 30 points and worse was to follow with the scheduled home leg falling victim to the weather on the last Sunday of the official season.

Attempts were made to install temporary floodlighting for the re-staging but that failed, forcing the Sabre Rockets to give up home advantage by switching the tie to neighbouring Arena-Essex.

Any chance of them pulling back the points to take the silverware had, effectively, been snuffed out and the season ended in something of an anti-climax.

1992 RIDER ROSTER

	Club Record								Career Record							
	M	R	Pts	BP	TPts	Ave	F	P	M	R	Pts	BP	TPts	Ave	F	P
Wayne Baxter	48	181	140.0	25.0	165.0	3.646	0	0	48	181	140.0	25.0	165.0	3.646	0	0
Mark Courtney	22	89	115.0	16.0	131.0	5.888	0	0	401	1773	3462.0	236.0	3698.0	8.343	43	16
Sean Courtney	24	108	137.0	29.0	166.0	6.148	0	0	324	1350	1707.0	345.0	2052.0	6.080	1	6
Martin Goodwin	33	163	357.0	21.0	378.0	9.276	3	1	268	1276	2606.5	135.0	2741.5	8.594	24	7
Robert Ledwith	16	63	65.0	11.0	76.0	4.825	0	0	26	98	97.0	14.0	111.0	4.531	0	0
Trevor O'Brien	79	410	548.5	75.0	623.5	6.083	1	0	79	410	548.5	75.0	623.5	6.083	1	0
Jan Pedersen	25	117	183.0	24.0	207.0	7.077	0	0	48	218	347.0	48.0	395.0	7.248	0	0
Jens Rasmussen	142	744	1586.0	64.0	1650.0	8.871	12	5	142	744	1586.0	64.0	1650.0	8.871	12	5
Chris Young	14	46	33.0	5.0	38.0	3.304	0	0	17	55	35.0	5.0	40.0	2.909	0	0

RYE HOUSE

Promoters: Ronnie Russell, Peter Redfern and Roger Shute.
Address: Rye House Stadium, Rye Road, Hoddesdon, Hertfordshire.
Telephone: 0992-450997.
Hotline: 0891 312155.
Track Length: 257 metres.
Track Record: 57.1 secs, Josh Larsen (Arena Essex), May 4, 1992, Heat 10, Rye House v Arena Essex, Inter League Challenge.
Seasons in Division Two: 19 (1974-1992).
Division Two Record: Champions (1), 1980. Runners-up (2), 1977, 1979. Third (1), 1978.
Division Two Cup Record: Winners (1), 1979. Runners-up (2), 1978, 1992.
Division Two Team Championship: Runners-up (1), 1980. Fourth (1), 1982. Qualified (5), 1976, 1979, 1980, 1982, 1992.
Appearances: Bob Garrad, 421 (1976-1986).
Points: Bob Garrad, 3805 (1976-1986).
World Finalists: None.
Division Two Riders' Championship Finalists: Brian Foote (1974-75), Ted Hubbard (1976, 1978), Kelvin Mullarkey (1977, 1980-81), Karl Fiala (1979), Bob Garrad (1982, 1984), Marvyn Cox (1983), Paul Woods (1986-87), Jens Rasmussen (1988-89-90), Melvyn Taylor (1991), Martin Goodwin (1992).

BERWICK (H), June 14, W46-44

1 †Martin Goodwin	0 3 2 2 2	9	1
2 §Sean Courtney	1 1 3 3 1	9	1
3 Jens Rasmussen	2 3 1 2	8	
4 §Jan Pedersen	3 2 1 1	7	1
5 §Mark Courtney	2 0 1 1	4	3
6 Trevor O'Brien	1 1 2 2 fx	6	3
7 §Chris Young	2 1 0 N	3	

Peterborough (A), June 19, L40-50

1 †Martin Goodwin	3 3 3 3 3 2	17	
2 Sean Courtney	0 1 0 1	2	
3 Jens Rasmussen	1 R 2 0	3	1
4 Jan Pedersen	3 1 2 0	6	
5 Mark Courtney	R 0 1 0	1	
6 Trevor O'Brien	2 1 3 3 1	10	1
7 Chris Young	1 R T 0	1	1

Exeter (A), June 22, L33-56

1 †Martin Goodwin	3 2 3 R 3 3	14	
2 Sean Courtney	0 1 T 0 1	2	1
3 Jens Rasmussen	1 1 2 2 2	8	2
4 Jan Pedersen	1 2 1 2 1 1	8	
5 Mark Courtney	0 0 0 0 1	1	
6 Trevor O'Brien	fxT T N	0	
7 Chris Young	R O T T 0	0	

SHEFFIELD (H), July 12, W59-31

1 †Martin Goodwin	**3 3 3 3 3**	**15**	
2 Sean Courtney	F 2 1 1	4	2
3 Jens Rasmussen	3 3 2 2	10	
4 Jan Pedersen	2 2 1 2	7	2
5 Mark Courtney	3 3 3 1 2	12	2
6 Chris Young	0 1 1 N	2	
7 Trevor O'Brien	3 2 2 1 1	9	3

Middlesbrough (A), July 16, W53-37

1 †Martin Goodwin	**3 2 3 3**	**11**	**1**
2 Sean Courtney	1 3 2 2	8	1
3 Jens Rasmussen	3 2 0 3 R	8	1
4 Jan Pedersen	2 2 2 1 2	9	2
5 Mark Courtney	3 3 R R	6	
6 §Mikael Teurnberg	3 3 fn3 0 2	11	
7 Chris Young	F 0 N O N	0	

GLASGOW (H), July 19, W47-43

1 †Martin Goodwin	3 3 2 3 1	12	1
2 Sean Courtney	2 0 1 1	4	2
3 Jens Rasmussen	2 3 3 2 2	12	
4 Jan Pedersen	1 2 2 2	7	2
5 Mark Courtney	0 3 3 1	7	1
6 Chris Young	1 0 0 N	1	
7 Mikael Teurnberg	0 3 0 1 0	4	

MIDDLESBROUGH (H), August 2, W52-35

1 †Martin Goodwin	3 2 2 3 2	12	2
2 Sean Courtney	1 1 1 3	6	1
3 Jens Rasmussen	3 3 2 0	8	
4 Jan Pedersen	2 1 2 3 3	11	2
5 Mikael Teurnberg	1 2 3 1	7	1
6 Chris Young	3 1 1 1 1	8	1
7 Mark Courtney	fnN N N	0	

Long Eaton (A), August 5, L27-63

1 †Martin Goodwin	2 3 2 3 3 1	14	
2 Sean Courtney	0 1 0 T 1	2	
3 Jens Rasmussen	0 R 1 0	1	
4 Jan Pedersen	0 1 2 2 0 0	5	1
5 Mikael Teurnberg	1 0 1 0	2	
6 §Robert Ledwith	0 1 0 T	1	
7 Chris Young	1 1 T 0	2	

STOKE (H), August 9, W51-39

1 †Martin Goodwin	3 2 2 3 3	13	1
2 Sean Courtney	1 1 1 3	6	1
3 Jens Rasmussen	2 3 3 2 0	10	
4 Jan Pedersen	1 2 0 3	6	
5 Mikael Teurnberg	3 1 2 1	7	3
6 Chris Young	2 1 1 3	7	1
7 Robert Ledwith	1 0 0 1	2	1

Newcastle (A), August 10, L33-57

1 †Martin Goodwin	3 1 1 fnN	5	1
2 Sean Courtney	0 0 2 0 1 0	3	1
3 Jens Rasmussen	2 fxN N	2	
4 Jan Pedersen	2 1 0 1 0	4	1
5 Mikael Teurnberg	0 2 0 2	4	
6 Robert Ledwith	3 2 2 2 1 1	11	
7 Chris Young	2 0 T 1 1	4	2

Sheffield (A), August 20, L32-58

1 Martin Goodwin	*rider replacement*		
2 Sean Courtney	0 0 N 0	0	
3 Jens Rasmussen	0 0 3 1 2	6	
4 Jan Pedersen	2 0 2 2 1 1	8	1
5 Mikael Teurnberg	1 1 0 0 T	2	
6 Mark Courtney	2 3 2 2 0 N	9	1
7 Robert Ledwith	1 1 1 3 0 1	7	2
8 Chris Young	0	0	

NEWCASTLE (H), August 31, W48-41

1 Martin Goodwin	*rider replacement*		
2 Sean Courtney	3 2 2 2 1 2	12	2
3 †Jens Rasmussen	2 2 1 0	5	
4 Jan Pedersen	2 3 3 3 3 1	15	1
5 Mikael Teurnberg	1 1 0 1 1	4	2
6 Robert Ledwith	E 1 1 2	4	2
7 Mark Courtney	R 1 3 3 1	8	1
8 Chris Young	*did not ride*		

Edinburgh (A), September 4, W46-43

1 †Martin Goodwin	1 3 1 3	8	1
2 Mikael Teurnberg	0 0 3 2	5	
3 Jens Rasmussen	2 3 fx0	5	
4 Jan Pedersen	3 1 2 1 3	10	1
5 Mark Courtney	0 2 1 2	5	
6 Sean Courtney	2 1 2 3 1 2	11	3
7 Robert Ledwith	1 1 N 0	2	2

Berwick (A), September 5, L38-52

1 †Martin Goodwin	3 2 3 3 1	12	1
2 Mikael Teurnberg	0 1 0 T	1	1
3 Jens Rasmussen	3 1 1 1 2	8	
4 Jan Pedersen	2 1 1 2	6	1
5 Mark Courtney	1 2 1 N 0 0	4	1
6 Sean Courtney	2 0 1 T 0 2	5	
7 Robert Ledwith	0 2 N R	2	1

LONG EATON (H), September 20, W50-39

1 †Martin Goodwin	3 1 3 3 3	13	
2 Mikael Teurnberg	E 3 3 E	6	
3 Jens Rasmussen	1 3 3 3 1	11	
4 Jan Pedersen	R 3 0 0	3	
5 Mark Courtney	2 1 1 0	4	1
6 Robert Ledwith	3 0 0 N 0	3	
7 Sean Courtney	1 2 2 2 1 2	10	2

EDINBURGH (H), October 4, W53-37

1 †Martin Goodwin	3 fx3 2	8	
2 Sean Courtney	0 3 0 1	4	
3 Jens Rasmussen	fx3 2 3	8	1
4 Jan Pedersen	1 3 E 2	6	1
5 Mark Courtney	2 1 3 2 3	11	1
6 Robert Ledwith	3 3 1 0	7	
7 Mikael Teurnberg	1 3 3 1 1 0	9	2

PETERBOROUGH (H), October 11, W62-28

1 †Martin Goodwin	3 3 2 2	10	1
2 Sean Courtney	2 1 2 1	6	3
3 Jens Rasmussen	2 3 3 3 2	13	1
4 Jan Pedersen	1 3 3 3 3	13	
5 Mark Courtney	3 1 3 2	9	1
6 Robert Ledwith	0 0 0 N	0	
7 Mikael Teurnberg	3 3 2 2 1	11	2

EXETER (H), October 18, W55-35

1 †Martin Goodwin	3 fx2 3 2	10	2
2 Mikael Teurnberg	0 3 2 3	8	
3 Jens Rasmussen	**3 3 3 3 3**	**15**	
4 Jan Pedersen	1 2 2 3	8	2
5 Mark Courtney	2 0 3 1	6	
6 Robert Ledwith	3 1 1 0 2	7	1
7 Chris Young	1 R 0 N	1	

Stoke (A), October 31, L33-57

1 †Martin Goodwin	2 0 N N	2	
2 Sean Courtney	0 1 3 R 2 1	7	1
3 Jens Rasmussen	2 1 1 R	4	
4 Jan Pedersen	2 1 0 1 2 2	8	
5 Mark Courtney	0 0 T 0	0	
6 Mikael Teurnberg	3 3 1 N 2 0 2	11	
7 Robert Ledwith	1 0 N 0	1	

The away match at Glasgow was never staged because of bad weather. The original staging of the match on July 17 was abandoned at the start of heat 12 because of heavy rain. Scorers were: GLASGOW 39.5 RYE HOUSE 26.5 (†Martin Goodwin 2-3-X-X- 5, Sean Courtney 1-0-2-2-2- 7:1, Jens Rasmussen 1-2-1.5-N-4.5, Jan Pedersen 1-0- 1:1, Mark Courtney 2-3-3- 8, Mikael Teurnberg 1-0-T-N-1, Chris Young 0-0-T-0-N- 0).

At-a-Glance Results

Berwick	W46-44	L38-52	84-96
Edinburgh	W53-37	W46-43	99-80
Exeter	W55-35	L33-56	88-91
Glasgow	W47-43	*not raced*	–
Long Eaton	W50-39	L27-63	77-102
Middlesbrough	W52-35	W53-37	105-72
Newcastle	W48-41	L33-57	81-98
Peterborough	W62-28	L40-50	102-78
Sheffield	W59-31	L32-58	91-89
Stoke	W51-39	L33-57	84-96

■ ***The away match against Glasgow was never staged and the Speedway Control Board ordered one point to each team but the bonus point was not awarded.***

WHO WAS WHO IN '92

Wayne BAXTER
Born: November 19, 1964, Adelaide, South Australia.
Younger brother of former Rockets' favourite Glen. He began the season at reserve but was dropped when Jens Rasmussen returned from injury.

Mark Vincent COURTNEY
Born: March 25, 1961, Braintree, Essex.
A shock eve-of-season signed from Berwick who was deprived of a fifth successive season as a Division Two everpresent when he hurt his back in a crash at home to Middlesbrough early in August.

Sean Joseph COURTNEY
Born: September 5, 1964, Braintree, Essex.
Agreed to join the Rockets on loan from Glasgow the same day that his elder brother Mark signed for the club.

Martin GOODWIN
Born: January 15, 1960, Pembury, Kent.
Missed only two League matches after suffering internal injuries in a crash at Newcastle in his second season at Hoddesdon and an unlucky faller in the Division Two Riders' Championship.

Robert Tience LEDWITH
Born: November 10, 1971, Forest Gate, London.
Former British Schoolboy Grass Track Champion who joined the Rockets on loan from First Division Arena Essex, making an impressive debut in August. Held onto a reserve team berth for the remainder of the season. Also rode for Arena in Division One.

Trevor O'BRIEN
Born: November 17, 1966, Tennent Creek, Northern Territory, Australia.
He was on his way to enjoying his best ever British season when he broke a thigh in the Westernapolis at Exeter on July 13. The injury kept him out for the rest of the season.

Jan PEDERSEN
Born: July 27, 1967, Brondekilde, Denmark.
On loan from sister First Division track Arena Essex.

Jens RASMUSSEN
Born: May 26, 1959, Odense, Denmark.
Made a hugely successful comeback after being out for a long spell with a broken leg sustained against Long Eaton in August, 1991. He returned to action in May and was an everpresent in the League.

Mikael TEURNBERG
Born: December 26, 1966, Hallstavik, Sweden.
Swedish international who made his British bow for Mildenhall after impressing during Rospiggarna's early season tour. Moved to Hoddesdon when the Fen Tigers closed down and rounded off a successful debut campaign with 16 points in the Phonesport Knock Out Cup Final.

Christopher YOUNG
Born: June 6, 1968, South Norwood, London.
Joined the Rockets on loan from Arena Essex and broke into the first team after a string of high-scoring performances in the Reserve League. Lost his team place to Robert Ledwith.

Tigers tale of doom

FOLLOWING the euphoria surrounding the return of the sport to Owlerton in 1991, former road racer turned promoter Cliff Carr ran into all sorts of financial problems in his second year.

Cash headaches piled up on him from the very beginning and with the BSPA threatening to withdraw his licence, he sold the promotional rights mid-term to a new consortium.

The writing was on the wall for Carr even before a wheel had been turned in anger on the track. He decided that Lars Gunnestad wouldn't be lining up for the Tigers for a second season despite a superb first year in British racing. Put quite simply he was a luxury Sheffield couldn't afford.

Loanees Ian Barney, Richie Musson and Richard Davison also failed to earn a recall, Carr preferring to rely on his own contracted riders. Louis and Peter Carr together with Neil Evitts were back to form a solid heat leader trio; Simon Green confirmed his return to fitness after recovering from the injuries that so nearly cost him his life; and Mark Hepworth was expected to continue the improvement he had shown the previous year.

The only new face belonged to Aussie Steve Johnston and with Carr convinced that he would be eligible for a two point assessed average in view of his British parentage, the search was on for another quality rider to complete the side.

That search was brought to an abrupt end when the authorities insisted that Johnston's average would be assessed at 7.00.

Another major pre-season problem arose when the City Council informed Carr that the entire track fence would have to be replaced to comply with safety standards. Delays to that work caused the cancellation of the first two scheduled home meetings and involved expense that the club could well have done without.

Not surprisingly the Tigers looked somewhat rusty when they did eventually take to the track but they soon slipped into the groove at home although their weakness at the bottom end was evident on their travels.

The heat leaders were doing their job but changes were obviously necessary particularly at reserve. Carr kept faith with Johnston who was struggling to adapt to British conditions at this early stage but axed reserve David Wolstenholme.

Coming in to replace him was teenager Steve Knott who had produced some impressive performances early on for the reserve side.

June was the crunch month: the cash flow problem was not helped at all by the fact that the Tigers had five away fixtures to fulfil and just three at home. With the situation regarding the finances becoming common knowledge team spirit suffered when it was announced that Carr had put the club up for sale.

By the time he sold out to the new consortium headed by Tim Lucking and Neil Machin, the Tigers were out of contention in all the major competitions. Rye House had dumped them out of the Phonesport Knock Out Cup; Kings Lynn proved far too strong for them in the BSPA Cup; and they had failed to qualify for the H.E.A.T. Team Championship Final.

Undeterred the new consortium immediately set about turning the season around and replaced Hepworth with Frenchman Thierry Hilaire. That move failed miserably but their next signing proved infinitely better. Tony Langdon, dropped by Poole, was persuaded to make the long journey north to join the Tigers on loan and immediately helped his new club to their first away success at Middlesbrough. Confidence was growing in the camp but a dispute developed between the club and Neil Evitts led to the former British Champion sitting out the rest of the season and the Tigers operating rider replacement in his absence.

Machin and Lucking stuck to their guns refusing to capitulate to the rider's demands. And they worked extremely hard behind the scenes to improve crowds with the Sheffield supporters rallying to the cause.

1992 RIDER ROSTER

	Club Record								Career Record							
	M	R	Pts	BP	TPts	Ave	F	P	M	R	Pts	BP	TPts	Ave	F	P
Louis Carr	43	194	290.0	29.0	319.0	6.577	1	1	**365**	**1539**	**2551.0**	**214.0**	**2765.0**	**7.186**	**21**	**16**
Peter Carr	43	223	490.0	35.0	525.0	9.417	3	8	**202**	**930**	**1674.0**	**123.0**	**1797.0**	**7.729**	**5**	**12**
Neil Evitts	36	171	406.0	11.0	417.0	9.754	13	0	95	402	748.0	50.0	798.0	7.940	15	0
Simon Green	24	96	94.0	15.0	109.0	4.542	0	0	119	508	515.0	78.0	593.0	4.669	0	0
Mark Hepworth	22	83	71.0	13.0	84.0	4.048	0	0	36	120	85.0	16.0	101.0	3.367	0	0
Thierry Hilaire	5	20	3.0	0.0	3.0	0.600	0	0	43	157	98.0	11.0	109.0	2.777	0	0
Rob Homer	5	18	6.0	2.0	8.0	1.778	0	0	5	18	6.0	2.0	8.0	1.778	0	0
Steve Johnston	22	99	84.0	14.0	98.0	3.960	0	0	22	99	84.0	14.0	98.0	3.960	0	0
Tony Langdon	8	43	92.0	7.0	99.0	9.209	1	1	96	481	791.0	122.0	913.0	7.593	1	5
Steve Knott	17	70	56.0	9.0	65.0	3.714	0	0	17	70	56.0	9.0	65.0	3.714	0	0
David Wolstenholme	4	12	4.0	1.0	5.0	1.667	0	0	5	14	5.0	1.0	6.0	1.714	0	0

SHEFFIELD

Promoters: Neil Machin and Tim Lucking.
Address: Owlerton Stadium, Penistone Road, Sheffield, South Yorkshire, S6 2DE.
Telephone: 0742 853142.
Information Line: 0891 800 602.
Track Length: 361 metres.
Track Record: 60.7 secs, Chris Morton (Belle Vue), August 29, 1988. Heat 6, Sheffield v Belle Vue, Cock of the North Trophy.
Seasons in Division Two: 2 (1991-92).
Division Two Record: Fifth, 1991.
Division Two Cup Record: Defeated first round, 1992.
Division Two Team Championship: Never qualified for the final.
Appearances: Louis Carr and Peter Carr, 43 (1991-92).
Points: Peter Carr, 525 (1991-92).
World Finalists: None.
Division Two Riders' Championship Finalists: Neil Evitts (1991), Peter Carr (1991), Tony Langdon (1992).
Other Honours: Division Three Champions, 1949.

Seasons in Division One: 24 (1965-1988).
Division One Record: Runners-up (2), 1973, 1985.
Speedway Star Cup Record: Winners (1), 1974. Runners-up (1), 1969.
Appearances: Reg Wilson, 469 (1969-1986).
Points: Reg Wilson, 3510.5 (1969-1986).
World Finalists: Jim Airey (1971), Shawn Moran (1984-85), Doug Wyer (1976).
Division One Riders' Championship Finalists: Jack Kitchen (1965), Charlie Monk (1968), Jim Airey (1969-70-71), Arnold Haley (1972-73), Bob Valentine (1974), Doug Wyer (1975-76-77-78), Shawn Moran (1981-82, 1984-85-86-87-88), David Bargh (1983), Kelly Moran (1987-88).

Stoke (A), April 25, L34-56

1 †Peter Carr	1 2 2 2 2	9	1
2 Simon Green	0 1 fx0	1	1
3 Neil Evitts	3 2 2 3 1	11	
4 §§Steve Johnston	0 0 0 0 0	0	
5 Louis Carr	3 2 fxR	5	
6 Mark Hepworth	3 0 T 2 1	6	
7 David Wolstenholme	1 0 T 1	2	

Berwick (A), May 9, L24-66

1 †Peter Carr	2 1 0 2 1 1	7	
2 Simon Green	1 R R R	1	1
3 Neil Evitts	1 1 2 2 R	6	
4 Steve Johnston	0 T 0 0	0	
5 Louis Carr	1 2 0 1 2 0	6	
6 §§Steve Knott	2 0 T 0	2	
7 Mark Hepworth	1 0 T 1	2	1

Edinburgh (A), May 29, L30-60

1 †Peter Carr	3 1 2 1 3 1	11	1
2 Simon Green	0 F F T	0	
3 Neil Evitts	2 2 1 3 1	9	
4 Steve Johnston	0 0 2 N	2	
5 Louis Carr	2 1 0 0 1 0	4	
6 Mark Hepworth	1 0 T 0	1	1
7 Steve Knott	2 0 1 0	3	1

EXETER (H), June 11, W51-38

1 †Peter Carr	**3 3 3 2 3**	**14**	**1**
2 Simon Green	2 0 2 2	6	2
3 Neil Evitts	**3 3 3 3**	**12**	
4 Louis Carr	0 1 3 2	6	
5 Steve Johnston	1 3 1 0 1	6	1
6 Mark Hepworth	R 2 0 E	2	1
7 Steve Knott	1 0 2 1 1	5	1

Glasgow (A), June 24, L32-58

1 †Peter Carr	1 1 2 3 fx	7	1
2 Simon Green	0 0 T 0	0	
3 Neil Evitts	3 3 3 2 1	12	1
4 Louis Carr	1 2 fxN 2 1	6	
5 Steve Johnston	0 0 2 0 0	2	
6 Mark Hepworth	0 0 N 1 T	1	
7 Steve Knott	2 1 T 0 1	4	

Newcastle (A), July 5, L32-58

1 †Peter Carr	3 1 2 3 2 1	12	1
2 Simon Green	0 0 T 0	0	
3 Neil Evitts	**3 3 3 3 3**	**15**	
4 Louis Carr	1 1 1 0 0	3	
5 Mark Hepworth	0 0 0 0	0	
6 Steve Johnston	0 0 0 1	1	
7 Steve Knott	1 0 T 0	1	

Rye House (A), July 12, L31-59

1 †Peter Carr	2 1 3 R 3 1	10	
2 Simon Green	1 0 0 3 2	6	1
3 Neil Evitts	fxN T T	0	
4 §Thierry Hilaire	0 0 fxR	0	
5 Louis Carr	1 2 1 0 3	7	
6 Steve Johnston	2 1 0 F	3	
7 Steve Knott	1 2 0 T 2 0	5	1

Long Eaton (A), July 15, L21-68

1 Peter Carr	2 fx3 2 2 3	12	
2 Simon Green	0 F 1 0 T R	1	
3 †Louis Carr	1 0 F 1 0	2	
4 Neil Evitts	*rider replacement*		
5 Thierry Hilaire	1 0 0 X	1	
6 Steve Johnston	0 1 1 F 1	3	
7 Steve Knott	1 0 T fx	1	
8 §§Rob Homer	1 0	1	

LONG EATON (H), JULY 16, D45-45

1 Peter Carr	3 3 R 3 3 3	15	
2 Thierry Hilaire	0 1 0 F	1	
3 Neil Evitts	*rider replacement*		
4 Simon Green	1 1 2 1 2	7	2
5 †Louis Carr	3 2 3 2 0 2	12	1
6 Steve Johnston	2 0 1 0	3	1
7 Steve Knott	3 1 2 0 1	7	1
8 Rob Homer	*did not ride*		

STOKE (H), July 23, W51-37

1 Peter Carr	**3 3 3 3 3**	**15**	
2 Simon Green	R 1 3 fx	4	
3 Neil Evitts	3 2 3 3	11	
4 Thierry Hilaire	F N fxN	0	
5 †Louis Carr	3 2 3 2 0	10	1
6 Steve Johnston	0 2 fx2 2	6	2
7 Steve Knott	2 0 1 2 R	5	1

PETERBOROUGH (H), July 30, L44-46

1 Peter Carr	2 3 3 2 3	13	1
2 Thierry Hilaire	0 0 X T	0	
3 Neil Evitts	3 3 3 3 3 E	15	
4 Simon Green	fx2 fx3 F	5	1
5 †Louis Carr	fnN R E 2	2	1
6 Steve Johnston	1 0 1 1 0	3	1
7 Steve Knott	2 1 1 T 0 2	6	

GLASGOW (H), August 6, W46-44

1 Peter Carr	3 3 3 R 3	12	
2 Steve Knott	0 1 1 1	3	
3 Neil Evitts	**3 3 3 3**	**12**	
4 Thierry Hilaire	0 fx1 N	1	
5 †Louis Carr	2 1 1 1 0	5	1
6 Steve Johnston	1 1 1 2 0	5	
7 Simon Green	3 3 1 1	8	

Middlesbrough (A), August 13, W46-43

1 Peter Carr	2 3 2 2 2 3	14	3
2 Steve Knott	0 0 0 T	0	
3 Neil Evitts	X 2 3 3 2	10	
4 §Tony Langdon	3 1 2 3 1	10	1
5 †Louis Carr	0 2 1 2	5	1
6 Steve Johnston	2 0 1 T 0 1	4	2
7 Simon Green	3 fxN N	3	

MIDDLESBROUGH (H), August 16, W63-27

1 Peter Carr	**3 3 3 2**	**11**	**1**
2 Steve Knott	1 1 1 2 0	5	2
3 Neil Evitts	**3 3 3 3**	**12**	
4 Tony Langdon	**2 3 3 3 3**	**14**	**1**
5 †Louis Carr	3 2 2 1	8	1
6 Steve Johnston	3 2 0 1 2	8	3
7 Simon Green	2 2 1 N	5	1

RYE HOUSE (H), August 20, W58-32

1 Peter Carr	3 2 R 2 2	9	2
2 Steve Knott	1 1 0 1	3	1
3 Neil Evitts	**3 3 3 3 3**	**15**	
4 Tony Langdon	**3 3 3 3**	**12**	
5 †Louis Carr	2 2 1 2	7	3
6 Steve Johnston	0 2 N 0	2	1
7 Simon Green	3 1 3 2 1	10	1

Peterborough (A), August 28, L41-49

1 Peter Carr	**3 3 3 3 3**	**15**	
2 Steve Knott	R fx0 T	0	
3 Neil Evitts	2 3 3 2 1	11	
4 Tony Langdon	2 1 2 0 1 0	6	1
5 †Louis Carr	3 0 0 1 T 2	6	1
6 Steve Johnston	2 0 0 T	2	
7 Simon Green	0 0 1 T	1	

BERWICK (H), September 10, W56-34

1 Peter Carr	**3 3 3 3 2**	**14**	**1**
2 Simon Green	0 1 2 1	4	
3 Neil Evitts	3 3 3 1 3	13	
4 Tony Langdon	3 3 2 R	8	1
5 †Louis Carr	2 2 0 3	7	2
6 Steve Johnston	2 2 1 3	8	1
7 Rob Homer	1 0 0 1	2	1

Exeter (A), September 14, L27-63

1 Peter Carr	1 R N T N	1	
2 Simon Green	0 0 T 3 0 1	4	
3 Neil Evitts	*rider replacement*		
4 Tony Langdon	2 1 3 3 2 3 0	14	
5 †Louis Carr	0 1 0 0 N 0	1	
6 Rob Homer	0 R 0 E 1	1	
7 Steve Johnston	2 1 1 1 1 T fx	6	
8 §§Rob Price	*0*	*0*	

NEWCASTLE (H), September 24, W52-38

1 Peter Carr	2 3 3 3 3 3	17	
2 Simon Green	0 1 3 2 2	8	1
3 Neil Evitts	*rider replacement*		
4 Tony Langdon	2 3 2 2 3 1	13	2
5 †Louis Carr	3 0 0 1 1	5	1
6 Steve Johnston	3 1 3 0 2	9	1
7 Rob Homer	R 0 0 N	0	
8 Dean Child	*did not ride*		

EDINBURGH (H), October 1, W53-37

1 Peter Carr	**3 3 3 3 3 2**	**17**	**1**
2 Simon Green	F 1 2 2	5	1
3 Neil Evitts	*rider replacement*		
4 Tony Langdon	1 3 3 2 3 3	15	1
5 †Louis Carr	3 0 1 2 1	7	
6 Steve Johnston	3 0 1 3 0	7	
7 Rob Homer	R 0 1 1	2	1
8 Dean Child	*did not ride*		

Mildenhall (A), June 7, L37-52

1 Rob Homer	R 0 T N	0	
2 Simon Green	2 2 2 0 2	8	
3 Neil Evitts	3 3 3 2 3	14	
4 †Louis Carr	1 2 0 1 1 2	7	2
5 Steve Johnston	2 1 2 1 0 0	6	1
6 Jason Gage	*1 0 T 0 T*	*1*	
7 Steve Knott	0 1 0 T	1	

At-a-Glance Results

Berwick	**W56-34**	**L24-66**	**80-100**
Edinburgh	**W53-37**	**L30-60**	**83-87**
Exeter	**W51-38**	**L27-63**	**78-101**
Glasgow	**W46-44**	**L32-56**	**78-100**
Long Eaton	**D45-45**	**L21-66**	**66-111**
Middlesbrough	**W63-27**	**W46-43**	**109-70**
Newcastle	**W52-38**	**L32-56**	**84-94**
Peterborough	**L44-46**	**L41-49**	**85-95**
Rye House	**W58-32**	**L31-59**	**89-91**
Stoke	**W51-37**	**L34-56**	**85-93**
Mildenhall		***L37-52***	

WHO WAS WHO IN '92

John Louis CARR
Born: January 28, 1960, Preston, Lancashire.
Took over as team skipper in July on the arrival of the new promoting team at Owlerton.

Peter CARR
Born: January 22, 1963, Preston, Lancashire.
Was unbeaten in five out of 10 home League matches and dropped only 12 League points at Owlerton – nine of them because of machine problems!

Dean Russell CHILD
Born: November 2, 1969, Morley, near Leeds, South Yorkshire.
Named as number eight in the Tigers' last two League matches of the season.

Neil EVITTS
Born: September 25, 1964, Birmingham West Midlands.
Walked out on the club in September after a contractual dispute. Before that he had been virtually unbeatable on his home track, dropping only six points in seven matches, including a tapes exclusion.

Simon Leslie GREEN
Born: November 8, 1969, Skipton, North Yorkshire.
Made a remarkable track return after the serious internal injuries which all but cost him his life following a crash in 1991.

Mark Alexander HEPWORTH
Born: September 22, 1967, Dewsbury, Yorkshire.
Axed by the new Sheffield promoters after missing the League match at Rye House because of a previously arranged trip to Poland to help England manager Eric Boocock in the World Under 21 qualifying round.

Thierry HILAIRE
Born: June 1, 1963, Suresnes, France.
Scored only three points in six matches for the Tigers after replacing Mark Hepworth as the first signing of the new promotion.

Robert (Rob) HOMER
Born: September 9, 1972, Birmingham, West Midlands.
Replaced injured reserve Steven Knott towards the end of the season after recovering from a serious back injury sustained in 1991. Son of former rider of the same name who rode for Birmingham and Scunthorpe in the early seventies.

Steven Paul JOHNSTON
Born: October 12, 1971, Kalgoorlie, Australia.
First season newcomer who made a favourable impression with his fighting spirit.

Steven Paul KNOTT
Born: March 29, 1975, Nocton Hall, near Lincoln, Lincolnshire.
Former Boston mascot who came through the ranks at Owlerton. Claimed a regular team place until he broke a collar bone towards the end of the season.

Anthony Michael (Tony) LANGDON
Born: June 20, 1969, Brisbane, Queensland, Australia.
Made an impressive return to the Second Division after being dropped by senior club Poole. Scored double figures in six of his eight League matches for the Tigers.

Robert Alan PRICE
Born: July 13, 1966, Birmingham, West Midlands.
Made a guest appearance for the Tigers as number eight at Exeter where he had been a member of their Reserve League side.

David WOLSTENHOLME
Born: July 30, 1973, Sheffield, South Yorkshire.
Had only limited team opportunities in the Gold Cup and subsequently moved to First Division Wolverhampton where he joined his elder brother Simon.

1992

SHEFFIELD

Back row: Simon Green, Neil Evitts, Louis Carr, Thierry Hilaire, Peter Carr, Steve Knott, Reg Wilson. Kneeling: Steve Johnston.

1992

STOKE

Left to right: Eric Monaghan, Andy Meredith, Gary Chessell, Nigel Crabtree, Garry Stead, Alan Grahame and Darren Standing.

Potters wheely struggle

IF EXPERIENCE is anything to go by Stoke should have romped to success in 1992 . In Alan Grahame, Nigel Crabtree and Eric Monaghan they boasted the most experienced heat leader trio anywhere in the second division.

Grahame had opted to sign for the Potters from Cradley Heath despite offers from several other clubs notably Long Eaton.

A new number one and a new team sponsor in the form of Mistral Boilers d gave promoter Dave Tattum every reason for confidence as he faced his second season at the helm of the club.

Gary Chessell and Garry Stead were expected to provide the necessary backing to the heat leaders and with Darren Standing at reserve there was every reason to believe that this might just be the Potters' year.

The Gold Cup campaign went according to plan – that is until the Final. Away victories in their group matches at Mildenhall and Milton Keynes meant that Stoke would reach the final IF they beat Peterborough by more than eight points at Loomer Road.

That target was achieved with ease as the Panthers were crushed 61-29 and the place in the Final was secured.

Any thoughts of celebrations went out the window six days later when Grahame crashed during the H.E.A.T. Team Championship qualifier at Peterborough sustaining back injuries that were to sideline him for nearly two months.

It was the second time that the Staffordshire club had gone home from Alwalton one rider light – reserve Ade Hoole broke his wrist their earlier in the season and that injury, arguably, was to cost him a regular team place for the first time in his career.

Gary Chessell too picked up an injury in the Fours when he crashed at Sheffield and collected an arm injury which was to rule him out for a month.

In their absence Newcastle warmed up for the Gold Cup Final by winning at Loomer Road in the League and the writing was on the wall.

Crowds began to dip and further financial strain was placed on the club when Reading visited in the BSPA Cup, making it a bumper pay-day with a 12 point win.

As Chessell returned, Standing replaced him on the sidelines having sustained a neck injury in the away League defeat at Newcastle.

Effectively his season was over – he tried an abortive track return – and Tattum moved swiftly to sign David Steen from the defunct Milton Keynes outfit to replace him.

Another home loss – this time against Glasgow – and defeats at Sheffield and Long Eaton left the Mistral Potters rooted to the bottom of the League table and it was hardly any consolation that they had ridden fewer matches than any of their Division Two rivals.

That was hardly the best of preparation for the Gold Cup Final and while Grahame returned in time for that, Newcastle easily won both legs to claim the trophy.

The 16 point defeat in the home leg hurt Tattum deeply. He said: "We just didn't rise to the occasion – none of our riders seemed to want to compete."

At least the consolation was the largest attendance of the season although Tattum admitted that the average gate at that stage was somewhere in the region of 250 down on 1991 levels.

It was obvious that he was feeling the pinch trying to balance the books at Stoke and combine that with running a business outside the sport.

He stuck by his team though who completed a fighting Phonesport Knock Out Cup victory over Exeter before losing out to Berwick in the quarter final.

The only thing left for the Potters by that stage was to avoid the wooden spoon in the League and avoid it they did winning their last six home matches on the trot.

The loss of Grahame and Chessell through injury within days of each other was obviously the turning point in a season that, until then, had promised a great deal.

Tattum admitted towards the end of the season that promoting speedway by himself at Loomer Road had taken it's toll and that he would need help if he were to continue – or be allowed to continue after the SCB annulled his retained list because of his mounting debts.

1992 RIDER ROSTER

	M	R	Pts	BP	TPts	Ave	F	P	**M**	**R**	**Pts**	**BP**	**TPts**	**Ave**	**F**	**P**
Gary Chessell	44	194	291.0	40.0	331.0	6.825	0	1	189	758	964.0	156.0	1120.0	5.910	0	2
Nigel Crabtree	276	1329	2945.0	143.0	3088.0	9.294	33	22	444	2012	3942.0	294.0	4236.0	8.421	37	23
Alan Grahame	16	78	150.0	13.0	163.0	8.359	1	1	76	294	489.0	58.0	547.0	7.442	5	6
Ade Hoole	6	16	6.0	1.0	7.0	1.750	0	0	18	55	32.0	6.0	38.0	2.764	0	0
Andy Meredith	22	74	51.0	13.0	64.0	3.459	0	0	22	74	51.0	13.0	64.0	3.459	0	0
Eric Monaghan	116	605	1204.0	79.0	1283.0	8.483	5	6	345	1584	2653.0	285.0	2938.0	7.419	5	17
Darren Standing	32	126	131.0	25.0	156.0	4.952	0	0	145	529	503.0	114.0	617.0	4.665	0	0
Garry Stead	48	217	246.0	45.0	291.0	5.364	0	0	48	217	246.0	45.0	291.0	5.364	0	0
David Steen	17	69	83.0	15.0	98.0	5.681	0	0	30	115	128.0	27.0	155.0	5.391	0	0

STOKE

Promoter: David Tattum.
Address: Newcastle Stadium, Loomer Road, Newcastle-under-Lyme, Staffordshire.
Telephone: 0782-561575.
Information Line: 0891 31 21 49.
Track Length: 336.5 metres.
Track Record: 59.1 secs, Andrew Silver (Arena Essex), August 8, 1987, heat 1, Stoke v Arena Essex (Division Two).
Seasons in Division Two: 20 (1973-1992).
Division Two Record: Third (2), 1975, 1984.
Division Two Cup Record: Semi-finalists, 1987.
Division Two Team Championship: Winners (1), 1990. Runners-up (3), 1978, 1984, 1989. Fourth (3), 1977, 1980, 1985. Qualified (9), 1977, 1978, 1980, 1984, 1985, 1986, 1988, 1989, 1990.
Gold Cup: Finalists (1), 1992. Southern Section Winners (1), 1992.
National Series: Third (1), 1990.
Appearances: Nigel Crabtree, 276 (1984-1992).
Points: Nigel Crabtree, 3088 (1984-1992).
World Finalists: None.
Division Two Riders' Championship Finalists: Mike Broadbank (1973-74), Alan Molyneux (1975), Les Collins (1976), Stuart Mountford (1977), Tony Lomas (1978), Ian Gledhill (1979), Tom Owen (1983-84-85), Paul Thorp (1986), Nigel Crabtree (1987, 1989), Graham Jones (1988), Eric Monaghan (1990-91), Alan Grahame (1992).
Other Honours: Division Three Champions, 1949.

SHEFFIELD (H), April 25, W56-34

1 §Alan Grahame	**3 3 3 2 3**	**14**	**1**
2 Gary Chessell	2 1 3 2	8	2
3 †Nigel Crabtree	1 3 3 3 2	12	2
4 Eric Monaghan	2 3 3 3	11	
5 Darren Standing	1 X 1 1	3	1
6 Garry Stead	2 2 1 0	5	
7 §§Andy Meredith	0 1 1 1	3	

Edinburgh (A), May 15, L44-46

1 Alan Grahame	3 2 3 2 1	11	1
2 Gary Chessell	0 R 1 1	2	
3 †Nigel Crabtree	2 3 F 1 3	9	1
4 Eric Monaghan	2 3 2 3 3 3	16	
5 Darren Standing	F 1 0 X	1	
6 Garry Stead	0 0 T 3	3	
7 Andy Meredith	1 1 T 0	2	1

Glasgow (A), May 27, L38-51

1 Alan Grahame	3 3 2 2 3 1	14	1
2 Gary Chessell	0 1 0 3	4	
3 †Nigel Crabtree	1 3 2 1 2 0	9	2
4 Eric Monaghan	1 2 2 0 2	7	
5 Darren Standing	0 1 0 T	1	1
6 §Ade Hoole	1 N F 0	1	
7 Andy Meredith	0 2 0 T T	2	

NEWCASTLE (H), June 20, L43-47

1 Alan Grahame	*rider replacement*		
2 Ade Hoole	0 N 2 3 0	5	1
3 †Nigel Crabtree	2 3 2 1 3 3	14	
4 Eric Monaghan	1 2 3 1 2 0	9	
5 Darren Standing	E 1 1 0 1	3	
6 Garry Stead	1 1 0 1 3 0	6	2
7 Andy Meredith	3 0 fn3 0	6	
8 Mark Walsh	*did not ride*		

Berwick (A), June 27, L30-60

1 Alan Grahame	*rider replacement*		
2 Ade Hoole	R 0 N 0	0	
3 †Nigel Crabtree	2 3 2 1 1 0 0	9	
4 Eric Monaghan	1 2 3 2 1 2 2	13	
5 Darren Standing	0 0 0 0	0	
6 Garry Stead	2 0 2 0 2	6	
7 Andy Meredith	1 0 1 F	2	2
8 Mark Walsh	*did not ride*		

BERWICK (H), June 28, W47-43

1 Alan Grahame	*rider replacement*		
2 Ade Hoole	0 0 N T	0	
3 †Nigel Crabtree	3 2 3 3 3 3 3	20	
4 Eric Monaghan	1 fx2 3 3 1	10	
5 Darren Standing	0 3 0 1 1	5	
6 Garry Stead	3 1 2 1 2	9	2
7 Andy Meredith	1 fxfx0 2	3	1
8 Mark Walsh	*did not ride*		

Newcastle (A), July 12, L39-50

1 Gary Chessell	1 1 2 1 R 0	5	1
2 Alan Grahame	*rider replacement*		
3 †Nigel Crabtree	0 3 3 3 1 1	11	2
4 Eric Monaghan	0 3 2 3 2 3	13	
5 Garry Stead	1 0 1 0 2 1 1	6	1
6 Darren Standing	fnT N T	0	
7 Andy Meredith	2 0 2 E	4	
8 Ade Hoole	*did not ride*		

GLASGOW (H), July 18, L42-47

1 Gary Chessell	1 1 3 3 fx1	9	1
2 Alan Grahame	*rider replacement*		
3 †Nigel Crabtree	3 2 1 3 3 2	14	1
4 Eric Monaghan	1 2 2 0 X 2 3	10	1
5 §David Steen	F 1 N N	1	1
6 Garry Stead	3 0 2 0 N 1 1	7	
7 Andy Meredith	1 T 0 T 0	1	
8 Ade Hoole	*did not ride*		

Sheffield (A), July 23, L37-51

1 Gary Chessell	1 1 1 N	3	1
2 Alan Grahame	*rider replacement*		
3 †Nigel Crabtree	2 1 2 1 fx3	9	
4 Eric Monaghan	2 3 3 2 1 R 1	12	1
5 David Steen	1 1 0 2 N 2	6	1
6 Andy Meredith	1 0 0 N	1	
7 Garry Stead	3 0 2 1 0 0	6	1
8 Ade Hoole	*did not ride*		

Long Eaton (A), July 29, L31-59

1 Gary Chessell	2 1 3 1 R T	7	
2 Alan Grahame	*rider replacement*		
3 †Nigel Crabtree	0 R 2 3 1 R R	6	
4 Eric Monaghan	2 0 2 2 3 1	10	
5 David Steen	1 0 2 0 R	3	1
6 Andy Meredith	0 0 T 1	1	
7 Garry Stead	2 1 0 1	4	1
8 Ade Hoole	*did not ride*		

Middlesbrough (A), August 6, L41-48

1 Alan Grahame	fx0 1 T	1	
2 Gary Chessell	2 1 1 3 1	8	
3 †Nigel Crabtree	3 1 3 3 2 2	14	
4 Eric Monaghan	2 2 2 2 3 0	11	1
5 Garry Stead	X 1 fx2	3	2
6 David Steen	1 0 T 3	4	
7 Andy Meredith	0 F T 0	0	

Rye House (A), August 9, L39-51

1 Alan Grahame	0 0 1 3	4	1
2 Gary Chessell	2 3 2 0 2	9	1
3 †Nigel Crabtree	3 3 3 0 2 2	13	
4 Eric Monaghan	2 2 1 0 1	6	1
5 Garry Stead	0 fx1 2	3	1
6 David Steen	3 F 1 N	4	
7 Andy Meredith	0 0 T T fx	0	

Exeter (A), August 17, L29-61

1 Alan Grahame	1 0 3 2 0	6	
2 Gary Chessell	0 1 2 1 1	5	
3 †Nigel Crabtree	3 R 1 T	4	
4 Eric Monaghan	0 0 0 1 0	1	1
5 Garry Stead	1 2 1 2 2 1	9	1
6 David Steen	2 0 2 fxN 0	4	
7 Darren Standing	R N N N	0	

PETERBOROUGH (H), September 5, W56-34

1 Alan Grahame	**3 3 3 3 3**	**15**	
2 Gary Chessell	2 2 2 2	8	3
3 †Nigel Crabtree	1 3 3 3 2	12	2
4 Eric Monaghan	2 fxN N	2	
5 Garry Stead	1 3 2 1	7	1
6 David Steen	fx2 1 1 F 3	7	1
7 Andy Meredith	1 1 1 2	5	2

MIDDLESBROUGH (H), September 12, W53-37

1 Alan Grahame	1 3 3 2 2	11	2
2 Gary Chessell	2 2 3 3 fx	10	1
3 Nigel Crabtree	2 3 3 2 2 2	14	1
4 Eric Monaghan	*rider replacement*		
5 Garry Stead	3 1 3 0 0	7	
6 David Steen	2 2 2 2 1 2	11	4
7 Andy Meredith	0 0 fnN	0	
8 Ade Hoole	0	0	

LONG EATON (H), September 26, W54-34

1 Alan Grahame	2 fx3 3 3 1	12	
2 Gary Chessell	0 2 3 2 0	7	2
3 †Nigel Crabtree	**3 3 3 3 3 3**	**18**	
4 Eric Monaghan	*rider replacement*		
5 Garry Stead	2 2 2 1 2	9	1
6 David Steen	3 1 0 0	4	
7 Andy Meredith	1 1 2 fx	4	1
8 Ade Hoole	*did not ride*		

Peterborough (A), October 3, L28-62

1 Alan Grahame	3 0 2 1 1 1 3	11	1
2 Gary Chessell	R 1 0 0	1	1
3 †Nigel Crabtree	1 1 2 0	4	
4 Eric Monaghan	*rider replacement*		
5 Garry Stead	1 2 1 2 1 0 0	7	
6 David Steen	3 0 1 0 1	5	1
7 Andy Meredith	0 0 T 0	0	
8 Ade Hoole	*did not ride*		

EXETER (H), October 10, W65-25

1 Alan Grahame	3 3 2 2	10	1
2 Gary Chessell	**2 2 3 3 2**	**12**	**3**
3 †Nigel Crabtree	**3 3 3 3 3**	**15**	
4 Eric Monaghan	2 3 0 2	7	1
5 David Steen	3 2 1 1	7	1
6 Garry Stead	3 1 1 3	8	
7 Andy Meredith	2 1 2 1	6	3

EDINBURGH (H), October 17, W50-40

1 Alan Grahame	1 2 2 3	8	1
2 Gary Chessell	2 1 fx0	3	1
3 †Nigel Crabtree	**3 3 3 3 2**	**14**	**1**
4 Eric Monaghan	**3 3 2 3 3**	**14**	**1**
5 David Steen	fx0 0 N	0	
6 Garry Stead	3 0 1 2 0	6	
7 Andy Meredith	2 2 1 0	5	1

RYE HOUSE (H), October 31, W57-33

1 Alan Grahame	3 2 3 3 3	14	
2 Gary Chessell	1 0 2 1	4	
3 †Nigel Crabtree	1 2 3 3 fx	9	1
4 Eric Monaghan	1 3 1 3	8	
5 David Steen	3 2 2 1	8	2
6 Garry Stead	2 3 3 3 2 1	14	1
7 Andy Meredith	0 F N N	0	

At-a-Glance Results

Berwick	W47-43	L30-60	77-103
Edinburgh	W50-40	L44-46	94-86
Exeter	W65-25	L29-61	94-86
Glasgow	L42-47	L38-51	80-98
Long Eaton	W54-34	L31-59	85-93
Middlesbrough	W53-37	L41-48	94-85
Newcastle	L43-47	L39-50	82-97
Peterborough	W56-34	L28-62	84-96
Rye House	W57-33	L39-51	96-84
Sheffield	W56-34	L37-51	93-85

WHO WAS WHO IN '92

Gary CHESSELL
Born: January 20, 1965, Ludlow, Shropshire.
Spent his second season at Loomer Road.

Nigel Robin CRABTREE
Born: March 15, 1960, Halifax, South Yorkshire.
An everpresent for the Mistral Boilers Potter in his ninth successive season with the club.

Alan William GRAHAME
Born: February 5, 1954, Birmingham, West Midlands.
A surprise winter signing after being transfer listed by First Division Cradley Heath. Missed seven successive League matches with a back injury.

Adrian Leslie (Ade) HOOLE
Born: August 28, 1970, Telford, Shropshire.
Started the season at reserve but lost his place after fracturing his wrist in an early season crash at Peterborough – the club he had originally agreed to join before being displaced by the signing of Jason Crump.

Andrew Colin MEREDITH
Born: December 28, 1973, Bradford, Yorkshire.
Joined the Potters as a reserve replacement for the injured Ade Hoole during their Gold Cup campaign and went on to become a regular first team choice.

Eric MONAGHAN
Born: October 31, 1957, Higher Whitley, Cheshire.
Broke his collar bone against Peterborough in September and missed three matches which prevented him having his third everpresent season at Loomer Road.

Darren STANDING
Born: June 20, 1969, Southampton, Hampshire.
Injured at Newcastle in July, he made an abortive comeback a nearly six weeks later but was forced to pull out after only one ride with spinal pain. He then missed the rest of the season.

Garry STEAD
Born: January 5, 1972, Meltham, Yorkshire.
Maintained his steady improvement with performances which certainly caught the eye of admiring rival promoters.

David Roscoe STEEN
Born: March 12, 1966, Maidstone, Kent.
Came into the side as a replacement for the injured Darren Standing against Glasgow in July and remained in the side for the rest of the summer. Had started off the season at Milton Keynes.

Mark Damian WALSH
Born: September 11, 1973, Middleton, Greater Manchester.
Son of Manchester businessman Peter Walsh, the guiding light behind attempts to stage speedway at Oldham. He had three meetings as the Potters number eight.

Dick's dream is broken

FORMER rider Dick Partridge had a dream. That was to bring speedway back to Mildenhall and he moved heaven and earth to make that dream come true only for it to turn into a nightmare.

For two years, having acquired the lease at West Row, he worked day and night at the stadium giving it a face-lift and introducing greyhound racing there for the first time.

Partridge felt that the revenue generated from that activity would subsidise any losses that may have been incurred running speedway in one of East Anglia's backwaters with the nearest substantial town a good 15 minute's drive away from West Row.

Joining forces with former Norwich second half rider Derek Hewitt, he submitted an application to join Division Two and that was gratefully accepted by the British Speedway Promoters' Association as it opened the door and enabled Swindon to get their wish of staying in Division One.

Having got the go ahead there was the small matter of putting together a team – and very little time in which to do so with the start of the season a mere seven weeks away.

David Smart and Nigel Leaver were the first riders put on contract and, after much speculation, Melvyn Taylor finally agreed to return to his roots and his hometown track.

Jamie Habbin was also snapped up together with Gary Tagg but two riders were still required as the season opened on March 22.

A reported 1,500 crowd flocked to the opener – the Autovalet Trophy – if only they had all returned each week the subsequent problems would never have arisen. Even two thirds of that opening Sunday crowd would have been enough to have kept the track afloat.

For the first team match – a challenge against powerful Swedish tourists Rospiggarna – guests Ian Barney and Savalas Clouting were drafted in. The visitors won that by four points with Mikael Teurnberg heading their scorechart and impressing Partridge no end.

Barney was signed on a month's loan from Exeter (via Milton Keynes) and, at last, the Fen Tigers had seven contracted riders when Jesper Olsen was signed, again on loan, from Eastbourne.

The plan had been to include the highly talented Clouting but his inclusion in the side would have dropped the Fen Tigers below the minimum points limit.

A shock win at Peterborough in the Gold Cup, after the Evening Telegraph Panthers had won the match at West Row, gave cause for optimism but the home attendances were already beginning to worry Partridge.

Undeterred he signed Teurnberg and Barney was the man to make way for the talented Swede. In only his third match for the club a paid 14 return helped the Fen Tigers to a mammoth 18-point Gold Cup victory at Rye House and that despite Gary Tagg refusing to ride after his mechanic had been refused admission to the stadium.

Partridge immediately slapped a three match suspension on Tagg and fined him in the process.

Not surprisingly mighty Oxford came, saw and conquered in the BSPA Cup and much money was lost on that particular fixture despite an increased attendance on earlier weeks.

A rift developed between Hewitt and Partridge although both remained tight-lipped on the situation. It soon became apparent though that the latter was now on his own.

It all proved too much for him with speedway attendances not matching the break-even figure and greyhound racing attendances proving even more disastrous.

He pulled the plug on both activities in mid-June and while there was some talk of former King's Lynn rider Graham Edmunds mounting a rescue operation, Mildenhall shut for good on Friday, July 3.

Two years of effort had ended with Partridge literally running out of money but, unlike other promotions, he didn't leave any outstanding debts.

He refused to be bitter though saying: "There simply weren't enough people coming through the turnstiles - it's a shame it didn't work."

MILDENHALL

Promoters: Derek Hewitt and Dick Partridge.
Address: Mildenhall Stadium, Hayland Drove, West Row, Mildenhall, Suffolk, IP28 8QU.
Telephone: 0638 711777.
Information Line: 0891 312144.
Track Length: 285 metres.
Track Record: 50.4 secs, Hans Nielsen (Oxford), May 10, 1992, Heat 1, Mildenhasll v Oxford, BSPA Cup.
Seasons in Division Two: 15 (1975-1989). ■ Mildenhall were expelled from the 1990 Second Division. They started the 1992 Second Division season but withdrew because of financial problems and all League results were expunged from the records.
Division Two Record: Champions (1), 1979. Runners-up (4), 1982, 1983, 1984, 1987.
Division Two Cup Record: Runners-up (2), 1986, 1987.
Division Two Team Championship: Winners (2), 1984, 1987. Runners-up (4), 1979, 1982, 1983, 1988. Finalists (8), 1979, 1981, 1982, 1983, 1984, 1986, 1987, 1988
Appearances: Robert Henry, 432 (1976-1986).
Points: Robert Henry, 3465.5 (1976-1986).
World Finalists: None.
Division Two Riders' Championship Finalists: Bob Coles (1975-76-77), Ray Bales (1978-79-80), Ian Gledhill (1981), Derek Harrison (1982), Richard Knight (1983), Carl Baldwin (1984-85), Dave Jessup (1986-87), Melvyn Taylor (1988), Preben Eriksen (1989).

1992 RIDER ROSTER

	Club Record								Career Record							
	M	R	Pts	BP	TPts	Ave	F	P	M	R	Pts	BP	TPts	Ave	F	P
Jamie Habbin									199	802	1013.0	128.0	1141.0	5.691	0	2
Nigel Leaver									147	700	850.0	166.0	1016.0	5.806	1	3
Jesper Olsen									11	51	54.0	7.0	61.0	4.784	0	0
David Smart									177	764	1164.5	142.0	1306.5	6.840	0	2
Gary Tagg									93	425	491.0	102.0	593.0	5.581	0	1
Melvyn Taylor	228	991	2115.0	120.0	2235.0	9.021	22	12	295	1330	2758.0	141.0	2899.0	8.719	23	12
Mikael Teurnberg									19	86	124.0	16.0	140.0	6.512	0	0
Jason Gage	3	11	6	4	10.0	3.636	0	0	0	0	0	0	0.0	n.a.	0	0

LONG EATON (H), May 24, W48-39

1 †David Smart	2 2 1 2 1	8	
2 Nigel Leaver	0 **1** 3 3	7	1
3 Melvyn Taylor	**2** 1 3 3 0	9	1
4 Gary Tagg	2 2 **1** 2	7	1
5 Mikael Teurnberg	0 **1** 3 1	5	1
6 Jamie Habbin	3 3 3 0	9	
7 Jason Gage	F **2** 0 **1**	3	2

Berwick (A), May 30, L22-68

1 †David Smart	1 2 2 1 1 1	8	
2 Jason Gage	0 0 T 0 0	0	
3 Melvyn Taylor	2 2 2 1 1 0	8	
4 Gary Tagg	1 F T T	1	
5 Mikael Teurnberg	0 2 2 N 0	4	
6 Jamie Habbin	0 0 0 0 0 T	0	
7 Jesper Olsen	1 0 F N	1	

GLASGOW (H), May 31, D45-45

1 †David Smart	3 1 0 2	6	
2 Nigel Leaver	**2** 3 2 3 1	11	1
3 Melvyn Taylor	3 **1** 2 **1** 0	7	2
4 Gary Tagg	fx1 **1** 1	3	1
5 Mikael Teurnberg	1 0 3 2	6	
6 Jamie Habbin	3 **2** 2 **2** R	9	2
7 Jason Gage	**2** F **1** N	3	2

SHEFFIELD (H), June 7, W52-37

1 †David Smart	3 **1** X 2	6	1
2 Nigel Leaver	fx2 3 3	8	
3 Melvyn Taylor	2 3 3 3 1	12	
4 Gary Tagg	0 1 0 1	2	
5 Mikael Teurnberg	3 3 **1** **2** 3	12	2
6 Jamie Habbin	3 R 0 2	5	
7 Jesper Olsen	**2** 1 1 3	7	1

At-a-Glance Results

Berwick		**L22-68**
Glasgow	**D45-45**	
Long Eaton	**W48-39**	
Sheffield	**W52-37**	

The above results were expunged from the League records.

WHO WAS WHO IN '92

Ian BARNEY – see Peterborough

Jason GAGE – see King's Lynn

Jamie HABBIN – see Coventry

Nigel LEAVER – see Wolverhampton

Jesper OLSEN – see Glasgow

David SMART – see Swindon

Gary Edward TAGG
Born: February 7, 1969, Wokingham, Berkshire.
Unable to claim a team place after Mildenhall's enforced closure. Had trials at King's Lynn but was not offered a contract. Had upset the Mildenhall management when he refused to race at Rye House and served a subsequent suspension.

Melvyn Roy TAYLOR
Born: April 26, 1961, West Row, Suffolk.
Resisted approached from a couple of clubs to continue racing after Mildenhall's closure. Had joined the Fen Tigers from Rye House at the beginning of the season.

Mikael TEURNBERG – see Rye House

1992

MILDENHALL

Back row: Ian Barney, Gary Tagg, Dick Partridge (co-promoter), Melvyn Taylor, Nigel Leaver. Front: Jamie Habbin, David Smart and Jesper Olsen.

Knights call it a day at last!

PROMOTING speedway at Milton Keynes has always been a struggle against the odds and those odds finally became too much even for a new-look regime which promised to ignore some of the excesses of the past.

After the running battles then-promoter Terry Cheney had with officialdom throughout 1991 there were serious doubts over Milton Keynes opening in 1992.

Cheney made it clear during the close season that he was looking for someone else to take over the running of the sport at Elfield Park but there seemed to be no takers.

That is until Exeter boss Colin Hill, together with Roger Jones, stepped in at the last minute much to everyone's relief – not just in Milton Keynes but at the British Speedway Promoters' Association headquarters in nearby Rugby for it enabled Swindon to retain their First Division status.

The turn out at a public meeting called by the new promoters was described as 'very encouraging' by the duo who set about the task of putting together a side in a very short space of time.

Veterans Gordon Kennett, Richard Hellsén and Peter Glanz were signed in a matter of days to provide a backbone of vast experience.

They were quickly followed by Ian Barney, Dave Steen and Lars Munkedal. Justin Walker and Frank Smart were the last two riders added to give the squad quite a solid look even if it did wear the look of a well-worn salesman.

Barney was the man to miss out at the start of the season (he moved to another of the troubled tracks Mildenhall) but it wasn't on-track results that were hogging the headlines in Buckinghamshire – it was what was happening off track.

Arguments and counter-arguments had soon developed between tenants and landlord over facilities, or rather the lack of progress in providing them at Elfield Park.

It was hardly a conducive atmosphere for the team to produce the goods on the track and the only bright spot on that score was a three point home victory over Exeter in the Gold Cup.

That was the last meeting for Munkedal whose request for more money was turned down prompting him to return home to Denmark.

Crowd levels were obviously a concern to Messrs Hill and Jones and a hefty 33 point home defeat at the hands of Arena-Essex in the BSPA Cup was little more than a financial disaster for them.

Speedway Control Board Manager John Eglese had already visited Elfield Park concerned about reports on track preparation and facilities especially after referee David Hughes had called off the proposed match on April 28 despite dry weather all day long.

The home Gold Cup match against Peterborough again ran into problems. The start time having to be put back by referee Frank Ebdon while the track was watered, with Peterborough's James Easter giving a hand with the all but ineffective hose!

A week later the re-arranged match against Long Eaton was called because of problems and enough was enough for the powers that be.

The SCB issued a statement to the effect that both the track and promoting licences were being suspended until such time as the stadium and track were brought up to standard.

Effectively that was the end although the Knights did contest the H.E.A.T. Team Championship rounds at Exeter, Mildenhall and Rye House although they were never able to stage their home leg.

Ironically the official announcement that the Knights were having to call it a day came at the same time as Mildenhall were also experiencing severe financial problems and was largely instrumental in Division Two promoters introducing a strict 1993 pay code.

The gamble had failed once again at Milton Keynes but it has to be said that the odds were always stacked against Colin Hill and Roger Jones succeeding where others, before them, had failed.

1992 RIDER ROSTER

	Club Record								Career Record							
	M	R	Pts	BP	TPts	Ave	F	P	M	R	Pts	BP	TPts	Ave	F	P
Ian Barney									382	1665	2520.0	229.0	2749.0	6.604	16	10
Peter Glanz	55	266	407.0	40.0	447.0	6.722	0	0	87	443	741.0	59.0	800.0	7.223	1	0
Richard Hellsén	79	413	831.0	39.0	870.0	8.426	1	2	101	516	1014.0	46.0	1060.0	8.217	2	2
Gordon Kennett	4	20	42.0	0.0	42.0	8.400	1	1	333	1535	3361.5	204.0	3565.5	9.291	30	27
Kieran McCullagh	9	26	14.0	4.0	18.0	2.769	0	0	9	26	14.0	4.0	18.0	2.769	0	0
Lars Munkedal									44	188	253.0	26.0	279.0	5.936	0	1
Frank Smart									29	128	158.0	26.0	184.0	5.750	0	1
David Steen									30	115	128.0	27.0	155.0	5.391	0	0
Justin Walker	11	52	55.0	7.0	62.0	4.769	0	0	74	274	283.0	60.0	343.0	5.007	0	0

MILTON KEYNES

Promoters: Colin Hill and Roger Jones.
Address: Elfield Park Stadium, Elfield Park, Milton Keynes, Buckinghamshire.
Telephone: 0908-669817.
Information Line: 0891 31 21 45.
Track Length: 265 metres.
Track Record: 55.4 secs, Darren Sumner (Middlesbrough), July 3, 1990, Heat 1, Milton Keynes v Middlesbrough (Division Two); Hans Nielsen (Oxford), March 31, 1991. Heat 1, Milton Keynes v Oxford, Inter Divisional Challenge.
Seasons in Division Two: 14 (1978-1988 [Groveway], 1989-1991 [Elfield Park]). ■ Milton Keynes started the 1992 Second Division season but were expelled from Division Two because of financial problems and all League results were expunged from the records.
Division Two Record: Third (1), 1987.
Division Two Cup Record: Quarter-finalists, 1979.
Division Two Team Championship: Third (2), 1983, 1984. Qualified (3), 1983, 1984, 1991.
Appearances: Keith White, 190 (1982-1987).
Points: Keith White, 1807 (1982-1987).
World Finalists: None.
Division Two Riders' Championship Finalists: Andy Grahame (1979), Bob Humphreys (1981), Keith White (1982-83-84), Nigel De'ath (1985), Trevor Banks (1987), Troy Butler (1988, 1991).

MIDDLESBROUGH (H), May 5, W48-42

1 Gordon Kennett	*rider replacement*		
2 Frank Smart	1 3 0 R 0	4	
3 †Richard Hellsén	3 3 2 2 2 1	13	
4 Peter Glanz	**3 3 3 3 3 3**	**18**	
5 Ian Barney	1 0 0 N	1	
6 David Steen	**1 1 2** 0 3 **1**	8	3
7 Justin Walker	2 1 0 1	4	
8 Kieran McCullagh	*did not ride*		

Glasgow (A), May 10, L35-55

1 Gordon Kennett	*rider replacement*		
2 Frank Smart	0 2 **1** 2 1	6	1
3 †Richard Hellsén	2 1 3 R T	6	
4 Peter Glanz	1 1 2 2 2 3 R	11	
5 Ian Barney	0 **1** 0 **1**	2	2
6 Justin Walker	2 0 0 N	2	
7 David Steen	**1 1** 2 0 2	6	2
8 Kieran McCullagh	**1** 1	2	1

At-a-Glance Results

Glasgow	L35-55
Middlesbrough	W48-42

The results above were expunged from the League records.

WHO WAS WHO IN '92

Ian BARNEY – see Peterborough

Peter Lybæk GLANZ
Born: May 3, 1962, Fredericia, Denmark.
Broke his leg in a crash in Denmark in May and never returned to a British team as he struggled to recover from the injury.

Richard HELLSÉN – see Long Eaton

Gordon KENNETT – see Wolverhampton

Kieran McCULLAGH – see Peterborough

Lars MUNKEDAL
Born: March 3, 1967, Copenhagen, Denmark.
Dropped by the Knights after only three Gold Cup matches because of a dispute over financial terms. He quietly slipped into British retirement.

Frank SMART – see Exeter

David STEEN – see Stoke

Justin WALKER – see Cradley Heath

HACKNEY 1991...

Promoter: Derek Howes.
Address: Hackney Stadium, Waterden Road, London E15.
Telephone: 081-985-9822.
Hotline: 0891 800 694.
Track Length: 292.6 metres.
Track Record: 59.5 secs, Andy Galvin (Hackney), May 4, 1990, Heat 1, Hackney v Long Eaton (Division Two).
Seasons in Division Two: 6 (1984-1986, 1988-1990).
Division Two Record: Champions (1), 1988.
Division Two Cup Record: Winners (2), 1984, 1988.
Division Two Team Championship: Third (3), 1985, 1986, 1990. Qualified (6), 1984, 1985, 1986, 1988, 1989, 1990.
Appearances: Paul Whittaker, 233 (1984-86, 1988-91).
Points: Andy Galvin 2152 (1984-86, 1988-90).
World Finalists: Dicky Case (1936), Morian Hansen (1936-37), Bengt Jansson (1967, 1971), Antonin Kasper (1983), Dag Lovaas (1974), Cordy Milne (1936-37), Zenon Plech (1975-76, 1979-80-81), Colin Pratt (1967), Finn Thomsen (1979-80).
Division Two Riders' Championship Finalists: Barry Thomas (1984), Trevor Banks (1985), Malcolm Simmons (1986), Mark Loram (1988), Steve Schofield (1989-90).
Other Honours: Division Two Champions, 1938. Speedway Star Knock-out Cup Winners, 1971.

■ Records above relate to Division Two unless otherwise stated.

Hackney closed down after their Sunbrite League Second Division match at Rye House on Sunday, July 14, 1991. The statistics listed above take into account the club's 1991 Phonesport Division Two Cup matches but not any of their League matches which were expunged from official records.

1992
MILTON KEYNES

Left to right: Kieran McCullagh, Gordon Kennett, mascot Jason Bunyan, David Steen, Richard Hellsén, Lars Munkedal, Peter Glanz and Justin Walker.

Red faces as Tigers roar and official boobs

EMBARRASSMENT filled the air in the aftermath of Poole's fighting BSPA Cup draw at their Southern neighbours Swindon...and once again speedway was held to ridicule by an administrative blunder.

After 15 heats of cut-and-thrust Cup racing the two teams were tied on 45 points each...and all sane-thinking people were already looking ahead to a replay.

But, no, this is speedway, and in one of the most incomprehensible decisions of the season referee Mick Barnes, after alleged telephonic liaison with the then British Speedway Promoters' Association Management Committee vice-chairman Tim Swales, ordered that the tie should be decided by a run-off between a nominated rider from each team!

Poole immediately lodged a protest against the decision and it was only under the threat of actually losing the match by default that they entered Steve Schofield in the race-off.

He lost to Leigh Adams and the Swindon fans who left Blunsdon that night were convinced that there team had won through to a quarter final tie at Eastbourne.

This belief was reinforced a couple of days later when it was announced that the match at Arlington would take place on Sunday, September 13 with the winners going through to the last four of the competition.

Poole and their promotional team of Mervyn Stewkesbury and Pete Ansell had other thoughts and swiftly sent in a written protest to the Speedway Control Board.

Their stand was vindicated as the Board ruled in their favour. In his judgement SCB Manager John Eglese ordered the match to be replayed at Poole and, to ensure there would be no repeats of the red-faced incident in future, deemed that if the two teams were, once again, level then there should be a second replay at a neutral venue.

Thankfully it was a relatively quick response to a situation that should never have happened with the final decision being handed down five days before the ADT Auctions Robins were due to travel to Eastbourne.

Not surprisingly, it was Poole who won the enforced replay and subsequently went forward to defeat Eastbourne in the quarter final and Wolverhampton in the semi final to reach what was their fourth successive Cup Final.

From 1989 the JTC Pirates had qualified for two National League Knock Out Cup Finals and the first two BSPA Cup Finals.

Having lost to Bradford a year earlier, they hoped to rub out the memory of that painful defeat and were confident of doing so when they travelled to team of the year Reading with a 10 point lead for the second leg of the Final.

It wasn't enough and Poole now have the unenviable record of only one victory in four successive Cup Final appearances – poor reward for the club's enterprise in recent years.

Reading duly completed a League and Cup double of sorts (they lost to Bradford in the Speedway Star Cup Final and so missed out on the treble) but the real winners of the BSPA Cup were undoubtedly Homefire League Second Division Glasgow who did what no other lower level club could do in 1992...

Success had been eluding the Clyde Two Tigers who had dipped out in the early season Gold Cup, and, in the week previous to Cradley Heath's July visit to Shawfield, lost interest in the Phonesport Division Two Knock Out Cup. Not only lost interest but also been beaten 39-51 in front of their own fans by the Gulf Oil Monarchs.

Add successive defeats at Sheffield and Peterborough and the Scottish club went into arguably their toughest test of the whole summer on the back of three successive losses.

Adding to Neil Macfarlane's woes was an injury that ruled out recent signing Mark Burrows.

The omens were not good...and when Simon Cross and rider replacement nomination Greg Hancock (instead of the injured Billy Hamill) swept to an opening race 5-1 there was little sign of any major upset.

By the end of heat four victory for the First Division visitors seemed a formality as they led 15-9 and, with only four races to go they still had the security of a six point cushion. Then came an inspired Glasgow fightback.

Hungarian Robert Nagy won heat 12; veteran Steve Lawson and Shane Bowes overpowered England Test stars Simon Cross and Andy Grahame in heat 13; Nagy won his fourth race out of five in heat 14 and, astonishingly, the two teams went into the last race tied 42-42.

Even so, who could have imagined a last race 4-2 from Nagy and Bowes?

But that is what happened as Glasgow joined the ranks of kilted giant-killers!

Until that sweet moment the competition had run true to form.

Even though a change in the tournament rules ensured that any Division Two side meeting senior League opposition would have the advantage of a home draw there hadn't been an upset in sight.

Newcastle, fancied by many to provide the shocks, went down to Belle Vue; champions-to-be Peterborough were always under the cosh against Ipswich; and not even Exeter's notorious County Ground strip could swing their tie against eventual First Division wooden spoonists Swindon their way.

First Round

Sunday, May 10

MILDENHALL 36

1 †David Smart	1 2 2 1 2 1	9	3
2 Nigel Leaver	F 1 3 2 0 2	8	1
3 Melvyn Taylor	2 2 1 0	5	1
4 Gary Tagg	1 0 T 2	3	
5 Mikael Teurnberg	0 1 2 1	4	
6 Jamie Habbin	3 1 3 0	7	1
7 Jason Gage	0 T 0 0	0	

OXFORD 54

1 †Hans Nielsen	**3 3 3 3 3**	**15**	
2 Mark Carlson	2 2 1 2 F	7	3
3 Martin Dugard	**3 3 3 3**	**12**	
4 Troy Butler	2 R 3 2	7	2
5 Dean Barker	3 1 1 3	8	
6 Spencer Timmo	1 0 1 1	3	1
7 Glenn Cunningham	2 0 0 0	2	

Sunday, May 10

NEWCASTLE 39

1 Mark Thorpe	3 1 2 2 3 0 2	13	
2 Phil Jeffrey	1 0 N N	1	
3 †David Bargh	0 0 3 3 3 1	10	1
4 Scott Norman	*rider replacement*		
5 Wayne Garratt	fx 0 0 N	0	
6 Richard Juul	2 1 2 1 1 0	7	
7 Max Schofield	1 1 1 2 1 2	8	3
8 David Nagel	*did not ride*		

BELLE VUE 51

1 Bobby Ott	F 1 0 2	3	
2 Frede Schøtt	2 3 0 2 3	10	
3 †Joe Screen	2 3 2 2 1	10	2
4 Jason Lyons	2 2 1 1	6	3
5 Shawn Moran	**3 3 3 3**	**12**	
6 Paul Smith	3 1 0 0	4	
7 Carl Stonehewer	0 3 3 fx	6	

Tuesday, May 12

MILTON KEYNES 28

1 Gordon Kennett	*rider replacement*		
2 Frank Smart	0 0 fx 0 N 1	1	1
3 †Richard Hellsén	2 2 R fx 1 1 2	8	1
4 Peter Glanz	3 3 2 2 N T	10	
5 Ian Barney	0 0 T N	0	
6 David Steen	1 0 3 1 1 1 2	9	
7 Justin Walker	fx R T R	0	
8 Kieran McCullagh	0	0	

ARENA ESSEX 61

1 Brian Karger	2 3 3 3	11	
2 Robert Ledwith	1 1 2 F 0	4	2
3 Bo Petersen	**3 3 3 2**	**11**	**1**
4 †Alan Mogridge	1 2 3 2 3	11	2
5 Allan Johansen	2 1 3 1	7	1
6 Troy Pratt	3 1 2 3	9	1
7 Josh Larsen	2 1 3 2	8	2

Wednesday, May 13

LONG EATON 39

1 †Jan Stæchmann	*rider replacement*		
2 Gary O'Hare	0 2 2 0	4	
3 Carl Blackbird	3 2 3 3 2 1	14	
4 Chris Readshaw	2 3 0 1 0	6	
5 Colin White	1 0 1 2 0 0	4	2
6 Deon Prinsloo	3 1 2 2 R 1	9	2
7 Paul Blackbird	1 1 R N	2	1
8 Jason Reed	*did not ride*		

EASTBOURNE 51

1 Andrew Silver	1 1 1 3	6	3
2 Olli Tyrvainen	2 2 0 2	6	
3 †Andy Grahame	**3 3 3 3 2**	**14**	**1**
4 Nathan Simpson	3 R 1 1	5	
5 Glenn Doyle	F 1 2 3 3	9	1
6 Neville Tatum	2 1 3 N 3 2	11	1
7 Darren Grayling	R R N 0 N	0	

First Round

Thursday, May 14

MIDDLESBROUGH 40

1 †Steve Regeling	2 2 3 2 3 1	13	1
2 Mark Lemon	1 0 F 1	2	1
3 Darren Sumner	2 3 1 1	7	
4 Donny Odom	1 0 T 1 2	4	
5 David Cheshire	3 3 2 0 0	8	
6 Duncan Chapman	2 1 N 3 N F	6	1
7 Paul Pickering	0 0 N 0 N T	0	

COVENTRY 50

1 Andy Smith	3 2 3 2 fx	10	1
2 Brian Andersen	0 1 1 N	2	2
3 †Tommy Knudsen	**3 3 3 3 3**	**15**	
4 Rick Miller	0 1 2 N	3	1
5 John Jørgensen	2 2 1 2	7	
6 Paul Bentley	3 1 1 2 3 fx	10	1
7 Michael Warren	1 F 2 0	3	

Thursday, May 14

SHEFFIELD 38

1 †Peter Carr	3 3 3 3 R 3	15	
2 Simon Green	1 0 1 T	2	
3 Neil Evitts	F 3 1 1 3	8	
4 Louis Carr	1 2 0 2 2 R	7	
5 Steve Johnston	0 R 0 N	0	
6 Mark Hepworth	2 2 0 1	5	
7 Steve Knott	1 T T R 0	1	1

KING'S LYNN 51

1 Bohumil Brhel	R N 2 1 1	4	3
2 Dennis Löfqvist	2 3 2 3 2	12	
3 †Mark Loram	3 2 2 3	10	1
4 Henrik Gustafsson	3 2 2 2	9	
5 Gary Allan	2 1 R 3	6	2
6 Alun Rossiter	3 1 1 3 1	9	1
7 Darren Spicer	fx 1 0 0	1	

Friday, May 15

PETERBOROUGH 35

1 Mick Poole	2 3 3 1 3 2	14	
2 Mark Blackbird	0 0 T 0	0	
3 †Stephen Davies	2 0 3 2 1	8	
4 Rodney Colquhoun	1 2 1 2 2 0	8	1
5 Paul Whittaker	0 1 T 0	1	1
6 Paul Hurry	2 0 T 0	2	
7 Jason Crump	1 0 0 1	2	2

IPSWICH 55

1 †Chris Louis	3 3 E 2 3	11	1
2 Jacek Rempala	1 0 2 1	4	
3 Tony Rickardsson	3 2 2 0	7	
4 Shane Parker	**3 2 3 3**	**11**	**1**
5 Zdenek Tesar	2 3 1 fx 1	7	1
6 Ben Howe	3 1 1 3 3	11	2
7 David Norris	0 1 1 2	4	2

Sunday, June 7

RYE HOUSE 37

1 †Martin Goodwin	2 3 3 2 R 2	12	2
2 Sean Courtney	0 1 T 3 3	7	
3 Jens Rasmussen	R 3 1 2 0	6	1
4 Jan Pedersen	2 1 1 1 1	6	
5 Mark Courtney	0 0 T 1	1	
6 Trevor O'Brien	1 1 1 2	5	
7 Chris Young	R T 0 0	0	

POOLE 53

1 †Marvyn Cox	**3 3 3 3**	**12**	
2 Tony Langdon	1 2 2 1	6	1
3 Steve Schofield	3 2 3 2	10	1
4 Craig Boyce	3 2 1 2	8	1
5 Jörgen Johansson	1 fx 3 3 0	7	
6 Andy Phillips	3 0 0 N 1	4	
7 Alastair Stevens	2 2 0 X 2	6	3

First Round

Saturday, July 4

STOKE 39

1 Alan Grahame	*rider replacement*		
2 Ade Hoole	0 1 0 T	1	
3 †Nigel Crabtree	1 2 2 0 2 2 3	12	1
4 Eric Monaghan	2 1 0 1 3 3 2	12	2
5 Darren Standing	1 0 2 2 0	5	1
6 Garry Stead	3 1 1 1 1	7	3
7 Andy Meredith	1 1 N 0	2	
8 Mark Walsh	*did not ride*		

READING 51

1 Per Jonsson	**2 3 3 3**	**11**	**1**
2 †David Mullett	**3 2 3 2**	**10**	**2**
3 Jan Andersson	3 2 0 1	6	1
4 Armando Castagna	3 3 3 1 0	10	
5 Garry Sweet	0 0 0 1	1	1
6 Ray Morton	2 3 3 2 1	11	
7 Phillip Morris	F 0 2 0	2	1

Monday, July 27

EXETER 37

1 †Peter Jeffery	2 1 2 1 0	6	2
2 Mark Simmonds	1 2 3 1	7	2
3 Frank Smart	2 1 F fx	3	1
4 Colin Cook	0 F 2 fx	2	
5 Richard Green	3 2 3 2 2 1	13	
6 Paul Fry	2 1 2 0 1	6	1
7 Ian Humphreys	R R N T	0	

SWINDON 53

1 †Mitch Shirra	**3 3 3 3 3**	**15**	
2 Matthew Cross	0 1 1 N	2	1
3 Leigh Adams	3 3 1 3 2	12	2
4 David Smart	1 0 R fn	1	1
5 Jimmy Nilsen	2 3 0 3	8	
6 Justin Elkins	1 0 2 1 N	4	
7 Kelly Moran	3 0 2 3 2 1	11	1

Second Round

Saturday, July 4

BERWICK 42

1 †Richard Knight	3 2 2 3	10	
2 Scott Lamb	1 1 1 0	3	1
3 David Blackburn	2 2 1 0 2	7	
4 Scott Robson	2 0 2 1	5	2
5 David Walsh	3 2 3 2 3 1	14	1
6 Michael Lowrie	3 E 0 F 0 0	3	
7 Chris Readshaw	fn N N T	0	

WOLVERHAMPTON 47

1 Ronnie Correy	2 3 3 3 0	11	
2 Charles Ermolenko	0 1 3 2	6	1
3 †Sam Ermolenko	3 3 2 X 3	11	
4 Graham Jones	1 3 3 1	8	
5 Peter Karlsson	0 1 1 2	4	
6 Simon Wolstenholme	2 0 1 0	3	1
7 Stephen Morris	fx 1 2 1	4	1

Sunday, July 5

GLASGOW 46

1 Neil Collins	1 0 T T	1	
2 Mick Powell	0 3 3 2	8	1
3 †Steve Lawson	1 3 1 3	8	
4 Robert Nagy	3 1 3 3 3 3	16	
5 Shane Bowes	0 3 2 1 2 1	9	1
6 Jason Straughan	3 0 0 0	3	
7 James Grieves	1 0 0 0	1	

CRADLEY HEATH 44

1 †Simon Cross	3 2 2 2 0	9	1
2 Billy Hamill	*rider replacement*		
3 Greg Hancock	2 2 2 3 2 0	11	2
4 Andy Grahame	2 2 1 3 1 2	11	
5 Frede Schøtt	1 0 1 E 2	4	2
6 Scott Smith	X 1 1 1	3	2
7 Andy Phillips	2 3 1 0 0	6	1
8 Geoff Powell	*did not ride*		

Second Round

Friday, July 10

EDINBURGH 32

1 Les Collins	2 3 3 1 1 2 0	12	2
2 Dariusz Fliegert	F 0 3 2 R	5	
3 Michael Coles	*rider replacement*		
4 Kenny McKinna	0 1 3 1 0 3 1	9	
5 †Brett Saunders	1 0 2 0 1	4	
6 Mike Lewthwaite	R 0 0 T	0	
7 Johnny Jørgensen	2 0 T 0	2	

BRADFORD 57

1 †Gary Havelock	**3 2 3 3 3**	**14**	**1**
2 Antal Kocso	1 3 2 2	8	1
3 Kelvin Tatum	2 2 3 3 2	12	1
4 Paul Thorp	3 1 0 2	6	2
5 Simon Wigg	2 2 1 2	7	1
6 Sean Wilson	3 1 1 1 3 1	10	4
7 Darren Pearson	fx N N N	0	

Sunday, July 19

EASTBOURNE 46

1 †Andrew Silver	2 3 2 1 2	10	1
2 Paul Dugard	0 1 0 N	1	
3 Glenn Doyle	3 3 1 1	8	
4 Peter Nahlin	3 2 2 F 0	7	
5 Olli Tyrvainen	1 0 1 N	2	
6 Nathan Simpson	3 1 2 3 1 3	13	2
7 Stefan Dannö	0 1 3 1	5	

ARENA ESSEX 44

1 Brian Karger	1 1 2 2 3	9	
2 Andy Galvin	3 3 3 0 0	9	
3 Allan Johansen	0 2 0 T 0	2	
4 †Alan Mogridge	0 fn N T	0	
5 Bo Petersen	2 E 2 3 3 1	11	1
6 Robert Ledwith	2 0 0 N 0 N	2	
7 Josh Larsen	1 2 1 T 2 3 2	11	2

Thursday, July 30

IPSWICH 51

1 †Chris Louis	3 1 2 1	7	1
2 Tony Olsson	1 2 1 1	5	2
3 Tony Rickardsson	3 3 0 3 1	10	1
4 Shane Parker	0 2 R 2	4	1
5 Zdenek Tesar	1 3 3 2 2	11	1
6 Ben Howe	2 1 2 1	6	2
7 David Norris	3 2 2 1	8	1

COVENTRY 39

1 Andy Smith	2 1 3 3 R 0	9	
2 Jamie Habbin	0 0 T N	0	
3 †Tommy Knudsen	2 3 3 2 2 3	15	1
4 Rick Miller	3 1 0 0 1	5	
5 John Jørgensen	2 0 0 3 3	8	1
6 Michael Warren	fx 0 T F	0	
7 Brian Andersen	1 0 T T 1	2	

Wednesday, August 5

OXFORD 48

1 †Hans Nielsen	2 3 3 3 2	13	1
2 Troy Butler	0 1 0 0	1	
3 Martin Dugard	2 3 3 3 3	14	
4 Morten Andersen	2 2 1 2	7	
5 Dean Barker	1 1 2 0	4	2
6 Glenn Cunningham	1 0 1 N	2	1
7 Mark Carlson	2 3 0 1 1	7	1

BELLE VUE 42

1 Bobby Ott	3 3 2 2 0	10	
2 Frede Schøtt	1 X 2 0	3	
3 †Joe Screen	3 2 3 2 1	11	
4 Jason Lyons	0 2 2 1	5	1
5 Shawn Moran	3 0 0 3	6	
6 Paul Smith	3 0 1 0	4	
7 Carl Stonehewer	0 1 1 1	3	2

THE CUP GIANT KILLERS

1975	April 13	Inter League KO Cup	First Round	BOSTON 40 Hackney 38
1975		Inter League KO Cup	Second Round	BOSTON v Swindon, walk over
1976	May 21	Inter League KO Cup	First Round	WORKINGTON 40 Ipswich 38
1976	August 22	Inter League KO Cup	Second Round	WORKINGTON 40 King's Lynn 38
1981	May 8	Speedway Star KO Cup	Preliminary Round	EDINBURGH 49 Sheffield 47
1981	May 8	Speedway Star KO Cup	Preliminary Round	PETERBOROUGH 50 Halifax 46
1991	July 20	BSPA Cup	Second Round	ARENA ESSEX 55 Eastbourne 35
1991	September 18	BSPA Cup	Third Round	ARENA ESSEX 48 Coventry 42
1992	July 5	BSPA Cup	Second Round	GLASGOW 46 Cradley Heath 44

Second Round

Monday, August 17

READING 54			
1 Per Jonsson	3 3 3 3	12	
2 David Mullett	2 1 2 2	7	3
3 †Jeremy Doncaster	3 1 2 2 2	10	2
4 Ray Morton	1 3 0 R 0	4	
5 Armando Castagna	0 2 F 3	5	1
6 Phillip Morris	fx 2 N N	2	1
7 Jan Andersson	3 3 3 3 2	14	

KING'S LYNN 33			
1 Bohumil Brhel	1 1 1 1	4	
2 Gary Allan	0 0 0 0	0	
3 †Mark Loram	E 2 X 2 1 3	8	
4 Dennis Löfqvist	2 0 1 0 1	4	1
5 Henrik Gustafsson	3 2 3 1 3	12	1
6 Emmerson Fairweather	1 0 0 T T	1	1
7 Kevin Brice	2 1 1 0	4	

Thursday, September 3

SWINDON 45			
1 †Mitch Shirra	3 2 3 0	8	
2 Dean Standing	0 1 3 0	4	1
3 Leigh Adams	3 3 3 3 3	15	
4 Kelly Moran	0 2 1 1	4	1
5 Jimmy Nilsen	2 3 3 1 1	10	
6 Justin Elkins	1 N 0 0	1	
7 David Smart	fx 1 2 0	3	1

POOLE 45			
1 †Marvyn Cox	2 1 2 2	7	
2 Alun Rossiter	1 0 1 1	3	2
3 Steve Schofield	2 3 2 2 2	11	1
4 Tom Knudsen	1 1 2 0	4	1
5 Craig Boyce	3 2 3 2 fx	10	1
6 Alastair Stevens	3 0 1 1 3	8	2
7 Jörgen Johansson	2 0 0 N	2	1

Referee Mick Barnes ordered a run-off to decide who should progress to the next round after consultation with BSPA vice chairman Tim Swales.
In the run-off Leigh Adams defeated Steve Schofield and Swindon were declared the winners. Poole lodged a protest with the Speedway Control Board and it was upheld and the two teams were ordered to replay at Poole.

Second Round Replay

Wednesday, September 23

POOLE 58			
1 †Marvyn Cox	2 3 3 3 2	13	
2 Alun Rossiter	1 2 2 2	7	3
3 Steve Schofield	2 2 2 2 0	8	3
4 Craig Boyce	3 2 1 3	9	
5 Tom Knudsen	2 0 0 1	3	2
6 Alastair Stevens	2 3 3 1	9	1
7 Jörgen Johansson	3 1 3 2	9	2

SWINDON 32			
1 Leigh Adams	3 3 3 1 3 3	16	
2 David Smart	0 1 0 0	1	
3 †Mitch Shirra	R 1 2 1 0	4	1
4 Kelly Moran	0 0 N 0	0	
5 Jimmy Nilsen	1 1 3 2 E 1	8	
6 David Clarke	0 0 N 0 N 1	1	
7 Justin Elkins	1 1 N N 0	2	

LEGEND

R = retired, engine failure; E = excluded for tapes offence; F = fell; fx = fell, excluded; X = excluded; fn = fell, unable to take part in re-run; T = replaced by tactical substitute; N = excluded under two minutes or replaced by a reserve.

Quarter Finals

Wednesday, September 9

WOLVERHAMPTON 49			
1 Ronnie Correy	E 3 3 3 3	12	
2 Gordon Kennett	1 1 2 2	6	2
3 Peter Karlsson	3 2 2 1	8	
4 †Sam Ermolenko	2 3 2 3 2	12	2
5 Charles Ermolenko	1 1 2 0	4	1
6 Stephen Morris	2 1 0 0	3	
7 Nigel Leaver	0 1 3 0 0	4	1

OXFORD 41			
1 †Hans Nielsen	3 2 1 2 0	8	1
2 Darren Sumner	2 0 0 T	2	1
3 Dean Barker	2 2 1 0	5	
4 Morten Andersen	fx 1 X N	1	
5 Martin Dugard	3 3 3 1 2 1	13	
6 Troy Butler	3 0 3 N 3 1	10	1
7 Mark Carlson	0 0 1 N 1	2	

Wednesday, September 23

READING 51			
1 Per Jonsson	2 3 2 3	10	2
2 David Mullett	3 fx 2 3 1	9	
3 †Jeremy Doncaster	2 1 2 3	8	1
4 Ray Morton	1 1 1 2	5	1
5 Armando Castagna	2 3 fx 2	7	1
6 Phillip Morris	2 1 0 N 0	3	2
7 Jan Andersson	3 1 1 3 1	9	2

BRADFORD 39			
1 †Gary Havelock	1 0 2 0 0	3	1
2 Sean Wilson	0 2 0 1 T	3	
3 Kelvin Tatum	3 2 T T	5	
4 Paul Thorp	0 2 3 1 1 2	9	2
5 Simon Wigg	3 3 3 2 3 3	17	
6 Antal Kocso	0 1 T 0 N	1	1
7 Darren Pearson	1 0 T N F	1	

Sunday, September 27

GLASGOW 42			
1 †Steve Lawson	3 2 0 3 0	8	
2 Mick Powell	2 0 2 2	6	1
3 Neil Collins	2 1 0 1	4	1
4 Robert Nagy	2 3 3 1 2 3	14	
5 Shane Bowes	R 2 1 2 2 1	8	1
6 Jesper Olsen	2 fx N T	2	
7 James Grieves	0 0 0 T T	0	

IPSWICH 48			
1 †Chris Louis	1 1 3 3 2	10	
2 Savalas Clouting	0 0 N N	0	
3 Tony Olsson	3 3 2 R	8	
4 David Norris	3 3 3 0 0	9	
5 Zdenek Tesar	1 2 2 3	8	1
6 Ben Howe	3 1 1 0 N	5	
7 Shane Parker	1 1 3 1 1 1	8	

Quarter Finals

Sunday, October 4

EASTBOURNE 41			
1 †Andrew Silver	3 2 2 fx 1 2	10	
2 Darren Grayling	0 1 0 N	1	1
3 Glenn Doyle	2 1 1 0	4	1
4 Peter Nahlin	fx 3 3 1 3 1	11	1
5 Nathan Simpson	3 1 2 1	7	1
6 Paul Woods	1 1 0 T 1	3	3
7 Olli Tyrvainen	2 1 2 T	5	

POOLE 49			
1 †Marvyn Cox	2 2 3 3 3	13	
2 Alun Rossiter	1 0 2 0	3	2
3 Steve Schofield	0 3 1 3 0	7	
4 Tom Knudsen	1 2 fx N	3	2
5 Craig Boyce	2 3 2 0	7	1
6 Alastair Stevens	3 3 N 3 N 3 2 2	16	1
7 Steve Leigh	0 N 0 N 0 N	0	

Semi Finals

Wednesday, October 7

POOLE 48			
1 †Marvyn Cox	2 3 3 3 0	11	
2 Alun Rossiter	F 1 1 1	3	1
3 Steve Schofield	3 1 3 2 1	10	
4 Craig Boyce	1 2 2 1	6	3
5 Tom Knudsen	3 3 0 0	6	
6 Alastair Stevens	2 N N 2 1 2	7	1
7 Jörgen Johansson	3 1 0 N 1 N	5	

WOLVERHAMPTON 42			
1 Ronnie Correy	3 1 2 3 2	11	1
2 Graham Jones	1 0 F N	1	
3 Peter Karlsson	0 0 2 1	3	1
4 Charles Ermolenko	0 3 3 2 1	9	
5 †Sam Ermolenko	2 2 2 0 3 3	12	1
6 Stephen Morris	0 N N 0 0	0	
7 Nigel Leaver	1 2 3 0	6	

Sunday, October 18

READING 49			
1 Per Jonsson	3 3 3 3 2	14	1
2 David Mullett	fx 1 0 0	1	
3 Jan Andersson	3 2 3 1 3	12	1
4 Lance Sealey	0 0 N 0	0	
5 †Jeremy Doncaster	3 2 2 3	10	
6 Phillip Morris	0 1 N 0	1	
7 Ray Morton	2 3 3 0 2 1	11	1

IPSWICH 41			
1 †Chris Louis	2 1 1 0 3	7	1
2 Tony Olsson	1 3 2 2 2	10	2
3 Tony Rickardsson	2 2 3 1 1	9	
4 Shane Parker	2 1 2 2 0	7	
5 Savalas Clouting	1 F N T	1	1
6 Ben Howe	1 0 1 T	2	
7 David Norris	3 fx 1 1 0	5	2

FINAL

Wednesday, October 21

POOLE 50			
1 †Marvyn Cox	2 1 3 3 2	11	
2 Alun Rossiter	0 0 N N	0	
3 Steve Schofield	3 3 3 2 1	12	1
4 Craig Boyce	3 3 2 2	10	1
5 Tom Knudsen	1 0 N N	1	
6 Alastair Stevens	3 1 0 R 2 0	6	1
7 Jörgen Johansson	1 3 3 2 N 0 1	10	2

READING 40			
1 Per Jonsson	3 2 2 1 3 3	14	
2 David Mullett	1 1 1 1	4	3
3 Jan Andersson	2 2 1 0	5	1
4 Armando Castagna	2 1 1 1 0	5	1
5 †Jeremy Doncaster	0 2 N 3	5	
6 Ray Morton	2 3 2 R 0	7	
7 Phillip Morris	0 0 N 0	0	

Monday, October 26

READING 52			
1 Per Jonsson	3 3 3 2 3	14	1
2 David Mullett	1 1 3 2	7	1
3 Jan Andersson	3 3 2 2 1	11	1
4 Armando Castagna	1 1 3 2	7	1
5 †Jeremy Doncaster	2 3 3 3	11	
6 Phillip Morris	1 0 1 0 N 0 0	2	
7 Ray Morton	R N N N	0	

POOLE 38			
1 †Marvyn Cox	2 2 3 1 3 2	13	
2 Alun Rossiter	0 0 N T	0	
3 Steve Schofield	1 2 1 1	5	2
4 Tom Knudsen	0 F 0 N	0	
5 Craig Boyce	3 2 1 0 1 0	7	
6 Alastair Stevens	3 0 2 N 1 0 T	6	
7 Jörgen Johansson	2 2 1 2 N	7	2

Aggregate: Reading 92 Poole 88

Roll of Honour

BSPA CUP

1991 BRADFORD 106 Poole 74
1992 READING 92 Poole 88

INTER LEAGUE KNOCK OUT CUP

1975 BELLE VUE 90 Halifax 65
1976 HULL 96 Wolverhampton 60
1977 IPSWICH 81 Cradley Heath 75
1978 KING'S LYNN 94 Exeter 62
1979 CRADLEY HEATH 85 King's Lynn 71
1980 KING'S LYNN 83 Swindon 73

† The Inter League Knock Out Cup was discontinued in 1981 when eight National League tracks were included in the Speedway Star Knock Out Cup.

THE amalgamation of the old British and National Leagues tempted promoters to revive the Inter League Knock Out Cup – dropped more than a decade earlier – as a renamed and slightly restyled BSPA Cup.

And Arena Essex dished out the shocks with successive home victories against two Division One sides.

Eastbourne succumbed to the Purfleet side with only Bobby Ott and reserve Jesper Olsen winning races and then mighty Coventry went the same way despite double figure returns from both American Rick Miller and fiery Czechoslovakian Roman Matousek.

The luck of the semi final draw took Arena to Odsal for their fourth tie and this time they were soundly thrashed by Bradford who went on to similar account for Poole in the two leg final, winning both home and away.

1991 BSPA Cup

First Round

Berwick 68 *Hackney 22*
***Rye House 37* Ipswich 52**
Belle Vue 56 *Edinburgh 34*
Coventry 54 *Middlesbrough 30*
Poole 46 Swindon 44
Oxford 63 *Peterborough 27*
Arena Essex 58 Newcastle 32
Byes: Bradford, Cradley Heath, Eastbourne, Exeter, Glasgow, King's Lynn, Milton Keynes, Reading, and Wolverhampton

Second Round

***Glasgow 39* Reading 51**
***Milton Keynes 42* Bradford 48**
Ipswich 60 *Exeter 30*
Poole 45 Wolverhampton 44
Cradley Heath 55 Belle Vue 35
Oxford 42 Berwick 48
***Arena Essex 55* Eastbourne 35**
Coventry 56 King's Lynn 34

Third Round

Bradford 59 Reading 31
Poole 51 Cradley Heath 39
Berwick 58 Ipswich 32
***Arena Essex 48* Coventry 42**

Semi Finals

Poole 50 Berwick 40
Bradford 61 *Arena Essex 29*

Final

Bradford 106 Poole 74

The Premiership

WOLVERHAMPTON made it a Premiership double...to claim the first trophy of the 1992 season.

They set up their victory with a two point win at Odsal despite a below par performance from Ronnie Correy who claimed only four points. The real match-winner was the unsung Graham Jones who grabbed a dozen points, including a crucial maximum with Sam Ermolenko.

In the return Sean Wilson (pictured above with colleague Paul Thorp) won the opening heat to level the overall scores but a Charles Ermolenko-Stephen Morris 5-12 in heat eight virtually settled the destination of the trophy.

First leg, Saturday, April 18

BRADFORD 44

1 †Gary Havelock	2 3 3 1 0	9	1
2 Sean Wilson	3 1 3 0	7	
3 Kelvin Tatum	3 3 3 3 2	14	
4 Paul Thorp	2 3 0 1	6	
5 Simon Wigg	1 1 1 0	3	1
6 Kevin Little	1 1 1 0	3	
7 Darren Pearson	0 2 fx0	2	1

WOLVERHAMPTON 46

1 Ronnie Correy	1 R R 2 1	4	1
2 Charles Ermolenko	0 2 1 N	3	
3 †Sam Ermolenko	2 2 2 2 3 3	14	1
4 Graham Jones	3 2 3 1 2 1	12	1
5 Peter Karlsson	0 R 2 3	5	1
6 Wayne Carter	3 0 T 2	5	1
7 Stephen Morris	2 fx1 T	3	2

Second leg, Monday, April 20

WOLVERHAMPTON 50

1 Ronnie Correy	2 2 3 3 1	11	
2 Charles Ermolenko	0 1 3 1	5	1
3 †Sam Ermolenko	R 3 2 3 3	11	
4 Graham Jones	2 3 0 3	8	1
5 Peter Karlsson	3 1 2 0	6	
6 Wayne Carter	3 2 1 0	6	
7 Stephen Morris	fx2 0 1	3	1

BRADFORD 40

1 †Gary Havelock	1 2 3 3 1 0	10	1
2 Sean Wilson	3 0 1 1	5	
3 Kelvin Tatum	3 3 1 2 2 2	13	
4 Paul Thorp	E 0 0 T	0	
5 Simon Wigg	1 2 1 2 2	8	1
6 Kevin Little	2 0 0 0	2	
7 Darren Pearson	1 1 N 0	2	1

Aggregate: Wolverhampton 96 Bradford 84

The original staging of the Bradford meeting on Saturday, March 28, was postponed because of a floodlighting failure at Odsal Stadium and the first attempt to stage the Monmore Green leg on Monday, March 30, was called off because of rain.

CHALLENGE MATCHES

IN THE following pages we take a look at the variety of challenge matches, individual meetings and Testimonials held during the 1992 season.

Suffolk Cup

Thursday, May 21

IPSWICH 51

1 †Chris Louis	**3 3 3 3 3**	**15**	
2 Shaun Tacey	0 0 N 0	0	
3 Shane Parker	**3 3 3 3 2**	**14**	**1**
4 David Norris	R 3 2 3	8	1
5 Lawrence Hare	1 0 0 0	1	
6 Savalas Clouting	1 1 0 1 N	3	1
7 Ben Howe	2 3 2 2 1	10	1

MILDENHALL 39

1 †David Smart	2 2 1 2 1	8	
2 Nigel Leaver	1 1 2 F	4	2
3 Melvyn Taylor	2 2 3 1 0	8	
4 Gary Tagg	2 1 2 1	6	3
5 Mikael Teurnberg	3 2 0 2 0	7	
6 Jamie Habbin	3 1 1 T	5	1
7 Jason Gage	0 0 fx1	1	1

Alan Wilkinson Trophy

Friday, June 5

BELLE VUE 63

1 Bobby Ott	3 1 3 3	10	
2 Frede Schøtt	2 3 1 2	8	2
3 †Joe Screen	3 3 3 2 2	13	1
4 Jason Lyons	**3 3 2 3 3**	**14**	**1**
5 Shawn Moran	2 1 3 1	7	2
6 Paul Smith	2 0 0 0	2	1
7 Carl Stonehewer	3 3 1 2	9	1

STOKE 27

1 Alan Grahame	1 2 1 2 3 1	10	1
2 Gary Chessell	0 0 0 0	0	
3 †Nigel Crabtree	2 2 2 2 1 0	9	
4 Eric Monaghan	1 2 1 0	4	
5 Darren Standing	0 1 0 1	2	1
6 Ade Hoole	0 0 T 0	0	
7 Andy Meredith	1 1 T 0	2	1

Anglian Cup

Saturday, March 21

KING'S LYNN 46

1 Bohumil Brhel	3 2 0 2 0	7	
2 Dennis Löfqvist	1 1 1 2	5	1
3 †Mark Loram	2 2 R 1	5	
4 Gary Allan	2 1 0 1	4	1
5 Henrik Gustafsson	3 3 3 3 2	14	
6 Darren Spicer	0 0 0 N	0	
7 Alun Rossiter	3 3 1 1 3	11	

IPSWICH 44

1 †Chris Louis	2 2 3 2 1	10	
2 Jacek Rempala	0 0 0 T	0	
3 Tony Rickardsson	N 3 2 2 3 3	13	1
4 Shane Parker	0 1 3 0	4	
5 Zdenek Tesar	1 3 1 R	5	
6 Ben Howe	1 1 0 0 N	2	1
7 David Norris	2 3 2 1 2	10	

Friday, May 15

ARENA ESSEX 48

1 Rick Miller	0 2 3 2	7	
2 Andy Galvin	2 1 1 2	6	3
3 Bo Petersen	3 1 3 3 2	12	
5 Robert Ledwith	F 0 N N	0	
4 †Alan Mogridge	2 3 0 2	7	
6 Troy Pratt	3 1 3 2 2 1	12	2
7 Josh Larsen	fx2 1 1 0	4	1

KING'S LYNN 41

1 Bohumil Brhel	3 2 2 fxE	7	
2 Dennis Löfqvist	1 1 3 0	5	1
3 †Mark Loram	2 3 3 3 3 3	17	
4 Tom Grinstead	1 0 F 1	2	
5 Gary Allan	3 2 1 1	7	
6 Alun Rossiter	fnN N N	0	
7 Darren Spicer	2 0 0 0 1 0	3	

Premiership Roll of Honour

1982 CRADLEY HEATH 84 Ipswich 72
1983 BELLE VUE 79 Cradley Heath 77
1984 CRADLEY HEATH 82 *Belle Vue 74*
1985 *Cradley Heath 81* IPSWICH 75
1986 *Coventry 86* OXFORD 70
1987 OXFORD 82 Cradley Heath 73
1988 Cradley Heath 43* COVENTRY 47
1989 Cradley Heath 112 COVENTRY 67
1990 Cradley Heath 95 OXFORD 85
1991 READING 95 *POOLE 85†*
1992 WOLVERHAMPTON 96 Bradford 84

■ In 1988 the Premiership was awarded to Cradley Heath when Coventry failed to stage the second leg.
■ Teams in CAPITALS were the previous season's Division One Champions, teams in *italics* won previous season's League Cup. Team in *CAPITAL ITALICS* were the previous season's National League champions.
■ In all other cases teams won the previous season's Speedway Star Knock Out Cup Final.
■ In 1991 Reading and Poole drew the first staging 90-90.

Bill Dore Trophy

First leg, Monday, April 20

OXFORD 46

1 †Hans Nielsen	2 3 3 3 3 3	17	
2 Mark Carlson	0 1 1 0	2	1
3 Martin Dugard	3 1 3 2 1 2 2	14	3
4 Troy Butler	*rider replacement*		
5 Dean Barker	3 2 2 0 0	7	
6 Glenn Cunningham	0 0 1 0	1	
7 Morten Andersen	1 2 2 0 N	5	-

READING 44

1 Per Jonsson	1 3 3 2 0	9	1
2 David Mullett	3 0 3 1	7	
3 Jan Andersson	2 R 3 2	7	
4 †Jeremy Doncaster	1 2 2 3 1	9	
5 Lance Sealey	0 0 N 0	0	
6 Ray Morton	3 2 1 1 1 1	9	2
7 Phillip Morris	2 1 0 N	3	2

Second leg, Monday, April 20

READING 46

1 Per Jonsson	2 3 3 3 1	12	1
2 David Mullett	1 2 3 2	8	3
3 Jan Andersson	3 3 3 1 2	12	
4 †Jeremy Doncaster	1 2 0 2	5	
5 Mike Tomlin	0 1 0 N	1	1
6 Lance Sealey	1 0 N 1	2	
7 Ray Morton	3 1 2 0 0 0	6	1

OXFORD 44

1 †Hans Nielsen	3 3 3 2 1 2 3	17	3
2 Mark Carlson	0 R 1 T	1	
3 Martin Dugard	2 1 3 2 2 3 0	13	
4 Troy Butler	*rider replacement*		
5 Dean Barker	2 2 1 1 3	9	2
6 Morten Andersen	2 X 0 0 1	3	
7 Glenn Cunningham	0 1 0 N	1	1

Aggregate: Reading 90 Oxford 90

Travelcare Trophy

Saturday, July 18

COVENTRY 55

1 Andy Smith	3 3 2 2 3 2	15	
2 Richard Musson	0 0 0 N	0	
3 Tommy Knudsen	*rider replacement*		
4 †Rick Miller	1 2 3 1 3	10	1
5 John Jørgensen	3 3 3 2 2 1	14	3
6 Michael Warren	2 2 2 0 1	7	3
7 Brian Andersen	0 2 3 3 1	9	
8 Chris Clarence	*did not ride*		

ARENA ESSEX 35

1 Brian Karger	*rider replacement*		
2 Andy Galvin	1 0 N N 0	1	1
3 Allan Johansen	0 1 1 1 2 0	5	1
4 †Alan Mogridge	0 1 0 T 1	2	
5 Bo Petersen	2 2 1 3 0 2 3	13	
6 Sean Wilson	1 3 3 2 0 0	9	
7 Josh Larsen	3 1 1 0	5	
8 Sean McCullagh	*did not ride*		

Northern Trophy

First leg, Saturday, March 21

BRADFORD 45

1 †Gary Havelock	2 3 3 1 0	9	1
2 Sean Wilson	3 2 1 2	8	2
3 Kelvin Tatum	3 2 3 3 2	13	
4 Paul Thorp	3 1 0 3	7	
5 Simon Wigg	R 0 2 0	2	
6 Kevin Little	2 1 0 0	3	1
7 Darren Pearson	3 0 0 0	3	

BELLE VUE 45

1 Bobby Ott	0 1 3 3 1 2	10	2
2 Jason Lyons	1 2 2 2 2 1 3	13	4
3 †Joe Screen	2 1 3 3 3 1	13	
4 Shawn Moran	*rider replacement*		
5 Kelly Moran	2 1 1 T 2	6	
6 Richard Musson	0 0 1 1	2	1
7 Mike Hampson	1 0 T 0	1	
8 Michael Howe	*did not ride*		

Second leg, Friday, March 27

BELLE VUE 47

1 Bobby Ott	1 3 3 3 1	11	1
2 Jason Lyons	2 2 2 2	8	2
3 †Joe Screen	2 3 2 1 3	11	1
4 Frede Schøtt	1 0 R R	1	
5 Kelly Moran	3 3 3 2	11	
6 Richard Musson	3 0 0 1 1	5	
7 Mike Hampson	R 0 0 N	0	

BRADFORD 43

1 †Gary Havelock	3 2 3 E 2 2	12	1
2 Sean Wilson	0 1 3 1	5	1
3 Kelvin Tatum	3 1 2 2 3 0	11	
4 Paul Thorp	0 1 1 T	2	1
5 Simon Wigg	2 2 1 3	8	1
6 Kevin Little	1 0 0 T	1	1
7 Darren Pearson	2 1 1 0 0	4	

Aggregate: Belle Vue 92 Bradford 88

Roll of Honour

1974 Sheffield
1975 Belle Vue
1976 Belle Vue
1977 Belle Vue
1978 Belle Vue
1979 Sheffield
1980 Halifax
1982 Belle Vue 92 Sheffield 64
1983 Belle Vue
1985 Sheffield 81 Belle Vue 75
1986 Sheffield
1987 Bradford
1989 Belle Vue 113 Bradford 67
1991 Belle Vue 95 Bradford 85
1992 Belle Vue 92 Bradford 88

Where no score is listed the competition was decided on a mini-League basis.

Clubcall Midlands Trophy

First leg, Saturday, June 13

CRADLEY HEATH 42

1 †Simon Cross	2 1 3 2 2	10	1
2 Dean Barker	*1 X 2 2 0*	*5*	*1*
3 Billy Hamill	2 0 2 3 2 3 2	14	
4 Jan O. Pedersen	*rider replacement*		
5 Greg Hancock	3 2 1 0 2 1	9	2
6 Scott Smith	3 F 1 N R	4	1
7 Mark Meredith	F fxF R N	0	

WOLVERHAMPTON 48

1 Ronnie Correy	3 3 3 1	10	
2 Charles Ermolenko	0 1 3 1	5	
3 †Sam Ermolenko	3 3 2 3 3	14	
4 Graham Jones	2 fx2 0	4	
5 Peter Karlsson	1 3 1 3 0	8	1
6 Simon Wolstenholme	2 0 0 N	2	
7 Stephen Morris	1 1 1 1 1	5	2

Second leg, Monday, July 27

WOLVERHAMPTON 45

1 Ronnie Correy	2 3 3 2 3 3	16	
2 Charles Ermolenko	0 0 1 T	1	
3 †Sam Ermolenko	3 3 1 3 3 2	15	1
4 Graham Jones	fnN N T	0	
5 Peter Karlsson	2 3 2 0 1	8	
6 Stephen Morris	1 F 0 0 0	1	1
7 Nigel Leaver	2 1 1 R N 0 T	4	1

CRADLEY HEATH 45

1 †Simon Cross	1 0 3 1 1	6	2
2 Billy Hamill	*rider replacement*		
3 Greg Hancock	3 2 2 3 3 1	14	
4 Andy Grahame	3 2 1 2 2 0	10	1
5 Sean Wilson	*0 2 2 1 0*	*5*	
6 Andy Phillips	3 1 2 1 2	9	2
7 Scott Smith	0 1 N 0	1	1
8 Justin Walker	*did not ride*		

Aggregate: Wolverhampton 93 Cradley Heath 87

Barclays Bank Trophy

First leg, Saturday, March 21

BERWICK 47

1 †Richard Knight	**3 3 3 3 3**	**15**	
2 Scott Robson	2 R 3 2 1	8	2
3 David Walsh	3 3 F 1	7	1
4 Scott Lamb	E 1 0 2	3	
5 David Blackburn	2 3 2 2	9	
6 Chris Readshaw	0 0 fx1	1	1
7 Michael Lowrie	1 0 2 1 0	4	1

NEWCASTLE 43

1 Mark Thorpe	R 2 3 3 2	10	
2 Phil Jeffrey	1 F 1 2	4	1
3 †David Bargh	2 2 fx1	5	1
4 Wayne Garratt	1 2 fxN	3	
5 Scott Norman	3 1 2 1	7	1
6 Richard Juul	3 1 3 3 0	10	1
7 Max Schofield	2 1 0 1 0	4	2

Second leg, Sunday, March 22

NEWCASTLE 53

1 Mark Thorpe	2 2 3 3	10	
2 Phil Jeffrey	1 0 2 1	4	2
3 †David Bargh	**3 3 3 3 3**	**15**	
4 Wayne Garratt	0 2 2 1	5	2
5 Scott Norman	3 3 X 2 2	10	2
6 Richard Juul	3 1 2 3	9	1
7 Max Schofield	fxN F 0 F	0	

BERWICK 36

1 †Richard Knight	3 1 2 1	7	
2 Scott Robson	F R R 1	1	1
3 David Walsh	2 3 2 0 0	7	1
4 Scott Lamb	1 0 2 0 1	4	1
5 David Blackburn	2 1 1 2	6	1
6 Chris Readshaw	2 1 3 3	9	
7 Michael Lowrie	1 0 1 0	2	1

Aggregate: Newcastle 96 Berwick 83

NEWS GROUP DUDLEY WOLVES TROPHY

First leg, Monday, August 31

CRADLEY HEATH 50

1 †Simon Cross	3 2 F R 2	7	
2 Andy Grahame	1 3 3 3 1	11	
3 Billy Hamill	3 2 2 3 1	11	2
4 Gert Handberg	*rider replacement*		
5 Greg Hancock	0 3 1 F 3 0	7	
6 Andy Phillips	3 2 3 3 1	12	1
7 Scott Smith	R 1 1 0	2	
8 Justin Walker	*did not ride*		

WOLVERHAMPTON 38

1 Ronnie Correy	2 1 E 2 2 3	10	
2 Gordon Kennett	0 0 T 0	0	
3 Peter Karlsson	1 2 2 2 1	8	
4 Charles Ermolenko	1 1 F 0 2	4	1
5 †Sam Ermolenko	3 1 F 3 3 2	12	2
6 Stephen Morris	R T T 0 2 T	2	
7 Nigel Leaver	2 0 0 N	2	

Second leg, Monday, August 31

WOLVERHAMPTON 41

1 Ronnie Correy	3 2 3 2 fx	10	
2 Gordon Kennett	0 1 1 2	4	2
3 Peter Karlsson	2 3 1 3	9	
4 †Sam Ermolenko	3 3 1 3 fx	10	1
5 Charles Ermolenko	2 0 2 1	5	1
6 Stephen Morris	F N N N	0	
7 Nigel Leaver	2 R 1 F F 0	3	

CRADLEY HEATH 47

1 Greg Hancock	2 1 3 2 2	10	2
2 Andy Grahame	1 2 2 2	7	3
3 Billy Hamill	**3 3 3 3 3**	**15**	
4 †Simon Cross	1 2 X 0	3	
5 Gert Handberg	0 0 0 1	1	1
6 Andy Phillips	3 0 3 1 1 2	10	
7 Scott Smith	1 fxN N	1	

Aggregate: Cradley Heath 97 Wolverhampton 79

Roll of Honour

1961 Wolverhampton 97 Cradley Heath 94
1962 Wolverhampton 81 Cradley Heath 74
1963 Cradley Heath 84 Wolverhampton 71
1964 Wolverhampton 103.5 Cradley Heath 88.5
1965 Wolverhampton 110 Cradley Heath 81
1966 Wolverhampton 115 Cradley Heath 89
1967 Wolverhampton 108 Cradley Heath 95
1968 Cradley Heath 112 Wolverhampton 103
1969 Cradley Heath 79 Wolverhampton 77
1970 Wolverhampton 82 Cradley Heath 74
1971 Cradley Heath 83 Wolverhampton 73
1972 Wolverhampton 86 Cradley Heath 69
1973 Wolverhampton 80 Cradley Heath 76
1974 Cradley Heath 79 Wolverhampton 77
1975 Wolverhampton 80 Cradley Heath 76
1976 Cradley Heath 45 Wolverhampton 33
1977 Wolverhampton 90 Cradley Heath 66
1978 Cradley Heath 81 Wolverhampton 75
1979 Cradley Heath 89 Wolverhampton 67
1980 Cradley Heath 84 Wolverhampton 71
1985 Cradley Heath 99 Wolverhampton 57
1986 Cradley Heath 84 Wolverhampton 72
1987 Cradley Heath 107 Wolverhampton 72
1988 Cradley Heath 95 Wolverhampton 85
1989 Wolverhampton 90 Cradley Heath 89
1990 Cradley Heath 91 Wolverhampton 87
1991 Cradley Heath 102 Wolverhampton 78
1992 Cradley Heath 97 Wolverhampton 79

◆ CRADLEY Heath and Wolverhampton met nine times during the season – twice in the First Division, twice in the Gold Cup and five times in challenge matches. Honours were shared with four wins each and a 45-45 draw!

Don Trent Trophy

Thursday, September

SHEFFIELD 49

1 Peter Carr	3 3 3 1 3	13	1
2 Simon Green	1 1 3 1	6	
3 Neil Evitts	**3 3 3 3**	**12**	
4 Tony Langdon	3 3 2 3	11	
5 †Louis Carr	2 0 2 1 0	5	1
6 Steve Knott	fxN N N	0	
7 Steve Johnston	fx1 0 1 fxR	2	

LONG EATON 37

1 Jason Lyons	*2 1 3 2 2 2*	*12*	*1*
2 Richard Hellsén	0 2 0 fx	2	
3 Carl Blackbird	2 2 1 0	5	
4 Martin Dixon	0 2 N 0	2	
5 Deon Prinsloo	1 1 2 3 2 1	10	2
6 Nigel Sparshott	3 0 T 1	4	1
7 Mark Lemon	fx0 2 0	2	

Wednesday, September 16

LONG EATON 48

1 †Jan Stæchmann	1 2 fx3 3	9	2
2 Richard Hellsén	2 3 2 3 0	10	
3 Carl Blackbird	2 2 2 1	7	
4 Martin Dixon	2 2 1 3	8	1
5 Deon Prinsloo	3 N 1 0	4	
6 Nigel Sparshott	2 1 1 1 0	5	4
7 Mark Lemon	3 1 0 1	5	1

SHEFFIELD 42

1 David Blackburn	***3 3 3 3 2***	***14***	***1***
2 Simon Green	0 N R T	0	
3 Shane Bowes	*3 1 2 1 2 1*	*10*	*2*
4 Tony Langdon	1 3 3 2 3 2	14	
5 †Louis Carr	0 fxN R	0	
6 Steve Johnston	1 0 T 1 0 2	4	1
7 Rob Homer	R 0 F T N	0	

Aggregate: Sheffield 91 Long Eaton 85

Scottish Team Championship

First leg, Friday, July 31

EDINBURGH 38

1 †Les Collins	3 3 3 2	11	
2 Deon Prinsloo	*1 2 0 0*	*3*	*1*
3 Michael Coles	3 3 3 2	11	
4 Johnny Jørgensen	1 0 1 1	3	
5 Kenny McKinna	2 3 2 F	7	
6 Brett Saunders	0 1 1 1	3	1
7 Stewart McDonald	*did not ride*		

BERWICK 30

1 Michael Lowrie	0 0 0 0	0	
2 David Walsh	2 2 3 3	10	
3 David Blackburn	2 2 2 3	9	
4 Chris Readshaw	1 fx0 X	1	
5 Scott Robson	3 0 2 fx	5	
6 Scott Lamb	1 1 1 2	5	1

GLASGOW 40

1 †Steve Lawson	2 1 X 1	4	1
2 Jesper Olsen	F 0 1 2	3	1
3 Neil Collins	3 2 3 3	11	
4 Mick Powell	0 1 1 2	4	2
5 Robert Nagy	3 3 0 3	9	
6 Peter Carr	*1 2 3 1*	*7*	*1*
7 Jason Straughan	2	2	

Second leg, Saturday, August 1

BERWICK 44

1 †Richard Knight	**3 3 3 3**	**12**	
2 David Walsh	2 2 1 1	6	2
3 David Blackburn	3 3 3 2	11	
4 Chris Readshaw	fx1 1 1	3	1
5 Scott Robson	1 0 3 1	5	2
6 Scott Lamb	2 2 1 2	7	
7 Michael Lowrie	*did not ride*		

EDINBURGH 28

1 †Les Collins	2 1 2 2	7	1
2 Brett Saunders	1 0 3 1	5	2
3 Michael Coles	2 2 1 0	5	
4 Johnny Jørgensen	0 0 0 3	3	
5 Kenny McKinna	2 2 2 2	8	
6 Stewart McDonald	0 0 0 0	0	
7 Wayne Park	*did not ride*		

GLASGOW 36

1 †Steve Lawson	1 3 1 3	8	
2 Jesper Olsen	0 1 F fx	1	
3 Neil Collins	3 3 2 3	11	
4 Mick Powell	1 1 0 0	2	
5 Robert Nagy	3 3 2 3	11	
6 Mark Lemon	*0 1 0 2*	*3*	*1*
7 Jason Straughan	*did not ride*		

Third leg, Sunday, August 2

GLASGOW 40

1 †Steve Lawson	3 2 R N	5	
2 Jason Straughan	0 0 1 1	2	
3 Neil Collins	3 3 3 2	11	
4 Mick Powell	2 1 2 0	5	2
5 Robert Nagy	3 0 3 3	9	
6 Peter Carr	1 3 2 2	8	2
7 James Grieves	0	0	

BERWICK 35

1 †Richard Knight	0 3 3 3	9	
2 David Walsh	1 1 1 1	4	
3 David Blackburn	3 2 3 1	9	
4 Chris Readshaw	1 0 0 N	1	
5 Scott Robson	0 3 1 2	6	1
6 Scott Lamb	2 1 fx3	6	
7 Michael Lowrie	0	0	

EDINBURGH 33

1 †Les Collins	1 3 2 3	9	1
2 Brett Saunders	2 1 0 1	4	
3 Michael Coles	2 1 0 2	5	1
4 Johnny Jørgensen	F 2 1 0	3	
5 Kenny McKinna	2 2 3 2	9	
6 Deon Prinsloo	*0 0 2 1*	*3*	*2*
7 Stewart McDonald	*did not ride*		

Aggregate: Glasgow 116 Berwick 109 Edinburgh 99

Scottish Cup

Friday, September 11

EDINBURGH 47

1 †Les Collins	3 1 3 2	9	
2 Brett Saunders	1 3 0 3	7	
3 Kenny McKinna	3 2 2 fx	7	
4 Johnny Jørgensen	1 F 0 3	4	
5 Michael Coles	3 3 2 1	9	1
6 Dariusz Fliegert	1 0 1 X	2	
7 Stewart McDonald	R 3 2	5	
8 Grant Blackie	2 1 1	4	1

GLASGOW 42

1 †Steve Lawson	2 1 0 3	6	
2 Peter Carr	*0 3 3 3 0*	*9*	
3 Neil Collins	2 2 2 3	9	
4 Mick Powell	0 1 1 2	4	2
5 Shane Bowes	2 2 1 2	7	
6 Jesper Olsen	0 F T 1	1	1
7 Jason Straughan	R 2 F	2	
8 James Grieves	3 E 1	4	1

Sunday, September 13

GLASGOW 41

1 †Steve Lawson	1 3 1 2	7	
2 Nigel Crabtree	*N 1 3 2*	*6*	
3 Neil Collins	2 1 2 2	7	
4 Mick Powell	0 T 1 3	4	1
5 Shane Bowes	2 2 0 fxfx	4	
6 Jesper Olsen	0 F 1 2	3	1
7 Jason Straughan	2 3 0	5	1
8 James Grieves	0 3 2 0	5	1

EDINBURGH 49

1 †Les Collins	**3 2 3 3**	**11**	**1**
2 Brett Saunders	2 3 2 1	8	2
3 Michael Coles	3 3 2 1	9	
4 Dariusz Fliegert	1 1 0 3	5	
5 Kenny McKinna	3 2 0 3	8	
6 Johnny Jørgensen	1 0 3 1	5	
7 Stewart McDonald	E 1 1	2	
8 Grant Blackie	1 0 0	1	

Aggregate: Edinburgh 96 Glasgow 83

Roll of Honour

1951 Edinburgh 108 Glasgow WC 106
1952 Glasgow WC 133 Glasgow Ashfield 83
1953 Glasgow WC 123 Motherwell 93
1964 Edinburgh 96 Glasgow 95
1965 Glasgow 96 Edinburgh 95
1966 Glasgow 99 Edinburgh 93
1967 Edinburgh 106 Glasgow 85
1968 Coatbridge 103 Glasgow 89
1969 Coatbridge 78 Glasgow 77
1974 Coatbridge 87 Berwick 69
1975 Coatbridge
1976 Coatbridge 95 Paisley 60
1977 Edinburgh 81 Glasgow 75
1978 Glasgow 85 Edinburgh 71
1979 Glasgow 81 Berwick 74
1984 Edinburgh 104.5 Glasgow 86.5
1985 Edinburgh 93 Glasgow 63
1989 Edinburgh 106 Glasgow 86
1989 Edinburgh 99 Glasgow 93
1990 Glasgow 101 Edinburgh 90
1991 Glasgow 101 Edinburgh 77
1992 Edinburgh 96 Glasgow 83

In 1975 the competition was staged as a mini-League. Glasgow WC indicates Glasgow White City when there was more than one club racing in the city.

Tyne Tees Trophy

Thursday, September 3

MIDDLESBROUGH 49

1 †Steve Regeling	0 1 3 3	7	
2 Donny Odom	3 0 2 F	5	1
3 Darren Sumner	2 1 2 2	7	2
4 Doug Nicol	3 0 3 1	7	1
5 Paul Whittaker	1 2 1 3	7	2
6 Duncan Chapman	2 3 0 3	8	
7 Paul Pickering	0 3 F	3	
8 Stuart Swales	3 2 fx	5	1

NEWCASTLE 41

1 Mark Thorpe	2 3 2 3 3	13	1
2 Phil Jeffrey	1 2 2 2	7	3
3 Scott Norman	0 fx0 2	2	
4 Sean Courtney	1 1 1 2	5	
5 †David Bargh	3 3 fxN	6	
6 Spencer Timmo	0 T 1 1	2	1
7 David Nagel	2 1 0 1	4	1
8 Andrew Howe	1 0 1	2	2

Sunday, October 11

NEWCASTLE 49

1 Mark Thorpe	**3 3 3 3**	**12**	
2 Phil Jeffrey	2 2 2 2	8	3
3 Scott Norman	0 2 3 0	5	
4 Richard Juul	1 0 2 2	5	1
5 †David Bargh	**3 3 3 2**	**11**	**1**
6 Max Schofield	1 0 1 2	4	
7 David Nagel	2 1 0	3	
8 Andrew Howe	1 0 0	1	1

MIDDLESBROUGH 41

1 †Steve Regeling	1 3 2 1	7	
2 Donny Odom	0 1 0 1	2	
3 Darren Sumner	2 2 1 3	8	1
4 Doug Nicol	3 1 0 1	5	1
5 Paul Whittaker	2 1 0 3	6	
6 Duncan Chapman	0 0 1 3	4	
7 Paul Pickering	3 2 0	5	1
8 Stuart Swales	fx3 1	4	

Aggregate: Newcastle 90 Middlesbrough 90

Mark Thorpe defeated Steve Regeling in a run-off.

Roll of Honour

1975 Newcastle 86 Middlesbrough 70
1976 Newcastle 98 Middlesbrough 58
1977 Newcastle 93 Middlesbrough 63
1978 Newcastle 87 Middlesbrough 68
1979 Newcastle 93 Middlesbrough 63
1980 Newcastle 83 Middlesbrough 73
1981 Newcastle 89 Middlesbrough 67
1982 Newcastle 98 Middlesbrough 94
1983 Newcastle 105 Middlesbrough 85
1986 Newcastle 82 Middlesbrough 73
1987 Newcastle 80 Middlesbrough 75
1989 Middlesbrough 107 Newcastle 85
1990 Newcastle 103 Middlesbrough 89
1991 Newcastle 108 Middlesbrough 72
1992 †Newcastle 90 Middlesbrough 90
†Newcastle won on a race-off.

Spring Trophy

First leg, Friday, March 27

EDINBURGH 49

1 Les Collins	1 1 3 3 2	10	2
2 †Brett Saunders	2 2 2 2	8	1
3 Michael Coles	3 3 3 3 0	12	
4 Kenny McKinna	3 2 1 3	9	
5 Dariusz Fliegert	2 0 0 0	2	1
6 Johnny Jørgensen	R 1 2 2 F	5	1
7 Stewart McDonald	2 0 N 1	3	

GLASGOW 41

1 †Steve Lawson	0 3 1 2	6	1
2 Mick Powell	3 1 1 2 2 1	10	
3 Neil Collins	2 3 3 3 2 3	16	
4 Robert Csillik	1 1 1 1	4	1
5 Robert Nagy	fx0 0 T	0	
6 Tim Korneliussen	3 0 1 0	4	
7 James Grieves	1 0 0 T	1	

Second leg, Sunday, May 20

GLASGOW 48

1 †Steve Lawson	0 3 1 3	7	1
2 Mick Powell	1 1 0 T	2	
3 Neil Collins	3 F 1 2 2	8	2
4 Robert Nagy	3 1 2 2 3 1	12	2
5 Shane Bowes	1 2 2 3 1 3	12	1
6 Geoff Powell	1 0 1 T	2	1
7 Jason Straughan	2 2 T 1	5	

EDINBURGH 42

1 Les Collins	2 3 3 1 3 2	14	1
2 Michael Coles	*rider replacement*		
3 Kenny McKinna	3 2 0 3 R 0	8	
4 Dariusz Fliegert	X 3 3 0 0	6	
5 †Brett Saunders	2 0 2 1 F	5	1
6 Mike McLuskey	0 2 F N	2	
7 Johnny Jørgensen	3 1 1 0 2	7	1
8 Stewart McDonald	*did not ride*		

Aggregate: Edinburgh 91 Glasgow 89

Tri Counties Championship

Thursday, September 17

SHEFFIELD 43

1 Peter Carr	**3 3 2 3**	**11**	**1**
2 Simon Green	1 2 3 1	7	1
3 David Blackburn	2 1 1 0	4	2
4 Tony Langdon	3 2 3 2	10	
5 †Louis Carr	3 2 2 0	7	
6 Steve Johnston	0 1 1 2	4	2
7 Rob Homer	*did not ride*		

PETERBOROUGH 39

1 Mick Poole	2 3 3 3	11	
2 Rodney Colquhoun	0 2 2 1	5	2
3 Mark Blackbird	2 3 2 3	10	
4 Paul Hurry	0 0 0 0	0	
5 Jason Crump	1 3 1 3	8	1
6 Neville Tatum	2 2 R N	4	1
7 Kieran McCullagh	1	1	

LONG EATON 26

1 Carl Blackbird	0 0 1 N	1	
2 Mark Lemon	1 1 0 2	4	
3 †Jan Stæchmann	3 3 2 3	11	
4 Richard Hellsén	1 0 0 1	2	
5 Martin Dixon	1 R 3 0	4	
6 Deon Prinsloo	0 1 R 2	3	
7 Nigel Sparshott	1	1	1

The first leg at Long Eaton on Wednesday, September 2, was abandoned after two races and never re-staged and the third leg at Peterborough was cancelled. Scorers at Long Eaton were: LONG EATON 4 (†Jan Stæchmann 3- 3, Richard Hellsén 1- 1, Carl Blackbird, Deon Prinsloo, Martin Dixon, Mark Lemon and Nigel Sparshott, did not ride SHEFFIELD 5 (Peter Carr 2- 2, Simon Green F- 0, Neil Evitts 1- 1:1, Tony Langdon 2- 2, †Louis Carr, Steve Knott, Steve Johnston, did not ride) PETERBOROUGH 4 (†Stephen Davies 3- 3, Paul Hurry 0- 0, Mick Poole, Rodney Colquhoun, Neville Tatum, Jason Crump and Mark Blackbird, did not ride).

◆ KIERAN McCullagh made his only first team appearance of the season for Peterborough in the Tri Counties Championship. McCullagh, signed when Milton Keynes closed down, had been included in the squad for the rained off leg at Long Eaton.

Auto Coachworks Trophy

Friday, September 18

EDINBURGH 66

1 †Les Collins	2 2 fx3	7	1
2 Brett Saunders	0 3 R 3	6	
3 Michael Coles	3 3 3 2 R	11	
4 Kenny McKinna	2 3 1 2 2	10	1
5 Johnny Jørgensen	3 1 R 1	5	1
6 Stewart McDonald	1 F N 1	2	1
7 Dariusz Fliegert	2 0 1 0 1	4	1
8 Mike Lewthwaite	0 3 2 2	7	2
9 Paul Taylor	2 3 3	8	
10 Grant Blackie	2 F 1	3	1
11 Wayne Park	1 N 2	3	1

NEWCASTLE 60

1 Mark Thorpe	1 0 2 3	6	
2 Phil Jeffrey	3 2 2 1 0 1	9	2
3 Scott Norman	2 1 3 0	6	
4 Richard Juul	1 1 1 T	3	2
5 †David Bargh	R 2 3 2 3 3	13	
6 Max Schofield	3 0 2 0	5	1
7 David Nagel	0 1 T 2	3	1
8 Paul Gould	3 0 3	6	
9 Andrew Howe	1 2 1	4	
10 James Grieves	3 1 R	4	
11 Chris Simpson	F 1 0	1	1

The second leg, scheduled for Newcastle, on Sunday, September 27, was postponed because of a waterlogged track and never staged.

Auto Coachworks 25th Anniversary Challenge

Sunday, October 18

NEWCASTLE 52

1 Mark Thorpe	**3 3 3 3**	**12**	
2 Phil Jeffrey	1 2 2 2 0	7	2
3 Scott Norman	2 3 2 2 1	10	1
4 Richard Juul	1 0 fx3	4	
5 †David Bargh	**3 3 3 3**	**12**	
6 Max Schofield	2 1 0 2	5	2
7 David Nagel	1 0 0 1	2	1

BERWICK 38

1 †Richard Knight	2 2 3 1 3	11	
2 Scott Robson	0 1 3 1 2	7	2
3 David Blackburn	3 1 1 2	7	
4 Scott Lamb	2 2 1 0	5	
5 David Walsh	0 1 1 2	4	2
6 Mike Smith	0 F 0 0	0	
7 Martin Dixon	*3 0 1 0*	*4*	

Farewell Challenge

Thursday, September 17

MIDDLESBROUGH 48

1 †Steve Regeling	1 2 2 2	7	1
2 Donny Odom	0 fx3 3	6	
3 Darren Sumner	2 3 3 2 1	11	1
4 Doug Nicol	1 3 0 3 F	7	1
5 Paul Whittaker	2 0 2 1	5	1
6 Duncan Chapman	3 3 2 1 0 2	11	3
7 Paul Pickering	1 fxN N	1	

EDINBURGH 42

1 †Les Collins	2 2 2 0 0	6	1
2 Brett Saunders	3 1 2 1	7	2
3 Michael Coles	1 3 3 3 3 3	16	
4 Johnny Jørgensen	0 1 1 T	2	
5 Kenny McKinna	3 X 1 1 2	7	1
6 Dariusz Fliegert	2 1 1 N T	4	1
7 Stewart McDonald	0 0 N 0 0	0	

Challenges

Monday, March 23

READING 46

1 Per Jonsson	**3 3 3 3 3**	**15**	
2 David Mullett	2 1 1 2	6	2
3 Jan Andersson	3 2 2 0 0	7	
4 Armando Castagna	3 0 0 3	6	
5 †Jeremy Doncaster	1 1 2 1	5	
6 Ray Morton	3 1 1 1 1	7	2
7 Phillip Morris	F 0 0 N	0	

CRADLEY HEATH 43

1 Greg Hancock	0 3 3 3 3 1	13	1
2 †Simon Cross	1 2 2 1	6	2
3 Billy Hamill	2 2 3 2	9	
4 Gert Handberg	0 0 1 2	3	1
5 Jan O. Pedersen	2 3 1 2 2	10	1
6 Mark Robinson	F 0 0 0	0	
7 Scott Smith	2 0 T 0	2	

Thursday, April 2

SWINDON 47

1 †Mitch Shirra	3 3 R 1	7	
2 Dean Standing	1 2 2 1	6	1
3 Jimmy Nilsen	3 3 2 3 1	12	1
4 John Davis	0 1 3 3	7	
5 Leigh Adams	3 3 3 1 2	12	
6 Peter Schroeck	2 0 R R	2	
7 Darren Boulton	1 0 0 0	1	1

POOLE 43

1 †Marvyn Cox	2 2 3 3 2 3	15	
2 Slawomir Drabik	R 0 T 1	1	
3 Steve Schofield	1 1 2 0	4	1
4 Tony Langdon	1 2 3 0	6	1
5 Craig Boyce	2 1 2 2 R	7	1
6 Tom Knudsen	3 0 1 1	5	2
7 Andy Phillips	R 2 1 2	5	1

Wednesday, April 1

POOLE 46

1 †Marvyn Cox	3 3 3 1 3 2	15	1
2 Slawomir Drabik	1 0 1 1	3	
3 Steve Schofield	3 3 1 1	8	
4 Craig Boyce	0 3 0 2 3	8	1
5 Tony Langdon	1 1 2 0	4	
6 Tom Knudsen	2 2 0 1	5	3
7 Andy Phillips	3 0 0 N	3	

SWINDON 44

1 †Mitch Shirra	2 2 2 2 3 0	11	2
2 Dean Standing	0 0 3 3	6	
3 Jimmy Nilsen	1 1 3 3	8	1
4 John Davis	2 1 2 2	7	3
5 Leigh Adams	3 2 2 2 1 1	11	1
6 Peter Schroeck	1 T R R	1	
7 Steve Camden	0 0 T fx	0	

Friday, April 17

SWINDON 42

1 †Mitch Shirra	1 3 2 3 0	9	
2 Dean Standing	X 1 3 1	5	1
3 Leigh Adams	3 2 3 0	8	
4 Jimmy Nilsen	2 1 2 0 3 2	10	1
5 John Davis	0 3 3 2	8	
6 Peter Schroeck	1 1 0 T	2	
7 Justin Elkins	0 0 0 0	0	

OXFORD 48

1 †Hans Nielsen	3 2 3 2 3 3	16	
2 Mark Carlson	2 0 2 1	5	2
3 Martin Dugard	3 2 2 1 2 1	11	
4 Troy Butler	*rider replacement*		
5 Dean Barker	1 3 1 1 2	8	1
6 Morten Andersen	3 0 1 0 1	5	1
7 Glenn Cunningham	2 0 1 0	3	2
8 Spencer Timmo	*did not ride*		

Friday, May 15

BELLE VUE 48

1 Bobby Ott	3 2 2 0	7	
2 Frede Schøtt	1 1 1 1	4	2
3 †Joe Screen	3 2 3 2 0	10	1
4 Jason Lyons	3 3 2 F 2	10	
5 Shawn Moran	fx0 2 3	5	
6 Paul Smith	2 1 0 1	4	2
7 Carl Stonehewer	3 0 2 3	8	1

WOLVERHAMPTON 42

1 Charles Ermolenko	0 1 0 0 1	2	2
2 Ronnie Correy	*rider replacement*		
3 †Sam Ermolenko	2 2 3 2 3 3 3	18	1
4 Graham Jones	1 2 3 3 3 1 1	14	1
5 Peter Karlsson	2 1 1 1 2	7	
6 Stephen Morris	0 0 0 T	0	
7 Simon Wolstenholme	1 0 T 0	1	
8 Mike Lewthwaite	*did not ride*		

Saturday, May 16

CRADLEY HEATH SELECT 56

1 †Greg Hancock	2 3 3 3 2	13	1
2 Paul Fry	1 2 3 1	7	2
3 Rick Miller	3 3 2 3	11	
4 Scott Smith	1 R R 2	3	
5 Billy Hamill	**3 3 3 2 3**	**14**	**1**
6 Wayne Garratt	3 1 1 0	5	
7 Troy Pratt	0 1 1 1	3	2

HOMEFIRE LEAGUE SELECT 34

1 Andy Grahame	3 2 2 3 1 1	12	
2 Josh Larsen	0 1 2 0	3	1
3 Troy Butler	2 R 1 1 R	4	2
4 Nigel Crabtree	0 0 2 T	2	
5 Alan Grahame	2 2 0 2 3 0	9	
6 Peter McNamara	2 1 T 0	3	
7 Donny Odom	1 0 0 T	1	1

Wednesday, July 15

POOLE 50

1 †Marvyn Cox	3 2 3 3 R	11	
2 Alastair Stevens	0 0 1 1	2	
3 Steve Schofield	**2 2 3 3 3**	**13**	**2**
4 Craig Boyce	3 1 2 3	9	1
5 Jörgen Johansson	1 0 1 1	3	
6 Tony Langdon	2 3 3 0	8	
7 Tom Knudsen	1 3 0 0	4	1

DIVISION TWO SELECT 40

1 Steve Regeling	1 3 2 2 1	9	2
2 Scott Norman	2 2 2 1	7	2
3 Richard Green	1 3 3 1 1 2	11	1
4 Eric Monaghan	2 1 2 0	5	
5 Nigel Crabtree	0 0 N N	0	
6 Jason Crump	3 1 2 0 2	8	1
7 Mark Lemon	0 0 0 0	0	

Saturday, August 15

CRADLEY HEATH 42

1 †Simon Cross	1 2 3 3 R	9	
2 Gert Handberg	*rider replacement*		
3 Greg Hancock	3 2 3 3 1 1	13	
4 Billy Hamill	1 1 1 2 3	8	1
5 Andy Grahame	0 2 1 2 0 0	5	1
6 Andy Phillips	3 1 fx0	4	1
7 Scott Smith	2 fx1 0	3	1

BELLE VUE 47

1 Bobby Ott	2 3 2 3 2	12	1
2 Peter Scully	0 0 2 0	2	
3 †Joe Screen	**3 3 3 3 3**	**15**	
4 Jason Lyons	3 1 2 2	8	2
5 Shawn Moran	2 2 1 2	7	1
6 Carl Stonehewer	1 R fx1 0 1	3	1
7 Paul Smith	0 0 fnN	0	

Wednesday, August 25

POOLE 57

1 †Marvyn Cox	3 3 3 1	10	
2 Alun Rossiter	2 2 0 2	6	3
3 Steve Schofield	2 3 3 2 2	12	1
4 Craig Boyce	3 2 3 2 1	11	1
5 Tom Knudsen	2 0 1 1	4	2
6 Alastair Stevens	3 3 1 3	10	
7 Jörgen Johansson	0 1 2 1	4	2

DANISH SELECT 33

1 Hans Nielsen	1 3 3 1 3 3	14	
2 Brian Andersen	0 1 2 0	3	1
3 Peter Ravn	1 1 0 0	2	
4 Frede Schøtt	0 0 1 N	1	
5 †Bo Petersen	1 2 2 2 3 0	10	
6 Jens Rasmussen	2 X N 0 0	2	
7 Jan Pedersen	1 0 0 N 0	1	1

Friday, September 18

ARENA ESSEX 55

1 Andy Galvin	*rider replacement*		
2 Josh Larsen	0 1 3 F 2 0	6	2
3 Peter Ravn	3 2 3 3 3	14	
4 Bo Petersen	**3 3 3 3 3**	**15**	
5 Troy Pratt	2 1 2 2 2 3	12	2
6 Colin White	0 0 1 0	1	
7 †Alan Mogridge	3 1 1 2	7	1

LONDON SELECT 34

1 Tony Olsson	1 0 0 E	1	1
2 Ray Morton	2 2 2 2 2	10	
3 †Steve Schofield	3 3 1 1 0 2	10	
4 Martin Goodwin	R fxN N	0	
5 Jan Pedersen	1 2 0 E 1	4	1
6 Paul Whittaker	2 0 3 1 0	6	
7 Michael Warren	1 1 0 F 1	3	1

Saturday, October 31

CRADLEY HEATH 42

1 Greg Hancock	2 3 3 3 2 2	15	
2 Gert Handberg	1 1 fx1 1	4	2
3 †Simon Cross	2 2 0 0	4	
4 Justin Walker	0 1 N T	1	1
5 Billy Hamill	2 2 2 2 2 1	11	2
6 Andy Phillips	1 0 0 T	1	
7 Scott Smith	3 1 2 0	6	

WOLVERHAMPTON 48

1 Ronnie Correy	3 3 3 3 0	12	
2 Graham Jones	0 0 3 1	4	
3 Peter Karlsson	3 2 1 3	9	
4 Charles Ermolenko	1 1 2 1	5	
5 †Sam Ermolenko	3 3 1 3 3	13	
6 Stephen Morris	0 0 0 N	0	
7 Nigel Leaver	2 1 2 0 0	5	1

◆ TEENAGER Richard Musson rode for three clubs during the 1992 season. He started off with his parent track Belle Vue, moved to Wolverhampton on loan and had a one match trial for Coventry – failing to score from three rides in their Travelcare Trophy challenge against Arena Essex.

Saturday, May 16

BERWICK 58

1 †Richard Knight	**3 3 3 3**	**12**	
2 Scott Lamb	0 1 3 2	6	1
3 David blackburn	3 2 3 3	11	
4 Scott Robson	3 2 1 3	9	1
5 David Walsh	2 3 2 2	9	2
6 Michael Lowrie	2 1 0 1	4	2
7 Chris Readshaw	3 1 1 2	7	1

THE SCOTS 26

1 †Les Collins	1 1 2 0	4	1
2 Mick Powell	2 0 2 0	4	
3 Shane Bowes	2 2 3 2	9	
4 Robert Nagy	0 3 1 1	5	
5 Dariusz Fliegert	1 1 0 1	3	
6 Mike McLuskey	0 0 0 0	0	
7 Troy Scott	1 0 0 F	1	

Wednesday, June 24

LONG EATON 42

1 †Jan Stæchmann	3 3 2 1 1	10	1
2 Scott Smith	0 0 1 3	4	1
3 Carl Blackbird	3 3 3 R 2	11	
4 Martin Dixon	1 0 2 0	3	
5 Gary O'Hare	3 2 1 1	7	1
6 Deon Prinsloo	2 1 0 fx	3	
7 Nigel Sparshott	1 0 2 1	4	2

HOMEFIRE LEAGUE SELECT 47

1 †Steve Regeling	1 1 3 3 0	8	2
2 Mark Lemon	2 2 0 2	6	1
3 David Bargh	R 3 3 3 3	12	
4 Richard Hellsén	2 1 2 2	7	2
5 David Walsh	0 2 1 2	5	2
6 Chris Readshaw	3 2 1 X 3	9	
7 Peter McNamara	R N F fn	0	

Wednesday, September 9

LONG EATON 52

1 †Jan Stæchmann	**3 3 3 3 3**	**15**	
2 Richard Hellsén	1 1 2 1	5	
3 Carl Blackbird	3 2 1 3	9	1
4 Martin Dixon	1 2 2 2 2	9	3
5 Deon Prinsloo	0 3 1 2	6	2
6 Nigel Sparshott	1 2 0 2	5	1
7 Mark Lemon	0 1 2 0	3	1

LEICESTER LIONS 38

1 Les Collins	2 1 3 0	6	
2 Jason Reed	0 0 N N	0	
3 Neil Collins	1 2 3 1	7	
4 David Blackburn	2 3 2 1 1	9	1
5 †Steve Regeling	3 1 0 3 0	7	
6 Mark Courtney	3 0 3 R 0 1	7	
7 Colin Cook	2 0 R 0	2	1

Thursday, October 8

SHEFFIELD 37

1 Peter Carr	2 2 1 1	6	2
2 Simon Green	0 1 1 2	4	
3 Steve Johnston	1 1 0 0	2	2
4 Sean Wilson	2 3 2 0	7	
5 †Louis Carr	1 2 1 2	6	1
6 Tony Langdon	**3 3 3 3**	**12**	

TRANSATLANTIC STARS 35

1 Ronnie Correy	1 2 2 3	8	1
2 Charles Ermolenko	3 3 3 2	11	
3 Greg Hancock	3 1 3 1	8	1
4 †Doug Nicol	0 0 0 1	1	
5 Billy Hamill	0 0 2 3	5	
6 Donny Odom	2 0 0 0	2	

Sunday, October 11

GLASGOW 40

1 †Steve Lawson	3 0 2 1	6	
2 Jason Straughan	0 1 F 1	2	
3 Neil Collins	3 3 1 1	8	1
4 Mick Powell	0 2 3 3	8	1
5 Shane Bowes	3 3 3 2	11	
6 James Grieves	2 0 1 2	5	1

JASON LYONS SELECT 32

1 †Jason Lyons	2 1 2 2	7	
2 Geoff Powell	1 0 0 0	1	1
3 Peter Carr	2 2 3 3	10	
4 Steve Johnston	1 1 1 0	3	2
5 Nigel Crabtree	1 3 2 0	6	
6 Stewart McDonald	0 2 0 3	5	1

Friday, June 12

ARENA ESSEX 54			
1 Brian Karger	*rider replacement*		
2 †Alan Mogridge	2 3 2 2	9	
3 Bo Petersen	**3 3 3 2**	**11**	**1**
4 Andy Galvin	**3 3 3 3**	**12**	
5 Allan Johansen	2 1 3 3	9	1
6 Troy Pratt	3 R 1 1	5	
7 Robert Ledwith	2 1 0 0 1 1	5	2
8 Roland Pollard	1 1 1 N 0	3	2

RYE HOUSE 36			
1 †Martin Goodwin	3 2 3 1 1 2	12	2
2 Sean Courtney	0 0 0 N	0	
3 Jens Rasmussen	2 R 0 1	3	1
4 Jan Pedersen	1 2 3 2 0 3	11	
5 Mark Courtney	0 0 N R	0	
6 Trevor O'Brien	R 2 2 2 2	8	
7 Chris Young	1 1 N 0	2	1

Wednesday, July 29

POOLE 64			
1 †Marvyn Cox	**3 3 3 2**	**11**	**1**
2 Alastair Stevens	**2 2 3 2**	**9**	**3**
3 Steve Schofield	2 3 2 3	10	1
4 Craig Boyce	**3 2 3 3**	**11**	**1**
5 Tony Langdon	2 3 1 2 3	11	2
6 Steve Leigh	0 R N 2 0	2	1
7 Tom Knudsen	2 2 N 3 2 1	10	2

PETERBOROUGH 26			
1 Mick Poole	1 1 1 1	4	
2 Rodney Colquhoun	0 0 1 0	1	
3 †Stephen Davies	3 1 3 0 2	9	
4 Neville Tatum	1 1 1 0	3	
5 Paul Hurry	0 0 1 0	1	
6 Mark Blackbird	1 R 2 1	4	1
7 Jason Crump	3 1 0 0	4	

Monday, August 31

EXETER 36			
1 †Peter Jeffery	F 2 3 0	5	
2 Mark Simmonds	2 1 2 0	5	1
3 Frank Smart	1 1 2 2 0	6	2
4 Colin Cook	0 1 1 2	4	1
5 Richard Green	2 2 2 1 3 1	11	1
6 Paul Fry	2 0 2 1	5	1
7 Ian Humphreys	fx0 T 0	0	

POOLE 54			
1 Marvyn Cox	*rider replacement*		
2 Alun Rossiter	3 3 1 3 2	12	1
3 Steve Schofield	**3 3 3 3 3**	**15**	
4 Tom Knudsen	3 3 2 1	9	
5 Craig Boyce	1 0 2 3	6	1
6 Alastair Stevens	3 R 0 N	3	
7 Jörgen Johansson	1 2 3 1 1	8	2
8 Martin Willis	1 0 0 0	1	

Monday, August 31

KING'S LYNN 48			
1 Bohumil Brhel	fx3 2 0	5	1
2 Gary Allan	fx2 3 3 0	8	1
3 †Mark Loram	3 3 3 3 2	14	
4 Bobby Ott	3 3 2 3	11	
5 Glenn Doyle	2 2 3 0	7	2
6 Robbie Fuller	0 0 0 0	0	
7 Kevin Brice	1 1 1 0	3	

PETERBOROUGH 41			
1 Mick Poole	3 N N T	3	
2 Rodney Colquhoun	2 0 0 2 1	5	2
3 Neville Tatum	1 1 1 1 2 3	9	2
4 Paul Hurry	0 1 1 3 1 1	7	2
5 †Stephen Davies	1 2 N N	3	
6 Mark Blackbird	2 1 N 2 N N	5	1
7 Jason Crump	3 2 0 2 0 2	9	

Thursday, September 10

MIDDLESBROUGH 34			
1 †Steve Regeling	2 2 3 2 2 3	14	
2 Donny Odom	R 1 1 T	2	1
3 Darren Sumner	1 2 1 1 1	6	1
4 Doug Nicol	0 0 0 T	0	
5 Paul Whittaker	1 1 1 0	3	1
6 Duncan Chapman	3 F 1 2 2 0	8	1
7 Paul Pickering	0 T 0 1	1	1

CRADLEY HEATH 56			
1 Greg Hancock	3 3 3 3 2	14	
2 Andy Grahame	1 2 2 2	7	2
3 †Simon Cross	3 3 3 1	10	
4 Gert Handberg	2 0 3 2	7	2
5 Billy Hamill	3 3 3 3 E	12	
6 Andy Phillips	2 0 0 0 1	3	1
7 Scott Smith	1 2 0 0	3	2

Wednesday, September 23

LONG EATON 48			
1 †Jan Stæchmann	3 2 3 3 2	13	1
2 Richard Hellsén	2 3 3 2 0	10	2
3 Carl Blackbird	3 2 R 2	7	
4 Martin Dixon	1 2 0 2	5	
5 Deon Prinsloo	0 0 2 1	3	1
6 Nigel Sparshott	1 N 0 1	2	1
7 Mark Lemon	3 0 2 2 1	8	2

BELLE VUE 42			
1 Bobby Ott	1 3 3 3 3 3	16	
2 Frede Schøtt	0 1 0 T	1	
3 †Joe Screen	2 1 F 2 1	6	
4 Jason Lyons	3 1 1 1 0	6	
5 Shawn Moran	2 3 0 1 R	6	2
6 Carl Stonehewer	2 0 T 3	5	
7 Paul Smith	0 1 1 T	2	1

Friday, October 9

EDINBURGH 35			
1 †Les Collins	1 2 3 3 1 1	11	
2 Jan Stæchmann	fx1 T T	1	1
3 Michael Coles	1 1 2 1 1	6	2
4 Kenny McKinna	0 2 2 0 2 X	6	1
5 Jan Andersen	1 1 1 0	3	2
6 Brett Saunders	3 0 2 2	7	
7 Dariusz Fliegert	1 T 0 N 0	1	

WOLVERHAMPTON 55			
1 Ronnie Correy	**3 3 3 3 3**	**15**	
2 Graham Jones	2 0 1 2	5	2
3 Peter Karlsson	**2 3 3 2 2**	**12**	**3**
4 Charles Ermolenko	2 fxfx2	4	2
5 Sam Ermolenko	**3 3 3 3**	**12**	
6 Stephen Morris	0 R 0 1	1	
7 Nigel Leaver	2 3 0 1	6	

Thursday, October 22

SHEFFIELD 41			
1 Peter Carr	R 3 2 2 2	9	2
2 Simon Green	1 0 T 2	3	1
3 Craig Boyce	2 3 2 3 0	10	1
4 †Louis Carr	1 1 T 3	5	1
5 Tony Langdon	2 2 3 3 1	11	
6 Steve Johnston	0 0 T 0	0	
7 Rob Homer	1 1 0	2	
8 Dean Child	0 R 1	1	

BELLE VUE 49			
1 Bobby Ott	3 2 1 2	8	1
2 Frede Schøtt	2 0 0 2	4	2
3 †Joe Screen	3 3 0 3	9	
4 Jason Lyons	0 1 1 1	3	
5 Shawn Moran	3 2 1 3	9	
6 Carl Stonehewer	1 1 0 3	5	1
7 Paul Smith	3 3 1	7	
8 Mike Lewthwaite	2 2 0	4	2

◆ A TOTAL of ten challenge matches between First and Second Division opposition were staged during the 1992 season – and only one featured a victory for the Division Two side!
Long Eaton defeated a full strength Belle Vue by six points in their last match of the season.

◆ FIVE First Division tracks played host to Second Division club sides during the summer – with Division Two champions Peterborough being the busiest, losing at both Poole and King's Lynn.

SWAPA Awards

RIDER OF THE YEAR

1978 Ole Olsen
1979 Ivan Mauger
1980 Dave Jessup
1981 Bruce Penhall
1982 Les Collins
1983 Michael Lee
1984 Erik Gundersen
1985 Erik Gundersen
1986 Hans Nielsen
1987 Hans Nielsen
1988 Erik Gundersen
1989 Hans Nielsen
1990 Todd Wiltshire
1991 Jan O. Pedersen

YOUNG RIDER OF THE YEAR

1983 Kelvin Tatum
1984 Lance King
1985 Kelvin Tatum
1986 Paul Thorp
1987 Jimmy Nilsen
1988 Mark Loram
1989 Joe Screen
1990 Chris Louis
1991 Tony Rickardsson

ORDER OF MERIT

1979 Barry Briggs
1980 Jack Parker
1981 Tommy Price
1982 Ove Fundin
1983 Freddie Williams
1984 Frank Varey
1985 Ivan Mauger
1986 Peter Collins
1987 Erik Gundersen
1988 Ole Olsen
1989 Chris Morton
1990 Colin Pratt
1991 Ronnie Moore

GRAHAM BAKER AWARD

1988 Frank Maclean
1989 Barrry Briggs

TRAVEL PLUS TOURS JOURNALIST OF THE YEAR

1990 Peter Oakes
1991 Tony Millard

Rider of the Year and Young Rider of the Year awards are voted for by members of the Speedway Writers' and Photographers' Association. The Order of Merit Award and the Graham Baker Award – in memory of the former SWAPA member – are at the discretion of the SWAPA Committee. Travel Plus Journalist of the Year is selected by James Easter, managing director of Travel Plus. No awards were made in 1992.

AUTOVALET TROPHY (Mildenhall, Sunday, March 22): Tony Rickardsson 15, Billy Hamill 14, Alan Grahame 11, Armando Castagna 10, Steve Schofield 10, David Norris 9, Jeremy Doncaster 8, David Smart 8, Chris Louis 6, Jamie Habbin 6, Jacek Rempala 6, Melvyn Taylor 5, Sean Wilson 5, Gary Tagg 2, Richard Hellsén 2, Nigel Leaver 1. *Reserves: Savalas Clouting 1, Jason Gage 1.*

Roll of Honour

1992 Tony Rickardsson (Ipswich)

BILLY SANDERS MEMORIAL TROPHY (Ipswich, Thursday, March 19): Tony Rickardsson 14+3, Kelvin Tatum 14+2, Jeremy Doncaster 12, Billy Hamill 11, Chris Louis 10, Greg Hancock 10, David Norris 8, Neville Tatum 8, Ben Howe 7, Josh Larsen 5, Jacek Rempala 5, Alan Mogridge 5, Steve Schofield 4, Zdenek Tesar 3, Paul Whittaker 2, Paul Hurry 1. *Reserves: Shaun Tacey 1, Lawrence Hare 0.*

Roll of Honour

1988 Armando Castagna (Ipswich)
1991 Jeremy Doncaster (Reading)
1992 Tony Rickardsson (Ipswich)

KEYLINE CLASSIC (Bradford, Saturday, June 6): Kelvin Tatum 14, Simon Cross 11+3, Joe Screen 11+2, Jason Lyons 11+1, Andy Grahame 10, Shawn Moran 10, Graham Jones 9, Shane Bowes 8, Peter Karlsson 7, Sean Wilson 7, Bobby Ott 6, Dean Barker 6, Frede Schøtt 5, David Norris 4, Kelly Moran 1, Robert Nagy 0. *Reserves: Darren Pearson 0, Richard Smith, did not ride.*

Roll of Honour

1986 Hans Nielsen (Oxford)
1988 Sam Ermolenko (Wolverhampton)
1989 Sam Ermolenko (Wolverhampton)
1990 Jan O. Pedersen (Cradley Heath)
1991 Glenn Doyle (Bradford)
1992 Kelvin Tatum (Bradford)

SCOTTISH RIDERS' CHAMPIONSHIP (Edinburgh, Friday, June 19): Kenny McKinna 15, Scott Lamb 14, Mike Lewthwaite 13, Michael Lowrie 12, Stewart McDonald 11 (Under 21 and Under 18 champion), James Grieves 9, Rob Homer 8, Paul Taylor 8, Grant Blackie 7, Brian Mercer 6, Stewart Crome 4, Stuart Coleman 3, Raymond Fosbury 3, Muir Templeton 3, George Wells 1, Wayne Park 0. *Reserves: Paul Gould 2, Ally Smith 0, Alan Hartley 0.*

Roll of Honour

1991 Scott Lamb (Newcastle)
1992 Kenny McKinna (Edinburgh)

Under 21 Champion

1991 Michael Lowrie (Berwick)
1992 Stewart McDonald (Edinburgh)

Under 18 Champion

1991 James Grieves (Glasgow)
1992 Stewart McDonald (Edinburgh)

BARUM TROPHY (King's Lynn, Sunday, June 28): 1 Henrik Gustafsson, 2 Brian Karger, 3 Mark Loram, 4 Gary Havelock. *Defeated semi finalists:* Hans Nielsen, Dennis Löfqvist, Gary Allan, Tony Olsson. *Qualifying scorers (15 heats):* Hans Nielsen 15, Henrik Gustafsson 12, Mark Loram 11, Brian Karger 10, Gary Havelock 9, Dennis Löfqvist 8, Gary Allan 5, Tony Olsson 5, Bo Petersen 5, Alun Rossiter 4, Ray Morton 4, Mikael Teurnberg 2. *Reserve: Emmerson Fairweather 0.*

Roll of Honour

1989 Hans Nielsen (Oxford)
1990 Jan O. Pedersen (Cradley Heath)
1991 Joe Screen (Belle Vue)
1992 Henrik Gustafsson (King's Lynn)

SUPER PINK PIZZA CLASSIC (Swindon, Sunday, July 5): 1 Zdenek Tesar, 2 Jimmy Nilsen, 3 Kelly Moran, 4 Brian Karger. *Defeated semi finalists:* Dean Standing, Peter Karlsson, Josh Larsen, Gary Allan. *Qualifying scorers (15 heats):* Jimmy Nilsen 13, Peter Karlsson 12, Brian Karger 11, Kelly Moran 10, Dean Standing 9, Zdenek Tesar 9, Shawn Moran 8, Gary Allan 6, Josh Larsen 4, Richard Green 3, Alun Rossiter 2, Tony Olsson 1. *Reserve: Steve Masters 1.*

Roll of Honour

1992 Zdenek Tesar (Ipswich)

LADBROKE OLYMPIQUE (Wolverhampton, Monday, July 6): Ronnie Correy 11, Sam Ermolenko 10+3, Gary Havelock 10+2, Greg Hancock 9, Chris Louis 8, Bobby Ott 8, Graham Jones 8, Charles Ermolenko 7, John Jørgensen 7, Jan Stæchmann 7, Dennis Löfqvist 7, Andy Grahame 6, Peter Karlsson 6, Andy Smith 6, Andy Phillips 5, Scott Norman 5. *Reserves: Stephen Morris and Simon Wolstenholme, did not ride.*

Roll of Honour

1966 Barry Briggs (Swindon)
1967 Anders Michanek (Long Eaton)
1970 Ole Olsen (Wolverhampton)
1971 Ole Olsen (Wolverhampton)
1972 Ole Olsen (Wolverhampton)
1973 Ole Olsen (Wolverhampton)
1974 Ole Olsen (Wolverhampton)
1975 Ole Olsen (Wolverhampton)
1976 Peter Collins (Belle Vue)
1977 Billy Sanders (Ipswich)
1978 Gordon Kennett (White City)
1979 Phil Crump (Swindon)
1980 Les Collins (Leicester)
1981 Mitch Shirra (Coventry)
1982 Hans Nielsen (Birmingham)
1984 Hans Nielsen (Oxford)
1987 Sam Ermolenko (Wolverhampton)
1988 Hans Nielsen (Oxford)
1989 Jan O. Pedersen (Cradley Heath)
1990 Ronnie Correy (Wolverhampton)
1991 Greg Hancock (Cradley Heath)
1992 Ronnie Correy (Wolverhampton)

■ *Meetings held at Newcastle (1966-67), Wolverhampton (1970-80, 1984-92) and Birmingham (1981-82).*

WESTERNAPOLIS (Exeter, Monday, July 13): Martin Goodwin 12, Peter Jeffery 11, Steve Regeling 11, Nigel Crabtree 10, Jan Stæchmann 9, Colin Cook 8, Stephen Davies 8, Deon Prinsloo 8, Jason Crump 7, Mark Simmonds 7, Carl Blackbird 6, Frank Smart 6, David Smart 4, Paul Fry 4, Trevor O'Brien 3, Richard Green 3. *Reserves: Ian Humphreys 2, Tommy Palmer 0.*

Roll of Honour

Division One

1967 Eric Boocock (Halifax)
1968 Eric Boocock (Halifax)
1969 Nigel Boocock (Coventry)
1970 Nigel Boocock (Coventry)
1971 Ivan Mauger (Belle Vue)
1972 Ivan Mauger (Belle Vue)
1973 Ivan Mauger (Exeter)
1974 Phil Crump (Newport)
1975 Ivan Mauger (Exeter)
1976 Peter Collins (Belle Vue)
1977 Michael Lee (King's Lynn)
1978 Phil Crump (Bristol)
1979 Zdenek Kudrna (Exeter)
1984 Phil Crump (Swindon)

Division Two

1990 John Williams (Exeter)
1991 Richard Green (Exeter)
1992 Martin Goodwin (Rye House)

THORNLEIGH FREIGHT GOLDEN HAMMER (Cradley Heath, Wednesday, July 22): Sam Ermolenko 15, Per Jonsson 11+3, Chris Louis 11+2, Joe Screen 10, Ronnie Correy 9, Andy Grahame 9, Armando Castagna 9, Brian Karger 8, Greg Hancock 7, Andy Smith 6, Kelvin Tatum 6, Simon Cross 5, Gert Handberg 5, Gary Havelock 5, Martin Dugard 4, Andy Phillips 0. *Reserves: Scott Smith and Justin Walker, did not ride.*

Roll of Honour

1977 Ole Olsen (Wolverhampton)
1978 Scott Autrey (Exeter)
1979 Bobby Schwartz (Cradley Heath)
1980 Chris Morton (Belle Vue)
1982 Kenny Carter (Halifax)
1983 Lance King (Cradley Heath)
1984 Alan Grahame (Cradley Heath)
1985 Kenny Carter (Halifax)
1986 Erik Gundersen (Cradley Heath)
1987 Erik Gundersen (Cradley Heath)
1988 Hans Nielsen (Oxford)
1989 Jan O. Pedersen (Cradley Heath)
1990 Simon Cross (Cradley Heath)
1991 Sam Ermolenko (Wolverhampton)
1992 Sam Ermolenko (Wolverhampton)

ELFORD'S DAIHATSU BLUE RIBAND (Poole, Wednesday, August 5): 1 Mitch Shirra 2 Marvyn Cox 3 Craig Boyce 4 Greg Hancock. *Qualifying scorers:* Craig Boyce 13, Mitch Shirra 13, Marvyn Cox 12, Greg Hancock 10, Steve Schofield 9, Mark Thorpe 9, Gary Allan 9, Tom Knudsen 8, Mark Loram 8, Bohumil Brhel 7, Andy Grahame 6, Simon Cross 5, Chris Louis 5, Armando Castagna 3, Josh Larsen 3, Kelly Moran 0.

Roll of Honour

1970 Barry Briggs (Swindon)
1971 Ole Olsen (Wolverhampton)
1972 Ray Wilson (Leicester)
1973 Anders Michanek (Reading)
1974 Ole Olsen (Wolverhampton)
1975 Malcolm Simmons (Poole)
1976 Malcolm Simmonds (Poole)
1977 Malcolm Simmons (Poole)
1978 Malcolm Simmons (Poole)
1979 Bobby Schwartz (Cradley Heath)
1980 Dave Jessup (King's Lynn)
1981 Bruce Penhall (Cradley Heath)
1982 Bobby Schwartz (Reading)
1983 Erik Gundersen (Cradley Heath)
1984 Mitch Shirra (Reading)
1985 Stan Bear (Poole)
1986 Kevin Smith (Poole)
1987 Melvyn Taylor (Mildenhall)
1988 Steve Schofield (Poole)
1989 Steve Schofield (Hackney)
1990 Chris Louis (Ipswich)
1991 Marvyn Cox (Poole)
1992 Mitch Shirra (Swindon)

BLUE RIBAND winner ... Mitch Shirra

SCOTTISH OPEN CHAMPIONSHIP (Edinburgh, Friday, August 28): Greg Hancock 14, Michael Coles 11+3, David Bargh 11+2, Steve Regeling 11+1, Jason Lyons 10, Richard Knight 9, Les Collins 9, Billy Hamill 9, Neil Collins 8, David Walsh 6, Kenny McKinna 6, Frede Schøtt 5, Brett Saunders 4, Robert Nagy 3, Eric Monaghan 2, Mark Thorpe 0. *Reserves: Dariusz Fliegert 1, Johnny Jørgensen 0.*

Roll of Honour

1960 Doug Templeton (Edinburgh)
1961 Trevor Redmond (Wolverhampton)
1962 Doug Templeton (Edinburgh)
1963 Maury Mattingley (Wolverhampton)
1964 George Hunter (Edinburgh)
1965 Arne Pander (Oxford)
1966 Bill Landels (Edinburgh)
1967 Barry Briggs (Swindon)
1968 Martin Ashby (Exeter)
1969 Reidar Eide (Coatbridge)
1970 Ivan Mauger (Belle Vue)
1971 Ivan Mauger (Belle Vue)
1972 Ivan Mauger (Belle Vue)
1973 Ivan Mauger (Exeter)
1975 Brian Collins (Coatbridge)
1976 Peter Collins (Belle Vue)
1977 Bert Harkins (Edinburgh)
1981 Wayne Brown (Berwick)
1983 Phil Collins (Cradley Heath)
1984 Mitch Shirra (Reading)
1985 Jamie Luckhurst (Wimbledon)
1986 Les Collins (Edinburgh)
1987 Neville Tatum (Wimbledon)
1988 Steve Lawson (Glasgow)
1989 Todd Wiltshire (Wimbledon)
1990 Les Collins (Edinburgh)
1981 Greg Hancock (Cradley Heath)
1992 Greg Hancock (Cradley Heath)

AT THE DOUBLE ... Greg Hancock

PRIDE OF THE POTTERIES (Stoke, Sunday, September 20): Simon Cross 14, Charles Ermolenko 12, Gary Chessell 12, Mark Carlson 10, Nigel Crabtree 10, Garry Stead 10, Frede Schøtt 8, Les Collins 8, Alan Grahame 7, Paul Thorp 7, David Steen 5, Louis Carr 5, Andy Grahame 5, Stephen Morris 4, Andy Meredith 3, Gary O'Hare 1. *Reserves:* Ade Hoole 1, Mark Walsh 0.

Roll of Honour

1976 Joe Owen (Newcastle)
1977 John Jackson (Ellesmere Port)
1978 Steve Finch (Ellesmere Port)
1979 Andy Grahame (Milton Keynes)
1980 Billy Burton (Stoke)
1981 Robert Lightfoot (Stoke)
1982 Steve Lawson (Glasgow)
1983 Alan Molyneux (Long Eaton)
1984 Martin Yeates (Weymouth)
1985 Gary Havelock (Middlesbrough)
1986 Paul Thorp (Stoke)
1987 Nigel Crabtree (Stoke)
1988 Mick Poole (Peterborough)
1989 Mick Poole (Peterborough)
1991 Sam Ermolenko (Wolverhampton)
1992 Simon Cross (Cradley Heath)

SILVER-SKI CHAMPIONSHIP OF SUSSEX (Eastbourne, Sunday, September 20): 1 Andrew Silver 2 Dean Barker 3 Josh Larsen 4 Nathan Simpson. Qualifying *scorers:* Glenn Doyle 8, Troy Pratt 8, Andrew Silver 8, Dean Barker 8, Nathan Simpson 8, Josh Larsen 7, Jörgen Johansson 7, Gordon Kennett 7, David Norris 6, Paul Woods 6, Craig Boyce 5, Tom Knudsen 5, Bo Petersen 4, Alan Mogridge 3, Olli Tyrvainen 3, Darren Grayling 3. *Reserve: Nathan Gaymer 0.* Run-off for Final place: Larsen, Johansson, Kennett. Final: Silver, Barker, Larsen, Simpson, Pratt (fx), Doyle (fx).

Roll of Honour

1969 Martyn Piddock (Canterbury)
1970 Richard May (Reading)
1972 Allen Emmett (Rayleigh)
1973 Roger Johns (Eastbourne)
1976 Steve Weatherley (Eastbourne)
1985 Jamie Luckhurst (Wimbledon)
1986 Neil Middleditch (Arena Essex)
1987 Nigel Crabtree (Stoke)
1989 Dean Standing (Ipswich)
1990 Alan Mogridge (Ipswich)
1991 Martin Dugard (Oxford)
1992 Andrew Silver (Eastbourne)

SABRE CLEANING SERVICES LTD 12 LAPPER (Arena Essex, Friday, October 16): 1 Mark Loram 2 Bo Petersen 3 Chris Louis 4 Andy Galvin. *Qualifying scorers:* Mark Loram 9, Zdenek Tesar 9, Bo Petersen 9, Brian Karger 8, Greg Hancock 8, Andy Galvin 7, Josh Larsen 7, Chris Louis 7, Andrew Silver 7, Bohumil Brhel 6, Troy Pratt 6, Jeremy Doncaster 5, Alan Mogridge 3, Martin Goodwin 3, Peter Ravn 2, Steve Schofield 0. *Final:* Loram, Petersen, Louis, Galvin, Hancock, Larsen, Karger, Tesar (F).

The original staging on Friday, October 2, was abandoned after 11 races because of heavy rain. Scorers at the time were: Sam Ermolenko 6, Martin Dugard 6, Mark Loram 6, Brian Karger 5, Chris Louis 5, Peter Ravn 5, Greg Hancock 5, Andrew Silver 4, Zdenek Tesar 4, Bo Petersen 4, Martin Goodwin 4, Troy Pratt 4, Josh Larsen 3, Andy Galvin 3, Craig Boyce 2, Alan Mogridge 0.

Roll of Honour

1984 Andrew Silver (Rye House)
1985 Gordon Kennett (Eastbourne)
1986 Martin Goodwin (Arena Essex)
1987 Andrew Silver (Arena Essex)
1988 Martin Goodwin (Arena Essex)
1989 Martin Goodwin (Arena Essex)
1990 Alan Mogridge (Ipswich)
1991 Brian Karger (Arena Essex)
1992 Mark Loram (King's Lynn)

G.A. WOODWARD STAR OF ANGLIA (Ipswich, Thursday, October 22): Sam Ermolenko 15, Brian Karger 13, Peter Ravn 10, Bohumil Brhel 9, Mark Loram 9, Tony Rickardsson 9, Charles Ermolenko 8, David Norris 8, Bo Petersen 7, Shane Parker 7, Chris Louis 6, Steve Schofield 6, Tony Olsson 6, Troy Pratt 4, Ronnie Correy 3, Ben Howe 0.

Roll of Honour

1979 John Louis (Ipswich)
1980 Ole Olsen (Coventry)
1991 Jeremy Doncaster (Reading)
1992 Sam Ermolenko (Wolverhampton)

R.T. STEWARD 16 LAPPER (Ipswich, Thursday, October 29): 1 Chris Louis 21, 2 Shane Parker 20, 3 Ben Howe 19, 4 Greg Hancock 18, 5 Josh Larsen 17, 6 Tony Olsson 11, 7 Jeremy Doncaster 9, 8 Billy Hamill 7. *16 Lap Final finishing positions:* Chris Louis, Ben Howe, Shane Parker, Josh Larsen, Tony Olsson, Greg Hancock, Jeremy Doncaster, Billy Hamill. *Qualifying scorers (12 heats):* Greg Hancock 12, Shane Parker 8, Billy Hamill 7, Josh Larsen 7, Chris Louis 7, Tony Rickardsson 7, Ben Howe 7, Jeremy Doncaster 7, Tony Olsson 5, Savalas Clouting 3, Zdenek Tesar 2, Bohumil Brhel 0.

Tony Rickardsson qualified for the Final but withdrew because of illness.

Roll of Honour

1979 Joe Owen (Hull)
1980 Billy Sanders (Ipswich)
1981 Phil Crump (Swindon)
1982 Phil Crump (Swindon)
1983 Kenny Carter (Halifax)
1984 Phil Crump (Swindon)
1985 Kenny Carter (Halifax)
1986 Hans Nielsen (Oxford)
1987 Jan O. Pedersen (Cradley Heath)
1989 Andy Galvin (Hackney)
1990 Craig Boyce (Poole)
1991 Sam Ermolenko (Wolverhampton)
1992 Chris Louis (Ipswich)

PETER CRAVEN MEMORIAL TROPHY (Belle Vue, Friday, October 30): Greg Hancock 15, Ronnie Correy 13+3, Hans Nielsen 13+2, Joe Screen 11, Bobby Ott 11, Shawn Moran 9, Sam Ermolenko 8, Billy Hamill 8, Josh Larsen 6, Kenny McKinna 6, Frede Schøtt 5, Graham Jones 5, Les Collins 4, Neil Collins 3, David Bargh 2, Carl Stonehewer 1. *Reserve: Jon Armstrong 0.*

Roll of Honour

1967 Ivan Mauger (Newcastle)
1969 Ole Olsen (Newcastle)
1970 Jim Airey (Sheffield)
1971 Ole Olsen (Wolverhampton)
1974 Chris Morton (Belle Vue)
1975 Chris Morton (Belle Vue)
1978 Peter Collins (Belle Vue)
1980 Dennis Sigalos (Hull)
1985 Andy Smith (Belle Vue)
1986 Chris Morton (Belle Vue)
1988 Kelly Moran (Sheffield)
1989 Shawn Moran (Belle Vue)
1990 Billy Hamill (Cradley Heath)
1991 Kelly Moran (Belle Vue)
1992 Greg Hancock (Cradley Heath)

PRIDE OF THE EAST (King's Lynn, Saturday, October 31): Henrik Gustafsson (above) 15, Hans Nielsen 14, Bohumil Brhel 12, Marvyn Cox 10, Mark Loram 9, Tomasz Gollob 9, Peter Ravn 8, Richard Knight 8, Troy Pratt 7, Kevin Brice 6, Gary Allan 6, Chris Manchester 4, Brian Karger 4, Bobby Ott 4, Josh Larsen 2, Jacek Gollob 2.

Roll of Honour

1966 Colin Pratt (Hackney)
1967 Bengt Larsson (Sheffield)
1968 Terry Betts (King's Lynn)
1969 Howard Cole (King's Lynn)
1970 Ole Olsen (Wolverhampton)
1971 Ole Olsen (Wolverhampton)
1972 Ole Olsen (Wolverhampton)
1973 Anders Michanek (Reading)
1974 Ivan Mauger (Exeter)
1975 John Louis (Ipswich)
1976 Peter Collins (Belle Vue)
1977 Ole Olsen (Coventry)
1978 Ole Olsen (Coventry)
1979 Dave Jessup (King's Lynn)
1980 Dave Jessup (King's Lynn)
1981 Michael Lee (King's Lynn)
1982 Tommy Knudsen (Coventry)
1983 Michael Lee (Poole)
1984 Hans Nielsen (Oxford)
1985 Jan Andersson (Reading)
1986 Sam Ermolenko (Wolverhampton)
1987 Kelvin Tatum (Coventry)
1989 Martin Dugard (Oxford)
1990 Kelvin Tatum (Coventry)
1991 Henrik Gustafsson (King's Lynn)
1992 Henrik Gustafsson (King's Lynn)

Northern Riders' Championship

Roll of Honour

1967 Ivan Mauger (Newcastle)
1968 Ivan Mauger (Belle Vue)
1969 Ivan Mauger (Belle Vue)
1970 Eric Boocock (Halifax)
1971 Jim Airey (Sheffield)
1972 Ivan Mauger (Belle Vue)
1973 Bob Valentine (Sheffield)
1974 Peter Collins (Belle Vue)
1975 Peter Collins (Belle Vue)
1976 Doug Wyer (Sheffield)
1977 Alan Wilkinson (Belle Vue)
1978 Reg Wilson (Sheffield)
1979 Doug Wyer (Sheffield)
1980 Ivan Mauger (Hull)
1981 Kenny Carter (Halifax)
1982 Shawn Moran (Sheffield)
1983 Chris Morton (Belle Vue)
1984 Peter Collins (Belle Vue)
1985 Shawn Moran (Sheffield)
1986 Peter Carr (Sheffield)
1987 Chris Morton (Belle Vue)
1992 Sam Ermolenko (Wolverhampton)

Sheffield, Thursday, October 15

Sam Ermolenko 13+3, Peter Carr 13+2, Tony Langdon 11+3, Shawn Moran 11+2, Joe Screen 10, Les Collins 9, Mark Thorpe 9, David Bargh 8, Steve Regeling 7, Sean Wilson 7, Paul Thorp 7, Simon Green 4, David Blackburn 4, Kenny McKinna 3, Nigel Crabtree 2, Neil Collins 2.

Pairs Meetings

GULF OIL PAIRS CLASSIC (Edinburgh, Friday, June 26): 1 Les Collins 14 & John Wainwright 4:2 = 18, 2 David Bargh 17 & Richard Juul 2 = 17, 3 David Walsh 8:1 & Scott Lamb 8:3 = 16, 4 Kenny McKinna 10 & Dariusz Fliegert 4:1 = 14, Scott Norman 9:1 & Phil Jeffrey 5:1 = 14, 6 Michael Coles 10 & Mike Lewthwaite 1 = 11. *Reserves: Brett Saunders and Stewart McDonald, did not ride.*

BEST PAIRS (Stoke, Thursday, October 29): 1 Andy Meredith 5:2 & Ade Hoole 17 = 22, 2 David Steen 6:3 & Mike Hampson 15 = 21, 3 Garry Stead 13:1 & Anthony Barlow 7:3 = 20, 4 Nigel Crabtree 13:1 & Jon Hughes 5:2 = 18, 5 Gary Chessell 15 & Matthew Powell 2:2 = 17, 6 Alan Grahame 14 & Harvey Bell 0 = 14, 7 Eric Monaghan 11 & Mark Walsh 1:1 = 12.

The meeting was run on a handicap basis with team members – named first in all pairings – starting from a 30 yard handicap.

REWARD-REAPING ... American Rick Miller , seen tussling with Hans Nielsen, staged one of the most successful Testimonial meetings of recent times with a full programme of off track entertainment for fans

MICHAEL COLES

Edinburgh, Sunday, October 4 Edinburgh

THE GREAT BRITS 43

1 Les Collins	3 1 2 **2**	8	1
2 Alun Rossiter	1 0 **1** 0	2	1
3 Kenny McKinna	3 2 2 1	8	
4 Scott Lamb	**2 1 1** 3	7	3
5 Michael Coles	2 3 2 3	10	
6 Garry Stead	0 1 F 3	4	
7 Stewart McDonald	1 0 0	1	
8 Grant Blackie	0 2 1	3	

EURO-ROOS 47

1 Brian Karger	2 3 3 0	8	
2 Dariusz Fliegert	0 0 1 **1**	2	1
3 Frede Schøtt	1 2 3 2	8	
4 Jan Andersen	F F 0 2	2	
5 David Blackburn	3 3 0 1	7	
6 Brett Saunders	1 **2** 3 0	6	1
7 Mike Lewthwaite	**2** 3 3	8	1
8 Michael Lowrie	3 1 **2**	6	1

MICHAEL COLES will never forget the day his Testimonial meeting was rained off...it was also his wedding day! Even though the original staging on Friday, October 2, was called off because of a waterlogged track Michael and his bride Michelle went ahead with their wedding in one of the Powderhall club rooms. The meeting itself subsequently took place two days later and marked his 11th season as an Exeter contracted rider even though he had spent six of those years with other clubs. Edinburgh opted to put on the Testimonial as Michael completed his fourth successive season on loan to the Scottish club.

RICK MILLER

Sunday, April 12, Coventry

INDIVIDUAL: 1 Rick Miller 2 Gary Havelock 3 Sam Ermolenko. *Qualifying scorers:* Rick Miller (Coventry) 3-3-1-3- 10, Sam Ermolenko (Wolverhampton) 2-3-3-2- 10, Jimmy Nilsen (Swindon) 3-2-3-1- 9, Hans Nielsen (Oxford) 1-3-3-1- 8, Billy Hamill 3-0-1-3- 7, Martin Dugard 1-3-2-1- 7, Gary Havelock (Bradford) 2-2-3-0- 7, Per Jonsson (Reading) 3-0-1-2- 6, Jan O. Pedersen (Cradley Heath) 0-1-2-3- 6, Ronnie Correy (Wolverhampton) 0-1-2-2- 5, Tommy Knudsen (Coventry) 2-1-2-0- 5, Bobby Schwartz 1-1-0-2- 4, Joe Screen (Belle Vue) 2-2-0-0- 4, Greg Hancock (Cradley Heath) 0-2-1-1- 4, Tony Rickardsson (Ipswich) 0-0-0-3- 3, Kelvin Tatum (Bradford) 1-F- 1. Reserves: Paul Bentley 0- 0, Andy Meredith 0- 0. *Semi Final 1:* Havelock, Nilsen, Miller, Hamill (R). *Semi Final 2:* Jonsson, Ermolenko, Dugard, Nielsen. *Repechage:* Miller, Nielsen, Dugard (R), Hamill (R). *Final:* Miller, Havelock, Ermolenko, Jonsson, Nilsen.

Special match races – 1: Ole Olsen, Bruce Penhall; 2: Penhall, Olsen; 3: Olsen, Penhall.

RICK MILLER celebrated 10 seasons with Coventry – having made his first appearance for the club at the beginning of 1983 when he arrived in Britain on the recommendation of fellow American Bruce Penhall. The former World Champion and Rick's first Coventry skipper Ole Olsen rode in three match races billed as The Last Showdown. His was a spectacular Testimonial meeting with a variety of extra events including the nerve-racking bungee jumping. The meeting was televised by satellite station Screensport.

■ DETAILS of 1993 Testimonial beneficiaries are given in the Day-to-Day Diary on page 49.

JAN O. PEDERSEN

Cradley Heath, Sunday, April 26

PAIRS: 1 WOLVERHAMPTON; 2 Cradley Heath A; 3 Cradley Heath B and Oxford. *Qualifying scorers:* Oxford 20 (**Hans Nielsen 4-3-4- 11:1**, Martin Dugard **3**-4-2- 9:1), Cradley Heath A 18 (**Billy Hamill 4-4-4- 12**, Greg Hancock **3**-0-**3**- 6:2), Wolverhampton 18 (Sam Ermolenko **3**-3-4- 10:1, Ronnie Correy 4-**2**-2- 8:1), Cradley Heath B 15 (Jan O. Pedersen 2-2-4- 8, Alan Grahame 4-0-3- 7:1), Coventry 10 (John Jørgensen 2-2-2- 6, Rick Miller R-4-R- 4), Reading 10 (Armando Castagna 0-3-0- 3, Per Jonsson 2-**2**-3- 7:1), Belle Vue 9 (Jason Lyons 3-0-0- 3, Joe Screen F-3-3- 6), Bradford 8 (Gary Havelock 2-4-0- 6, Kelvin Tatum 0-0-2- 2). *Semi final 1:* Ermolenko, Nielsen, Correy, Dugard. *Semi final 2:* Pedersen, Hamill, Hancock, Grahame. *Final:* Correy, Ermolenko, Hamill, Hancock. Scoring: 4-3-2-0.

JAN O. PEDERSEN celebrated his 10 seasons as a Cradley Heath asset as the reigning World Champion. After a second half trial in 1982 he signed for the Heathens and made his debut for them in 1983 when he rode in 36 matches in their British League title winning campaign. Other than one season on loan to Sheffield ion 1984, he has spent the remainder of his British career at Dudley Wood.

DAVID MULLETT

Reading, Monday, September 21

DAVE'S TESTIMONIAL RACERS 52

1 Per Jonsson	2 2 3 **2**	9	2
2 David Mullett	**1** 3 3 2 1	10	2
3 Jan Andersson	2 1 2 3	8	
4 Jeremy Doncaster	**2** 2 3 2	9	1
5 Armando Castagna	3 **1** 3 1 0	8	1
6 Phillip Morris	0 **1** 0 0	1	1
7 Jason Crump	3 **2 1 1**	7	3

COCKER'S MAGNIFICENT SEVEN 38

1 Marvyn Cox	3 3 3 2 **2**	13	1
2 Ben Howe	0 0 1 0	1	
3 David Norris	3 1 2 0	6	
4 Tony Olsson	0 **2** 1 0	3	1
5 Leigh Adams	1 3 1 3 3	11	
6 David Steen	2 0 **1** 0	3	1
7 Darren Spicer	**1** 0 0 0	1	1

DAVID MULLETT celebrated his 10th season as a regular team member– with a Testimonial at his only First Division track Reading. He had actually made his debut for Canterbury in the National League in 1981 but didn't establish himself in he Crusaders' line-up until 1983. He spent five seasons at Kingsmead before the track's closure and then moved permanently to Reading, where he had ridden occasionally from the beginning of 1985.

COLIN COOK

Exeter, Monday, September 28

PAIRS: 1 Joe Screen & David Smart; 2 Steve Schofield & Ian Humphreys; 3 Gary Havelock & Mark Simmonds; 3 Jason Crump & Paul Fry. *Qualifying scorers:* Joe Screen (Belle Vue) 4-4-4-4-R- 16 & Frank Smart (Exeter) **3**-2-2-0-3- 10 = 26; Steve Schofield (Poole) 4-4-4-4-4- 20 & Ian Humphreys (Exeter) 0-2-2-0-2- 6 = 26; Gary Havelock (Bradford) 3-0-4-3-**2**- 12 & Mark Simmonds (Exeter) **2**-3-2-**2**-3- 12 = 24; Jason Crump (Peterborough) N-4-3-4-**2**- 13 & Paul Fry (Exeter) 3-2-0-2-3- 10 = 23; Richard Green (Exeter) 4-3-3-3-3- 16 & Paul Thorp (Bradford) 0-0-0-R-0- 0 = 16; Martin Dugard (Exeter) 0-3-4-3-4- 14 & Steve Regeling (Middlesbrough) 2-0-0-0-N- 2 = 16. Reserve: Justin Elkins 2-2- 4. *Semi final 1:* Havelock, Screen, Smart, Simmonds. *Semi final 2:* Schofield, Crump, Humphreys, Fry (fell). *Final:* Schofield, Screen, Smart, Humphreys (ret). Scoring: 4-3-2-0.

COLIN COOK was awarded a Benefit meeting after eight seasons with Exeter – and 13 seasons in the sport. He began his career in the second half at Ipswich, joined National League Scunthorpe in 1975 and saw First Division service with Ipswich (1976-79), Leicester (1979-83) and Division Two duty with Scunthorpe (1975-76, Boston (1977, 1984, 1986) and Exeter (1985-1992). The appearance of World Champion Gary Havelock helped attract one of the biggest crowds of the season to the County Ground.

Alan WILKINSON Benefit

Belle Vue, Friday, May 29

ALAN WILKINSON was awarded a richly deserved Benefit meeting by his old track Belle Vue. Wilky, a former England international, has been confined to a wheelchair after being paralysed in a crash at the old Hyde Road track on July 1, 1978, in a British League match for the Aces against Swindon. The 43-year-old Cumbrian was in his eighth season with Belle Vue, having made his debut in 1971. He also rode for sister Division Two track Rochdale in 1970 and 1971.

1 Joe Screen	3 3 3 3 3	15
2 Frede Schøtt	3 3 3 3 2	14
3 David Bargh	3 3 2 2 3	13
4 Tony Olsson	2 2 3 3 F	10
5 Darren Sumner	3 2 2 2 1	10
6 Alan Grahame	0 1 1 3 3	8
7 Shawn Moran	2 2 3 1 0	8
8 Eric Monaghan	1 3 2 0 2	8
9 Carl Stonehewer	1 2 1 2 2	8
10 Neil Collins	2 1 1 1 1	6
11 Nigel Crabtree	1 0 2 1 1	5
12 Richard Hellsén	0 1 0 0 3	4
13 David Walsh	2 0 0 1 1	4
14 Paul Smith	1 1 1 0 0	3
15 Nigel Leaver	0 0 0 0 2	2
16 Gordon Kennett	0 0 0 2 0	2

Division One Gold Cup Northern Section

Friday, March 20
Belle Vue 16 (Peter Scully **2**-**1**-0- 3:2, Mike Hampson 3-1-1- 5, Michael Howe 0-2-R- 2, Jon Armstrong 3-0-3- 6) **Oxford 19** (Glenn Cunningham 1-3-**2**- 6:1, Wayne Parker F-**1**-3-2- 6:1, Spencer Timmo 2-**2**-3- 7:1, Paul Regan N-N-N- 0)

Friday, March 27
Oxford 17 (**Glenn Cunningham 3-2-3- 8:1**, Wayne Parker 0-R- 0, **Spencer Timmo 3-3-2- 8:1**, Paul Regan R-1-F- 1) **Coventry 16** (David Haynes 1-**2**-F- 3:2, Chris Clarence 2-1-3- 6, Andy Meredith R-3-F- 3, Scott Wormleighton 2-0-**2**- 4:1)

Saturday, March 28
Coventry 15 (David Haynes 1-2-1- 4, Chris Clarence 3-R- 3, Andy Meredith 3-X-3- 6, Scott Wormleighton 0-1-0-1- 2) **Belle Vue 21** (Peter Scully F-3-3-2- 8, Mike Hampson 2-1-**2**- 5:1, Steve Cope 1-**2**-0- 3:2, Jon Armstrong 2-E-3- 5)
Cradley Heath 23 (Mark Robinson **2**-**2**-F- 4:2, Anthony Boyd 3-2-3- 8, Scott Smith 3-3-**1**- 7, Mark Meredith 1-**1**-**2**- 4:2) **Oxford 13** (Glenn Cunningham 1-fx-3- 4, Wayne Parker N-N- 0, Spencer Timmo 2-3-**2**- 7:1, Paul Regan F-0-1-1- 2)

Friday, April 3
Belle Vue 13 (Steve Cope F-3-0- 3, Peter Scully 1-0-0- 1, Mike Hampson 2-N-3- 5, Jon Armstrong **1**-0-1-2- 4:1) **Cradley Heath 23** (**Mark Robinson 3-2-3- 8:1**, Mark Meredith **2**-2-**1**- 5:2, Scott Smith 3-3-1- 7, Anthony Boyd F-**1**-2- 3:1)
Oxford 17 (Glenn Cunningham 3-0-3- 6, Wayne Parker F-2-2- 4, Spencer Timmo 3-2-**2**- 7:1, Paul Regan fx-fx-N- 0) **Bradford 17** (Stuart Parnaby 2-fx-1- 3, Darren Pearson **1**-3-1- 5:1, Simon Bean R-3-0- 3, Richard Smith 2-1-3- 6)

Saturday, April 4
Bradford 27 (Stuart Parnaby **2**-3-R- 5:1, **Darren Pearson 3-3-3- 9. Simon Bean 2-2-3- 7:2,** Richard Smith 3-1-**2**- 6:1)
Coventry 8 (Chris Clarence 1-2-2- 5, Scott Wormleighton 0-0-1- 1, Andy Meredith 1-R-R- 1, Paul Bromwich R-1-0- 1)
Cradley Heath 28 (**Mark Robinson 2-3-2- 7:2, Mark Meredith 3-2-2- 7:2**, Scott Smith 3-R-3- 6, **Anthony Boyd 2-3-3- 8:1**) **Belle Vue 8** (Steve Cope 0-0-0- 0, Peter Scully 1-**1**-1- 3:1, Mike Hampson 0-1-1- 2, Jon Armstrong 1-2-0- 3)

Monday, April 6
Wolverhampton 21 (**Stephen Morris 3-3-2- 8:1**, Shane Cooper 0-3-fx- 3, **Simon Wolstenholme 3-2-3- 8:1**, Craig Taylor 1-1-fx- 2) **Cradley Heath 12** (Mark Robinson N-N- 0, Mark Meredith 1-fx-R-3-1- 5:1, Scott Smith X-N- 0, Anthony Boyd 2-2-1-2-X- 7)

Saturday, April 11
Bradford 30 (**Stuart Parnaby 2-2-3- 7:2, Darren Pearson 3-3-3- 9, Simon Bean 3-3-2- 8:1, Richard Smith 2-2-2- 6:3**) **Belle Vue 6** (Steve Cope 0-0-0- 0, Peter Scully 1-0-0- 1, Mike Hampson 1-1-1- 3, Jon Armstrong 0-1-1- 2)
Coventry 10 (Chris Clarence F-3-1- 4, Scott Wormleighton 1-1-F- 2, David Haynes 1-1-2- 4, Paul Bromwich 0-0-0- 0)
Wolverhampton 26 (**Stephen Morris 3-3-3- 9**, Shane Cooper 2-2-3- 7:1, **Simon Wolstenholme 3-2-2- 7:2**, Craig Taylor **2**-0-1- 3:1)

Monday, April 13
Wolverhampton 24 (**Stephen Morris 3-3-3- 9**, Shane Cooper 1-fx-2- 3, **Simon Wolstenholme 3-2-2- 7:2,** Craig Taylor **2**-2-1- 5:1) **Belle Vue 11** (Steve Cope 0-fx-fx-0, Peter Scully 2-0-3- 5, Mike Hampson 0-3-1- 4, Jon Armstrong 1-1-0- 2)

Friday, April 17
Belle Vue 7 (Steve Cope 0-1-1- 2, Peter Scully 1-fx-F- 1, Mike Hampson fx-fx-3- 3, Jon Armstrong 1-F-fx- 1) **Wolverhampton 27** (Stephen Morris **2-3-3- 8:1**, Shane Cooper **3-3-2- 8:1**, Simon Wolstenholme 3-**2**-2- 7:1, Craig Taylor **2**-**2**-R- 4:2)

Monday, April 20
Cradley Heath 23 (Mark Robinson R-N-R-0, Mark Meredith 3-3-N- 6, **Scott Smith 3-3-2- 8:1**, Anthony Boyd **2**-1-N-3-3- 9:1)
Coventry 11 (Chris Clarence 2-2-0- 4, Colin Thorpe **1**-2-1- 4:1, David Haynes 0-fx-N- 0, Scott Wormleighton 1-0-2- 3)
Coventry 11 (Chris Clarence 0-3-3- 6, Colin Thorpe 1-1-0- 2, Scott Wormleighton 1-0-X- 1, Paul Bromwich 0-0-2- 2) **Cradley Heath 24** (Mark Robinson **2**-**2**-N- 4:2, Mark Meredith 3-2-3-**1**- 9:1, Scott Smith 3-3-2- 8, Anthony Boyd **2**-**1**-fn- 3:2)

Friday, April 24
Belle Vue 22 (Steve Cope F-**1**-3- 4:1, Peter Scully 2-**2**-2- 6:1, Mike Hampson **2**-2-**2**- 6:2, Jon Armstrong 3-3-R- 6) **Coventry 14** (Chris Clarence 1-1-F-1- 3, **Colin Thorpe 3-3-3- 9**, David Haynes R-1-1- 2, Scott Wormleighton fn-0-F- 0)

Saturday, April 25
Bradford 21 (**Stuart Parnaby 3-3-3- 9,** Darren Pearson 1-2-3- 6, Kevin Little 2-**2**-F- 4:1, Richard Smith **1**-0-1- 2:1)
Wolverhampton 15 (Stephen Morris 2-3-2- 7, Shane Cooper 0-R-2- 2, Simon Wolstenholme 3-1-**1**- 5:1, Craig Taylor R-1-0- 1)
Coventry 13 (Chris Clarence 0-3-1- 4, Colin Thorpe 2-1-0- 3, Scott Wormleighton 1-0-0- 1:1, Paul Bromwich 2-0-3- 5) **Oxford 23** (**Glenn Cunningham 3-3-3- 9**, Wayne Parker 1-**1**-2- 4:1, **Spencer Timmo 3-2-2- 7:2**, Nick Upton 0-2-1- 3:1)

Wednesday, April 29
Oxford 22 (**Glenn Cunningham 3-3-3- 9**, Nick Upton 0-0-0- 0, **Spencer Timmo 3-2-2- 7:2**, Wayne Parker 1-3-2- 6) **Belle Vue 14** (Steve Cope 2-2-0- 4, Peter Scully **1**-0-1- 2:1, Mike Hampson 0-**1**-3- 4:1, Jon Armstrong 2-1-1- 4)

Friday, May 1
Belle Vue 9 (Steve Cope 0-R-0- 0, Peter Scully 1-0-2- 3, Mike Hampson **1**-1-0- 2:1, Jon Armstrong 2-1-1- 4) **Bradford 27** (**Stuart Parnaby 3-3-2- 8:1, Darren Pearson 2-3-3- 8:1, Kevin Little 3-2-3- 8:1,** Richard Smith 0-**2**-1- 3:1)

Saturday, May 2
Bradford 20 (Stuart Parnaby **2**-3-0- 5:1, Darren Pearson 3-3-2- 8, Kevin Little 2-1-3- 6, Richard Smith R-0-1- 1) **Cradley Heath 16** (Mark Robinson 1-**1**-2- 4:1, Mark Meredith 0-0-0- 0, Scott Smith 3-2-3- 8, Peter McNamara 1-2-1- 4)

Monday, May 4
Wolverhampton 19 (Stephen Morris 3-3-fx- 6, Shane Cooper fx-N- 0, **Simon Wolstenholme 3-2-3- 8:1**, Craig Taylor 1-1-**2**-1- 5:1) **Coventry 17** (Chris Clarence 2-3-**2**- 7:1, Scott Wormleighton **1**-0-0- 1:1, Colin Thorpe 2-**2**-3- 7:1, Paul Bromwich F-1-1- 2)

Monday, May 18
Wolverhampton 20 (Stephen Morris 2-3-3- 8, Colin Thorpe fx-0-3- 3, **Simon Wolstenholme 3-2-2- 7:2**, Craig Taylor 0-1-1- 2) **Oxford 16** (Glenn Cunningham 3-3-1- 7, Nick Upton 1-fx-0- 1, Spencer Timmo 2-**2**-0- 4:1, Wayne Parker **1**-1-2- 4:1)

Friday, May 22
Oxford 15 (Glenn Cunningham 3-3-F- 6, Nick Upton 0-0-0- 0, Spencer Timmo **1**-**2**-1- 4:2, Wayne Parker 2-1-2- 5) **Wolverhampton 21** (Stephen Morris 2-**2**-**2**- 6:2, Craig Taylor 0-0-3- 3, **Simon Wolstenholme 3-3-3- 9**, Colin Thorpe **1**-1-1- 3:1)

Saturday, May 23
Bradford 19 (Stuart Parnaby 2-**2**-1- 5:1, Darren Pearson **1**-2-3- 6:1, Kevin Little 2-3-R- 5, Richard Smith **1**-0-**2**- 3:2) **Oxford 17** (Glenn Cunningham 3-1-**2**- 6:1, Nick Upton 0-0-0- 0, **Spencer Timmo 3-3-3- 9,** Wayne Parker 0-1-1- 2)

Cradley Heath 18 (Anthony Boyd 3-**2**-1-6:1, Shaun Naylor 1-**1**-1-1- 4:1, Scott Smith N-N-N- 0, Peter McNamara 2-3-N-3- 8)
Wolverhampton 18 (Stephen Morris 2-**2**-3- 7:1, Colin Thorpe 0-1-0- 1, **Simon Wolstenholme 3-3-2- 8:1**, Craig Taylor F-R-2- 2)

Monday, May 25
Coventry 8 (Chris Clarence fx-2-2- 4, Scott Wormleighton 1-1-0- 2, Paul Bromwich R-0-1- 1, Andy Oliver 1-F-F- 1) **Bradford 28** (**Stuart Parnaby 2-2-3- 7:2, Darren Pearson 3-3-3- 9**, Kevin Little **2**-3-1- 6:1, Richard Smith 3-1-**2**- 6:1)

Wednesday, June 3
Wolverhampton 20 (**Stephen Morris 3-3-3- 9**, Shane Cooper fx-N-N- 0, Simon Wolstenholme 3-**2**-1- 6:1, Craig Taylor **2**-2-1- 5:1) **Bradford 16** (Stuart Parnaby **1**-3-0-4:1, Darren Pearson 2-1-2- 5, Kevin Little 1-1-3- 5, Richard Smith 0-0-**2**- 2:1)

Wednesday, June 10
Cradley Heath 16 (Scott Smith 3-2- 5, Mark Meredith 1-X-2- 3, Shaun Naylor N-0-0- 0, Peter McNamara 3-3-2- 8) **Bradford 20** (Stuart Parnaby 0-2-2-3-1- 8, Darren Pearson 2-3-3- 8, Kevin Little N-N- 0, Richard Smith **1**-1-**1**-1- 4:2)

Friday, June 12
Oxford 14 (Glenn Cunningham 2-3-1- 6, Nick Upton 0-0-1- 1, Spencer Timmo 3-**2**-0-5:1, Wayne Parker F-2-N- 2) **Cradley Heath 22** (**Scott Smith 3-3-3- 9**, Mark Meredith X-1-3- 4, Shaun Naylor **1**-1-**2**-4:2, Peter McNamara 1-2-0-**2**- 5:1)

DIVISION ONE GOLD CUP NORTHERN SECTION LEAGUE TABLE

	M	W	D	L	PtsF	PtsA	BP	TPts
BRADFORD	10	8	1	1	225	132	5	22
Wolverhampton	10	8	1	1	211	143	4	21
Cradley Heath	10	6	1	3	205	149	3	16
Oxford	10	4	1	5	173	181	2	11
Belle Vue	10	2	0	8	127	229	1	5
Coventry	10	0	0	10	123	230	0	0

COVENTRY went through the complete Gold Cup competition without claiming a single victory. The closest they came to winning was a one point defeat at Oxford.

BRADFORD completed a white wash against Belle Vue in the Gold Cup – the only full score recorded in the competition. The Yorkshire club came close to repeating the performance at Coventry where two third places denied them an away maximum performance.

THE Northern Section of the Gold Cup was the only First Division Reserve League competition to be completed in full!

MICHAEL Howe made his debut for Belle Vue in the first Reserve League match of the season – and never rode for them again as he joined Second Division Peterborough.

All The 1992 Results

	BELLE VUE	BRADFORD	COVENTRY	CRADLEY HEATH	OXFORD	WOLVES
BELLE VUE		9-27	22-14	13-23	16-19	7-27
BRADFORD	30-6		27 8	20-16	19-17	21-15
COVENTRY	15-21	8-28		11-24	13-23	10-26
CRADLEY HEATH	28-8	16-20	23 11		23-13	18-18
OXFORD	22-14	17-17	17-16	14-22		15-21
WOLVERHAMPTON	24-11	20-16	19-17	21-12	20-16	

Division One Gold Cup Southern Section

Friday, March 28
King's Lynn 21 (Tom Grinstead 2-2-R- 4:1, Emmerson Fairweather 1-2-3- 6:1, Jason Gage 3-3-2- 8, Andrew Mountain 2-1-0- 3:2) **Arena Essex 15** (**Troy Pratt 3-3-3- 9**, Terry Giles 0-1-2- 3, Roland Pollard R-0-1- 1:1, Ricky Sandford 1-0-1- 2)

Friday, April 3
Arena Essex 15 (Robert Ledwith R-3-2- 5, Terry Giles 1-0-1- 2:1, Roland Pollard 2-2-F- 4:1, Ricky Sandford 1-1-2- 4:1) **King's Lynn 21** (**Tom Grinstead 3-2-3- 8:1**, Emmerson Fairweather 2-0-F- 2:1, Jason Gage 3-3-1- 7, Andrew Mountain R-1-3- 4)

Saturday, April 4
King's Lynn 25 (Tom Grinstead 0-1-3- 4, Emmerson Fairweather 2-3-2- 7:1, **Jason Gage 3-3-3- 9**, Andrew Mountain 2-1-2- 5:2) **Swindon 11** (Matthew Cross 1-2-1- 4, Darren Boulton 3-2-0- 5, Robert Vincent R-0-0- 0, Scott Broad 1-0-1- 2)

Sunday, April 5
Eastbourne 11 (Nathan Gaymer X-2-2- 4, Scott Swain E-1- 1, Mike Randall F-X-C- 0, Paul Mitchell 2-1-0-2-1- 6:1) **Arena Essex 24** (Troy Pratt fx-3-3- 6, Robert Ledwith 3-3-X- 6, **Roland Pollard 3-2-3- 8:1**, Ricky Sandford 2-1-1- 4:1)

Monday, April 6
Reading 24 (**Phillip Morris 3-2-3- 8:1**, Jason Green 0-1-F- 1:1, **Lance Sealey 2-3-2- 7:2**, Mick Tomlin 3-2-3- 8) **King's Lynn 12** (Tom Grinstead 2-0-2- 4, Emmerson Fairweather 1-1-1- 3:1, Jason Gage fx-3-0- 3, Andrew Mountain -0-1- 2:1)

Wednesday, April 8
Poole 15 (Steve Leigh 0-0-2- 2, Justin Elkins 2-2-3- 7, Jonathon Gould 3-2-1- 6, Martin Willis fx-R-0- 0) **Arena Essex 20** (Troy Pratt 3-3-2- 8, Ricky Sandford 1-1-1- 3, Roland Pollard 2-1-R- 3, Robert Ledwith R-3-3- 6)

Thursday, April 9
Ipswich 23 (Lawrence Hare F-1-3- 4:1, Savalas Clouting 2-1-2- 5:1, Ben Howe 3-2-3- 8, Shaun Tacey 2-3-1- 6:1) **Poole 13** (Anthony Blake 1-0-1- 2, Justin Elkins 3-3-2- 8, Jonathon Gould 1-2-0- 3, Martin Willis 0-F-0- 0)
Swindon 11 (Matthew Cross 3-N- 3, Scott Broad 1-3-2-fx- 6, Darren Boulton fn-N- 0, Robert Vincent fx-1-0-1- 2) **Reading 24** (Phillip Morris 2-3-3- 8, Lance Sealey 0-E-2- 2:1, Jason Green 2-2-1-2- 7:2, Mick Tomlin 1-3-3- 7:1)

Friday, April 10
Arena Essex 25 (**Robert Ledwith 3-3-2- 8:1**, Terry Giles 1-fx-3- 4, **Roland Pollard 3-2-3- 8:1**, Ricky Sandford 2-2-1- 5:1)
Eastbourne 11 (Nathan Gaymer 2-3-1- 6, Mike Randall R-R-X- 0, Justin Shaw 1-1-0- 2, Paul Mitchell 0-1-2- 3)

Saturday, April 11
King's Lynn 24 (Tom Grinstead 1-2-2- 5:1, Emmerson Fairweather 3-3-1- 7:1, Jason Gage 1-3-1- 5:1, Andrew Mountain 3-2-2- 7:1) **Poole 12** (Anthony Blake 0-0-N- 0, Justin Elkins 2-R-3- 5, Jonathon Gould 2-1-3-0- 6, Martin Willis R-1-0- 1)

Sunday, April 12
Eastbourne 17 (Nathan Gaymer fx-1-2- 3:2, Scott Swain 2-fx-3- 5, Darren Grayling 3-2-R- 5, Paul Mitchell 1-2-1- 4) **Poole 18** (Anthony Blake X-1-1- 2, **Justin Elkins 3-3-3- 9**, Jonathon Gould 2-3-2- 7:1, Martin Willis F-fx-0- 0)

Monday, April 13
Reading 21 (**Phillip Morris 3-3-3- 9**, Jason Green 0-N-0- 0, Lance Sealey 3-1-2- 6, Mick Tomlin 2-3-1- 6:1) **Poole 15** (Anthony Blake 1-1-0- 2:2, Justin Elkins 2-2-2- 6, Jonathon Gould fx-2-3- 5, Martin Willis 1-0-1- 2)

Friday, April 17
Ipswich 22 (Lawrence Hare 1-0-R- 1, Savalas Clouting 3-2-2- 7, **Ben Howe 3-3-3- 9**, Shaun Tacey 2-1-2- 5:3) **King's Lynn 14** (Tom Grinstead 2-fx-3- 5, Emmerson Fairweather F-1-1- 2:1, Jason Gage 0-3-1- 4, Andrew Mountain 1-2-R- 3)
Poole 14 (Darren Boulton 0-3-2- 5, Anthony Blake 1-2-0- 3, Jonathon Gould fx-2-3- 5:1, Martin Willis fx-1-N- 1:1) **Reading 21** (**Phillip Morris 3-3-3- 9**, Lance Sealey 2-1-1- 4:1, Jason Green 2-0-1- 3:2, Mick Tomlin 3-R-2- 5)

Sunday, April 19
Eastbourne 24 (**Nathan Gaymer 3-2-3- 8:1**, Scott Swain 2-0-3- 5:1, Darren Grayling 3-3-0- 6, Paul Mitchell 2-1-2- 5:2) **Reading 11** (Phillip Morris 1-3-2- 6, Jason Green 0-0-1- 1, Lance Sealey 1-2-0- 3:1, Mick Tomlin 0-1-0- 1)

Monday, April 20
Swindon 16 (Matthew Cross 2-2-2- 6:2, Robert Vincent 0-1-1- 2, Justin Elkins 2-3-3- 8, Scott Broad 0-F- 0) **Ipswich 20** (Lawrence Hare 1-2-3- 6:1, Savalas Clouting 3-1-1- 5, Ben Howe 3-3-0- 6, Shaun Tacey 1-0-2- 3:1)

Wednesday, April 22
Poole 14 (Darren Boulton 2-3-1- 6:1, Anthony Blake 0-2-2- 4, Jonathon Gould 2-0-2- 4, Martin Willis 0-0-0- 0) **Ipswich 22** (Lawrence Hare 1-1-1- 3, Savalas Clouting 3-2-fx- 5, **Ben Howe 3-3-3- 9**, Shaun Tacey 1-1-3- 5:1)

Thursday, April 23
Ipswich 26 (Lawrence Hare 3-3-1- 7, Savalas Clouting 2-2-3- 7:1, **Ben Howe 3-2-3- 8:1**, Shaun Tacey 1-1-2- 4:2)
Swindon 10 (Matthew Cross 1-0-0- 1, Steve Camden 0-1-0- 1, Justin Elkins 2-3-2- 7, Scott Broad 0-fx-1- 1)

Friday, April 24
Arena Essex 17 (Robert Ledwith 3-2-X- 5:1, Terry Giles fx-0-2- 2:1, Roland Pollard 1-3-F- 4:1, Ricky Sandford 2-1-3- 6)
Swindon 18 (Matthew Cross 2-3-3- 8, Steve Camden 1-1-1- 3:1, **Justin Elkins 3-2-2- 7:2**, Robert Vincent 0-0-0- 0)

Saturday, April 25
King's Lynn 26 (**Tom Grinstead 3-2-2- 7:2**, Emmerson Fairweather 2-fx-3- 5:1, Jason Gage R-3-2- 5:1, **Andrew Mountain 3-3-3- 9**) **Eastbourne 9** (Nathan Gaymer 0-2-0- 2, Scott Swain 1-R-R- 1, Mike Randall 1-fx-1- 2:1, Paul Mitchell 2-1-1- 4)

Sunday, April 26
Swindon 19 (Matthew Cross 2-2-2- 6:1, Steve Camden 1-2-3- 6:1, Justin Elkins 3-3-1- 7:1, Scott Broad fx-F-fx- 0) **Arena Essex 17** (**Troy Pratt 3-3-3- 9**, Ricky Sandford 0-0-1- 1:1, Roland Pollard 1-1-2- 4:1, Robert Ledwith 2-1-F- 3)

Wednesday, April 29
Poole 23 (Darren Boulton 3-3-1- 7:1, Anthony Blake 2-2-2- 6:1, Jason Smith 0-2-3- 5:1, Martin Willis 3-R-2- 5:1) **Eastbourne 13** (Nathan Gaymer 1-3-fx- 4, Mike Randall 0-0-R- 0, Scott Swain 2-1-3- 6, Paul Mitchell 1-1-1- 3:1)

Friday, May 1
Arena Essex 12 (Robert Ledwith F-2-fx- 2, Terry Giles 1-0-1- 2, Roland Pollard 2-1-0- 3:1, Ricky Sandford 1-3-1- 5:1) **Ipswich 24** (Lawrence Hare 3-1-2- 6:2, **Savalas Clouting 2-3-2- 7:2**, Ben Howe 3-2-3- 8, Shaun Tacey 0-0-3- 3)
Eastbourne 14 (Nathan Gaymer F-X- 0, Scott Swain 1-2-0- 3, **Darren Grayling 3-3-3- 9**, Paul Mitchell 0-0-1-1- 2:1)
King's Lynn 22 (Darren Spicer 3-3-2- 8, Emmerson Fairweather 2-1-1- 4:3, Tom Grinstead 2-0-2- 4:1, Andrew Mountain 1-2-3- 6:1)

Monday, May 4
Reading 24 (**Phillip Morris 3-3-3- 9**, Gary Sweet 1-3-2- 6:1, Lance Sealey 2-0-2- 4:1, Mick Tomlin 1-1-3- 5:1)
Swindon 12 (Steve Masters 2-2-2-1- 7, Steve Camden 0-1-1- 2:1, Justin Elkins 3-0-0- 3, Robert Vincent R-N-0- 0)

Wednesday, May 6
Poole 11 (Darren Boulton 2-0-1- 3, Anthony Blake 1-1-2- 4:1, Steve Leigh 2-2-fx- 4, Martin Willis 0-fx- 0) **King's Lynn 24** (Tom Grinstead F-N- 0, **Emmerson Fairweather 3-3-2- 8:1**, **Darren Spicer 3-3-3- 9**, Andrew Mountain 1-1-2-3- 7:1)

Thursday, May 7
Ipswich 20 (Lawrence Hare 2-2-1- 5:1, Savalas Clouting 1-2-3- 6:1, **Ben Howe 3-3-3- 9**, Gary Wells 0-0-0- 0) **Arena Essex 16** (Robert Ledwith 3-3-0- 6, Terry Giles 0-0-1- 1:1, Roland Pollard 1-1-2- 4:1, Ricky Sandford 2-1-2- 5)
Swindon 23 (Steve Masters 3-3-1- 7, Steve Camden 2-R-3- 5:1, **Justin Elkins 3-2-3- 8:1**, Robert Vincent 1-1-1- 3)
Eastbourne 13 (Nathan Gaymer 0-2-0- 2:1, Justin Shaw 1-1-0- 2, Scott Swain 2-3-2- 7, Paul Mitchell R-F-2- 2)

Friday, May 8
Arena Essex 26 (**Robert Ledwith 3-3-3- 9**, Terry Giles 2-fx-2- 4:2, **Roland Pollard 3-2-2- 7:2**, Ricky Sandford 1-2-3- 6) **Poole 10** (Darren Boulton F-1-F- 1, Anthony Blake 1-1-1- 3, Steve Leigh 2-3-F- 5, Martin Willis 0-fx-1- 1)

Sunday, May 10
King's Lynn 20 (Tom Grinstead 1-1-1- 3, Emmerson Fairweather 3-1-2- 6:1, Darren Spicer 2-3-0- 5, Andrew Mountain 1-2-3- 6:1) **Ipswich 16** (Lawrence Hare 2-F-1- 3, Savalas Clouting 0-2-2- 4, **Ben Howe 3-3-3- 9**, Shaun Tacey F-0-N- 0)

Monday, May 11
Reading 19 (Phillip Morris 3-2-1- 6, Gary Sweet F-1-2- 3:2, Lance Sealey 3-1-0- 4:1, Mick Tomlin 1-2-3- 6) **Ipswich 16** (Lawrence Hare 2-R-R- 2, Savalas Clouting F-3-3- 6, Ben Howe 2-3-2- 7:1, Gary Wells 0-0-1- 1)

Wednesday, May 13
Poole 9 (Steve Leigh 2-1-0- 3:1, Anthony Blake 0-R-0- 0, Darren Boulton 1-2-1- 4, Martin Willis 0-1-1- 2) **Swindon 27** (Matthew Cross 1-2-3- 6:1, **Steve Masters 3-3-2- 8:1**, **Justin Elkins 3-3-3- 9**, Steve Camden 2-0-2- 4:2)

Friday, May 15
Eastbourne 16 (Nathan Gaymer 0-1-0-3- 4, Scott Swain 1-2-0- 3, **Darren Grayling 3-3-3- 9**, Paul Mitchell fx- 0) **Swindon 19** (Matthew Cross 2-3-1- 6:2, Justin Elkins 3-2-2-2- 9, Steve Camden 1-0-1-2- 4:1)

Saturday, May 16
King's Lynn 28 (Tom Grinstead 2-2-3-3- 10:1, Emmerson Fairweather 1- 1, **Darren Spicer 3-3-2- 8:1**, **Andrew Mountain 2-2-2-3- 9:3**) **Reading 8** (Phillip Morris 3-1-1- 5, Gary Sweet fx-1- 1, Lance Sealey 1-0-1- 2, Mick Tomlin 0-R-0-0- 0)

Monday, May 18
Reading 25 (**Phillip Morris 3-3-3- 9**, Gary Sweet 2-1-1- 4:2, Lance Sealey 2-2-2- 6:2, Mick Tomlin 1-2-3- 6:1) **Eastbourne 11** (Mike Randall 0-0-0- 0, Scott Swain 1-1-2- 4, Darren Grayling 3-3-fx- 6, Justin Shaw 0-0-1- 1)

Thursday, May 28
Swindon 19 (Matthew Cross 3-2-0- 5:1, Steve Camden 1-2-R- 3, **Justin Elkins 3-3-3- 9**, Robert Vincent 0-0-2- 2) **King's Lynn 17** (Tom Grinstead F-1-1- 2, Emmerson Fairweather 2-1-2- 5, Darren Spicer 2-3-1- 6:1, Andrew Mountain 1-0-3- 4:1)

Thursday, June 11
Ipswich 29 (Lawrence Hare 2-3-1- 6:1, **Savalas Clouting 3-2-3- 8:1**, **Ben Howe 2-2-3- 7:2**, **Shaun Tacey 3-3-2- 8:1**)
Eastbourne 6 (Nathan Gaymer 1-1-1-E- 3, Scott Swain 0-1-2- 3, Darren Grayling N- 0, Paul Mitchell 0-0-N- 0)
Swindon 28 (**Justin Elkins 3-3-3- 9**, **Steve Masters 2-3-2- 7:2**, **Matthew Cross 3-2-3- 8:1**, Steve Camden 1-1-2- 4:1)
Poole 8 (Darren Boulton fx-N- 0, Jason

All The 1992 Results

	ARENA ESSEX	EASTBOURNE	IPSWICH	KING'S LYNN	POOLE	READING	SWINDON
ARENA ESSEX		25-11	12-24	15-21	26-10		17-18
EASTBOURNE	11-24		10-25	14-22	17-18	24-11	16-19
IPSWICH	20-16	29-6		22-14	23-13	22-13	26-10
KING'S LYNN	21-15	26-9	20-16		24-12	28-8	25-11
POOLE	15-20	23-13	14-22	11-24		14-21	9-27
READING	22-14	25-11	19-16	24-12	21-15		24-12
SWINDON	19-17	23-13	16-20	19-17	28-8	11-24	

DIVISION ONE GOLD CUP SOUTHERN SECTION LEAGUE TABLE

	M	W	D	L	PtsF	PtsA	BP	TPts
IPSWICH	12	10	0	2	265	163	6	26
King's Lynn	12	9	0	3	254	176	5	23
Reading	11	8	0	3	212	179	3	19
Swindon	12	7	0	5	213	216	3	17
Arena Essex	11	4	0	7	201	192	2	10
Poole	12	2	0	10	162	266	1	5
Eastbourne	12	1	0	11	155	270	0	2

Smith 1-0-0-0-1- 2, Jonathon Gould N-N- 0, Martin Willis 2-1-2-1- 6)

Thursday, June 25
Ipswich 22 (Lawrence Hare 0-2-**1**- 3:1, Savalas Clouting 2-3-**2**- 7:1, Ben Howe **2**-R-2- 4:1, **Shaun Tacey 3-2-3- 8:1**) **Reading 13** (Phillip Morris 3-F-N- 3, Gary Sweet 1-R-3-1- 5, Lance Sealey 0-1-0- 1, Mick Tomlin 1-3-0- 4)

Sunday, June 28
Eastbourne 10 (Nathan Gaymer 2-2-fx- 4, Scott Swain **1**-R-R- 1:1, Darren Grayling 3-fx-fx- 3, Justin Shaw 0-1-1- 2) **Ipswich 25** (Lawrence Hare N-**2**-3- 5:1, **Savalas Clouting 3-3-3- 9**, Ben Howe 2-3-**2**- 7:1, Shaun Tacey F-**1**-1-**2**- 4:2)

THE scheduled Reserve League Gold Cup match between Arena Essex and Reading was never staged. It was originally programmed for May 29 but became a victim of heavy overnight rain. The subsequent re-staging on July 7 was abandoned because of floodlighting failure at the Purfleet track.

All the 1992 Results & Scorers

Division One Reserve League

Friday, April 10
Belle Vue 11 (Steve Cope fx-N- 0, Peter Scully 1-1-0- 2, Mike Hampson 2-F-2- 4, Jon Armstrong **1**-**1**-E-1-**2**- 5:2) **Reading 25** (**Phillip Morris 2-3-3- 8:1**, Lance Sealey 3-3-1- 7, Jason Green 0-**2**-0- 2:1, **Mick Tomlin 3-2-3- 8:1**)

Saturday, April 11
Cradley Heath 22 (Mark Robinson 3-**2**-2- 7:1, Mark Meredith **2**-1-X- 3:1, Scott Smith R-N-N- 0, Anthony Boyd 3-3-3-3-R- 12) **Eastbourne 14** (Nathan Gaymer 1-2-1- 4, Mike Randall 0-0-fn- 0, Justin Shaw **1**-0-**1**- 2:2, Paul Mitchell 2-1-2-3- 8)

Friday, April 17
Arena Essex 15 (Robert Ledwith X-3-3- 6, Terry Giles 2-1-0- 3:1, Roland Pollard 2-0-2- 4, Ricky Sandford 0-2-0- 2) **Cradley Heath 20** (Mark Robinson F-3-3- 6, Mark Meredith 3-1-**1**- 5:2, Scott Smith 1-N- 1, Anthony Boyd 3-2-F-1-2- 8)

Saturday, April 18
Cradley Heath 19 (Mark Robinson 1-1-2- 4, Mark Meredith 3-2-1- 6, **Scott Smith 3-3-3- 9**, Anthony Boyd R-0-R- 0) **King's Lynn 17** (Tom Grinstead 0-3-0- 3, Emmerson Fairweather 2-2-2- 6, Jason Gage 2-1-3- 6, Andrew Mountain 1-0-1- 2)

Saturday, April 18
Coventry 23 (**Chris Clarence 3-3-3- 9**, **Colin Thorpe 2-3-2- 7:2**, David Haynes 3-**2**-2- 7:1, Scott Wormleighton R-0-0- 0) **Reading 13** (Phillip Morris R-**1**-3- 4:1, Jason Green 1-0-1- 2, Lance Sealey **1**-2-1- 4:1, Mick Tomlin 2-1-0- 3)

Monday, April 27
Wolverhampton 25 (**Stephen Morris 3-3-2- 8:1**, Shane Cooper **2**-2-3- 7:1, **Simon Wolstenholme 3-2-3- 8:1**, Craig Taylor 1-**1**-fx- 2:1) **Reading 11** (Phillip Morris 1-3-1- 5, Jason Green 0-0-**1**- 1:1, Lance Sealey F-0-2- 2, Mick Tomlin 2-1-0- 3)

Saturday, May 2
King's Lynn 23 (Tom Grinstead 1-3-3- 7, Emmerson Fairweather 3-2-0- 5, Darren Spicer 3-**2**-2- 7:1, Andrew Mountain 1-**1**-**2**- 4:2) **Oxford 13** (Glenn Cunningham 2-3-3- 8, Nick Upton 0-0-0- 0, Spencer Timmo 2-0-1- 3, Wayne Parker 0-1-1- 2)

Monday, May 4
King's Lynn 22 (Tom Grinstead 3-1-**2**-**1**- 7:3, Emmerson Fairweather **2**-**2**-**2**- 6:3, Darren Spicer N-N- 0, Andrew Mountain 2-**1**-3-3-0- 9:1) **Bradford 14** (Stuart Parnaby 0-1-0- 1, Darren Pearson 1-3-3- 7, Kevin Little 3-R-R-**2**- 5:1, Richard Smith 0-N-1- 1)

Friday, May 8
Belle Vue 18 (Jon Armstrong F-3-**2**- 5:1, Mike Hampson 2-1-X- 3, Peter Scully **1**-**2**-2- 5:2, Mike Lewthwaite 2-0-3- 5) **Swindon 17** (Steve Masters 3-**2**-fn- 5:1, Steve Camden 1-1-0- 2, **Justin Elkins 3-3-3- 9**, Robert Vincent F-0-1-R- 1)

Sunday, May 10
Eastbourne 20 (Nathan Gaymer 2-**2**-0- 4:1, Scott Swain 1-1-3- 5, Darren Grayling 2-3-3- 8, Paul Mitchell **1**-0-**2**- 3:2) **Wolverhampton 16** (Stephen Morris 3-**2**-2- 7:1, Colin Thorpe 0-1-F- 1, Simon Wolstenholme 3-3-**1**- 7:1, Craig Taylor 0-F-1- 1)

Wednesday, May 13
Oxford 20 (Glenn Cunningham 2-3-3- 8, Nick Upton **1**-0-**1**- 2:1, Spencer Timmo 3-**2**-1- 6:1, Wayne Parker 2-2-X- 4:1) **Arena Essex 16** (Robert Ledwith 3-3-2- 8, Terry Giles 0-1-3- 4, Roland Pollard 1-1-0- 2, Ricky Sandford 0-0-**2**- 2:1)

Thursday, May 14
Ipswich 23 (Lawrence Hare 1-1-F- 2, **Savalas Clouting 3-3-2- 8:1**, **Ben Howe 3-3-3- 9**, Shaun Tacey 0-1-3- 4) **Belle Vue 13** (Steve Cope 0-0-**1**- 1:1, Mike Hampson 2-0-2- 4, Peter Scully **1**-2-0- 3:1, Mike Lewthwaite 2-2-1- 5)

Saturday, May 16
Bradford 19 (Stuart Parnaby 1-1-**2**- 4:1, **Darren Pearson 3-3-3- 9**, Kevin Little **1**-F-3- 4:1, Richard Smith 2-F-0- 2) **Belle Vue 17** (Steve Cope 0-N-0- 0, Mike Hampson 2-3-**1**- 6:1, Peter Scully 0-1-**1**- 2:1, Mike Lewthwaite 3-**2**-2-2- 9:1)

Wednesday, May 20
Poole 19 (Jonathon Gould 0-3-2- 5, Anthony Blake 2-2-**1**- 5:1, Darren Boulton 3-**2**-2- 7:1, Martin Willis 0-1-**1**- 2:1) **Coventry 17** (**Chris Clarence 3-3-3- 9**, Scott Wormleighton 1-1-0- 2, Paul Bromwich 1-0-3- 4, Andrew Oliver 2-F-fx-2)

Friday, May 22
Arena Essex 22 (Robert Ledwith **1**-3-F-4:1, Terry Giles 2-3-2- 7, Roland Pollard 3-fx-**2**- 5:1, Ricky Sandford **1**-**2**-3- 6:1) **Belle Vue 12** (Steve Cope R-fx-fx- 0, Mike Hampson 3-2-3- 8, Peter Scully F-1-1- 2, Mike Lewthwaite 2-F-N- 2)

Saturday, May 23
Coventry 9 (Chris Clarence 3-2-1- 6, Scott Wormleighton 0-1-R- 1, Paul Bromwich 1-**1**-0- 2:1, Andrew Oliver fx-fx-N- 0) **Ipswich 26** (Lawrence Hare **1**-**2**-**2**- 5:3, Savalas Clouting 2-3-**2**- 7:1, **Ben Howe 3-3-3- 9**, Shaun Tacey **2**-E-3- 5:1)
King's Lynn 25 (Tom Grinstead **1**-**2**-3- 6:2, Emmerson Fairweather 2-**2**-1- 5:1, **Darren Spicer 3-3-3- 9**, Andrew Mountain 1-3-1- 5) **Swindon 11** (Matthew Cross 0-0-2- 2, Steve Masters 3-0-0- 3, Justin Elkins 2-1-2- 5, Steve Camden 0-1-0- 1)

Sunday, May 24
Eastbourne 15 (Nathan Gaymer 2-1-0- 3, Scott Swain R-1-3- 4, Darren Grayling 3-3-1- 7, Mike Randall 0-0-1- 1) **Bradford 21** (Stuart Parnaby 1-3-2- 6, Darren Pearson 3-2-3- 8, Kevin Little 2-**2**-**2**- 6:2, Richard Smith **1**-0-fx- 1:1)

Monday, May 25
Cradley Heath 21 (Anthony Boyd **1**-**1**-**2**- 4:3, Mark Meredith 2-2-3- 7, Scott Smith **1**-2-3- 6:1, Peter McNamara 2-**1**-1- 4:1) **Swindon 15** (Matthew Cross 0-3-2- 5, Steve Masters 3-3-1- 7, Justin Elkins 3-F-N- 3, Steve Camden F-F-fx-N- 0)
Swindon 22 (Matthew Cross 0-3-**2**- 5:1, Steve Masters 2-2-1-**1**- 6:1, Justin Elkins **2**-3- 5:1, Steve Camden **1**-3-2- 6:1) **Cradley Heath 14** (Anthony Boyd 3-3-2-3- 11, Mark Meredith 1-1-fx- 2, Scott Smith R- 0, Shaun Naylor E-0-0-1- 1)
Wolverhampton 17 (**Stephen Morris 3-3-3- 9**, Colin Thorpe 0-1-0- 1, Simon Wolstenholme 3-1-**2**- 6:1, Craig Taylor 0-F-1- 1) **Ipswich 19** (Lawrence Hare **1**-**2**-0- 3:2, Savalas Clouting 2-2-3- 7, Ben Howe 2-3-1- 6, Shaun Tacey **1**-0-**2**- 3:2)

Wednesday, May 27
Poole 10 (Jason Smith 0-0-X- 0, Jonathon Gould 2-0-1- 3, Darren Boulton 2-2-0- 4, Martin Willis 0-1-2- 3) **Bradford 25** (Stuart Parnaby 1-3-3- 7, **Darren Pearson 3-3-2- 8:1**, **Kevin Little 3-2-3- 8:1**, Richard Smith 1-1-R- 2)

Saturday, May 30
Bradford 21 (Stuart Parnaby 0-0-0- 0, **Darren Pearson 3-3-3- 9**, Kevin Little **2**-3-0- 5:1, Richard Smith 3-01-3- 7) **King's Lynn 15** (Tom Grinstead **1**-2-2- 5:1, Emmerson Fairweather 2-2-**1**- 5:1, Andrew Mountain 1-**1**-0-1-**2**- 5:2)

Saturday, June 6
King's Lynn 28 (**Tom Grinstead 2-3-2- 7:2**, **Emmerson Fairweather 3-3-3- 9**, Darren Spicer **2**-R-3- 5:1, **Andrew Mountain 3-2-2- 7:2**) **Poole 8** (Darren Boulton 1-fx-1- 2, Jason Smith 0-0-**1**-0-0- 1:1, Martin Willis 1-2-1-1- 5)

Sunday, June 7
Eastbourne 19 (Nathan Gaymer 3-0-2- 5, Scott Swain 0-3-0- 3, Darren Grayling 3-3-2- 8, Justin Shaw 1-1-**1**- 3:1) **Belle Vue 17** (Steve Cope 1-fx-N- 1:1, Mike Hampson 2-**1**-1- 4:1, Peter Scully fx-2-0- 2, Mike Lewthwaite 2-2-3-3- 10)

Monday, June 8
Wolverhampton 21 (**Stephen Morris 3-3-3- 9**, Craig Taylor 1-1-3- 5, Simon Wolstenholme R-**2**-**2**- 4:2, Dean Felton 2-0-1- 3) **Coventry 15** (Chris Clarence 2-3-1- 6, Scott Wormleighton 0-1-2- 3, Colin Thorpe 3-**2**-0- 5:1, Paul Bromwich 1-0-0- 1)

DIVISION ONE RESERVE LEAGUE TABLE

	M	W	D	L	PtsF	PtsA	BP	TPts
IPSWICH	23	22	0	1	536	288	11	55
Swindon	24	17	0	7	493	365	10	44
Wolverhampton	24	16	1	7	485	375	8	41
King's Lynn	21	13	0	8	423	326	8	34
Bradford	24	13	2	9	465	395	7	35
Cradley Heath	23	13	1	9	424	400	7	34
Reading	23	11	1	11	428	391	5	28
Belle Vue	24	9	0	15	400	446	5	23
Oxford	24	9	0	15	362	484	3	21
Arena Essex	24	7	3	14	391	468	3	20
Eastbourne	24	7	1	16	355	502	1	16
Poole	24	6	1	17	344	514	3	16
Coventry	24	5	0	19	355	507	3	13

Roll of Honour

1987	1 SHEFFIELD	2 Bradford	3 Coventry
1988	1 BRADFORD	2 Belle Vue	3 Sheffield
1989	1 BELLE VUE	2 Oxford	3 Swindon
1990	1 WOLVERHAMPTON	2 Reading	3 King's Lynn
1991	1 CRADLEY HEATH	2 Oxford	3 Ipswich
1992	1 IPSWICH	2 Swindon	3 Wolverhampton

Wednesday, June 10
Poole 14 (Darren Boulton 2-3-0- 5, Jason Smith 0-0-**1**- 1:1, Jonathon Gould **1**-1-2- 4:1, Martin Willis 2-1-1- 4) **Oxford 22** (**Glenn Cunningham 3-3-2- 8:1**, Nick Upton 1-0-R- 1, **Spencer Timmo 3-2-3- 8:1**, Wayne Parker 0-2-3- 5)

Friday, June 12
Belle Vue 13 (Steve Cope 1-**1**-F- 2:1, Mike Hampson fx-0-3- 3, Peter Scully **1**-2-0- 3:1, Mike Lewthwaite 2-1-2- 5) **Bradford 23** (Stuart Parnaby 3-**2**-2- 7:1, Dean Child **2**-3-1- 6:1, **Darren Pearson 3-3-3- 9**, Martin Jones R-C-**1**- 1:1)

Saturday, June 13
Bradford 24 (Stuart Parnaby 3-R-3-3- 9, **Darren Pearson 2-3-3- 8:1**, Dean Child 3-**2-2**-R- 7:2) **Eastbourne 11** (Mike Randall R-1-0-2-1- 4, Paul Mitchell 1-2-1-1-2- 7) **King's Lynn 30** (**Tom Grinstead 3-2-3- 8:1**, **Emmerson Fairweather 2-3-2- 7:2**, **Darren Spicer 2-3-2- 7:2**, **Andrew Mountain 3-2-3- 8:1**) **Belle Vue 6** (Steve Cope R-0-0- 0, Mike Hampson 1-1-1- 3, Peter Scully 0-1-0- 1, Mike Lewthwaite 1-0-1- 2)

Monday, June 15
Wolverhampton 29 (**Stephen Morris 3-3-3- 9**, Shane Cooper **2-2**-1- 5:2, **Simon Wolstenholme 3-2-2- 7:2**, **Craig Taylor 2-3-3- 8:1**) **Eastbourne 7** (Nathan Gaymer 0-fx-0- 0, Scott Swain 1-1-1- 3, Justin Shaw 0-1-0- 1, Paul Mitchell 1-0-2- 3)

Wednesday, June 17
Poole 21 (**Steve Leigh 3-3-3- 9**, Jason Smith 0-fx-**2**- 2:1, Jonathon Gould **1**-fx-3- 4:1, Martin Willis 2-3-1- 6) **Belle Vue 15** (Jon Armstrong **1**-2-0- 3:1, Mike Hampson 2-1-R- 3:1, Peter Scully 0-**1**-1- 2:1, Mike Lewthwaite 3-2-2- 7)

Friday, June 19
Belle Vue 16 (Steve Cope **2**-2-**1**- 5:2, Mike Hampson 3-1-2- 6, Peter Scully **1**-0-0- 1:1, Jon Armstrong 2-0-2- 4) **Wolverhampton 20** (Stephen Morris 0-**2**-3- 5:1, Shane Cooper 1-3-0- 4, **Simon Wolstenholme 3-3-3- 9**, Craig Taylor 0-1-1- 2)

Wednesday, June 24
Poole 12 (**Steve Leigh 3-3-3- 9**, Jason Smith 0-0-0- 0, Jonathon Gould 1-0-fx- 1, Martin Willis 0-1-1- 2) **King's Lynn 24** (Tom Grinstead **1**-3-**2**- 6:2, Emmerson Fairweather 2-2-3- 7, Darren Spicer **2-2-1**- 5:3, Andrew Mountain 3-**1**-2- 6:1)

Saturday, June 27
Coventry 6 (Chris Clarence 1-0-1- 2, Scott Wormleighton 0-0-1-0- 1, Colin Thorpe 1-1-1- 3, Paul Bromwich N-N-N- 0) **King's Lynn 30** (**Tom Grinstead 3-3-2- 8:1**, **Emmerson Fairweather 2-2-3- 7:2**, **Darren Spicer 3-2-3- 8:1**, **Andrew Mountain 2-3-2- 7:2**)
Cradley Heath 16 (Shaun Naylor F-0-2- 2, **Justin Walker 3-3-3- 9**, Mark Meredith 3-2-X- 5, Carl Checketts 0-0-0- 0) **Reading 20** (Phillip Morris **1**-2-2- 5:1, Gary Sweet 2-1-3- 6, Lance Sealey 2-**1**-1- 4:1, Mick Tomlin **1**-3-**1**- 5:2)

Monday, June 29
Reading 27 (**Phillip Morris 3-3-3- 9**, Gary Sweet **2**-2-3- 7:1, Lance Sealey **2-2**-1- 5:2, Mick Tomlin 3-1-**2**- 6:2) **Cradley Heath 9** (Justin Walker 0-3-2- 5, Mark Meredith 1-1-0- 2, Shaun Naylor 1-0-1- 2, Carl Checketts 0-0-0 0)
Wolverhampton 18 (Stephen Morris **2**-R-3- 5:1, Shane Cooper 3-1-1- 5, Simon Wolstenholme 2-3-0- 5, Craig Taylor **1**-0-**2**- 3:2) **Swindon 16** (Justin Elkins R-**2**-R- 2:1, Steve Camden 1-2-**2**- 5:1, **Steve Masters 3-3-3- 9**, Steven Woolley fx-F-F- 0)

Saturday, July 4
Cradley Heath 19 (Carl Checketts 1-0-**1**- 2:1, Justin Walker 3-2-2- 7, Mark Meredith 3-3-0- 6, Shaun Naylor 0-**2**-2- 4:1) **Oxford 17** (Glenn Cunningham 2-3-1- 6, Wayne Parker **1**-1-3- 5:1, Spencer Timmo 2-1-3- 6, Nick Upton 0-0-0- 0)

Sunday, July 5
Eastbourne 28 (Paul Mitchell 1-**2**-3- 6:1, **Darren Grayling 3-3-3- 9**, Scott Swain 1-3-**2**- 6:1, **Nathan Gaymer 3-2-2- 7:2**) **Coventry 8** (Chris Clarence 2-0-1- 3, Paul Bromwich 0-1-0- 1, Colin Thorpe 2-1-0- 3, Scott Wormleighton 0-F-1- 1)

Wednesday, July 8
Poole 9 (Steve Leigh R-2-1- 3, Darren Boulton 1-1-2- 4, Martin Willis X-**1**-0-1-0- 2:2,) **Wolverhampton 26** (**Stephen Morris 3-2-2- 7:2**, **Shane Cooper 2-3-3- 8:1**, **Simon Wolstenholme 3-3-3- 9**, Craig Taylor **2**-0-R- 2:1)

Friday, July 10
Arena Essex 19 (Robert Ledwith 3-3-1- 7, Terry Giles F-0-1- 1, Roland Pollard 3-1-3- 7, Ricky Sandford **2**-2-0- 4:1) **Swindon 17** (Justin Elkins **1**-3-3- 7:1, Steve Masters 2-**2**-2- 6:1, Steve Camden 1-0-1-2- 4, Steve Woolley F-N-N- 0)

Saturday, July 11
Coventry 7 (Chris Clarence 1-F-1- 2, Sean McCullagh fx-N- 0, Colin Thorpe 0-1-0-0- 1, Scott Wormleighton 2-1-1- 4) **Wolverhampton 29** (**Stephen Morris 3-2-3- 8:1**, **Shane Cooper 2-3-3- 8:1**, **Simon Wolstenholme 3-3-2- 8:1**, Craig Taylor 1-**2-2**- 5:2)

Sunday, July 12
Eastbourne 23 (Paul Mitchell fx-**2**-3- 5:1, Scott Swain N-R-**2**- 2:1, Darren Grayling 3-N-3- 6, Nathan Gaymer 3-**2**-3-F-**2**- 10:2) **Poole 12** (Steve Leigh 2-3-1- 6, Darren Boulton 1-F-1-0- 2, Martin Willis 1-F-**2**-1- 4:1)

Monday, July 13
Reading 21 (**Phillip Morris 3-3-3- 9**, Mick Tomlin **2**-1-1- 4:1, Lance Sealey 1-**2**-3- 6:1, Gary Sweet fx-0-**2**- 2:1) **Belle Vue 15** (Steve Cope 1-**2**-fx- 3:1, Mike Hampson F-fx-1- 1, Peter Scully **2**-3-2- 7:1, Jon Armstrong 3-1-0- 4)

Thursday, July 16
Arena Essex 18 (Robert Ledwith 3-**2**-fx- 5:1, Terry Giles 1-0-0- 1, Roland Pollard 3-3-1- 7, Ricky Sandford 0-2-3- 5) **Wolverhampton 18** (Stephen Morris 2-3-**2**- 7:1, Shane Cooper fx-1-**1**- 2:1, Simon Wolstenholme 2-1-3- 6, Craig Taylor **1**-0-2- 3:1)
Ipswich 25 (Lawrence Hare **2**-1-**2**-**1**- 6:3, **Savalas Clouting 3-3-2- 8:1**, Ben Howe 2-3-3- 8, Shaun Tacey **1**-E-2- 3:1) **Oxford 11** (Glenn Cunningham 1-0-3- 4, Wayne Parker 0-2-0- 2, Spencer Timmo 3-1-1- 5, John Clayton 0-0-0- 0)
Swindon 25 (**Steve Masters 3-2-2- 7:2**, Steve Camden 0-**1**-3- 4:1, **Justin Elkins 3-3-3- 9**, Robert Vincent 1-2-**2**- 5:1) **Eastbourne 11** (Paul Mitchell **1**-3-0- 4:1, Scott Swain 2-2-1-1- 6, Mike Randall 0-R-0-1- 1)

Saturday, July 18
Coventry 15 (Chris Clarence 2-**2**-1- 5:1, Sean McCullagh 0-0-2- 2, Colin Thorpe 3-3-0- 6, Scott Wormleighton 0-1-**1**- 2:1) **Oxford 21** (**Glenn Cunningham 3-2-2- 7:2**, Wayne Parker 1-1-3- 5, Spencer Timmo 2-3-3- 8, John Clayton **1**-0-R- 1:1)

Wednesday, July 22
Poole 25 (Steve Leigh 3-3-1- 7, Darren Boulton **2**-fx-**2**- 4:2, Martin Willis 3-1-3- 7, Mick Tomlin **2**-3-2- 7:1) **Eastbourne 11** (Paul Mitchell 0-**1**-1- 2:1, Scott Swain 1-2-3- 6, Nathan Gaymer 1-2-fx- 3, Mike Randall 0-0-0- 0)

Thursday, July 23
Ipswich 22 (Lawrence Hare **1**-**1**-3- 5:2, Savalas Clouting 2-3-X- 5, Ben Howe **2**-2-**2**- 6:2, Shaun Tacey 3-**2**-1- 6:1) **Bradford 14** (Stuart Parnaby 0-0-0- 0, **Darren Pearson 3-3-2- 8:1**, Lance Sealey 1-1-3- 5, Richard Smith 0-0-1- 1)
Swindon 24 (Steve Masters F-**2**-3- 5:1, Matthew Cross 2-3-**2**- 7:1, Justin Elkins 3-3-2- 8, Steve Camden **2-2**-0- 4:2) **Arena Essex 12** (Robert Ledwith 3-1-3- 7, Terry Giles 1-0-1- 2, Roland Pollard 1-0-1- 2, Ricky Sandford 0-1-0- 1)

Friday, July 24
Belle Vue 29 (Steve Cope 1-**2-2**- 5:2, **Mike Hampson 3-2-3- 8:1**, **Peter Scully 2-3-2- 7:2**, **Jon Armstrong 3-3-3- 9**) **Poole 7** (Steve Leigh R-R-N- 0, Jason Green 2-1-0- 3, Martin Willis 1-1-1- 3, Lee Rowlinson F-fx-1- 1)
Oxford 19 (Glenn Cunningham 3-**2**-2- 7:1, Wayne Parker 1-2-2- 5, Spencer Timmo 3-3-0- 6, John Clayton 1-0-F- 1) **Swindon 17** (Steve Masters 2-1-N- 3, Matthew Cross F-1-3-1- 5, Justin Elkins 2-3-3- 8, Steve Camden 0-0-1- 1)

Saturday, July 25
Cradley Heath 18 (Justin Walker 3-3-2- 8, Anthony Boyd 1-2-2- 5, Mark Meredith 2-1-**1**-**1**- 5:2, Shaun Naylor fx-N-N- 0) **Bradford 18** (Stuart Parnaby 0-3-3- 6, Darren Pearson 2-2-3- 7, Richard Smith 1-N-N- 1, Dean Child 3-0-0-1-0- 4)

Monday, July 27
Reading 25 (**Phillip Morris 2-3-2- 7:2**, **Mick Tomlin 3-3-3- 9**, Lance Sealey 3-**2**-fx- 5:1, Gary Sweet 0-1-3- 4) **Poole 11** (Steve Leigh 1-2-1- 4, Jason Green 0-0-2- 2, Martin Willis 2-0-**1**- 3:1, Paul Mitchell **1**-1-0- 2:1)

Thursday, July 30
Ipswich 24 (Lawrence Hare 1-2-**2**- 5:1, **Savalas Clouting 3-3-3- 9**, Ben Howe 3-R-3- 6, Shaun Tacey **2-2**-F- 4:2) **Coventry 12** (Chris Clarence 0-1-1- 2, Jamie Habbin 2-3-N- 5, Gary Frankum 0-0-0-**1**- 1:1, Colin Thorpe 1-1-2- 4)
Swindon 24 (**Justin Elkins 3-2-2- 7:2**, Steve Camden **2**-3-R- 5:1, **Matthew Cross 3-3-3- 9**, Robert Vincent 1-1-1- 3) **Belle Vue 12** (Steve Cope 1-2-0- 3, Mike

All The 1992 Results

	ARENA ESSEX	BELLE VUE	BRADFORD	COVENTRY	CRADLEY HEATH	EASTBOURNE	IPSWICH	KING'S LYNN	OXFORD	POOLE	READING	SWINDON	WOLVERHAMPTON
ARENA ESSEX		22-12	18-18	24-12	15-20	21-15	10-26	19-17	27-9	23-13	16-20	19-17	18-18
BELLE VUE	25-11		13-23	20-16	21-15	24-10	9-27	21-15	†17-7	29-7	11-25	18-17	16-20
BRADFORD	26-10	19-17		24-12	15-21	24-11	15-21	21-15	28-8	24-12	21-15	17-19	20-16
COVENTRY	22-14	16-20	22-14		15-21	29-7	9-26	6-30	15-21	16-20	23-13	13-22	7-29
CRADLEY HEATH	23-13	19-16	18-18	22-14		22-14	15-21	19-17	19-17	25-11	16-20	21-15	23-13
EASTBOURNE	18-18	19-17	15-21	28-8	21-14		13-23	17-19	19-17	23-12	20-16	11-25	20-16
IPSWICH	24-11	23-13	22-14	24-12	25-11	27-9		28-8	25-11	25-11	27-9	24-12	21-14
KING'S LYNN	22-14	30-6	22-14	28-8		30-5			23-13	28-8	0-30	25-11	20-16
OXFORD	20-16	19-17	14-21	13-23	10-26	21-14	14-21	13-23		22-13	19-17	19-17	9-27
POOLE	24-12	21-15	10-25	19-17	20-15	25-11	16-20	12-24	14-22		18-18	15-20	9-26
READING	21-14	21-15	22-13	21-15	27-9	19-17	16-20		17-18	25-11		12-24	16-20
SWINDON	24-12	24-12	23-13	26-10	22-14	25-11	19-17	24-12	21-14	28-08	19-17		23-13
WOLVERHAMPTON	22-14	20-16	19-17	21-15	20-16	29-7	17-19	21-15	24-12	21-15	25-11	18-16	

†Abandoned after four heats, result to stand.

Hampson F-1-3- 4, Peter Scully 2-F-1- 3, Jon Armstrong 0-0-**2**- 2:1)

Friday, July 31

Belle Vue 25 (Steve Cope **1**-**2**-**2**- 5:3, Mike Hampson 2-3-**1**- 6:1, Peter Scully **2**-3-2- 7:1, Jon Armstrong 3-1-3- 7) **Arena Essex 11** (Robert Ledwith 3-2-3- 8, Terry Giles 0-0-0- 0, Roland Pollard 0-0-1- 1, Ricky Sandford 1-1-0- 2)

Oxford 22 (Glenn Cunningham 2-3-**2**- 7:1, Wayne Parker **1**-2-3- 6:1, **Spencer Timmo 3-2-3- 8:1**, John Clayton 1-0-0- 1) **Poole 13** (Steve Leigh 3-3-1- 7, Darren Boulton 0-F-N- 0, Martin Willis 0-1-**1**-0- 2:1, Jason Green 2-F-2- 4)

Saturday, August 1

Arena Essex 10 (Robert Ledwith 2-R-3- 5, Ricky Sandford 0-1-0- 1, Roland Pollard 1-2-0- 3, Terry Giles 0-0-1 1) **Ipswich 26** (Lawrence Hare 1-**2**-**2**- 5:2, Savalas Clouting 3-3-**1**- 7:1, Ben Howe 3-3-2- 8, Shaun Tacey **2**-1-3- 6:1)

Bradford 24 (**Stuart Parnaby 2-3-3- 8:1**, **Darren Pearson 3-3-2- 8:1**, Richard Smith 1-R-2- 3, Dean Child 3-1-**1**- 5:1) **Coventry 12** (Chris Clarence 1-2-R- 3, Colin Thorpe 2-2-0-0- 4, Scott Wormleighton 0-0-**1**-3-1- 5:1)

Sunday, August 2

Eastbourne 17 (Nathan Gaymer **1**-2-F- 3:1, Darren Grayling 2-3-3- 8, Paul Mitchell fx-0-0- 0, Scott Swain 2-1-3- 6) **King's Lynn 19** (Darren Spicer 3-0-1- 4, Tom Grinstead 0-3-2- 5, Andrew Mountain 1-1-1- 3, Emmerson Fairweather 3-2-2- 7)

Monday, August 3

Wolverhampton 24 (Stephen Morris 2-3-3- 8, Shane Cooper **1**-**1**-3- 5:2, **Simon Wolstenholme 3-2-2- 7:2**, Craig Taylor 1-2-1- 4) **Oxford 12** (Glenn Cunningham 3-3-0- 6, Wayne Parker 0-1-2- 3, Spencer Timmo 2-R-1- 3, Nick Upton 0-0-0- 0)

Wednesday, August 5

Oxford 19 (Glenn Cunningham 2-3-3- 8, Wayne Parker 0-3-2- 5, Spencer Timmo 3-**2**-1- 6:1, Nick Upton 0-0-0- 0) **Belle Vue 17** (Peter Scully 1-2-R- 3, Mike Hampson 3-0-1- 4, Jon Armstrong 2-**1**-2- 5:1, Steve Cope **1**-1-3- 5:1)

Thursday, August 6

Ipswich 21 (Lawrence Hare 2-**2**-0- 4:1, Savalas Clouting fx-R-3- 3, **Ben Howe 3-3-3- 9**, Shaun Tacey **2**-1-**2**- 5:2) **Wolverhampton 14** (Stephen Morris 3-3-**1**- 7:1, Shane Cooper fx-1-fx- 1, Simon Wolstenholme 1-**2**-**2**- 5:1, Craig Taylor 0-0-1- 1)

Swindon 19 (**Justin Elkins 3-3-2- 8:1**, Steve Camden 1-1-1- 3, **Matthew Cross 3-2-3- 8:1**, Robert Vincent 0-N- 0) **Reading 17** (Phillip Morris N-N- 0, Mick Tomlin fx-1-3- 4, Gary Sweet **1**-**2**-**2**-1- 6:3, Lance Sealey 2-2-0-3-0- 7)

Friday, August 7

Arena Essex 23 (Colin White **2**-3-2- 7:1, Ricky Sandford 3-2-3- 8, Roland Pollard 3-**2**-**1**- 6:2, Terry Giles 1-0-1- 2) **Poole 13** (Scott Swain 1-3-3- 7, Martin Willis 0-1-2- 3, Jason Green 2-1-0- 3, Jason Smith E-E-R- 0)

Belle Vue 20 (Peter Scully 2-**1**-**1**- 4:2, Mike Hampson 0-3-3- 6, Jon Armstrong 3-2-2- 7, Steve Cope 1-0-**2**- 3:1) **Coventry 16** (Chris Clarence 1-**1**-0-0- 2:1, **Jamie Habbin 3-3-3- 9**, Colin Thorpe 2-0-2-1-E- 5, Sid Cooper fx- 0)

Oxford 13 (Glenn Cunningham 3-2-3- 8, Wayne Parker 0-1-1- 2, Spencer Timmo 3-0-R- 3, Nick Upton 0-0-0- 0) **King's Lynn 23** (Darren Spicer 2-3-X- 5, Tom Grinstead **1**-3-3- 7:1, Emmerson Fairweather 2-**2**-2- 6:1, Andrew Mountain **1**-**1**-2-**1**- 5:3)

Saturday, August 8

King's Lynn 30 (**Tom Grinstead 3-2-2- 7:2**, **Emmerson Fairweather 2-2-3- 7:2**, **Darren Spicer 3-3-3- 9**, **Andrew Mountain 2-3-2- 7:2**) **Eastbourne 5** (Nathan Gaymer R-1-0-F- 1, Darren Grayling N-N- 0, Paul Mitchell 1-0-1- 2, Mark Bruton R-1-R-1-0- 2)

Monday, August 10

Wolverhampton 22 (**Stephen Morris 3-3-3- 9**, Shane Cooper fx-N-N- 0, **Simon Wolstenholme 3-2-2- 7:2**, Craig Taylor **2**-2-2- 6:1) **Arena Essex 14** (Colin White 2-3-1- 6, Ricky Sandford **1**-1-0- 2:1, Roland Pollard 0-1-3- 4, Terry Giles 1-0-1- 2)

Friday, August 14

Arena Essex 27 (**Colin White 2-2-3- 7:2**, **Ricky Sandford 3-3-3- 9**, **Roland Pollard 3-3-2- 8:1**, Terry Giles 1-1-1- 3) **Oxford 9** (Glenn Cunningham 1-fx-2- 3, Wayne Parker F-1-F- 1, Danny O'Brien F-2-R- 2, Nick Upton 2-0-1- 3)

Belle Vue 24 (**Peter Scully 3-3-2- 8:1**, Mike Hampson fx-3-3- 6, **Jon Armstrong 3-2-3- 8:1**, Steve Cope **2**-fx-0- 2:1)

Eastbourne 10 (Nathan Gaymer 2-2-R- 4, Mike Randall F-1-1- 2, Paul Mitchell 1-fx-2- 3, Mark Bruton 0-F-**1**- 1:1)

Saturday, August 15

Bradford 24 (Stuart Parnaby 1-3-1- 5, Darren Pearson 3-2-3- 8, Richard Smith **2**-1-**2**- 5:2, Dean Child 3-0-3- 6) **Poole 12** (Steve Leigh 2-3-2- 7, Martin Willis 0-2-0- 2, Jonathon Gould 0-1-1- 2, Jason Green 1-0-0- 1)

Sunday, August 16

Eastbourne 19 (Nathan Gaymer 2-3-2- 7, Mike Randall N-2-N- 2, Paul Mitchell 3-1-**1**- 5:1, Mark Bruton 1-1-**1**-2- 5:1) **Oxford 17** (**Glenn Cunningham 3-3-3- 9**, Wayne Parker fx-fx-3- 3, Danny O'Brien 0-0-1- 1, Nick Upton 2-2-0- 4)

Monday, August 17

Reading 12 (Lance Sealey 0-**1**-2- 3:1, Gary Sweet 1-1-1- 3, Mick Tomlin 2-2-fx- 4, Mark Sayer 1-0-**1**- 2:2) **Swindon 24** (**Justin Elkins 2-2-3- 7:2**, **Matthew Cross 3-3-3- 9**, **Steve Masters 3-3-2- 8:1**, Steve Camden R-0-X- 0)

Wednesday, August 19

Poole 18 (Steve Leigh 3-3-2- 8, Jonathon Gould R-N-1- 1, Martin Willis 2-**2**-**1**- 6:2, Jason Green 0-0-3- 3) **Reading 18** (Phillip Morris 2-3-0- 5, Gary Sweet **1**-1-2- 4:1, **Mick Tomlin 3-2-3- 8:1**, Lance Sealey 1-0-0- 1)

Thursday, August 20

Ipswich 25 (Lawrence Hare 3-**2**-0- 5:1, Savalas Clouting 1-3-3- 7, **Ben Howe 3-3-3- 9**, Shaun Tacey **2**-0-**2**- 4:2) **Cradley Heath 11** (Justin Walker 2-2-2- 6, Shaun Naylor 0-R-1- 1, Anthony Boyd 1-**1**-**1**- 3:2, Gary Wells 0-1-0- 1)

Friday, August 21

Arena Essex 19 (**Colin White 2-3-3- 8:1**, Ricky Sandford 3-2-1- 6, Roland Pollard 2-fx-2- 4, Terry Giles fx-0-**1**- 1:1) **King's Lynn 17** (Andrew Mountain 1-**1**-1-3- 6:1, Tom Grinstead 0-fn- 0, Emmerson Fairweather 3-3-2- 8, Jason Gage 1-2-R-0- 3)

Oxford 13 (Glenn Cunningham 2-2-3- 7, Wayne Parker 0-0-2- 2, Danny O'Brien 2-0-0- 2, Nick Upton **1**-1-0- 2:1) **Coventry 23** (Chris Clarence 1-**2**-3- 6:1, Jamie Habbin 3-3-N- 6, Colin Thorpe 3-1-3-2- 9, Adrian Mountain R-X-1-**1**- 2:1)

Saturday, August 22

Bradford 15 (Dean Child 1-1-2- 4, Simon Bean 0-0-1- 1, Stuart Parnaby 3-3-1- 7, Stuart Swales **2**-1-R- 3:1) **Cradley Heath 21** (**Scott Smith 3-2-3- 8:1**, Jon Armstrong **2**-**2**-2- 6:2, Justin Walker 1-3-3- 7, Carl Checketts 0-0-0- 0)

Coventry 29 (Chris Clarence **2**-3-3-1- 9:1, Jamie Habbin 3-3-N- 6, **Spencer Timmo 2-2-2- 6:3**, **Colin Thorpe 3-2-3- 8:1**) **Eastbourne 7** (Nathan Gaymer N-1-2- 3, Darren Grayling R-0-1- 1, Paul Mitchell 0-R-R- 0, Mark Bruton 1-1-1-0- 3)

Sunday, August 23

Eastbourne 13 (Nathan Gaymer 1-2-1- 4, Darren Grayling 0-3-3- 6, Paul Mitchell 0-1-0- 1, Mark Bruton 1-0-1- 2) **Ipswich 23** (Lawrence Hare **2**-**1**-3- 6:2, Savalas Clouting 3-3-2- 8, Ben Howe 3-2-0- 5, Shaun Tacey **2**-F-2- 4:2)

Monday, August 31

Coventry 22 (Chris Clarence 1-**2**-**1**-2- 6:2, Jamie Habbin 3-2-N- 5, Spencer Timmo 3-3-N- 6, Colin Thorpe 1-**1**-2-**1**- 5:2) **Arena Essex 14** (Colin White 2-3-3- 8, Ricky Sandford 0-1-3- 4, Roland Pollard 2-0-0- 2, Terry Giles 0-0-0- 0)

Oxford 19 (**Glenn Cunningham 3-3-3- 9**, Danny O'Brien 0-1-1- 2, Wayne Parker 1-**2**-**2**- 5:2, Nick Upton 0-0-3- 3) **Reading 17** (Phillip Morris N-N-N- 0, Gary Sweet **1**-1-2-4:1, Mick Tomlin 3-3-1- 7, Lance Sealey **2**-**2**-fx-2-0- 6:2)

Reading 17 (Lance Sealey 2-3-**1**- 6:1, Gary Sweet F-2-3- 5, Mick Tomlin 2-**2**-2- 6:1, Mark Sayer 0-R-0- 0) **Oxford 18** (**Glenn Cunningham 3-3-3- 9**, Danny O'Brien R-0-2- 2, Wayne Parker 3-1-0- 4, Nick Upton 1-1-**1**- 3:1)

Swindon 19 (Matthew Cross **2**-3-0- 5:1, Justin Elkins 3-2-2- 7, Steve Masters 2-1-3- 6, Steve Camden **1**-0-0- 1:1) **Ipswich 17** (Lawrence Hare 0-1-2- 3, Savalas Clouting 1-2-1- 4, **Ben Howe 3-3-3- 9**, Shaun Tacey 0-X-**1**- 1:1)

Wednesday, September 2

Oxford 9 (Glenn Cunningham 2-2-0- 4, Danny O'Brien 0-0-0- 0, Wayne Parker 1-0-1- 2, Nick Upton F-1-2- 3) **Wolverhampton 27** (**Stephen Morris 3-3-3- 9**, Shane Cooper 1-3-3- 7, **Simon Wolstenholme 3-2-2- 7:2**, Craig Taylor **2**-1-1- 4:1)

Poole 20 (**Steve Leigh 3-3-3- 9**, Scott Swain 0-1-3- 4, Martin Willis 2-**2**-1- 5:1, Jason Green **1**-0-1- 2:1) **Cradley Heath 15** (Justin Walker 2-2-0- 4:1, Mark Meredith **1**-fx-2- 3:1, Anthony Boyd 3-3-2- 8, Shaun Naylor N-0-0- 0)

Thursday, September 3

Ipswich 27 (Lawrence Hare 1-0-3- 4, **Savalas Clouting 3-3-2- 8:1**, **Ben Howe 2-3-2- 7:2**, **Shaun Tacey 3-2-3- 8:1**) **Eastbourne 9** (Darren Grayling 2-**1**- 3:1, Nathan Gaymer 0-fx-1-0- 1, Mark Bruton 1-2-0-1-1- 5)

Friday, September 4

Arena Essex 21 (Colin White 3-2-3- 8, Ricky Sandford 1-2-3- 6, Roland Pollard 2-**1**-0- 3:1, Terry Giles 1-**1**-2- 4:2) **Eastbourne 15** (Paul Mitchell 0-3-**1**- 4:1, Darren Grayling 2-3-2- 7, Nathan Gaymer 3-0-1- 4, Mark Bruton R-N-N- 0)

Saturday, September 5

Bradford 26 (Michael Graves 1-**2**-3- 6:1, **Darren Pearson 3-3-3- 9**, Richard Smith 3-3-0- 6, Stuart Swales **2**-**1**-2- 5:2) **Arena Essex 10** (Colin White 2-2-2- 6, Ricky Sandford 0-1-1- 2, Roland Pollard 1-0-**1**- 2:1, Terry Giles 0-0-0- 0)

Cradley Heath 22 (Justin Walker 3-3-2- 8, Mark Meredith **2**-3-2- 7:1, Anthony Boyd 3-**2**-**1**- 6:2, Shaun Naylor 1-0-0- 1) **Coventry 14** (Chris Clarence 1-2-3- 6, Jamie Habbin 0-1-N- 1, Colin Thorpe 0-**1**-1- 2:1, Scott Kirton 2-0-3-F- 5)

Monday, September 7

Wolverhampton 21 (Stephen Morris 2-3-3- 8, Shane Cooper **1**-**1**-2- 4:2, Simon Wolstenholme 3-**2**-1- 6:1, Craig Taylor 0-2-**1**- 3:1) **King's Lynn 15** (Andrew Mountain 0-0-0- 0, Darren Spicer 3-1-0- 4, Emmerson Fairweather **1**-3-2- 6:1, Jason Gage 2-0-3- 5)

Wednesday, September 9

Poole 24 (**Steve Leigh 3-3-3- 9**, Martin Willis 1-**2**-**1**- 4:2, Jason Green 0-**2**-2- 4:1, Scott Swain 3-3-1- 7) **Arena Essex 12** (Colin White 2-1-2- 5, Ricky Sandford 0-**1**-N-3- 4:1, Roland Pollard 2-0-0- 2, Terry Giles N-1-0- 1)

Thursday, September 10

Swindon 23 (Matthew Cross **2**-R-3- 5:1, **Justin Elkins 3-3-3- 9**, Steve Masters 3-2-**2**- 7:1, Steve Camden 0-1-1- 2) **Bradford 13** (Michael Graves N-N- 0, Darren Pearson 1-3-0- 4, Richard Smith **1**-1-fx-fn-2:1, Stuart Swales 0-2-N-2-2-1- 7)

Friday, September 11

Arena Essex 16 (**Colin White 3-3-3- 9**, Ricky Sandford **2**-1-1- 4:1, Roland Pollard 1-1-1- 3, Terry Giles 0-0-0- 0) **Reading 20** (Phillip Morris F-3-3- 6, Gary Sweet 1-2-**2**-5:1, Mick Tomlin 3-**2**-0- 5:1, Lance Sealey 2-0-2- 4:1)

Belle Vue 21 (Stuart Parnaby 1-1-2- 4, Jason Handley 2-2-**1**- 5:1, **Mike Hampson 2-3-3- 8:1**, Peter Scully 3-**1**-F- 4:1) **Cradley Heath 15** (Justin Walker 3-3-2- 8, Mark Meredith 0-2-**1**- 3:1, Anthony Boyd 1-0-3-4, Carl Checketts 0-0-0- 0)

Oxford 14 (**Glenn Cunningham 3-3-3- 9**, Danny O'Brien 0-0-0- 0, Wayne Parker 1-0-1- 2, Nick Upton 0-1-**2**- 3:1) **Ipswich 21** (Lawrence Hare **1**-3-R- 4:1, Savalas Clouting 2-2-**2**- 6:1, Ben Howe **2**-**2**-R- 4:2, Shaun Tacey 3-**1**-3- 7:1)

Saturday, September 12

Coventry 13 (Chris Clarence F-1-2- 3, Jamie Habbin 3-3-N- 6, Paul Bromwich E-0-**1**-0- 1:1, Scott Kirton 2-0-1- 3) **Swindon 22** (Matthew Cross **1**-**2**-**1**-**2**- 6:4, Steve Masters 2-3-3- 8, Justin Elkins 3-2-3- 8, Steve Camden F-N-N- 0)

Cradley Heath 23 (**Justin Walker 3-3-3- 9**, Mark Meredith 1-2-**1**- 4:1, Anthony Boyd 3-**2**-1- 6:1, Carl Checketts 1-**1**-2- 4:1)

Arena Essex 13 (Colin White 2-3-2- 7, Ricky Sandford 0-1-3- 4, Roland Pollard 2-F-0- 2, Terry Giles 0-0-0- 0)

Wednesday, September 16

Poole 16 (Steve Leigh 3-2-E- 5, Martin Willis **2**-2-1- 5:1, Scott Swain 1-**1**-3- 5:1, Jason Green 0-**1**-0-0- 1:1) **Ipswich 20** (Lawrence Hare 1-R-2- 3, Savalas Clouting 0-3-**2**- 5:1, **Ben Howe 3-3-3- 9**, Shaun Tacey **2**-0-**1**- 3:2)

Thursday, September 17

Ipswich 25 (Lawrence Hare 1-**2**-**2**-3- 8:2, Savalas Clouting 3-3-**1**- 7:1, Ben Howe 3-3-2- 8, Shaun Tacey 1-N-1- 2) **Poole 11** (Steve Leigh 2-fx-3- 5, Martin Willis 0-1-2-3, Scott Swain 0-1-0- 1, Jason Green 2-0-0- 2)

Swindon 26 (Steve Masters 3-**2**-R-3- 8:1, **Justin Elkins 3-3-3- 9**, Matthew Cross 0-N-**2**-3-**2**-**2**- 9:3) **Coventry 10** (Chris Clarence 1-2-1- 4:1, Jamie Habbin 2-R- 2, Colin Thorpe 0-**1**-1- 2:1, Scott Kirton 1-1-E-0- 2)

Friday, September 18

Belle Vue 21 (Mike Hampson **1**-2-1- 4:1, Jon Armstrong 2-**2**-3- 7:1, Jason Handley 0-**1**-3- 4:1, Peter Scully 2-3-1- 6) **King's Lynn 15** (Adrian Mountain 0-1-0- 1, Emmerson Fairweather 3-3-0- 6, Darren Spicer 3-0-N- 3, Jason Gage 1-fx-2-2- 5)

Wednesday, September 23

Cradley Heath 23 (Justin Walker 3-2-**2**- 7:1, **Mark Meredith 2-3-3- 8:1**, Anthony Boyd 2-3-3- 8, Carl Checketts 0-0-0- 0)

Wolverhampton 13 (Stephen Morris N-N-0, Craig Taylor F-fx-**1**-2- 3:1, Simon Wolstenholme 3-2-1- 6, Phil Ashcroft 1-1-1-N-**1**- 4:1)

Reading 22 (**Phillip Morris 3-3-2- 8:1**, Gary Sweet 1-1-0- 2, Mick Tomlin 2-F- 2, Lance Sealey **1**-3-3-3- 10:1) **Bradford 13** (Mark Sayer 0-0-2- 2, Darren Pearson 2-R-**1**- 3:1, Wayne Parker 0-2-0- 2, Stuart Swales 3-2-1- 6)

Thursday, September 24

Ipswich 24 (Lawrence Hare **1**-1-**2**- 4:2, Savalas Clouting 2-3-1- 6, **Ben Howe 2-3-3- 8:1**, Shaun Tacey 3-0-3- 6) **Swindon 12** (Matthew Cross 3-2-2-2- 9, Steve Masters

N-N-N- 0, Justin Elkins 1-**1**-F- 2:1, Dean Ing 0-0-R-1- 1)

Friday, September 25
Belle Vue 17 (Mike Hampson fx-**2**- 2:1, Jon Armstrong 2-3- 5, **Jason Handley 3-3-6, Peter Scully 2-2- 4:2) Oxford 7** (Glenn Cunningham 3-N- 3, Danny O'Brien 1-0- 1, Wayne Parker 0-1- 1, Nick Upton 1-1- 2)
†Abandoned after four heats, result to stand.

Saturday, September 26
Coventry 15 (Chris Clarence 1-3-F- 4, Adrian Mountain 0-0-0- 0, Colin Thorpe **1-2**-2- 5:2, Scott Kirton 2-1-3- 6) **Cradley Heath 21** (Justin Walker 3-3-3- 9, Mark Meredith **2**-1-2- 5:1, Anthony Boyd 3-**2**-1- 6:1, Carl Checketts 0-0-**1**- 1:1)
Eastbourne 11 (Paul Mitchell 0-2-1-0- 3, Nathan Gaymer **1**-fx-**1**- 2:2, Mark Bruton 1-2-0-2-1- 6) **Swindon 25** (**Steve Masters 3-3-3- 9, Matthew Cross 2-3-2- 7:2, Justin Elkins 3-2-3- 8:1**, Dean Ing R-1-0- 1)
King's Lynn 20 (Andrew Mountain 2-**2**-**1**- 5:2, Emmerson Fairweather **1**-fx-3- 4:1, Darren Spicer 3-3-2- 8, Shaun Tacey 1-2-F- 3) **Wolverhampton 16** (**Stephen Morris 3-3-3- 9**, Craig Taylor E-0-**1**- 1:1, Simon Wolstenholme 2-1-0- 3, Phil Ashcroft 0-0-1-2- 3)

Monday, September 28
Reading 16 (**Phillip Morris 3-3-3- 9**, Gary Sweet 0-1-0- 1, Lance Sealey 2-**2**-1- 5:1, Mark Sayer 0-0-1- 1) **Wolverhampton 20** (Stephen Morris 2-3-2- 7, Craig Taylor 1-0-3- 4:1, Simon Wolstenholme 1-**2**-**2**- 5:2, Phil Ashcroft 3-1-0- 4)

Tuesday, September 29
Bradford 28 (Darren Pearson 2-3-1- 6:1, **Michael Graves 3-2-3- 8:1**, Simon Bean 3-**2**-1- 6:1, **Stuart Swales 2-3-3- 8:1**) **Oxford 8** (Glenn Cunningham 1-1-2- 4, Danny O'Brien fx-F-0- 0, Wayne Parker 1-0-0- 1), Nick Upton 0-1-2- 3)
Bradford 20 (Darren Pearson 3-3-2- 8, Michael Graves 1-N- 1, Stuart Swales 3-**2**-2-3-1- 11:2, Simon Bean 0- 0) **Wolverhampton 16** (Stephen Morris 2-3-3- 8, Craig Taylor 0-1-1- 2, Simon Wolstenholme 2-1-0- 3, Phil Ashcroft 0-0-2)

Wednesday, September 30
Oxford 21 (**Glenn Cunningham 3-3-3- 9**, Danny O'Brien F-0-**2**- 2:1, Wayne Parker 3-1-1- 5, Nick Upton 0-2-3- 5) **Eastbourne 14** (Paul Mitchell **1**-**1**-1-N- 3:2, Darren Grayling 2-2-2- 6, Nathan Gaymer N-N- 0, Mark Bruton 2-0-3- 5)
Poole 15 (Steve Leigh N-N-N- 0, Jason Green 2-1-2- 5, Scott Swain 2-3-2- 7, Chris Strong 1-0-2- 3) **Swindon 20** (Matthew Cross N-1-3- 4, Justin Elkins 3-2-3- 8, Steve Masters 3-3-1- 7, Dean Ing N-R-N- 0)
Wolverhampton 19 (Stephen Morris fx-**1**-**2**- 3:2, Craig Taylor 2-0-3- 5, Simon Wolstenholme 3-2-**1**- 6:1, Phil Ashcroft **2**-1-2- 5:1) **Bradford 17** (**Darren Pearson 3-3-3- 9**, Jonathan Swales 1-0-0- 1, Simon Bean 0-N-1- 1, Stuart Swales 1-3-**2**-0- 6:1)
Wolverhampton 20 (Stephen Morris N-0-3- 3, Craig Taylor **1**-2-F- 3:1, **Simon Wolstenholme 2-3-3- 8:1**, Phil Ashcroft 2-3-R-1- 6) **Cradley Heath 16** (Justin Walker 3-3-2- 8, Mark Meredith fx-2-2- 4, Anthony Boyd 1-1-0- 2, Carl Checketts 0-**1**-**1**- 2:2)

Thursday, October 1
Ipswich 24 (Shaun Tacey **2**-**2**-**1**- 5:3, Ben Howe 3-2-3- 8, **Savalas Clouting 3-3-2- 8:1**, Lawrence Hare X-1-2- 3:1) **Arena Essex 11** (Colin White 1-3-fx- 4, Ricky Sandford 0-1-3-1- 5, Roland Pollard fx-N-N- 0, Terry Giles 2-0-0-0- 2)
Swindon 24 (**Matthew Cross 3-2-2- 7:2**, Steve Masters **2**-2-3- 7:1, **Justin Elkins 3-3-3- 9**, Dean Ing 0-0-1- 1) King's Lynn 12 (Andrew Mountain 1-1-3-0- 5, Darren Spicer fn- 0, Emmerson Fairweather **1**-1-1- 3:1, Jason Gage 0-2-R-2- 4)

Sunday, October 4
King's Lynn 28 (Andrew Mountain 2-3-3- 8, Darren Spicer **1**-3-**2**- 6:2, **Emmerson Fairweather 2-2-3- 7:2, Jason Gage 3-2-2- 7:2) Coventry 8** (Chris Clarence 3-1-X- 4, Jamie Habbin R-N- 0, Colin Thorpe 1-0-0-0- 1, Scott Kirton R-1-1-1- 3)

Monday, October 5
Reading 21 (Phillip Morris F-3-3- 6, Gary Sweet 2-3-**2**- 7:1, Lance Sealey 3-1-3- 7, Mark Sayer 1-F-0- 1) **Arena Essex 14** (Colin White 3-F-2- 5, Ricky Sandford 1-2-2-1- 6, Roland Pollard N-N- 0, Terry Giles 0-0-2-1-0- 3:1)
Wolverhampton 21 (Stephen Morris **1**-fx-3- 4:1, Craig Taylor 2-0-1- 3, **Simon Wolstenholme 3-3-3- 9**, Phil Ashcroft **2**-1-2- 5:2) **Poole 15** (Steve Leigh 3-**2**-0- 5:1, Chris Strong 0-1-0- 1:1, Scott Swain 0-3-1-4, Jason Green 1-2-2- 5)

Tuesday, October 6
Bradford 15 (Darren Pearson 3-**2**-**1**- 6:2, Simon Bean 0-0-1- 1, Stuart Parnaby 2-3-2- 7, Stuart Swales 0-1-0- 1) **Ipswich 21** (Shaun Tacey **1**-**2**-0- 3:2, Ben Howe 2-0-3- 5, **Savalas Clouting 3-3-3- 9**, Lawrence Hare 1-1-2- 4:1)

Wednesday, October 7
Reading 19 (Mark Seabright 3-R-**2**- 5:1, Gary Sweet **2**-**1**-1- 4:2, Lance Sealey 3-2-0- 5, Mark Sayer E-2-3- 5) **Eastbourne 17** (Paul Mitchell 1-0-1- 2, Darren Grayling fx-3-3- 6, Nathan Gaymer **1**-3-**2**- 6:2, Mark Bruton 2-1-F- 3)

Thursday, October 8
Ipswich 28 (Shaun Tacey **2**-1-**2**- 5:2, **Ben Howe 3-3-3- 9, Savalas Clouting 3-3-2- 8:1**, Lawrence Hare 1-2-3- 6:1) **King's Lynn 8** (Andrew Mountain 0-0-0-1- 1, Justin Walker 1-2-0- 3, Emmerson Fairweather 2-1-1- 4, Jason Gage F- 0)
Swindon 21 (**Matthew Cross 3-2-3- 8:1**, Justin Elkins 1-3-3- 7, Steve Masters 3-3-6, Dean Ing fx-0-R- 0) **Oxford 14** (Glenn Cunningham 2-2-2- 6, Nick Upton 0-0-**1**- 1:1, Wayne Parker 2-**1**-**1**- 4:2, Danny O'Brien F-1-2- 3)
Swindon 23 (**Matthew Cross 2-3-3-2- 10:2**, Justin Elkins 3-2-3- 8, Steve Masters 1-1-3- 5, Dean Ing N-R- 0) **Wolverhampton 13** (Dean Felton 0-N-**1**- 1:1, Craig Taylor 1-0-2- 3, Simon Wolstenholme 2-3-0- 5, Phil Ashcroft 0-2-1-1- 4)

Friday, October 9
Arena Essex 24 (Colin White **1**-3-3- 7:1, Ricky Sandford 2-3-1- 6, Chris Young 3-0-3- 6, Terry Giles **2**-1-**2**- 5:2) **Coventry 12** (Chris Clarence R-F-N- 0, Jamie Habbin 3-2-2- 7, Scott Kirton 1-**1**-2-1- 5:1)
Belle Vue 9 (Mike Hampson 1-F-1- 2, Jason Handley 0-1-0- 1, Jon Armstrong 2-1-0- 3, Peter Scully **1**-0-2- 3:1) **Ipswich 27** (**Shaun Tacey 3-2-3- 8:1**, Ben Howe **2**-3-1- 6:1, **Savalas Clouting 3-3-3- 9**, Lawrence Hare 0-**2**-**2**- 4:2)
Oxford 10 (Glenn Cunningham 3-1-3- 7, Nick Upton 0-0-N- 0, Wayne Parker 1-0-0-1, Danny O'Brien 0-1-1- 2) **Cradley Heath 26** (Anthony Boyd **1**-**2**-**2**- 5:3, Scott Smith 2-3-3- 8, Justin Walker 3-3-**1**- 7:1, Mark Meredith **2**-**2**-2- 6:2)

Saturday, October 10
Bradford 21 (**Darren Pearson 3-3-3- 9**, Simon Bean 1-0-1- 2, Stuart Parnaby R-**2**-3- 5:1, Stuart Swales 3-2-X- 5) **Reading 15** (Phillip Morris 2-3-2- 7, Gary Sweet 0-1-2-3, Lance Sealey 2-1-**1**- 4:1, Mark Sayer **1**-0-0- 1:1)
Coventry 16 (Gary Frankum 0-0-1- 1, **Jamie Habbin 3-3-3- 9**, Colin Thorpe **1**-2-0- 3:1, Scott Kirton 2-1-R- 3) **Belle Vue 20** (Mike Hampson **1**-2-2- 5:1, Jason Handley 2-3-**1**- 6:1, Jon Armstrong 3-0-3- 6, Peter Scully 0-1-**2**- 3:1)
Cradley Heath 25 (Anthony Boyd **2**-**2**-1- 5:2, Scott Smith 3-2-3- 8, **Justin Walker 3-3-3- 9**, Mark Meredith 1-fx-**2**- 3:1) **Poole 11** (Steve Leigh 1-01-2- 4, Martin Willis 0-1-1- 2, Scott Swain 2-3-0- 5, Jason Green 0-0-0- 0)

Sunday, October 11
Eastbourne 20 (Paul Mitchell 0-1-**2**- 3:1, Darren Grayling 2-3-R- 5, Nathan Gaymer 3-3-2- 8, Mark Bruton 0-1-3- 4) **Reading 16** (Phillip Morris 1-N- 1, Gary Sweet 3-2-3- 8, Lance Sealey 2-2-1- 5, Mark Sayer **1**-0-R-1- 2:1)

Monday, October 12
Wolverhampton 20 (Stephen Morris 3-2-**1**- 6:1, Craig Taylor **1**-0-0- 1:1, Simon Wolstenholme **2**-**1**-3- 6:2, Phil Ashcroft 3-2-2- 7) **Belle Vue 16** (Mike Hampson 2-3-0- 5, Mike Lewthwaite 0-3-3- 6, Jon Armstrong 1-1-2- 4, Peter Scully 0-0-**1**- 1:1)

Thursday, October 15
Ipswich 27 (Shaun Tacey 1-1-**2**- 4:1, **Ben Howe 3-3-2- 8:1, Savalas Clouting 3-3-3- 9**, Lawrence Hare **2**-1-3- 6:1) **Reading 9** (Phillip Morris 2-2-1- 5, Gary Sweet 0-2-0- 2, Lance Sealey 1-0-1- 2, Mark Sayer F-0-0- 0)
Swindon 28 (**Matthew Cross 2-3-2-2-2- 11:4, Justin Elkins 3-3-3- 9, Steve Masters 2-3-3- 8:1**, Dean Ing N-N-R- 0) **Poole 8** (Steve Leigh 1-1-1- 3, Martin Willis 0-0-**1**- 1:1, Scott Swain 1-0-F- 1, Jason Green 0-1-2- 3)

Friday, October 16
Oxford 14 (**Glenn Cunningham 3-3-3- 9**, Nick Upton 0-N- 0, Wayne Parker 1-fx-F- 1, Danny O'Brien 0-1-3- 4) **Bradford 21** (Dean Child 2-E-F- 2, Simon Bean **1**-**1**-2- 4:2, Stuart Parnaby 3-3-2- 8, Stuart Swales **2**-**2**-2-**1**- 7:3)

Saturday, October 17
Bradford 17 (Dean Child 1-2-2- 5, Simon Bean 0-0-**1**- 1:1, Stuart Parnaby 3-**1**-**1**- 5:2, Stuart Swales **2**-2-2- 6:1) **Swindon 19** (**Matthew Cross 3-3-3- 9**, Justin Elkins **2**-3-R- 5:1, Steve Masters 1-1-3- 5, Dean Ing 0-F-0- 0)
Coventry 16 (Adrian Mountain 1-0-0-1- 2, Jamie Habbin R-N-N- 0, Colin Thorpe 1-3-3- 7, Scott Kirton 3-3-R-1- 7) **Poole 20** (Steve Leigh N-**1**-**2**- 3:2, Martin Willis 3-0-2-2- 7, Scott Swain 2-2-3- 7, Jason Green **2**-E-**1**-fx- 3:2)
Cradley Heath 15 (Mark Meredith 0-**1**-2-3:1, Scott Smith 2-2-2- 6, Justin Walker 3-2-**1**- 6:1, Carl Checketts 0-0-R- 0) **Ipswich 21** (Shaun Tacey 1-3-E- 4, **Ben Howe 3-3-3- 9**, Savalas Clouting **1**-1-3- 5:1, Lawrence Hare 2-0-1-0- 3)

Sunday, October 18
Eastbourne 21 (Paul Mitchell 0-**2**-**1**-3- 6:2, Nathan Gaymer 3-3-2- 8, Mark Bruton 2-**2**-2-1- 7:2) **Cradley Heath 14** (**Scott Smith 3-3-3- 9**, Ricky Sandford 1-1-0- 2, Mark Meredith 1-0-fn- 1, Carl Checketts 0-0-2- 2)

Friday, October 23
Arena Essex 18 (**Colin White 3-3-3- 9**, Ricky Sandford **2**-1-1- 4:1, Chris Young E-1-3- 4, Terry Giles 1-0-0- 1) **Bradford 18** (Richard Smith 0-**2**-2- 4:1, Simon Bean 1-0-**1**- 2:1, Stuart Parnaby 3-3-0- 6, Stuart Swales **2**-2-2- 6:1)

Saturday, October 17
King's Lynn 22 (Andrew Mountain 1-3-3-**2**-2- 11:1, Emmerson Fairweather 3-3-R- 6, Darren Spicer N-N- 0, Sid Cooper F-**2**-E-3-5:1) **Arena Essex 14** (Colin White 2-1-3- 6, Ricky Sandford 0-1-2- 3, Chris Young 2-0-1- 3, Terry Giles **1**-0-**1**- 2:2)

Sunday, October 18
Reading 16 (Phillip Morris 2-3-3- 8, Jason Green 1-1-0- 2:1, Lance Sealey 2-1-2- 5, Mark Sayer **1**-N-0- 1:1) **Ipswich 20** (Lawrence Hare 0-3-3- 6, Ben Howe 3-2-**1**- 6:1, Savalas Clouting 3-**2**-2- 7:1, Gary Wells 0-0-1- 1)

Monday, October 19
Reading 21 (**Phillip Morris 3-3-3- 9**, Gary Sweet **2**-2-1- 5:1, Lance Sealey 2-1-2- 5, Mark Sayer 0-**1**-**1**- 2:2) **Coventry 15** (Adrian Mountain 1-0-0-0- 1, Jamie Habbin N-N- 0, Colin Thorpe 3-3-2- 8, Scott Kirton fx-1-2-3-0- 6)

Saturday, October 24
Cradley Heath 19 (**Scott Smith 3-3-3- 9**, Anthony Boyd 0-X-R- 0, **Justin Walker 3-2-2- 7:2**, Carl Checketts 0-1-2- 3) **Belle Vue 16** (Mike Hampson 2-1-**2**- 5:1, Jason Handley **1**-N-N- 1:1, Jon Armstrong 2-3-1-6, Peter Scully **1**-F-3- 4:1)

Sunday, October 25
Eastbourne 18 (Paul Mitchell 0-1-**1**- 2:1, Darren Grayling 3-2-2- 7, Nathan Gaymer 3-3-**1**- 7:1, Mark Bruton F-R-2- 2) **Arena Essex 18** (Colin White 2-3-3- 8, Ricky Sandford **1**-**2**-F- 3:2, Simon Wolstenholme 1-1-3- 5, Terry Giles 2-0-0- 2)

Saturday, October 31
Coventry 22 (Scott Wormleighton 1-R- 1, Jamie Habbin 3-3- 6, Colin Thorpe 3-2-1-6, Scott Kirton 1-**2**-3-3- 9:1) **Bradford 14** (Stuart Parnaby 2-1-0- 3, Simon Bean 0-1-**1**- 2:1, Richard Smith 0-0- 0, Stuart Swales 2-3-2-2- 9)

KING'S Lynn were awarded the unstaged match against Reading 30-0 following the Speedway Control Board ruling although points were not awarded to the riders.

IPSWICH lost only three matches in all Reserve team competitions. They were beaten once in the Reserve League (at Swindon) and twice in the Gold Cup (at Reading and King's Lynn). They won all their Knock Out Cup matches to finish the season with a record of 40 wins out of 43 official matches.

IN THE Reserve League match between Eastbourne and Bradford only five riders competed! Bradford tracked only three riders and visitors Eastbourne went into action with only two riders with Mike Randall and Paul Mitchell sharing 10 outings between them.

THE matches between King's Lynn and Cradley Heath and King's Lynn and Ipswich were never staged as the Norfolk club ran out of dates following their mid-season closure.

KING'S Lynn featured in three whitewash results during the season – winning 30-6 at Coventry and at home to Belle Vue and claiming a 30-5 victory over Eastbourne.

Division One Reserve League Knock Out Cup

First Round

Saturday, April 25, First leg
Cradley Heath 27 (**Mark Robinson 3-2-2-7:2**, Mark Meredith **2**-0-**2**- 4:2, **Scott Smith 3-3-3- 9**, Peter McNamara **2**-2-3- 7:1) **Poole 9** (Darren Boulton X-1-1- 2, Anthony Blake 1-1-1- 3, Jonathon Gould 1-3-0- 4, Martin Willis 0-0-0- 0)

Wednesday, June 3, Second leg
Poole 1 (Darren Boulton fx- 0, Jason Smith 1- 1, Jonathon Gould and Martin Willis, did not ride) **Cradley Heath 5** (Anthony Boyd **2**- 2:1, Mark Meredith 3- 3, Peter McNamara, did not ride)

Meeting abandoned after one race, Poole concede tie.

Cradley Heath win 32-10 on aggregate

Thursday, April 30, First leg
Swindon 14 (Matthew Cross N-2-3- 5, Steve Masters 1-2-N-N- 3, Justin Elkins 2-R-N- 2, Robert Vincent F-0-**1**-2-1- 4:1) **Wolverhampton 21** (Stephen Morris 3-fx-3- 6, Shane Cooper 2-3-**2**- 7:1, Simon Wolstenholme 3-3-R- 6, Craig Taylor 1-1-fx- 2)

Monday, May 11, Second leg
Wolverhampton 26 (**Stephen Morris 3-3-3- 9**, Colin Thorpe 1-0-3- 4, **Simon Wolstenholme 3-2-2- 7:2**, Craig Taylor **2**-2-**2**- 6:2) **Swindon 10** (Steve Masters 2-1-0- 3, Steve Camden fx-1-1-1- 3, Justin Elkins F-3-1- 4)

Wolverhampton win 47-24 on aggregate

Monday, July 6, First leg
Reading 19 (Phillip Morris 3-3-2- 8, Mick Tomlin 1-1-**2**- 4:1, Lance Sealey 2-**2**-0- 4:1, Gary Sweet 0-0-3- 3) **Oxford 17** (Glenn Cunningham 2-3-3- 8, Wayne Parker 0-fx-1- 1, Spencer Timmo 3-**2**-1- 6:1, Nick Upton 1-1-N- 2)

Friday, July 10, Second leg
Oxford 20 (Glenn Cunningham 2-3-3- 8, Wayne Parker 0-2-2- 4, **Spencer Timmo 3-2-2- 7:2**, John Clayton 1-0-0- 1) **Reading 16** (Phillip Morris 3-3-F- 6, Lance Sealey 1-0-1- 2, Mick Tomlin 0-1-3- 4, Gary Sweet 2-1-1- 4)

Oxford win 37-35 on aggregate

Friday, July 10, 1st leg
Belle Vue 21 (Steve Cope fx-1-**1**- 2:1, Mike Hampson 1-3-3- 7, Peter Scully 0-3-2- 5, **Jon Armstrong 3-2-2- 7:2**) **Coventry 15** (Chris Clarence 3-0-1- 4, Paul Bromwich **2**-0-0- 2:1, Colin Thorp 2-1-3- 6, Scott Wormleighton **1**-2-0- 3:1)

Saturday, July 25, Second leg
Coventry 18 (Chris Clarence R-N- 0, **Jamie Habbin 3-3-3- 9**, Sean McCullagh 1-1-R- 2, Colin Thorpe 3-3-0-1-0- 7) **Belle Vue 18** (Steve Cope **1**-0-0-**2**- 3:2, Mike Hampson 2-N-3- 5, Peter Scully E-2-2- 4, Jon Armstrong 2-2-**1**-**1**- 6:2)

Belle Vue win 39-33 on aggregate

Thursday, June 4
Ipswich 28 (Lawrence Hare R-N- 0, **Savalas Clouting 3-2-2- 7:2**, **Ben Howe 2-2-3- 7:2**, **Shaun Tacey 3-3-3-2-3- 14:1**) **King's Lynn 8** (Tom Grinstead 2-0-1- 3, Emmerson Fairweather **1**-1-0- 2:1, Darren Spicer 0-1-1- 2, Andrew Mountain 1-0-0- 1)

Sunday, August 16, Second leg
King's Lynn 10 (Tom Grinstead 2-0-0- 2, Andrew Mountain 0-1-0- 1, Emmerson Fairweather 2-2-2- 6, Jason Gage 0-fx-1-1) **Ipswich 26** (Lawrence Hare 3-**2**-1- 6:1, Savalas Clouting 1-1-3- 5, **Ben Howe 3-3-3- 9**, Shaun Tacey 1-3-**2**- 6:1)

Ipswich win 54-18 on aggregate

Second Round

Saturday, July 11, First leg
Bradford 28 (Stuart Parnaby 3-3-1- 7, Peter Scully **2**-1-**2**- 5:2, **Richard Smith 2-2-3- 7:2**, **Dean Child 3-3-3- 9**) **Eastbourne 8** (Paul Mitchell fx-0-1- 1, Mike Randall 1-1-0- 2, Nathan Gaymer 1-2-2- 5, Mark Smith 0-fx-0- 0)

Friday, July 24, Second leg
Eastbourne 14 (Paul Mitchell **1**-**1**-1- 3:2, Scott Swain 2-1-2- 5, Mark Smith F-0-0- 0, Nathan Gaymer 3-2-**1**- 6:1) **Bradford 22** (Stuart Parnaby fx-3-3- 6, **Darren Pearson 3-3-3- 9**, Lance Sealey 2-**2**-0- 4:1, Richard Smith 1-0-**2**- 3:2)

Bradford win 50-22 on aggregate

Friday, July 24, First leg
Arena Essex 20 (Robert Ledwith 3-3-fx- 6, Terry Giles 0-F-0- 0, Roland Pollard 3-1-3-7, Ricky Sandford **2**-3-2- 7:1) **Cradley Heath 16** (Justin Walker 2-2-3- 7, Anthony Boyd **1**-2-1- 4:1, Mark Meredith 1-**1**-2- 4:1, Shaun Naylor fx-0-**1**- 1:1)

Wednesday, July 29, Second leg
Cradley Heath 17 (Justin Walker **1**-2-3-6:1, Anthony Boyd 2-**2**-2- 6:1, Mark Meredith E-fx-3- 3, Shaun Naylor 1-R-1- 2) **Arena Essex 19** (Robert Ledwith 3-3-1- 7, Terry Giles 0-1-fx- 1, Roland Pollard **2**-1-2-5:1, Ricky Sandford 3-3-0- 6)

Arena Essex win 39-33 on aggregate

Wednesday, September 2, First leg
Oxford 14 (Glenn Cunningham 2-3-3- 8, Danny O'Brien 0-0-1- 1, Wayne Parker 2-0-**2**- 4:1, Nick Upton 0-1-0- 1) **Wolverhampton 22** (Stephen Morris 3-3-F- 6, Shane Cooper 1-2-3- 6, Simon Wolstenholme 3-**2**-1- 6:1, Craig Taylor 1-**1**-**2**- 4:2)

Wednesday, September 9, Second leg
Wolverhampton 26 (**Stephen Morris 3-3-3- 9**, Shane Cooper 1-2-**2**- 5:1, **Simon Wolstenholme 3-2-2- 7:2**, Craig Taylor **2**-fx-3- 5:1) **Oxford 10** (Glenn Cunningham 2-3-1- 6, Danny O'Brien 0-0-1- 1, Wayne Parker 1-1-0- 2, Nick Upton 0-1-0- 1)

Wolverhampton win 48-24 on aggregate

Friday, September 4, First leg
Belle Vue 15 (Stuart Parnaby F-0-1- 1, Mike Hampson 2-2-3- 7, Jon Armstrong 1-3- 4, Peter Scully 0-2-F-1- 3) **Ipswich 20** (Lawrence Hare fx-1-R- 1, Savalas Clouting 3-3-X- 6, Ben Howe 2-3-2- 7, Shaun Tacey 3-1-2- 6)

Thursday, September 10, Second leg
Ipswich 24 (Lawrence Hare 1-1-1- 3, Savalas Clouting 3-2-1- 6, **Ben Howe 2-3-3- 8:1**, Shaun Tacey 3-**1**-3- 7:1) **Belle Vue 12** (Stuart Parnaby 0-0-0- 0, Anthony Boyd 2-2-0- 4, Mike Hampson 1-3-2- 6, Peter Scully 0-0-2- 2)

Ipswich win 44-27 on aggregate

Semi Final

Friday, September 18, First leg
Arena Essex 10 (Colin White 1-3-3- 7, Ricky Sandford 0-1-0- 1, Roland Pollard 1-0-1- 2, Terry Giles 0-0-0- 0) **Ipswich 26** (Lawrence Hare **2**-**2**-**1**- 5:3, Savalas Clouting 3-2-**2**- 7:1, Ben Howe **2**-3-2- 7:1, Shaun Tacey 3-**1**-3- 7:1)

Thursday, October 1, Second leg
Ipswich 24 (Shaun Tacey **2**-**2**-1- 5:3, Ben Howe 3-2-3- 8, **Savalas Clouting 3-3-2-8:1**, Lawrence Hare X-1-**2**- 3:1) **Arena Essex 11** (Colin White 1-3-fx- 4, Ricky Sandford 0-1-3-1- 5, Roland Pollard fx-N-N- 0, Terry Giles 2-0-0-0- 2)

Ipswich win 50-21 on aggregate

Tuesday, September 29, First leg
Bradford 20 (Darren Pearson 3-3-2-8, Michael Graves 1-N- 1, Simon Bean 0- 0, Stuart Swales 3-**2**-2-3-1-11:1) **Wolverhampton 16** (Stephen Morris 2-3-3- 8, Craig Taylor 0-1-**1**-2:1, Simon Wolstenholme 2-1-0- 3, Phil Ashcroft 1-0-2- 3)

Wednesday, September 30, Second leg
Wolverhampton 19 (Stephen Morris fx-**1**-**2**- 3:2, Craig Taylor 2-0-3- 5, Simon Wolstenholme 3-2-1- 6:1, Phil Ashcroft **2**-1-2- 5:1) **Bradford 17** (**Darren Pearson 3-3-3- 9**, Jonathan Swales 1-0-0- 1, Simon Bean 0-N-1- 1, Stuart Swales 1-3-**2**-0- 6:1)

Bradford win 37-35 on aggregate

SHAUN Tacey created a Cup record when he completed a paid 15 point maximum against King's Lynn...riding in each of the last five races. The only heat he missed was the first as he replaced the unavailable Lawrence Hare in heat three and then rode in both the nominated riders' races!

Roll of Honour

1987 BRADFORD 91 Sheffield 87
1988 CRADLEY HEATH 102 Reading 77
1989 BELLE VUE 99 Swindon 78
1990 WOLVERHAMPTON 46 Bradford 25
1991 KING'S LYNN 41 Bradford 30
1992 IPSWICH 47 Bradford 25

FINAL

Tuesday, October 6, First leg
Bradford 15 (Darren Pearson 3-**2**-**1**- 6:2, Simon Bean 0-0-1- 1, Stuart Parnaby 2-3-2- 7, Stuart Swales 0-1-0- 1) **Ipswich 21** (Shaun Tacey **1**-**2**-0- 3:2, Ben Howe 2-0-3-5, **Savalas Clouting 3-3-3- 9**, Lawrence Hare 1-1-**2**- 4:1)

Thursday, October 15, Second leg
Ipswich 26 (Shaun Tacey 3-0-3- 6, **Ben Howe 2-3-3- 8:1**, **Savalas Clouting 3-3-2-8:1**, Lawrence Hare 1-1-**2**- 4:1) **Bradford 10** (Jonathan Swales 0-N-0- 0, Stuart Parnaby 1-2-1- 4, Simon Bean 0-0-1- 1, Stuart Swales 2-**1**-2-0- 5:1)

Ipswich win 47-25 on aggregate

Division Two Northern Section

Friday, April 3
Edinburgh 22 (Mike McLuskey 2-3-3- 8, Grant Blackie **1**-**1**-**1**- 3:3, **Stewart McDonald 3-2-2- 7:2**, Paul Taylor 0-2-2- 4) **Middlesbrough 14** (Paul Pickering 3-fx-F-3, Martin Jones 0-2-0-3- 5, Stuart Swales **1**-1-3-1- 6:1)

Saturday, April 4
Berwick 21 (Michael Lowrie 3-**2**-1- 6:1, Jonathan Swales 1-0-0- 1, Chris Readshaw **1**-3-3- 7:1, Stuart Swales 2-2-3- 7) **Newcastle 15** (Paul Gould fx-1-2- 3, Andrew Howe 2-1-0- 3, David Nagel 3-3-2-8, Neil Taylor 0-0-**1**- 1:1)

Sunday, April 5
Glasgow 16 (Jason Straughan 0-3-**2**- 5:1, James Grieves 1-3-3- 7, Stuart Coleman 1-fx-2- 3, Raymond Fosbury 0-1-0- 1) **Berwick 20** (Chris Readshaw 3-N-3- 6, Michael Lowrie **2**-2-1- 5:1, Paul Pickering 3-X-1- 4, Craig Rathbone **2**-1-**2**-fx- 5:2)

Thursday, April 9
Middlesbrough 15 (Paul Pickering 2-3-2-7, Stuart Swales **1**-2-0- 3:1, Martin Jones 2-0-2- 4, Jason Handley 0-F-**1**- 1:1) **Berwick 21** (**Chris Readshaw 3-3-3- 9**, Michael Lowrie 0-2-3- 5, Troy Scott 1-1-R-2, David Nagel 3-**1**-1- 5:1)

Friday, April 10
Edinburgh 17 (Mike McLuskey 3-0-3-fx- 6, Grant Blackie fx-1-2- 3, Stewart McDonald 2-**2**-2- 6:1, Paul Taylor 1-0-**1**- 2:2) **Newcastle 19** (Paul Gould 1-**1**-**2**-1- 5:2, Andrew Howe 2-0-3- 5, **Max Schofield 3-3-3- 9**, Chris Simpson fx- 0)

Saturday, April 11
Berwick 24 (**Michael Lowrie 3-2-2- 7:2**, Troy Scott 0-3-3- 6, **Chris Readshaw 3-3-3- 9**, William Beveridge 1-0-1- 2) **Sheffield 12** (Steve Knott **1**-**1**-2- 4:2, Rob Homer 2-R-1-1- 4, David Wolstenholme 2-2-0- 4, Steve Battle N-R-0- 0)

Sunday, April 12
Glasgow 19 (Jason Straughan 3-3-0- 6, James Grieves 1-1- 2, Stuart Coleman 3-**2**-3-2- 10:1, Raymond Fosbury F-0-1- 1) **Middlesbrough 17** (Paul Pickering 2-3-3-8, Jonathan Swales 0-0-2- 2, Martin Jones 2-**2**-1- 5:1, Stuart Swales **1**-1-0- 2:1) **Newcastle 21** (Andrew Howe 2-1-3- 6, Paul Gould 1-2-1- 4:1, **David Nagel 3-3-3- 9**, Chris Simpson 1-0-1- 2) **Sheffield 15** (Steve Knott 3-2-2- 7, Rob Homer R-3-R-3, Steve Battle 0-2-F-1-2- 5)

Friday, April 17
Edinburgh 17 (Mike McLuskey 2-3-3- 8, Grant Blackie 0-0-fx- 0, Stewart McDonald 2-**2**-1- 5:1, Paul Taylor **1**-1-2- 4:1) **Berwick 17** (Michael Lowrie 3-**2**-2- 7:1, Jason Handley 0-1-3- 4, Chris Readshaw 3-3-0-6, Craig Rathbone 0-0-fx- 0) **Sheffield 22** (**Steve Knott 2-3-3- 8:1**, David Wolstenholme 3-2-R- 5, Rob Homer R-1-3- 4, Steve Battle 2-1-**2**- 5:2) **Middlesbrough 14** (Jonathan Swales 0-fx-1- 1, Stuart Swales 1-2-1- 4:1, Martin Jones 3-3-2- 8, William Beveridge 1-0-0- 1)

Saturday, April 18
Berwick 22 (**Chris Readshaw 3-3-3- 9**, Michael Lowrie **2**-2-3- 7:1, Jason Handley 2-**2**-1- 5:1, Craig Rathbone **1**-0-fx- 1:1) **Glasgow 14** (Jason Straughan X-1-2- 3, Stuart Coleman 1-1-2- 4, James Grieves 3-3-0- 6, Raymond Fosbury fx-F-**1**- 1:1)

Sunday, April 19
Glasgow 18 (Jason Straughan 3-**2**-**1**- 6:2, Stuart Coleman F-1-2- 3, James Grieves 3-3-2- 8, Raymond Fosbury 1-F-fx- 1)

DIVISION TWO NORTHERN SECTION LEAGUE TABLE

	M	W	D	L	PtsF	PtsA	BP	TPts
MIDDLESBROUGH	20	12	0	8	390	322	7	31
Berwick	20	10	2	8	373	337	7	29
Sheffield	20	10	1	9	369	345	6	27
Newcastle	20	10	2	8	346	370	4	26
Edinburgh	20	8	3	9	340	368	3	22
Glasgow	20	5	2	13	315	391	3	15

Newcastle 18 (Paul Gould 2-**2**-0- 4:1, Andrew Howe **1**-1-3- 5:1, David Nagel 2-3-3- 8, Chris Simpson fx-0-1- 1) **Middlesbrough 23** (**Paul Pickering 3-3-3- 9**, Stuart Swales 1-3-F- 4, Martin Jones 3-1-2- 6, Jason Handley **2**-1-1- 4:2) **Edinburgh 13** (Mike McLuskey 2-2-2- 6, Paul Taylor 0-0-0- 0, Stewart McDonald 0-0-3- 3, Grant Blackie 1-2-**1**- 4:1)

Monday, April 20
Newcastle 21 (Paul Gould 0-1-**2**- 3:1, Andrew Howe 1-2-3- 6, **David Nagel 3-3-3- 9**, Neil Taylor **2**-**1**-0- 3:2) **Glasgow 14** (Jason Straughan 3-3-2- 8, James Grieves **2**-2-**1**- 5:2, Chris Simpson R-0-0- 0, Raymond Fosbury R-0-1- 1)

Thursday, April 23
Middlesbrough 20 (**Martin Jones 3-3-3- 9**, William Beveridge 0-1-**2**- 3:1, Stuart Swales 3-X-1- 4, Jason Handley 1-F-3- 4) **Glasgow 12** (Jason Straughan 2-3-2- 7, Stuart Coleman **1**-0-0- 1:1, James Grieves 2-**2**-0- 4:1, Raymond Fosbury N-N-E- 0) **Sheffield 25** (**Rob Homer 2-3-3- 8:1**, **Steve Knott 3-3-3- 9**, David Wolstenholme 3-**2**-E- 5:1, Steve Battle 1-0-**2**-0- 3:1) **Newcastle 11** (Andrew Howe 1-**1**-**1**- 3:2, Paul Gould 0-1-1- 2, David Nagel 2-2-2- 6, Chris Simpson 0-0-0- 0)

Friday, April 24
Edinburgh 17 (Mike McLuskey fx-3-3- 6, Grant Blackie 2-2-1-1- 6, Stewart McDonald N-1-0- 1, Paul Taylor **1**-0-3- 4:1) **Glasgow 16** (Jason Straughan 3-3-2- 8, Wayne Park 1-2-0- 3, James Grieves 3-**2**-0- 5:1, Raymond Fosbury 0-0-0- 0)

Saturday, April 25
Berwick 19 (Michael Lowrie 2-**2**-1- 5:1, Craig Rathbone **1**-**1**-0- 2:2, **Chris Readshaw 3-3-3- 9**, William Beveridge 0-2-1- 3) **Middlesbrough 17** (Martin Jones 0-fx-3- 3, Paul Pickering 3-fx-2- 5, Stuart Swales 2-3-0- 5, Jason Handley **1**-1-**2**- 4:2)

Sunday, April 26
Newcastle 19 (Paul Gould 0-F-1-2- 3, Andrew Howe 3-3-1- 7, **David Nagel 3-3-3- 9**, Chris Simpson R-N-N- 0) **Middlesbrough 17** (Stuart Swales **1**-3-R- 4:1, Martin Jones 2-2-2- 6, Jason Handley 2-2-0- 4, William Beveridge **1**-**1**-1- 3:2)

Friday, May 1
Edinburgh 22 (**Mike McLuskey 3-3-3- 9**, Grant Blackie 0-2-**2**- 4:1, Stewart McDonald 2-1-1- 4, Paul Taylor **1**-**1**-3- 5:2) **Sheffield 14** (Rob Homer **1**-F-fx- 1:1, Steve Knott 2-2-0- 4, David Wolstenholme 3-3-2- 8, Steve Battle F-0-1- 1)

Saturday, May 2
Berwick 11 (Michael Lowrie 0-3-2- 5, Craig Rathbone 1-2-N- 3, Chris Readshaw N-N-N- 0, William Beveridge 0-1-1-1- 3) **Edinburgh 25** (**Mike McLuskey 3-3-3- 9**, Grant Blackie 1-F-**2**- 3:1, Stewart McDonald 3-**2**-1- 6:1, Paul Taylor **2**-2-3- 7:1)

Sunday, May 3
Glasgow 14 (Jason Straughan 3-N-2- 5, Stuart Coleman 0-2-1-1- 4, James Grieves 3-**1**-0- 4:1, Stuart Crome F-0-**1**- 1:1) **Sheffield 22** (Rob Homer **1**-**2**-3- 6:2, Steve Knott 2-3-3- 8, David Wolstenholme 2-3-**2**- 7:1, Steve Battle **1**-0-0- 1:1) **Newcastle 24** (Andrew Howe 3-**2**-1-1- 7:2, Dean Child **2**-2-3- 7:1, **David Nagel 3-3-3- 9**, Paul Gould 1- 1) **Edinburgh 12** (Mike McLuskey 1-3-2- 6, Paul Taylor fx-**1**-**1**- 2:1, Stewart McDonald 2-0-0- 2, Grant Blackie fx-R-2- 2)

Thursday, May 7
Sheffield 19 (Rob Homer 1-3-3- 7, Steve Knott 3-1-3- 7, David Wolstenholme 3-**2**-0- 5:1, Steve Battle R-0-F- 0) **Berwick 17** (Michael Lowrie 2-**2**-**1**- 5:2, Craig Rathbone 0-1-2- 3, Chris Readshaw 2-3-2- 7, William Beveridge **1**-0-**1**- 2:2)

Saturday, May 9
Berwick 24 (**Michael Lowrie 3-2-3- 8:1**, Craig Rathbone 1-**1**-3- 5:1, **Chris Readshaw 3-3-2- 8:1**, William Beveridge 1-2-fx- 3) **Sheffield 11** (Steve Knott 2-1-0- 3, Mark Hepworth 2-3-1- 6, Steve Battle 0-fx-0-F-2- 2. *David Wolstenholme and Rob Homer did not arrive after being involved in a road accident en route*)

Sunday, May 17
Glasgow 17 (Stuart McDonald 1-3-3-1- 8, **James Grieves 3-2-3- 8:1**, Raymond Fosbury 0-0-1-F- 1) **Middlesbrough 19** (Paul Pickering 3-R-3- 6, Stuart Swales **2**-R-2- 4:1, Jason Handley 2-2-**2**- 6:1, Jonathan Swales **1**-1-**1**- 3:2)

Thursday, May 21
Middlesbrough 26 (Paul Pickering 3-fx-3- 6, **Martin Jones 2-3-3- 8:1**, Stuart Swales 3-E-**2**- 5:1, Jason Handley 2-1-**2**-**2**- 7:3) **Sheffield 9** (Rob Homer N-N- 0, Steve Knott 1-3-1- 5, Dean Child 1-**2**-fx-0- 3:1, Steve Battle 0-F-N-F-1- 1)

Saturday, May 23
Berwick 17 (**Michael Lowrie 3-3-2- 8:1**, Craig Rathbone 1-fx-F- 1, Chris Readshaw 3-fx-3- 6, William Beveridge 0-1-1- 2) **Newcastle 18** (Andrew Howe 2-**2**-0- 4:1, Neil Taylor 0-E-**2**- 2:1, David Nagel 2-3-1- 6, Paul Gould **1**-2-3- 6:1)

Thursday, May 28
Sheffield 23 (Rob Homer 3-3-1- 7, Dean Child 0-1-3- 4, **Steve Knott 3-2-3- 8:1**, Steve Battle **2**-0-**2**- 4:2) **Edinburgh 13** (Mike McLuskey 2-3-2- 7, Paul Taylor 1-1-0- 2:1, Stewart McDonald 1-**2**-0- 3:1, Grant Blackie 0-0-1- 1)

Friday, May 29
Edinburgh 20 (Wayne Park 1-1-0- 2, Grant Blackie 0-1-3- 4, **Stewart McDonald 3-3-3- 9**, Paul Taylor 2-3-0- 5) **Sheffield 16** (Rob Homer 3-2-2- 7, Steve Knott 2-2-**1**- 5:1, Dean Child 0-0-2- 2, Steve Battle 1-F-**1**- 2:1)

Thursday, June 4
Sheffield 27 (**Dean Child 2-2-3- 7:2**, **Rob Homer 3-3-2- 8:1**, **Steve Knott 3-3-3- 9**, Steve Battle F-1-**2**- 3:1) **Glasgow 8** (Damon Cowell R-R-N-R- 0, Stuart Coleman 1-N-fx- 1, James Grieves 2-2-N- 4, Wayne Park **1**-1-0-1- 3:1)

Friday, June 12
Edinburgh 18 (Mike McLuskey 2-**2**-**1**- 5:2, Grant Blackie 2-1-3- 6, Stewart McDonald fx-3-2- 5, Paul Taylor R-R-**2**- 2:1) **Middlesbrough 17** (**Paul Pickering 3-3-3- 9**, Jonathan Swales 1-0-1- 2, Stuart Swales 3-**2**-F- 5:1, William Beveridge F-1-0- 1)

Sunday, June 14
Newcastle 14 (Andrew Howe 2-1-fx- 3, Paul Gould 0-2-F- 2, **David Nagel 3-3-3- 9**, Neil Taylor 0-fn- 0) **Edinburgh 20** (Mike McLuskey 3-3-2- 8, Paul Taylor 1-2-**1**- 4:1,

All The 1992 Results	BERWICK	EDINBURGH	GLASGOW	MIDDLESBRO'	NEWCASTLE	SHEFFIELD
BERWICK		11-25 †17-17	22-14 23-10	19-17 15-21	21-15 17-18	24-12 24-11
EDINBURGH	17-17 21-15		17-16 17-18	22-14 18-17	17-19 18-18	22-14 20-16
GLASGOW	16-20 14-22	21-15 23-13		19-17 17-19	18-18 20-16	14-22 15-20
MIDDLESBROUGH	15-21 13-23	23-13 22-13	20-12 25-11		19-17 23-13	26-9 23-12
NEWCASTLE	19-17 20-16	24-12 14-20	21-14 19-17	19-17 11-25		21-15 20-16
SHEFFIELD	19-17 23-12	23-13 26-10	27-8 18-18	22-14 16-20	25-11 23-13	

Stewart McDonald 2-fx-3- 5, Wayne Park **1**-0-**2**- 3:2)

Wednesday, June 17
Glasgow 14 (Jason Straughan 2-2-2- 6, Stuart Coleman **1**-fx-2- 3:1, James Grieves 2-R-**1**- 3:1, Wayne Park 0-1-**1**- 2:1) **Berwick 22** (Michael Lowrie 3-3-R- 6, Craig Rathbone 0-1-0- 1, **Chris Readshaw 3-2-3- 8:1**, David Nagel 1-3-3- 7)

Saturday, June 20
Berwick 23 (Michael Lowrie 3-1-3- 7, Craig Rathbone F-F-R- 0, **Chris Readshaw 2-3-3- 8:1**, **David Nagel 3-3-2- 8:1**) **Glasgow 10** (Paul Coward F-1-2- 3:1, James Grieves 2-2-1- 5, Stuart Coleman R-N-N- 0, Wayne Park fx-0-2-F-R- 2)

Sunday, June 24
Glasgow 15 (Stuart Coleman fx-1-3- 4, Wayne Park 2-2-1- 5, James Grieves 2-3-F- 5, Raymond Fosbury **1**-R-F- 1:1) **Sheffield 20** (Steve Battle R-1-**1**- 2:1, Dean Child 3-**2**-2- 7:1, **Steve Knott 3-3-3- 9**, Daimon Cowell 0-0-2- 2)

Thursday, July 2
Middlesbrough 19 (Jason Handley 2-**2**-0- 4:1, William Beveridge **1**-0-2- 3:1, **Stuart Swales 3-3-3- 9**, Jonathan Swales 1-1-**1**- 3:1) **Newcastle 17** (Paul Gould F-0-**2**-3- 5:1, Andrew Howe 3-1-**1**- 5:1, David Nagel 2-3-2- 7, Chris Simpson E-0-fx- 0)
Newcastle take bonus point. David Nagel defeated Stuart Swales (fell) in a run-off.

Sunday, July 5
Newcastle 20 (Paul Gould **1**-1-2- 4:1, Andrew Howe 2-2-1- 5, **David Nagel 3-3-3- 9**, Chris Simpson 1-**1**-0- 2:1) **Sheffield 16** (Dean Child 0-3-2- 5, Rob Homer 3-2-R- 5, Steve Knott 2-fx-0-3- 5, Steve Battle 0-0-1- 1)

Saturday, July 11
Berwick 17 (Michael Lowrie 2-F-3- 5, Craig Rathbone F-2-1- 3, **David Nagel 3-3-3- 9**, Paul Coward F-N-N- 0) **Edinburgh 17** (Mike McLuskey 3-3-0- 6, Stewart McDonald 2-2-fx-2- 6, Grant Blackie 1-**1**-**1**-2- 5:2)

†Result as amended by the Speedway Control Board following the illegal use of Craig Rathbone in heat five when he was used as a supplementary reserve to replace the injured Paul Coward. His third place finish was deducted from the final result. The decision did not affect the placings of any Edinburgh rider.

Friday, July 17
Edinburgh 21 (Grant Blackie **1**-0-1-R- 2:1, Mike McLuskey 2-3-3- 8, Stewart McDonald 3-3-fx- 6, Mike Lewthwaite **2**-3- 5:1) **Berwick 15** (Michael Lowrie 3-2-2- 7, Paul Coward 0-2-1- 3:1, Paul Taylor 1-0-2- 3, Craig Rathbone 0-**1**-**1**- 2:2)

Sunday, July 19
Newcastle 19 (Paul Gould R-1-2- 3, Andrew Howe 2-2-1- 5, **David Nagel 3-3-3- 9**, Chris Simpson 1-0-**1**- 2:1) **Berwick 17** (Michael Lowrie 3-3-2- 8, Craig Rathbone 1-2-3- 6, Paul Coward 2-1-fx- 3, John Routledge 0-0-0- 0)

Thursday, July 23
Middlesbrough 13 (Jason Handley 2-1-0- 3, William Beveridge 0-2-2- 4, Stuart Swales 2-3-1- 6, Jonathan Swales 0-0-0- 0) **Berwick 23** (**Michael Lowrie 3-3-3- 9**, Craig Rathbone 1-fx-3- 4, Paul Coward 1-1-1- 3, Mike Smith 3-2-**2**- 7:1)

Thursday, August 6
Sheffield 18 (Steve Battle 0-2-1-2- 5, Dean Child 2-2-1- 5, Rob Homer E-3-3- 6, Richard Moss **1**-F-**1**- 2:2) **Glasgow 18** (Jason Straughan 3-1-0- 4, Stuart Coleman 1-2-3- 6, James Grieves 3-3-2- 8, Raymond Fosbury 0-0-F- 0)

Thursday, August 13
Middlesbrough 23 (Paul Pickering 2-1-3- 6, Jason Handley **1**-fx-**2**- 3:2, **Stuart Swales 3-3-3- 9**, William Beveridge 1-3-1- 5) **Sheffield 12** (Steve Battle 0-2-fx- 0- 2, Dean Child 3-2-2- 7, Rob Homer E-N- 0, Richard Moss fx-0-2-1- 3)

Saturday, August 15
Berwick 15 (**Michael Lowrie 3-3-3- 9**, Craig Rathbone 0-1-2- 3, Paul Coward 0-fx-0-0- 0, Mike Smith 3-R-N- 3) **Middlesbrough 21** (Paul Pickering **1**-3-**1**- 5:2, Stuart Swales 2-**1**-3- 6:1, Jason Handley 2-**2**-2- 6:1, William Beveridge **1**-2-1- 4:1)

Sunday, August 16
Sheffield 16 (Steve Battle 2-1-F- 3, Dean Child 1-1-R- 2:1, **Rob Homer 3-3-3- 9**, Richard Moss 1-F-1- 2) **Middlesbrough 20** (Paul Pickering 3-3-**1**- 7:1, Jason Handley 0-2-3- 5, Stuart Swales 2-**2**-2- 6:1, Jonathan Swales R-X-**2**- 2:1)

Roll of Honour

1988	1 POOLE	2 Stoke	3 Milton Keynes
1989	1 HACKNEY	2 Middlesbrough	3 Eastbourne
		Central League	
1990	1 STOKE	2 Rye House	3 Milton Keynes
1991	1 SHEFFIELD	2 Milton Keynes	3 Peterborough
		Northern League	
1990	1 MIDDLESBROUGH	2 Edinburgh	3 Newcastle
1991	1 MIDDLESBROUGH	2 Glasgow	3 Edinburgh
1992	1 MIDDLESBROUGH	2 Berwick	3 Sheffield
		Southern League	
1990	1 POOLE	2 Arena Essex	3 Hackney
1991	1 ARENA ESSEX	2 Exeter	3 Rye House
1992	1 EXETER	2 Rye House	3 Stoke

Thursday, August 20
Middlesbrough 25 (**Paul Pickering 3-3-3-9**, Jason Handley **2**-2-3- 7:1, **Stuart Swales 3-2-2- 7:2**, William Beveridge 1-**1**-F- 2:1) **Glasgow 11** (Jonathan Swales 1-0-0- 1, Stuart Coleman fx-1-2- 3, James Grieves 2-3-1- 6, Raymond Fosbury F-0-**1**- 1:1)

Friday, August 21
Edinburgh 18 (Stewart McDonald 3-3-0- 6, Paul Taylor 0-1-2- 3, Grant Blackie 3-1-3- 7, Wayne Park 1-0-**1**- 2:1) **Newcastle 18** (Paul Gould 2-**2**-**1**- 5:2, Andrew Howe **1**-2-3- 6:1, David Nagel 0-3-2- 5, Chris Simpson 2-0-0- 2)

Sunday, August 23
Newcastle 11 (David Nagel 2-2-2- 6, Andrew Howe 0-1-2- 3, Paul Gould fx-**1**-0- 1:1, Chris Simpson 1-0-0- 1) **Middlesbrough 25** (**Paul Pickering 3-3-3- 9**, Jason Handley 1-3-3-1- 8, Stuart Swales E-**2**-3- 5:1, William Beveridge **2**-0-1- 3:1)

Thursday, August 27
Middlesbrough 23 (**Paul Pickering 3-3-3-9**, Jason Handley **2**-2-**2**- 6:2, Stuart Swales 2-2-3- 7:1, William Beveridge F-F-1- 1) **Newcastle 13** (Paul Gould 1-1-1- 3, Andrew Howe F-1-2- 3, David Nagel 3-3- 6, Chris Simpson 1-0-0-0- 1)

Sunday, August 30
Newcastle 19 (Paul Gould 0-1-3- 4, Andrew Howe 2-2-1- 5, **David Nagel 3-3-3-9**, Chris Simpson 1-0-0- 1) **Glasgow 17** (Stuart Coleman 1-1-**1**- 3:1, James Grieves 3-2-2- 7, Jason Straughan 2-3-0- 5, Raymond Fosbury X-0-2- 2)

Thursday, September 10
Sheffield 23 (Steve Battle 1-2-**2**- 5:1, **Dean Child 3-3-3- 9**, Rob Homer 3-R-3- 6, Richard Moss 1-**2**-0- 3:1) **Berwick 12** (Michael Lowrie 2-F-**1**- 3:1, Craig Rathbone 0-R-N- 0, Paul Coward R-1-1- 2, Mike Smith 2-3-2- 7)

Sunday, September 13
Glasgow 21 (Geoff Powell 3-3-2- 8, James Grieves **2**-2-3- 7:1, Stuart Coleman 3-**2**-1-6:2, Raymond Fosbury 0-0-0- 0) **Edinburgh 15** (Stewart McDonald 1-3-3- 7, Paul Taylor R-fx-2- 2, Grant Blackie **1**-1-**1**-3:2, Wayne Park 2-1-0- 3)

Newcastle 20 (Paul Gould 1-1-3- 5, Andrew Howe 3-2-**1**- 6:1, David Nagel 3-3-2- 8, Chris Simpson 0-0-1- 1) **Berwick 16** (Michael Lowrie 0-3-3- 6, Paul Coward 2-0-2- 4, Craig Rathbone **1**-2-1-R- 4:1, Mike Smith 2-N-N- 2)

Thursday, September 17
Middlesbrough 22 (Jonathan Swales **1**-0-R- 1:1, Jason Handley 2-3-**2**- 7:1, **Stuart Swales 3-3-3- 9**, William Beveridge **2**-0-3-5:1) **Edinburgh 13** (Stewart McDonald 3-2-1- 6, Paul Taylor 0-**1**-**1**- 2:2, Wayne Park F-2-**1**-2-fx- 5:1)

Sunday, September 20
Glasgow 20 (**Jason Straughan 2-3-3- 8:1**, James Grieves 3-R-1- 4, Stuart Coleman fx-F-3- 3, Geoff Powell 2-2-1- 5) **Newcastle 16** (Paul Gould 1-1-F-0- 2, Andrew Howe 0-2-2- 4, David Nagel 3-3-2- 8, Chris Simpson 1-**1**-N- 2:1)

Thursday, September 24
Sheffield 23 (**Steve Battle 2-2-3- 7:2**, Dean Child 3-3-F- 6, **Rob Homer 3-3-3- 9**, Richard Moss 0-0-1- 1) **Newcastle 13** (Paul Gould 0-**1**-2- 3:1, Andrew Howe 1-1-**1**- 3:1, David Nagel 2-2-2- 6, Chris Simpson **1**-0-0- 1:1)

Friday, September 25
Edinburgh 17 (Stewart McDonald 3-3-2- 8, Paul Taylor 0-fx-3- 3, Grant Blackie **1**- 1:1, Wayne Park 2-**2**-1-fx- 5:1) **Glasgow 18** (Jason Straughan 2-**2**-1- 5:1, Stuart Coleman **1**-0-2- 3:1, **James Grieves 3-3-3-9**, Raymond Fosbury fx-0-**1**- 1:1)

Thursday, October 1
Sheffield 26 (**Steve Cope 2-2-2- 6:3**, Dean Child 3-2-3- 8, **Rob Homer 3-3-3- 9**, Steve Battle **2**-**1**-fx- 3:2) **Edinburgh 10** (Stewart McDonald 1-3-1- 5, Paul Taylor 0-0-1- 1, Grant Blackie 0-0-2- 2, Wayne Park 1-1-0- 2)

Sunday, October 18
Glasgow 23 (Geoff Powell **2**-**2**-1- 5:2, Stuart Coleman 3-2-3- 8, **James Grieves 3-3-3- 9**, Raymond Fosbury 0-**1**-fx- 1:1) **Edinburgh 13** (Stewart McDonald 1-3-2- 6, Paul Taylor 0-1-**1**- 2:1, Grant Blackie **1**-R-2- 3:1, Wayne Park 2-0-fx- 2)

Division Two Southern Section

Saturday, March 28
Stoke 22 (**Ade Hoole 3-3-3- 9**, Mark Walsh F-0-fn- 0, **Matthew Powell 3-2-2-7:2**, Anthony Barlow 1-2-3- 6) **Nottingham 13** (Jason Reed 2-3-fn- 5, Richard Webb **1**-R- 1:1, Shaun Naylor 2-1-fx-fx- 3, Mark Geary 0-1-2-1- 4)

Friday, April 3
Peterborough 20 (**Michael Howe 3-2-2-7:2**, Lee Coleman 2-3-3- 8, Jason Wilby 0-0-0- 0, Dean Garrod 0-2-3- 5) **Stoke 16** (Mark Walsh 1-0-2-0- 3:1, Matthew Powell 3-1-1- 5, Anthony Barlow 2-1-1-3-**1**- 8:1)

Saturday, April 4
Stoke 12 (Drew Wheeldon 0-0-0- 0, Matthew Walsh 1-0-2- 3, Matthew Powell 0-2-2- 4, Anthony Barlow 3-1-**1**- 5:1)
Exeter 24 (**Tommy Palmer 3-3-3- 9**, Richard Knight **2**-3-0- 5:1, Scott Pegler **1**-**2**-3- 6:2, Dean Garton 2-1-1- 4)

Sunday, April 5
Rye House 13 (Chris Young 3-3-F- 6, Steve Reynolds 0-0-F- 0, Martin Cobbin 2-**2**-2- 6:1, Graham Barker 0-1-fx- 1) **Exeter 22** (Richard Knight 2-3-3- 8, Dean Garton **1**-0-2- 3:1, Scott Pegler 1-**2**-3- 6:1, Sean McCullagh 3-1-1- 5)

Monday, April 6
Exeter 21 (Darren Matthews 2-**2**-**2**- 6:2, Scott Pegler 3-3-fx-3- 9, Dean Garton **1**-1-1-3- 6:1) **Rye House 14** (Chris Young 3-3-2- 8, Steve Reynolds R-1-R- 1, Martin Cobbin 2-**2**-**1**- 5:2, Graham Barker F-F-fx-0)

Wednesday, April 8
Nottingham 19 (Jason Reed 2-3-2- 7, Shaun Naylor **1**-2-**1**- 4:2, Richard Webb 1-**2**-2- 5:1, Daz Santos 3-0-R- 3) **Stoke 17** (**Andy Meredith 3-3-3- 9**, Mark Walsh 0-1-1- 2, Matthew Powell F-1-3- 4, Anthony Barlow 2-0-0- 2)

Sunday, April 12
Rye House 16 (**Chris Young 3-3-3- 9**, Steve Reynolds 0-E-1- 1, Martin Cobbin 3-**2**-1- 6:1, Graham Barker 0-fx-E- 0)
Peterborough 19 (Michael Howe 1-**2**-N-3:2, Jason Wilby 2-0-3- 5, Lee Coleman 2-3-2- 7, Dean Garrod **1**-1-**2**- 4:2)

Friday, April 17
Peterborough 16 (Michael Howe 2-3-2- 7, Jason Wilby 0-0-fx- 0, Dean Garrod **1**-**2**-0-3:2, Lee Coleman 2-1-3- 6) **Rye House 19** (Chris Young 3-**2**-1- 6:1, Martin Cobbin 1-1-2- 4, **Wayne Baxter 3-3-3- 9**, Graham Barker R-N-N- 0)

Monday, April 20
Peterborough 20 (Michael Howe 0-3-3- 6, Jason Wilby 1-0-**1**- 2:1, Dean Garrod 1-1-2- 4, **Lee Coleman 3-3-2- 8:1**) **Long Eaton 16** (Jason Reed **2**-2-1- 5:1, Shaun Naylor 3-0-3- 6, Richard Webb 2-**1**-0- 3:1, Daz Santos R-2-F- 2)

Friday, April 24
Peterborough 24 (**Michael Howe 3-3-3- 9**, Jason Wilby 0-0-1- 1, **Dean Garrod 2-2-3-7:2**, Lee Coleman 3-3-1- 7) **Exeter 12** (Rob Price **1**-**1**-0- 2:2, Gavin Pell 0-0-2- 2, Scott Pegler 1-2-2- 5, Chris Storey 2-1-0- 3)

Wednesday, April 29
Nottingham 9 (Jason Reed N-**1**-F- 1:1, Mark Geary 1-0-2- 3, Richard Webb 2-2-1-E- 5, Daz Santos R-F- 0) **Rye House 22** (Chris Young **2**-3-3-fx- 8:1, **Wayne Baxter 3-2-3- 8:1**, Martin Cobbin 3-R-0-3- 6)

Saturday, May 2
Stoke 12 (Andy Meredith 3-N- 3, Mark Walsh 1-0-3- 4, Matthew Powell fx-N- 0, Anthony Barlow 1-2-1-1- 5) **Rye House 23** (Mark Jolly 0-1-**2**-2- 5:1, **Wayne Baxter 3-3-3- 9**, Martin Cobbin 2-**2**-3-**2**- 9:2)

Sunday, May 10
Rye House 27 (**Chris Young 3-3-3- 9**, Mark Jolly 1-**2**-**2**-3- 8:2, **Martin Cobbin 2-3-3-2- 10:2**) **Nottingham 7** (Jason Reed fx- 0, Daz Santos fx-N- 0, Richard Webb 2-1-1-1- 5, Mark Geary 0-0-2- 2)

Monday, May 18
Exeter 22 (Scott Pegler 3-3-3-**1**- 10:1, Tommy Palmer 3-**2**-2- 7:1, Dean Garton 1-1-0-3- 5) **Peterborough 14** (Michael Howe 2-**1**-3- 6:1, Gavin Pell R-0-**1**- 1:1, Lee Coleman 2-2-0- 4, Dean Garrod 0-1-2- 3)

Wednesday, May 20
Nottingham 15 (Jason Reed 3-3-1- 7, Daz Santos 1-1-3- 5, Richard Webb 2-R-R- 2, Mark Geary 0-0-1- 1) **Exeter 21** (Scott Pegler 2-3-3- 8, Tommy Palmer 3-2-**2**-**2**-9:2, Dean Garton 0-1-**1**-2- 4:1)

Monday, May 25
Exeter 20 (**Scott Pegler 3-3-3- 9**, Dean Garton 1-0-3- 4, Tommy Palmer 3-**2**- 5:1, Rob Price 1-1-0- 2) **Stoke 16** (Andy Meredith 2-3-2- 7, Mark Walsh 0-0-**1**- 1:1, Anthony Barlow 0-**2**-2- 4:1, Ade Hoole 2-1-**1**- 4:1)

Wednesday, May 27
Nottingham 22 (Jason Reed 3-2-3- 8, Daz Santos 1-3-**2**- 6:1, Richard Webb 2-**1**-2-5:1, Mark Geary **1**-**1**-**1**- 3:2) **Peterborough 14** (Michael Howe 2-F-3- 5, Gavin Pell 0-0-0- 0, Dean Garrod E-2-1- 3, Lee Coleman 3-3-N- 6)

Sunday, May 31
Rye House 20 (**Chris Young 3-2-3- 8:1**, Mark Jolly **2**-0-2- 4:1, Martin Cobbin 2-3-**2**-7:1, Carl Johnson 0-1-0- 1) **Stoke 16** (Mark Walsh fx-0-**2**-3- 5:1, Anthony Barlow 1-1-1-1-1- 5, Ade Hoole 3-3-fx- 6)

Saturday, June 6
Stoke 19 (Andy Meredith 3-3-**1**- 7:1, Mark Walsh F-0-3- 3, Anthony Barlow 2-0-0- 2:1, Ade Hoole 3-2-2- 7) **Peterborough 17** (Michael Howe 2-3-3- 8, Lee Coleman **1**-2-F- 3:1, Dean Garrod E-1-2- 3, Gavin Pell 1-**1**-**1**- 3:2)

Wednesday, June 10
Nottingham 17 (Jason Reed **1**-3-**1**- 5:2, Richard Webb 2-2-2- 6, Mark Geary 0-1-2-3, Daz Santos 2-**1**-N- 3:1) **Exeter 19** (Scott Pegler 3-0-fx- 3, Chris Storey 0-0-3- 3, **Tommy Palmer 3-3-3- 9**, Rob Price 1-2-1-4)

Friday, June 19
Peterborough 14 (Michael Howe 0-3-F- 3, Lee Coleman 2-2-2- 6, Dean Garrod 2-0-2-4, Nathan Wilson 0-0-**1**- 1:1) **Rye House 22** (**Chris Young 3-3-3- 9**, Mark Jolly 1-3-2-1- 7, Martin Cobbin 1-**1**-**1**-3- 6:1)
Rye House awarded bonus point after the failure to stage a run-off.

Wednesday, July 29
Nottingham 17 (Jason Reed 2-3-2- 7, Richard Webb **1**-2-3-**1**- 7:2, Mark Geary 0-fx-0- 0, Daz Santos 2-**1**-fn- 3:1) **Stoke 19** (**Ade Hoole 3-3-3- 9**, Mark Walsh 0-1-2-3:1, Matthew Powell 1-0-1- 2, Anthony Barlow 3-2-X- 5)

Friday, July 31
Peterborough 17 (Kieran McCullagh 3-3-1- 7, Scott Burland 0-0-3- 3, Dean Garrod 2-**2**-0- 4:1, Carl Johnson 0-1-**2**- 3:1) **Exeter 19** (Scott Pegler 2-**2**-**2**- 6:2, Rob Price **1**-0-0- 1:1, **Tommy Palmer 3-3-3- 9**, Chris Storey 1-1-1- 3)

Monday, August 3
Exeter 26 (**Scott Pegler 3-3-2- 8:1**, Rob Price **2**-**1**-1- 4:2, **Tommy Palmer 3-2-3-8:1**, Dean Garton 1-2-3- 6) **Peterborough 10** (Kieran McCullagh 2-3-1- 6, Dean Garrod 0-1-0- 1, Scott Burland 0-0-0- 0, Carl Johnson 1-0-2- 3)

Wednesday, August 5
Long Eaton 16 (Jason Reed 1-3-3- 7, Scott Wormleighton R-fx-2- 2, Richard Webb 3-**2**-1- 6:1, Mark Geary 0-1-0- 1) **Rye House 20** (Chris Young **2**-3-2- 7:1, Robert Ledwith 3-0-3- 6, Martin Cobbin 2-**2**-0- 4:1, Mark Jolly **1**-1-1- 3:1)

Sunday, August 9
Rye House 16 (Chris Young **2**-3-fx- 5:1, Robert Ledwith 3-0-**2**- 5:1, Martin Cobbin 1-**2**-fx- 3:1, Mark Jolly 0-1-2- 3) **Stoke 19** (Ade Hoole 1-3-3- 7, Mark Walsh 0-F-1- 1, Andy Meredith 3-**2**-1- 6:1, Anthony Barlow **2**-fx-3- 5:1)

Monday, August 10
Exeter 20 (**Scott Pegler 3-3-2- 8:1**, Rob Price 1-fx-2- 3, **Tommy Palmer 3-2-3- 8:1**, Graham Gordon fx-1- 1) **Nottingham 15** (Jason Reed 2-3-1- 6, Scott Wormleighton 0-1-**2**-3-fx- 6:1, Mark Geary 2-E-1- 3)

Wednesday, August 12
Nottingham 14 (Jason Reed fx- 0, Scott Wormleighton 2-2-2- 6, Richard Webb 2-3-1- 6:1, Mark Geary 0-0-0-2- 2) **Peterborough 21** (**Kieran McCullagh 3-3-3- 9**, Dean Garrod 1-2-3- 6, Scott Burland 1-1-F-2, Carl Johnson 3-**1**-R- 4:1)

DIVISION TWO SOUTHERN SECTION LEAGUE TABLE

	M	W	D	L	PtsF	PtsA	BP	TPts
EXETER	16	13	0	3	320.5	250.5	7	33
Rye House	15	10	0	5	293	229	4	24
Stoke	15	8	0	7	275.5	261.5	3	19
Peterborough	16	5	0	11	260	312	3	13
Nottingham	16	3	0	13	234	330	1	7

Monday, August 17
Exeter 23.5 (**Scott Pegler 3-2-3- 8:1** Dean Garton R-2-3- 5, Tommy Palmer 3-3-.5-6.5, Rob Price **2**-0-**2**- 4:2) **Stoke 12.5** (Andy Meredith 2-3-2- 7, Mark Walsh **1**-0-1- 2:1, Ade Hoole 1-1-.5- 2.5, Anthony Barlow 0-1-0- 1)

Friday, August 21
Peterborough 17 (Kieran McCullagh 2-3-R- 5, Scott Burland 0-0-0- 0, Dean Garrod 3-1-3- 7, Carl Johnson **2**-2-1- 5:1) **Nottingham 19** (**Jason Reed 3-3-3- 9**, Scott Wormleighton 1-2-**2**- 5:1, Gavin Pell fx-1-**1**- 2:1, Mark Geary 1-0-2- 3)

Saturday, September 5
Stoke 26 (Ade Hoole 2-**2**-**2**- 6:2, Mark Walsh **1**-2-3- 6:1, **Andy Meredith 3-3-3- 9**, Anthony Barlow **2**-1-**2**- 5:3) **Peterborough 10** (Kieran McCullagh 3-3-fx- 6, Dean Garrod 0-1-1- 2, Carl Johnson fx-0-0- 0, Scott Burland 1-0-1- 2)

Sunday, September 20
Rye House 25 (**Chris Young 3-2-2- 7:2**, Martin Cobbin 1-3-3- 7, **Robert Ledwith 3-3-3- 9**, Mark Jolly R-R-**2**- 2:1) **Nottingham 9** (Jason Reed 0-2-1- 3, Scott Wormleighton **1**-0-F- 1:1, Richard Webb 2-2-1-0- 5)

Saturday, September 26
Stoke 26 (**Ade Hoole 3-3-3- 9**, **Mark Walsh 2-3-2-3- 10:2**, Matthew Powell N-N-0, Anthony Barlow **2**-**2**-3-0- 7:2) **Nottingham 10** (Jason Reed R-0-**1**- 1:1, Richard Webb 1-0-2- 3, Scott Wormleighton 0-1-**1**- 2:1, Daz Santos 1-1-2- 4)

Saturday, October 3
Peterborough 14 (Kieran McCullagh 3-3-1- 7, Carl Johnson 1-1-R- 2, Dean Garrod 0-1-**1**- 2:1, Gavin Pell 1-0-2- 3) **Stoke 22** (Andy Meredith 2-**2**-3- 7:1, Mark Walsh 0-0-0- 0, **Ade Hoole 2-3-3- 8:1**, Anthony Barlow 3-2-**2**- 7:1)

Monday, October 5
Exeter 23 (**Scott Pegler 3-2-3- 8:1**, Rob Price **2**-fx-**2**- 4:2, Tommy Palmer 2-3-fx- 5, Graham Gordon E-3-3- 6) **Rye House 12** (Mark Geary 0-**1**-1- 2:1, Darren Matthews 1-1-N-2-**1**- 5:1, Mark Fry fn-N- 0, Robert Ledwith 3-fx-2- 5)
Exeter 20 (Scott Pegler 2-2-2- 6:1, Rob Price R-2-**1**- 3:1, Tommy Palmer 3-3-**1**-7:1, Graham Gordon **2**-R-2- 4:1) **Nottingham 16** (**Jason Reed 3-3-3- 9**, Scott Wormleighton 1-1-0- 2, Richard Webb 1-1-3- 5, Daz Santos F-0-R- 0)

Saturday, October 10
Stoke 21 (Ade Hoole 3-3-2- 8, Mark Walsh fx-E-**2**- 2:1, Andy Meredith 3-**2**-**1**- 6:2, Anthony Barlow 1-1-3- 5) **Exeter 15** (Scott Pegler 2-**2**-0- 4:1, Tommy Palmer 2-3-3- 8, Rob Price **1**-0-1-1- 3:1)

Sunday, October 11
Rye House 22 (Chris Young 3-3-**1**- 7:1, Martin Cobbin **2**-E-3- 5:1, Robert Ledwith 3-fx-2- 5, Mark Jolly 1-2-**2**- 5:1) **Peterborough 13** (Kieran McCullagh fx-3-3- 6, Carl Johnson 1-fx-1- 2, Dean Garrod 2-1-0- 3, Gavin Pell 0-2-0- 2)

Sunday, October 18
Rye House 22 (Chris Young 3-**2**-1- 6:1, Martin Cobbin **2**-2-fx- 4:1, **Robert Ledwith 3-3-3- 9**, Mark Jolly 0-0-3- 3) **Exeter 13** (Scott Pegler 0-1-2- 3, Rob Price 1-**1**-1-fx-3:1, Tommy Palmer 2-3-2- 7)

Saturday, October 31
Stoke 18 (Ade Hoole 3-3-2- 8, Mark Walsh **2**-2-0-0- 4:1, Andy Meredith N-N- 0, Anthony Barlow **1**-**1**-1-3- 6:1) **Rye House 17** (Martin Cobbin 1-2-**2**-1- 6:1, **Robert Ledwith 3-3-3- 9**, Mark Jolly F-0-0-2- 2)

PETERBOROUGH were the only club in the Division Two Reserve League who tracked their own four riders in each of their official matches. Everyone else either turned up short-handed or with guests. In Rye House's visit to Exeter on October 5, they had only one of their own riders in their squad.

All The 1992 Results

	EXETER	NOTTINGHAM (LONG EATON)	PETERBORO'	RYE HOUSE	STOKE	MILDENHALL	MILTON KEYNES
EXETER		20-15 20-16	22-14 26-10	21-14 23-12	20-16 23.5-12.5	*25-9*	*13-22*
NOTTINGHAM	15-21 17-19		22-14 14-21	9-22 16-20	19-17 17-19	*17-17*	*11-25*
PETERBOROUGH	24-12 17-19	20-16 17-19		16-19 14-22	20-16 14-22	*22-14*	*11-24*
RYE HOUSE	13-22 22-13	27-7 25-9	16-19 22-13		20-16 16-19	*25-9*	
STOKE	12-24 21-15	22-13 26-10	19-17 26-10	12-23 18-17			*24-12*
MILDENHALL	*26-10*	*19-17*	*15-21*	*10-25*	*21-14*		*13-22*
MILTON KEYNES	*27-7*				*22-14*		

IN THE results chart alongside we list those results involving both Mildenhall and Milton Keynes even though they were subsequently expunged from official records on the closure of the two tracks.
Below are the full details from those matches which are not included in the Reserve League averages.

Wednesday, April 1
Nottingham 11 (Daz Santos R-**1**-R- 1:1, Shaun Naylor 2-1-1- 4, Richard Webb 2-2-0- 4, Mark Geary 0-0-2- 2) **Milton Keynes 25** (**Kieran McCullagh 3-3-3- 9**, Tony Kingsbury 1-3-3- 7, **Sean McCullagh 3-2-2- 7:2**, Chris Strong 1-0-1- 2)

Sunday, April 5
Mildenhall 15 (Savalas Clouting 2-3-2- 7, Jason Nieberding fx-R-0- 0, Clive Clark 0-0-N- 0, Nathan Wilson 3-2-2-**1**- 8:1) **Peterborough 21** (Michael Howe 3-3-3- 9, Jason Wilby 1-2-0- 3, Lee Coleman 2-1-3- 6, Dean Garrod **1**-**1**-1- 3:2)

Friday, April 10
Peterborough 22 (**Michael Howe 3-3-3- 9**, Jason Wilby 1-2-1- 4, Dean Garrod **2**-1-0- 3:1, Lee Coleman 3-F-3- 6) **Mildenhall 14** (Adrian Mountain 2-1-2- 5, Clive Clark X-2-3-2- 7, Nathan Wilson 0-1-F-0-1- 2)

Sunday, April 12
Mildenhall 15 (Adrian Mountain 2-2-**1**- 5:1, Gavin Pell 0-0-**1**- 1:1, Clive Clark **1**-fx-2-3:1, Nathan Wilson 2-2-2- 6) **Nottingham 20** (**Jason Reed 3-3-3- 9**, Shaun Naylor 1-3-3- 7, Richard Webb 3-1-R- 4, Daz Santos F-fx-R- 0)

Sunday, April 19
Mildenhall 10 (Adrian Mountain 1-2-2- 5, Gavin Pell N-N- 0, Clive Clark 1-**1**-N-0-2-2:1, Nathan Wilson 0-F-1-2- 3) **Rye House 25** (**Chris Young 3-2-3- 8:1**, Martin Cobbin **2**-**2**-3-1- 8:2, **Wayne Baxter 3-3-3- 9**)

Monday, April 20
Exeter 13 (Darren Matthews 1-1-1-3-fx- 6, Scott Pegler N-0- 0, Dean Garton 0-3-**2**-2-7:1) **Milton Keynes 22** (Kieran McCullagh **2**-R-3- 5:1, **Tony Kingsbury 3-3-2- 8:1**, Sean McCullagh 2-**2**-3- 7:1, Chris Strong fx-N-1-1- 2)

Rye House 25 (Chris Young **2**-3-R- 5:1, **Wayne Baxter 3-3-3- 9**, Mark Jolly fx-1-**2**-3:1, **Martin Cobbin 3-2-3- 8:1**) **Mildenhall 9** (Adrian Mountain 1-1-1- 3, Clive Clark R-0-R-R- 0, Nathan Wilson 0-2-2-2- 6)

Tuesday, April 21
Milton Keynes 27 (**Kieran McCullagh 3-3-3- 9**, Tony Kingsbury 1-3-3-3- 10, **Sean McCullagh 2-2-2-2- 8:4**) **Exeter 7** (Scott Pegler 2-F-N- 2, Chris Storey 1-1-1- 3, Chris Strong 0-R-0-2- 2)

Sunday, April 26
Mildenhall 26 (**Adrian Mountain 2-3-3- 8:1**, **Jason Gage 3-3-2- 8:1**, Clive Clark 2-E-**2**- 4:1, Nathan Wilson 0-**2**-1-3- 6:1)
Exeter 10 (Rob Price 1-R-1- 2, Gavin Pell R-1-fx- 1, Scott Pegler 3-2-1- 6, Chris Storey 1-fx-0- 1)

Sunday, May 3
Mildenhall 13 (Adrian Mountain 1-2-0- 3, Jason Gage 3-2-1- 6, Clive Clark F-F-R- 0, Nathan Wilson 2-0-2- 4) **Milton Keynes 22** (Kieran McCullagh 2-3-3- 8, Tony Kingsbury 0-3-3- 6, Sean McCullagh 3-1-**2**-6:1, Chris Strong F-1-1- 2)

Wednesday, May 6
Nottingham 17 (Jason Reed 3-2-**1**- 6:1, Mark Geary 1-2-2- 5, Richard Webb 3-**1**-2-6:1, Daz Santos R-fx- 0) **Mildenhall 17** (Adrian Mountain 2-3-0- 5, Jason Gage fx-3-3- 6, Clive Clark F-F-1- 1, Nathan Wilson 2-0-3- 5)

Friday, May 8
Peterborough 11 (Michael Howe 1-3-3- 7, Gavin Pell 0-0-2- 2, Dean Garrod R-1-1- 2, Lee Coleman R-N- 0) **Milton Keynes 24** (Kieran McCullagh **2**-**2**-2- 6:2, Tony Kingsbury 3-2-3- 8, Sean McCullagh 3-3-1-7, Chris Strong **2**-0-1- 3:1)

Saturday, May 9
Stoke 24 (**Andy Meredith 3-3-3- 9**, Mark Walsh 0-**1**-3- 4:1, Ade Hoole 3-**2**-**1**- 6:1, Anthony Barlow **2**-2-1- 5:1) **Milton Keynes 12** (Kieran McCullagh 2-3-2- 7, Tony Kingsbury **1**-0-2- 3:1, Sean McCullagh 1-1-0-0- 2, Rob Price fx-N-0- 0)

Monday, May 18
Mildenhall 21 (Adrian Mountain 1-3-0- 4, **Jason Gage 3-3-3- 9**, Clive Clark **2**-1-F-3:1, Nathan Wilson 3-0-2- 5) **Stoke 14** (Ade Hoole 2-2-2- 6, Mark Walsh 0-2-**1**-3:1, Anthony Barlow E-**1**-3- 4:1, Matthew Powell fx-0-1- 1)

Tuesday, May 19
Milton Keynes 22 (**Kieran McCullagh 3-2-3- 8:1**, **Tony Kingsbury 2-3-3- 8:1**, Sean McCullagh 3-3-0- 6, Chris Strong R-N-N- 0) **Stoke 14** (Ade Hoole 1-2-2- 5, Mark Walsh F-R-2- 2, Matthew Powell **1**-**1**-**1**- 3:3, Anthony Barlow 2-1-**1**- 4:1)

Sunday, May 24
Mildenhall 19 (Adrian Mountain **2**-1-1- 4:1, **Jason Gage 3-3-3- 9**, Clive Clark **1**-R-**1**-2:2, Nathan Wilson 2-0-2- 4) **Nottingham 17** (Jason Reed F-2-3- 5, Daz Santos 1-3-2- 6, Richard Webb 3-1-**0**- 4:1, Mark Geary R-**2**-0- 2:1)

Monday, June 1
Exeter 25 (**Scott Pegler 3-2-2- 7:2**, Dean Garton 1-3-3- 7, **Tommy Palmer 3-3-3- 9**, Rob Price 2-N- 2:1) **Mildenhall 9** (Adrian Mountain 0-2-0- 2, Jason Gage 2-1-1- 4, Clive Clark 1-N-N- 1, Nathan Wilson 0-0-2-2)

BEFORE their closure Milton Keynes were well placed to win the Southern Section of the Division Two Reserve League. They had completed their first set of away matches with the exception of the match at Rye House and had lost only one, at Stoke. Of the successful Milton Keynes reserve side only Kieran McCullagh, who signed for Peterborough, held down a regular Reserve League team place. Of the Mildenhall side that also withdrew from the League, Jason Gage returned to parent track King's Lynn and became a regular in their Division One Reserve League squad.

Division One Reserve League

All the 1992 League Averages

Division One Reserve League

No.	Rider	Team/s	M.	R.	Pts	BP	TPts	Ave
1	David Haynes	Coventry	1	3	7.0	1.0	8.0	10.667
2	Darren Pearson	Bradford	19	57	143.0	8.0	151.0	10.596
3	Ben Howe	Ipswich	23	69	171.0	10.0	181.0	10.493
4	Stephen Morris	Wolverhampton	22	65	155.0	13.0	168.0	10.338
5	Justin Walker	Cradley Heath	17	51	124.0	7.0	131.0	10.275
6	Justin Elkins	Swindon	24	70	167.0	11.0	178.0	10.171
7	Savalas Clouting	Ipswich	23	69	160.0	12.0	172.0	9.971
8	Scott Smith	Cradley Heath	11	27	64.0	2.0	66.0	9.778
9	Darren Spicer	King's Lynn	13	34	74.0	9.0	83.0	9.765
10	Matthew Cross	Swindon	20	67	140.0	23.0	163.0	9.731
11	Glenn Cunningham	Oxford	24	70	165.0	5.0	170.0	9.714
	Phillip Morris	Reading	17	49	111.0	8.0	119.0	9.714
	Michael Graves	Bradford	3	7	15.0	2.0	17.0	9.714
14	Simon Wolstenholme	Wolverhampton	24	72	152.0	22.0	174.0	9.667
15	Colin White	Arena Essex	16	48	110.0	5.0	115.0	9.583
16	Steve Masters	Swindon	21	62	135.0	11.0	146.0	9.419
17	Tom Grinstead	King's Lynn	13	38	76.0	13.0	89.0	9.368
18	Emmerson Fairweather	King's Lynn	20	60	121.0	17.0	138.0	9.200
19	Jamie Habbin	Coventry	13	27	62.0	0.0	62.0	9.185
20	Darren Grayling	Eastbourne	14	40	86.0	2.0	88.0	8.800
21	Robert Ledwith	Arena Essex	8	24	50.0	2.0	52.0	8.667
22	Spencer Timmo	Oxford & Coventry	13	38	74.0	7.0	81.0	8.526
23	Kevin Little	Bradford	5	16	28.0	6.0	34.0	8.500
24	Steve Leigh	Poole	18	52	103.0	4.0	107.0	8.231
25	Mick Tomlin	Reading	14	41	74.0	9.0	83.0	8.098
26	Stuart Swales	Bradford	13	46	80.0	12.0	92.0	8.000
	Mark Robinson	Cradley Heath	3	9	17.0	1.0	18.0	8.000
	Anthony Blake	Poole	1	3	5.0	1.0	6.0	8.000
	Mark Seabright	Reading	1	3	5.0	1.0	6.0	8.000
30	Shaun Tacey	Ipswich	22	65	100.0	28.0	128.0	7.877
31	Shane Cooper	Wolverhampton	12	34	57.0	9.0	66.0	7.765
32	Anthony Boyd	Cradley Heath	17	56	93.0	14.0	107.0	7.643
33	Jon Armstrong	Belle Vue	17	52	90.0	8.0	98.0	7.538
34	Mike Lewthwaite	Belle Vue	9	28	51.0	1.0	52.0	7.429
35	Lawrence Hare	Ipswich	23	72	104.0	28.0	132.0	7.333
36	Stuart Parnaby	Bradford	18	55	94.0	6.0	100.0	7.273
37	Andrew Mountain	King's Lynn	20	70	103.0	24.0	127.0	7.257
38	Jason Handley	Belle Vue	6	15	23.0	4.0	27.0	7.200
39	Mark Meredith	Cradley Heath	20	59	88.0	15.0	103.0	6.983
40	Lance Sealey	Reading	22	71	108.0	14.0	122.0	6.873
41	Mike Hampson	Belle Vue	24	72	110.0	10.0	120.0	6.667
	Peter McNamara	Cradley Heath	1	3	4.0	1.0	5.0	6.667
43	Gary Sweet	Reading	18	55	78.0	12.0	90.0	6.545
44	Scott Swain	Eastbourne & Poole	19	57	89.0	4.0	93.0	6.526
45	Dean Child	Bradford	8	27	39.0	4.0	43.0	6.370
46	Nathan Gaymer	Eastbourne	21	66	95.0	10.0	105.0	6.364
47	Chris Clarence	Coventry	20	62	91.0	7.0	98.0	6.323
48	Peter Scully	Belle Vue	24	71	87.0	21.0	108.0	6.085
49	Sid Cooper	King's Lynn	1	4	5.0	1.0	6.0	6.000
50	Phil Ashcroft	Wolverhampton	9	31	41.0	5.0	46.0	5.935
51	Colin Thorpe	Wolves & Coventry	22	73	96.0	11.0	107.0	5.863
52	Jason Gage	King's Lynn	7	22	30.0	2.0	32.0	5.818
53	Ricky Sandford	Arena Essex	24	74	99.0	8.0	107.0	5.784
54	Chris Young	Arena Essex	3	9	13.0	0.0	13.0	5.778
55	Scott Kirton	Coventry	10	38	49.0	2.0	51.0	5.368
56	Darren Boulton	Poole	8	24	28.0	4.0	32.0	5.333
57	Roland Pollard	Arena Essex	19	55	67.0	6.0	73.0	5.309
58	Martin Willis	Poole	22	73	81.0	14.0	95.0	5.205
59	Paul Mitchell	Eastbourne	21	68	72.0	15.0	87.0	5.118
60	Craig Taylor	Wolverhampton	24	73	74.0	17.0	91.0	4.986
61	Steve Cope	Belle Vue	15	41	35.0	14.0	49.0	4.780
62	Wayne Parker	Oxford	24	71	76.0	7.0	83.0	4.676
63	Jonathon Gould	Poole	7	20	21.0	2.0	23.0	4.600
64	Richard Smith	Bradford	13	35	35.0	5.0	40.0	4.571
65	Mark Bruton	Eastbourne	13	47	45.0	5.0	50.0	4.255
66	Steve Camden	Swindon	15	44	38.0	7.0	45.0	4.091
67	Simon Bean	Bradford	10	27	20.0	7.0	27.0	4.000
	Justin Shaw	Eastbourne	3	9	6.0	3.0	9.0	4.000
	Chris Strong	Poole	2	6	4.0	2.0	6.0	4.000

A TOTAL of 149 riders appeared in Reserve League matches during the 1992 season – although not all of them were technically eligible to compete in the competition under the published rules.

Top of the Division Two averages was Rye House's Wayne Baxter who was neither English nor under 25!

There were other examples of riders who didn't qualify under at least one of the three major restrictions.

TON-UP BOYS

THE following riders topped the century points mark in the Division One Reserve League. It includes all four regular members of the successful Ipswich side.

Ben Howe	171
Justin Elkins	167
Glenn Cunningham	165
Savalas Clouting	160
Stephen Morris	155
Simon Wolstenholme	152
Darren Pearson	143
Matthew Cross	140
Steve Masters	135
Justin Walker	124
Emmerson Fairweather	121
Phillip Morris	111
Mike Hampson	110
Colin White	110
Lance Sealey	108
Lawrence Hare	104
Steve Leigh	103
Andrew Mountain	103
Shaun Tacey	100

STUART Swales was the busiest junior in Britain – riding in a total of 33 League matches.

He appeared to double up between his Second Division club Middlesbrough (for whom he was an everpresent in League competition) and First Division Bradford for whom he made 13 League appearances!

GUESTS

THE following riders appeared as guests for other Division One clubs during the 1992 season.

	M	R	Pts	BP	TPts	Ave
Jon Armstrong	1	3	6.0	2.0	8.0	10.667
Lawrence Hare	1	3	8.0	0.0	8.0	10.667
Mick Tomlin	1	3	7.0	1.0	8.0	10.667
Simon Wolstenholme	1	3	5.0	1.0	6.0	8.000
Stuart Parnaby	1	3	4.0	1.0	5.0	6.667
Lance Sealey	1	3	5.0	0.0	5.0	6.667
Justin Walker	1	4	5.0	1.0	6.0	6.000
Shaun Tacey	1	3	3.0	0.0	3.0	4.000
Paul Mitchell	1	3	2.0	1.0	3.0	4.000
Mark Sayer	1	3	2.0	0.0	2.0	2.667
Wayne Parker	1	3	2.0	0.0	2.0	2.667
Ricky Sandford	1	3	2.0	0.0	2.0	2.667
Shane Cooper	1	1	0.0	0.0	0.0	0.000

No.	Rider	Team/s	M.	R.	Pts	BP	TPts	Ave
	Dean Felton	Wolverhampton	2	5	4.0	1.0	5.0	4.000
71	Jason Green	Reading & Poole	19	60	47.0	8.0	55.0	3.667
72	Robert Vincent	Swindon	4	11	9.0	1.0	10.0	3.636
73	Terry Giles	Arena Essex	24	74	47.0	10.0	57.0	3.081
74	Paul Bromwich	Coventry	5	16	9.0	3.0	12.0	3.000
75	Mark Sayer	Reading	10	30	15.0	7.0	22.0	2.933
76	Nick Upton	Oxford	20	55	35.0	5.0	40.0	2.909
77	Scott Wormleighton	Coventry	10	32	20.0	2.0	22.0	2.750
78	Martin Jones	Bradford	1	3	1.0	1.0	2.0	2.667
79	Mike Randall	Eastbourne	7	21	10.0	2.0	12.0	2.286
80	Danny O'Brien	Oxford	13	39	21.0	1.0	22.0	2.256
81	Shaun Naylor	Cradley Heath	8	23	11.0	1.0	12.0	2.087
82	Carl Checketts	Cradley Heath	12	36	14.0	4.0	18.0	2.000
	Sean McCullagh	Coventry	2	4	2.0	0.0	2.0	2.000
84	Adrian Mountain	Coventry	4	14	5.0	1.0	6.0	1.714
	Gary Frankum	Coventry	2	7	2.0	1.0	3.0	1.714
86	Andrew Oliver	Coventry	2	5	2.0	0.0	2.0	1.600
87	Jason Smith	Poole	6	20	4.0	3.0	7.0	1.400
88	John Clayton	Oxford	4	12	3.0	1.0	4.0	1.333
	Gary Wells	Cradley Heath & Ipswich	2	6	2.0	0.0	2.0	1.333
	Jonathan Swales	Bradford	1	3	1.0	0.0	1.0	1.333
	Lee Rowlinson	Poole	1	3	1.0	0.0	1.0	1.333
92	Dean Ing	Swindon	8	20	4.0	0.0	4.0	0.800
93	Steve Woolley	Swindon	2	4	0.0	0.0	0.0	0.000

Listed below are the individual club averages of those riders who appeared for more than one team.

Rider	Team	M.	R.	Pts	BP	TPts	Ave
Spencer Timmo	Coventry	2	5	12.0	3.0	15.0	12.000
Spencer Timmo	Oxford	11	33	62.0	4.0	66.0	8.000
Scott Swain	Poole	10	30	48.0	1.0	49.0	6.533
Scott Swain	Eastbourne	9	27	41.0	3.0	44.0	6.519
Colin Thorpe	Coventry	20	67	94.0	11.0	105.0	6.269
Jason Green	Poole	15	48	40.0	5.0	45.0	3.750
Jason Green	Reading	4	12	7.0	3.0	10.0	3.333
Colin Thorpe	Wolverhampton	2	6	2.0	0.0	2.0	1.333
Gary Wells	Cradley Heath	1	3	1.0	0.0	1.0	1.333
Gary Wells	Ipswich	1	3	1.0	0.0	1.0	1.333

PROMOTERS voted to end the Reserve League at their 1992 Winter Conference – a decision that produced a welter of complaints from both fans and riders.

Reserve League team managers, in particular, were angered by the decision to scrap a competition introduced on a national basis in 1987.

In reality, though, there were serious question marks about the effectiveness of the Reserve League.

Only a handful of riders have progressed from the Reserve League to a permanent first team place in recent seasons, particularly in the First Division.

And there was also a marked deterioration in commitment to the League in 1992 with many clubs tracking either guest riders or turning up for meetings short-handed, sometimes even on their home track!

To appease the supporters of the Reserve League it was agreed to include two young riders at reserve (number seven and eight) in both the First and Second Divisions in 1993.

Tracks are also allowed to stage up to three junior races in their 1993 race programme although there was even talk, early in 1993, of the British Speedway Promoters' Association revising some of their winter decisions.

All the 1992 League Averages

Division Two Reserve League

No.	Rider	Team/s	M.	R.	Pts	BP	TPts	Ave
1	Wayne Baxter	Rye House	3	9	26.0	1.0	27.0	12.000
	Max Schofield	Newcastle	1	3	9.0	0.0	9.0	12.000
	Steve Cope	Sheffield	1	3	6.0	3.0	9.0	12.000
	Mike Lewthwaite	Edinburgh	1	2	5.0	1.0	6.0	12.000
5	Chris Readshaw	Berwick	12	35	92.0	4.0	96.0	10.971
6	Tommy Palmer	Exeter	13	39	97.5	7.0	104.5	10.718
7	Darren Matthews	Exeter	1	3	6.0	2.0	8.0	10.667
8	Andy Meredith	Stoke	9	25	61.0	5.0	66.0	10.560
9	David Nagel	Newcastle/Berwick	23	68	175.0	2.0	177.0	10.412
10	Chris Young	Rye House	13	40	95.0	9.0	104.0	10.400
11	Ade Hoole	Stoke	12	36	83.5	4.0	87.5	9.722
12	Mike McLuskey	Edinburgh	13	39	92.0	2.0	94.0	9.641
13	Paul Pickering	Middlesbrough	14	42	98.0	3.0	101.0	9.619
14	Scott Pegler	Exeter	16	50	107.0	12.0	119.0	9.520
15	Michael Lowrie	Berwick	20	60	128.0	12.0	140.0	9.333
	Richard Knight	Exeter	2	6	13.0	1.0	14.0	9.333
17	Steve Knott	Sheffield	14	42	92.0	5.0	97.0	9.238
18	Robert Ledwith	Rye House	7	21	48.0	0.0	48.0	9.143
19	Michael Howe	Peterborough	9	26	54.0	5.0	59.0	9.077
20	Mike Smith	Berwick	4	9	19.0	1.0	20.0	8.889
	Geoff Powell	Glasgow	3	9	18.0	2.0	20.0	8.889
22	Lee Coleman	Peterborough	9	26	55.0	2.0	57.0	8.769
23	Kieran McCullagh	Peterborough	7	21	46.0	0.0	46.0	8.762
24	James Grieves	Glasgow	20	58	116.0	8.0	124.0	8.552
25	Jason Straughan	Glasgow	13	38	76.0	5.0	81.0	8.526
26	Rob Homer	Sheffield	17	50	98.0	6.0	104.0	8.320
27	Martin Cobbin	Rye House	15	50	88.0	15.0	103.0	8.240
28	David Wolstenholme	Sheffield	6	18	34.0	3.0	37.0	8.222
29	Stuart Swales	Middlesbrough	20	61	111.0	13.0	124.0	8.131
30	Jason Reed	Long Eaton	16	42	80.0	5.0	85.0	8.095
31	Martin Jones	Middlesbrough	9	28	53.0	3.0	56.0	8.000
	Mark Hepworth	Sheffield	1	3	6.0	0.0	6.0	8.000
33	Dean Child	Newcastle & Sheffield	13	40	72.0	6.0	78.0	7.800
34	Jason Handley	Middlesbro' & Berwick	18	56	88.0	18.0	106.0	7.571

Division Two Reserve League

THE following riders appeared for teams in both the Division One and Division Two Reserve Leagues.

Dean Child, Steve Cope, Jason Handley, Martin Jones, Robert Ledwith, Mike Lewthwaite, Sean McCullagh, Jonathan Swales, Stuart Swales, Scott Wormleighton and Chris Young.

Details of their performance are listed in the Division averages.

GUESTS

THE following riders appeared as guests for other Division Two clubs during the 1992 season.

	M	R	Pts	BP	TPts	Ave
Stuart Swales	1	3	7	0	7	9.333
Stewart McDonald	1	4	8	0	8	8.000
Darren Matthews	1	4	5	1	6	6.000
Paul Pickering	1	3	4	0	4	5.333
Paul Coward	1	3	3	1	4	5.333
Paul Taylor	1	3	3	0	3	4.000
Mark Geary	1	3	2	1	3	4.000
Gavin Pell	2	6	4	1	5	3.333
Jonathan Swales	2	6	2	0	2	1.333
Carl Johnson	1	3	1	0	1	1.333
Chris Simpson	1	3	0	0	0	0.000
Damon Cowell	1	3	0	0	0	0.000
Mark Fry	1	0	0	0	0	–

No.	Rider	Team/s	M.	R.	Pts	BP	TPts	Ave
35	Stewart McDonald	Edinburgh	20	61	106.0	6.0	112.0	7.344
36	Andrew Howe	Newcastle	20	61	94.0	10.0	104.0	6.820
37	Sean McCullagh	Exeter	1	3	5.0	0.0	5.0	6.667
38	Anthony Barlow	Stoke	16	55	78.0	12.0	90.0	6.545
39	Richard Webb	Long Eaton	14	45	64.0	8.0	72.0	6.400
40	Matthew Powell	Stoke	6	16	22.0	3.0	25.0	6.250
41	Dean Garton	Exeter	8	27	37.0	4.0	41.0	6.074
42	Shaun Naylor	Long Eaton	3	10	13.0	2.0	15.0	6.000
	Graham Gordon	Exeter	3	8	11.0	1.0	12.0	6.000
44	Stuart Coleman	Glasgow	17	49	65.0	7.0	72.0	5.878
45	Mark Jolly	Rye House	10	34	42.0	7.0	49.0	5.765
46	Dean Garrod	Peterborough	16	49	60.0	9.0	69.0	5.633
47	Troy Scott	Berwick	2	6	8.0	0.0	8.0	5.333
48	Grant Blackie	Edinburgh	18	55	59.0	13.0	72.0	5.236
49	Paul Taylor	Edinburgh	18	54	54.0	16.0	70.0	5.185
50	Paul Gould	Newcastle	20	62	68.0	12.0	80.0	5.161
51	Rob Price	Exeter	11	35	33.0	12.0	45.0	5.143
52	Scott Wormleighton	Long Eaton	7	23	24.0	4.0	28.0	4.870
53	Mark Walsh	Stoke	16	51	49.0	10.0	59.0	4.627
54	Daz Santos	Long Eaton	10	26	26.0	3.0	29.0	4.462
55	William Beveridge	Berwick & Middlesbro'	18	55	50.0	10.0	60.0	4.364
56	Carl Johnson	Peterborough	7	21	20.0	2.0	22.0	4.190
57	Steve Battle	Sheffield	20	67	55.0	14.0	69.0	4.119
58	Wayne Park	Edin/Glasgow	13	45	39.0	7.0	46.0	4.089
59	Neil Taylor	Newcastle	4	10	6.0	4.0	10.0	4.000
	Chris Storey	Exeter	3	9	9.0	0.0	9.0	4.000
61	Craig Rathbone	Berwick	17	52	41.0	9.0	50.0	3.846
62	Paul Coward	Berwick	7	20	17.0	1.0	18.0	3.600
63	Richard Moss	Sheffield	5	16	11.0	3.0	14.0	3.500
64	Gavin Pell	Peterborough	5	15	9.0	3.0	12.0	3.200
65	Jonathan Swales	Middlesbrough	8	24	14.0	5.0	19.0	3.167
66	Mark Geary	Long Eaton	11	36	25.0	2.0	27.0	3.000
67	Damon Cowell	Sheffield	1	3	2.0	0.0	2.0	2.667
	Nathan Wilson	Peterborough	1	3	1.0	1.0	2.0	2.667
	Stuart Crome	Glasgow	1	3	1.0	1.0	2.0	2.667
70	Jason Wilby	Peterborough	5	15	8.0	1.0	9.0	2.400
71	Chris Simpson	Newcastle	15	42	16.0	4.0	20.0	1.905
72	Scott Burland	Peterborough	5	15	7.0	0.0	7.0	1.867
73	Raymond Fosbury	Glasgow	14	43	12.0	5.0	17.0	1.581
74	Steve Reynolds	Rye House	3	9	2.0	0.0	2.0	0.889
75	Graham Barker	Rye House	4	10	1.0	0.0	1.0	0.400
76	Drew Wheeldon	Stoke	1	3	0.0	0.0	0.0	0.000
	John Routledge	Berwick	1	3	0.0	0.0	0.0	0.000

Listed below are the individual club averages of those riders who appeared for more than one team.

	Rider	Team	M.	R.	Pts	BP	TPts	Ave
	Dean Child	Newcastle	1	3	7.0	1.0	8.0	10.667
	David Nagel	Newcastle	19	56	146.0	0.0	146.0	10.429
	David Nagel	Berwick	4	12	29.0	2.0	31.0	10.333
	Jason Handley	Middlesbrough	16	50	79.0	17.0	96.0	7.680
	Dean Child	Sheffield	12	37	65.0	5.0	70.0	7.568
	Jason Handley	Berwick	2	6	9.0	1.0	10.0	6.667
	William Beveridge	Middlesbrough	12	36	35.0	8.0	43.0	4.778
	Wayne Park	Edinburgh	8	27	24.0	5.0	29.0	4.296
	Wayne Park	Glasgow	5	18	15.0	2.0	17.0	3.778
	William Beveridge	Berwick	6	19	15.0	2.0	17.0	3.579

BEE-LINE LUBRICANTS JUNIOR CLASSIC (Swindon, Thursday, May 21): Glenn Cunningham 15, Robert Ledwith 13, Stephen Morris 12, Spencer Timmo 11, Justin Elkins 9, Scott Swain 8, Andrew Mountain 8, Matthew Cross 8, Steve Masters 8, Phillip Morris 6, Mark Meredith 6, Chris Clarence 5, Steve Camden 4, Darren Boulton 3, Chris Young 3, Lance Sealey 0. *Reserve: Robert Vincent 0.*

DEVON INTERMEDIATE PAIRS (Exeter, Monday, June 15): 1 Justin Elkins 19 & Tony Kingsbury 14:2 = 33, 2 Scott Pegler 22 & Martin Willis 9:2 = 31, 3 Sean McCullagh 18:2 & Dean Garton 13:1 = 31, 4 Jason Reed 17 & Rob Price 10:2 = 27, 5 Matthew Cross 24 & Chris Strong 2 = 26, 6 Tommy Palmer 19 & Chris Storey 6:2 = 25, 7 Kieran McCullagh 3 & Darren Boulton 0 = 3. *Reserves: Graham Gordon 11.*

Berwick, Saturday, June 13

THE THISTLE 40

1 †Michael Lowrie	**3 3 3 3**	**12**	
2 Stuart Coleman	F 1 fx N	1	
3 Mike McLuskey	3 3 2 **1**	9	1
4 Stewart McDonald	F 1 0 3	4	
5 James Grieves	2 0 2 2	6	
6 Paul Taylor	3 1 0 3 0 1	8	
7 Grant Blackie	fx N N N	0	

THE ROSE 43

1 †Chris Readshaw	2 3 3 3	11	
2 Troy Scott	**1 2 1** 1	5	3
3 David Nagel	2 2 3 **1**	8	1
4 Stuart Swales	fx **1 1** 0	2	2
5 Jason Straughan	3 2 2 2	9	
6 Craig Rathbone	2 F 1 2 fx	5	
7 William Beveridge	**1** 0 2 N	3	1

Middlesbrough, Thursday, June 25

BORO BEAR CUBS 49

1 †Paul Pickering	**3 3 3 3 3**	**15**	
2 Jonathan Swales	F 1 0 1	2	
3 Stuart Swales	3 3 fx 2 **2**	10	1
4 Craig Rathbone	N 0 0 1	1	
5 Jason Handley	3 2 fx N	5	
6 William Beveridge	**2** 0 1 1 **1**	5	2
7 Andrew Howe	3 **2** 3 1 2	11	1

NOTTINGHAM ARCHERS 41

1 Stuart Parnaby	2 3 3 3 3 0	14	
2 Richard Webb	**1** 1 **1** T	3	2
3 David Nagel	2 2 **2 2** 2 1	11	2
4 Chris Clarence	1 2 0 F	3	
5 †Jason Reed	0 fx **1** 3	4	1
6 Mark Geary	1 0 T 0	1	
7 Colin Thorpe	R **1** 2 2	5	1

Berwick, Saturday, October 17

BANDITS JUNIORS 40

1 Michael Lowrie	*rider replacement*		
2 Andrew Howe	0 **1** 2 **2** 1	6	2
3 David Nagel	R 2 3 3 1	9	
4 Jason Handley	1 **1** 3 3 3	11	1
5 Mike Smith	2 3 2 3 0	10	
6 Craig Rathbone	fx 2 **2** F	4	1
7 William Beveridge	fx fx 0 fx	0	

LINLITHGOW LIONS 37

1 James Grieves	3 3 2 3	11	
2 Paul Taylor	1 0 F **1**	2	1
3 Stewart McDonald	3 3 R 0 **2**	8	1
4 Grant Blackie	0 fx N T	0	
5 Paul Gould	2 fx 2 F	4	
6 Wayne Park	3 0 F 0 N	3	
7 †Brian Mercer	**2** 1 3 1 2	9	1

SOUTH WEST JUNIOR CHAMPIONSHIP (Exeter, Monday, October 5): 1 Scott Pegler, 2 Jason Reed, 3 Tommy Palmer, 4 Robert Ledwith. *Defeated semi finalists:* Scott Wormleighton, Richard Webb, Dean Garton, Darren Matthews. *Qualifying scorers (6 heats):* Robert Ledwith 6, Tommy Palmer 6, Scott Pegler 5, Jason Reed 4, Dean Garton 4, Jason Reed 4, Scott Wormleighton 3, Darren Matthews 2, Daz Santos 1, Graham Gordon 1, Mark Geary 0, Rob Price 0.

Roll of Honour

1987 Peter Jeffery (Exeter)
1988 Trevor Williams (Reading)
1989 Mark Simmonds (Exeter)
1990 Scott Swain (Eastbourne)
1991 Frank Smart (Exeter)
1992 Scott Pegler (Exeter)

SOUTH WEST SPEEDTRACK CHAMPIONSHIP (Exeter, Monday, October 12): Graham Gordon 13+2, Chris Dix 13+2, Paul Fudge 12, Mark Dimmer 11, Darren Matthews 10, David Plain 10, Jock Davidson 9, Mark Rowe 8, Jason Prynne 8, Mike Bowden (sen) 8, Dave Threadingham 5, Kevin Wajknecht 5, Steve Hoare 3, Clive Stoneman 1, Barry Woodruff 0, Dave Wright 0. *Reserves: Steve James 1, Alan Hosie 0, Michael Bowden (jun) 0, Matthew Shepherd 0.*

The meeting is confined to non-contracted grass track riders.

RESERVE LEAGUE RIDERS' CHAMPIONSHIP (Poole, Sunday, October 18): Justin Walker 13, Glenn Cunningham 12, Chris Readshaw 10, Scott Swain 10, Justin Elkins 9, Darren Grayling 9, Jon Armstrong 8, Emmerson Fairweather 8, Steve Leigh 8, Paul Pickering 7, Shaun Tacey 7, Colin White 7, Andy Meredith 4, Gary Sweet 3, Stephen Morris 2, Colin Thorpe 1. *Reserve: Martin Willis 2, Chris Strong, did not ride.*

Roll of Honour

1984 Lawrie Bloomfield (Ipswich)
1985 Jamie Habbin (King's Lynn)
1986 Sean Wilson (Sheffield)
1987 Mark Loram (Hackney)
1989 Carl Stonehewer (Belle Vue)
1990 Richard Musson (Belle Vue)
1991 Ben Howe (Ipswich)
1992 Justin Walker (Cradley Heath)

CHRIS PRIME MEMORIAL TROPHY (Newcastle, Sunday, June 7): 1 Stuart Parnaby, 2 David Nagel, 3 Stuart Swales, 4 Martin Jones, 5 Mike McLuskey, 6 Jason Handley, 7 James Grieves, 8 Paul Pickering, 9 Richard Smith, 10 Michael Howe, 11 Jason Reed, 12 Mark Meredith, 13 Wayne Park & Neil Taylor, 15 Lee Coleman & Ali Smith, 17 Paul Gould, 18 Stewart McDonald, 19 Daz Santos, 20 Andrew Howe, 21 Steve Battle & Dean Child, 23 William Beveridge & Craig Rathbone.

The meeting was staged under the proposed FIM Grand Prix formula under which riders progressed throughout the meeting based on performance.

Roll of Honour

1978 Tom Owen (Newcastle)
1979 Alan Emerson (Workington)
1980 Robbie Blackadder (Newcastle)
1981 David Bargh (Newcastle)
1982 Rod Hunter (Newcastle)
1983 Steve McDermott (Berwick)
1984 John Louis (King's Lynn)
1985 Charlie McKinna (Berwick)
1986 Dave Perks (Newcastle)
1987 Nigel Crabtree (Stoke)
1989 Duncan Chapman (Middlesbrough)
1991 Chris Readshaw (Middlesbrough)
1992 Stuart Parnaby (Bradford)
■ From 1989 the meeting has been for juniors.

STARS OF TOMORROW '92 (Berwick, Saturday, August 29): Mike Smith 15, James Grieves 14, Stewart McDonald 11+3, Stuart Swales 11+2, Stuart Coleman 10, Grant Blackie 9, Jason Handley 9, Andrew Howe 7, Paul Gould 7, Craig Rathbone 5, Wayne Park 5, Paul Taylor 5, Jonathan Swales 4, Raymond Fosbury 2, Paul Coward 2, William Beveridge 0.

Roll of Honour

1970 Jim Gallacher (Berwick)
1971 Malcolm McPhie (Middlesbrough)
1972 Wattie Robertson
1973 Robin Dixon (Berwick)
1974 Vic Harding (Sunderland)
1975 Peter Waite (Berwick)
1976 Jon Bower (Berwick)
1977 Ian Darling (Berwick)
1978 Rob Grant (Berwick)
1979 Neil Farnish (Swindon)
1980 Paul Henderson (Berwick)
1982 Martin McKinna (Glasgow)
1983 Peter Erskine (Berwick)
1984 Jackson Irving (Berwick)
1985 Jackson Irving (Berwick)
1986 Scott Lamb (Edinburgh)
1987 Steve Wicks (Newcastle)
1990 Mike McLuskey (Edinburgh)
1991 Troy Scott (Berwick)
1992 Mike Smith (Berwick)

Speedtrack Roll of Honour

1990 Richard Knight
1991 Dean Garton
1992 Graham Gordon

1991 SUNBRITE LEAGUE DIVISION ONE TABLE

		Home			Away						
	P	W	D	L	W	D	L	PtsF	PtsA	BP	TPts
1 WOLVERHAMPTON	24	11	1	0	8	0	4	1205.5	952.5	10	49
2 Bradford	24	11	1	0	4	3	5	1184.5	973.5	9	43
3 Cradley Heath	24	12	0	0	3	1	8	1118	1032	10	41
4 Belle Vue	24	9	2	1	3	1	8	1042	1082	6	33
5 Berwick	24	10	0	2	3	0	9	1073	1053	6	32
6 Ipswich	24	9	0	3	3	1	8	1065.5	1089.5	7	32
7 Coventry	24	9	0	3	3	0	9	1076	1079	6	30
8 King's Lynn	24	8	1	3	4	0	8	1013.5	1139.5	5	30
9 Oxford	24	6	1	5	2	2	8	1069	1085	6	25
10 Poole	24	8	0	4	0	2	10	1053	1103	5	23
11 Reading	24	8	0	4	1	0	11	1030	1123	3	21
12 Eastbourne	24	4	3	5	2	0	10	1027	1125	3	18
13 Swindon	24	5	1	6	0	0	12	1018	1138	2	13

Roll of Honour

DIVISION ONE CHAMPIONS
Wolverhampton

SPEEDWAY STAR
KNOCK OUT CUP WINNERS
Bradford

GOLD CUP WINNERS
Berwick

DIVISION ONE RIDERS' CHAMPION
Sam Ermolenko
(Wolverhampton)

FIRST TIMERS

CHAMPIONS ... the successful 1991 Wolverhampton squad Graham Jones, Wayne Carter, team manager Peter Adams, Charles Ermolenko, Sam Ermolenko, Andy Phillips, Ronnie Correy and Scott Norman

BRADFORD had the most successful season in the club's history in 1991 winning both the BSPA Cup and the Speedway Star Knock Out Cup

BERWICK were one of four National League tracks to join Division One in 1991 and the most successful on track, winning the Gold Cup.

1991 SUNBRITE LEAGUE DIVISION TWO TABLE

		Home			Away						
	P	W	D	L	W	D	L	PtsF	PtsA	BP	TPts
1 ARENA ESSEX	22	11	0	0	10	0	1	1194	784	11	53
2 Glasgow	22	10	0	1	4	0	7	1051	925	8	36
3 Newcastle	22	8	0	3	5	1	5	1001	960	8	35
4 Edinburgh	22	9	0	2	3	0	8	1038	938	7	31
5 Sheffield	22	10	0	1	2	0	9	1017	957	7	31
6 Long Eaton	22	10	0	1	1	0	10	983	991	5	27
7 Exeter	22	9	0	2	0	0	11	1008	967	8	26
8 Middlesbrough	22	8	0	3	1	0	10	921	1054	2	20
9 Rye House	22	7	0	4	1	0	10	893	1065	4	20
10 Stoke	22	7	1	3	0	1	10	941	1036	2	18
11 Milton Keynes	22	7	0	4	0	0	11	905	1066	3	17
12 Peterborough	22	7	1	3	0	0	11	883	1092	1	16

■ HACKNEY withdrew mid-season because of financial problems and all results were expunged from the League table.

Roll of Honour

DIVISION TWO CHAMPIONS
Arena Essex

PHONESPORT KNOCK OUT CUP WINNERS
Arena Essex

GOLD CUP WINNERS
Newcastle

DIVISION TWO RIDERS' CHAMPION
Jan Stæchmann (Long Eaton)

ARENA COP THE LOT

WINNERS ... the victorious Arena Essex squad that completed an historic 1991 treble of the Sunbrite League Division Two, the Phonesport Knock Out Cup and the H.E.A.T. Division Two Team Championship. Back row: Colin White, Paul Hurry, co-promoter Ivan Henry, Ricky Sandford and Tommy Palmer. Middle row: Peter Thorogood (team manager), Alan Mogridge and Terry Russell (co-promoter). Front: Bo Petersen, Troy Pratt and Andy Galvin

THE WORLD crown fitted new Track King Jan O. Pedersen as snugly as a golden glove....as years of misfortune were buried in the time vaults of distant memories.

And no wonder. For the tiny Dane – the smallest rider in world speedway – had twice had his heart broken when injuries ruled him out of successive World Finals in 1989 and 1990.

This time around he was taking no chances as he ordered a pair of ultra-lightweight racing leathers (made from a material usually used for ladies' gloves) that also incorporated his World Final race-jacket in another bid to reduce his overall weight.

Jan O. explained: "I wanted to save as much weight as I could. I've put a little bit on in the last year or so."

Even so the tiny racer from Middelfart, still only tipped the scale at 56.2 kilos – in his leathers, by far the lightest of the 16 World Finalists.

Jan O.'s build up to the big day had been unerringly similar to that in previous years when all his hopes and ambitions had been snapped like a brittle bone.

He rode for his club Cradley Heath in home and away Dudley-Wolves Trophy challenges against Black Country rivals Wolverhampton on the Bank Holiday Monday preceding the World Final.

A year earlier he had stumbled at a kart centre in Birmingham and broken his wrist. Twelve months previous to that he had crashed at Wolverhampton and fractured his wrist.

Pedersen could have been excused for keeping out of the traffic at Dudley Wood and Monmore Green. But that's not his way and he was beaten just once by an opponent (Ronnie Correy) in nine races as he prepared for his first World Final since his third place at Vojens in 1988.

He admitted in his build-up: "I don't even like to tempt fate by saying too much. I have got to stay in one piece and actually take part in the final before I can think of winning it."

But becoming the 1991 World Champion at Ullevi Stadium, Gothenburg, Sweden, was certainly on Jan O.'s mind as he mentally relaxed on the eve of the biggest meeting of his career.

He joined the holiday-making World Final fans and fun-seeking locals at the Liseberg, Gothenburg's famous entertainment complex a few miles down the road from the track.

He explained: "I wanted to relax and not think too much about the next day."

It was a philosophy that was to reap the richest dividend of all for everyone's favourite as he studiously ignored one of the most upsetting behind-the-scenes rows to hit a World Final for many, many years.

Acrimony filled the Swedish air as Pedersen's rivals queued up for the compulsory machine examination on the Friday afternoon with the meeting little more than 24 hours away.

Twenty-six machines failed first time around when they were tested on the noise meter.

All were above the 102 decibel limit and while some registered below that figure at a second, third or even fourth attempt others were still over the limit a day later with the first race approaching too rapidly for the nerves.

The turnstiles were opened on Saturday evening and pop music cascaded from the loudspeakers around Ullevi as Jeremy Doncaster, Billy Hamill, Paul Thorp and Sam Ermolenko were still desperately waiting for clearance.

The widely-used, British manufactured King silencer appeared to be the main culprit – and that was the muffler that was generally first choice of the majority of the World Finalists.

There were hurried centre green conversations between high-ranking FIM officials as they realised they had a major problem on their hands but despite pleas from riders for everyone to be allowed to use the King silencer (irrespective of its decibel rating) they refused to bow down and there was deep resentment among most of the riders.

And there was cheating!

Some riders privately admitted they pushed blocks of wood, wire brushes and other noise-deadening implements into their silencers to get through the test...and swiftly removed them as they prepared for their opening race.

Others were not so lucky and debutant Billy Hamill was forced to go out into the stadium concourse to borrow a silencer from a bike being used as part of a public display!

Six-time World Champion Ivan Mauger was later to insist: "It is the most unfair World Final I have ever known."

But not even the unfairness of it all – and more of that later – could detract from the head-and-shoulders supremacy of the new World Champion.

Jan O. had to wait for the fourth race to resume his World Final challenge and he made light work of a tough on-paper challenge from England's best hope Kelvin Tatum and American Sam Ermolenko whose own chances had been severely harmed by not only the silencer row but a crash at Ipswich some 16 nights earlier when he tore ligaments in his knee.

For the first year the route to the World Final had included two semi-finals, from which the top eight scorers would qualify.

It was a change of qualification which pleased most people who were convinced it would rid the sport of the seemingly top-heavy bias towards Continental riders.

The first semi-final was held at Rovno in the Soviet Union and provided a totally unexpected winner in American Billy Hamill who could afford to drop two points in his last ride and yet still claim first place.

The big Ukraine track – 40 metres longer than Bradford – claimed only one major name victim: 1990 World Finalist Henrik Gustafsson.

He was beaten in a run-off for World Final reserve by his fellow countryman Mikael Blixt who was just edged out of becoming the first rider to qualify for the big night while under contract to a Division Two club.

The Continental rounds had supplied seven of the 16 Rovno semi-finalists...and only two, Coventry's Roman Matousek and the Italian Armando Castagna, reached the World Final.

Justification for the change?

The second semi-final, held a week later at Abensberg, Germany, provided further evidence that it was a fairer method of qualification with only Gerd Riss finishing in the top eight.

The round went to Nielsen with a 15 point maximum ahead of Pedersen and Knudsen in a Danish clean sweep.

Tony Rickardsson, who had come into the meeting instead of England's Andy Smith, ruled out with a broken neck, made the best of his second chance to qualify for his first World Final.

His girlfriend Anna, an international gymnast, cried for joy. The tears in Gert Handberg's game were of despair.

The former World Under 21 Champion appeared to be coasting towards the World Final with six points from his first three rides but in heat 16 he crashed heavily, unable to avoid Kelly Moran who had stopped midtrack after his engine seized solid.

Shaken, Handberg returned for the re-run but could manage only third place and still needed a point from his last race. He had it in the palm of his throttle hand when his chain snapped throwing him off and out of the 1991 World Final.

It was a cruel blow, and it was little or no consolation when he beat the Yugoslavian Jozsef Petrikovics for the reserve slot at Ullevi.

There were, as usual, a couple of slices of controversy.

Belle Vue's Kelly Moran missed two ferries at Dover, arrived at Abensberg hours after official practice had ended, and then signed in late on the Sunday morning.

He was fined £100 but avoided the ultimate penalty of exclusion from the meeting because no-one was prepared to make an official protest.

Had he been ruled out (as many riders and officials privately felt he ought to have been) his place would, ironically, have gone to his Aces team-mate Joe Screen.

And during the meeting itself another American, Wolverhampton's Ronnie Correy was excluded after falling in an incident with home rider Gerd Riss which, almost everyone in the stadium except the man who mattered most, referee Graham Brodie, believed was the fault of the German.

Correy was incensed and refused to leave the track as he argued the decision. Former World Champion Michael Lee, one of his mechanical team, was violently manhandled by four burly policemen as he tried to support Correy's vain plea.

It was only when FIM Track Commission President Gunter Sorber warned him that he could be thrown out of the World Championship if he continued his protests, that Correy retired to the pits. Fortunately for him results in the remaining three races meant he retained his interest in the title chase for the last lap of all....

Controversy is rarely far away when it comes around to the World Championship – and the heated debate began during the European winter, in Australasia.

The bone of contention was the qualification method adopted by both Australia and New Zealand who retained their right to ignore results in their national championships.

David Bargh returned home to win the Kiwi title but was overlooked as one of his country's two seeded Commonwealth Finalists and Middlesbrough's David Cheshire was furious when he was overlooked as one of Australia's four representatives even though he had finished ahead of 1990 bronze medallist Todd Wiltshire, whom he had beaten in an Australian Final run-off!

Cheshire's family threatened to take legal action but it all blew over when Cheshire fractured a scaphoid and the authorities produced black and white evidence that they were certainly in their right to seed riders although no-one could defend their actions morally.

Leigh Adams, who had missed the Aussie Final because of injury, was also selected ahead of Cheshire and the six Colonials were joined at the Ancit Commonwealth Final at King's Lynn by the top ten scorers from the Homefire British Final where Bradford's Gary Havelock glittered on his way to a first national title.

The unattached Andy Smith – who had won his semi-final round at Ipswich where Simon Wigg departed – eased through even though he didn't have, at that time, a British club.

John Davis, in his 16th successive British Final, fell by the wayside at Brandon and defending British kingpin Tatum saw his title slip away when he finished third in his opener.

The Commonwealth Final saw the elimination of in-form Martin Dugard, his Oxford team-mate Craig Boyce and Chris Louis. And it also saw the end of the career of 1980 World Champion Michael Lee who had, earlier, been eliminated through injury and circumstances in the re-arranged British quarter final at Hackney.

Lee responded to a call from his King's Lynn promoter Bill Barker to act as supplementary reserve...a decision he was to deeply regret.

Dugard never recovered from a first race exclusion after he had clouted the fence trying to ride around Gary Allan, and Boyce bowed out after a heavy fall in heat 12 which saw him taken to hospital with a back injury.

That crash was, coincidentally, to lead to Lee's eventual downfall as he was called out to replace the Aussie champion in heat 19.

He finished last but was subsequently chosen for a random drugs test which he failed to take despite being aware that his name had been picked out.

He was initially suspended pending a hearing and never rode again although he was only given a suspended sentence when he appeared before the Speedway Control Board, explaining that because he was only reserve he had stopped on the way to the track for a lunchtime drink and was fearful that would show up at the drugs check.

BRITISH QUARTER FINAL 2 (Newcastle, Sunday, April 14): **Peter Carr 14, Louis Carr 12+3, Nigel Crabtree 12+2, Neil Evitts 11+3,** David Blackburn 11+2, David Walsh 10, Les Collin 10, Eric Monaghan 10, Paul Dugard 7, Scott Robson 5, Wayne Carter 4, Andy Philslips 4, Matthew Cross 4, Max Schofield 3, David Nagel 2, Ray Taaffe 0. *Reserve: Paul Coward, did not ride.*

David Nagel replaced Kevin Little and Ray Taaffe replaced Bryan Larner.

BRITISH QUARTER FINAL 3 (Exeter, Monday, April 15): **Steve Schofield 14, Gordon Kennett 12, Richard Green 11+3, Melvyn Taylor 11+2,** Nigel Leaver 11+1, Jamie Luckhurst 10, Martin Goodwin 10, Alun Rossiter 10, Paul Fry 7, Wayne Garratt 7, Darren Sumner 4, Alastair Stevens 3, Andy Meredith 3, Scott Smith 3, Kevin Brice 2, Darren Grayling 2. *Reserves: Richard Knight 0, Frank Smart 0.*

BRITISH QUARTER FINAL 1 (Hackney, Sunday, April 21): **Andy Grahame 15, Alan Mogridge 14, Nathan Simpson 11, Chris Louis 10+3,** Martin Dixon 10+2, Ray Morton 10+F, Paul Bentley 8, Neville Tatum 7, Andy Hackett 6, Peter Jeffery 6, David Norris 6, Ben Howe 5, Paul Whittaker 5, Michael Lee 4, Dean Standing 2, David Steen 1. *Reserve: Michael Warren 0.*

The meeting was originally scheduled for Friday, April 12, but abandoned after 5 heats because of heavy rain. Scorers were: Morton 5, Norris 4, Lee 3, Grahame 3, Whittaker 3, Mogridge 3, Tatum 3, Louis 2, Jeffery 1, McKinna 1, Howe 1, Simpson 1, Steen 0, Parnaby 0, Hackett 0, Standing 0.

Martin Dixon replaced Kenny McKinna and Paul Bentley replaced Stuart Parnaby.

SEMI FINAL 1 (Ipswich, Thursday, May 2): **Andy Smith 11, Jeremy Doncaster 11, Sean Wilson 10, Joe Screen 9, Chris Louis 9, Richard Knight 8, David Mullett 8, Mark Loram 8,** Alan Mogridge 8, Dean Barker 8, Simon Wigg 7, Marvyn Cox 7, Gordon Kennett 6, Richard Green 5, Melvyn Taylor 3, Nathan Simpson 2.

Five riders tied for the last three qualifying places on 8 points and a series of races were needed to determine the finishing positions. The results of those races were: Run-Off 1: Loram, Mogridge, Mullett. Run-off 2: Knight, Barker. Run-off 3: Mullett, Mogridge, Barker (ret). Run-off 4: Knight, Mullett, Loram, Mogridge (fell).

SEMI FINAL 2 (Cradley Heath, Sunday, May 5): **Steve Schofield 12, Alan Grahame 11+3, Martin Dugard 11+2, Kelvin Tatum 10, Neil Collins 10, John Davis 9, Gary Havelock 9, Paul Thorp 8,** Andy Grahame 7+3, Neil Evitts 7+2, Carl Stonehewer 6, Louis Carr 5, Graham Jones 5, Andrew Silver 5, Peter Carr 4, Nigel Crabtree 0. *Track Reserve: Mark Meredith 0.*

HOMEFIRE BRITISH FINAL (Coventry, Sunday, May 19): **Gary Havelock 15, Kelvin Tatum 13, Chris Louis 11, Paul Thorp 10, Jeremy Doncaster 10, Neil Collins 9, Martin Dugard 8, Andy Smith 8, Joe Screen 7, Sean Wilson 7,** Mark Loram 5, John Davis 5, Alan Grahame 4, Richard Knight 3, David Mullett 3, Steve Schofield 2. *Track reserve: Lee Coleman 0.*

AUSTRALIAN FINAL (Alice Springs, Sunday, January 27): **Craig Boyce 15, Glenn Doyle 14,** Glyn Taylor 12, David Cheshire 10+3, **Todd Wiltshire 10+2,** Shane Bowes 10+1, Phil Crump 9, Troy Butler 8, Shane Parker 8, Scott Norman 5, Damon Richardson 5, Mark Lemon 5, Wayne Bridgeford 3, Darrin Winkler 2, Glen Baxter 2, Jason Lyons 2. Track reserve: Kelvin Willis 0.

Todd Wiltshire and Leigh Adams, who missed the Australian Final because of injury, were seeded to the Commonwealth Final.

NEW ZEALAND FINAL (Gisborne, Saturday, January 26): David Bargh 15, Chris Martin 14, Mark Thorpe 12, John Tuffley 11, Justin Monk 10, Michael Long 10, Greg Fisher 8, John Roberts 7, Nathan Murray 5, Ricky Bennett 5, Jacqui Mauger 5, Dean Sullivan 5, Nick Young 4, Gary Marsh 3, Michael Hollow 3, Steve Etchers 0.

Mitch Shirra and Gary Allan were seeded to the Commonwealth Final.

ANCIT COMMONWEALTH FINAL (King's Lynn, Sunday, June 2): **Jeremy Doncaster 13, Leigh Adams 10, Paul Thorp 10, Joe Screen 10 (after ballot), Kelvin Tatum 9, Glenn Doyle 9, Neil Collins 8, Gary Havelock 8, Todd Wiltshire 7, Andy Smith 7, Mitch Shirra 7,** Chris Louis 6, Sean Wilson 5, Gary Allan 4, Martin Dugard 4, Craig Boyce 1. *Track reserves: Paul Fry 0, Michael Lee 0.*

AMERICAN FINAL (Long Beach, California, Saturday, March 2): **Rick Miller 15, Sam Ermolenko 14, Ronnie Correy 13, Kelly Moran 11, Billy Hamill 10+3,** Bobby Ott 10+2, Gary Hicks 9, Bobby Schwartz 7, Mike Faria 7, Greg Hancock 6, Lance King 5, Louis Rosso 4, Steve Lucero 3, Brad Oxley 3, Andy Northrup 2, John Kehoe 0. *Reserve: Josh Larsen 1.*

HOMEFIRE OVERSEAS FINAL (Bradford, Sunday, June 23): **Kelvin Tatum 13, Sam Ermolenko 12+3, Billy Hamill 12+2, Andy Smith 11, Paul Thorp 10, Ronnie Correy 9, Jeremy Doncaster 7, Mitch Shirra 7,** Kelly Moran 7, Todd Wiltshire 6+3, Glenn Doyle 6+2, Joe Screen 5, Rick Miller 4, Gary Havelock 4, Leigh Adams 4, Neil Collins 3. *Reserves: Chris Louis and Bobby Ott, did not ride.*

DANISH FINAL (Fladbro, Sunday, May 19): **Jan O. Pedersen 15, Tommy Knudsen 14, Hans Nielsen 12+3, John Jørgensen 12+2, Gert Handberg 10, Bo Petersen 9,** Jan Jacobsen 8, Brian Karger 6, Jan Stæchmann 6, Jens Henry Nielsen 6, Allan Johansen 5, Tom Knudsen 5, Per Sørensen 4, Lars Munkedal 3, Jan Pedersen 3, Lars Henrik Jørgensen 1.

SWEDISH FINAL OVERALL SCORERS: **Henrik Gustafsson 40, Per Jonsson 36, Tony Rickardsson 33, Jimmy Nilsen 33, Mikael Blixt 29,** Erik Stenlund 27, Conny Ivarsson 26, Peter Karlsson 23, Stefan Dannö 19, Claes Ivarsson 18, Tony Olsson 15, Mikael Karlsson 15, Mikael Teurnberg 15, Peter Nahlin 13, Mikael Löfqvist 10, Mikael Rittervall 8.

SCANDINAVIAN FINAL (Brovst, Denmark, Sunday, June 22): **Hans Nielsen 13, Jan O. Pedersen 12, Jimmy Nilsen 11, Henrik Gustafsson 10, Per Jonsson 9, Lars Gunnestad 9, Gert Handberg 9, Tommy Knudsen 8, Mikael Blixt 8,** Tony Rickardsson 7+3, Einar Kyllingstad 7+3, Vesa Ylinen 7+1, Bo Petersen 4, John Jørgensen 4, Juha Moksunen 1, Tor Einar Hjelm 1.

Kai Niemi withdrew through injury and was replaced by Vesa Ylinen. A qualifying race after practice on Friday, June 20, resulted in Vesa Ylinen and Tor Einar Hjelm being seeded to the meeting.

SEMI-FINAL 1 (Abensberg, Germany, Sunday, August 18): **Hans Nielsen 15, Jan O. Pedersen 14, Tommy Knudsen 12, Sam Ermolenko 11, Tony Rickardsson 10, Ronnie Correy 8, Gerd Riss 8, Kelvin Tatum 8,** Gert Handberg 7+3, Jozsef Petrikovics 7+2, Kelly Moran 6, Wojciech Zaluski 5, Vaclav Milik 3, Zdenek Schneiderwind 3, Klaus Lausch 2, Mikhail Starostin 1.

SEMI FINAL 2 (Rovno, Soviet Union, Sunday, August 11): **Billy Hamill 12, Jimmy Nilsen 11, Per Jonsson 10+3, Paul Thorp 10+2, Armando Castagna 9, Roman Matousek 9, Jeremy Doncaster 9, Mitch Shirra 9,** Mikael Blixt 8+3, Henrik Gustafsson 8+2, Vladimir Kalina 7, Lars Gunnestad 6, Zoltan Adorján 4, Petr Vandirek 4, Robert Nagy 1, Rif Saitgareev 0, Antonin Kasper 0.

1991 WORLD FINAL

Ullevi Stadium, Gothenburg, Sweden

Saturday, August 31, 1991

1 Jan O. Pedersen	**3**	**3**	**3**	**3**	**3**	**15**
2 Tony Rickardsson	2	3	3	2	2	12
3 Hans Nielsen	2	3	1	3	2	11 +3
4 Tommy Knudsen	3	1	1	3	3	11 +2
5 Jimmy Nilsen	0	2	2	3	3	10
6 Paul Thorp	3	2	2	2	1	10
7 Sam Ermolenko	2	3	2	R	2	9
8 Kelvin Tatum	1	2	3	2	0	8
9 Per Jonsson	1	2	R	1	3	7
10 Ronnie Correy	3	0	0	1	2	6
11 Armando Castagna	1	1	3	1	0	6
12 Billy Hamill	2	E	2	1	1	6
13 Mitch Shirra	0	0	1	2	1	4
13 Roman Matousek	0	1	1	0	0	2
15 Jeremy Doncaster	1	1	0	R	0	2
15 Gerd Riss	0	R	0	0	1	1
17 Michael Blixt	0					0

Reserve: Gert Handberg, did not ride.

HIGH-FLYING Denmark kept their feet on the ground even though their thoughts were in the clouds to win a record-breaking ninth World Team Cup Final!

World Champion Jan O. Pedersen made it a clean sweep of the gold medals as he powered to yet another World Final maximum to round off the most memorable year in his career with yet another title.

As he stood on the rostrum at Vojens he could look back on a World Final record that was as close to perfection as it is possible to come.

He was deprived of immortality by a burnt out plug cap lead in the World Pairs Final – otherwise he would have gone through all three World Finals without dropping a single point!

On the eve of his solo victory in Gothenburg, Jan O. had gone up in the world at the Liseberg funfair.

Before going out to lead Denmark to victory in the World Team Cup Final he and his team-mates were guests of the Danish Royal Air Force and photographed in and alongside an F-16 Fighter

The Danes plainly have a head for heights and a hunger for gold medals.

Team manager Kjell Lund brought in Arena Essex's Brian Karger to supplement his four World Finalist and gambled bravely on a team formation which meant their potential weakest link, Gert Handberg, going out in the first race.

It was a ploy which reaped its own reward as the Cradley rider outgated and outsmarted his rivals to record an opening heat win.

The Danes never looked back and it wasn't until heat seven that another nation was able to provide a heat winner! Greg Hancock broke the spell by defeating his Cradley Heath team-mate but, by then, it was all over bar the official trophy presentation.

At that early stage the Danes led with a maximum 18 points, the United States had eight, Sweden were on six and England were staring relegation in the face with only four points.

The Sunbrite Lions, forced to bring Marvyn Cox in for his fifth World Team Cup Final appearance as a replacement for injured skipper Kelvin Tatum, never recovered from their dismal opening and were the only nation not to provide at least one race winner.

Their 11 point total (from 20 heats) was also the country's lowest ever in World Team Cup competition and sentenced the Sunbrite Lions to a place in the 1992 semi-final round.

Overall it was a shabby display, particularly as it came hard on the heels of yet another disappointing World Final. After the Danish powerhouse start to the meeting the only real medal placings in any doubt beyond the halfway stage were for silver and bronze.

America had the better of the first half but Sweden came on strongly the longer the meeting lasted. After eight heats the Yanks had a two point advantage. After 12 races that had been prised open to five points and with the last stanza of four races to go the two countries were level.

GLITTERING PRIZES ....Denmark's 1991 World Team Cup winning squad. Back: Jan O. Pedersen, Tommy Knudsen and Gert Handberg. Front: Brian Karger, Hans Nielsen and team manager Kjell Lund

Everything hinged on the last four races when riders were allocated according to their scores.

Jimmy Nilsen got the better of Rick Miller in heat 17 to give the Swedes the edge; Henrik Gustafsson was second behind Hans Nielsen in heat 18 and Hancock was tailed off in last place to see Sweden three points to the better.

Sam Ermolenko won heat 19 but with Tony Rickardsson close behind it meant that the only way the Americans could finish in second place overall was if Billy Hamill ruined Jan O. Pedersen's maximum in the final race with former World Champion Per Jonsson in last place.

Hamill did everything he could but had to bow down to his Dudley Wood colleague but Jonsson's third place in front of Martin Dugard meant the Swedes had secured their highest

World Team Cup placing since they finished runners-up to England at Chorzow, Poland, in 1974!

Nothing, though, could take it away from Denmark.

Critics were ready to write them off as the dominant force after their World Team Cup eclipse at Odsal in 1989 when they also lost the services of Erik Gundersen.

Now they had bounced back with a vengeance, providing all speedway's World Champions in the same season.

Ominously the same night they were winning in Denmark one of their own, Long Eaton's Jan Stæchmann, was winning the Division Two Riders' Championship Final at Coventry.

And for the depressed England management team of Eric Boocock and Colin Pratt there was nothing over which they could enthuse.

They had picked what was universally accepted as the strongest team but, to use Eric Boocock's own words, were never in the race.

He said: "After four races we went rapidly downhill and never improved. It is frustrating, believe me. We have, for the last six years, asked for international matches abroad but everything revolves around cost and until there is a majority of people who want to do something we will get nowhere."

They were comments that fell, like chaff, on stony ground and as the Danes celebrated the biggest ever winning World Team Cup margin the Brits were left to reflect on how they had been left behind in the race....

GROUP D

ROUND 1 (Leipzig, Germany, Monday, April 22): Holland 29 (Robert-Jan Munnecom 14, Rene Elzinga 6, Rob Steman 5, Ron Koppe 4) Yugoslavia 28 (Gregor Pintar 16, Gerhard Lekse 9, Kreso Omerzel 3) East Germany 27 (Thomas Diehr 15, Thomsen Hopp 10, Herbert Mussehl 1, Thomas Koch 1) France 18 (11, David Ochocki 7, Christian Ianotto 0) Bulgaria 16 (Zdravko Jordanov 9, Nikolai Manev 7).

ROUND 2 (Ljubljana, Yugoslavia, Sunday, April 28): Yugoslavia 33 (Gregor Pintar 15, Kreso Omerzel 12, Gerhard Lekse 6) Bulgaria 27 (Giorgi Petranov 12, Zdravko Jordanov 9, Nikolai Manev 6) East Germany 22 (Thomas Diehr 11, Herbert Mussehl 6, Roland Saß 5) Holland 19 (Ron Koppe 8, Rene Elzinga 8, Robert-Jan Munnecom 3) France 19 (David Ochocki 11, Christophe Dubernard 7, Christian Ianotto 1).

*Aggregate: **YUGOSLAVIA 61,** East Germany 49, Holland 48, Bulgaria 43 France 37.*
YUGOSLAVIA progress to Group C.
East Germany were allowed to compete as a separate nation to West Germany in the competition.

GROUP C

ROUND 1 (Lonigo, Italy, Sunday, May 19): Italy 31 (Armando Castagna 13, Valentino Furlanetto 10, Armando dal Chiele 8) Norway 28 (Lars Gunnestad 18, Einar Kyllingstad 8, Tor Einar Hjelm 2) Austria 26 (Franz Leitner 13, Andreas Bössner 9, Heinrich Schatzer 4) Poland 25 (Piotr Swist 14, Tomasz Gollob 8, Dariusz Sledz 3) Yugoslavia 9 (Kreso Omerzel 7, Gregor Pintar 2, Gerhard Leske 0).

ROUND 2 (Tarnow, Poland, Sunday, May 26): Norway 36 (Lars Gunnestad 16, Einar Kyllingstad 14, Tor Einar Hjelm 6) Poland 30 (Piotr Swist 14, Tomasz Gollob 11, Jacek Rempala 5) Italy 26 (Armando dal Chiele 12, Armando Castagna 9, Valentino Furlanetto 5) Austria 17 (Andreas Bössner 9, Heinrich Schatzer 5, Franz Leitner 3) Yugoslavia 10 (Gerhard Lekse 6, Gregor Pintar 4, Kreso Omerzel 0).

*Aggregate: **NORWAY 64,** Italy 57 Poland 55, Austria 43, Yugoslavia 30.*

GROUP B

ROUND 1 (Diedenbergen, Germany, Sunday, July 7): Hungary 38 (Zoltan Adorján 11, Jozsef Petrikovics 10, Zoltan Hajdu 8, Sándor Tihányi 6, Robert Nagy 3) West Germany 33 (Gerd Riss 11, Klaus Lausch 10, Tommy Dunker 8, Robert Barth 4, Andre Pollehn 0) Norway 28 (Lars Gunnestad 13, Tor Einar Hjelm 7, Arnt Førland 4, Einar Kyllingstad 4, Odd Pettersen, did not ride) Finland 21 (Vesa Ylinen 8, Mika Pellinen 8, Juha Moksunen 3, Olli Tyrvainen 2, Tomi Havu 0).

ROUND 2 (Debrecen, Hungary, Sunday, July 14): Hungary 53 (Zoltan Adorján 14, Jozsef Petrikovics 14, Zoltan Hajdu 10, Sándor Tihányi 10, Robert Nagy 5) West Germany 27 (Gerd Riss 9, Andre Pollehn 8, Klaus Lausch 7, Robert Barth 3, Peter Schroeck 0) Norway 26 (Lars Gunnestad 11, Einar Kyllingstad 6, Tor Einar Hjelm 6, Arnt Førland 3, Odd Pettersen 0) Finland 14 (Vesa Ylinen 8, Tomi Havu 3, Mika Pellinen 2, Juha Moksunen 1, Janne Moksunen 0).

*Aggregate: **HUNGARY 91,** West Germany 60, Norway 54, Finland 35.*

GROUP A

ROUND 1 (Pardubice, Czechoslovakia, Sunday, August 25): Sweden 49 (Per Jonsson 15, Henrik Gustafsson 15, Jimmy Nilsen 13, Tony Rickardsson 6, Peter Nahlin 0) Australia 35 (Steve Regeling 11, Craig Hodgson 9, Shane Bowes 6, Troy Butler 5, Leigh Adams 4) Czechoslovakia 21 (Zdenek Tesar 7, Vaclav Milik 7, Petr Vandirek 4, Antonin Kasper 3, Vladimir Kalina 0) Hungary 15 (Sándor Tihányi 8, Zoltan Adorján 3, Antal Kocso 2, Jozsef Petrikovics 1, Zoltan Hajdu 1).

*Aggregate: **SWEDEN 49,** Australia 35, Czechoslovakia 21, Hungary 15.*

1991 WORLD TEAM CUP FINAL

Vojens, Denmark
Saturday, September 14, 1991

1 DENMARK 51						
Jan O. Pedersen	3	3	3	3	3	15
Hans Nielsen	3	3	2	3	3	14
Tommy Knudsen	3	3	3	3	1	13
Gert Handberg	3	2	1	2	N	8
Brian Karger	1					1
2 Sweden 30						
Per Jonsson	2	2	3	1	1	9
Tony Rickardsson	1	1	1	2	2	7
Henrik Gustafsson	1	1	0	3	2	7
Jimmy Nilsen	0	1	2	1	3	7
Peter Nahlin	did not ride					
3 United States of America 28						
Sam Ermolenko	2	2	2	0	3	9
Billy Hamill	2	2	2	1	2	9
Greg Hancock	0	3	3	0	0	6
Rick Miller	1	1	2			4
Ronnie Correy	0	0	N			0
4 England 11						
Martin Dugard	2	0	0	2	0	4
Gary Havelock	1	1	1	0	0	3
Marvyn Cox	0	0	N	2	1	3
Chris Louis	1	0	0	N	0	1
Paul Thorp	0	0				0

JAN O. PEDERSEN, Billy Hamill and Olli Tyrvainen left it late...but for a distraught England it was a case of never!

For the first time since 1973, the Sunbrite Lions were knocked out of the World Pairs championship at the semi-final stage, an ignominious elimination behind speedway minnows from Norway and Czechoslovakia.

The England trio of Kelvin Tatum, Jeremy Doncaster and Gary Havelock (following the accidents in the 1990 World Pairs Final the FIM decided that all nations could take a third rider to meetings) argued bitterly that two vital decisions by referee Peter Von Koelln cost them a place in the World Final – but they had little sympathy from the folk back home appalled by another below-par performance on a world stage.

Tatum seethed: "It was the worst refereeing I have seen in eight years."

Incident number one: England's opening race where Tatum claimed he wasn't ready for the start because the green light stayed on from when he was leaving the pits.

Incident number two: A vital race for England against Hungary when they insisted that Zoltan Adorján had touched the tapes but got away with it to take a flier.

Team manager Eric Boocock agreed with Tatum: "It was a disgrace. This is the referee's first year as an FIM official and he was weak. In the first race the green light was on all the time and when I spoke to him about it he said he was sorry. I was on the centre green when Adorján got his flyer and threw my arms up in the air.

"The referee being sorry has cost us a World Final place."

Boocock worked tirelessly in the pits switching and changing his pairing.

He began the meeting with Gary Havelock and Kelvin Tatum; switched to a Havelock-Jeremy Doncaster partnership after the first race; and ended the meeting with Tatum and Doncaster in harness.

All to no avail as England recorded only one heat maximum all afternoon – against Austria!

Australia was also having a torrid time at Pardubice and after their silver medal in 1990 finished one point behind England as the semi-finals were dominated by the Scandinavians.

It was no surprise that Sweden and Denmark were the

respective winners but who could have forecast that little Norway would finish in front of both England and the Aussies in Czechoslovakia?

Their inspiration was 20-year-old Lars Gunnestad who was a model of consistency, winning his last two races and picking up four second places to confirm his status as his country's most exciting prospect since Dag Lovaas.

With Czechoslovakia pinching points when they were needed, England went into their last race knowing they had to claim at least three points against Sweden who had dropped only two points in their first five races: Gunnestad and Aussie Glenn Doyle splitting the highly impressive Per Jonsson-Henrik Gustafsson pairing.

It looked on as Tatum swept into a lead, followed by Gustafsson, the reigning World Champion and Doncaster at the back.

There was no way the Swedes were going to give England an easy passage to the World Final and, on the last lap, Gustafsson rounded Tatum to dump the Sunbrite Lions out of the competition. Embarrassing for England. Embarrassing for Australia.

And embarrassing for America in the other semi final at Pocking, Germany, where Pedersen, Hamill and Tyrvainen arrived 90 minutes after signing-in time and were barred from riding.

It raised the interesting thought: would similar punitive action have been taken if the nations hadn't had three riders on parade?

Jan O.'s absence didn't faze the Danes with Hans Nielsen and Tommy Knudsen dropping their only points to New Zealand and Germany in their last two races.

Gerd Riss's victory over the Dane sent the crowd wild and booked him a place in the final but America – with Sam Ermolenko having an unaccustomary off day – and the Kiwis were squeezed out by the solid Germans and an inspirational Armando Castagna who scored all but four of Italy's 20 points.

On the evidence of the two semi-finals the shoot-out for gold was between Denmark and Sweden.

That's exactly how it worked out with the Danes even more dominant than their four point winning margin suggested.

Had Jan O. Pedersen not stopped in heat four while leading then they would have recorded a full score.

Much interest centred on the battle for third place with Norway, Germany and Czechoslovakia all in contention up to the last three races.

The Czechs did themselves a power of good with a maximum over woeful Poland to finish on 18 points to temporarily take third place. Lars Gunnestad and Einar Kyllingstad swept to a 5-1 over Italy in heat 20 to give them 19 points.

That left Germany needing three points against Sweden to strike bronze – or two points to force a run-off.

They got neither as Gustafsson and Nilsen took the major placings to give Norway their first FIM medal since Sverre Harrfeldt was runner up to Barry Briggs in the 1966 World Final.

Qualifying Round

Wiener Neustadt, Austria, Sunday, April 7

1 NORWAY 28 (Lars Gunnestad 15, Einar Kyllingstad 13) 2 Soviet Union 26 (Rif Saitgareev 14, Mikhail Starostin 12, Oleg Kurguskin, did not ride) 3 Austria 20 (Anton Pilotto 11, Heinrich Schatzer 6, Andreas Bössner 3) 4 Finland 17 (Vesa Ylinen 13, Kai Niemi 4, Petri Vaatsio, did not ride) 5 Yugoslavia 14 (Gregor Pintar 7, Kreso Omerzel 7) 6 Holland 11 (Robert-Jan Munnecom 7, Rene Elzinga 4, Ron Koppe 0) 7 Bulgaria 10 (Giorgi Petranov 8, Nikolai Manev 2, Zdravko Jordanov 0).

Semi Finals

Pardubice, Czechoslovakia, Sunday, June 16

1 SWEDEN 27 (Per Jonsson 14, Henrik Gustafsson 13, Jimmy Nilsen, did not ride) 2 Norway 20 (Lars Gunnestad 14, Einar Kyllingstad 6, Tor Einar Hjelm, did not ride) 3 Czechoslovakia 20 (Bohumil Brhel 16, Zdenek Tesar 4, Antonin Kasper, did not ride) 4 England 19 (Kelvin Tatum 9, Gary Havelock 6, Jeremy Doncaster 4) 5 Australia 18 (Glenn Doyle 8, Todd Wiltshire 5, Leigh Adams 5) 6 Hungary 16 (Zoltan Adorján 8, Sándor Tihányi 8, Antal Kocso, did not ride) 7 Austria 6 (Franz Leitner 5, Andreas Bössner 1, Anton Pilotto, did not ride).

Pocking, Germany, Sunday, June 16

1 DENMARK 26 (Hans Nielsen 14, Tommy Knudsen 12, Jan O. Pedersen, did not ride) 2 Italy 20 (Armando Castagna 16, Valentino Furlanetto 4) 3 Germany 20 (Gerd Riss 12, Klaus Lausch 7, Tommy Dunker 1), 4 United States of America 19 (Ronnie Correy 12, Sam Ermolenko 7, Billy Hamill, did not ride) 5 New Zealand 17 (Mitch Shirra 15, Gary Allan 2) 6 Soviet Union 14 (Rif Saitgareev 9, Oleg Kurguskin 5, Mikhail Starostin 0) 7 Finland 10 (Vesa Ylinen 6, Juha Moksunen 4, Olli Tyrvainen, did not ride).

Jan O. Pedersen, Billy Hamill and Olli Tyrvainen arrived 90 minutes after the official signing on time and were barred from competing in the meeting. David Bargh (New Zealand) did not travel because of mechanical problems.

1991 WORLD PAIRS FINAL

Poznan, Poland
Saturday, July 20, 1991

1 DENMARK 28							
Hans Nielsen	**2**	3	**2**	3	**2**	**2**	14:4
Jan O. Pedersen	3	R	3	**2**	3	3	14:1
Tommy Knudsen, did not ride							
2 Sweden 24							
Henrik Gustafsson	3	**2**	N	N	1	3	9:1
Per Jonsson	**2**	N	3	2	0	N	7:1
Jimmy Nilsen	3	**2**	**1**	**2**			8:3
3 Norway 19							
Lars Gunnestad	2	0	3	3	0	3	11
Einar Kyllingstad	0	1	**2**	**2**	1	**2**	8:3
Tor Einar Hjelm, did not ride							
4 Germany 18							
Gerd Riss	1	3	1	**2**	1	1	9:1
Klaus Lausch	3	0	0	3	3	0	9
Tommy Dunker, did not ride							
5 Czechoslovakia 18							
Bohumil Brhel	2	2	0	3	2	3	12
Roman Matousek	**1**	**1**	1	N	**1**	**2**	6:4
Zdenek Tesar	0						0
6 Italy 10							
Armando Castagna	0	3	1	1	3	1	9
Valentino Furlanetto	1	0	0	0	N	0	1
Fabrizio Vesprini	0						0
7 Poland 9							
Ryszard Dolomisiewicz	1	**1**	R	1	2	0	5:1
Wojciech Zaluski	0	N	N	0	N	1	1
Piotr Swist	2	1	0				3

SIMON WIGG'S hopes of a first-ever World Long Track hat-trick disappeared, lost somewhere in the foliage surrounding the Marianske-lazne track.

For Wigg, gold medal winner in both 1989 and 1990, blamed the trees outside the 1,000 metre circuit for his carburation problems which reduced the power output from his Jawa.

Wigg offered the bizarre excuse as one of the reasons he looked strangely below full power after going to Czechoslovakia convinced he could achieve what had eluded Ivan Mauger, Egon Müller and Karl Maier before him...a third successive title success.

The England star, victorious in three of the previous six years, was virtually resigned to handing over the winner's laurels after his first two rides.

He scored only two fourth places and knew then that his dream had faded.

He improved later but couldn't even make it into the final six so had to watch uncomfortably from over the fence as the last race decided his successor.

Four of the six finalists had a realistic chance of the crown with Gerd Riss, using a lay-down engine, leading the scoreboard.

He had 19 points after the semi-finals, Jan O. Pedersen had 18, veteran Ales Dryml and Switzerland's Marcel Gerhard had 17 apiece.

The German, without a top three placing to his name, kept his nerve to blast around the outside of the unfortunate Dryml who, after being fastest in practice, had to be content for the second time in three years, with a silver medal.

Pedersen, who already had a World Pairs gold medal by this time, had to be content with a bronze for his collection after losing a run-off to the evergreen Dryml.

Britain's challenge had been soured from the moment the Auto-Cycle Union named our contestants, ignoring the claims of acknowledged world-class operators on shale to give further opportunities to the likes of Martin Hagon and Clayton Williams on the strength of their grass-track exploits.

Only after a lot of complaining was Andy Smith given a wild card entry – winning the preliminary round, finishing third in his semi-final and claiming eighth place overall, level on points with the defrocked Wigg.

Countrymen Mark Loram, Marvyn Cox and Steve Schofield also won through to the World Final to give the speedway fraternity a 100% record in the championship with all five entrants making it.

That, surely, must be food for thought for the blinkered A-C.U. officials who nominate the British riders.

1991 WORLD LONG TRACK FINAL

Marianske-lazne, Czechoslovakia
Sunday, July 28, 1991

1 GERD RISS	**5**	**5**	**4**	**5**	**5**	**24**
2 Ales Dryml	5	4	5	3	4	21
3 Jan O. Pedersen	4	4	5	5	3	21
4 Marcel Gerhard	5	4	4	4	1	18
5 Mitch Shirra	4	5	5	1	2	17
6 Stefan Dannö	3	5	0	4	R	12
7 Karl Maier	4	3	3	R		10
8 Andy Smith	2	2	4	2		10
9 Simon Wigg	2	2	3	3		10
10 Mark Loram	1	3	2	2		8
11 Klaus Lausch	3	3	1	0		7
12 Marvyn Cox	2	2	2	1		7
13 Steve Schofield	3	1	1			5
14 Erik Stenlund	1	0	3			4
15 Hans-Otto Pingel	0	1	2			3
16 Walter Scherwitzki	R	R	1			1
17 Jan Holub	1	0	R			1
18 Borivoj Hadek	R	1	0			1

JOE SCREEN and Dean Barker were on parade at Coventry in the Homefire World Under 21 Final...but were still counting the cost nine months later!

The two Brits had failed to arrive at their scheduled semi-final at Tcherkessk in the old Soviet Union after hanging about at the border awaiting the arrival of their entry visas.

By the time they arrived, flown out by travel agent Gareth Parry and delivered to their Warsaw Hotel, the plane taking riders to the meeting had already left.

Screen and Barker, unaware that the Russians had arranged for a second charter to wait at the airport for them, gave up at the border, turned round, headed back to Britain and straight into an unholy row!

The British authorities blamed the Russians. The Russians, in turn, blamed the Brits.

And the World Under 21 Final was threatened as Maurice Ducker, Chief Executive of the British Speedway Promoters' Association, delivered the ultimatum: if you don't seed our two riders we'll not stage the meeting.

It appeared to be hard-line diplomacy with an end result when FIM Track Commission President Gunter Sorber announced that the two British riders would face the Poles Adam Labedzki and Jacek Rempala in two pre-World Final races, with the best placed Englishman definitely going through to be joined by the top scorer of the remaining three riders.

A couple of weeks later that decision was overruled by FIM Secretary General Guy Maitre who ordered that only one Englishman could be seeded to the meeting.

Consequently Screen defeated Barker 2-0 in a race-off at Brandon and lined up as favourite to succeed Chris Louis as Under 21 Champion.

His chances evaporated when his engine seized while he was leading the opening race and, not for the first time, the principal contenders were two Danes.

Brian Andersen, who had agreed to join Newcastle during the 24 hours the meeting was delayed because of rain, beat Morten Andersen in a decider with Glasgow's Jason Lyons overcoming a slow start to grab third place ahead of the luckless Screen who had suffered another setback to his hopes when he missed the re-arranged practice.

He insisted another administrative cock-up had denied him valuable practice time on the track claiming: "I was told the practice would be at three o'clock on the Monday but when I arrived I was told I was two hours late.

"Apparently there had been a riders' briefing at which they were told to report at 1 p.m. If I'd be allowed to practice my motor would have blown then instead of when I was leading the first race."

EDITOR'S NOTE: As of February 1, 1992, Dean Barker and Joe Screen were still awaiting payment of their expenses for the aborted trip to Tcherkessk.

1991 WORLD UNDER 21 FINAL

Coventry, England
Monday, September 30

1 BRIAN ANDERSEN	**3**	**2**	**3**	**3**	**3**	**14**	**+3**
2 Morten Andersen	2	3	3	3	3	14	+2
3 Jason Lyons	1	2	2	3	3	11	
4 Shane Parker	3	3	3	1	R	10	
5 Joe Screen	R	3	3	2	2	10	
6 Jacob Olsen	3	2	2	0	2	9	
7 Niklas Klingberg	0	1	1	3	3	8	
8 Frede Schøtt	1	2	2	2	1	8	
9 Joakim Karlsson	2	3	fx	0	1	6	
10 Jimmy Engman	2	1	0	1	2	6	
11 Viktor Gaidym	2	0	1	2	1	6	
12 Piotr Paluch	3	1	1	0	0	5	
13 Robert Kuzdzal	1	1	1	1	0	4	
14 Marek Hucko	1	0	2	R	0	3	
15 Zsolt Böszörmenyi	F	0	0	1	1	2	
16 Adam Labedzki	0	0	fn	N	N	0	
Reserves							
Dean Barker	2					2	
Jacek Rempala	0	2				2	

■ FOR full details of the 1992 World Championship events please consult the World Championship section at the front of the *1993 SPEEDWAY YEARBOOK*.

■ Also included in that section are the complete past results of the individual, pairs, team, long-track and Under 21 World Finals.

ENGLAND bosses Eric Boocock and Colin Pratt suffered a shock defeat in the inaugural Sunbrite Inter Nations Championship – but could at least look back on the series as the launchpad for two promising international careers.

World Under 21 Champion Chris Louis and Belle Vue's British Junior title-holder Joe Screen were both given their debut Sunbrite Lions' caps in the opening match of a three-Test series against Sweden and Australia as the Sunbrite Inter Nations Championship splashed off to a watery and abandoned start at Glasgow's Shawfield Park, the first official senior international in Scotland for nearly two decades.

Louis didn't have to wait long to become only the second son of a former international to represent his country (Neil Middleditch had been the other when he joined his father Ken as an England Test rider) as he had been named for the second match little more than 48 hours later at Poole where his father John saw him win his first two rides in an England race-jacket.

But teenager Screen had to be a little more patient. He had originally been picked for the planned third in the series at Oxford but was withdrawn, along with Louis, so that they could race for their respective club sides in a Sunbrite League Division One match. He didn't get his chance until the following month when he dropped only four points from six rides against America.

That series, also sponsored by Coal Products Limited who continued their backing for the national team, punctuated the Inter Nations Championship as it was decided to re-stage the rained off first Test back at Shawfield Park in the autumn when it became the deciding match of a top-heavy triangular tournament in which Australia began and ended as makeweights to the more powerful English and Swedish squads.

There was considerable confusion over the way the eventual winners would be decided.

Initially it was announced that the three countries would carry points forward to the third Test when double points would be at stake but this quite farcical proposal was quietly dropped without any beating of the drums.

Instead it was agreed that the rubber would rest with the finishing positions of each nation after the three matches had been completed.

With England winning narrowly at Poole, thanks to a last race 5-1 against Australia from home favourite Marvyn Cox and Jeremy Doncaster, and Sweden gaining ample revenge at Oxford where there was the rarity of two unbeaten riders on different sides (Martin Dugard for England and Jimmy Nilsen for the Swedes) everything was set up for a final showdown back at Shawfield.

This time the weather was favourable and England called up another debutant in Ipswich's David Norris who had wholly impressed the England management duo throughout the summer but particularly at the H.E.A.T. Team Championship Final at Peterborough.

Norris was happy to make the long trip from his Sussex home to Scotland even though he was only reserve and was rewarded with his first two international outings as a replacement for tape-toucher Paul Thorp and, later, the out of sorts Sean Wilson.

Under the competition formula each nation met each other six times during the meeting and England and Sweden squared their clashes 18-18.

But a shock 5-1 to Australia against the Sunbrite Lions in heat 15 when local reserve Jason Lyons took the win, and a subsequent race maximum for Sweden against Steve Regeling and Shane Bowes determined the series in Sweden's favour.

Sandwiched between the Oxford and Glasgow Tests, the Sunbrite Lions resumed hostilities with the United States after a year off the international calendar.

It was another opportunity to blood the younger faces with Louis being picked for all three Tests, Second Division Andy Galvin collecting his first cap at Monmore Green and Dean Standing completing a fairy-tale revival!

He had joined Second Division Stoke at the beginning of the season, slumped to reserve and then been allowed to join First Division Swindon where his form rocketed so meteorically that he was brought in as a late, late replacement for the injured Joe Screen in front of his own home fans.

How many other riders have soared from Second Division reserve to England international in a matter of only 86 days?

The three-match series began badly in the opening race at Bradford when, in a crash reminiscent of the first heat of the fateful 1990 World Team Cup Final, Andy Smith and Rick Miller came down heavily in the first and second turn and were unable to continue.

Miller damaged his knee but was soon back in action but it was to be Smudger's last race of the season as he cracked a couple of bones in his neck and also suffered painful rib injuries.

American manager John Scott was already under severe pressure with only nine Californians racing in the 1991 Sunbrite League of whom one, Shawn Moran, was ruled out because he had taken out a British ACU licence.

Kelly Moran was again missing – this time suffering mechanical problems at the World Championship semi-final in Germany – and when skipper Sam Ermolenko aggravated a knee injury in the same meeting the United States had to bring in holiday-making Donny Odom to track a rider in each race at Wolverhampton!

They had five scorers only but fought manfully although the final scoreline was somewhat flattering as they trailed by 16 points with five races to go and then staged a fighting recovery to collected two 5-1s and a couple of 4-2s in heats 14 to 17!

At Swindon, England built up a 14-point lead after only seven heats but once again the Americans staging a late revival, sparked off by Bobby Ott's dramatic change of fortune.

The Eastbourne star didn't score a point in his first three rides but then was headed only by an unbeaten Gary Havelock in the second half of the meeting.

Once again Odom was called up but this time he didn't need to go on track with reserve Dukie Ermolenko covering all six programmed rides that his injured brother missed.

Kelly Moran? He was absent again. This time at the christening of his daughter Chelsea!

SUNBRITE INTER NATIONS CHAMPIONSHIP

First Test, at Poole, Tuesday, July 9

ENGLAND 46			
1 †Kelvin Tatum	**3 3 3 3**	**12**	
2 Martin Dugard	1 1 2 2	6	2
3 Gary Havelock	2 1 3 1	7	1
4 §Chris Louis	3 3 0 fx	6	
5 Marvyn Cox	1 1 3 2	7	3
6 Jeremy Doncaster	2 2 1 3	8	
7 Paul Thorp	*did not ride*		
SWEDEN 45			
1 †Per Jonsson	2 2 3 2	9	2
2 Tony Rickardsson	0 3 2 3	8	1
3 Henrik Gustafsson	3 3 2 3	11	
4 Mikael Blixt	0 0 1 2	3	2
5 Jimmy Nilsen	3 2 0 2	7	2
6 Peter Nahlin	R 3 1 3	7	
7 Tony Olsson	*did not ride*		
AUSTRALIA 16			
1 †Todd Wiltshire	1 0 1 fx	2	
2 Steve Regeling	0 2 0 N	2	
3 Leigh Adams	1 2 0 1	4	1
4 Craig Hodgson	2 0 N 0	2	
5 Glenn Doyle	0 fx N 0	0	
6 Shane Bowes	1 1 0 N	2	
7 Mick Poole	2 1 1 R	4	

Second Test, at Oxford, Friday, July 12

ENGLAND 36			
1 †Kelvin Tatum	3 1 3 2	9	
2 Richard Knight	1 F N N	1	
3 Martin Dugard	**3 3 3 3**	**12**	
4 Gary Havelock	1 1 0 0	2	
5 Marvyn Cox	3 2 E 0	5	1
6 Dean Barker	1 3 X N	4	
7 Sean Wilson	0 1 2	3	1
SWEDEN 40			
1 †Per Jonsson	2 N 2 3	7	
2 Tony Rickardsson	X 2 1 0	3	2
3 Henrik Gustafsson	0 0 3 3	6	
4 Mikael Blixt	2 N N N	2	
5 Jimmy Nilsen	**3 3 2 3**	**11**	**1**
6 Peter Nahlin	F 2 3 0	5	1
7 Dennis Löfqvist	3 2 0 1	6	
AUSTRALIA 31			
1 Stephen Davies	2 1 3 2	8	1
2 Troy Butler	X 2 0 1	3	1
3 Leigh Adams	1 1 1 2	5	1
4 Craig Hodgson	3 0 2 1	6	1
5 Glenn Doyle	2 N 2 2	6	
6 Steve Regeling	0 1 1 1	3	2
7 Shane Bowes	F	0	

Third Test, at Glasgow, Sunday, October 6

ENGLAND 39			
1 Paul Thorp	3 E 1 0	4	
2 Sean Wilson	0 2 0 N	2	
3 Martin Dugard	1 2 3 1	7	1
4 Joe Screen	3 3 0 3	9	
5 Gary Havelock	2 3 1 3	9	
6 Mark Loram	0 2 3 1	6	1
7 §David Norris	1 1	2	1
SWEDEN 44			
1 †Jimmy Nilsen	2 3 1 2	8	
2 Peter Nahlin	1 1 3 0	5	1
3 Henrik Gustafsson	3 1 2 3	9	
4 Tony Rickardsson	2 0 1 2	5	3
5 Per Jonsson	1 3 3 3	10	
6 Tony Olsson	3 0 2 2	7	2
7 Dennis Löfqvist	*did not ride*		
AUSTRALIA 25			
1 †Steve Regeling	0 0 N 0	0	
2 Shane Bowes	2 3 0 1	6	
3 Tony Langdon	0 1 N 0	1	
4 Craig Hodgson	1 0 0 N	1	
5 Leigh Adams	2 2 2 2	8	1
6 Glenn Doyle	0 1 X N	1	1
7 Jason Lyons	2 1 3 2	8	

ENGLAND v UNITED STATES OF AMERICA

First Test, at Bradford, Sunday, August 4

ENGLAND 64			
1 †Kelvin Tatum	2 1 3 3 2 3	14	1
2 Andy Smith	fnN N N N N	0	
3 Gary Havelock	3 3 2 2 3 3	16	1
4 Jeremy Doncaster	0 2 1 3 1 1	8	2
5 Paul Thorp	3 1 1 1 3 1	10	3
6 Chris Louis	0 0 2 2 0 2	6	
7 Marvyn Cox	*did not arrive*		
8 Sean Wilson	3 3 0 1 1 2	10	2
UNITED STATES OF AMERICA 44			
1 †Sam Ermolenko	1 1 3 2 2 3	12	
2 Rick Miller	fnN N N N N	0	
3 Billy Hamill	1 3 1 1 2 1	9	2
4 Greg Hancock	2 2 2 0 1 0	7	2
5 Ronnie Correy	2 2 3 R 3 2	12	
6 Bobby Ott	1 0 0 3 0 0	4	1
7 Charles Ermolenko	F 0 0 0 0 0	0	

Second Test, at Wolverhampton, Monday, August 19

ENGLAND 56			
1 †Kelvin Tatum	2 0 2 2 0 0	6	
2 Chris Louis	0 3 1 1 2 2	9	2
3 §Joe Screen	2 3 3 1 2 1	12	2
4 Martin Dugard	3 2 2 3 1 2	13	3
5 Gary Havelock	2 1 2 2 1 1	9	2
6 Paul Thorp	1 N N N N N	1	1
7 Mark Loram	2 1 3 0	6	1
8 §Andy Galvin	0	0	
UNITED STATES OF AMERICA 52			
1 †Sam Ermolenko	N N N N N N	-	
2 Greg Hancock	3 1 3 3 3 3	16	
3 Billy Hamill	1 3 3 2 2 3	14	1
4 Kelly Moran	N N N N N N	-	
5 Ronnie Correy	3 1 0 R 1 3	8	1
6 Bobby Ott	R 2 1 1 3 fx	7	
7 Charles Ermolenko	1 0 F 0 3 2 1	7	1
8 Donny Odom	0 0 0 0 0	0	

Third Test, at Swindon, Sunday, August 25

ENGLAND 57			
1 †Kelvin Tatum	2 3 2 2 0 0	9	1
2 Mark Loram	3 2 F N N N	5	1
3 Jeremy Doncaster	3 1 1 N 2 1	8	2
4 Martin Dugard	0 2 3 0 R N	5	
5 Gary Havelock	**3 3 2 3 3 2**	**16**	**2**
6 Chris Louis	2 0 3 0 1 3	9	1
7 Andrew Silver	1 1 2	4	
8 §Dean Standing	0 1	1	
UNITED STATES OF AMERICA 51			
1 †Sam Ermolenko	N N N N N N	-	
2 Ronnie Correy	1 3 1 3 3 1	12	
3 Billy Hamill	2 1 1 2 2 2	10	3
4 Greg Hancock	1 2 3 3 0 3	12	1
5 Rick Miller	1 1 2 1 2 R	7	2
6 Bobby Ott	0 0 0 2 3 3	8	
7 Charles Ermolenko	R 0 0 1 1 0	2	
8 Donny Odom	*did not ride*		

The original staging of the First Test at Glasgow on Sunday, July 7, was abandoned after five heats because of heavy rain and a waterlogged track. The scores were: ENGLAND 6** (1 †Kelvin Tatum 0- 0, 2 §Joe Screen 2- 2, 3 Gary Havelock fx- 0, 4 Mark Loram 3- 3, 5 Paul Thorp R- 0, 6 §Chris Louis 1- 1, 7 Sean Wilson, did not ride) **SWEDEN 15** (1 †Per Jonsson 3- R- 3, 2 Tony Rickardsson 1-2- 3, 3 Henrik Gustafsson 3- 3, 4 Mikael Blixt 1- 1, 5 Jimmy Nilsen **2**- 2:1, 6 Peter Nahlin 3- 3, 7 Tony Olsson, did not ride) **AUSTRALIA 8** (1 †Todd Wiltshire 2- 2, 2 Jason Lyons **1**- 1:1, 3 Leigh Adams 2- 2, 4 Craig Hodgson fx- 0, 5 Glenn Doyle F- 0, 6 Steve Regeling 3- 3, 7 Shane Bowes, did not ride). **The Test was re-staged at Glasgow on Sunday, October 6.

HUNGARIAN TOUR OF DIVISION TWO

First match, Milton Keynes, Tuesday, April 16

MILTON KEYNES 59			
1 Gordon Kennett	2 2 3 3 1	11	1
2 Paul Woods	1 3 3 2	9	2
3 Troy Butler	F 3 3 3 3	12	
4 Nigel De'ath	1 3 2 2	8	1
5 †Peter Glanz	3 2 1 2	8	3
6 Jon Cooper	2 3 0 2	7	1
7 Paul Blackbird	3 1 R F	4	
HUNGARY 31			
1 †Zoltan Adorján	0 1 2 R	3	
2 Sándor Tihányi	3 0 2 T	5	
3 Jozsef Petrikovics	2 0 3 1 0	6	1
4 Robert Nagy	fx 1 1 1 2	5	1
5 Lászlo Bódí	2 2 1 1 0	6	
6 Zoltan Hajdu	1 1 0 3	5	
7 Csaba Hell	0 1 0 0	1	

Second match, at Middlesbrough, Thursday, April 18

MIDDLESBROUGH 57			
1 Darren Sumner	1 R 2 3	6	1
2 Mark Lemon	0 2 2 3	7	
3 Paul Bentley	3 R 3 2	8	1
4 David Cheshire	3 2 2 3 1	11	3
5 †Jamie Luckhurst	2 3 3 3 2	13	1
6 Simon Green	2 2 3 F	7	1
7 Duncan Chapman	1 1 1 2	5	3
HUNGARY 32			
1 †Zoltan Adorján	3 1 3 2 1 3	13	
2 Sándor Tihányi	2 0 0 1 fx	3	2
3 Jozsef Petrikovics	0 1 T N	1	
4 Robert Nagy	0 X 0 0 0	0	
5 Zoltan Hajdu	1 2 0 N	3	
6 Lászlo Bódí	3 3 2 1 1 1	11	
7 Csaba Hell	0 1 T T 0	1	

Third match, at Edinburgh, Friday, April 19

EDINBURGH 58			
1 Les Collins	3 3 2 1	9	
2 Darrin Winkler	F F 1 fx	1	
3 †Brett Saunders	**3 3 2 2**	**10**	**2**
4 Michael Coles	**2 2 3 2 3**	**12**	**3**
5 Frede Schøtt	**3 3 3 3**	**12**	
6 Carsten Schøtt	R 1 1 0	2	
7 Nigel Alderton	3 3 3 3 fx	12	
HUNGARY 32			
1 †Zoltan Adorján	1 1 0 0	2	1
2 Robert Nagy	2 R 2 1 1 2	8	
3 Zoltan Hajdu	2 2 2 3 2 1	12	1
4 Jozsef Petrikovics	1 0 1 T	2	
5 Lászlo Bódí	0 2 1 0 1	4	1
6 Robert Csillik	1 1 T 0 0	2	2
7 Csaba Hell	2 0 0 T	2	

Fourth match, at Glasgow, Sunday, April 21

GLASGOW 39			
1 †Steve Lawson	3 0 0 1	4	
2 Sean Courtney	0 2 3 1	6	
3 Shane Bowes	3 1 1 3 1	9	
4 Jason Lyons	2 2 0 F	4	1
5 Kenny McKinna	3 0 3 3 R	9	
6 Martin McKinna	2 fx 0 1	3	
7 Mick Powell	1 0 T 3 0	4	1
HUNGARY 51			
1 †Zoltan Adorján	2 3 2 1 2	10	2
2 Sándor Tihányi	1 1 2 0	4	1
3 Jozsef Petrikovics	fnN 0 N	0	
4 Robert Nagy	0 3 2 2 3	10	1
5 Lászlo Bódí	1 2 2 1	6	3
6 Robert Csillik	0 1 1 2 2	6	1
7 Zoltan Hajdu	3 2 3 1 3 3	15	1

Fifth match, at Newcastle, Monday, April 22

NEWCASTLE 54			
1 David Bargh	2 3 3 3 2 2	15	
2 Richard Juul	*rider replacement*		
3 Jamie Habbin	2 1 3 0 3	9	
4 Brian Nixon	fx 1 N 0 N	1	
5 †Martin Dixon	0 3 1 2 2 1	9	4
6 Mark Thorpe	2 1 2 2 2	9	4
7 Scott Lamb	3 2 1 2 3	11	1
HUNGARY 36			
1 †Sándor Tihányi	1 0 T 1	2	
2 Robert Nagy	3 1 2 1 1 0	8	
3 Zoltan Adorján	3 2 3 3 3 3	17	
4 Zoltan Hajdu	2 1 0 0	3	
5 Csaba Hell	3 0 1 0	4	
6 Robert Csillik	1 0 0 1	2	
7 Lászlo Bódí	0 0 0 N	0	

● **LISTED below are the number of amendments to the best-selling The Complete History of the British League. Owing to a computer malfunction which forced the cancellation of publication of the 1992 Speedway Yearbook some amendments may have been lost from the records.**

● **If you are aware of any not listed below please contact Front Page Books with details and they will be included in the 1994 Speedway Yearbook.**

■ *On page 3 Roll of Honour it is inadvertently stated that Peter Collins was the 1977 World Champion. This is, of course, a typographical error and should read Ivan Mauger.*

■ *On Page 14 Division Two Tables and Results the result of the 1981 National League Riders' Championship Final has been omitted:*

1981 National League Riders' Championship Final

Saturday, September 26, Wimbledon:
1 Mike Ferreira 15, 2 Simon Wigg 13, 3 Bruce Cribb 11, 4 Dave Perks 10, Neil Collins 10, 6 Steve Wilcock 9, 7 Steve Lawson 8, 8 Barry Thomas 8, Kelvin Mullarkey 8, 10 Steve Finch 6, 11 Wayne Brown 5, 12 Ian Gledhill 4, 13 Robert Maxfield 4, 14 David Gagen 3, 15 David Bargh 3, 16 Bob Humphreys 2.*Track reserves: John Barclay 1, Neville Moore 0. Sponsors: Mirror Newspapers.*

■ *On page 19 in some editions the team names are not at the top of the Results charts. The missing teams should read, left to right: Arena Essex, Berwick, Birmingham, Boston, Canterbury, Eastbourne, Edinburgh, Exeter, Glasgow, Hackney, Long Eaton, Middlesbrough, Mildenhall, Milton Keynes, Newcastle, Peterborough, Poole, Rye House, Stoke and Wimbledon.*

■ *On Page 21 Division Two Tables and Results the result of the 1988 National League Riders' Championship Final has been omitted:*

1988 National League Riders' Championship Final

Saturday, September 10, Coventry:
1 Troy Butler 15, 2 Mark Loram 11, 3 Kenny McKinna 11, 4 Graham Jones 10, 5 Melvyn Taylor 10, 6 Steve Schofield 9, 7 Kevin Jolly 9, 8 Gordon Kennett 8, 9 Mark Fiora 7, 10 Ian Barney 6, 11 Steve Regeling 6, 12 Jens Rasmussen 5, 13 Martin Goodwin 5, 14 Jamie Luckhurst 4, 15 Keith White 3, 16 Mark Courtney 1. *Track reserve: Mike Bacon 0. Sponsors: Jawa-Barum.*

■ *On page 21 Division Two Tables and Results the following results have been omitted:*

Mildenhall 52.5 Arena Essex 43.5; Poole 50.5 Eastbourne 45.5.

■ *On page 21 in some editions the team names are not at the top of the Results charts. The teams should read, left to right: Arena Essex, Berwick, Eastbourne, Edinburgh, Exeter, Glasgow, Hackney, Long Eaton, Middlesbrough, Mildenhall, Milton Keynes, Peterborough, Poole, Rye House, Stoke and Wimbledon.*

■ *Division One Averages, page 9, Nigel Boocock's 1965 Coventry average should read as follows:*

	M	R	Pts	BP	TPts	Ave	F	P	Total
§§Nigel Boocock	**35**	**150**	**395.0**	**22.0**	**417.0**	**11.120**	**10**	**8**	**18**

■ *The following seasonal averages are missing from the Division One Averages section.*

WIMBLEDON...WIMBLEDON
1974...1974...1974...1974...1974...1974

	M	R	Pts	BP	TPts	Ave	F	P	Total
§Barry Briggs	30	129	294.0	6.0	300.0	9.302	3	1	4
Trevor Hedge	**34**	**137**	**225.0**	**18.0**	**243.0**	**7.095**	**3**		**3**
Graeme Stapleton	**34**	**138**	**205.0**	**24.0**	**229.0**	**6.638**			
Bert Harkins	32	122	144.0	34.0	178.0	5.836	1	1	2
§Roger Johns	23	88	98.0	22.0	120.0	5.455			
Neil Cameron	**34**	**109**	**126.0**	**15.0**	**141.0**	**5.174**			
Reg Luckhurst	33	121	128.0	24.0	152.0	5.025			
Rob Jones	13	33	21.0	4.0	25.0	3.030			
§§Paul Dowdall	1	3	1.0	0.0	1.0	1.333			

WOLVERHAMPTON...WOLVERHAMPTON
1978...1978...1978...1978...1978...1978

	M	R	Pts	BP	TPts	Ave	F	P	Total
Hans Nielsen	32	146	309.0	18.0	327.0	8.959	5	1	6
Jim McMillan	38	169	355.0	11.0	366.0	8.663	3		3
§Dave Morton	37	160	328.0	12.0	340.0	8.500	1	1	2
Dave Trownson	3	12	16.0	3.0	19.0	6.333			
§Edgar Stangeland	26	93	83.0	12.0	95.0	4.086			
Carl Askew	2	7	6.0	1.0	7.0	4.000			
§Sean Willmott	1	3	2.0	1.0	3.0	4.000			
§Mike Spink	1	2	1.0	1.0	2.0	4.000			
§§Hasse Danielsson	29	100	79.0	17.0	96.0	3.840			
§Brian Woodward	38	130	100.0	22.0	122.0	3.754			
§§Knud Ellegaard	27	85	61.0	16.0	77.0	3.624			
§§Dave Allen	2	4	2.0	1.0	3.0	3.000			
Steve Lomas	12	39	21.0	4.0	25.0	2.564			
§§Ivan Blacka	1	4	1.0	1.0	2.0	2.000			
Mark Stokes	1	2	1.0	0.0	1.0	2.000			
§Steve Wilcock	4	10	4.0	0.0	4.0	1.600			
§John Barker	1	3	0.0	0.0	0.0	0.000			
Robert Hollingworth	1	2	0.0	0.0	0.0	0.000			
Arthur Browning	1	1	0.0	0.0	0.0	0.000			

SUBSCRIBERS

I WOULD like to offer my personal thanks and appreciation to all the Subscribers listed below who showed their faith in Front Page Books and myself and waited patiently for this edition of THE SPEEDWAY YEARBOOK.
I would also like to apologise for the non-publication of the 1992 edition for reasons beyond the control of either myself or Front Page Books.

PETER OAKES

Kevin Hammond
Geoff Hingley
Paul Church
David Kinvig
Ken Weaver
Colin Roy Pheasant
Sue & Dave Farthing
Alan Hunt
Bob Hipkiss
Graham & Marion Pigney
Mark & Deb Harvey
Bridget Brockman
David Coulson
Ben Henshaw
Neil Reynolds
Anthony Brown
Mike & Jessica Berry
Anne & Trevor Kimberley
Michael & Dorothy Aris
Kevyn Raymond Jones
Tony Webb
David J. Carter
Roy Nuttall
Rebecca Jarvis
Mike Noble
Darren Evans
T.A. Griffiths
Paul & Rosie Brown
Stuart Brownhill
Steve Brown
Graham S. Rowland
G.F. Russell
Michael Hodson
Paul Frankum
David Hood
Sam Fowler
Garry Chance
Gerald Quinney
Colin Marshall
Nigel John Palmer
Gary Marshall
Mick Richardson
Maria Vockins
Michael Piggins
John Oughton
Gary Bird
Joseph Allan Green
Bob Tasker
Michael & Margaret Colman
David Armstrong
Peter Pickup
Roger Airey
Peter Corderoy
Nigel Whitworth
Patricia A. Palmer
Geoff Wilson
Michael Stockham
Tim Robinson, Strapleford
Phil Edwards
Neil Howard Southam
Ian Smith
David Shadbolt
Claire Vockins
Brian J. Deakin
Alan Marriott
William J. Playle
Dave Eaton
Mike Hunter
Sally Prodger (Eastbourne Speedway)
Barry Bowles
Bryan Alan Utley
James Wilson
Richard Smethurst
Peter Alan Scully
Leslie Ring
James Charles Purchase
Ron Bursill
Graham L. Smith
Paul M. Markham
Mark A. Robinson
I.R. Willis
Mrs. L.C. Martin
Wayne Nation & Sarah Dunford
Sharon J. Fisher
Sid Kent
David Whurr
Jem Cole
Graham Smith
Dave Bone
Les Hughes
Alan Hickson
Leslie O'Keeffe
Keith Knapton
Chris Knights
Joy Evans
John Henry Hilton
David Jones
Raymond Brewer
Mr. R.J. Norman (Bob)
Andrew Pinfield
Craig Saul
J.C. Vine
Claire Elston
David Wright
David Bishop
Grahame E. Andrews
John Bonner
Andrew Bayliss
Colin Pratt
Geoff Shelton
Mr. B. Coe
James Sutherland
David W. Stimpson
Paul L. Jeffries
Jerry Harrison
Julie Brady
Terry Hunt
Jayne Higgins
Alan Barwick
Stephen Arthur Hopkins
David Greaves
Eddie Baker
Melvin England
Andrew Shurey
John R. Clarkson
David Kemp
Malcolm Owen
A. John Moore
Robert T. Bamford
Keith & Les Burden
Andrew Townshend
Vic Butcher
Peter Charles Scaife
Paul Eggett
Trevor James
Mike 'Mimmo' Moseley
Tony Jackson
Janey Brown
David G. Murray
Richard & Tina Butler
Christopher M. Weston
George Sheridan
Keith Farman - Yarmouth Bloater
David Woodley
The Sales Family
Frank Billington
James Edward Gooderham
Geoff Ledger
Ray Allan
Charles McKay
Malcolm Preen
Kevin Stuart Rutter
The Colven Family & Ian Rickards
Mel Homer
Michael Williams
Gail Hood
Chris & Lorraine Durno
John Plumbley
Nigel Pearson
Chiefy Lee
Mike Treadwell
Gary Crapper
Ron Haglington
Tony Hambidge
Adrian Bell
Neil Hubbert
Terry Warren
Deidre & Peter Cuckow
Barrie J. Wood
R. Payne
Eileen & Russell Large
Jeff Lukomiak
Brian A. Pearson
Dave Wildman
Keith James Halliwell
E.V. Walder
Jeremy Frosdick
Steve 'P.E.P. Talk' Allen
Graham Jarvis
Terry Catley
Carol Garland
Mr. W.A. Giles
Trevor Webb
S.C. Manton
John Vaughan
David Macdonald
Peter H. Gardner
John Treadwell
Dawn & Peter Gardner
BBD120 NLM831
Nigel Platt
Marianne Batten
Stephen Rowland
Scott & Martin Somerville
Peter & Ann Foster
Stan & Judy Ward
Nicholas Jennings
John Charles Smith
Dodgson Family
Derek & Sandra Richardson
Mr. R.W. Dredge
Janet & Gerry Shoesmith
Julie & Bill Gordon
Gary Hicks
Stanley Simpson
Steve Wilkes
Bob Boardman
F. Dacey
A.P. Reader
Paul Fiddes
Jonathan Crawford
H.W. Jones
Philip John Allen
Kevin Neil Maynell
Adrian Fenwick
Mark Aspinall
Peter Amass
Derek J. Hosie
Bob Lyon & Sally Hicks
Alan Beckett
John Richardson
Dave Day
John Hutton
Mr. J.J. McCormacaigh
Michael C. Tandy
Kelvin Thompson
Peter Foster
Brian & Marcia Dolbear
John William Rolfe
Craig McCurdy
Martyn Neil Green
Gary Thompson
Andy Marlow
John Hill
Roger Rose
Stefan Nodesjo
Jeff Bone
Nicholas S. Gardner
Dave Bauer
R.G. Newton
D.R. Howarth
Ken Taylor
Barry Richardson
Len Webster
Trevor John Mundon
Paul Cureton
Diane Smith & Linda Smith
Stephen Chaloner
Rob Brading
M.C. Fotty
Rosemary Mellers
Neil Girdham
J.H. Woods
In Memory of H.H. Howard

1993 DIARY DATES

WORLD UNDER 21 CHAMPIONSHIP

Holder: Leigh Adams

Qualifying Round 1 (Pfaffenhofen, Germany, Sunday, May 16): CIS 2, Czechoslovakia 2, Denmark 2, Germany 2, Great Britain 2, Hungary 2, Norway 2, Sweden 2.
Qualifying Round 2 (Lonigo, Italy, Sunday, May 16): Austria 2, CIS 2, Czechoslovakia 2, Germany 2, Holland 2, Hungary 2, Italy 2, Poland 2.
Qualifying Round 3 (Brokstedt, Germany, Saturday, May 1): Australia 2, Czechoslovakia 2, Denmark 2, Germany 2, Poland 2, Sweden 2, Ukraine 2, Finland 1, New Zealand 1.
Qualifying Round 4 (Fjelsted, Denmark, Sunday, May 16): Denmark 3, Sweden 3, Finland 2, Great Britain 2, Norway 2, Poland 2, Latvia 1, United States of America 1.
Semi Final 1 (Olching, Germany, Tuesday, June 10): Qualifiers from Qualifying rounds.
Semi Final 2 (Wroclaw, Poland, Sunday, July 11)

WORLD FINAL (Pardubice, Czechoslovakia, Sunday, August 15): Eight qualifiers from each semi final.

WORLD LONG TRACK CHAMPIONSHIP

Holder: Marcel Gerhard

Qualifying Round (Pfarrkirchen, Germany, Sunday, June 6): Germany 3, CIS 2, France 2, Poland 2, Ukraine 2, Australia 1, Czechoslovakia 1, Great Britain 1, Holland 1, Hungary 1, Italy 1, Latvia 1.
Semi Final 1 (Herxheim, Germany, Sunday, July 4): Germany 4, Great Britain 3, Czechoslovakia 2, Sweden 2, Denmark 1, Italy 1, Norway 1, Switzerland 1, United States of America 1, two qualifiers from Qualifying round.
Semi Final 2 (Marianske-lazne, Czechoslovakia, Sunday, July 4): Czechoslovakia 4, Germany 3, Great Britain 3, CIS 2, New Zealand 2, Austria 1, Hungary 1, two qualifiers from Qualifying round.
Semi Final 3 (Scheeßel, Germany, Sunday, July 4): Germany 3, Great Britain 3, Finland 2, Sweden 2, Argentina 1, Australia 1, Czechoslovakia 1, Denmark 1, Norway 1, United States of America 1, two qualifiers from qualifying round.

WORLD FINAL (Mühldorf, Germany, Sunday, September 26): Six qualifiers from each of the three semi finals.

CHAMPIONS CUP

Holder: Gert Handberg

FINAL (Tampere, Finland, Saturday, May 29): National champs from Australia, Austria, CIS, Czechoslovakia, Denmark, Finland, Germany, Great Britain, Holland, Hungary, Italy, Latvia, Norway, Poland, Slovenia, Sweden.

WORLD INDIVIDUAL CHAMPIONSHIP

Holder: Gary Havelock (England)

Preliminary Round 1 (Ludwigslust, Germany, Sunday, April 25): Qualifiers: Germany 3, Austria 2, CIS (Russia) 2, Hungary 2, Italy 2, Slovenia 2, Argentina 1, Holland 1, Latvia 1.
Preliminary Round 2 (Tcherkessk, Russia, Sunday, April 25): Qualifiers: CIS 3, Germany 3, Austria 2, Czechoslovakia 2, Latvia 2, Poland 2, Ukraine 2.
Preliminary Round 3 (Marmande, France, Sunday, April 25): Qualifiers: Czechoslovakia 3, Germany 3, Austria 2, France 2, Holland 2, Italy 2, Slovenia 2.
Preliminary Round 4 (Ljubljana, Slovenia, Sunday, April 25): Qualifiers: CIS 3, Germany 3, Austria 2, France 2, Hungary 2, Italy 2, Slovenia 2.
Qualifying Round A (Landshut, Germany, Sunday, May 23): Qualifiers: Czechoslovakia 3, Hungary 2, Poland 2, Germany 1, eight qualifiers Preliminary round 1.
Qualifying Round B (Wiener-Neustadt, Austria, Sunday, May 23): Qualifiers: Poland 3, Czechoslovakia 2, Hungary 2, Italy 1, eight qualifiers from Preliminary round 2.
Qualifying Round C (Gorzow, Poland, Sunday, May 23): Qualifiers: Czechoslovakia 3, Poland 3, CIS 2, eight qualifiers from Preliminary round 3.
Qualifying Round D (Kaposvar, Hungary, Sunday, May 23): Hungary 3, Czechoslovakia 2, Poland 2, Italy 1, eight qualifiers from Preliminary round 4.
Commonwealth Final (King's Lynn, England, Sunday, May 23): Ten qualifiers from the British Final, four from Australia and two from New Zealand.
Continental Semi Final 1 (Prague, Czechoslovakia, Sunday, June 13): Eight qualifiers from each of the Qualifying Rounds A and B.
Continental Semi Final 2 (Zielona Gora, Poland, Sunday, June 13): Eight qualifiers from each of the Qualifying Rounds C and D.
Scandinavian Final (Seïnajoki, Finland, Sunday, June 13): Six qualifiers from Denmark, five from Sweden, two from Norway and two from Finland with the 16th qualifier being the winner of a race off between one rider from each of the four Scandinavian nations.
Overseas Final (Coventry, England, Sunday, June 13): Eleven qualifiers from the Commonwealth Final, five from the North American Final.
Semi Final 1 (Vetlanda, Sweden, Friday, August 6): see below.
Semi Final 2 (Lonigo, Italy, Saturday, July 24): see below.
The two semi finals will be drawn by ballot with qualifiers from the Continental Semi Finals (14), Scandinavian Final (9) and Overseas Final (9).

WORLD FINAL (Pocking, Germany, Sunday, August 29): 8 qualifiers from each semi final.

WORLD TEAM CUP

Holders: United States of America

Group D, Round 1 (Krsko, Slovenia - to be confirmed): Slovenia, Latvia, France, Russia, Ukraine.
Group D, Round 2 (Rovno or Lvov, Ukraine - to be confirmed): CIS, France, Latvia, Slovenia, Ukraine.
Group C, Round 1 (Neustadt-Donau, Germany, Sunday, May 9): Austria, Germany, Italy, Winners Group D.
Group C, Round 2 (To be confirmed): Austria, Germany, Italy, Winners Group D.
Group B, Round 1 (Torun, Poland, Sunday, June 27): Hungary, Norway, Poland, Winners Group C.
Group B, Round 2 (To be confirmed): Hungary, Norway, Poland, Winners Group C.
Group A, Round 1 (Slangerup, Denmark, Sunday, August 22): Australia, Czechoslovakia, Denmark, Winners Group B.

WORLD FINAL (Bradford, England, Sunday, September 19): England, Sweden, United States of America and Winners, Group A.

WORLD PAIRS CHAMPIONSHIP

Holders: United States of America

Qualifying Round (Wiener-Neustadt, Austria, Saturday May 1): Austria, CIS, France, Holland, Latvia, Slovenia, Ukraine.
Semi Final 1 (Miskolc, Hungary, Sunday, June 6): Australia, Czechoslovakia, Germany, Hungary, Italy, United States of America, one nation from the Qualifying round.
Semi Final 2 (Bydgoszcz, Poland, Sunday, June 6): Finland, Great Britain, New Zealand, Norway, Poland, Sweden, one nation from the qualifying round.

WORLD FINAL (Vojens, Denmark, Sunday, August 1) Denmark and top three nations from each of the two semi finals.

■ **All dates and venues subject to alteration.**